D1130022

Coders at Work

Reflections on the Craft of Programming

Peter Seibel

Apress®

Coders at Work

Copyright © 2009 by Peter Seibel

All rights reserved. No part of this work may be reproduced or transmitted in any form or by any means, electronic or mechanical, including photocopying, recording, or by any information storage or retrieval system, without the prior written permission of the copyright owner and the publisher.

ISBN-13 (pbk): 978-1-4302-1948-4
ISBN-13 (electronic): 978-1-4302-1949-1

Printed and bound in the United States of America 9 8 7 6 5 4 3 2 1

Trademarked names may appear in this book. Rather than use a trademark symbol with every occurrence of a trademarked name, we use the names only in an editorial fashion and to the benefit of the trademark owner, with no intention of infringement of the trademark.

Lead Editor: Jeffrey Pepper
Technical Reviewer: John Vacca

Editorial Board: Clay Andres, Steve Anglin, Mark Beckner, Ewan Buckingham, Tony Campbell, Gary Cornell, Jonathan Gennick, Michelle Lowman, Matthew Moodie, Jeffrey Pepper, Frank Pohlmann, Ben Renow-Clarke, Dominic Shakeshaft, Matt Wade, Tom Welsh

Coordinating Editor: Anita Castro
Copy Editor: Candace English
Production Manager: Frank McGuckin
Cover Designer: Anna Ishschenko
Manufacturing Managers: Tom Debolsky; Michael Short

Distributed to the book trade worldwide by Springer-Verlag New York, Inc., 233 Spring Street, 6th Floor, New York, NY 10013. Phone 1-800-SPRINGER, fax 201-348-4505, e-mail `orders-ny@springer-sbm.com`, or visit `http://www.springeronline.com`.

For information on translations, please contact us by e-mail at info@apress.com, or visit `http://www.apress.com`.

Apress and friends of ED books may be purchased in bulk for academic, corporate, or promotional use. eBook versions and licenses are also available for most titles. For more information, reference our Special Bulk Sales–eBook Licensing web page at `http://www.apress.com/info/bulksales`.

The information in this book is distributed on an “as is” basis, without warranty. Although every precaution has been taken in the preparation of this work, neither the author(s) nor Apress shall have any liability to any person or entity with respect to any loss or damage caused or alleged to be caused directly or indirectly by the information contained in this work.

For Amelia

Contents

About the Author

Peter Seibel is either a writer turned programmer or programmer turned writer. After picking up an undergraduate degree in English and working briefly as a journalist, he was seduced by the web. In the early '90s he hacked Perl for *Mother Jones Magazine* and Organic Online. He participated in the Java revolution as an early employee at WebLogic and later taught Java programming at UC Berkeley Extension. In 2003 he quit his job as the architect of a Java-based transactional messaging system, planning to hack Lisp for a year. Instead he ended up spending two years writing the Jolt Productivity Award–winning *Practical Common Lisp*. Since then he's been working as chief monkey at Gigamonkeys Consulting, learning to train chickens, practicing Tai Chi, and being a dad. He lives in Berkeley, California, with his wife Lily, daughter Amelia, and dog Mahlanie.

Acknowledgments

First of all I want to thank my subjects who gave generously of their time and without whom this book would be nothing but a small pamphlet of unanswered questions. Additional thanks go to Joe Armstrong and Bernie Cosell, and their families, for giving me a place to stay in Stockholm and Virginia. Extra thanks also go to Peter Norvig and Jamie Zawinski who, in addition to taking their own turns speaking into my recorders, helped me get in touch with other folks who became my subjects.

As I traveled around the world conducting interviews several other families also welcomed me into their homes: thanks for their hospitality go to Dan Weinreb and Cheryl Moreau in Boston, to Gareth and Emma McCaughan in Cambridge, England, and to my own parents who provided a great base of operations in New York city. Christophe Rhodes helped me fill some free time between interviews with a tour of Cambridge University and he and Dave Fox rounded out the evening with dinner and a tour of Cantabrigian pubs.

Dan Weinreb, in addition to being my Boston host, has been my most diligent reviewer of all aspects of the the book since the days when I was still gathering names of potential subjects. Zach Beane, Luke Gorrie, Dave Walden and my mom also all read chapters and provided well-timed encouragement. Zach additionally—as is now traditional with my books—provided some words to go on the cover; this time the book's subtitle. Alan Kay made the excellent suggestion to include Dan Ingalls and L Peter Deutsch. Scott Fahlman gave me some useful background on Jamie Zawinski's early career and Dave Walden sent historical materials on Bolt Beranek and Newman to help me prepare for my interview with Bernie Cosell. To anyone I have forgotten, you still have my thanks and also my apologies.

Thanks to the folks at Apress, especially Gary Cornell who first suggested I do this book, John Vacca and Michael Banks for their suggestions, and my copy editor Candace English who fixed innumerable errors.

Finally, deepest thanks to my family, extended and nuclear. Both of my moms, biological and in-law, came on visits to watch the the kid and let me get some extra work done; my parents gave my wife and kid a place to escape for a week so I could make another big push. And most of all, thanks to the wife and kid themselves: Lily and Amelia, while I may occasionally need some time to myself to do the work, without you guys in my life, it wouldn't be worth doing. I love you.

Introduction

Leaving aside the work of Ada Lovelace—the 19th century countess who devised algorithms for Charles Babbage's never-completed Analytical Engine—computer programming has existed as a human endeavor for less than one human lifetime: it has been only 68 years since Konrad Zuse unveiled his Z3 electro-mechanical computer in 1941, the first working general-purpose computer. And it's been only 64 years since six women—Kay Antonelli, Jean Bartik, Betty Holberton, Marlyn Meltzer, Frances Spence, and Ruth Teitelbaum—were pulled from the ranks of the U.S. Army's "computer corps", the women who computed ballistics tables by hand, to become the first programmers of ENIAC, the first general-purpose electronic computer. There are many people alive today—the leading edge of the Baby Boom generation and all of the Boomers' parents—who were born into a world without computer programmers.

No more, of course. Now the world is awash in programmers. According to the Bureau of Labor Statistics, in the United States in 2008 approximately one in every 106 workers—over 1.25 million people—was a computer programmer or software engineer. And that doesn't count professional programmers outside the U.S. nor the many student and hobbyist programmers and people whose official job is something else but who spend some or even a lot of their time trying to bend a computer to their will. Yet despite the millions of people who have written code, and the billions, if not trillions of lines of code written since the field began, it still often feels like we're still making it up as we go along. People still argue about what programming is: mathematics or engineering? Craft, art, or science? We certainly argue—often with great vehemence—about the best way to do it: the Internet overflows with blog articles and forum postings about this or that way of writing code. And bookstores are chock-a-block with books about new programming languages, new methodologies, new ways of thinking about the task of programming.

This book takes a different approach to getting at what programming is, following in the tradition established when the literary journal *The Paris*

Review sent two professors to interview the novelist E.M. Forster, the first in a series of Q&A interviews later collected in the book *Writers at Work.*

I sat down with fifteen highly accomplished programmers with a wide range of experiences in the field—heads down systems hackers such as Ken Thompson, inventor of Unix, and Bernie Cosell, one of the original implementers of the ARPANET; programmers who combine strong academic credentials with hacker cred such as Donald Knuth, Guy Steele, and Simon Peyton Jones; industrial researchers such as Fran Allen of IBM, Joe Armstrong of Ericsson, and Peter Norvig at Google; Xerox PARC alumni Dan Ingalls and L Peter Deutsch; early Netscape implementers Jamie Zawinski and Brendan Eich; folks involved in the design and implementation of the languages the present-day web, Eich again as well as Douglas Crockford and Joshua Bloch; and Brad Fitzpatrick, inventor of Live Journal, and an able representative of the generation of programmers who came of age with the Web.

I asked these folks about programming: how they learned to do it, what they've discovered along the way, and what they think about its future. More particularly, I tried to get them to talk about the issues that programmers wrestle with all the time: How should we design software? What role do programming languages play in helping us be productive or avoid errors? Are there ways we can make it easier to track down hard-to-find bugs?

As these are far from settled questions, it's perhaps unsurprising that my subjects sometimes had quite varied opinions. Jamie Zawinski and Dan Ingalls emphasized the importance of getting code up and running right away while Joshua Bloch described how he designs APIs and tests whether they can support the code he wants to write against them before he does any implementation and Donald Knuth described how he wrote a complete version of his typesetting software TeX in pencil before he started typing in any code. And while Fran Allen lay much of the blame for the decline in interest in computer science in recent decades at the feet of C and Bernie Cosell called it the "biggest security problem to befall modern computers", Ken Thompson argued that security problems are caused by programmers, not their programming languages and Donald Knuth described C's use of pointers as one of the "most amazing improvements in notation" he's seen. Some of my subjects scoffed at the notion that formal proofs could be useful in improving the quality of software, but Guy Steele gave a very nice illustration of both their power and their limitations.

There were, however, some common themes: almost everybody emphasized the importance of writing readable code; most of my subjects have found that the hardest bugs to track down are in concurrent code; and nobody seemed to think programming is a solved problem: most are still looking for a better way to write software, whether by finding ways to automatically analyze code, coming up with better ways for programmers to work together, or finding (or designing) better programming languages. And almost everyone seemed to think that ubiquitous multi-core CPUs are going to force some serious changes in the way software is written.

These conversations took place at a particular moment in our field's history, so no doubt some of the topics discussed in this book will fade from urgent present-day issues to historical curiosities. But even in a field as young as programming, history can hold lessons for us. Beyond that, I suspect that my subjects have shared some insights into what programming is and how we could do it better that will be useful to programmers today *and* to programmers several generations from now.

Finally, a note on the title: we chose *Coders at Work* for its resonance with the previously mentioned *Paris Review's Writers at Work* series as well as Apress's book *Founders at Work*, which does for starting a technology company what this book tries to do for computer programming. I realize that "coding" could be taken to refer to only one rather narrow part of the larger activity of programming. Personally I have never believed that it is possible to be a good coder without being a good programmer nor a good programmer without being a good designer, communicator, and thinker. Certainly all of my subjects are all of those and much more and I believe the conversations you are about to read reflect that. Enjoy!

CHAPTER

1

Jamie Zawinski

Lisp hacker, early Netscape developer, and nightclub owner Jamie Zawinski, a.k.a. jwz, is a member of the select group of hackers who are as well known by their three-letter initials as by their full names.

Zawinski started working as a programmer as a teenager when he was hired to hack Lisp at a Carnegie Mellon artificial intelligence lab. After attending college just long enough to discover that he hated it, he worked in the Lisp and AI world for nearly a decade, getting a strange immersion in a fading hacker subculture when other programmers his age were growing up with microcomputers.

He worked at UC Berkeley for Peter Norvig, who has described him as "one of the of the best programmers I ever hired," and later at Lucid, the Lisp company, where he ended up leading the development of Lucid Emacs, later renamed XEmacs, which eventually led to the great Emacs schism, one of the most famous open source forks.

In 1994 he finally left Lucid and the Lisp world to join Netscape, then a fledgling start-up, where he was one of the original developers of the Unix version of the Netscape browser and later of the Netscape mail reader.

In 1998 Zawinski was one of the prime movers, along with Brendan Eich, behind mozilla.org, the organization that took the Netscape browser open source. A year later, discouraged by the lack of progress toward a release, he quit the project and bought a San Francisco nightclub, the DNA Lounge, which he now runs. He is currently devoting his energies to battling the California Department of Alcoholic Beverage Control in an attempt to convert the club to an all-ages venue for live music.

In this interview we talked about, among other things, why C++ is an abomination, the joy of having millions of people use your software, and the importance of tinkering for budding programmers.

Seibel: How did you learn to program?

Zawinski: Wow, it was so long ago I can barely remember it. The first time I really used a computer in a programming context was probably like eighth grade, I think. We had some TRS-80s and we got to goof around with BASIC a little bit. I'm not sure there was even a class—I think it was just like an after-school thing. I remember there was no way to save programs so you'd just type them in from magazines and stuff like that. Then I guess I read a bunch of books. I remember reading books about languages that I had no way to run and writing programs on paper for languages that I'd only read about.

Seibel: What languages would that have been?

Zawinski: APL, I remember, was one of them. I read an article about it and thought it was really neat.

Seibel: Well, it saves having to have the fancy keyboard. When you were in high school did you have any classes on computers?

Zawinski: In high school I learned Fortran. That's about it.

Seibel: And somehow you got exposed to Lisp.

Zawinski: I read a lot of science fiction. I thought AI was really neat; the computers are going to take over the world. So I learned a little bit about that. I had a friend in high school, Dan Zigmond, and we were trading books, so we both learned Lisp. One day he went to the Apple Users Group meeting at Carnegie Mellon—which was really just a software-trading situation—because he wanted to get free stuff. And he's talking to some college student there who's like, "Oh, here's this 15-year-old who knows Lisp; that's novel; you should go ask Scott Fahlman for a job." So Dan did. And Fahlman gave him one. And then Dan said, "Oh, you should hire my friend too," and that was me. So Fahlman hired us. I think his motivation had to be something along the lines of, Wow, here are two high school kids who are actually interested in this stuff; it doesn't really do me much harm to let them hang out in the lab." So we had basic grunt work—this set of stuff needs to be recompiled because there's a new version of the compiler; go figure out how to do that. Which was pretty awesome. So there are the two of us—these two little kids—surrounded by all these grad students doing language and AI research.

Seibel: Was that the first chance you actually had to run Lisp, there at CMU.

Zawinski: I think so. I know at one point we were goofing around with XLISP, which ran on Macintoshes. But I think that was later. I learned how to program for real there using these PERQ workstations which were part of the Spice project, using Spice Lisp which became CMU Common Lisp. It was such an odd environment. We'd go to weekly meetings, learning how software development works just by listening in. But there were some really entertaining characters in that group. Like the guy who was sort of our manager—the one keeping an eye on us—Skef Wholey, was this giant blond-haired, barbarian-looking guy. Very intimidating-looking. And he didn't talk much. I remember a lot of times I'd be sitting there—it was kind of an open-plan cubicle kind of thing—working, doing something, writing some Lisp program. And he'd come shuffling in with his ceramic mug of beer, bare feet, and he'd just stand behind me. I'd say hi. And he'd grunt or say nothing. He'd just stand there watching me type. At some point I'd do something and he'd go, "Ptthh, wrong!" and he'd walk away. So that was kind of getting thrown in the deep end. It was like the Zen approach—the master hit me with a stick, now I must meditate.

Seibel: I emailed Fahlman and he said that you were talented and learned very fast. But he also mentioned that you were kind of undisciplined. As he put it, "We tried gently to teach him about working in a group with others and about writing code that you, or someone else, could understand a month from now." Do you remember any of those lessons?

Zawinski: Not the learning of them, I guess. Certainly one of the most important things is writing code you can come back to later. But I'm about to be 39 and I was 15 at the time, so it's all a little fuzzy.

Seibel: What year did that start?

Zawinski: That must have been '84 or '85. I think I started in the summer between 10th and 11th grade. After high school, at 4:00 or so I'd head over there and stay until eight or nine. I don't think I did that every day but I was there a fair amount.

Seibel: And you very briefly went to CMU after you finished high school.

Zawinski: Yeah. What happened was, I hated high school. It was the worst time of my life. And when I was about to graduate I asked Fahlman if he'd hire me full-time and he said, "No, but I've got these friends who've got a startup; go talk to them." Which was Expert Technologies—ETI. I guess he was on their board. They were making this expert system to automatically paginate the yellow pages. They were using Lisp and I knew a couple of the people already who had been in Fahlman's group. They hired me and that was all going fine, and then about a year later I panicked: Oh my god, I completely lucked into both of these jobs; this is never going to happen again. Once I no longer work here I'm going to be flipping burgers if I don't have a college degree, so what I ought to do is go get one of those.

The plan was that I'd be working part-time at ETI and then I'd be going to school part time. That turned into working full-time and going to school full-time and that lasted, I think, six weeks. Maybe it was nine weeks. I know it lasted long enough that I'd missed the add/drop period, so I didn't get any of my money back. But not long enough that I actually got any grades. So it's questionable whether I actually went.

It was just awful. When you're in high school, everyone tells you, "There's a lot of repetitive bullshit and standardized tests; it'll all be better once you're in college." And then you get to your first year of college and they're like, "Oh, no—it gets better when you're in grad school." So it's just same shit, different day—I couldn't take it. Getting up at eight in the morning, memorizing things. They wouldn't let me opt out of this class called Introduction to Facilities where they teach you how to use a mouse. I was like, "I've been working at this university for a year and a half—I know how to use a mouse." No way out of it—"It's policy." All kinds of stuff like that. I couldn't take it. So I dropped out. And I'm glad I did.

Then I worked at ETI for four years or so until the company started evaporating. We were using TI Explorer Lisp machines at ETI so I spent a lot of my time, besides actually working on the expert system, just sort of messing around with user-interface stuff and learning how those machines worked from the bottom up. I loved them—I loved digging around in the operating system and just figuring out how it all fit together.

I'd written a bunch of code and there was some newsgroup where I posted that I was looking for a job and, oh, by the way, here's a bunch of code. Peter Norvig saw it and scheduled an interview. My girlfriend at the time had moved out here to go to UC Berkeley, so I followed her out.

Seibel: Norvig was at Berkeley then?

Zawinski: Yeah. That was a very strange job. They had a whole bunch of grad students who'd been doing research on natural language understanding; they were basically linguists who did some programming. So they wanted someone to take these bits and pieces of code they'd left behind and integrate them into one thing that actually worked.

That was incredibly difficult because I didn't have the background to understand what in the world they were doing. So this would happen a lot: I'd be looking at something; I'd be completely stuck. I have no idea what this means, where do I go from here, what do I have to read to understand this. So I'd ask Peter. He'd be nice about it—he'd say, "It totally makes sense that you don't understand that yet. I'll sit down and explain it to you Tuesday." So now I've got nothing to do. So I spent a lot of time working on windows system stuff and poking around with screen savers and just the kind of UI stuff that I'd been doing for fun before.

After six or eight months of that it just felt like, wow, I'm really just wasting my time. I'm not doing anything for them, and I just felt like I was on vacation. There have been times when I was working really a lot when I'd look back at that and I'm like, "Why did you quit the vacation job? What is wrong with you? They were paying you to write screen savers!"

So I ended up going to work for Lucid, which was one of the two remaining Lisp-environment developers. The thing that really made me decide to leave was just this feeling that I wasn't accomplishing anything. And I was surrounded by people who weren't programmers. I'm still friends with some of them; they're good folks, but they were linguists. They were much more interested in abstract things than solving problems. I wanted to be doing something that I could point to and say, "Look, I made this neat thing."

Seibel: Your work at Lucid eventually gave rise to XEmacs, but when you went there originally were you working on Lisp stuff?

Zawinski: Yeah, one of the first projects I worked on was—I can't even remember what the machine was, but it was this 16-processor parallel computer and we had this variant of Lucid Common Lisp with some control structures that would let you fork things out to different processors.

I worked a little bit on the back end of that to make the overhead of spawning a thread lower so you could do something like a parallel implementation of Fibonacci that wasn't just completely swamped by the overhead of creating a new stack group for each thread. I really enjoyed that. It was the first time I'd gotten to use a fairly bizarre machine like that.

Before that I was bringing up Lisp on new machines. Which means basically someone's already written the compiler back end for the new architecture and then they've compiled the bootstrap piece of code. So I've got this file full of binary, supposedly executable code for this other machine and now I've got to decipher their loader format so that I can write a little C program that will load that in, make the page executable, and jump to it. Then, hopefully, you get a Lisp prompt and at that point you can start loading things in by hand.

Which for every architecture was bizarre, because it's never documented right. So it's a matter of compiling a C program and then looking at it byte by byte—byte-editing it in Emacs. Let's see what happens if I change this to a zero; does it stop running?

Seibel: When you say it wasn't documented right, was it that it wasn't documented correctly, or it wasn't documented at all?

Zawinski: It was usually documented and it was usually wrong. Or maybe it was just three revisions behind—who knows? But at some point you tweak a bit and then it would no longer believe this was an executable file and you had to figure out what was going on there.

Seibel: So that's something that comes up all the time, from the lowest-level systems programming to high-level APIs, where things just don't work the way you expect or the way they are documented. How do you deal with that?

Zawinski: Well, you just come to expect it. The sooner you realize that your map is wrong, the sooner you'll be able to figure out where it went wrong. In my case, I'm trying to produce an executable file. Well, I know the C compiler will produce one. Take the good one and start converting it into the bad one until it stops working. That's primary tool of reverse engineering.

The hardest bug I've ever fixed, I think, was probably during that period at Lucid. I'd gotten to the point where it's running the executable and it's trying to bootstrap Lisp and it gets 500 instructions in and crashes. So there I am leaning on the S key, stepping through trying to figure out where it crashes. And it seems to be crashing at a different place each time. And it doesn't make any sense. I'm reading the assembly output of this architecture I only barely understand. Finally I realize, "Oh my god, it's doing something different when I step; maybe it's timing-based." Eventually I figure out that what's going on is this is one of the early machines that did speculative execution. It would execute both sides of the branch. And GDB would always take the branch if you single-stepped past a branch instruction. There was a bug in GDB!

Seibel: Nice.

Zawinski: Right. So then that takes me down into, "Oh my god; now I'm trying to debug GDB, which I've never looked at before." The way to get around that is you're coming up to a branch instruction and you stop before the branch, set a break point on both sides, and continue. So that was how I proved that really was what was going on. Spent like a week trying to fix GDB; couldn't figure it out. I assume a register was getting stomped somewhere, so it always thought there was a positive value in the branch check or something like that.

So I changed the step-by-instruction command to recognize when it was coming up on a branch instruction and just say, "No, don't do that." Then I can just lean on the S key and it would eventually stop and I'd set the break point by hand and continue. When you're debugging something and then you figure out that not only is the map wrong but the tools are broken—that's a good time.

Working on Lisp systems was especially weird because GDB was completely nonfunctional on Lisp code because it doesn't have any debug info—it's written by a compiler GDB has never heard of. I think on some platforms it laid out the stack frames in a way GDB didn't understand. So GDB was pretty much an assembly stepper at that point. So you wanted to get out of the GDB world just as quickly as you could.

Seibel: And then you'd have a Lisp debugger and you'd be all set.

Zawinski: Right, yeah.

Seibel: So somewhere in there Lucid switched directions and said, "We're going to make a C++ IDE".

Zawinski: That had been begun before I started working there—it was in progress. And people started shifting over from the Lisp side to the Energize side, which is what the development environment was called. It was a really good product but it was two or three years too early. Nobody, at least on the Unix side, had any idea they wanted it yet. Everyone uses them now but we had to spend a lot of time explaining to people why this was better than vi and GCC. Anyway, I'd done a bit of Emacs stuff. I guess by that point I'd already rewritten the Emacs byte compiler because—why did I do that? Right, I'd written this Rolodex phone/address-book thing.

Seibel: Big Brother Database?

Zawinski: Yeah. And it was slow so I started digging into why it was slow and I realized, oh, it's slow because the compiler sucks. So I rewrote the compiler, which was my first run-in with the intransigence of Stallman. So I knew a lot about Emacs.

Seibel: So the change to the byte compiler, did it change the byte-code format or did it just change the compiler?

Zawinski: It actually had a few options—I made some changes at the C layer, the byte-code interpreter, added a few new instructions that sped things up. But the compiler could be configured to emit either old-style byte-code or ones that took advantage of the new codes.

So I write a new compiler and Stallman's response is, "I see no need for this change." And I'm like, "What are you talking about? It generates way faster code." Then his next response is, "Okay, uh, send me a diff and explain each line you changed." "Well, I didn't do that—I rewrote it because the old one was crap." That was not OK. The only reason it ever got folded in was because I released it and thousands of people started using it and they loved it and they nagged him for two years and finally he put it in because he was tired of being nagged about it.

Seibel: Did you sign the papers assigning the copyright to the Free Software Foundation?

Zawinski: Oh yeah, I did that right away. I think that was probably the first thing in the email. It was like, send me a diff for each line and sign this. So I signed and said, "I can't do the rest; can't send you a diff; that's ridiculous. It's well documented; go take a look." I don't think he ever did.

There's this myth that there was some legal issue between Lucid and FSF and that's absolutely not true—we assigned copyrights for everything we did to them. It was convenient for them to pretend we hadn't at certain times. Like, we actually submitted the paperwork multiple times because they'd be like, "Oh, oh, we seem to have lost it." I think there was some kind of brouhaha with assignments and XEmacs much later, but that was way after my time.

Seibel: So you started with Lisp. But you obviously didn't stick with it for your whole career. What came next?

Zawinski: Well, the next language I did any serious programming in after Lisp was C, which was kind of like going back to the assembly I programmed on an Apple II. It's the PDP-11 assembler that thinks it's a language. Which was, you know, unpleasant. I'd tried to avoid it for as long as possible. And C++ is just an abomination. Everything is wrong with it in every way. So I really tried to avoid using that as much as I could and do everything in C at Netscape. Which was pretty easy because we were targeting pretty small machines that didn't run C++ programs well because C++ tends to bloat like crazy as soon as you start using any libraries. Plus the C++ compilers were all in flux—there were lots of incompatibility problems. So we just settled on ANSI C from the beginning and that served us pretty well. After that

Java felt like going back to Lisp a bit in that there were concepts that the language wasn't bending over backwards trying to make you avoid—that were comfortable again.

Seibel: Like what?

Zawinski: Memory management. That functions felt more like functions than subroutines. There was much more enforced modularity to it. It's always tempting to throw in a goto in C code just because it's easy.

Seibel: So these days it seems like you're mostly doing C and Perl.

Zawinski: Well, I don't really program very much anymore. Mostly I write stupid little Perl scripts to keep my servers running. I end up writing a lot of goofy things for getting album art for MP3s I have—that kind of thing. Just tiny brute-force throw-away programs.

Seibel: Do you like Perl or is it just handy?

Zawinski: Oh, I despise it. It's a horrible language. But it is installed absolutely everywhere. Any computer you sit down on, you're never going to have to talk someone through installing Perl to run your script. Perl is there already. That's really the one and only thing that recommends it.

It has an OK collection of libraries. There's often a library for doing the thing you want. And often it doesn't work very well, but at least there's something. The experience of writing something in Java and then trying to figure out—I myself have trouble installing Java on my computer—it's horrible. I think Perl is a despicable language. If you use little enough of it, you can make it kind of look like C—or I guess more like JavaScript than like C. Its syntax is crazy, if you use it. Its data structures are a mess. There's not a lot good about it.

Seibel: But not as bad as C++.

Zawinski: No, absolutely not. It's for different things. There's stuff that would be so much easier to write in Perl or any language like Perl than in C just because they're text-oriented—all these so-called "scripting languages". Which is a distinction I don't really buy—"programming" versus "scripting". I think that's nonsense. But if what you're doing is fundamentally manipulating text or launching programs, like running wget and pulling some HTML out and pattern-matching it, it's going to be easier to do that in Perl than even Emacs Lisp.

Seibel: To say nothing of, Emacs Lisp is not going to be very suitable for command-line utilities.

Zawinski: Yeah, though I used to write just random little utilities in Emacs all the time. There was actually a point, early on in Netscape, where part of our build process involved running "emacs -batch" to manipulate some file. No one really appreciated that.

Seibel: No. I imagine they wouldn't. What about XScreenSaver—do you still work on that?

Zawinski: I still write new screen savers every now and then just for kicks, and that's all C.

Seibel: Do you use some kind of IDE for that?

Zawinski: I just use Emacs, mostly. Though recently, I ported XScreenSaver to OS X. The way I did that was I reimplemented Xlib in terms of Cocoa, the Mac graphics substrate, so I wouldn't have to change the source code of all the screen savers. They're still making X calls but I implemented the back end for each of those. And that was in Objective C, which actually is a pretty nice language. I enjoyed doing that. It definitely feels Java-like in the good ways but it also feels like C. Because it's essentially C, you can still link directly with C code and just call the functions and not have to bend over backwards.

Seibel: At Lucid, leaving aside the politics of Emacs development, what technical stuff did you learn?

Zawinski: I definitely became a better programmer while I was there. Largely because that was really the smartest group of people I've been around. Everyone who worked there was brilliant. And it was just nice to be in that kind of environment where when someone says, "That's nonsense," or "We should do it this way," you can just take their word for it, believe that they know what they were talking about. That was really nice. Not that I hadn't been around smart people before. But it was just such a high-quality group of people there, consistently.

Seibel: And how big was the development team?

Zawinski: I think there were like 70 people at the company so probably; I don't know, 40 or so on the development team. The Energize team was maybe 25 people, 20. It was divided up into pretty distinct areas. There were the folks working on the compiler side of things and the back-end database side of things. The GUI stuff that wasn't Emacs. And then there was, at one point, me and two or three other people working on integrating Emacs with the environment. That eventually turned into mostly me working on mostly Emacs stuff, trying to make our Emacs 19 be usable, be an editor that doesn't crash all the time, and actually runs all the Emacs packages that you expect it to run.

Seibel: So you wanted the Emacs included in your product to be a fully capable version of Emacs.

Zawinski: The original plan was that we wouldn't include Emacs with our product. You have Emacs on your machine already and you have our product and they work together. And you had GCC on your machine already and our product, and they work together. I think one of the early code names for our product was something like Hitchhiker because the idea was that it would take all the tools that you already have and integrate them—make them talk to each other by providing this communication layer between them.

That didn't work out at all. We ended up shipping our version of GCC and GDB because we couldn't get the changes upstream fast enough, or at all in some cases. And same thing with Emacs. So we ended up shipping the whole thing. We ended up going down the path of, "Well, we're replacing Emacs. Shit. I guess we have to do that so we better make it work." One thing I spent a bunch of time on was making the vi emulation mode work.

Seibel: And that's several weeks of your life you're never going to get back.

Zawinski: That's true, yeah. It was challenging. I think it ended up working OK. The real problem with that wasn't so much that it was emulating vi wrong as that vi users quit and restart vi all the time. And no amount of coding on my part is going to get them out of that mindset. So they're like, "I expected this to launch in half a second and it's taking 14 seconds. That's ridiculous. I can't use this."

Seibel: Why did you leave Lucid?

Zawinski: Lucid was done. There'd been a bunch of layoffs. I sent mail to a bunch of people I know saying, "Hey, looks like I'm going to need a new job soon" and one of those people was Marc Andreessen and he said, "Oh, funny you should mention that, because we just started a company last week." And that was that.

Seibel: So you went to Netscape. What did you work on there?

Zawinski: I pretty much started right away doing the Unix side of the browser. There had been maybe a few days' worth of code written on it so far. A little bit more of the Windows and Mac sides had been started. The model was a big pile of back-end code and then as small as possible a piece of front-end code for each of the three platforms.

Seibel: And was this all new code?

Zawinski: It was all new code. Most of the Netscape founders had been NCSA/Mosaic developers so they had written the various versions of NCSA/Mosaic, which was actually three different programs. And all six of those people were at Netscape. They weren't reusing any code but they had written this program before.

Seibel: So they started with an empty disk and started typing?

Zawinski: Exactly. I never looked at the Mosaic code; still haven't. We actually were sued over that at one point; the university claimed that we were reusing their code and I guess that was settled one way or the other. There's always been that rumor that we started that way, but we didn't.

And really, why would we? Everyone wants to write version two, right? You were figuring it out while you wrote it and now you've got a chance to throw that away and start over—of course you're going to start over. It's going to be better this time. And it was. With the design that the other ones had, there was basically no way to load images in parallel, things like that. And that was really important. So we had a better design for the back end.

Seibel: Yet that's also a classic opportunity to fall into the second-system syndrome.

Zawinski: It is, it is.

Seibel: How did you guys avoid that?

Zawinski: We were so focused on deadline it was like religion. We were shipping a finished product in six months or we were going to die trying.

Seibel: How did you come up with that deadline?

Zawinski: Well, we looked around at the rest of the world and decided, if we're not done in six months, someone's going to beat us to it so we're going to be done in six months.

Seibel: Given that you picked the date first, you had to rein in scope or quality. How did that work?

Zawinski: We spent a long time talking about features. Well, not a long time, but it seemed like a long time because we were living a week every day. We stripped features, definitely. We had a whiteboard; we scribbled ideas; we crossed them out. This was a group of like six or seven people. I don't remember exactly the number. A bunch of smart, egotistical people sitting in a room yelling at each other for a week or so.

Seibel: Six or seven being the whole Netscape development team or the Unix development team?

Zawinski: That was the whole client team. There were also the server folks who were implementing their fork of Apache, basically. We didn't talk to them much because we were busy. We had lunch with them, but that was it. So we figured out what we wanted to be in the thing and we divided up the work so that there were, I guess, no more than two people working on any part of the project. I was doing the Unix side and Lou Montulli did most of back-end network stuff. And Eric Bina was doing layout and Jon Mittelhauser and Chris Houck were doing the Windows front end and Aleks Totić and Mark Lanett were doing the Mac front end for the pre–version 1.0 team. Those teams grew a little bit after that. But we'd have our meetings and then go back to our cubicles and be heads-down for 16 hours trying to make something work.

It was really a great environment. I really enjoyed it. Because everyone was so sure they were right, we fought constantly but it allowed us to communicate fast. Someone would lean over your cubicle and say, "What the fuck did you check in; that's complete bullshit—you can't do it that way. You're an idiot." And you'd say, "Fuck off!" and go look at it and fix it and check it in. We were very abrasive but we communicated fast because you didn't have to go blow sunshine up someone's ass and explain to them what you thought was wrong—you could say, "Hey, that's a load of shit! I can't use that." And you'd hash it out very quickly. It was stressful but we got it done pretty quickly.

Seibel: Are the long hours and the intensity required to produce software quickly?

Zawinski: It's certainly not healthy. I know we did it that way and it worked. So the way to answer that question is, is there another example of someone delivering a big piece of software that fast that's of reasonable quality where they actually had dinner at home and slept during the night? Has that ever happened? I don't actually know. Maybe it has.

But it's not always about getting it done as quickly as possible. It also would be nice to not burn out after two years and be able to continue doing your job for ten. Which is not going to happen if you're working 80-plus hours a week.

Seibel: What is the thing that you worked on that you were most proud of.

Zawinski: Really just the fact that we shipped it. The whole thing. I was very focused on my part, which was the user interface of the Unix front end. But really just that we shipped the thing at all and that people liked it. People converted immediately from NCSA Mosaic and were like, "Wow, this is the greatest thing ever." We had the button for the What's Cool page up in the toolbar and got to show the world these crazy web sites people had put up already. I mean, there were probably almost 200 of them! It's not so much that I was proud of the code; just that it was done. In a lot of ways the code wasn't very good because it was done very fast. But it got the job done. We shipped—that was the bottom line.

That first night when we put up the .96 beta, we were all sitting around the room watching the downloads with sound triggers hooked up to it—that was amazing. A month later two million people were running software I'd written. It was unbelievable. That definitely made it all worthwhile—that we'd had an impact on people's lives; that their day was more fun or more pleasant or easier because of the work we'd done.

Seibel: After this relentless pace, at some point that has to start to catch up with you in terms of the quality of the code. How did you guys deal with that?

Zawinski: Well, the way we dealt with that was badly. There's never a time to start over and rewrite it. And it's never a good idea to start over and rewrite it.

Seibel: At some point you also worked on the mail reader, right?

Zawinski: In 2.0 Marc comes into my cubicle and says, "We need a mail reader." And I'm like, "OK, that sounds cool. I've worked on mail readers before." I was living in Berkeley and basically I didn't come into the office for a couple weeks. I was spending the whole time sitting in cafes doodling, trying to figure out what I wanted in a mail reader. Making lists, crossing it off, trying to decide how long it would take me. What should the UI look like?

Then I came back and started coding. And then Marc comes in again and says, "Oh, so we hired this other guy who's done mail stuff before. You guys should work together." It's this guy Terry Weissman, who was just fantastic—we worked together so well. And it was a completely different dynamic than it had been in the early days with the rest of the browser team.

We didn't yell at each other at all. And the way we divided up labor, I can't imagine how it possibly worked or could ever work for anyone. I had the basic design done and I'd started doing a little coding and every day or every couple of days we'd look at the list of features and I'd go, "Uhhh, maybe I'll work on that," and he'd go, "OK, I'll work on that," and then we'd go away.

Check-ins would happen and then we'd come back and he'd say, "Alright, I'm done with that, what are you doing?" "Uh, I'm working on this." "OK, well, I'll start on that then." And we just sort of divided up the pieces. It worked out really well.

We had disagreements—I thought we had to toss filtering into folders because we just didn't have time to do it right. And he was like, "No, no, I really think we ought to do that." And I was like, "We don't have time!" So he wrote it that night.

The other thing was, Terry and I rarely saw each other because he lived in Santa Cruz and I lived in Berkeley. We were about the same distance from work in opposite directions and because the two of us were the only two who ever needed to communicate, we were just like, "I won't make you come in if you don't make me come in." "Deal!"

Seibel: Did you guys email a lot?

Zawinski: Yeah, constant email. This was before instant messaging—these days it probably all would have been IM because we were sending one-liner emails constantly. And we talked on the phone.

So we shipped 2.0 with the mail reader and it was well-received. Then we're working on 2.1, which is the version of the mail reader that I'm starting to consider done—this is the one with all the stuff that we couldn't ship the first time around. Terry and I are halfway through doing that and Marc comes in and says, "So we're buying this company. And they make a mail-reader thing that's kind of like what you guys did." I'm like, "Oh. OK. Well, we have one of those." And he says, "Well, yeah, but we're growing really fast and it's really hard to hire good people and sometimes the way you hire good people is you just acquire another company because then they've already been vetted for you." "OK. What are these people going to be working on?" "They're going to be working on your project." "OK, that kind of sucks—I'm going to go work on something else."

So basically they acquired this company, Collabra, and hired this whole management structure above me and Terry. Collabra has a product that they had shipped that was similar to what we had done in a lot of ways except it was Windows-only and it had utterly failed in the marketplace.

Then they won the start-up lottery and they got acquired by Netscape. And, basically, Netscape turned over the reins of the company to this company. So rather than just taking over the mail reader they ended up taking over the entire client division. Terry and I had been working on Netscape 2.1 when the Collabra acquisition happened and then the rewrite started. Then clearly their Netscape 3.0 was going to be extremely late and our 2.1 turned into 3.0 because it was time to ship something and we needed it to be a major version.

So the 3.0 that they had begun working on became 4.0 which, as you know, is one of the biggest software disasters there has ever been. It basically killed the company. It took a long time to die, but that was it: the rewrite helmed by this company we'd acquired, who'd never accomplished much of anything, who disregarded all of our work and all of our success, went straight into second-system syndrome and brought us down.

They thought just by virtue of being here, they were bound for glory doing it their way. But when they were doing it their way, at their company, they failed. So when the people who had been successful said to them, "Look, really, don't use C++; don't use threads," they said, "What are you talking about? You don't know anything."

Well, it was decisions like not using C++ and not using threads that made us ship the product on time. The other big thing was we always shipped all platforms simultaneously; that was another thing they thought was just stupid. "Oh, 90 percent of people are using Windows, so we'll focus on the Windows side of things and then we'll port it later." Which is what many other failed companies have done. If you're trying to ship a cross-platform product, history really shows that's how you don't do it. If you want it to really be cross-platform, you have to do them simultaneously. The porting thing results in a crappy product on the second platform.

Seibel: Was the 4.0 rewrite from scratch?

Zawinski: They didn't start from scratch with a blank disk but they eventually replaced every line of code. And they used C++ from the beginning. Which I fought against so hard and, dammit, I was right. It bloated everything; it introduced all these compatibility problems because when you're programming C++ no one can ever agree on which ten percent of the language is safe to use. There's going to be one guy who decides, "I have to used templates." And then you discover that there are no two compilers that implement templates the same way.

And when your background, your entire background, is writing code where multiplatform means both Windows 3.1 and Windows 95, you have no concept how big a deal that is. So it made the Unix side of things—which thankfully was no longer my problem—a disaster. It made the Mac side of things a disaster. It meant it was no longer possible to ship on low-end Windows boxes like Win16. We had to start cutting platforms out. Maybe it was time to do that, but it was a bad reason. It was unnecessary.

It really felt—this is my bitter, selfish way of looking at it—like Terry and I built this great thing and were punished for our success by having it handed over to idiots. That was a very unhappy time for me at Netscape. That began the period where I was only there waiting to vest.

Seibel: So you lasted there five years?

Zawinski: Yeah. A year past vesting, because just before vesting day mozilla.org stared and that was really interesting again, so I stuck around for that.

Seibel: Did you ultimately get dragged into using C++?

Zawinski: Well, there was the Java thing. At one point, we were going to rewrite the browser in Java. We were like, "Yes! We're going to get to ditch that 4.0 code base which is going to destroy our company and this is gonna actually work because, like, we know what we're doing!"

And it didn't work.

Seibel: Did it just not work because Java wasn't ready?

Zawinski: No. We were all broken up into fairly well-defined groups again. There were three of us working on the mail reader. And we were done. We had a really nice mail reader that was fast and had a lot of really nice features and was better about saving your data—there were never any stalls where it was writing some big file. We took really good advantage of multithreading in Java, which was less painful than I had expected it to be. It was just really pleasant to work on. From the API we had designed we saw all these directions it could grow.

Except the one thing that it couldn't do was display messages. Because what it did was, it generated HTML and to display HTML you need an HTML display layer, which wasn't done and was never finished. The layout group just completely went down a rat hole and they were the reason that that project got canceled.

Seibel: So they were presumably wrestling with the—at that time—immature Java GUI technology.

Zawinski: I don't think so. Because all the chrome worked. There was just this big blank rectangle in the middle of the window where we could only display plain text. They were being extremely academic about their project. They were trying to approach it from the DOM/DTD side of things. "Oh, well, what we need to do is add another abstraction layer here and have a delegate for this delegate for this delegate. And eventually a character will show up on the screen."

Seibel: Overengineering seems to be a pet peeve of yours.

Zawinski: Yeah. At the end of the day, ship the fucking thing! It's great to rewrite your code and make it cleaner and by the third time it'll actually be pretty. But that's not the point—you're not here to write code; you're here to ship products.

Seibel: Folks engaged in overengineering usually say, "Well, once I've got this framework in place everything will be easy after that. So I'll actually save time by doing this."

Zawinski: That is always the theory.

Seibel: And there are times when that theory is true, when someone has good sense and the framework isn't too elaborate, and it does save time. Is there any way you can tell which side of the line you're on?

Zawinski: I know it's kind of a cliché but it comes back to worse is better. If you spend the time to build the perfect framework that's going to do what you want and that's going to carry you from release 1.0 through release 5.0 and everything's going to be great; well guess what: release 1.0 is going to take you three years to ship and your competitor is going to ship their 1.0 in six months and now you're out of the game. You never shipped your 1.0 because someone else ate your lunch.

Your competitor's six-month 1.0 has crap code and they're going to have to rewrite it in two years but, guess what: they can rewrite it because you don't have a job anymore.

Seibel: There must have been times, perhaps on a shorter time frame, where you've ripped out a big chunk of code because you thought it would be faster to start over.

Zawinski: Yes, there are definitely times when you have to cut your losses. And this always feels wrong to me, but when you inherit code from someone else, sometimes it's faster to write your own than to reuse theirs. Because it's going to take a certain amount of time to understand their code and learn how to use it and understand it well enough to be able to debug it. Where if you started from scratch it would take less time. And it might only do 80 percent of what you need, but maybe that's the 80 percent you actually need.

Seibel: Isn't it exactly this thing—someone comes along and says, "I can't understand this stuff. I'll just rewrite it"—that leads to the endless rewriting you bemoan in open-source development?

Zawinski: Yeah. But there's also another aspect of that which is, efficiency aside, it's just more fun to write your own code than to figure out someone else's. So it's easy to understand why that happens. But the whole Linux/GNOME side of things is straddling this line between someone's hobby and a product. Is this a research project where we're deciding what desktops should look like and we're experimenting? Or are we competing with Macintosh? Which is it? Hard to do both.

But even phrasing it that way makes it sounds like there's someone who's actually in charge making that decision, which isn't true at all. All of this stuff just sort of happens. And one of the things that happens is everything get rewritten all the time and nothing's ever finished. If you're one of those developers, that's fine because there's always something to play around with if your hobby is messing around with your computer rather than it being a means to an end—being a tool you use to get whatever you're actually interested in done.

Seibel: Speaking of messing around with a computer for its own sake, do you still enjoy programming?

Zawinski: Sometimes. I end up doing all the sysadmin crap, which I can't stand—I've never liked it. I enjoy working on XScreenSaver because in some ways screen savers—the actual display modes rather than the XScreenSaver framework—are the perfect program because they almost always start from scratch and they do something pretty and there's never a version 2.0. There's very rarely a bug in a screen saver. It crashes—oh, there's a divide-by-zero and you fix that.

But no one is ever going to ask for a new feature in a screen saver. "I wish it was more yellow." You're not going to get a bug report like that. It is what it is. So that's why I've always written those for fun. They make this neat result and you don't have to think about them too much. They don't haunt you.

Seibel: And do you enjoy the puzzle of doing some math and figuring out geometry and graphics?

Zawinski: Yeah. What's this abstract little equation going to look like if I display it this way? Or, how can I make these blobs move around that looks more organic and less rigid, like a computer normally moves things? Stuff like that. What do I do to these sine waves to make it look more like something bouncing?

And then I end up writing all these stupid little shell scripts—self-defense stuff. I know I could do this by clicking on 30,000 web pages and doing it by hand, but why don't I write this script—little time-saver things. Which barely feels like programming to me. I know to people who aren't programmers, that seems like a black art.

I really enjoyed doing the Mac port of the XScreenSaver framework. That was actually writing a lot of new code that required thinking about APIs and the structure of the thing.

Seibel: Was that your APIs—how you were structuring your code?

Zawinski: Both. Both figuring out the existing APIs and figuring out the best way to build a layer between the X11 world and the Mac world. How should I structure that? Which of the Mac APIs is most appropriate? It was the first time in a long time that I'd done something like that and it was just like, "Wow, this is kind of fun. I think I might be kind of good at this."

It had been forever because I got completely burned out on the software industry. That part of it I just couldn't take anymore—the politics of it both in the corporate world and in the free-software world. I'd just had too much. I wanted to do something that didn't involve arguing online about trivia. Or having my product destroyed by bureaucratic decisions that I had no input in.

Seibel: Are you ever tempted to go back and hack on Mozilla?

Zawinski: Nah. I just don't want to be arguing with people and having pissing matches in Bugzilla anymore. That's not fun. That kind of thing is necessary to build big products. If it's something that requires more than one person working on it, which obviously Mozilla does, that's the way you have to do it. But I don't look forward to that kind of fight anymore. That's been beaten out of me by too many years of it. And the other alternative, as a programmer, is go work for someone else. And I don't have to do that, so I can't. My first bad day I'd just leave. And were I to start my own company I couldn't be a programmer—I'd have to run the company.

Seibel: Other than having two million people using your software, what about programming do you enjoy?

Zawinski: It's a hard question. The problem-solving aspect of it, I guess. It's not quite like it's a puzzle—I don't really play many puzzle-type games. Just figuring out how to get from point A to point B—how to make the machine do what you want. That's the basic element that the satisfaction of programming comes from.

Seibel: Do you find code beautiful? Is there an aesthetic beyond maintainability?

Zawinski: Yeah, definitely. Anything expressed just right, whether it's being really concise or just capturing it—like anything, a really well-put-together sentence or a little doodle, a caricature that looks just like someone but only used four lines, that kind of thing—it's the same sort of thing.

Seibel: Do you find that programming and writing are similar intellectual exercises?

Zawinski: In some ways, yeah. Programming is obviously much more rigid. But as far as the overall ability to express a thought, they're very similar. Not rambling, having an idea in your head of what you're trying to say, and then being concise about it. I think that kind of thinking is the overlap between programming and writing prose.

It feels like they use similar parts of my brain, but it's hard to express exactly what it is. A lot of times I'll read things that just look like bad code. Like most contracts. The really rigid style they use—it's so repetitive. I look at that and I'm like, why can't you break this out into a subroutine—which we call paragraphs. And the way they usually begin with definitions, like, so and so, referred to as blah blah blah.

Seibel: Lets talk a little bit about the nitty-gritty of programming. How do you design your code? How do you structure code? Maybe take your recent work on the OS X XScreenSaver as an example.

Zawinski: Well, first I messed around and made little demo programs that never ended up being used again. Just to figure out here's how you put a window on the screen, and so on. Since I'm implementing X11, the first thing to do is pick one of the screen savers and make the list of all the X11 calls it makes.

Then I create stubs for each of those and then I slowly start filling them in, figuring out how am I going to implement this one, how am I going to implement this one.

At another level, on the Mac side of things, there's the start-up code. How is the window getting on the screen? And at some point that's going to call out to the X code. One of the trickier parts of that was really figuring out how to set up the build system to make that work in any kind of sane way. So a bunch of experimentation. Moving things around. At some point, maybe I'd had this piece of code on top and this piece of code being called by it. And then maybe those need to be turned inside out. So there's a lot of cut-and-pasting until I kind of wrapped my head around a flow of control that seemed sensible. Then I went in and cleaned things up and put things in more appropriate files so this piece of code is together with this piece of code.

That was sort of the broad strokes, building the infrastructure. After that it was just a matter of moving on to the next screen saver; this one uses these three functions that the previous one hadn't used before, so I've got to implement those. And each of those tasks was fairly straightforward. There were some that ended up being really tricky because the X11 API has a ton of options for putting text on the screen and moving rectangles around. So I kept having to make that piece of code hairier and hairier. But most of them were fairly straightforward.

Seibel: So for each of these X11 calls you're writing an implementation. Did you ever find that you were accumulating lots of bits of very similar code?

Zawinski: Oh, yeah, definitely. Usually by the second or third time you've cut and pasted that piece of code it's like, alright, time to stop cutting and pasting and put it in a subroutine.

Seibel: If you were doing something on the scale of writing a mail reader again, you mentioned starting with a few paragraphs of text and a list of features. Is that the finest granularity that you would get to before you would just start writing code?

Zawinski: Yeah. Maybe there'd be a vague description of the division between library and front end. But probably not. If I was working alone I wouldn't bother with that because that part is just kind of obvious to me. And then the first thing I would do with something like that is either start at the top or at the bottom. So start with either, put a window on the screen that has some buttons on it, and then dig down and start building the stuff that those buttons do. Or you can start at the other side and start writing the thing that parses mailboxes and that saves mailboxes. Either way. or both and meet in the middle.

I find that getting something on the screen as soon as possible really helps focus the problem for me. It helps me decide what to work on next. Because if you're just looking at that big to-do list it's like, eh, I don't know which one I should do—does it matter which one I do? But if there's something you can actually look at, even if it's just the debug output of your mailbox parser, it's like, OK, there! That's something; what's the next direction this needs to go in? OK, instead of just displaying a tree structure, now maybe I should be emitting HTML or something along those lines. Or parsing the headers in a more detailed way. You just look for the next thing to build on from there.

Seibel: Do you refactor to keep the internal structure of the code coherent? Or do you just have a very good sense at the beginning how it's all going to fit together?

Zawinski: I usually have a pretty good sense of that. I don't remember too many occasions where I thought, "Oh, I did this whole thing inside out. I'm going to have to move everything around." That does happen sometimes.

When I'm just writing the first version of the program, I tend to put everything in one file. And then I start seeing structure in that file. Like there's this block of things that are pretty similar. That's a thousand lines now, so why don't I move that into another file. And the API sort of builds up organically that way. The design process is definitely an ongoing thing; you never know what the design is until the program is done. So I prefer to get my feet wet as early as possible; get something on the screen so I can look at it sideways.

Also, once you start writing the code, you're gonna realize, "No, that was a dumb idea. Why did I think that this module was going to be really easy when actually it's way more complicated than I thought?"

Which is something you're not going to clue into until you actually start writing code and you feel it getting away from you.

Seibel: What are the signs that something is getting away from you?

Zawinski: When you go into something and you have in your head, "Oh, this is going to take me half a day and it's gonna be a chunk of code this size," and then you start doing it and you get that sinking feeling like, "Oh, right, I need this other piece too; well, I'd better go off and do that. Oh, and that's kind of a big problem."

Seibel: I've noticed that one thing that separates good programmers from bad programmers is that good programmers are more facile at jumping between layers of abstraction—they can keep the layers distinct while making changes and choose the right layer to make changes in.

Zawinski: There's definitely got to be some style in where you decide to put things—it can matter a lot down the line. Being able to just hack it out somewhere up near the user versus making a maybe larger change that may have repercussions down at the bottom—either of those can be the right answer and it is tricky to know which is which. This change I need to make, is it really one little special case or are there eventually going to be 12 of these?

I think one of the most important things, for me anyway, when building something from the ground up like that is, as quickly as possible, getting the program to a state that you, the programmer, can use it. Even a little bit. Because that tells you where to go next in a really visceral way. Once the thing's on the screen and you've got the one button hooked up that does one thing, now you kind of know, which button is next. Obviously that's a GUI-centric description of what I'm talking about.

Seibel: We talked a bit about some of the really hideous bugs you had to track down like that thing with GDB. But let's talk a little bit more about debugging. For starters, what's your preferred debugging tool? Print statements? Symbolic debuggers? Formal proofs of correctness?

Zawinski: That's changed over the years a lot. When I was using the Lisp machines it was all about running the program and stopping it and exploring the data—there was an inspector tool that let you browse through memory and I changed it so basically the Lisp listener became an inspector. So anytime time it printed out an object there was a context menu on it so you could click on this thing here and have that value returned. Just to make it easier to follow around chains of objects and that sort of thing. So early on that was how I thought about things. Getting down in the middle of the code and chasing it around and experimenting.

Then when I started writing C and using GDB inside of Emacs I kind of tried to keep up that same way of doing things. That was the model we built Energize around. And that just never seemed like it worked very well. And as time went by I gradually stopped even trying to use tools like that and just stick in print statements and run the thing again. Repeat until done. Especially when you get to more and more primitive environments like JavaScript and Perl and stuff like that, it's the only choice you have—there aren't any debuggers.

People these days seem confused about the notion of what a debugger is. "Oh, why would you need that? What does it do—put print statements in for you? I don't understand. What are these strange words you use?" Mostly these days it's print statements.

Seibel: How much of that was due to the differences between Lisp and C, as opposed to the tools—one difference is that in Lisp you can test small parts—you can call a small function you're not sure is working right and then put a break in the middle of it and then inspect what's going on. Whereas C it's like, run the whole program in all of its complex glory and put a break point somewhere.

Zawinski: Lisp-like languages lend themselves more to that than C. Perl and Python and languages like that have a little more of the Lisp nature in that way but I still don't see people doing it that way very much.

Seibel: But GDB does give you the ability to inspect stuff. What about it makes it not usable for you?

Zawinski: I always found it unpleasant. Part of it is just intrinsic to being C. Poking around in an array and now I'm looking at a bunch of numbers and now I have to go in there and cast the thing to whatever it really is. It just never managed that right, the way a better language would.

Seibel: Whereas in Lisp, if you're looking at a Lisp array, they'll just be printed as those things because it knows what they are.

Zawinski: Exactly. It always just seemed in GDB like bouncing up and down, the stack things would just get messed up. You'd go up the stack and things have changed out from under you and often that's because GDB is malfunctioning in some way. Or, oh well, it was expecting this register to be here and you're in a different stack frame, so that doesn't count anymore.

It just always felt like I couldn't really trust what the debugger was actually telling me. It would print something and, look, there's a number. Is that true or not? I don't know. And a lot of times you'd end up with no debug info. So you're in a stack frame and it looks like it has no arguments and then I'd spend ten minutes trying to remember the register that argument zero goes in is. Then give up, relink and put in a print statement.

It seemed like as time went by the debugging facilities just kept getting worse and worse. But on the other hand now people are finally realizing that manual memory allocation is not the way to go; it kind of doesn't matter as much any more because the sorts of really complicated bugs where you'd have to dig deep into data structures don't really happen as often because those, often, in C anyway, were memory-corruption issues.

Seibel: Do you use assertions or other more or less formal ways of documenting or actually checking invariants?

Zawinski: We went back and forth about what to do about assertions in the Netscape code base. Obviously putting in assert statements is always a good idea for debugging and like you said, for documentation purposes. It expressed the intent. We did that a lot.

But then the question is, well, what happens when the assertion fails and you're in production code; what do you do? And we sort of decided that what you do is return zero and hope it keeps going. Because having the browser go down is really bad—it's worse than returning to the idle loop and maybe having leaked a bunch of memory or something. That's going to upset people less than the alternative.

A lot of programmers have the instinct of, "You've got to present the error message!" No you don't. No one cares about that. That sort of stuff is a lot easier to manage in languages like Java that actually have an exception system. Where, at the top loop of your idle state, you just catch everything and you're done. No need to bother the user with telling them that some value was zero.

Seibel: Did you ever just step through a program—either to debug it or, as some people recommend, to just step through it once you've written it as a way of checking it?

Zawinski: No, not really. I only really do stepping when I'm debugging something. I guess sometimes to make sure I wrote it right. But not that often.

Seibel: So how do you go about debugging?

Zawinski: I just eyeball the code first. Read through it until I think, well, this can't happen because that's going on right there. And then I put in something to try and resolve that contradiction. Or if I read it and it looks fine then I'll stop in the middle or something and see where it is. It depends. It's hard to generalize about that.

Seibel: As far as the assertions—how formally do you think? Some people just use ad hoc assertions—here's something that I think should be true here. And some people think very formally—functions have preconditions and postconditions and there are global invariants. Where are you on that scale?

Zawinski: I definitely don't think about things in a mathematically provable way. I'm definitely more ad hoc than that. You know, it's always helpful when you've got inputs to a function to at least have an idea in your head what their bounds are. Can this be an empty string? That sort of thing.

Seibel: Related to debugging, there's testing. At Netscape, did you guys have a separate QA group or did you guys test everything yourselves?

Zawinski: We did both. We were all running it all the time, which is always your best front-line QA. Then we had a QA group and they had formal tests they went through. And every time there was a new release they'd go down the list and try this thing. Go to this page, click on this. You should see this. Or you shouldn't see this.

Seibel: What about developer-level tests like unit tests?

Zawinski: Nah. We never did any of that. I did occasionally for some things. The date parser for mail headers had a gigantic set of test cases. Back then, at least, no one really paid a whole lot of attention to the standards. So you got all kinds of crap in the headers. And whatever you're throwing at us, people are going to be annoyed if their mail sorts wrong. So I collected a whole bunch of examples online and just made stuff up and had this giant list of crappily formatted dates and the number I thought that should turn into. And every time I'd change the code I'd run through the tests and some of them would flip. Well, do I agree with that or not?

Seibel: Did that kind of thing get folded into any kind of automated testing?

Zawinski: No, when I was writing unit tests like that for my code they would basically only run when I ran them. We did a little bit of that later with Grendel, the Java rewrite, because it was just so much easier to write a unit test when you write a new class.

Seibel: In retrospect, do you think you suffered at all because of that? Would development have been easier or faster if you guys had been more disciplined about testing?

Zawinski: I don't think so. I think it would have just slowed us down. There's a lot to be said for just getting it right the first time. In the early days we were so focused on speed. We had to ship the thing even if it wasn't perfect. We can ship it later and it would be higher quality but someone else might have eaten our lunch by then.

There's bound to be stuff where this would have gone faster if we'd had unit tests or smaller modules or whatever. That all sounds great in principle. Given a leisurely development pace, that's certainly the way to go. But when you're looking at, "We've got to go from zero to done in six weeks," well, I can't do that unless I cut something out. And what I'm going to cut out is the stuff that's not absolutely critical. And unit tests are not critical. If there's no unit test the customer isn't going to complain about that. That's an upstream issue.

I hope I don't sound like I'm saying, "Testing is for chumps." It's not. It's a matter of priorities. Are you trying to write good software or are you trying to be done by next week? You can't do both. One of the jokes we made at Netscape a lot was, "We're absolutely 100 percent committed to quality. We're going to ship the highest-quality product we can on March 31st."

Seibel: That leads to another topic, maintaining software. How do you tackle understanding a piece of code that you didn't write?

Zawinski: I just dive in and start reading the code.

Seibel: So where do you start? Do you start at page one and read linearly?

Zawinski: Sometimes. The more common thing is learning how to use some new library or toolkit. If you're lucky there's some documentation. There's an API. So you figure out the piece of it you might be interested in using. Or work out how that was implemented. Thread your way through. Or with something like Emacs, maybe start at the bottom. What are cons cells made of? How's that look? And then skip around from there. Sometimes starting with the build system can give you an idea how things fit together. I always find that a good way to sort of immerse yourself in a piece of code is pick a task you want to accomplish and then try and do it.

With something like Emacs you might do that by taking an existing module and gutting it. OK, now I've got this piece of code. Rip out the part that actually does anything and now I've got the boilerplate. OK, now I know what a component of this system looks like and I can start putting my stuff back in. Sort of stripping it down to the frame.

Seibel: In Emacs you ended up rewriting the byte-code compiler and bits of the byte-code VM. And we've talked about how it's more fun to rewrite stuff than to fix it, but it's not always a good idea. I wonder how do you draw that line? Do you think that you chose to rewrite the whole compiler because it was really easier than fixing it more locally? Or was it just, "Hey! It'd be fun to write a compiler."

Zawinski: It sort of just turned into a rewrite. It started with me just fixing it and trying to add optimizations to it. And then eventually there wasn't any of the original left. I ended up using the same APIs until then they were gone. I think the byte-code compiler worked out fine. Partly because that was such an isolated module. There's only one entry point: compile and save.

There was definitely a lot of stuff that I put into Lucid Emacs that was more gratuitous than that. Really, a lot of the stuff I did was motivated by wanting it to be more like Lisp machines. Wanting it to be more like the Emacs I was familiar with. Which really was the Lisp environment I was familiar with. So I put in a lot of stuff to try to make Emacs be a less half-assed Lisp in a lot of ways: there should be event objects instead of a list with a number in it. Having an event object be a list with a number in it—that's just tasteless. It's icky. And in retrospect, those changes were some of the biggest problems. Those kind of changes caused compatibility problems with third-party libraries.

Seibel: Of course you didn't know there were going to be two Emacs at that point.

Zawinski: Sure. But even without that, even if there had only been one Emacs, there were still two Emacs—there was Emacs 18 and Emacs 19. There was still going to be a compatibility problem. In hindsight those were changes that if I'd realized what an impact it was going to make, I probably would have done that differently. Or spent a lot more time on making the old way work as well. That kind of thing.

Seibel: Earlier you said something about writing code in order to make it easier to read, which ties into maintenance. What are the characteristics that make code easier to read?

Zawinski: Well, comments obviously. Writing down what the assumptions are and what this does. If it's building up a data structure, describing the layout of it. A lot of times I find that pretty helpful. Especially in writing Perl code when it's like, uh, well, it's a hash table and values are bunch of references to lists, because the data structures in Perl are just nuts. Do I need a right arrow here to get to this? I find examples like that to be helpful.

I always wish people would comment more, though the thing that makes me cringe is when the comment is the name of the function rephrased. Function's called push_stack and the comment says, "This pushes to the stack." Thank you.

You've got to say in the comment something that's not there already. What's it for? Either a higher-level or a lower-level description, depending on what's most important. Sometimes the most important thing is, what is this for? Why would I use it? And sometimes the most important thing is, what's the range of inputs that this expects?

Long variable names. I'm not a fan of Hungarian notation, but I think using actual English words to describe things, except for loop iterators, where it's obvious. Just as much verbosity as possible, I guess.

Seibel: What about organization—ultimately there's some linear organization but programs are not really linear. Do you organize your code top-down or bottom-up?

Zawinski: I usually end up putting the leaf nodes up at the top of the file—try to keep it basically structured that way. And then usually up at the top, document the API. What are the top-level entry points of this file, this module, whatever? With an object-y language, that's done by the language for you. With C you've got to be a little more explicit about that. In C I do tend to try to have a .h file for every .c file that has all the externs for it. And anything that's not exported in the .h file is static. And then I'll go back and say, "Wait, I need to call that," and I change it. But you're doing that explicitly rather than just by accident.

Seibel: You put the leaves first in the file, but is that how you write? Do you build up from leaves?

Zawinski: Not always. Sometimes I start at the top and sometimes I start at the bottom. It depends. One way is, I know I'm going to need these building blocks and I'll put those together first. Or another way of thinking about it is, you've sort of got an outline of it in your head and you dig down. I do it both ways.

Seibel: So suppose for the sake of argument that you were going to come out of retirement and build a development team. How would you organize it?

Zawinski: Well, I think you want to arrange for there to be no more than three or four people working really closely together on a day-to-day basis. Then that can scale up a lot. Say you've got a project where you can divide it up into twenty-five really distinct modules. Well, you can have twenty-five tiny teams—maybe that's a little much. Say ten. And as long as they can coordinate with each other, I don't think there's a whole lot of limit to how big you can scale that. Eventually it just starts looking like multiple projects instead of like one project.

Seibel: So you've got multiple teams of up to four people. How do you coordinate the teams? Do you have one grand architect who's managing the dependencies and mediating between those teams?

Zawinski: Well, there's got to be agreement about what the interface between modules is. For that very modular approach to work at all, the interface between modules has to be clear and simple. Which, hopefully, means it won't take too much screaming for everyone to agree on it and it won't be too difficult to follow the module contract. I guess what I'm getting at is the best way to make interaction between modules be easy is to just make it be really simple. Make there be fewer ways for that to go wrong.

And what lines you divide on depends entirely on a project. With some kind of web app you've probably got the UI and you've got your database and the part that runs on the server and the part that runs on the machine behind the server. And if it's a desktop application it's similar division of labor. There's file formats and GUI and basic command structure.

Seibel: How do you recognize talent?

Zawinski: That I don't know. I've never really been the person who had to hire people. And when I've been involved in interviews I've always just felt like I had no idea. I can tell from the interview whether I'd get along with this person, but I can't tell whether they're any good or not just by talking to them. I always found that difficult.

Seibel: How about if they're bad? Are there reliable clues then?

Zawinski: Sometimes. Normally I would think that someone who is a big fan of C++ templates—keep me away from that guy. But that might just be a snap judgment on my part. Maybe in the context they've used them, they actually work fine. Certainly with the folks I've worked with, ability to argue their point was important because we all ended up being a pretty argumentative bunch. With that environment, that helped a lot. That certainly doesn't have anything to do with programming ability. That's just interpersonal-dynamics stuff.

Seibel: And on a different team, that would actually be detrimental.

Zawinski: Yeah, absolutely.

Seibel: It sounds like at Netscape you guys divided things up so people owned different parts of the software. Some people think that's really important. Other folks say it's better for a team to collectively own all the code. Do you have an opinion on that?

Zawinski: I've done it both ways. They both have their merits. The idea that everyone should own all the code, I don't think is really practical because there's going to be too much of it. People are going to have to specialize; you need an expert sometimes. It's just always going to work out that way. There's always going to be the code you're familiar with because you happened to write more of that module than some other guy did. Or there's just going to be parts that resonate with you more. It's certainly good for other people to have their hands in it, if only because you're not going to be maintaining it yourself forever. It's going to have to be handed off to someone else for one reason or another. And for that knowledge to be spread around is good. But it's also good to have someone to blame. If everybody is responsible for it then there's no one to put their foot down.

Seibel: Have you ever been a manager?

Zawinski: Not really. When I was doing the Emacs stuff at Lucid, there would be a lot of modules that were included in Lucid Emacs that were written by other people. Those people didn't really work for me but it was a little bit like management. And a lot of those people were definitely less experienced and the way that worked out well was they were doing their favorite thing and I was basically giving them feedback: "Well, I want to include this but first I need this, this, and this from it."

Seibel: And did you give them a free rein? You tell them you want X, Y, and Z and then they get to figure out how to do it?

Zawinski: Yeah. If I'm trying to decide whether to include this module in the thing that I'm going to ship, I'm going to have requirements about it. Does the damn thing work is really the bottom line there. So I would give them advice on, "I think you're going to have better luck if you try it this rather than this way." But I wanted it to work and I wanted to not have to be the one to write it. If they wanted to go do it in some crazy way but it worked, that was OK because that gave me point two: I didn't have to write it. But mostly the feedback I was giving them was just, does it work and does it make sense.

Seibel: On the flip side, when you were the less-experienced programmer, what did your mentors do that was helpful?

Zawinski: I guess the most important thing is they'd recognize when it was time to level up. When I went to work for Fahlman I was given some silly little busy work. And eventually got given tasks that were a little more significant—not that they were significant at all really.

Seibel: I think you talked about Skef, who just hovered and said, "Wrong!" Was that balanced, perhaps, by someone else who was a little more nurturing?

Zawinski: Well, he wasn't completely a cave man. He would actually tell me things, too. I know I ended up doing a lot of reading of code and asking questions. I think one thing that's really important is to not be afraid of your ignorance. If you don't understand how something works, ask someone who does. A lot of people are skittish about that. And that doesn't help anybody. Not knowing something doesn't mean you're dumb—it just means you don't know it yet.

Seibel: Did you read code mostly because it was something you were working on, or was it just something you wanted to know how it worked?

Zawinski: Yeah. Just poking around—"I wonder how that works." The impulse to take things apart is a big part of what gets people into this line of work.

Seibel: Were you actually one of those kids who took toasters apart?

Zawinski: Yeah. I made a telephone and learned how to dial with a telegraph tapper that I made out of a tin can. When I was little I had these old books I got at a garage sale or something, like *Boy's Own Science Book* from the '30s, and I remember getting a really big kick out of those. That was really hacker culture in the '20s and '30s where they're showing how to wire up a telegraph between your room and the barn and making Leyden jars.

Seibel: That brings me to another of my standard questions: do you, as a programmer, think of yourself as a scientist or an engineer or an artist or a craftsman or something else?

Zawinski: Well, definitely not a scientist or engineer because those have very formal connotations. I don't do a lot of math; I don't draw blueprints; I don't prove things. I guess somewhere between craftsman and artist, depending on what the project is. I write a lot of screen savers—that's not craftsman; that's making pretty pictures. Somewhere in that area.

Seibel: Do you feel like you taught yourself computer science or did you just learn to program?

Zawinski: Well, I certainly picked up a bunch of computer science over the years. But learning to program was the goal. Making the machine do something was the goal and the computer-science side of it was a means to an end.

Seibel: Did you ever feel that as a lack—did you ever wish you had been exposed to things in a more systematic way?

Zawinski: There were definitely times, especially at Lucid, where it'd be obvious that there's this whole big black hole that these guys are talking about that I just completely missed because I never needed to know it. And I'd then I'd pick up the terminology and have a basic idea what they're talking about and maybe do a little bit of reading on it if it was something I needed to know. So there were definitely times, especially early on, where I felt like, "Oh my god, I don't know anything." It would just be embarrassing—but that was just being insecure. Being the young kid around all these people with PhDs—"Aaah, I don't know anything! I'm an idiot! How did I bluff my way into this?"

Though my life certainly would have turned out very differently if I had spent a lot more time in school—it was a moment in time when I got to do the things I did.

Seibel: Did you ever feel the opposite, where you felt like the computer scientists around you just didn't understand actual programming as well as you did?

Zawinski: I felt like that a lot, but really that's not so much about thinking, "Wow, you guys have been barking up the wrong tree." as, "Wow, we're just not interested in the same things." I don't want to be a mathematician but I'm not going to criticize someone who is a mathematician.

It's weird that people often confuse those two pursuits. People who are into very theoretical computer science are thought of in this same way as people who are shipping desktop applications. And they don't really have a lot to do with each other.

Seibel: You're largely self-taught. Do you have any advice for self-taught programmers?

Zawinski: That's a really hard question because the world's so different now. I always feel weird talking about, "Here's what I did." I don't know if that was the right way to do it. But people always hear it as, "Be like me."

I stumbled into this—it all just sort of happened. I made some decisions and they led to others and here we are.

Every now and then I get an email from someone that's basically, "I want to be a programmer; what do I do?" Or, "Should I go to college or not?" How can I answer that? I would have had very strong opinions about this if you asked me in 1986. But someone today couldn't take the same path that I took because that path doesn't even exist anymore.

Ten years ago I would have said absolutely the first thing you have to do is learn assembly language. You have to learn how the machine actually works. Does that matter any more? I don't even know. Maybe it does. But possibly not. If the way software is going to be ten years from now is all web applications or a piece of distributed code in some rented computing cluster that's moving around between a dozen different Google servers and spawning other copies of itself and then merging back together once it's got results, does anyone need to know assembly language any more? Is that so abstracted away that it doesn't matter? I don't know.

I was kind of freaked out when I realized that there are people graduating with CS degrees who'd never written C. They started in Java and they stayed there. That just seemed bizarre and wrong. But I don't know. Maybe it's not wrong. Maybe that's the caveman thoughts: "Back in my day, we programmed with a nine-volt battery and a steady hand!"

Seibel: What about books? Are there particular computer-science or programming books that everyone should read?

Zawinski: I actually haven't read very many of those. The one I always recommend is *Structure and Interpretation of Computer Programs*, which a lot of people are afraid of because it's Lispy, but I think does a really good job of teaching programming without teaching a language. I think a lot of introductory-level stuff focuses on syntax and I definitely saw that in the classes I had in high school and in the intro classes at Carnegie-Mellon during my brief time there.

This is not teaching people to program; this is teaching people where the semicolon goes. That seems like the kind of thing that's going to scare people away from it more than anything, because that's not the interesting part. Not even to someone who knows what they're doing.

There was another book—what was it called?—about debugging, written by someone from Microsoft. It was about how to use asserts effectively. I remember thinking that was a really good book, not because I learned anything from it, but because it was the book you wish your idiot coworker had read.

Then there was another book that everybody thought was the greatest thing ever in that same period—*Design Patterns*—which I just thought was crap. It was just like, programming via cut and paste. Rather than thinking through your task you looked through the recipe book and found something that maybe, kinda, sorta felt like it, and then just aped it. That's not programming; that's a coloring book. But a lot of people seemed to love it. Then in meetings they'd be tossing around all this terminology they got out of that book. Like, the inverse, reverse, double-back-flip pattern—whatever. Oh, you mean a loop? OK.

Seibel: Is there a key skill programmers must have?

Zawinski: Well, curiosity—taking things apart. Wanting to know what's going on under the hood. I think that's really the basis of it. Without that I don't think you get very far. That's your primary way of acquiring knowledge. Taking something apart and looking at it is how you learn to build your own. At least for me. I've read very few books about computers. My experience has been digging through source code or reference manuals. I've got a goal and, alright, to do this I need to know what this thing does and what this thing does. And I'll just sort of random-walk through that until I find where I'm going.

Seibel: Have you read Knuth's, *The Art of Computer Programming?*

Zawinski: I haven't. And that's one of those things where, I really probably should have. But I never did.

Seibel: It's tough going—you need a lot of math to really grok it.

Zawinski: And I'm not a math person at all.

Seibel: That's interesting. Lots of programmers come out of mathematics and lots of computer-science theory is very mathematical. So you're an existence proof that it's not absolutely necessary. How much math or mathy kind of thinking is necessary to be a good programmer?

Zawinski: Well, it depends on where you draw the line as to what's mathy and what's not. Is being good at pattern matching mathy? Having an understanding of orders of magnitude and combinatorics is important at a gut level. But I'm sure I would completely flunk if I had to take a basic intro quiz on that kind of stuff. It's been so long since I've had to do anything formal like that.

Really the only math classes I had were in high school. I had algebra. A little bit of calculus. I wasn't terribly good at it. I got through it but it didn't really come naturally to me. I had a physics class in high school where we were doing mechanics and doing labs dragging blocks across sandpaper and stuff like that. I did terribly in that class and felt like an idiot because I actually enjoyed the class. I did the labs really well—the procedure was spot on—and then I just couldn't do the math.

I'd get an answer that I knew was three orders of magnitude off. I'd show my work—I don't know what I did wrong. I'd get half credit since the data was collected properly and I cleaned up afterwards. So math was never really my forte.

But I wouldn't go so far as to say you don't need that to be a programmer. There's obviously different kinds of programming. Without people who are not like me none of this would exist. But I've always seen much more in common with writing prose than math. It feels like you're writing a story and you're trying to express a concept to a very dumb person—the computer—who has a limited vocabulary. You've got this concept you want to express and limited tools to express it with. What words do you use and what does your introductory and summary statement look like? That sort of thing.

The issue of taste really fits in there. You can have a piece of text describing something that describes it correctly or it can describe it well, with some flair. And the same thing's true of programs. It can get the job done or it can also make sense, be put together well.

Seibel: And why does that matter? Is that just for the satisfaction of it or is tasteful code also better in some practical way?

Zawinski: To a large degree, tasteful and maintainable are similar. Or very closely related. One of the things that makes a piece of writing tasteful is if it's structured in a way that's easy to grasp. Are the facts loaded up at the front or are they scattered around? If you're referring back—if you're flipping through a book, can you figure out where in the book is the thing you kind of remember? "This was somewhere near the middle because that's where he talked about this thing." Or is it just scattered all through. And that's the same sort of thing that goes on with programming a lot.

Seibel: Do you think the kind of people who can be successful at programming has changed?

Zawinski: Certainly these days it's impossible to just write a program from scratch that doesn't have any dependencies. The explosion of toolkits and libraries and frameworks and that sort of thing—even the most basic piece of software needs those these days. It's just exploded. These days, everything's got to be a web app. And that's just a whole different way of going about it.

So, if anything, that makes the part of the skill set that is being able to dive into someone else's code and figure out how to make use of it even more important. "I don't understand this, so I'm going to write my own" worked better in the past. Whether it was ever a good idea or not, you could do it. It's much harder to get away with that now.

Seibel: I wonder if the inclination to take things apart and understand everything also needs to be a little more tempered these days. If you try to take apart every piece of code you work with, it'll never end—these days you've got to have a little capacity for saying, "I sort of understand how this works and I'm going to let it go at that until it becomes urgent that I understand it better."

Zawinski: Yeah. My first instinct, because things work that way, is you're breeding a generation of programmers who don't understand anything about efficiency or what's actually being allocated. When they realize, "Oh, my program's getting gigantic," what are they going to do? They're not going to know where to start. That's my first instinct because I'm a caveman. Really that probably doesn't even matter because you'll just throw more memory at it and it'll be fine.

Seibel: Or perhaps people will actually learn a more sophisticated view of what all those things mean. Like, maybe it doesn't really matter whether we allocated six bytes or four bytes here—what matters is whether we've sized this thing so it fits in one node of the cluster versus having to spill over onto a second node.

Zawinski: Right, exactly. I think programming has definitely changed in that sense. The things you had to focus on before were different. Before you would focus on counting bytes, and "How big are my objects? Maybe I should do something different here because that array header is really going to add up." Things like that. No one is ever going to care about that stuff again. Tricks like XORing your forward and back pointers into the same word are voodoo—why would anyone do that; it's crazy. But there's this whole different set of skills now that were always around but come more to the front. People who can dig into an API and figure out which parts you need and which parts you don't, is, I think, one of those important things now.

Seibel: If you were 13 today, would you be drawn to programming the way programming is today?

Zawinski: So hard to say. I don't know any 13-year-olds. I don't know what the world looks like. Things are harder to take apart now. There's not going to be some 10-year-old who pops open his cell phone and figures out how the speaker works like I did with a phone when I was a little kid. There are no user-serviceable parts anymore.

I feel like that kind of tinkering, taking the back of the tape deck off and seeing how the gears fit together, that sort of exploration is what led to this for me. Aside from things like LEGO Mindstorms, I don't think there's a lot of opportunity for people to follow that path these days. But maybe I'm wrong—like I said, I don't know any 13-year-olds. I don't know what the toys are like. There's a lot of video games; there's a lot of things with remote controls. I haven't seen any really good construction kinds of toys. Which seems sad.

Seibel: On the flip side, programming itself is much more accessible. You don't have to master all the intricacies of assembly programming right off the bat just to making a computer do something neat.

Zawinski: Yeah. I imagine that today's kids who are getting into programming start off building some web app or writing a Facebook plugin or something. Brad Fitzpatrick, who wrote LiveJournal, is a friend of mine. When he wrote LiveJournal he was goofing around and wrote this Perl script where he and his friends could say, "I'm going to get lunch." The way he started out was he wrote a little Perl script and put it on a web server. Probably things will go more in that direction.

CHAPTER

2

Brad Fitzpatrick

Brad Fitzpatrick is the youngest person I interviewed and the only one who has never lived in a world without the Internet or personal computers. Born in 1980, he got an early start as a programmer, learning to program at age five on a home-built Apple II clone. By his teenage years the Internet revolution was in full swing and he was deep into it, building his first commercial web site while still in high school and starting work on the popular community site LiveJournal the summer before he went to college.

Keeping up with LiveJournal's ever-growing popularity forced Fitzpatrick to learn the hard way about building scalable web sites and along the way he and the programmers at the company he founded, Danga Interactive, ended up building several pieces of open source software, including memcached, Perlbal, and MogileFS, which are now used on the servers of many of the world's busiest web sites.

Fitzpatrick is a prototypical—if exceptionally accomplished—turn-of-the-century web programmer: his primary programming languages have been Perl and C, though he also works in Java, C++, Python, JavaScript, and C# as needed. And almost all the programming he does is somehow network-related, whether it's building better back-end infrastructure for web sites, designing protocols and software to improve the way blog-reading software knows when blogs have been updated, or programming his cell phone to automatically open his garage door when he rides up on his motorcycle.

We talked about learning to program at the same age as he was reading Clifford the Big Red Dog, why he was glad he stayed in college while running LiveJournal, and how he learned not to be afraid of reading other people's code.

Seibel: How did you become a programmer?

Fitzpatrick: My dad was working at Mostek. They made memory and he was into computers. He built an Apple II from spare parts, pretty much. He and my mom would sit around the TV soldering it all together. It took them months, just soldering it. Then he was able to get ROMs from work that they weren't going to sell because they had a bit, or multiple bits, stuck high or stuck low. Somehow they got the Apple II ROM and they just kept burning it onto these dead chips until they got one that worked, where the stuck bits just happened to be right. Eventually he and a bunch of his coworkers managed to make homemade Apple IIs. I was playing on that from age two or so and watching him program.

Seibel: Was he a programmer or a hardware guy?

Fitzpatrick: He was an electrical engineer; he dabbled in programming. He taught me to program when I was five and jokes that I passed him up around six or seven. My mom says I was reading the Apple II programmers' manual from the library at the same time as *Clifford the Big Red Dog*. Instead of "variables," I would say, "valuables." Some of my first memories are programming with my dad. Like he pulled me into the kitchen and he was writing down a program on paper. He asked, "What do you think it does?" I remember it was like, "`10 PRINT HELLO, 20 GOTO 10`."

Seibel: So you started with BASIC?

Fitzpatrick: Yeah, that was BASIC. I couldn't do stuff with the mouse, or stuff with higher graphics modes and colors, until a friend of our family introduced me to C and gave me Turbo C. This was maybe when I was eight or ten. My dad moved to Intel in '84 and we moved to Portland. He helped design the 386 and 486. He's still at Intel. We always had new, fun computers.

Seibel: Did you get into assembly programming at all?

Fitzpatrick: I did assembly a little on calculators. Like Z80 on the TI calculators, but that was about it.

Seibel: Do you remember what it was that drew you to programming?

Fitzpatrick: I don't know. It was just always fun. My mom had to cut me off and give me computer coupons to make me go outside and play with friends. My friends would come over: "Brad's on the computer again. He's so boring." My mom's like, "Go outside and play."

Seibel: Do you remember the first interesting program that you wrote?

Fitzpatrick: We had this Epson printer and it came with big, thick manuals with a programmers' reference at the end. So I wrote something—this was back on an Apple—where I could draw something in the high graphics mode, and then, once my program finished drawing whatever it was drawing—lines or patterns or something—I'd hit control C and be typing in the background, in a frame buffer that's not showing, and load my other program, which read the screen off and printed it.

Before that I remember writing something that every time I hit a key, it moved the head and I had wired backspace up to go backwards so as I typed it felt like a typewriter.

This was one of my first programs—it was something like K equals grab the next char. Then I said if K equals "a", print "a"; if K is "b", print "b". I pretty much did every letter, number, and some punctuation. Then at one point I was like, "Wait, I could just say, 'Print the variable!'" and I replaced 40 lines of code with one. I was like, "Holy shit, that was awesome!" That was some major abstraction for a six-year-old.

Those are the notable early ones. Then in middle school I would make games and I would make the graphics editors and the level editors for my friends, and my friends would make the graphics into levels, and then we would sell it to our classmates. I remember having to make games that detected EGA versus VGA. If one of 'em failed on VGA, it would fault back to EGA and use a different set of tiles that fit on the screen, so we'd have to have two sets of graphics for everything. People from school would buy it for like five bucks and they would go to install it and it wouldn't work, and their parents would call my parents and yell, "Your son stole five dollars from my kid for this crap that doesn't work." My mom would drive me over there and sit in the cul-de-sac while I went in and debugged it and fixed it.

Seibel: During that time did you take any classes on programming?

Fitzpatrick: Not really. It was all one or two books from the library, and then just playing around. There weren't really forums or the Internet. At one point I got on a BBS, but the BBS didn't really have anything on it. It wasn't connected to the Net, so it was people playing board games.

Seibel: Did your school have AP computer science or anything?

Fitzpatrick: Well, we didn't have AP C.S., but we had a computer-programming class. There was a guy teaching it but then I would teach sort of an advanced class in the back. They still use the graphics editor and the graphics library I wrote—their final project is to make a game. I still occasionally run into that C.S. teacher—he's a friend of my family's and I'll see him at my brother's soccer games—he'll be like, "Yep, we still use your libraries."

I did take the AP C.S. test. It was the last year it was in Pascal before they switched to C, which was one year before they switched to Java or something like that. I didn't know Pascal so I went to a neighboring high school that had AP C.S. and I went to some night classes, like three or four of them. Then I found a book and learned the language, and I spent most of my time building asteroids in Pascal because I had just learned trig. I was like, "Oooh, sin and cosin; these are fun. I can get thrust and stuff like that."

Seibel: How'd you do?

Fitzpatrick: Oh, I got a five. I had to write bigint classes. Now that's one of the interview questions I give people. "Write a class to do arbitrary, bigint manipulation with multiplication and division." If I did it in high school on an AP test, they should be able to do it here.

Seibel: Your freshman year in college you worked at Intel during the summer. Did you also work as a programmer during high school?

Fitzpatrick: Yeah, I worked at Tektronix for a while. Before I had any official job, I got some hosting account. I got kicked off of AOL for writing bots, flooding their chat rooms, and just being annoying. I was scripting the AOL client from another Windows program. I also wrote a bot to flood their online form to send you a CD. I used every variation of my name, because I didn't want their duplicate suppression to only send me one CD, because they had those 100 free hours, or 5,000 free hours. I submitted this form a couple thousand times and for a week or so the postman would be coming with bundles of CDs wrapped up.

My mom was like, "Damn it, Brad, you're going to get in trouble." I was like, "Eh—their fucking fault, right?" Then one day I get a phone call and I actually picked up the phone, which I normally didn't, and it was someone from AOL. They were just screaming at me. "Stop sending us all these form submissions!" I'm not normally this quick and clever, but I just yelled back, "Why are you sending me all this crap? Every day the postman comes! He's dropping off all these CDs!" They're like, "We're so sorry, sir. It won't happen again." Then I used all those and I decorated my dorm room in college with them. I actually still have them in a box in the garage. I can't get rid of them because I just remember them being such a good decoration at one point.

After I got kicked off of AOL, I got a shell account on some local ISP. That's basically where I learned Unix. I couldn't run CGI scripts, but I could FTP up, so I would run Perl stuff on my desktop at home to generate my whole website and then upload it. Then I got a job at Tektronix, like a summer intern job. I knew Perl really well and I knew web stuff really well, but I had never done dynamic web stuff. This was probably '95, '94—the web was pretty damn new.

Then I go to work at Tektronix and on my first day they're introducing me to stuff, and they're like, "Here's your computer." It's this big SPARCstation or something running X and Motif. And, "Here's your browser." It's

Netscape 2 or something—I don't remember. And, "If you have some CGIs, they go in this directory." I remember I got a basic hello-world CGI, like three lines working that night and I was like, "Holy shit, this is so fun." I was at work the next day at six in the morning and just going crazy with CGI stuff.

Then I started doing dynamic web-programming stuff on my own. Maybe at that point I had found a web server for Windows that supported CGI. I finally convinced my ISP—I'd made friends with them enough, or sent enough intelligent things that they trusted me—so they said, "OK, we'll run your CGIs but we're going to audit them all first." They'd skim them and toss them in their directory. So I started running this Voting Booth script where you created a topic like, "What's your favorite movie?" and you could add things to it and vote them up. That got more and more popular. That was going on in the background for a couple of years.

Seibel: That was FreeVote?

Fitzpatrick: Yeah, that turned into FreeVote after it flooded my host. Banner ads were really popular then, or they were just getting really popular, and I kept getting more and more money from that, better contracts, more cost per click. At the height I was getting 27 cents per click of banner ads, which I think is pretty ridiculous even by today's standards. So at the height, I was making like 25, 27 grand per month on fucking clicks on banner ads.

This was all through high school—I did this in the background all of high school. And I worked at Intel two summers, and then started doing LiveJournal my last summer, right before college. So then my first year of college, I was just selling FreeVote, which I basically sold for nothing to a friend, for like 11 grand just because I wanted to get rid of it and get rid of legal responsibility for it.

Seibel: When you got on your ISP and got to use Unix, did that change your programming much?

Fitzpatrick: Yeah. It didn't drive me crazy. I couldn't understand what was going on with Windows. You've probably seen the Windows API—there are like twenty parameters to every function and they're all flags and half of them are zero. No clue what's going on. And you can't go peek underneath the covers when something's magically not working.

Seibel: Are there big differences you can identify between your early approach to programming or programming style to the way you think about programming now?

Fitzpatrick: I went through lots of styles, object-oriented stuff, and then functional stuff, and then this weird, hybrid mix of object-oriented and functional programming. This is why I really love Perl. As ugly as the syntax is and as much historical baggage and warts as it has, it never fucks with me and tells me what style to write in. Any style you want is fine. You can make your code pretty and consistent, but there's no language-specified style. It's only since I've been at Google that I've stopped writing much Perl.

I've also done a lot of testing since LiveJournal. Once I started working with other people especially. And once I realized that code I write never fucking goes away and I'm going to be a maintainer for life. I get comments about blog posts that are almost 10 years old. "Hey, I found this code. I found a bug," and I'm suddenly maintaining code.

I now maintain so much code, and there's other people working with it, if there's anything halfway clever at all, I just assume that somebody else is going to not understand some invariants I have. So basically anytime I do something clever, I make sure I have a test in there to break really loudly and to tell them that they messed up. I had to force a lot of people to write tests, mostly people who were working for me. I would write tests to guard against my own code breaking, and then once they wrote code, I was like, "Are you even sure that works? Write a test. Prove it to me." At a certain point, people realize, "Holy crap, it does pay off," especially maintenance costs later.

Seibel: When did you start working with other people?

Fitzpatrick: It was pretty much towards the end of college when I started hiring other people, and especially once I moved back to Portland after college.

Then the early employees were customer support, so they didn't write any code. Then slowly I started hiring programmers. The first person I hired was a friend of mine from online. His name is Brad Whitaker and we both had websites called BradleyLand or BradleyWorld, so we found each other's websites. I was a couple of years ahead of him web programming–wise, or maybe a year, and he was asking me, "Hey, how do you that," whether it was HTML, or frames, or CGI, or Perl stuff. So then I started getting a bunch of contract projects and I would give the ones I didn't want to him. And then we had a project that was too big for either of us so we told the guy, "It's going to take two people to do this project." And he flew us out to Pennsylvania. Pittsburgh? I don't know the east coast at all; I'm a west-coast guy. Philadelphia? The cheesesteak place.

Seibel: Philadelphia.

Fitzpatrick: Yeah, and we met for the first time at some cheapo hotel and it felt like I knew him already. He was like, "Hey, what up?" He came in and took a piss in my hotel bathroom without even closing the door as I'm standing right there. I'm like, "Alright. You're comfortable." It was like we knew each other for four or five years, even though we had never met. We started working on this stuff together.

He moved up into my spare bedroom and we basically moved all the stuff out of my kitchen, set up a bunch of tables, and worked on computers. We would wake up around 10 or 11 and work until noon, and watch some TV—sit around in our boxers and watch TV, and hack, and stay up until 3 or 4 in the morning just working nonstop. Then another friend of mine moved down for the summer from UW. This was after my freshman year in college and then there were three of us working there. The third friend was living downtown. He would come on the light rail in the morning and skateboard over to my house. He would sit outside on Wi-Fi, just hacking until we woke up, opened the door, and let him in.

Once there were three of us, it was a little crowded in my house, so I was like, "Oh, OK, let's get an office." So we got an office and we were like, "Oh, we have all this space! Let's hire more people." We slowly got up to 12 over the next couple of years, and LiveJournal got more and more popular, and then more stressful too, because I was dealing with HR.

Or my mom was dealing with HR and my mom was fighting with me because she worked for me. I had to make rules for my mom, like, "If you call me, it has to be personal or business; whatever one you start with, that's how you end it. You can't switch from work to personal or personal to work." I just started hanging up on her if she switched. Then she'd call back and I'm like, "Nope, you lost." So that was really stressful. She was really happy when I sold it, and she could stop working for me and we could stop fighting.

Seibel: Was your company still doing contract work or was it all LiveJournal at that point?

Fitzpatrick: It was pretty much all LiveJournal. We were also trying to start a photo hosting-service, which Flickr beat us to. Ours was probably overdesigned: beautifully abstract and plugged into everything. But each new infrastructure thing we did for LiveJournal, we were like, "How is this going to work on FotoBilder?" so we started building everything abstract. Memcached was abstract because there was no reason to tie it into LiveJournal. Then we built a file system like GFS, and we built a job queue. So we kept building all these infrastructure components for scaling that would work for either of our products, but also because the less intertwined spaghetti dependency-wise, the easier it is to maintain something. Even if it's a little bit more work, if you can cut some dependencies, it was great, so we started building all that generic infrastructure.

Seibel: I'm curious about the process that you went through of scaling LiveJournal, in terms of where you started and how you learned the lessons you needed to learn along the way.

Fitzpatrick: So it started on one shared Unix box with other customers and pretty much killed that.

Seibel: Running as CGIs?

Fitzpatrick: Yes. Yeah. I think it was probably a literal CGI, fork up the whole world and die. There was a guy assigned to me at this ISP. I was having problems with my server dying all the time. I'm like, "I paid my

$10.00 a month. Why isn't it working?" So he would say, "Oh, do this." Pretty soon I was learning Unix and learning what was actually going on.

Then I converted to FastGCI. Then I tuned Apache and turned off reverse DNS lookups. All these steps you go through. Finally, I was I/O-bound or CPU-bound. Then I got my own dedicated server, but it was still just one and it was dying and I was out of capacity. I had originally opened it up for my friends and I just left the signup page alive. Then they invited their friends who invited their friends—it was never really supposed to be a public site. It just had an open signup page on accident. So then I put something up on the LiveJournal news page and I said, "Help. We need to buy servers."

I think that raised maybe six or seven thousand dollars or something to buy these two big Dells and put them in Speakeasy in downtown Seattle. Somebody recommend some servers, Dells, these huge 6U things, like ninety pounds each. The logical split was the database server and the web server. That was the only division I knew because I was running a MySQL process and an Apache process.

That worked well for a while. The web servers spoke directly to the world and had two network cards and had a little crossover cable to the database server. Then the web server got overloaded, but that was still fairly easy. At this point I got 1U servers. Then we had three web servers and one database server. At that point, I started playing with three or four HTTP load balancers—mod_backhand and mod_proxy and Squid and hated them all. That started my hate for HTTP load balancers.

The next thing to fall over was the database, and that's when I was like, "Oh, shit." The web servers scale out so nicely. They're all stateless. You just throw more of them and spread load. So that was a long stressful time. "Well, I can optimize queries for a while," but that only gives you another week until it's loaded again. So at some point, I started thinking about what does an individual request need.

That's when—I thought I was the first person in the world to think of this—I was like, we'll shard it out—partition it. So I wrote up design doc with pictures saying how our code would work. "We'll have our master database just for metadata about global things that are low traffic and all the per-blog and per-comment stuff will be partitioned onto a per-user database cluster. These user IDs are on this database partition." Obvious in retrospect—it's what everyone does. Then there was a big effort to port the code while the service was still running.

Seibel: Was there a red-flag day where you just flipped everything over?

Fitzpatrick: No. Every user had a flag basically saying what cluster number they were on. If it was zero, they were on the master; if it was nonzero, they were partitioned out. Then there was a "Your Account Is Locked" version number. So it would lock and try to migrate the data and then retry if you'd done some mutation in the meantime—basically, wait 'til we've done a migration where you hadn't done any write on the master, and then pivot and say, "OK, now you're over there."

This migration took months to run in the background. We calculated that if we just did a straight data dump and wrote something to split out the SQL files and reload it, it would have taken a week or something. We could have a week of downtime or two months of slow migration. And as we migrated, say, 10 percent of the users, the site became bearable again for the other ones, so then we could turn up the rate of migration off the loaded cluster.

Seibel: That was all pre-memcached and pre-Perlbal.

Fitzpatrick: Yeah, pre-Perlbal for sure. Memcached might have come after that. I don't think I did memcached until like right after college, right when I moved out. I remember coming up with the idea. I was in my shower one day. The site was melting down and I was showering and then I realized we had all this free memory all over the place. I whipped up a prototype that night, wrote the server in Perl and the client in Perl, and the server just fell over because it was just way too much CPU for a Perl server. So we started rewriting it in C.

Seibel: So that saved you from having to buy more database servers.

Fitzpatrick: Yeah, because they were expensive and slow to migrate. Web servers were cheap and we could add them and they would take effect immediately. You buy a new database and it's like a week of setup and validation: test its disks, and set it all up and tune it.

Seibel: So all the pieces of infrastructure you built, like memcached and Perlbal, were written in response to the actual scaling needs of LiveJournal?

Fitzpatrick: Oh, yeah. Everything we built was because the site was falling over and we were working all night to build a new infrastructure thing. We bought one NetApp ever. We asked, "How much does it cost?" and they're like, "Tell us about your business model." "We have paid accounts." "How many customers do you have? What do you charge?" You just see them multiplying. "The price is: all the disposable income you have without going broke." We're like, "Fuck you." But we needed it, so we bought one. We weren't too impressed with the I/O on it and it was way too expensive and there was still a single point of failure. They were trying to sell us a configuration that would be high availability and we were like, "Fuck it. We're not buying any more of these things."

So then we just started working on a file system. I'm not even sure the GFS paper had published at this point—I think I'd heard about it from somebody. At this point I was always spraying memory all over just by taking a hash of the key and picking the shard. Why can't we do this with files? Well, files are permanent. So, we should record actually where it is because configuration will change over time as we add a more storage nodes. That's not much I/O, just keeping track of where stuff is, but how do we make that high availability? So we figured that part out, and I came up with a scheme: "Here's all the reads and writes we'll do to find where stuff is." And I wrote the MySQL schema first for the master and the tracker for where the files are. Then I was like, "Holy shit! Then this part could just be HTTP. This isn't hard at all!"

I remember coming into work after I'd been up all night thinking about this. We had a conference room downstairs in the shared office building—a really dingy, gross conference room. "All right, everyone, stop. We're going downstairs. We're drawing." Which is pretty much what I said every time we had a design—we'd go find the whiteboards to draw.

I explained the schema and who talks to who, and who does what with the request. Then we went upstairs and I think I first ordered all the hardware because it takes two weeks or something to get it. Then we started writing the code, hoping we'd have the code done by the time the machines arrived.

Everything was always under fire. Something was always breaking so we were always writing new infrastructure components.

Seibel: Are there things that if someone had just sat you down at the very beginning and told you, "You need to know X, Y, and Z," that your life would have been much easier?

Fitzpatrick: It's always easier to do something right the first time than to do a migration with a live service. That's the biggest pain in the ass ever. Everything I've described, you could do on a single machine. Design it like this to begin with. You no longer make assumptions about being able to join this user data with this user data or something like that. Assume that you're going to want to load these 20 assets—your implementation can be to load them all from the same table but your higher-level code that just says, "I want these 20 objects" can have an implementation that scatter-gathers over a whole bunch of machines. If I would have done that from the beginning, I'd have saved a lot of migration pain.

Seibel: So basically the lesson is, "You have to plan for the day when your data doesn't all fit into one database."

Fitzpatrick: Which I think is common knowledge nowadays in the web community. And people can go overkill on assuming that their site is going to be huge. But at the time, the common knowledge was, Apache is all you need and MySQL is all you need.

Seibel: It does seem that while you were writing all this stuff because you needed it, you also enjoyed doing it.

Fitzpatrick: Oh, yeah. I definitely try to find an excuse to use anything, to learn it. Because you never learn something until you have to write something in it, until you have to live and breathe it. It's one thing to go learn a language for fun, but until you write some big, complex system in it, you don't really learn it.

Seibel: So what languages would you say you've really lived and breathed with enough to claim as your own?

Fitzpatrick: Perl. C. Back in the day, BASIC, but I'm not even sure BASIC counts. I wrote a lot of Logo too. In our Logo class in elementary school, people were doing pen up, pen down and I would be not in graphics mode—there's some key to get out of graphics mode—writing functions. My teacher would come over and say, "What are you doing? You're doing the wrong thing. You're supposed to be drawing houses." "No, I'm writing Logo. Look," "No, you're not." Then at the end of the class I'd do something—I had a library that drew every letter of the alphabet, but at arbitrary scales and rotations. So I could print entire messages on wavy banners going into the distance and stuff, and everyone was like, "What the fuck?" I don't know if that one counts either.

But a lot of Perl and C, and then a lot of C++ in college for work and for Windows stuff. Then I forgot C++, or it atrophied, and now at Google, in the last year, it's a lot of C++, Python, and Java. I also wrote a lot of Java back in the day when it first came out, but then I got sick of it. Now I'm writing a lot of Java again, and I'm kinda sick of it.

Seibel: Does it matter much to you what language you use?

Fitzpatrick: I'm still not happy with any of them. I don't know what exactly would make me totally happy. I hate that for a given project you have to jump around all the time. I want something that lets me have static types and checks all that stuff at compile time, when I want. Perl gets me pretty close in that it lets me write in any style I want. It doesn't let me do enough static checking at compile time but I can make it blow up pretty hard when I want to a runtime. But it's still not good enough.

I want optional static typing. In Perlbal, there's no reason for half the things to be performant except for the core, copying bytes around. I would like to give the runtime hints in certain parts of the code and declare types. But if I want to be lazy and mock something out, I want to write in that style.

Seibel: So you want types mostly so the compiler can optimize better?

Fitzpatrick: No. I also want it to blow up at compile time to tell me like, "You're doing something stupid." Then sometimes I don't care and I want it to coerce for me at runtime and do whatever. I don't want to be too optimistic about Perl 6, but they're preaching a lot of things I want to see. But I don't think it'll ever come out.

Seibel: Do you like C++?

Fitzpatrick: I don't mind it. The syntax is terrible and totally inconsistent and the error messages, at least from GCC, are ridiculous. You can get 40 pages of error spew because you forgot some semicolon. But—like anything else—you quickly memorize all the patterns. You don't even read the words; you just see the structure and think, "Oh, yeah, I probably forgot to close the namespace in a header file." I think the new C++ spec, even though it adds so much complexity, has a lot of stuff that'll make it less painful to type—as far as number of keystrokes. The auto variables and the for loops. It's more like Python style. And the lambdas. It's enough that I could delude myself into thinking I'm writing in Python, even though it's C++.

Seibel: And you use C++ for efficiency.

Fitzpatrick: Yeah, pretty much. I mostly use it at Google. Anything that's halfway performant is in C++ there. I also write a ton of Java at Google.

Seibel: From what I understand, Google has a C++-centric culture because that's what they used originally and they've built a whole bunch of software infrastructure around it. While you can't undo all that history, there's probably a lot of code written at Google in C++ where it's not really necessary for performance.

Fitzpatrick: Especially because, over time, Java has gotten faster and the JVM has gotten a lot smarter. The thing that annoys me about Java is that everyone has such a strong aversion to JNI stuff. Sometimes a library is in C++. The Python people—in the outside community and inside Google—don't care. They're like, "Oh, we'll, SWIG-wrap it." They get on their way and they're happy. Python gets support for something right away if it's in C++ because they're not religious about what the source language is.

Java people are like, "Must be pure Java. We cannot use JNI because then if the JVM crashes, we don't know why." The problem with that is you end up writing everything twice, once for C++ and Python and all the other languages, and then once for Java. So if they could come up with a good embedding story or get over this fear of JNI, then I wouldn't mind it.

Seibel: What about explicit memory management versus garbage collection? People still argue about that. Do you have a strong opinion one way or the other?

Fitzpatrick: No, not really. I'm amused to watch other people's strong opinions when generally they're not backed up by anything. I personally don't find it that annoying to manage memory, at least in C++ with like scoped pointers. I can write in C++ for days and never actually say "new" or "delete". It seems to just all kind of work.

I rewrote memcached inside Google to work with Google infrastructure and to add it to App Engine. That was all written in C++ because I needed a very exclusive control of memory to reduce fragmentation. So I really appreciated having it there.

Seibel: The original memcached was in C. Did you redo it in C++ because C++ is more accepted within Google, or were there other advantages?

Fitzpatrick: I started to take the existing one and port it but it turned out to be more work. Memcached isn't that much code to begin with, so it was a lot quicker to just rewrite in C++. It was like half as much code, rewriting it in C++.

Seibel: Do you think that was because of C++ or just because you were smarter this time around?

Fitzpatrick: It could be. Once, when I was 11 or 12, we were on a trip around the US and I wrote that game Mastermind on a TI-85 calculator. I'm writing this program—a couple hundred lines—on this tiny little screen trying to remember where I am. I ended up deleting the damn thing twice. So I wrote the thing three times. But then it got so easy. That's a good point—the second time around it was a lot easier.

Seibel: You've done a lot of your work in Perl, which is a pretty high-level language. How low do you think programmers need to go—do programmers still need to know assembly and how chips work?

Fitzpatrick: I don't know. I see people that are really smart—I would say they're good programmers—but say they only know Java. The way they think about solving things is always within the space they know. They don't think end-to-end as much. I think it's really important to know the whole stack even if you don't operate within the whole stack.

When I was doing stuff on LiveJournal, I was thinking about things from JavaScript to how things were interacting in the kernel. I was reading Linux kernel code about epoll and I was like, "Well, what if we have all these long TCP connections and JavaScript is polling with these open TCP connections that are going to this load balancer?" I was trying to think of how much memory is in each structure here. That's still somewhat high-level, but then we were thinking about things like, we're getting so many interrupts on the Ethernet card—do we switch to this NAPI thing in the kernel where rather than the NIC sending an interrupt on every incoming packet it coalesces them to boundaries that were equivalent to 100 megabits speed even though it was a gigabit NIC. We were collecting numbers to see at what point this made sense and freed up the processor.

We were getting a lot of wins for really low-level stuff. I had somebody recently tell me about something: "Java takes care of that; we don't have to deal with that." I was like, "No, Java can't take care of this because I know what kernel version you're using and the kernel doesn't support it. Your virtual machine may be hiding that from you and giving you some abstraction that makes it look like that's efficient, but it's only efficient when you're running it on this kernel." I get frustrated if people don't understand at least the surface of the whole stack.

In practice, nothing works. There are all these beautiful abstractions that are backed by shit. The implementation of libraries that look like they could be beautiful are shit. And so if you're the one responsible for the cost of buying servers, or reliability—if you're on call for pages—it helps to actually know what's going on under the covers and not trust everyone else's libraries, and code, and interfaces.

I almost don't think I would be a programmer today if I was starting off. It's just too ugly. This is why I'm so excited about things like App Engine. Someone described Google's App Engine as this generation's BASIC. Because this generation, everything is networked. When I was programming, it was one language, and it was on my own machine, and the deploy was up enter, or RUN enter. Kids today don't want to write something stupid like a "bounce a ball" app on their own machine. They want a web site to interact with.

I still have people mailing me who are like, "Hey, I have this idea—I want to make Wikipedia meets YouTube, meets—" Everyone wants to do a web site where their favorite four web sites aren't quite right and they want to make one that looks kind of like that.

The fact that App Engine gives you one button, "Put this on the Web," and you write in one language, arguably a pretty easy-to-learn one, Python, is perfect. It's a great intro to programming—there are so many layers and layers of bullshit that it gets rid of.

Seibel: How does that fit with your dismay at the Java guys who tell you, "Oh, Java takes care of that for you." Isn't that the same? "Well, App Engine will take care of that for you."

Fitzpatrick: I don't know. Maybe it's because I know what's going on. Actually the JVM isn't that bad. I guess it's when people have blind faith in their abstractions without understanding what's going on.

Seibel: You had a lot of programming experience by the time you got to college and studied computer science. How did that work out?

Fitzpatrick: I skipped a lot of my early C.S. classes, because they were just really boring. I would go and take the tests. Then towards the end they got kind of fun, once you get to the 300- and 400-level classes. But right when it got interesting, I graduated. And they wouldn't let me take the fun grad-level classes, because I wasn't a grad student.

I remember in the compiler class, the final project was we had to take this existing language that we had been playing with and add a whole bunch of features, including one feature of our own choosing as the bonus part of the project. So I chose to implement run-time array bounds checking. Anyway, the professor took our compiled binary and ran his test suite against it, and it failed a couple of his tests. He was like, "Sorry, you get a C because you failed my unit test," When I went to look at it, I was like, "You have off-by-ones in your test suite." So he gave me the grade back and I got an A, but I never got the bonus points for adding a feature to the language. I was angry at school at that point.

And I remember our database class was taught by someone who, it seemed, had no real-world experience with databases. At this point I'd worked with Oracle, Microsoft Server, and tons of MySQL. So I was asking all these real-world questions I actually wanted answers to—things that were melting right now—they would just give me some textbook answer. I'm like, "No, no. That doesn't work."

Seibel: You graduated in 2002. Do you have any greater appreciation now of what they were trying to teach you?

Fitzpatrick: Half the classes I totally loved, and either I learned something totally new that I wouldn't have learned at the time, or I learned the proper background material and the proper terminology. Prior to that, I knew programming pretty well but I didn't have the vocabulary to describe what it was I was doing. Or I would make up my own terminology for it and people would think I didn't know what I was talking about. Formal C.S. education helped me be able to talk about it.

Seibel: Do you have any regrets about combining running a business with school? Would you rather have just done one or the other?

Fitzpatrick: No, I think that was the best way. I had friends who went to college and just did college, but I knew so much of it already, I would've been bored. I had one friend who also knew a whole bunch of it but he was of this school of thought that he's at college to learn, not for grades, so he was, on the side, studying Arabic and Chinese and Japanese. And all the crazy programming languages. Every week it was like, "I have a new favorite language. This week I'm only going to write in OCaml." So he kept himself busy that way. I kept myself busy and not bored other ways.

Then I had friends who dropped out after their freshman year just to do web stuff. A couple were doing a porn web site or something. They were like, "Oh, we're making all this money." But they just worked a whole bunch; they were always in their basement working. College was awesome for meeting people and partying. If I *just* did LiveJournal, I would've killed myself stresswise.

Seibel: Are you glad you studied computer science?

Fitzpatrick: I probably could have done without it. I did a lot of things I wouldn't have done normally, so I guess it was good. I wish maybe I would have like done something else as well, maybe stayed another year and double-majored in something totally unrelated. Did linguistics more. I'm kind of sad I left college and I felt I only did half studying because so much of it I already knew. My early C.S. classes I barely attended and it was only towards the end where things just started to get interesting when it was like, "OK, you're done."

Seibel: Did you ever think about going to grad school?

Fitzpatrick: Yeah. It would have been fun, but I was busy.

Seibel: Do you try to keep up with the C.S. literature?

Fitzpatrick: Me and my friends still forward each other papers around, neat papers. I read something the other day about some new technique for resizing Bloom filters at runtime. It was pretty awesome. The papers that come out of the storage conferences, some out of industry and some from academics, about different cool systems—I try to read those. There are different reading groups at Google—systems reading groups or storage reading groups. I'll see something on Reddit or a friend will forward a paper or something like that or link it on a blog.

Seibel: You just mentioned papers from the academy and from industry. Do you have any sense of whether those two meet in the right place these days?

Fitzpatrick: They kind of feel about the same to me. But it's more interesting, a lot of times, to read the industry ones because you know they did it to solve a problem and their solution works as opposed to, "We'd think it would be cool if—" There's a lot of crazier stuff that comes out of academia and it doesn't actually work, so it's just a crazy idea. Maybe they turn it into commercial things later.

Seibel: How do you design software?

Fitzpatrick: I start with interfaces between things. What are the common methods, or the common RPCs, or the common queries. If it's storage, I try to think, what are the common queries? What indexes do we need? How are the data going to be laid out on disk? Then I write dummy mocks for different parts and flesh it out over time.

Seibel: Do you write mocks in the test-first sense so you can test it as you go?

Fitzpatrick: More and more. I always designed software this way, even before testing. I would just design interfaces and storage first, and then work up to an actual implementation later.

Seibel: What form would the design take? Pseudocode? Actual code? Whiteboard scribbles?

Fitzpatrick: Generally I would bring up an editor and just write notes with pseudocode for the schema. After it got good, I would make up a real schema and then I would copy-paste it in just to make sure that "create table" works. Once I got that all going, I'd actually go implement it. I always start with a spec.txt first.

Seibel: After you write a bunch of code do you ever discover that you really need to reconsider your original plan?

Fitzpatrick: Sometimes. But I've started with the hard bits or the parts I was unsure of, and tried to implement those parts first. I try not to put off anything hard or surprising to the end; I enjoy doing the hard things first. The projects that I never finish—my friends give me shit that it's a whole bunch—it's because I did the hard part and I learned what I wanted to learn and I never got around to doing the boring stuff.

Seibel: Do you have any advice for self-taught programmers?

Fitzpatrick: Always try to do something a little harder, that's outside your reach. Read code. I heard this a lot, but it didn't really sink in until later. There were a number of years when I wrote a lot of code and never read anyone else's. Then I get on the Internet and there's all this open source code I could contribute to but I was just scared shitless that if it wasn't my code and the whole design wasn't in my head, that I couldn't dive in and understand it.

Then I was sending in patches to Gaim, the GTK instant-messenger thing, and I was digging around that code and I just saw the whole design. Just seeing parts of it, I understood. I realized, after looking at other people's code, that it wasn't that I memorized all my own code; I was starting to see patterns. I would see their code and I was like, "Oh, OK. I understand the structure that they're going with."

Then I really enjoyed reading code, because whenever I didn't understand some pattern, I was like, "Wait, why the fuck did they do it like this?" and I would look around more, and I'd be like, "Wow, that is a really clever way to do this. I see how that pays off." I would've done that earlier but I was afraid to do it because I was thinking that if it wasn't my code, I wouldn't understand it.

Seibel: And how do you tackle reading other people's code? For starters, do you read code just to see how it works overall, or do you always go in with some change you want to make?

Fitzpatrick: Generally I wanted to change something. Or if you really respect some programmer, go read some of their code. Maybe that'll make you realize that they're mortal and they're not really someone you should be idolizing. Or you learn something about their code.

Seibel: So say you've got a change you want to make; how do you tackle it?

Fitzpatrick: First step, take a virgin tarball or check out from svn, and try to get the damn thing to build. Get over that hurdle. That tends to be the hugest hurdle for most people—dependencies in the build system or they're assuming this library is installed. I almost wish that these large projects just came with a virtual machine that was the build environment.

Seibel: You mean like a VMware virtual machine?

Fitzpatrick: Yeah, so if you just want to get into hacking on it really quickly, here's all the dependencies. People's connections are getting quick enough. That's totally viable.

Anyway, once you have one clean, working build, kill it, and just make one damn change. Change the title bar to say, "Brad says, 'Hello world.'" Change something. Even if everything's ugly, just start making changes.

Then send out patches along the way. I find that's the best way to start a conversation. If you get on a mailing list and you're like, "Hey, I want to add a feature X," the maintainer is probably going to be like, "Oh fuck, I'm so busy. Go away. I hate feature X." But if you come to them and you're like, "I want to add feature X. I was thinking something like the attached patch," which is totally wrong but you say, "But I think it's totally wrong. I'm thinking the right way might be to do X," which is some more complex way, generally they'll be like, "Holy crap, they tried, and look, they totally did it the wrong way."

Maybe that pains the maintainer. They're like, "Oh man, I can't believe they went through all that effort to do it. It's so easy to do it the right way." Or, "Oh, wow, they did all this work in the wrong direction. I hope they don't go in that direction any more." And then they reply.

That's always the best way to start a conversation. Even at Google, that's the way I start a lot of conversations to a team I don't know. When I fix a bug in their product the first thing I do is send them a patch in the mail and just say, "What do you guys think of this?" Or on the internal code-review tool I'd be like, "Here is a review. What do you think?" They could just say, "Fuck no, that's totally the wrong fix."

Seibel: Do you still read code for fun, as opposed to reading it because you need to work with it?

Fitzpatrick: Sometimes. I checked out Android source code for no real reason. The same with Chrome; when it went open source, I mirrored the repo and just looked around. I did the same thing with Firefox and Open Office. Some program you've been using and all of a sudden you have access and you might as well look.

Seibel: Programs like that, the code base is pretty huge. When you look at something like that for fun, how deeply do you get into it?

Fitzpatrick: Generally, I'll just pipe `find` into `less` and try to understand the directory structure. Then either something grabs my eye or I don't understand what something is. So I pick a random file and get a feel for it. Then I bounce around and wander aimlessly until I'm bored and then pick a new random spot to jump in.

A lot of times, I'll work on building it in parallel with reading it because they're very parallelizable tasks, especially if it's hard to build. By the time it's finally built, then I can start tweaking it if I want to.

Seibel: So when you read good code it either fits into patterns that you already understand, or you'd discover new patterns. But not all code is good. What are the first warning signs of bad code?

Fitzpatrick: Well, I'm particularly snooty now, having worked at Google with really strict style guidelines in all languages. On our top six or seven languages, there's a really strict style guide that says, "This is how we lay out our code. This is how we name variables. This is how we do spacing and indentation, and these patterns and conventions you use, and this is how you declare a static field."

We've started putting these online too, just as a reference for external contributors contributing to our projects. We wanted to have a documented policy so we don't just say, "We don't like your style."

Now when I work on projects in C, the first thing I do is add a style guide. Once a project is mature and has a lot of people hacking on it, they'll have a style guide. It's not even always written, but the programmer just respect the style of code written already. Maybe they don't like the brace style, but fuck it, it's more important to have it consistent within a file, within a project, than to do it your favorite way.

Seibel: Do you ever do any pair programming?

Fitzpatrick: I think it's pretty fun. It's good for lots of things. Sometimes you just need to think and want to be left alone. I don't subscribe to it all the time, but it's definitely fun.

I start too many projects. I finish them because I have guilt if I don't finish them, but I definitely context-switch way too often and I'm spread too thin. This is why I really need pair programming—it forces me to sit down for three solid hours, or even two or one solid hour, and work on one thing with somebody else, and they force me to not be bored. If I hit a bored patch, they're like, "Come on. We've got to do it," and we finish.

I like working alone but I just bounce all over the place when I do. On a plane I'll bring extra laptop batteries and I have a whole development environment with local web servers and I'll be in a web browser, testing stuff. But I'll still be hitting new tabs, and typing "reddit" or "lwn"—sites I read. Autocomplete and hit Enter, and then—error message. I'll do this multiple times within a minute. Holy fuck! Do I do this at work? Am I reading web sites this often that I don't even think about it? It's scary. I had a friend, who had some iptables rule, that on connection to certain IP addresses between certain hours of the day would redirect to a "You should be working," page. I haven't got around to doing that, but I need to do something like it, probably.

Seibel: What about code ownership? Is it important for people to own code individually or is it better for a team to share ownership?

Fitzpatrick: I don't think code should be owned. I don't think anyone really thinks that. The way it works within Google is that it's one massive source tree, one root, and one unified build system across all of it. And so anyone can go and change anything. But there are code reviews, and directories have owners, always at least two people, just in case some quits or is on vacation.

To check in you need three conditions met: You need someone to review it and say it looks good. You need to be certified in the language—basically you've proven you know the style of this language—called "readability." And then you also need the approval above from somebody in the owner's file in that directory. So in the case that you already are an owner of that directory and you have readability in that language, you just need someone to say, "Yeah, it looks good." And it's a pretty good system, because there tends to be a minimum of two, up to twenty, thirty owners. Once you work on a code base for a while, someone just adds you to owners. I think it's a great system.

Seibel: So let's go back in time a bit—how did LiveJournal start?

Fitzpatrick: It was just fucking around with my friends—what I wanted and what we thought would be funny. Commenting on LiveJournal was a practical joke. I was checking my LiveJournal right before I ran into class. We had just introduced friend pages and I saw something my friend wrote and it was really stupid and I wanted to make fun of him. "Oh, but I can't reply." So I went to class and all throughout class I was thinking, "How can I add a reply system?" I was thinking of the existing schema and how we could render it. I had a two-hour break between classes, so I add commenting and I reply something smartass and sarcastic and go to my other class. When I came back from my second class, and he's like, "What the fuck? We can comment now?"

Everything on LiveJournal was pretty much a joke. The whole security thing, like friends-only posts and private posts, was because a friend wrote that he went to a party and woke up drunk in a ditch the next day. His parents read it and were like, "What? You're drinking?" He was like, "Brad, we need a way to lock this shit down!" I was like, "On it!" We already had friends, so we just made it so some posts are friends only and then your parents—just don't be friends with them.

Seibel: In the early days of LiveJournal it seems your life was an endless series of late nights, sleeping late, and overall working long hours. How much of that is a necessary part of programming?

Fitzpatrick: I just thought it was the least stressful time. During the day, there's always something coming up, like another meal is coming up, or a class, or maybe you get a phone call. There's always some interruption. I can't relax. If I go into work two hours before some meeting, that two hours is less productive than if I didn't have that meeting that day or if the meeting was the first thing in the morning. Knowing that I have nothing coming up to bug me, I'm so much more relaxed.

At night I feel like this is my time and I'm stealing this time because everyone else is sleeping. There's no noise and no interruptions, and I can do whatever. I still stay up late sometimes. I did it this weekend; I was up quite a bit working on different things. But that screws me up for days sleepwise. I did that mostly when I had to in college, because I had some project, and I was also doing LiveJournal on the side. The only time to do it was at night and also all our server maintenance had to be at night. And then in the summer, just because why not? There's no reason to wake up early in the morning to go to a class or anything, so might as well work at night.

Seibel: What about the length and intensity? I'm sure you've done the 80-, 100-, 120-hour weeks. Is that necessary? Under what circumstances is that really necessary and when is it just a macho thing that we do?

Fitzpatrick: In my case, I'm not sure it was either necessary or a macho thing. I was having fun and it was what I wanted to be doing. Sometimes things were breaking, but even when they weren't breaking, I was still doing it just because I was working on a new feature that I really wanted to see happen.

Seibel: Have you ever been in a situation where you really had to estimate how long things were going to take?

Fitzpatrick: Once I got to Six Apart. I guess that was my first experience, three and a half years ago. We had started doing migration—we'd have a customer and they'd say, "Can you move this data?" That requires adding this support for this code and testing, and pushing it out. I was terrible at it. I probably still am terrible at it, because I always forget a factor, like the bullshit multiplier of having to deal with interruptions and the fact that I'm never going to get away from maintaining a dozen projects on the side.

I think I'm getting better, but fortunately they don't ask for that too often. And now when I actually do get a deadline for something, I'm like, "Yay! A deadline!" and I get so excited that the adrenaline kicks in, and I work, and I finish the damn thing. Nothing with Google is really a deadline. With Google it's like, "What do you think about launching this? How does that feel?" It's rare that there's some real deadline. Most of them, we think it'd be nice to launch on this date and so everyone tries really hard. But you're only letting down other people that want to see it launch by that day if you don't finish something. And most of the things I work on are very "When it's done, it's done."

Seibel: When you were hiring programmers at LiveJournal, did you manage them?

Fitzpatrick: Well, I kind of assumed that none of them would need managing; that they would just all be self-driven like me. That was a learning experience in HR, that some people just do what they're told and don't really have a passion for excellence. They're just like, "Done. Next assignment," Or they don't tell you and just browse the Web. So I had a couple of painful experiences. But I think after a year or two of that, I learned that people are different.

Some are purists. They would just do abstraction on abstraction on abstractions. They would go really slowly and are very religious about their style. They're like, "I'm an artisan programmer." And I was like, "Your code doesn't run. It's not efficient and it doesn't look like any of the other code that you're interacting with."

Seibel: Did you figure out how to make good use of people like that?

Fitzpatrick: One person, I tried dozens of different things. I think he might've been ten years older than me. I don't know how much, because I never ask that—I was afraid of legal hiring questions. But I got the feeling that he didn't want to work for some young punk. I was like 22. That one eventually didn't work out. That was the only person I let go.

Other people I eventually figured out what motivated them. One guy was really good at tinkering and getting a prototype working. He wrote sysadmin Perl. He could wire stuff together, write shell scripts, and write really bad Perl and really bad C, but kind of get it working. Then we would be like, "Holy crap, you researched all this stuff, you got all these components talking to each other?"

We were setting up a voice bridge to LiveJournal so you record something and post it to LiveJournal. There were just so many moving parts involved. I thought it was painful as hell. He loved it. He figured it all out and got it working. Then we just rewrote it all. And we figured out that was the way it worked with him. He figured out the interface and we would fix it all up. Once I figured out that was his role, we got along great.

Seibel: So you've hired for your own company, and I assume you've been involved in hiring at Google. How do you recognize a great programmer?

Fitzpatrick: I often look for people that have done, like, a lot of stuff on their own that wasn't asked of them. Not just their school project or just what their previous employer had them do. Somebody who was passionate about something and had some side project. How did they maintain it and how serious did they get with it? Or do they do a lot of quick hacks and abandon them?

Seibel: Do you have favorite interview questions?

Fitzpatrick: One of the ones I've given a few times because it was on my AP programming test is given two decimal numbers as a strings of arbitrary length, multiply them. There are a lot of different ways that they could do it. If they're really good at math—like I'm not—they can find some clever ways to do it really efficiently. Worst case, they can make a class that does just addition repeatedly.

I tell them from the beginning, "Don't stress out. You don't have to do it efficiently. Just get it done somehow." Some people stress out and have no clue where to begin. That's kind of a bad sign. The worst case, you just implement the algorithm you do in grade school.

I actually wrote a program in grade school to do my long division and multiplication and show the work. Including all the steps and where to cross out. So then we would get these problems, like ten per page or something, and I would type it into the computer and then just reproduce the problems in scribbles. I did the same thing in chemistry to find the orbitals of electrons. But the thing I find is by writing a program to cheat, you learn because you have to learn it really in depth to write that program.

Seibel: Do you think that would work for anyone? Instead of teaching kids long division, should we teach them how to program and then say, "OK, now your task is to write a program to do this long-division procedure"? By the time they've actually written that program, they'll understand division. Or does that only work if you have some natural inclination that way?

Fitzpatrick: It worked for me. A lot times, someone could teach you something and you're like, "Yeah, yeah, sure. I understand." You delude yourself but once you actually have to get down and do it at a real level and understand all the corner cases, it forces you to actually learn the thing. But I don't know if that would work for everyone.

Seibel: Google has a bit of a reputation, as Microsoft also does, of interviewers using puzzle questions.

Fitzpatrick: I think those are kind of banned. Or strongly discouraged. Maybe some people still do them, but I think, in general, they're discouraged.

Seibel: What did they ask you in your interview?

Fitzpatrick: One question was, imagine you have a bunch of computers on a switch and they turn on the whole rack; come up with an algorithm so every machine on the rack knows the status of all the other ones about whether they're on or off. So basically a presence thing. That was pretty much the constraint. Basically, they described Ethernet: you could send a broadcast to everyone, or you could send it to a specific MAC address. So I just kind of walked through all the different strategies to minimize bandwidth and to minimize latency discovering when something's dead. That was a fun one.

Seibel: What's the worst bug you ever had to track down?

Fitzpatrick: I try not to remember them. I hate it when it's something where your assumptions are so far off. The other day—this is definitely not an example of the worst one ever—I spent 90 minutes debugging something because I was writing to one output file and reading another file named the same thing but with one path component missing. I kept rerunning this huge MapReduce and seeing the output and putting it in GDB and stepping through it. "What the fuck? It's not changing!" Finally I looked at the paths and I was like, "Holy crap." I don't know why I spent 90 minutes on it; I was so obsessed that I didn't step back and check, is my command line correct?

There's a lot of that. We always had some good stuff with Perl like the $_ isn't lexically scoped. So if you fuck with $_ in a sort, you can mess with somebody else's far away. So we had this bug that took us forever and we had a bunch of corruption going on. We finally figured that out. Then I audited all our code we had a new policy of "never do this."

Seibel: What are your debugging tools? Debuggers? Printlns? Something else?

Fitzpatrick: Println if I'm in an environment where I can do that. Debugger, if I'm in an environment that has good debuggers. GDB is really well maintained at Google and is kind of irreplaceable when you need it. I try not to need it too often. I'm not that great at it, but I can look around and kind of figure things out generally. If I have to go in there, I generally can find my way out. I love strace. Strace, I don't think I could live without. If I don't know what some program is doing, or what my program is doing, I run it under strace and see exactly what's happening. If I could only have one tool, it would probably be that. All the Valgrind tools, Callgrind and all that, those are good.

But a lot of times lately, if there's something weird going on, I'm like, "OK, that function is too big; let's break that up into smaller parts and unit-test each one of them separately to figure out where my assumptions are wrong, rather than just sticking in random printlns."

Then maybe in the process of refactoring, I have to think about the code more, and then it becomes obvious. I could, at that point, go back to the big, ugly state where it was one big function and fix it but I'm already halfway there; I might as well continue making it simpler for the next maintainer.

Seibel: How do you use invariants in your code? Some people throw in ad hoc asserts and some people put in invariants at every step so they can prove formal properties of their programs, and there's a big range in the middle.

Fitzpatrick: I don't go all the way to formal. My basic rules is, if it could possibly come from the end user, it's not a run-time crash. But if it is my code to my code, I crash it as hard as possible—fail as early as possible.

I try to think mostly in terms of preconditions, and checking things in the constructor and the beginning of a function. Debug checks, if possible, so it compiles away. There are probably a lot of schools of thought and I'm probably not educated about what the proper way to do it is. There are languages where all this stuff is actually a formal part of the language. Pretty much all the languages I write in, it's up to you.

Seibel: You wrote once that optimization is your favorite part of programming. Is that still true?

Fitzpatrick: Optimization is fun because it's not necessary. If you're doing that, you've got your thing working and nothing else is more important and you're either saving money or doing it because it's like a Perl golf contest—how short can I make this or how much faster. We would identify hotspots in LiveJournal, and I would send out some contests. "Here's some code. Here's the benchmark. Make it fast." I sent our load balancer's header parsing. We were all writing crazy regexps that didn't backtrack and tried to capture things with the most efficient capture groups. And we were all competing, getting faster and faster and faster. Then one guy comes over the next day. He had written it all in C++ with XS, and so he was like, "I win."

Seibel: The flip side of that these days is . . .

Fitzpatrick: Programmers' time is worth more and all that crap? Which can be true. This is true for a small number of machines. Once you get to a lot of machines, all of a sudden the programmers' time is worth less than the number of machines that this will be deployed against, so now write it in C and profile the hell out of it, and fix the compiler, and pay people to work on GCC to make this compile faster.

Seibel: But even Google uses C++ rather than assembly, so there's some point at which trying to squeeze the maximum performance isn't worth it. Or is the theory that a good C++ compiler generates better code than all but the most freakishly rare assembly coders?

Fitzpatrick: We still have some stuff in assembly, but it's very rare. We have profiling for lots and lots of stuff and it has to really be justified to rewrite it even from Perl to C, and then from C to assembly. Even if it's all x86, there are all different variations of x86. Do you really want to write assembly for every variation of x86? This one uses SSE 2 and that one uses SSE 3.1. Let the compiler deal with it.

Seibel: You learned to program from programming manuals when you were a little kid. Are there any books that you strongly recommend to new programmers now or think that everyone should read?

Fitzpatrick: Back when I was doing Perl—even for people that knew Perl really well—I would recommend MJD's *Higher-Order Perl*. The book is really fun in that it starts somewhat simple and you're like, "Yeah, yeah, I know what a closure is." And then it just continues to fuck with your head. By the end of the book, you're just blown away. Even though I knew all that stuff, in theory, just watching it taken to the extreme really changed how I thought. I recommended that to a bunch of my friends and it blew their minds. In general, any book that gives people a different style to think in. That's the most recent example I can think of.

Seibel: I see you've got *The Art of Computer Programming* up there; it doesn't look too worn. How much of it have you read?

Fitzpatrick: Oh, I didn't get it until less than five years ago, maybe five years ago. I bounce around and read parts of it for fun. But at the time I got it, I had already learned a lot of it through C.S.. So it probably would have been more valuable early on, but I didn't really know about it prior to the Internet.

Seibel: How much math do you think is necessary to be a programmer? To read Knuth and really understand it, you've got to be pretty mathematically sophisticated, but do you actually need that to be a programmer?

Fitzpatrick: You don't need that much math. For most programmers, day to day, statistics is a lot more important. If you're doing graphics stuff, math is a lot more important but most people doing Java enterprise stuff or web stuff, it's not. Logic helps and statistics comes up a lot.

Seibel: You obviously still enjoy programming. But reading some of your LiveJournal entries from when you were in college, it seems like there were times when you were pretty stressed out and hating computers.

Fitzpatrick: Oh, well, I always hate computers. I don't think we've really made any progress in quite a long time. Computers seem slower, and crashier, and buggier than ever. But I'm such an optimist, I keep thinking that they'll get better. It seems like my computing experience was happier ten years ago than it is today. It seems like my computer was faster ten years ago; like my computer worked better ten years ago. Things have gotten faster but the software has gotten slower and buggier in the meantime.

Seibel: Why do you think that is?

Fitzpatrick: I don't know. Has the bar been lowered? Or are computers faster so you don't need to be efficient or you don't need to know what you're doing? I have no clue. Some combination of all of the above, or maybe there are so many layers of abstraction that people don't know what the hell is going on underneath because the computers are so damn fast that it hides your stupidity.

Seibel: So maybe things are not as fast as they ought to be given the speed of computers. But ten years ago there was no way to do what people, as users, can do today with Google.

Fitzpatrick: Yeah. So some people are writing efficient code and making use of it. I don't play any games, but occasionally I'll see someone playing something and I'm like, "Holy shit, that's possible?" It just blows me away. Obviously, some people are doing it right.

I guess I'm mostly dissatisfied with the state of my desktop. It seems like there is a lot of good interesting stuff going on in the back end. But as I'm using my computer I'm more and more frustrated with it. It seems like my Mac shouldn't have a beach ball spinning all the time.

Seibel: Do you have any interest in writing better desktop software?

Fitzpatrick: The problem is, no one uses it. You want to write stuff people use, which comes down to web apps. I lost my laptop the other day and people were like, "Oh, my God, did you lose stuff?" I had no files on there. It was an Internet terminal. And it was an encrypted disk so I'm not worried about my password or cookies or anything like that. People won't download programs, I don't think.

Seibel: Are you more motivated by having users or just by the fun of programming?

Fitzpatrick: There's definitely some stuff I write for me and I write it explicitly for me as the only user and I could care less if I get patches and stuff. But a lot of times I want to work with other people. Having users is a key to getting contributors. More users find more bugs and find more use cases. It's more fun to work with other people, especially on open source stuff.

It always feels good when someone writes in to tell you, "Hey, we're now using your software for *x*." That's pretty cool. When I see the number of web sites that use memcached or the load balancer or something, I'm like, "Ah, that's cool." I remember all these porn sites started telling me they're using my file system. Well, that says something. I'm helping serve up porn. On Craigslist, every request goes through a web server that is basically a front end to memcached. OK. That's cool.

Seibel: Do you think programmers are overenamored of new things? New languages, new tools, new whatever?

Fitzpatrick: They might be. I don't know if that's desperation in hoping the new thing doesn't suck, like the new programming language does what we all want. But users are the same way. Users always like to get the one with the higher version number even if it sucks more.

I don't know if programmers are statistically different than humans in general. New must be better. Which is not always the case, but people hope it is. They want it to be.

I remember talking to my dentist a while back and she was going on and on about, like, the advances in dentistry over the last, like, five years, and she was really excited about them.

Seibel: A lot of being a modern programmer requires finding the right pieces that you need to use and understanding them just well enough to use them. How do you deal with that?

Fitzpatrick: CPAN has everything. There are 14 ID3 parsers. Pick one.

Seibel: So that, in a way, is the problem facing the modern programmer—there are 14 of them. How do you pick?

Fitzpatrick: Google search—which one's highest? Which one do people tend to like? And knowing people. I got so much more involved in the open source community once I started going to all these conferences because then I would meet people and see who was respected, and who was cool.

Then I would see their code: I remember that guy. He was awesome. He was fun, friendly, and attentive, and he really cared about his code. He was really passionate when people complained about it. I'm going to use that one because if I find any bugs, I know he'll be crazy about fixing them. As opposed to the grumpy guy who maybe writes great code, but he's grumpy and not fun to interact with if you have a question or a bug. So you pick maintainers you trust or respect.

Seibel: Then is there any trick to quickly figuring out whether something's going to suit your needs?

Fitzpatrick: I just start. I don't plug it right into my code—first I write a test program that uses the couple functions I know I'm going to need, make sure they work. Or write a unit test for just that library on just the data I plan to use with it. A lot of libraries out there don't even have their own tests. Even if it does, maybe you read the doc and you don't really trust that it does what it says it does, or the doc wasn't clear about how it behaves. So I write my own tests for the shit I care about. I figure since I'm going to have to write something to learn the library anyway, my first Hello, World program might as well be a unit test against it.

Seibel: What about the actual tools you use—you're still an Emacs user, right?

Fitzpatrick: I'm still an Emacs user. I wish I were better at Emacs. But I know all the keystrokes but I don't really customize it much. I steal other people's customizations and I can kind of read it. But I find myself getting annoyed by something and saying, "I should go write some Elisp to bind it to a key." And then I don't.

Steve Yegge is working on project to basically replace all of Elisp with JavaScript. So I keep saying, I'll wait for him to do that so I don't have to learn another language. I'll just write it in JavaScript. I don't mind JavaScript as a language. It's browsers that suck. At Google I write a lot of stuff in JavaScript that I then embed in Java and C++. I figure JavaScript is a good embedding language.

Seibel: Are there any tools that you are forced to use regularly that you just hate? Other than your whole desktop?

Fitzpatrick: Yeah, the whole desktop. There are a whole lot of things on my desktop. All these browsers are always hanging and crashing and using tons of memory. My whole operating system hanging. My coworkers try to tell me—if they see me doing something in Emacs—that Eclipse or IntelliJ does it for them automatically. So every six months I try out one of them, Eclipse or IntelliJ. And the damn thing just sits there spinning forever, consuming memory and maybe crashes in the middle of me typing or can't keep up with me typing. Come on—syntax-highlight in the background or compile in a different thread. Why are you blocking my typing to do this? OK, I'll try it again in six months, guys. So I'm glad I'm not forced to use that. I should really get better at Emacs, though.

My learning curve is, I learn something pretty rapidly until I get to this point where I'm pretty productive and good enough. Then I kind of plateau at like maybe 90 percent or 80 percent, where I'm productive and I don't have to look things up and I'm happy. And then it slowly gets better after that. It's only after I'm supercomfortable with something that I'm like, "I'm going to go dig around the docs for this language—the man pages—and learn every nook and cranny."

Seibel: Is that maybe wise these days? There are so many things you could learn. You could spend forever just learning how to use your editor, and how much software would you write then?

Fitzpatrick: Yeah, but I've always found—at least for your editor—it always pays off. Whenever I learn something, it pays off within, I don't know, a week or two. Whenever I write a stupid little shell script in my bin directory, or a little Perl script, or something to automate my life, it always pays off.

Seibel: So you've never gotten trapped in the pit of endless toolsmithing?

Fitzpatrick: Nah. I tend to do it for a purpose. I definitely know people who are just always working on their personal tools and never get anything done. I can go a little bit more in that direction and be safe, though.

Seibel: What do you think is the most important skill for a programmer to have?

Fitzpatrick: Thinking like a scientist; changing one thing at a time. Patience and trying to understand the root cause of things. Especially when you're debugging something or designing something that's not quite working. I've seen young programmers say, "Oh, shit, it doesn't work," and then rewrite it all. Stop. Try to figure out what's going on. Learn how to write things incrementally so that at each stage you could verify it.

Seibel: Is there anything that you did specifically to improve your skill as a programmer?

Fitzpatrick: Sometimes I'll go out of my way to write something in a language that I would rather not write it in—and I know it'll take me longer to write in that language—because I know I'll be better in the end. Like when I got to Google, there were a lot of times where I was writing one-off things and I'd go to write it in Perl. Then I'd be like, "Ah, no, I should write this in Python." Now I write tons of Python and it doesn't bother me—I barely have to look things up. Perlbal was originally written in C# just to learn that.

Seibel: And are there skills apart from programming itself that you think would-be programmers should develop?

Fitzpatrick: There's communication, but I'm not sure that's something you can really practice. Deal with people on mailing lists a lot. Written communication style goes a long way. But that's a general life thing, right? There was some study about who was successful after high school. Was it the smart kids or the social kids? It turned out that it was the social kids who ended up making all the money in life, not the people with the good grades. I thought that was interesting.

Seibel: That seems to be a bit of a change from the past. It used to be programmers could be gnomes hiding in an office. These days it's all mailing lists and collaboration.

Fitzpatrick: Well, at the places I've worked, either on open source or at companies, everyone depends on each other. The motivating factor is, "I'm going to write this code because I know you're going to be needing it in two weeks or I'm going to be needing yours in two weeks." There's always a human level.

Seibel: People have claimed that there are orders of magnitude differences in productivity between the best and worst programmers. Has that been your experience?

Fitzpatrick: Yeah, but it's probably like that in every field. It's how much experience you have. It's not often the case where I know of two people who do the same sort of programming and have been doing it the same amount of time, but differ by a factor of ten times. It seems like if you're not getting better all the time, you're probably getting frustrated and you drop out.

I guess there are the people who just do it for a job but don't really enjoy it. Which is OK. But it's kind of weird to compare those people with people who are hardcore programmers. What's ten times more productive when one person works ten times the hours and thinks about it nonstop and the other person just does it at his job?

Seibel: You just mentioned taking a scientist's approach to debugging. Do you consider yourself a scientist, an engineer, an artist, or a craftsman?

Fitzpatrick: Either scientist or engineer. Probably more engineer. I would say scientist was second, but only in the sense of the scientific method of changing one thing at a time and how you diagnose problems. Engineer for the design aspect of things. I definitely have friends who call themselves artists or craftsmen. I've never thought of myself as that.

Seibel: On the other hand, there's a lot of engineering envy in software. You hear the jokes about, "If people built skyscrapers the way we build software, the first woodpecker would destroy civilization." Do you think building software is a well-understood engineering discipline?

Fitzpatrick: No. I don't think it's there yet. You don't need a license, right, to write code. Not that I want tons of regulation, but it would be nice to know that some of these PHP programmers with these XSS exploits aren't the same people writing the air-traffic-control system. I'd like there to be some official line between those people.

I have a friend who's a structural engineer and he went to school forever and took all this engineering certification stuff. It's kind of comforting to know that the people who build the bridges I'm on studied this shit forever and took tons of tests and stayed up all the time studying.

Seibel: But what test could you give a programmer that would give you confidence that they can write software that will work?

Fitzpatrick: I don't know. It's kind of scary.

Seibel: Even without licensing, do you think programmers have any sort of special ethical responsibilities to society? We're arguably a profession, and professions have codes of conduct.

Fitzpatrick: You shouldn't kill anyone. Like with flight-control software. But that's kind of a rare case. I would like to ask that everyone is consistent on their credit-card forms to like let me put in fucking spaces or hyphens. Computers are good at removing that shit. Like don't tell me how to format my numbers. But there's no ethics there. Just stupidity.

Seibel: You're 28 now. Do you have any worries that programming is sort of a young person's game, that you're going to lose a step as you get older?

Fitzpatrick: No. The worst case, I could always just stop and work on fun things on my own. I don't feel like I'm competing with anyone right now and I don't really care if other people are better because I feel like there are tons of people who are better already. I figure we are always in the middle anyway, so I'm happy to stay in the middle.

Seibel: So programming is what you'd do for fun, even if you quit working?

Fitzpatrick: Oh, yeah. I'd still do stupid shit. I have this silly board game on my phone. I was kind of tired—I couldn't work on anything serious, so I wrote a solver for that game. Tried to do some dynamic programming and did different board sizes and did a bunch of random boards and made a histogram of how many moves it takes to solve the board for different board sizes. I sent it to the author because the game has a really bad estimate of par. Basically, to advance in the game you have to do better than par. And everyone on the mailing list was noticing that the game got easier as you went on because his estimate of par he kind of pulled out of nowhere. So I sent him the histograms at every board size. I think in the new version of the game he adjusted par. That was a fun hack, just on the shuttle home. I could retire and just do dumb shit like that all day.

CHAPTER

3

Douglas Crockford

A senior JavaScript Architect at Yahoo!, Douglas Crockford has been a programmer since the early '70s when he took a Fortran course in college after being unable to get studio time for his major in television broadcasting. Over the course of his career, he has combined computers with media in various ways at places like Atari, Lucasfilm, Electric Communities, and now Yahoo!

Crockford is, by nature, a simplifier and a tidier. He invented JSON, the data interchange format widely used in Ajax applications, because he found XML too complicated. His recently published book, JavaScript: The Good Parts, argues that JavaScript is actually quite a nice language if one avoids certain features. When I talked to him he stressed the importance of subsetting as a way of managing complexity and described a code-reading process he uses that starts with simply tidying up the code.

At the time of our interview, Crockford had become well known as an outspoken critic of the proposed ECMAScript 4 (ES4) revision to the ECMAScript (JavaScript) language standard, on the grounds that it was too complex. He was in favor of a more modest proposal labeled ES3.1, and since then he and the other ES3.1 advocates have largely prevailed—ES3.1 has been renamed ES5, and the ES4 effort has been officially abandoned.

Crockford and I talked about what he disliked about the ES4 proposal, the importance of code reading as a team activity, and how to move the Web forward despite the legacy of existing systems.

Seibel: How did you start programming?

Crockford: I went to San Francisco State University. I went there because they had a really good television program. My first year I couldn't get into the studio so I looked for other things to take and sort of as a fluke I took a Fortran class in the math department. And it turned out I was really good at it so I took the second-semester class.

That was '71, '72. It was punch cards in the basement of the library. Timesharing had just come to the school. At San Francisco State we didn't have a strong engineering department that owned all the computers. Instead they got distributed all over the school. Natural sciences had a lab; school of business had a lab; school of education had a lab; and humanities had a lab. Which was really interesting in that you had all these disciplines all playing with computers.

I went to work first in the science lab and then in the humanities lab. So I'd have people coming in who were economists or psychologist or geographers—they were the most interesting people. I'd learn about the problems that they were working on and I developed a lot of sensitivity really early on to the concerns of normal people as they play with these terrible machines and started looking at how we can make this stuff better for them.

Eventually I got into the studios and did all the TV stuff and that was fun but in the end I decided to go the computer way. But all along I spent a lot of time thinking about the two things together. I anticipated a lot of what would become multimedia and now digital media, and at various times in my career I've gone back and done the media part and then returned to the programming part.

Seibel: So you started with Fortran and discovered that you were good at it. Was there anything that drew you to programming other than, "Oh, I seem to be good at this."?

Crockford: That's all it was. It was my first semester, and I had to take a math class and I had picked one of those at random and it happened to have Fortran in it. So I didn't go into it intending to learn how to program. It was just what happened.

Seibel: What was the first interesting program you remember writing?

Crockford: That's going way back. I think it was a program I wrote to disassemble the runtime of the Fortran system on the timesharing system I was using. By doing that, I was able to read how that system worked and taught myself a lot about programming based on that model, something which would not ordinarily have been published.

Seibel: What do you think is the biggest change in the way you think about programming compared to back then?

Crockford: There was a period of maybe a decade where efficiency was really, really important. I guess it was in the early microprocessor era when memory was still really small and the CPUs were still really slow. We'd get down into assembly language in order to do things like games and music to make it fit and to make it fast. Eventually we got over that, so today we're writing big applications in JavaScript that run in a browser. It's such a profoundly inefficient environment compared to the stuff that we used to do, but Moore's Law sort of made it all OK.

Seibel: And is there anything that you regret about the path that you took learning the program?

Crockford: There are some languages that I was aware of that I never got a chance to use. I've read a lot about APL and I understand why it lost, but it was really neat and I never spent any time with it and that was unfortunate. There are other languages like that, where I'm aware of them, I've read what I can about them, but I never got a chance to actually think in them.

Seibel: So you actually ended up doing your degree in broadcasting; after that what did you do?

Crockford: I started a master's program in educational technology. But I felt like I was so far ahead of where the program was that I was just wasting time. I left that after about a year and went to work at SRI in Menlo Park, as a researcher. Then I went to a company called Basic Four, which was making small business minicomputers and spent a lot of years there. I developed a word-processing system for them and started doing some research into portable machines and PCs. I tried to push that company into PCs; I bought the first PC in the company and left it open on my desk so that the engineers could come look at it and see what IBM had done, but ultimately I couldn't change the culture there—they were pretty set in what they were doing.

Then one Christmas, maybe it was Christmas of '81, I bought an Atari 800. I went to the computer store and there was an Apple II and an 800 and the 800 looked to be snazzier so I got that one. I thought that I'd write a word processor on it or a programming language for it. But the 6502 was just not up to doing anything. So I'd spent two thousand dollars for the thing—what can it do? Well, obviously it can do games. So I started writing computer games and I sold one to Atari and then got an offer to work in their research laboratory in Sunnyvale. That was the research lab that Alan Kay had started, his first thing since PARC. So I went there and it was great. I was there for two years and watched the company melt down. But I managed to do some interesting work there. Worked with some really good people.

Seibel: Had you ever been a game aficionado before that?

Crockford: I'd thrown some quarters at Space Invaders and Pac-Man. I liked the games; I wasn't hard-core. The interesting thing about games for me was it was another place where television interacted with computers. It was the first place where the public got to participate in that interaction. I thought that was really interesting.

Seibel: After Atari melted down, what next?

Crockford: Then I went to Lucasfilm and was there for eight years.

Seibel: And Habitat started while you were there.

Crockford: It sure did. A friend of mine, Chip Morningstar, started that project. He invented the avatar; he invented the graphical virtual world. He did all that stuff first. It ran on Commodore 64s and off-peak x25 networks. Just amazing foresight in the design of that thing—he got so much right, It was amazing. I was sort of a spectator. I saw them doing it and encouraged them. But I can't take any credit for what they did.

Seibel: And then you went with them to found Electric Communities, which built upon those ideas?

Crockford: Right. Morningstar and Randy Farmer left Lucasfilm to start a company called the American Information Exchange, which took their idea of a social server and applied it to the idea of online markets. Brilliant idea, but ahead of their time. Had they been a little bit later, they could have been eBay.

Then we got the idea of well, let's do that again and come up with a common platform which does the entertainment thing and the social thing and the business thing and the commercial thing and everything and we'll do the platform for the whole world. And we had some ideas about how to make it fully distributed so that there is no single server—that it all spreads over the Net. And we would come up with security models that would allow it to be fully decentralized. It was a really powerful idea and that was the idea behind Electric Communities.

Seibel: And that's where the first versions of E came from.

Crockford: Right. We needed a secure programming language to develop the platform and the applications in. And our first attempt at that was something called Joule which was being developed at another company called Agorics. Joule was an actor language and was pretty odd in the way that it did things—it was brilliant but unconventional.

We had concerns about Joule. Were we going to be able to get people to use this language; is it too freaky? Then we came up with the idea of E, which was taking the core actor concepts out of Joule and reimplementing them on top of Java.

Seibel: Did E ever have any adoption by anyone other than its inventors?

Crockford: Not the original language. The old E was a Java dialect. We had all sorts of problems with Sun about that. We then came up with an E scripting language that was lighter but had similar properties. And that is the language which is now called E.

We developed that language at Electric Communities but I don't think we ever made use of it. But at one point we decided that we weren't using it, but it was good stuff so we spun it out and I'm really happy to see that it survived.

One of the things that was good for me in being at Electric Communities is it taught me to think in terms of closures. So when I started doing web stuff I looked at JavaScript and said, "There's something familiar about this." Because a lot of JavaScript's heritage comes from Scheme but you look at the documentation and there's nothing there that tells you that there are closures in the language. So I kind of discovered it by accident and went, "Whoa! This is great." And I've been promoting that idea that you can actually do serious programming in this silly little language.

Seibel: So that sort of brings us to the recent controversy about ECMAScript 4. I gather that you like the simplicity of the ES3 version of JavaScript.

Crockford: Well, ultimately, the significance of the changes you can make to a language is related to the success of the language. The more successful the language is, the greater the cost of changing it. You have greater re-education costs and you have the potential costs of disruption which, as you become bigger, become unacceptable. When you're really successful, you need to be extremely cautious in any changes that you make. Whereas if you haven't made it yet, you have a lot more freedom in changing it around.

JavaScript, purely by accident, has become the most popular programming language in the world. There are more JavaScript processors in the world than any other language by far. And for all of its problems with its security model, JavaScript is the only language where you can write code and run it on any machine.

And if that weren't enough, it's now being embedded in a lot of applications. Most of the Adobe applications have JavaScript in them so you can script them locally. And other applications as well. So it's become hugely popular.

The problem with the language is that it was rushed to market way too fast and standardized way too fast. So most of its defects are not in the current implementations—they are in the specification. The standard says *do this incorrectly*. Which is appalling. But that's the state of it. It got frozen in 1999 and then should have gone into neglect and died. But instead, by accident, Ajax happened and suddenly it's the world's most important programming language.

So now we're thinking that we need to fix it. But the time to have fixed it should have been in 2000. But it didn't get fixed then, back when everyone was paying no attention to it. Now it's huge.

There's another thing that's odd about JavaScript in the web context: If you're doing a server application or a desktop application or an embedded application, you get to choose not only the language but which specific compiler you're going to use, which specific runtime you're going to use. You don't get that choice in JavaScript. You have to run on everything that's out there.

Because we have to run on everything, bugs don't get fixed. If a browser maker ships a bug and goes, "Oops, we screwed up," and the next month they ship another one, we cannot depend on all of their users doing the upgrade. The mainstream, once they get IE installed on their machine, that's it; they don't upgrade. Those bugs stay there for years.

Seibel: So that's the current situation. Yet you want the Web to be a better platform for developing applications. If we can't fix the problems we have unless all the browsers fix it and even that doesn't help, we're just stuck. What's the way forward?

Crockford: That's the thing I struggle with. I can see the ideal. I know what it needs to be. And I know where we are and I can see all the obstructions in the way. And so I'm trying to figure out how do we take this forward. We're in a trap, in a sense, in that we have developed these huge systems—I'm more concerned with the economic systems and the social systems, but also the technological systems—that are dependent on this system which was not thought through very well.

The worst feature of JavaScript, without question, is its dependence on a global object. It doesn't have linkers, it doesn't have any kind of information hiding between compilation units. It all gets dumped together into a common global object. So all the components see everything else; all the components have equal access to the DOM; they all have equal access to the network. If any script gets onto your page it can go to the server and represent itself as your script and there's absolutely no way the server can tell the difference.

It has access to the screen; it can go to the user and represent itself as your script and the user can't tell the difference. All of the new antiphishing things that they're putting in the chrome don't work if the page came from your server and all scripts come with the same authority no matter where they came from.

But it's even worse than that because there are other ways that script can get onto your page. The architecture of the Web has several languages in it—there's HTTP, there's HTML, URLs are a language, there's CSS, and there's the scripting language. They're all in there and they can all be embedded in each other and they all have different quoting and escaping and commenting conventions. And they are not consistently implemented in all of the browsers. Some of them are not specified anywhere. So it's really easy for an evildoer to take some script and put it in a URL, put it in a piece of style and put that in some HTML and put that in another script, and so on.

Seibel: Those are the classic cross-site scripting attacks, taking advantage of bugs in the browser.

Crockford: Right. That's horrible; we have to fix that—it's intolerable that we keep going this way.

On top of that we've discovered mash-ups. And mash-ups realize something that we've been trying to do in software for 20 years: to have interesting reusable components that we can snap together like LEGO and make new applications out of, instantly. And we're doing that stuff in mash-ups and it's brilliant, where you can take something from Yahoo and something from Google and something of yours and something of someone else's and put them all together and make an application, and it's great. And it all happens on the browser, right in front of your eyes. Except that each of those components has access to the same stuff. So now we are intentionally creating XSS exploits. And the browser's security model did not anticipate any of this goodness and does not provide any way of allowing for cooperation with mutual suspicion. The whole Web is built on one mistake after another. We have this big pile of accidents.

Seibel: So given all that, is the cost of the ES4 effort just the opportunity cost, that everyone is going to spend time thinking about that instead of some way to fix these problems?

Crockford: Right. It's solving the wrong problem. It's solving the problem that people hate JavaScript. And I can appreciate Brendan Eich's position there because he did some brilliant work but he rushed it and he was mismanaged and so bad stuff got out. And he's been cursed and vilified for the last dozen years about how stupid he is and how stupid the language is and none of that's true. There's actually brilliance there and he's a brilliant guy. So he's now trying to vindicate himself and prove, I'm really a smart guy and I'm going to show it off with this language that has every good feature I've ever seen and we're going to put them all together and it's going to work.

I don't think that's the problem we need to be solving right now. I think the problem we need to be solving is: The Web is broken and we need to fix it. So we need to figure out a way to go forward. And my biggest objection with what Brendan is trying to do is it's a distraction.

I'm looking at this stuff incrementally. If we can get a module; if we can get a choice of programming language, we've gone way forward. We're still not done yet, but we're in much better shape than we are now. Then there are things like Caja and ADsafe which are trying to do that using today's technology. We can't wait.

What ADsafe does is it creates a safe subset of JavaScript. So it disallows access to anything that's global and anything that's dangerous. And it turns out there's still a useful language in that subset. Because all the lambda power is there. And lambdas can do a lot. So it's an unconventional language because it doesn't let you use prototypes in the way we have up until now. But it's a full lambda language, so hugely powerful.

Seibel: Leaving aside that it may be solving the wrong problem, are there any bits of ES4 that you like, just from a language point of view?

Crockford: There are some bug fixes that are good that I think we should have. But there's too much stuff in the language that hasn't been tried. And our experience with ES3 is that once an error gets into the spec, it's impossible to take it out. And we have no experience with this language. No one has ever written a big application with it.

It will be standardized and deployed before we know that it works. So I think we're doing this way too fast. I'd be much more comfortable if we had multiple reference implementations and people doing useful applications with it and then go, OK, the language seems to work; now let's standardize it, now let's deploy it worldwide. I think we're doing it all backwards.

Seibel: So Google's GWT compiles Java into JavaScript. And other folks have played around with compiling other languages to JavaScript. Is that a path forward?

Crockford: It's sort of interesting to see JavaScript turning into the universal runtime. That's not a role we ever expected for it.

Seibel: But, as you said, it's everywhere; it *is* the universal runtime.

Crockford: Which I think puts even more pressure on getting JavaScript to go fast. Particularly as we're now going into mobile. Moore's law doesn't apply to batteries. So how much time we're wasting in interpreting stuff really matters there. The cycles count. So I think that's going to put more pressure on improving the quality of the runtime.

As far as GWT goes, and other transforming things, I'm really pragmatic. This environment is so hard to work in—if you can find something that works, then great. I'm fearful of using it myself because I worry about the abstraction leakage. If there's a problem in your Java code or in GWT or in what it produces on the other side, you may or may not have a place to stand to deal with that. Particularly if you took the approach that you can afford to be completely ignorant about JavaScript because the language is hidden from you. Then you're going to be in a world of hurt if anything goes wrong. I hadn't heard of that happening to anybody, so so far they appear to be doing it right. But there is that risk.

Seibel: What would you like to see happen with JavaScript?

Crockford: I think the best way to make JavaScript better would be to make it smaller. If we could just get it down to what it does really well and remove the features that add little or no value, it's actually a better language. And I think we can take that approach to HTML; I think we can take that approach to HTTP and to CSS. I think all of the standards that we're working with, we need to figure out what do they do right and what is it missing and refocus them, rather than just piling new features on top.

Seibel: Yet there's often a tension between small, elegant jewels and sprawling, practical balls of mud. A small, perfect jewel is easy to understand and it doesn't have warts but then you have to build more stuff on top of it to do anything. So everybody reimplements the same things over and over and that leads to a different kind of bloat and ugliness.

Crockford: But that's not what's happening. We have a number of Ajax library developers who are doing that and some of them are getting very sophisticated in their use of the language. And then the communities out there are building sloppy stuff on top of it and that's working. So it's not necessary for every application programmer to understand how to fully exploit lambda in order to take advantage of the lambda nature of the language. So we're already doing that. We don't need to abandon the language in order to fix that—that's not where it's broken.

Where we do have a problem there is that there are too many Ajax libraries. That was a consequence of the fact that JavaScript is so powerful and the need is so profound and that they're easy to make. So for a while everybody was making them. I've been expecting that we're going to have a shake-out but it hasn't happened yet. So we still have a whole lot of libraries. So we have an alternative problem now—because there are so many libraries to choose from, developers don't know which one to use. I think there will be a shake-out eventually.

One thing that we're seeing now is that the Ajax libraries are converging. jQuery came up with a notation for using CSS selectors for getting a list of objects from the DOM and then providing methods for manipulating the objects en masse. And that turns out to be a really good idea and it's something that JavaScript does very effectively. There's an inefficiency there in that the interface to the DOM is horrible but they hide it all. They've really simplified the programming model—it's brilliant.

So everybody's doing that now—we're seeing feature convergence. Which makes the problem even harder for the user community because it makes it harder to decide which library to use because they're all becoming more similar. But eventually they're going to coalesce down to a couple, maybe one. I had been predicting that one of the winners was going to be Microsoft with their Atlas framework, just because Microsoft is always one of the winners. But they don't appear to be getting traction. The open frameworks seem to be doing much better. So I'm expecting one or two of the open frameworks will ultimately win.

Seibel: These days you're a JavaScript architect and evangelist here at Yahoo!, so part of your job, presumably, is to tell Yahoo! JavaScript programmers, "Here's how you should do it." Does your job also cover general good design practice and good coding practice?

Crockford: One of the things I've been pushing is code reading. I think that is the most useful thing that a community of programmers can do for each other—spend time on a regular basis reading each other's code. There's a tendency in project management just to let the programmers go off independently and then we have the big merge and if it builds then we ship it and we're done and we forget about it.

One of the consequences of that is that if you have weak or confused programmers you're not aware of their actual situation until much too late. And so the risks to the project, that you're going to have to build with stuff that's bad and the delays that that causes, that's unacceptable. The other thing is that you may have brilliant programmers on the project who are not adequately mentoring the other people on the team. Code reading solves both of those problems.

Seibel: Can you talk a bit about how you conduct a code reading?

Crockford: At each meeting, someone's responsible for reading their code, and they'll walk us through everything, and the rest of us will observe. It's a really good chance for the rest of the team to understand how their stuff is going to have to fit with that stuff.

We get everybody around the table; everybody gets a stack of paper. We also blow it up on the screen. And we all read through it together. And we're all commenting on the code as we go along. People say, "I don't understand this comment," or, "This comment doesn't seem to describe the code." That kind of stuff can be so valuable because as a programmer you stop reading your own comments and you're not aware that you're misdirecting the reader. Having the people you work with helping to keep your code clean is a huge service—you find defects that you never would've found on your own.

I think an hour of code reading is worth two weeks of QA. It's just a really effective way of removing errors. If you have someone who is strong reading, then the novices around them are going to learn a lot that they wouldn't be learning otherwise, and if you have a novice reading, he's going to get a lot of really good advice.

And it shouldn't be something that we save for the end. Back in the old days, we would schedule a code reading just as we were finishing a project and usually it would be canceled because we were late. I now believe that code reading should be happening all the time throughout the life of the project. That's something that took me a while to figure out but there are so many benefits that come from that.

For one thing it makes it easier to track the project, because we can actually see what progress people are making. And we can see much sooner if they're going off the rails or not.

I've managed projects where we're up against a deadline and we had people saying, "Yeah, I'm almost done," and then you get the code, and there's nothing there, or it's crap, or whatever, and they're nowhere close to done. In management, those are the experiences you hate the most and I think code reading is the best way of not getting trapped like that.

Seibel: So say we're doing a code reading of some of my code. I bring printouts and we put it up on the screen. Then what? Do I literally read it out loud?

Crockford: Yeah, go through it line by line, and you'll be doing commentary on it. This is what's supposed to be happening here. If we have time, we'll go line by line.

Seibel: Do you find that you have to teach people how to do code readings? I can imagine it'd be hard to find the right balance of being critical enough to be worthwhile without making the code's author feel personally attacked.

Crockford: Yeah, it requires a lot of trust on the part of the team members so there have to be clear rules as to what's in bounds and what's not. If you had a dysfunctional team, you don't want to be doing this, because they'll tear themselves apart. And if you have a dysfunctional team and you're not aware of it, this will reveal it pretty quickly. There's a lot that you can learn, a lot that's revealed by this process. It feels unnatural at first, although once you get into the rhythm of it, it feels extremely natural.

Another aspect is writing your code such that it can be read. Neatness counts, as it turns out, and style is important. And all of those things will increase the quality of the code base going forward and increase the competence of the programming community.

Seibel: What makes code readable for you?

Crockford: It happens at a number of levels. The simplest is just being consistent in the presentation so you always indent everything properly; you have white space in all the right places. One habit that I still struggle with, something I learned back in the Fortran days, is I tend to use too many one-letter variable names, which I believe is a bad thing. And I'm trying really hard to break it, but it's difficult—it's still something I struggle with.

Seibel: How hard is it? Do you write the code and then you come back later and say, "Oh, look at all these one-character variable names."?

Crockford: I think in terms of one letter. Also in JavaScript, there's an indefensible efficiency argument that you're actually paying for the download cost of those extra characters, and so you can make programs smaller by making your variable names smaller.

Seibel: There are tools for that, right?

Crockford: Well, you can gzip it and that pretty much takes it all out, so I have no defense. When I'm going back through my old code and I see the names are too short, if I have time, I'll change them. Some things, like my loop counters, will probably always be `i`. I don't think I'll ever fix that, but there are a lot of others that are just inexcusable.

That's the first level, the grammatical stuff. It's similar to writing in English or any language, getting the punctuation right, getting the capitalization right, putting the commas in the right place. Then you start looking at higher-level things like how you structure the sentences and where you break the paragraphs. In a programming language, it takes the form of how do you decompose the problem into a set of functions or a set of classes?

Seibel: What are the concrete things that programmers should focus on to make their code readable?

Crockford: The subset idea is really important, especially for JavaScript because it contains so many bad features. But it's true for all languages. When I was a journeyman, I would read the language manual and I would understand every feature. And I would figure out how to use them all. And I'd use them all all the time. It turns out a lot of them were not well thought through.

I'm thinking back to Fortran now, but it was true in all languages. Sometimes language designers get it wrong. C has a whole bunch of errors in it, from my perspective now.

Seibel: For instance?

Crockford: Like the switch statement having fall-through be the default was wrong—they shouldn't have done that. ++ has huge security problems—it encourages you to be way too tricky, to try to do too much in one line. In that compulsion to do it in one line, you make code which is hard to understand and which is likely to lead to things like buffer overrun errors. So most of the security problems that we've seen in operating systems over the last few years are a consequence of ++.

In my programming style now I don't use ++ anymore, *ever.* I can make the case that it's good to use it here and it's bad to use it there but it's hard for me to find the good pieces and the bad pieces in my code.

Seibel: Couldn't one argue that the security problem with ++ really has nothing to do with ++ but with unchecked array bounds or raw pointers? It isn't a security risk in Java because if you ++ off the end of the array you just get an exception.

Crockford: Yeah, it's certainly less dangerous in Java. And that danger doesn't exist at all in JavaScript because it doesn't have arrays. But even so, I found that the quality of my code got better when I stopped doing it, just because it invited me to write one-liners and that's usually a bad idea.

Another example of that is the `continue` statement. I have never seen a piece of code that I could not improved by taking the `continue` out. It makes certain kinds of complicated structures easier to write. But I found that I can always improve the structure if I can find a way to factor it out. So as part of my personal discipline, I don't use `continue` ever. If I see a `continue` in my code, then I assume I haven't thought it through carefully.

Seibel: How do you read code you didn't write?

Crockford: By cleaning it. I'll throw it in a text editor and I'll start fixing it. First thing I'll do is make the punctuation conform; get the indentation right; do all that stuff. I have programs that can do that for me, but I find doing that myself is more efficient in the long run because it gets me more acquainted with the code. Morningstar taught me to do this. He's brilliant at refactoring other people's code and that's the approach he takes and I find it works.

Seibel: Have you ever found that code that was, at that level, a mess, then you cleaned it all up and discovered it was actually good code underneath?

Crockford: I've never actually seen that. I think it's really difficult to write good code in a sloppy manner. By good code, I mean it's going to be readable. At one level, it doesn't matter what it does to a machine if I can't figure out what it does, so it might turn out that the code is amazing in terms of its efficiency, or its compactness, or some other metric which I don't care about.

Readability of code is now my first priority. It's more important than being fast, almost as important as being correct, but I think being readable is actually the most likely way of making it correct. So I think it's probably not good code and they probably made the wrong trade-offs if the code turned out to be in the state that it's not easily readable.

Seibel: What about in the inner loop of the inner loop where it's just got to be blazing-fast? Can all code be readable or are there times when you must sacrifice readability to gain efficiency?

Crockford: I suppose, but I would write a novel on both ends of that and explain this is why we're doing what we're doing. Usually that gets left out. I also see a lot of folks struggling to try to make stuff fast in situations where it absolutely doesn't need to go fast. They're unaware of how their own program is spending its time and so they're optimizing things which don't require optimization and which will never be big enough going through that path to ever make any difference so there's no reward, no benefit at all, for having done that optimization. All the optimization did was introduce cruft. I see a lot of that.

Seibel: In curly-brace languages, there are endless religious wars about what's the proper place to put the braces, and people argue that one style or the other makes it easier to read. Is part of what you're doing when you "clean up" code just putting it in the form that's easy for you to absorb?

Crockford: Yeah, definitely, because I believe I'm using the only correct style and everybody else got it wrong! I think Thompson and Ritchie did the world a disservice by not defining the pretty-print presentation for C. Saying, "This is how we do it, but you can do it some other way," has had a huge toll on humanity, and it will probably continue to always have one.

Seibel: So your preferred style is K&R?

Crockford: Yeah, I think they got it right. Their initial style is right. Particularly in JavaScript. JavaScript does semicolon insertion, and so there are places where the meaning of a program will change in a drastically bad way if you put the braces on the left instead of on the right. It turns out the K&R style is not subject to that problem, but the flush style is.

So I can argue in the case of JavaScript, there absolutely is a correct way of placing the braces. In other C-flavored languages I can't make that same case. Some people like to have their braces flush and I've seen people argue for hours about which way is right, and none of the explanations make any sense on either side, because what they're really arguing is, what I used in school, or what I used at my first job, or the style that's used by someone who impressed me, now looks right to me and everything else looks wrong.

It's similar, I suppose, to an argument about, should we be driving on the left side of the street or the right. Ultimately there's not a good case for doing it one way or another. If you live on an island, you can do it the wrong way and it doesn't matter, but ultimately the community benefits if we can all figure out how to drive on the same side.

Seibel: So if you changed jobs and went somewhere where they programmed C or Java in a different style than you prefer, would you say, "Well, I'll switch and I know that after a little bit, I'll be happy to see this style"? Or would you just not take the job?

Crockford: Maybe that's something that people should look at—what is the house of style here? Are we on the left or the right? And maybe not go work at a place that gets them on the wrong side. It does take on a Dr. Seuss quality where you get really upset about whether you've got a star on your belly or not. Ultimately you have to embrace the house style and you hope that the people who put the house style together knew what they were doing. They probably didn't; maybe it doesn't matter. It's more important that everybody be on the same page.

Seibel: So when you're reading code you start with a typographical cleanup, how deeply or dramatically do you refactor things?

Crockford: I'll rearrange code so that everything is declared and set up before it's called. Some languages give you a lot of flexibility around that so you don't have to. I don't want that flexibility.

Seibel: So you want no forward references?

Crockford: Right, or if there is a forward reference, I want it to be explicit. I don't want code to come in any random order unless I'm doing a literate programming thing in which I'm explicitly breaking the code in terms of a presentational order rather than the order that the language wants, and I like that a lot. But unless you're actually using literate tools, you shouldn't be doing that.

Seibel: In one of your talks you quoted Exodus 23:10 and 11: "And six years thou shalt sow thy land, and shalt gather in the fruits thereof: But the seventh year thou shalt let it rest and lie still" and suggested that every seventh sprint should be spent cleaning up code. What is the right time frame for that?

Crockford: Six cycles—whatever the cycle is between when you ship something. If you're on a monthly delivery cycle then I think every half year you should skip a cycle and just spend time cleaning the code up.

Seibel: So if you don't clean up every seventh cycle you may be faced with the choice of whether or not to do a big rewrite. How do you know when, if ever, it's time for a big rewrite?

Crockford: Generally the team knows when it's time. Management finds out a lot later. The team is getting beat up pretty regularly, making too many bugs; the code's too big, it's too slow; we're falling behind. They know why. It's not because they became stupider or lazier. It's because the code base is no longer serving the purpose that it needs to.

It's a really difficult thing for management to see, particularly managers who are not programmers. But even programming managers have trouble with this because you've seen that you've invested so much time to get to this point. And starting over means we've got to go all the way back to there and bring it up. And in the meantime we're not going to be going forward on anything else and it's just impossible. No, we go forward with what we have.

The fallacy is that it's going to take that amount of time again, though there are counterexamples. You've got the second-system problem where people who've had some success are given a blank slate and allowed to do whatever they want. Generally, they will fail because they'll be too ambitious, they won't understand the limits. And you get nothing out of that. You have to have extreme discipline to say, "It's not a blank slate; it's reimplementing what we had here; it's doing what we knew."

Part of what makes programming difficult is most of the time we're doing stuff we've never done before. If it was stuff that had been done before we'd be reusing something else. For most of what we do, we're doing something that we haven't done before. And doing things that you haven't done before is hard. It's a lot of fun but it's difficult. Particularly if you're using a classical methodology you're having to do classification on systems that you don't fully understand. And the likelihood that you're going to get the classification wrong is high.

Seibel: By "classical" you mean using classes.

Crockford: Right. I've found it's less of a problem in the prototypal world because you focus on the instances. If you can find one instance which is sort of typical of what the problem is, you're done. And generally you don't have to refactor those. But in a classical system you can't do that—you're always working from the abstract back to the instance. And then making hierarchy out of that is really difficult to get right. So ultimately when you understand the problem better you have to go back and refactor it. But often that can have a huge impact on the code, particularly if the code's gotten big since you figured it out. So you don't. So you keep bundling these new things on top of it to try to patch the problems that were in the original hierarchy and it gets cruftier and worse.

Seibel: But you do think that refactoring can work, if you take every seventh interval to do it? You don't *have* to end up needing a big rewrite?

Crockford: I think it can work. Throw it out and start over should only be considered in the cases where you didn't do that or you did it badly or something went wrong and you've got a code base that has become unworkable. And you can make a reasonable judgment that it will be faster to replace it than to fix it.

Seibel: What about the risk that you don't fully understand what the code you want to rewrite actually does. Because any piece of code contains bits of embedded knowledge—little bits of cruft that are hard-won functionality that you don't think of when you say, "Oh, we can just rewrite this."

Crockford: That is a real problem. One of the reasons that we're in the mess that we're in is that the Web is so poorly specified. The specifications were incomplete and were largely misinterpreted and many of those misinterpretations have become part of the canon. So these systems are way more complicated than they should be due to those historical reasons. Working at that level, yeah, I have huge sympathy for that, that there is a lot of undocumented knowledge that is reflected in the code base.

Microsoft has a similar problem with their operating systems, in that they shipped crap for too many years and then they had to remain compatible with all the bad stuff that was based on the bad stuff that they had done. And so the constraints that puts on the design of their next system are just horrendous. So it's really hard going forward with that. Ultimately they may find that they can't go forward anymore either.

Those sort of specification errors are really, really hard. And we have them in the Ajax world. Most of our problems in the Ajax world are due to the differences at the browser level. Doing the cross-browser stuff is much harder than it should be because the Web is not specified well and because the implementations are so variable.

We've gotten a lot better at that over the last few years, particularly with the advent of the Ajax libraries. Most of them do a very good job—not a complete job yet—but a pretty good job of boosting the level of programming that you do. So we're not having to deal directly with the browser guts; we have a sort of virtualized application layer that we can work on that is fairly resilient and pretty portable. We have one group here at Yahoo! which is primarily responsible for dealing with the pain that the browser causes. And when they do their job right, it makes it easier for all the other developers here. So that's good.

Seibel: On the other hand, rewrites don't always work out. You just mentioned the second-system effect and in one of your talks, you described seeing it in action as "heartbreaking." When was that?

Crockford: It was at Electric Communities. We got together the smartest team of programmers I've ever seen assembled anywhere. And we had enough money and we were going to reimplement the stuff that Chip and Randy had already done and knew exactly how to do it. Except it was grander.

Seibel: So that was basically Habitat, redone.

Crockford: Yeah, we were going to redo Habitat except it was now going to be globally distributed. And it turned out to be really hard. We actually got it built but it was painful. Not something I'd like to do again.

Seibel: Would the advice you gave before—to be very disciplined about only reimplementing what you already understand—would that have been sufficient to head off the disaster?

Crockford: I think it could have helped. We didn't think about it in stages properly. We didn't have an incremental approach. Had we taken an incremental approach, I would have started with two parallel efforts. One, work out a secure distributed platform which doesn't do anything but has the infrastructure for doing the messaging and the object management. Two, let's rebuild Habitat. Knowing what we know, with modern languages, let's just rebuild it.

Then the second phase would be, OK let's merge them together. Can we hoist this one on top of that one and still have a working system? OK, now distribute it.

Had we taken that kind of incremental approach, I think we would have been very successful with it. But we tried to do all of those in one step and that was too hard.

Seibel: And you think you were led into trying to do it in one step because you knew big chunks of it.

Crockford: Because we were so smart and we had so much experience. We had it wired. Couldn't miss. Programmers are optimistic. And we have to be because if we weren't optimists we couldn't do this work. Which is why we fall prey to things like second systems, why we can't schedule our projects, why this stuff is so hard.

Seibel: Is programming getting easier? In the future will more people be able to do something that we would recognize as programming?

Crockford: My interest in programming is helping other people to do programming, designing a language or a programming tool specifically so that it's more accessible to more people—the thing that got Smalltalk started. Smalltalk went in a different direction, but the initial direction was really attractive to me. How do we build a language specifically for children or how do we build a language specifically for people who don't think of themselves as programmers?

Seibel: Is that because you think should everybody learn to program, at least a little bit?

Crockford: I think you have to. The world has been pretty much taken over by computers now and in order to defend yourself, or to be a full citizen, you have to have some understanding of how these things work.

Seibel: Some folks would also argue that learning to program teaches a way of thinking that's important, like reading and math are different ways of thinking, and both important.

Crockford: I used to think so. I had these amazing insights when I started programming: everything became orderly, and I saw structures and things I had never seen before. I thought, "Wow, this is amazing. Everybody should learn how to do this," because suddenly I was feeling a lot smarter. Except pretty quickly I'd find, talking to other programmers, that somehow they didn't get it. Programmers are capable of completely misunderstanding the world in exactly the same way everybody else does. I was really sad to figure that out.

Seibel: Do you still enjoy programming as much as you always did?

Crockford: Oh, yeah.

Seibel: Do you think that programming is at all biased toward being young?

Crockford: I used to think so. A few years ago I had sleep apnea, but I didn't know it. I thought I was just getting tired and old, and I got to the point where it was so difficult to concentrate that I couldn't program anymore because I just couldn't keep enough stuff in my head. A lot of programming is you keep stuff in your head until you can get it written down and structured properly. And I just couldn't do it.

I had lost that ability and I thought it was just because I was getting older. Fortunately, I got better and it came back and so I'm programming again. I'm doing it well and maybe a little bit better now because I've learned how not to depend so much on my memory. I'm better at documenting my code now than I used to be because I'm less confident that I'll remember next week why I did this. In fact, sometimes I'll be going through my stuff and I'm amazed at stuff that I had written: I don't remember having done it and it's either really either awful or brilliant. I had no idea I was capable of that.

Seibel: I read somewhere where you said that literate programming, a la Donald Knuth, is a brilliant idea. Do you use literate tools?

Crockford: No. I've been thinking about it and I've been designing literate tools for some of the languages that I'm using but I'm currently not doing any literate programming.

Seibel: Is that just a tool-chain problem? If the tools existed you think you would write literate programs?

Crockford: I would. I think JSLint, for example, would be easier for me to maintain if I had written it in a literate style. The thing I like about the literate style is that you're designing the program specifically for reading and I think that provides tremendous value to the program.

Seibel: What are the key features of a literate programming tool, as you see it?

Crockford: The principal thing that Knuth found or provided was the ability to write out of order. So if I'm concerned with a particular thing which touches code in a lot of places, I can collect all that code together and describe it together, and then the tool will distribute the details out to where it needs to go.

Another of the things he frees you from is the size of a function. Ideally, you want a function to be no bigger than a screen's worth so that you can read it all at once. And if it doesn't fit, then you're making a lot more functions, and if the functions aren't actually contributing anything to the structure of the program, they're just introducing noise.

Knuth allows you to take each of the aspects of that function, which may be closely related—it might have good coherence but it's just big; sometimes stuff is big—and he allows you to represent each of those collections of stuff with an extremely descriptive label and then say, "This function is:" and then list those labels. You could do that with functions, but it's not quite the same and then you have to deal with communication between the pieces, and so on. So it's introducing more structure which doesn't exactly match the problem.

Ultimately I would like to see new languages designed specifically to be literate languages. Knuth has been very good at applying the idea to Pascal and C, but I'd really like to see a new language which is, from the bottom, designed to be used in that fashion.

Seibel: Have you read Knuth's literate programs?

Crockford: Sure.

Seibel: How do you read them? Like a novel?

Crockford: Yeah, I read it like a novel. I tend to be reading his prose rather than his program, but I really like the way he lays it out and he writes really well, and occasionally he'll slip a little joke in there. I enjoy reading his stuff.

Seibel: And what do you get out of it? So you've read *TeX: The Program*, and you get to the end. Now are you ready to go add features into TeX or do you just have an overall sense of wow, Knuth's a brilliant guy?

Crockford: That's a really good question. I've read TeX, but I didn't read it with an intention that I wanted to modify TeX. I was just reading it to see what he had done. I had a particular interest in how he was doing line-breaking, so I read that part with particular interest, more to understand his algorithm than to understand how the code works so that I can modify it or reuse it. If I were reading it with the expectation that I was going to mess with the program, I'm sure I would've read it differently.

Seibel: Do you often read code, literate or otherwise, for fun?

Crockford: Yeah. There's not much code out there that's good enough that you could read it for fun. Knuth wrote some. Fraser and Hanson have a C compiler that is literate; it's very good. But there are not a lot of examples of that yet. That's kind of a shame. That could indicate that maybe literate programming has failed, because there aren't very many examples of it.

Seibel: What about Knuth's magnum opus, *The Art of Computer Programming*? Are you the kind of person who read it cover to cover, who dips into it for reference, or who put it on the shelf and never looked at it?

Crockford: All except the last one. When I was in college, there were a couple of months where I didn't pay rent in order to buy copies of his books. And I read them and found jokes in them, like there's a TUG joke in the index of Volume I. I have not been able to make sense out of all of it. There are places where he goes really a lot deeper than I can go, but I enjoy the books a lot, and I've also used them as reference books.

Seibel: Did you literally read them cover to cover, skimming over the math that you couldn't understand?

Crockford: Yeah, the part when there are too many stars, I would read it very quickly.I tried to make familiarity with Knuth a hiring criteria, and I was disappointed that I couldn't find enough people that had read him. In my view, anybody who calls himself a professional programmer should have read Knuth's books or at least should have copies of his books.

Seibel: To read Knuth, it seems to me, you have to be able to read the math and understand it. To what extent do you think having that kind of mathematical training is necessarily to be a programmer?

Crockford: Obviously it's not, because most of them don't have it. In the sorts of applications that I'm working on, we don't see that much application of the particular tools that Knuth gives us. If we were writing operating systems or writing runtimes, it'd be much more critical. But we're doing form validations and UIs. Generally performance is not that important in the things that we do. We spend most of our time waiting for the user or waiting for the network.

I would like to insist that it's absolutely necessary for people to understand this stuff, but it's not. And maybe that's why web programming has taken off and why it's so accessible and why JavaScript works. This stuff really isn't that hard. And most of the things that make it hard are unnecessarily hard. If we just cleaned up the platform a little bit, this work gets a lot easier.

Seibel: So there's the nitty-gritty stuff that Knuth will teach you how to do and then there's the big picture. Even if you clean up the platform, building big systems and designing them in a way that's comprehensible will still be hard. How do you design your code?

Crockford: It's not so much about writing the program as making iterations on the program's survival. Generally the reason we're doing software is because we know we're going to have to change it and changing anything is hard because there's a likelihood that, in changing it, you're going to break it.

You can't anticipate everything that's going to be done with it but you try to build in enough flexibility that it's likely to adapt to whatever you're going to do. So that's what I'm thinking. How do I not write myself into a corner too much? How do I give myself the flexibility to adapt as I need to?

That's one of the things that I discovered I really like about JavaScript. Refactoring in JavaScript, I find, is really easy. Whereas refactoring a deep class hierarchy can be really, really painful.

For example, JSLint has transformed quite a lot since I started writing it in 2000, 2001. And its goals have changed significantly—it's doing a lot of stuff now that I never thought it would do. And a lot of that's because JavaScript is so flexible. I can fiddle with it and allow the program to grow without becoming sloppy.

Seibel: What makes it so much easier?

Crockford: I've become a really big fan of soft objects. In JavaScript, any object is whatever you say it is. That's alarming to people who come at it from a classical perspective because without a class, then what have you got? It turns out you just have what you need, and that's really useful. Adapting your objects . . . the objects that you want is much more straightforward.

Seibel: Presumably the problem, working with a class-based language, is that it's too static—you've got a big class hierarchy and if you want to change that structure you've got to take it apart and put it back together. In JavaScript it seems the danger is that it can be too dynamic—you've stuck little kludges everywhere and the actual structure of your program is determined by lots of things that happen at runtime; there's no static thing you can look at and say, "OK, this is the program and how it's structured."

Crockford: That is the scary part of it and it's good to be scared because it is scary and it is real. It requires discipline. In most of the classical languages, the language is the thing imposing the discipline. In JavaScript you have to bring your own discipline.

Part of what I do to keep my code from falling apart is to be really rigorous myself in how I put it together because I know the language is not providing that rigor for me. So today I would not consider undertaking something as complicated as JSLint without JSLint. JavaScript does not scale very well on its own, but with that tool I become a lot more confident that I'm going to be able to keep it working.

Seibel: So the softness of JavaScript objects can be dangerous. But if you never availed yourself of the ability to augment objects, then you might as well just be writing classes in Java. Is there some way you think about structuring your JavaScript programs to take good advantage of the flexibility the language gives you?

Crockford: For me it was years of trial and error. When I started working with JavaScript, I didn't read anything about it. I just started. I found a sample program, which was awful, and started fiddling with it until it worked more like the way I thought it should. So I began programming in the language, having no understanding about what the language was, or how it worked, or how you needed it to think about it.

I understand why people are frustrated with the language. If you try to write in JavaScript as though it is Java, it'll keep biting you. I did this. One of the first things I did the in the language was to figure out how to simulate something that looked sort of like a Java class, but at the edges it didn't work anything like it. And I would always eventually get pushed up against those edges and get hurt.

Eventually I figured out I just don't need these classes at all and then the language started working for me. Instead of fighting it, I found I was being empowered by it.

Seibel: When you're designing software, do you prefer to think top-down or bottom-up or middle-out?

Crockford: All at once. That's the thing about keeping the system in your head. Ultimately you need to divide and conquer and get it down into something you can manage. I find I'm on all parts of the problem and using all those techniques simultaneously. And I keep struggling with it until I become clear on what the structure is. Once you figure out what the structure is, then the rest of it falls out.

Seibel: How do design and coding relate for you? Do you start coding immediately and then iteratively refine it, or do you do something that's separate from writing code?

Crockford: They used to be separate. They're becoming more similar now. I used to work in a design language or a meta language—something semi-English, a little structured, which is more descriptive of what you're going to write. But if I'm writing in JavaScript, that language has turned into JavaScript.

Seibel: What tools do you actually use for writing code?

Crockford: I use a little freeware text editor. It doesn't do anything tricky. That's about all I need. There is much less need of formal tools like you have in other languages. The browser just wants a source file, and so you send it a source file, and the compiler is built into the browser, so there's really nothing to do. You don't have a linker. You don't have a compiler. You don't have any of that stuff. It just all runs on the browser.

Seibel: You use JSLint, presumably.

Crockford: I do use JSLint. I use it a lot. I try to use it every time before I run a program, so if I've gone through and I've done some edits, I'll run it through JSLint first before I run it.

Seibel: So you edit in your text editor, run JSLint on the program, and then run it in a browser. How about debugging?

Crockford: It depends on the browser. If it's Firefox, then you use Firebug. If it's IE, then you use the Visual Studio debugger. They're both actually very good. We have surprisingly good debuggers in the browser.

I've used frameworks in which there were inspectors built out of DOM elements that could then go into objects, and open them up, and inspect through that set of frames. But I found I really don't need that. Just a debugger is enough.

Seibel: Do you ever step through code just as a way of checking it when you're not tracking down a specific bug?

Crockford: Only if I have something that's really intricate. I'll step through it as part of my testing, but generally I only step if I know I have problems.

Seibel: How about other debugging techniques, like assertions, or proofs. Do you use any of those? Do you think in terms of invariants?

Crockford: I like them. I was disappointed that Eiffel was not the winner in the object-oriented-language contest; that C++ won instead. I thought Eiffel was a much more interesting language and I liked the precondition/postcondition contract stuff that it did. I would like to see that built into my language, whatever language I'm using, but that's another one of those ideas that hasn't really caught on.

Seibel: What's the worst bug you ever had to track down?

Crockford: It would've been a real-time bug. It might've been in a video game. We've got interrupts popping all over the place, and no memory management at all, and the program suddenly goes away and you don't know why. That kind of stuff is really hard. And generally there wouldn't be a debugger around either.

At Basic Four we had developed a word-processing terminal. It was a Z80-based terminal with a full-page display and 64K, which wasn't nearly enough memory for a display that big. And it had a local network connection to our server where it would send up the pages.

And we had this problem where every once in a while the screen would go blank. We had this architecture in which we had a line of text and then it would have a stop code, and then the address of the next line, and a little DMA processor that would follow those links. And at some point a link would go away—there was some race that was happening.

From our perspective, looking at it logically, all of the links were good, but we hadn't considered the real-time interaction with the DMA processor, which might not be looking at memory at the same time that we were. I just puzzled it out. I remember I was working at home that day and I was on the phone with my team and suddenly the lightbulb went on; I knew what the problem was and I was able to tell them how to fix it and we never had that problem again.

In my experience, the worst bugs are the real-time bugs, which have to do with interactions with multiple threads. My approach to those bugs is to avoid making them. So I don't like threads. I think threads are an atrocious programming model. They're an occasionally necessarily evil, but they're not necessary for most of the things we use threads for.

One of the things I like about the browser model is that we only get one thread. Some people complain about that—if you lock up that thread, then the browser's locked up. So you just don't do that. There are constantly calls for putting threads into JavaScript and so far we've resisted that. I'm really glad we have.

The event-based model, which is what we're using in the browser, works really well. The only place where it breaks down is if you have some process that takes too long. I really like the approach that Google has taken in Gears to solving that, where they have a separate process which is completely isolated that you can send a program to and it'll run there. When it's finished, it'll tell you the result and the result comes back as an event. That's a brilliant model.

Seibel: Have you ever been interested in formal proofs?

Crockford: I watched it closely during the '70s, looking to see if they were going to come up with anything. And I didn't see it paying off. Software is so complicated and can go wrong in so many ways.

Basically, software is the specification for how the software is supposed to work. And anything less than the complete specification doesn't really tell you anything about how it's ultimately going to behave. And that just makes software really, really hard.

Seibel: How do you test code? Are you, as they say these days, test-infected?

Crockford: I tend to be more ad hoc. That's another place where I'm considering changing my style, but I haven't accomplished that yet.

Seibel: There is a JsUnit, right?

Crockford: There is a JsUnit. Testing of UI code is really difficult because it's really dependent on a whole lot of stuff, so breaking it down into units tends to be less effective. Also, I found because of the style that I'm writing in JavaScript, it doesn't break in an orderly way into units the way classes do, so you can think about testing a class in isolation.

In JavaScript, testing a function in isolation maybe doesn't make much sense because there's the state that it needs in order to be interesting. I haven't figured out a sufficiently useful way of testing units of JavaScript yet.

Seibel: In places that have separate QA groups, how should developers and QA groups work together?

Crockford: I've had companies where there was an antagonism between the development teams and the testing teams, which I thought was extremely unhealthy. There was this theory that you keep the two separate and one would rat out the other, basically. And I just think it's a horrible model.

It worked much better when we put the two teams together and made the testers responsible for helping the developers to make their programs better, rather than ratting out the developers. It changed the way they reported and was much more effective. Also, cycling the developers into testing, so you weren't exclusively one or the other.

The place where I found that to be most effective was taking testing, sort of, to the ultimate: going to visit customers. I did some of that early in my career and that was a great experience, having to go live with a customer for a week, helping them to install a new system, and helping them to work out the problems with using it.

It gave me a huge amount of insight into what it's like to actually use our stuff and what I want to be doing for the benefit of the people who are going to be using my stuff. Going back afterwards, developers who had not had that experience all seemed arrogant to me in a way which was completely inexcusable. The lack of respect they had for the people who used our stuff was appalling and it was basically a consequence of their having never met those people.

Seibel: Do you consider yourself a scientist, an engineer, an artist, a craftsman, or something else?

Crockford: I think of myself as a writer. Sometimes I write in English and sometimes I write in JavaScript.

It all comes down to communication and the structures that you use in order to facilitate that communication. Human language and computer languages work very differently in many ways, but ultimately I judge a good computer program by its ability to communicate with a human who reads that program. So at that level, they're not that different.

Seibel: And if it can communicate well to a human, you feel like the communicating-with-the-computer part will fall out?

Crockford: You hope so. Computers are arbitrary and not very smart, so you have to make special efforts to make sure that they get it. Because that's so hard, it's easy to overlook the other part, but I think it is at least as important.

Seibel: So Dijkstra had a famous paper, "On the cruelty of really teaching computing science," that basically said computer programming is a branch of applied math. Do you agree?

Crockford: Mathematics is important in programming, but it's just one of a lot of things that are important. I think if you overemphasize the math then you underemphasize stuff which might be even more important, such as literacy.

I mentioned I wanted to have the hiring requirement that they had to have read Knuth and I couldn't do that because I couldn't find enough people who had. The other thing I wanted was that they be really literate in whatever language they write to other humans. I want people who can write, because we spend a lot of time writing to each other. We're writing email or documentation. We're writing plans. We're writing specifications. I want to know that the people on my team are capable of doing that, and that turns out to be a really difficult skill. So I would actually rather see people start as English majors than as math majors to get into programming.

Seibel: I think Dijkstra had another quote about that along the lines of, "If you can't write in your native language, give it up."

Crockford: I agree with that one.

Seibel: An aspect of programming that you seem to keep running up against is that while we are unbound by physical constraints we get tied down by accidents of history. A lot of your proposals for subsetting JavaScript and your version of HTML5 seem to be attempts to fix these kinds of historical accidents.

Crockford: Yeah, and some of it is quixotic. I know that a lot of the things that I'm hoping to accomplish are not achievable. I'm aware of that. But every once in a while something works. Like when XML was proposed as a data-interchange format, my first impression of that was, "My god, this is way, way, way too complicated. We don't need all of this stuff just to move data back and forth." And so I proposed another way to do it, and it won. JSON is now the preferred way of doing data transfer in Ajax applications and it's winning in a whole lot of other applications. And it's just really simple. So that restores my faith in humanity, that maybe we can finally get some of these things right.

But you can't have everybody going off, making up their own thing. That doesn't work. That doesn't do anybody any good. But one person has to make up a thing and everyone else has to figure out how to agree which one of those we're all going to get behind. JSON was a different kind of accident of history.

Seibel: Overall, do you think that the software industry is a brilliant engine of innovation or a horrible mess?

Crockford: I'm trying to think of a nice way to say, "Horrible mess." I'd think generally software has gotten better. Not at the same pace that Moore lets the hardware got better. We track way, way slow compared to him, so it takes us 20 years to double our efficiency in software development. But we have seen improvement. Most of our improvement is due to the fact that we don't have to make it fit anymore. We don't have to make it fast anymore. So that should have liberated us to just making it good. But we don't spend enough time doing that, I think.

Seibel: So if we are, however nicely you put it, a horrible mess, what could we do to not be such a mess?

Crockford: That's what I'm trying to figure out. A lot of it I think has to do with the way that we create standards. The reason why things are working as well as they are now is because the Net works; all the benefits that came, came from being able to tie everything together and have that happen pretty reliably.

But you don't have to scratch it very deep to find places where we got that wrong, where we could've got it better. The dilemma is, how do we fix this stuff in place? Anytime we change a software standard, it's an act of violence. It is disruptive. It will cause stuff to fail. It will cause cost and harm to people. So we need to be really careful when we revise the standards because there is that cost. We have to make sure that we're adding so much value to offset that cost. From what I see of the way that standards are being manipulated right now, that's not occurring. Standard changes are being motivated by "we want to do it" or "because it'd be neat" or some other motivation which is not necessarily closely related to creating a lot of value for the world. So I'm struggling with that. How do we get better at that?

Seibel: You seem to lean toward specifying less. That, obviously, is a way to avoid over specifying things and standardizing things that you're going to regret later. But if less is specified in standards, then people have to make more stuff up and you're going to have a big pile of de facto standards as people try to settle on OK ways of getting stuff done. Is making standards simpler really going to fix the problem, if the complexity just pops up elsewhere?

Crockford: What we really need to be doing is getting better at predicting what we're really going to need in the future. Maybe we have to wait for time travel before we finally start getting this stuff right. In the meantime, I look on that experimentation and proliferation of possible approaches as a positive thing in that maybe the right approach to take to standardization is to figure out which of those are the best thought out, which are the most maintainable, which are the most growable, and pick that. Rather than a standards committee trying to guess the best way to do it, we pick from examples in the marketplace what is actually demonstrably the best way to do it.

Seibel: But you feel like overall we're making some progress?

Crockford: Progress isn't always forward. Sometimes we're leaping forward and sometimes we're leaping backwards. When we leaped to the PC, we lost a whole lot of stuff. In the timesharing era, we had social systems online. A timesharing system was a marketplace. It was a community and everybody who was a part of that system could exchange email, they could exchange files, they could chat, they could play games. They were doing all this stuff and all that got lost when we went to PCs. It took another 20 years or so to get that back.

We also took a huge step backwards in terms of security. Timesharing systems were starting to understand how to defend the system and the users of the system from each other. When we went to PCs, you owned your machine and everything running in that machine had the same privileges, the same rights to do whatever it had to do, and it turned out that not all the software running in your machine is acting in your interest. We're still struggling with that. We've seen lots of improvements going into the PC operating systems, but we're still not at the point where some of the more forward-looking timesharing systems were way, way back.

Seibel: Which ones are you thinking of?

Crockford: MULTICS was doing some really interesting stuff in cooperative processes, and having multiple address spaces which were able to communicate with each other but couldn't get into each other's stuff. That's the basic baseline you need in order to start doing cooperative computing. And we're now trying to figure out how to get that into the browser. It's a long time between MULTICS and here. We're starting now to catch up to insights that were being acted on way back then.

Seibel: I've noticed a similar thing with languages—PCs were programmed in assembly because even C was too high-level and only now are we getting back to languages with some of the power of languages like Smalltalk and Lisp that existed when PCs came out. I wonder if programmers are as aware of the relatively short history of our field as they could be, or do we keep reinventing the wheel?

Crockford: I think we're tragically unaware of our history, and I'm often really disappointed to see that people who are now practicing this craft having no intellectual curiosity about where this stuff came from and just assume that some committee got it right and presented them with a set of tools or languages, and all they have to do is use it properly.

There are amazing stories about where this stuff came from, and what influenced what, and who did what, and what is now considered a mistake, and what *should* be considered a mistake, but hasn't yet. I think of myself sometimes as an archaeologist of software technology and over the years I've accumulated this collection of underappreciated technology, things that I think were really, really good, which are significantly in advance of the state of the art of what we're doing now. I keep hoping that we will somehow rediscover this stuff and learn to appreciate it and benefit from having done it, but it's a really slow process. I see folks are really entrenched in the way that things are working right now and it's really difficult to move.

Seibel: What are some of those technologies?

Crockford: Lisp and Smalltalk, you've just mentioned. That's brilliant stuff, and we're now finally seeing those ideas being factored into modern languages, so we're doing a lot of work now in JavaScript and trying to modernize that. It turns out JavaScript already anticipated a bunch of that stuff; it's got functions which are lexically scoped and first-class, which was brilliant. Now we're trying to figure out how to get more of the goodness of Smalltalk and Scheme into this language without breaking it. You could argue that we'd be better off if we just threw out everything we're working on now and go back to Smalltalk and Scheme, and we probably would be better off than we are right now, but that doesn't appear to be an option.

As we're getting more and more into mash-ups, we want to have code from all over the place—stuff that we'll never, ever test with—actually run out in the field. Which is a new kind of programming. We've never done that before. I think that's the future of programming and we're getting to it in JavaScript first and it's working here because the language, in spite of all the stuff it got wrong, got this other stuff right.

Looking at where we've come on the timeline of programming, we started with machine codes and then we took a leap to symbolic assembly language and then we took a leap to high-level languages and then we took a leap to structured programming and then we took a leap to object-oriented programming. And each of these leaps takes about a human generation.

We're overdue on the next one. We've been at object for a while. You could argue it was Smalltalk-80. You could go back a little bit earlier, but we've been sitting on these ideas for a long time.

I think the next leap, we don't know what the name of it is yet, but I think it's something related to mash-ups where we can casually take bits of program and put them together and immediately make new programs. We've been talking for decades about a model of programming in which we snapped programs together like LEGO and make stuff. That hasn't happened yet. But I think it is starting to happen now and the place it's happening is in JavaScript, which is the least likely place.

Seibel: When you're hiring programmers, how do you recognize the good ones?

Crockford: The approach I've taken now is to do a code reading. I invite the candidate to bring in a piece of code he's really proud of and walk us through it.

Seibel: And what are you looking for?

Crockford: I'm looking for quality of presentation. I want to see what he thinks is something he's proud of. I want to see evidence that in fact he is the author of the thing that he's defending. I find that is much more effective than asking them to solve puzzles or trivia questions. I see all that kind of stuff as useless. But how effectively they can communicate, that's a skill that I'm hiring for.

Seibel: Do you have any advice for self-taught programmers?

Crockford: Yeah, read a lot. There are good books out there. Find the good ones and read those. And if you're doing web development, find the best sites and look at their code. Although I'm a little reluctant to give that advice yet. Most web developers learned to do web development by doing "view source," and until fairly recently, most of the source that was out there was very bad. So you had a generation of programmers who were raised on really bad examples, thinking bad code was the way to write.

That's getting better now, but there's still so much bad stuff out there that I'm reluctant to give that advice yet.

Seibel: What about advice for someone who's actually getting a C.S. degree who wants to work as a programmer?

Crockford: I would focus on the communication aspect. Learn to write; learn to read.

My advice to everybody is pretty much the same, to read and write. I generally don't hire for specific skills. Until very recently, you couldn't hire good JavaScript programmers. They were extremely rare. There are a lot of really good ones out there now, but that's a fairly recent thing. So until that happened, I would just hire for quality. Are you a good Java programmer, a good C programmer, or whatever? I don't care. I just want to know that you know how to put an algorithm together, you understand data structures, and you know how to document it. If you can do that, you should be able to figure out JavaScript.

Seibel: Have you ever had problems with that? People who've been successful in one language sometimes have a hard time giving up their old ways, even when working in a new language where they don't really make sense.

Crockford: I have with, say, Windows programmers. Windows has a number of very complicated APIs and you can spend years just understanding how those APIs work. And that's pretty much all you do, is you know that one API. You can write a window handle but there's not much else you can do. I tend not to look for that kind of overspecialization unless I have a really specific niche. Generally, I prefer generalists. I want someone who's capable of learning any of those APIs but isn't necessarily skilled in any one.

Seibel: You said earlier that you got into computers because you thought they would make the world a better place.

Crockford: That's my intention.

Seibel: How's that working out?

Crockford: For the most part, we've done pretty good. I think the world is a better place, although it's not always moving forward. Looking at, say, international politics over the last ten years, the consolidation of big media and the corrupting effects of that have not been compensated for by the open network. That's a big disappointment.

Hundreds of thousands of people have died as a direct consequence of that. That's really sad. I would like for the network to be doing a better job so that kind of stuff doesn't happen again. It's not clear yet what transformations to the network have to occur in order to accomplish that. And maybe it'll be fine on its own, but I'm more pessimistic. I think we need to figure out the next leap in order to overcome whatever is not working now.

Seibel: Wouldn't the gazillion bloggers out there say, "Hey, we're out here blogging about everything and the mainstream media is taking it in the pants."

Crockford: Yeah, that's great. We still got it wrong. We've got this great thing where we can all get wired together and we can all get the message out to each other, but it's not working. It's just a lot of noise at this point.

Seibel: And do you think that part of that solution of that problem will be technical? Is there something programmers or system designers can do to tweak the architecture that will help? Or is it a social problem?

Crockford: It may be that new social systems have to evolve on top of this new network infrastructure and it's just immature at this point and that's why it's not working. Maybe it just solves itself. I'm hoping that's the case. But I think there may be more involved. Right now, the network does an extremely poor job of identity, does an extremely poor job of security, and those are a necessary component, I think, of building robust social systems. So that aspect of the Web is still deficient and maybe that's why it's so noisy still.

CHAPTER

4

Brendan Eich

Creator of JavaScript, perhaps the most widely used and most reviled programming language on the modern Web, Brendan Eich is now CTO of the Mozilla Corporation, the subsidiary of the Mozilla Foundation responsible for continuing development of the Firefox browser.

With an appreciation of both elegant theory and good pragmatic engineering, Eich spent the early days of his career hacking network and kernel code at Silicon Graphics and MicroUnity. After MicroUnity, he moved to Netscape, where he worked on the Netscape browser and, under intense time pressure, invented JavaScript.

In 1998, along with Jamie Zawinski, he was one of the leaders of the effort to convince Netscape to open-source its browser, leading to the formation of mozilla.org, where he was chief architect.

In recent years Eich has been involved in both high-level direction setting for the Mozilla platform and in low-level hacking on a new JIT'ing JavaScript virtual machine called TraceMonkey. And, as he explains in this interview, he has also been trying to find ways for the Mozilla project to "move the research needle," bringing practical-minded academics into the Mozilla fold in order to bridge the gap between academic theory and industrial practice.

Other topics we touched on include why JavaScript had to look somewhat like Java but not too much, why JavaScript does still need to grow as a language despite the failure of the ECMAScript 4 project, and the need for more kinds of static code analysis.

Seibel: When did you learn to program?

Eich: I was a physics major as an undergraduate at Santa Clara in the late '70s, early '80s. We used to go over to Stanford and hack into LOTS-A and LOTS-B, which were the two big timesharing DEC TOPS-20 systems and Santa Clara had a TOPS-20 system: a nice 36-bit processor from DEC, great OS, wonderful macro assembler. C is "portable assembler" but the macro processing is terrible, whereas back then you had real macros for assembly and you could do a lot of fairly structured programming if you were disciplined about it. No type system, but C doesn't have much of one to speak of. And a rich set of system calls, system services, memory-mapped I/O, all the stuff that didn't make it into Unix originally.

Eich: I was doing physics but I was starting to program more and I was liking the math and computer-science classes I was taking, dealing with automata theory and formal languages. At that point there was a research race to develop the best bottom-up parser generator, what yacc was doing and others would do. It was easy to see the formal purity translate into fairly clean code, which has almost always been the case with the front end of compiler construction. The back end back then was a mess of lore and heuristics, but I really liked the formal language theory and the theory of regular languages and so on.

Seibel: And what languages and environments were you programming in—presumably in physics you were doing Fortran?

Eich: That's the funny thing. I was so pure physics, I wasn't taking the engineering classes that would've had me carrying the deck and risking spilling it and using the collator. I actually bypassed Fortran. Pascal was big then and we were getting into C. And assembly. So I was doing low-level coding, writing assembly hash tables and stuff like that. Which was good. You get better appreciation for different trade-offs. You can tell the programmers who've actually been down to bit-banging level versus the ones who've been shielded all their lives.

I also was interested in C and Unix but we were only just getting into it with this old DEC iron. We had the Portable C Compiler yacc-based mess and we were just starting to generate code and play around with Unix utility porting. Since physics wasn't getting me summer jobs and I was doing a lot of hacking and being a lab assistant I ended up switching in my senior year to math/computer science, and that's what I got my undergraduate degree in.

Seibel: What was the first interesting program that you remember writing?

Eich: This is going to be embarrassing. There was a terrible graphics terminal DEC made; it was like an evolution of VT100 because it understood the escape sequences, but it also had some pathetic color depth and some sort of early '80s resolution. So I started writing game knockoffs for it: Pac-Man, Donkey Kong. I wrote those games in Pascal and they emitted escape sequences. But it was kind of hobby programming that grew and grew. I think that was the first nontrivial programming I did where I had to think about modularity and protecting myself.

This was while I was a physics major, probably third year. Fourth year I became math/computer science and I was starting to study formal languages and write parser generators. So those were the kinds of programs I wrote: either games or serious nerd parser generator type programs. Then I started thinking about compilers and writing macro processor knock offs, like m4 knockoffs or CPP knockoffs. I remember when we got some version of the Unix source and reading some of the really crufty C code. The John Reiser C preprocessor—probably the original—was just an amazing mess. It was very efficient; it was using a global buffer and it was a huge pointer stew, and it would try to avoid copying. I thought, "There has to be a better way to do this."

So that's how I ended up getting out of physics and into computer science and programming. I wasn't really programming before that; it was all math and science. My parents didn't let me get an Apple II. I tried once. I didn't beg but I was saying, "I could learn a foreign language with this," which was a complete smoke screen. "No. You'll probably waste time playing games." And they were right. So they saved me from that fate.

Seibel: Other than providing more summer employment than physics, what about programming drew you in?

Eich: The connection between theory and practice, especially at the front end of the compiler construction process, was attractive to me. Numerical methods I didn't get into too much. They're less attractive because you end up dealing with all sorts of crazy trade-offs in representing real numbers as finite precision floating-point numbers and that's just hellish. It still bites JavaScript users because we chose this hardware standard from the '80s and it's not always operating the way people expect.

Seibel: Because, like the Spanish Inquisition, no one really expects floating point.

Eich: No one expects the rounding errors you get—powers of five aren't representable well. They round badly in base-two. So dollars and cents, sums and differences, will get you strange long zeros with a nine at the end in JavaScript. There was a blog about this that blamed Safari and Mac for doing math wrong and it's IEEE double—it's in everything, Java and C.

Physics was also less satisfying to me because it has kind of stalled. There's something not quite right when you have these big inductive theories where people are polishing corners and inventing stuff like dark energy, which is basically unfalsifiable. I was gravitating toward something that was more practical but still had some theoretical strength based in mathematics and logic.

Then I went to University of Illinois Champaign-Urbana to get a master's degree, at least. I was thinking of going all the way but I got stuck in a project that was basically shanghaied by IBM. They had a strange 68020 machine they had acquired from a company in Danbury, Connecticut, and they ported Xenix to it. It was so buggy they co-opted our research project and had us become like a QA group. Every Monday we'd have the blue suit come out and give us a pep talk. My professors were kind of supine about it. I should've probably found somebody new, but I also heard Jim Clark speak on campus and I pretty much decided I wanted to go work at Silicon Graphics.

Seibel: What were you working on at SGI?

Eich: Kernel and networking code mostly. The amount of language background that I used there grew over time because we ended up writing our own network-management and packet-sniffing layer and I wrote the expression language for matching fields and packets, and I wrote the translator that would reduce and optimize that to a short number of mask-and-match filters over the front 36 bytes of the packet.

And I ended up writing another language implementation, a compiler that would generate C code given a protocol description. Somebody wanted us to support AppleTalk in this packet sniffer. It was a huge, complex grab bag of protocol syntax for sequences and fields of various sizes and dependent types of . . . mostly arrays, things like that. It was fun and challenging to write. I ended up using some of the old Dragon book—Aho and Ullman—compiler skills. But that was it. I think I did a unifdef clone. Dave Yost had done one and it didn't handle `#if` expressions and it didn't do expression minimization based on some of the terms being pound-defined or undefined, so I did that. And that's still out there. I think it may have made its way into Linux.

I was at SGI from '85 to '92. In '92 somebody I knew at SGI had gone to MicroUnity and I was tired of SGI bloating up and acquiring companies and being overrun with politicians. So I jumped and it was to MicroUnity, which George Gilder wrote about in the '90s in *Forbes ASAP* as if it was going to be the next big thing. Then down the memory hole; it turned into a $200 million crater in North Sunnyvale. It was a very good learning experience. I did some work on GCC there, so I got some compiler-language hacking. I did a little editor language for MPEG2 video where you could write this crufty pseudospec language like the ISO spec or the IEC spec, and actually generate test bit streams that have all the right syntax.

Seibel: And then after MicroUnity you ended up at Netscape and the rest is history. Looking back, is there anything you wish you had done differently as far as learning to program?

Eich: I was doing a lot of physics until I switched to math and computer science. I was doing enough math that I was getting some programming but I had already studied some things on my own, so when I was in the classes I was already sitting in the back kind of moving ahead or being bored or doing something else. That was not good for personal self-discipline and I probably missed some things that I could've studied.

I've talked to people who've gone through a PhD curriculum and they obviously have studied certain areas to a greater depth than I have. I feel like that was the chance that I had then. Can't really go back and do it now. You can study anything on the Internet but do you really get the time with the right professor and the right coursework, do you get the right opportunities to really learn it? But I've not had too many regrets about that.

As far as programming goes, I was doing, like I said, low-level coding. I'm not an object-oriented, design-patterns guy. I never bought the Gamma book. Some people at Netscape did, some of Jamie Zawinski's and my nemeses from another acquisition, they waved it around like the Bible and they were kind of insufferable because they weren't the best programmers.

I've been more low-level than I should've been. I think what I've learned with Mozilla and Firefox has been about more test-driven development, which I think is valuable. And other things like fuzz testing, which we do a lot of. We have many source languages and big deep rendering pipelines and other kinds of evaluation pipelines that have lots of opportunity for memory safety bugs. So we have found fuzz testing to be more productive than almost any other kind of testing.

I've also pushed us to invest in static analysis and that's been profitable, though it's fairly esoteric. We have some people we hired who are strong enough to use it.

Seibel: What kind of static analysis?

Eich: Static analysis of C++, which is difficult. Normally in static analysis you're doing some kind of whole-program analysis and you like to do things like prove facts about memory. So you have to disambiguate memory to find all the aliases, which is an exponential problem, which is generally infeasible in any significant program. But the big breakthrough has been that you don't really need to worry about memory. If you can build a complete control-flow graph and connect all the virtual methods to their possible implementation, you can do a process of partial evaluation over the code without actually running it. You can find dead code and you can find redundant tests and you can find missing null tests.

And you can actually do more if you go to higher levels of discourse where we all operate, where there's a proof system in our head about the program we're writing. But we don't have a type system in the common languages to express the terms of the proof. That's a real problem. The Curry-Howard correspondence says there's a correspondence between logic systems and type systems, and types are terms and programs are proofs, and you should be able to write down these higher-level models that you're trying to enforce. Like, this array should have some constraint on its length, at least in this early phase, and then after that it maybe has a different or no constraint. Part of the trick is you go through these nursery phases or other phases where you have different rules. Or you're inside your own abstraction's firewall and you violate your own invariants for efficiency but you know what you're doing and from the outside it's still safe. That's very hard to implement in a fully type-checked fashion.

When you write Haskell programs you're forced to decide your proof system in advance of knowing what it is you're doing. Dynamic languages became popular because people can actually rapidly prototype and keep this latent type system in their head. Then maybe later on, if they have a language that can support it, or if they're recoding in a static language, they can write down the types. That was one of the reasons why in JavaScript we were interested in optional typing and we still are, though it's controversial in the committee. There's still a strong chance we'll get some kind of hybrid type system into a future version of JavaScript.

So we would like to annotate our C++ with annotations that conservative static analysis could look at. And it would be conservative so it wouldn't fall into the halting-problem black hole and take forever trying to go exponential. It would help us to prove things about garbage-collector safety or partitioning of functions into which control can flow from a script, functions from which control can flow back out to the script, and things to do with when you have to rematerialize your interpreter stack in order to make security judgments. It would give us some safety properties we can prove. A lot of them are higher-level properties. They aren't just memory safety. So we're going to have to keep fighting that battle.

Seibel: So that's a very high-level view of programming. How close to the metal do you think programmers today need to be able to go? If someone is going to be writing most of their applications in JavaScript, is it still important that they grok assembly?

Eich: I know a lot of JavaScript programmers who are clever programmers, and the best ones have a good grasp of the economics. They benchmark and they test as they go and they write tight JavaScript. They don't have to know about how it maps to machine instructions.

A lot of them are interested in that when they hear about these JITing, tracing VMs that we're building. And we're getting more and more people who are pushing pixels. If you give people enough programming-language performance and enough pixel-pushing power I think JavaScript programmers will start using JavaScript at a lower level. And machine economics or the virtual-machine economics—what really matters? Maybe it's the virtual-machine economics.

Abstraction is powerful. What I'm really allergic to, and what I had a bad reaction to in the '90s, was all the CORBA, COM, DCOM, object-oriented nonsense. Every startup of the day had some crazy thing that would take 200,000 method calls to start up and print "hello, world." That's a travesty; you don't want to be a programmer associated with that sort of thing. At SGI, the kernel, of course, was where the real programmers with chest hair went, and there you couldn't screw around. Kernel `malloc` was a new thing; we still used fixed-sized tables, and we panicked when we filled them up.

Staying close to the metal was my way of keeping honest and avoiding the bullshit, but now, you know, with time and better, faster hardware and an evolutionary winnowing process of good abstractions versus bad, I think people can operate above that level and not know assembly and still be good programmers and write tight code.

Seibel: Do you think, conversely, that the people who, back in the day, could write intricate, puzzle-box assembly code, would be just as great programmers in today's world doing high-level programming? Or does that kind of programming require different skills?

Eich: I would say for certain aspects of programming there is a correspondence between the two. There's a difference between raw pointers and this happy, fun JavaScript world. That kind of still separates the chest hair—gender-independent—programmers from those who don't quite have it.

Keeping it all in your head is important. Obviously people have different-sized heads. Somebody with a big head could keep track of higher-level invariants in a memory-safe architecture and not have to worry about pointers. But there's something still that bothers me if over time we lose the ability to write to the metal. Somebody's doing it; the compiler is generating the code. The compiler writers have to be doing a better job over time.

Seibel: So there will always be a place for that kind of programming. But are there people who can be successful programmers now who just couldn't when all programming was low-level hacking? Or is there one fixed population of people who have the right kind of brain for programming and now they're split with some people doing low-level stuff and some people doing high-level stuff?

Eich: I haven't hacked kernel code in a long time, so I would have to go for there's some ability to migrate. There's more code to write. And sound abstractions give you leverage over problems you couldn't address before.

Seibel: Let's go back to those ten days when you implemented the original JavaScript. I know that at some point someone had turned you on to Abelson and Sussman and your original idea was to put Scheme in the browser.

Eich: The immediate concern at Netscape was it must look like Java. People have done Algol-like syntaxes for Lisp but I didn't have time to take a Scheme core so I ended up doing it all directly and that meant I could make the same mistakes that others made.

I didn't have total dynamic scope, like Stallman insisted was somehow important for Emacs and infested Elisp with. JavaScript has mostly lexical scope with some oddness to it—there are a few loopholes that are pretty much dynamic: the global object, the `with` statement, eval. But it's not like dollar variables in Perl before `my` or `upvar`, `uplevel` in Tcl. The '90s was full of that—it was trendy.

But I didn't stick to Scheme and it was because of the rushing. I had too little time to actually think through some of the consequences of things I was doing. I was economizing on the number of objects that I was going to have to implement in the browser. So I made the global object be the window object, which is a source of unknown new name bindings and makes it impossible to make static judgments about free variables. So that was regrettable. Doug Crockford and other object-capabilities devotees are upset about the unwanted source of authority you get through the global object. That's a different way of saying the same thing. JavaScript has memory-safe references so we're close to where we want to be but there are these big blunders, these loopholes.

Making those variables in the top level actually become mutable properties of an object that you can alias and mess around with behind the back of somebody—that's no good. It should've been lexical bindings. Because if you go down from there into the functions and nested functions, then it is much more Scheme-like. You don't quite have the rich binding forms, the fluid lets or whatever; you have more like set-bang. But the initial binding you create with a local variable is a lexical variable.

Seibel: So basically now people make a top-level function to get a namespace.

Eich: Yeah. You see people have a function and they call it right away. It gives them a safe environment to bind in, private variables. Doug's a big champion of this. It was not totally unknown to the Schemers and Lispers but a lot of JavaScript people had to learn it and Doug and others have done a valuable service by teaching them. It's not like you're getting everybody to be high-quality Scheme programmers, unfortunately, but to some extent they've succeeded, so people now do understand more functional idioms at some patterny level, not necessarily at a deep level.

Seibel: So that's the JavaScript that's been out there for over a decade. And now there's this big renaissance due to Ajax. So folks say, "OK, we really need to take another look at this." You recently went through the drama of the ECMAScript 4 proposal and the competing ECMAScript 3.1 proposal and now things seem to have settled down with the "Harmony" plan for unifying the two. Was the ES4 proposal your chance to show the world that, "Look, I'm a really smart guy and JavaScript is a really a good language"?

Eich: No, I don't think so. I know Doug may think that. I don't think Doug knows me that well, but the thing is, I'm not really looking for respect, especially from the Java-heads or the trailing edge.

Seibel: Was ES4 your brainchild? Was it your take on, knowing all that you know now, what you want JavaScript to be?

Eich: No. It was definitely a collaborative effort and in some ways a compromise because we were working with Adobe, who had done a derivative language called ActionScript. Their version three was the one that was influencing the fourth-edition proposals. And that was based on Waldemar Horwat's work on the original JavaScript 2/ECMAScript fourth-edition proposals in the late '90s, which got mothballed in 2003 when Netscape mostly got laid off and the Mozilla foundation was set up.

Waldemar did a good job—I gave him the keys to the kingdom in late '97 when I went off to found mozilla.org with Jamie. Waldemar is a huge brain—I think he won the Putnam in '87. MIT PhD. He did try and keep the dynamic flavor of the language, but he struggled to add certain programming-in-the-large facilities to it, like namespaces.

There's a contrary school which is more pedantic: "We should have just a few primitives we can de-sugar our spec to; we can lambda code everything. That's how people should write anyway because that's how I think of things" or, "That's the best way to think of things." It's very reductionistic and it's not for everybody. Obviously one way to do your own mental proof system is to reduce things, to subset languages. Subsetting is powerful. But to say everyone has to program in this sort of minuscule subset, that's not usable.

Seibel: In some of the discussion about ES4, you cited Guy Steele's paper, "Growing a Language." Speaking as a Lisper, to me the take-away from that paper was, step one, put a macro system in your language. Then all of this special sugar goes away.

Eich: There are two big problems, obviously. C syntax means that you have a much harder time than with s-expression, so you have to define your ASTs and we're going to have to standardize them and that's going to be a pain. Then there's the other problem, which is hygiene is still not quite understood. Dave Herman, who's working with us is doing his thesis—or was last I checked—on a kind of logic for proving soundness for hygiene, which is, I hope, beneficial. Because we will get to macros.

I said this to Doug Crockford a couple years ago when he had me speak at Yahoo! I started talking about the sugar that I was enthusiastic about. He said, "Gee, maybe we should do a macro system first," and I said, "No, because then we'll take nine years." At the time there was a real risk politically that Microsoft was just not going to cooperate. They came back into ECMA after being asleep and coasting. The new guy, who was from Hyderabad, was very enthusiastic and said, "Yes, we will put the CLR into IE8 and JScript.net will be our new implementation of web JavaScript." But I think his enthusiasm went upstairs and then he got told, "No, that's not what we're doing." So it led to the great revolt and splitting the committee.

So we were concerned that if we went off to do macros we were doing research, and if we were doing research we were not going to have Microsoft engaged and we were not going to be putting competitive pressure on them. So macros have had to wait. I'm fine with that so long as we do the right automated grammar checks and we do make sure we can recast all of the sugar as macros when we have macros. But in the meantime there's no reason to starve the users for sugar. It doesn't rot their teeth and it helps them avoid mistakes.

Seibel: Back in 1995, what other languages influenced your original design of JavaScript?

Eich: Self was big, mainly because of the papers that Dave Ungar had just written. I never played with any Self code, but I was just inspired by them. I like Smalltalk and here was somebody taking one idea applied to Smalltalk, which was prototype-based delegation—multiple prototypes unlike JavaScript—and just running with it as hard as they could. That was inspiring to me because there was both good compiler, VM-level engineering and, I thought, good language design.

Because, like Crock and others, I think you do want to simplify and I do like the languages designers who take fewer primitives and see how far they can go. I think there's been kind of a Stockholm syndrome with JavaScript: "Oh, it only does what it does because Microsoft stopped letting it improve, so why should we want better syntax; it's actually a virtue to go lambda-code everything." But that Stockholm syndrome aside, and Microsoft stagnating the Web aside, language design can do well to take a kernel idea or two and push them hard.

Seibel: Were you aware of NewtonScript at all?

Eich: Only after the fact did someone point it out to me and I realized, "Hey, they've got something like our scope chain in their parent link and our single prototype." I think it was convergent evolution based on Self. And the DOM event handlers—part of the influence there was HyperTalk and Atkinson's HyperCard. So I was looking not only at Self and Scheme, but there were these onFoo event handlers in HyperTalk, and that is what I did for the DOM onClick and so on.

One more positive influence, and this is kind of embarrassing, was awk. I mean, I was an old Unix hacker and Perl was out, but I was still using awk for various chores. And I could've called these first-class functions anything, but I called them "function" mainly because of awk. An eight-letter keyword—it's kind of heavy, but there it is.

Seibel: At least it wasn't "lambda"—JavaScript would've been doomed from the start. Were there any languages that negatively influenced JavaScript, in the sense of, "I don't want to do that"?

Eich: It was such a rush job that I wasn't, like, worried about, "Oh, I can't make it into Ada or Common Lisp." Java was in some ways a negative influence. I both had to make it look like Java and not let in those crazy things like having a distinction between primitive types and objects. Also, I didn't want to have anything classy. So I swerved from that and it caused me to look at Self and do prototypes.

Seibel: Did you ever consider making a language more closely related to Java—take Java and make some kind of simple subset; get rid of the primitive types and other needless complexities?

Eich: There was some pressure from management to make the syntax look like Java. There was also some pressure to make it not too big, because after all, people should use Java if they're doing any real programming; this is just Java's dumb little brother.

Seibel: So you wanted to be like Java, but not too much.

Eich: Not too much. If I put classes in, I'd be in big trouble. Not that I really had time to, but that would've been a no-no.

Seibel: Coming back to the present, ES4 has been officially abandoned and everyone is now working toward ES-Harmony, which will somehow combine ES3.1 with ideas from ES4? Do you think that's ultimately a good decision?

Eich: Doug was a little triumphalist in first blog post: "We've won. The devil has been vanquished." I had a joke slide I gave in London a year ago about Doug being Gandalf on the bridge, at Khazad-dûm facing down the ES4rog. He liked that a lot. It was the first time I poked fun at him because he's a little serious sometimes when he gets on this topic and he liked it a lot. He can be the hero; ES4 wasn't quite the monster.

ES4 looks, in retrospect, too big. But we need to be practical about standards. We can't just say all you need are lambdas—Alonzo Church proved it, so we're not going to add any more to the language. That's the sort of impoverished approach that tries to make everybody into an expert and it will not work on the large number of programmers out there who have been mistrained in these Java schools. JavaScript *will* fall someday but we can keep evolving it and keep it competitive in both the theoretical and the practical sense if we don't try to hold back the sugar for purity's sake.

It needs to evolve to solve the problems that programmers face. Programmers can solve some of them by writing their own library abstractions. But the ability to write abstractions in the language is limited without the extensions—you can't write getters and setters. You can't make objects look native, have properties turn into code; things like that. And you can't solve some of these security problems in an implicit or automated way.

Seibel: In general do you feel like languages are getting better over time?

Eich: I think so, yeah. Maybe we're entering the second golden age; there's more interest in languages and more language creation. We talk about programming: we need to keep practicing the craft—it's like writing or music. But the language that you use—the tonal system—matters too. Language matters. So we should be evolving programming languages; we shouldn't be sitting still. Because the Web demands compatibility, JavaScript may have to sit still too much. But we shouldn't get stuck by that; we should either make a better JavaScript, even if it doesn't replace the one on the Web, or we should move beyond that.

You see stuff like Ruby, which took influences from Ada and Smalltalk. That's great. I don't mind eclecticism. Though Ruby does seem kind of overhyped. Nothing bad about it, just sometimes the fan boys make it sound like the second coming and it's going to solve all your problems, and that's not the case. We should have new languages but they should not be overhyped. Like the C++ hype, the whole "design patterns will save us." Though maybe they were reacting to the conservatism of the Unix C world of the '80s.

But at some point we have to have better languages. And the reason is to have proof assistants or proof systems, to have some kind of automatic verification of some claims you're making in your code. You won't get all of them, right? And the dynamic tools like Valgrind and its race detectors, that's great too. There's no silver bullet, as Brooks said, but there are better languages and we should migrate to them as we can.

Seibel: To what extent should programming languages be designed to prevent programmers from making mistakes?

Eich: So a blue-collar language like Java shouldn't have a crazy generic system because blue-collar people can't figure out what the hell the syntax means with covariant, contravariant type constraints. Certainly I've experienced some toe loss due to C and C++'s foot guns. Part of programming is engineering; part of engineering is working out various safety properties, which matter. Doing a browser they matter. They matter more if you're doing the Therac-25. Though that was more a thread-scheduling problem, as I recall. But even then, you talk about better languages for writing concurrent programs or exploiting hardware parallelism. We shouldn't all be using synchronized blocks—we certainly shouldn't be using mutexes or spin locks. So the kind of leverage you can get through languages may involve trade-offs where you say, "I'm going, for safety, to sacrifice some expressiveness."

With JavaScript I think we held to this, against the wild, woolly Frenchmen superhackers who want to use JavaScript as a sort of a lambda x86 language. We're not going to add call/cc; there's no reason to. Besides the burden on implementers—let's say that wasn't a problem—people would definitely go astray with it. Not necessarily the majority, but enough people who wanted to be like the superhackers. There's sort of a programming ziggurat—the Right Stuff, you know. People are climbing towards the top, even though some of the tops sometimes fall off or lose a toe.

You can only borrow trouble so many different ways in JavaScript. There are first-class functions. There are prototypes, which are a little confusing to people still because they're not the standard classical OOP.

That's almost enough. I'm not a minimalist who says, "That's it; we should freeze the language." That's convenient cover for Microsoft, and it kind of outrages me, because I see people wasting a lot of time and still having bugs. You know, you can still have lots of hard-to-find bugs with lambda coding.

Doug has taught people different patterns, but I do agree with Peter Norvig: those patterns show some kind of defect in the language. These patterns are not free. There's no free lunch. So we should be looking for evolution in the language that adds the right bits. Adding optional types probably will happen. They might even be more like PLT contracts.

Seibel: A lot of the stuff you're dealing with, from static analysis of your C++ to the tracing JITs and new features for JavaScript, seems like you're trying to keep up with some pretty cutting-edge computer-science research.

Eich: So we're fighting the good fight but we're trying to be smart about it. We're also trying to move the research needle because—this is something else that was obvious to me, even back when I was in school, and I think it's still a problem—there are a lot of problems with academic research. It's widely separated from industry.

So there's something wrong that we'd like to fix. We've been working with academics who are practically minded. That's been great. We don't have much money so we're going to have to use leverage—partly it's just getting people to talk and network together.

You lose something when the academics are all off chasing NSF grants every year. The other thing is, you see the rise in dynamic languages. You see crazy, idiotic statements about how dynamic language are going to totally unseat Java and static languages, which is nonsense. But the academics are out there convinced static type systems are the ultimate end and they're researching particular kinds of static type systems like the ML, Hindley-Milner type inferences and it's completely divorced from industry.

Seibel: Why is that? Because it's not solving any real problems or because it's only a partial solution?

Eich: We did some work with SML New Jersey to self-host the reference implementation of JavaScript, fourth edition, which is now defunct. We were trying to make a definitional interpreter. We weren't even using Hindley-Milner. We would annotate types and arguments to avoid these crazy, notorious error messages you get when it can't unify types and picks some random source code to blame and it's usually the wrong one. So there's a quality-of-implementation issue there. Maybe there's a type-theoretic problem there too because it is difficult, when unification fails, to have useful blame.

Now you could do more research and try to develop some higher-level model of cognitive errors that programmers make and get better blame coordinates. Maybe I'm just picking on one minor issue here, but it does seem like that's a big one.

Academia has not been helpful in leading people toward a better model. I think academia has been kind of derelict. Maybe it's not their fault. The economics that they subsist on aren't good. But we all knew we were headed toward this massively parallel future. Nobody has solved it. Now they're all big about transactional memory. That's not going to solve it. You're not going to have nested transactions rolling back and contending across a large number of processors. It's not going to be efficient. It's not going to actually work correctly in some cases. You can't map all your concurrent or parallel programming algorithms on to it. And you shouldn't try.

People like Joe Armstrong have done really good work with the shared-nothing approach. You see that a lot in custom systems in browser implementations. Chrome is big on it. We do it our own way in our JavaScript implementation. And shared nothing is not even interesting to academics, I think. Transactional memory is more interesting, especially with the sort of computer-architecture types because they can figure out ways to make good instructions and hardware support for it. But it's not going to solve all the problems we face.

I think there will be progress and it should involve programming languages. That's why I do think the talk about the second golden age isn't wrong. It's just that we haven't connected the users of the languages with the would-be developers with the academics who might research a really breakthrough language.

Seibel: You got a Masters but not a PhD. Would you generally recommend that people who want to be programmers should go get a PhD. in computer science? Or should only certain kinds of people do that?

Eich: I think only certain kind of people. It takes certain skills to do a PhD, and sometimes you wonder if it's ultimately given just because you endured. But then you get the three letters to put after your name if you want to. And that helps you open certain doors. But my experience in the Valley in this inflationist boom of 20 years or so that we've been living through—though that may be coming to an end—was certainly it wasn't a good economic trade-off. So I don't have regrets about that.

The ability to go study something in a systematic, and maybe even leisurely, way is attractive. The go-to-market, ride Moore's law, and compete and deal with fast product cycles and sometimes throwaway software—seems like a shame if that's all everybody does. So there's a role for people who want to get PhDs, who have the skills for it. And there is interesting research to do. One of the things that we're pushing at Mozilla is in between what's respected in academic research circles and what's already practice in the industry. That's compilers and VM stuff, debuggers even—things like Valgrind—profiling tools. Underinvested-in and not sexy for researchers, maybe not novel enough, too much engineering, but there's room for breakthroughs. We're working with Andreas Gal and he gets these papers rejected because they're too practical.

Of course, we need researchers who are inclined that way, but we also need programmers who do research. We need to have the programming discipline not be just this sort of blue-collar thing that's cut off from the people in the ivory towers.

Seibel: How do you feel about proofs?

Eich: Proofs are hard. Most people are lazy. Larry Wall is right. Laziness should be a virtue. So that's why I prefer automation. Proofs are something that academics love and most programmers hate. Writing assertions can be useful. In spite of bad assertions that should've been warnings, we've had more good assertions over time in Mozilla. From that we've had some illumination on what the invariants are that you'd like to express in some dream type system.

I think thinking about assertions as proof points helps. But not requiring anything that pretends to be a complete proof—there are enough proofs that are published in academic papers that are full of holes.

Seibel: On a completely different topic, what's the worst bug you ever had to track down?

Eich: Oh, man. The worst bugs are the multithreaded ones. The work I did at Silicon Graphics involved the Unix kernel. The kernel originally started out, like all Unix kernels of the day, as a monolithic monitor that ran to completion once you entered the kernel through a system call. Except for interrupts, you could be sure you could run to completion, so no locks for your own data structure. That was cool. Pretty straightforward.

But at SGI the bright young things from HP came in. They sold symmetric multiprocessing to SGI. And they really rocked the old kernel group. They came in with some of their new guys and they did it. They stepped right up and they kept swinging until they knocked the ball pretty far out of the field. But they didn't do it with anything better than C and semaphores and spin locks and maybe monitors, condition variables. All hand-coded. So there were tons of bugs. It was a real nightmare.

I got a free trip to Australia and New Zealand that I blogged about. We actually fixed the bug in the field but it was hellish to find and fix because it was one of these bugs where we'd taken some single-threaded kernel code and put it in this symmetric multiprocessing multithreaded kernel and we hadn't worried about a particular race condition. So first of all we had to produce a test case to find it, and that was hard enough. Then under time pressure, because the customer wanted the fix while we were in the field, we had to actually come up with a fix.

Diagnosing it was hard because it was timing-sensitive. It had to do with these machines being abused by terminal concentrators. People were hooking up a bunch of PTYs to real terminals. Students in a lab or a bunch of people in a mining software company in Brisbane, Australia in this sort of '70s sea of cubes with a glass wall at the end, behind which was a bunch of machines including the SGI two-processor machine. That was hard and I'm glad we found it.

These bugs generally don't linger for years but they are really hard to find. And you have to sort of suspend your life and think about them all the time and dream about them and so on. You end up doing very basic stuff, though. It's like a lot of other bugs. You end up bisecting—you know "wolf fence." You try to figure out by monitoring execution and the state of memory and try to bound the extent of the bug and control flow and data that can be addressed. If it's a wild pointer store then you're kinda screwed and you have to really start looking at harder-to-use tools, which have only come to the fore recently, thanks to those gigahertz processors, like Valgrind and Purify.

Instrumenting and having a checked model of the entire memory hierarchy is big. Robert O'Callahan, our big brain in New Zealand, did his own debugger based on the Valgrind framework, which efficiently logs every instruction so he can re-create the entire program state at any point. It's not just a time-traveling debugger. It's a full database so you see a data structure and there's a field with a scrogged value and you can say, "Who wrote to that last?" and you get the full stack. You can reason from effects back to causes. Which is the whole game in debugging. So it's very slow. It's like a hundred times slower than real time, but there's hope.

Or you can use one of these faster recording VMs—they checkpoint only at system call and I/O boundaries. They can re-create corrupt program states at any boundary but to go in between those is harder. But if you use that you can probably close in quickly at near real time and then once you get to that stage you can transfer it into Rob's Chronomancer and run it much slower and get all the program states and find the bug.

Debugging technology has been sadly underresearched. That's another example where there's a big gulf between industry and academia: the academics are doing proofs, sometimes by hand, more and more mechanized thanks to the POPLmark challenge and things like that. But in the real world we're all in debuggers and they're pieces of shit from the '70s like GDB.

Seibel: In the real world one big split is between people who use symbolic debuggers and people who use print statements.

Eich: Yeah. So I use GDB, and I'm glad GDB, at least on the Mac, has a watch-point facility that mostly works. So I can watch an address and I can catch it changing from good bits to bad bits. That's pretty helpful. Otherwise I'm using `printf`s to bisect. Once I get close enough usually I can just try things inside GDB or use some amount of command scripting. But it's incredibly weak. The scripting language itself is weak. I think Van Jacobson added loops and I don't even know if those made it into the real GDB, past the FSF hall monitors.

But there's so much more debugging can do for you and these attempts, like Chronomancer and Replay, are good. They certainly changed the game for me recently. But I don't know about multithreading. There's Helgrind and there are other sort of dynamic race detectors that we're using. Those are producing some false positives we have to weed through, trying to train the tools or to fix our code not to trigger them. The jury is still out on those.

The multithreaded stuff, frankly, scares me because before I was married and had kids it took a lot of my life. And not everybody was ready to think about concurrency and all the possible combinations of orders that are out there for even small scenarios. Once you combine code with other people's code it just gets out of control. You can't possibly model the state space in your head. Most people aren't up to it. I could be like one of these chest-thumpers on Slashdot—when I blogged about "Threads suck" someone was saying, "Oh he doesn't know anything. He's not a real man." Come on, you idiot. I got a trip to New Zealand and Australia. I got some perks. But it was definitely painful and it takes too long. As Oscar Wilde said of socialism, "It takes too many evenings."

Seibel: How do you design code?

Eich: A lot of prototyping. I used to do sort of high-level pseudocode, and then I'd start filling in bottom up. I do less of the high-level pseudocode because I can usually hold it in my head and just do bottom-up until it joins. Often I'm working with existing pieces of code adding some new subsystem or something on the side and I can almost do it bottom-up. When I get in trouble in the middle I do still write pseudo-code and just start working bottom up until I can complete it. I try not to let that take too long because you've got to be able to test it; you've got to be able to see it run and step through it and make sure it's doing what it's supposed to be doing.

Before that level of design, there may be some entity relationships or gross modularization. There's probably an algorithm or three that we're thinking of where you're reasoning about the complexity of it—is it linear? Is it constant? Every time I've written some kind of linear search that's going to compound quadratically, and unleashed it on the Web, web developers have found that to be a problem. They've written enough stuff it stresses it. So we tend to do a lot of data structures that are constant time. And even then, constant can be not one—it can be big enough that you care.

So we do lots of prototyping, we do lots of bottom-up and top-down and they meet in the middle. And I think actually we, at Mozilla, don't do enough rewriting. We're very conservative. We are open source, so we have community we try to build and bring new people into. We certainly have value that users benefit from, and we don't want to take a three-year break rewriting, which is what would happen if we tried too much.

But if you really are trying to move a needle and you don't know exactly what you're doing, rewrite. It's going to take several tries to know what the hell you're doing. And then when you have a design more firm you'll stick with it and you'll start patching it more, and you'll get to this mature state where we creak with patches. It's kind of an evolutionary dead-end for code. You know, maybe it's a good sunk cost and you can stand on it for years. Maybe it's this thing that's crying out for replacement. Maybe in the open-source world some better standard library has emerged.

And that gets back to the craft of programming, I think. You don't just write code based on some old design. You want to keep practicing, and the practicing involves thinking about design and feeding back your experience in coding to the design process.

I have this big allergy to ivory-tower design and design patterns. Peter Norvig, when he was at Harlequin, he did this paper about how design patterns are really just flaws in your programming language. Get a better programming language. He's absolutely right. Worshipping patterns and thinking about, "Oh, I'll use the X pattern."

Seibel: So newer experiences can show you better ways going forward. But what about when writing the code shows you big flaws in your existing design?

Eich: That does happen. It happens a lot. Sometimes it's difficult to throw out and go back to square one. You've already made commitments, and you get into this trap. I did this with JavaScript, In a great big hurry, I wrote a byte-code interpreter. Even at the time I knew I was going to regret some of the things I'd done. But it was a design that was understandable to other people and I could hope to get other people helping me work on. So I question design all the time. I just realize that we don't always get the luxury of revisiting our deepest design decisions. And that is where we then attempt to do a big rewrite, because you really would have a hard time incrementally rewriting to change deep design decisions.

Seibel: How do you decide when it's right to do a big rewrite? Thanks to Joel Spolsky, Netscape is in some ways the poster child for the dangers of the big rewrite.

Eich: There was an imperative from Netscape to make the acquisition that waved the *Design Patterns* book around feel like they were winners by using their new rendering engine, which was like My First Object-Oriented Rendering Engine. From a high level it sounded good; it used C++ and design patterns. But it had a lot of problems.

But the second reason we did the big rewrite—I was in mozilla.org and I really was kind of pissed at Netscape, like Jamie, who was getting ready to quit. I thought, you know, we need to open up homesteading space to new contributors. We can't do it with this old hairball of student code from 1994. Or my fine Unix kernel-style interpreter code.

We needed to do a fairly big reset. Yeah, we were going to be four years from shipping. At that point I don't think we were telling upper management that because they didn't want to hear it, so we were optimizing to them. And that cost some of the management their heads. Though they all made out fabulously on the options—much better than I did. But for Mozilla that was the right trade.

We were lucky in hindsight, because we could have had a more rapid evolution of the Web. Microsoft was—some people claim this was due to the antitrust case more than their nature—inclined to sit on the Web and stagnate it. So that gave us time to wave the standards flag—which is two-edged and half bullshit—and go rewrite. Like Joel, I'm skeptical of rewrites. I think it's rare to find that kind of an alignment of interests and get enough funding to live through it and not miss the market. The exceptions are very rare.

The rewrites I was speaking of earlier, though, were when you're prototyping. That's critical and smaller-scale. It may be a cross-cutting change to a big pile of code so it's small in lines, but it's big in reach and all the invariants you have to satisfy. Or maybe it's a new JIT or whatever, and that you can get away with.

Seibel: Have you ever done any literate programming, a la Knuth?

Eich: I followed the original stuff. It was very neat. I liked it. It was word retrieval. He had some kind of a hash-trie data structure and it was all literately programmed. Then Doug McIlroy came along and did it all with a pipeline.

Our programs are heavily commented but we don't have any way of extracting the prose and somehow making it be checked by humans, if not automatically, against the code. Python people have done some more interesting work there. I have not done anything more than heavily comment. I do go back and maintain comments—it's a real pain and sometimes I don't do it and then I regret it because somebody gets a bum steer.

I actually like McIlroy's rejoinder. It wasn't a rebuttal of literate programming—but it was kind of. You don't want to write too many words, prose or code. In some ways the code should speak for itself at the small level. It's at the bigger level, the big monster function or the module boundary, that you need docs. So doc comments or things like them—doc strings. Embedding the test in the comment. I guess that's the big Python thing. That's good.

There is something to literate programming, especially these integrated tests and doc strings. I'd like to see more of that supported by languages. We tried to add doc comments of some sort to ES4 with first-class metadata hooks or reflection hooks and it was just impossible to get everybody to agree.

Seibel: Do you read code you're not working on?

Eich: I do it as part of my job. Code review is a mandatory pre-check-in step, mostly to compensate for Netscape's bad hiring, but we kept it and still use it for integration review. We have a separate "super review" for when you're touching a lot of modules and you don't know all the hidden invariants that Joe Schmoe, who no longer works on Mozilla, knew in his head. Somebody else may have figured them out so you have somebody experienced to look at the big picture. Sometimes you can bypass it if you know what you're doing and you're in the sort of Jedi council, but we're not trying to cheat on it too much.

We don't have design reviews, so sometimes this causes a delayed design review to happen. They say, "Oh, back to the drawing board. You wrote too much code. You should have designed it this other way." That's the exception. We aren't going to impose any kind of waterfall, design then implementation. That was the big thing when I was getting into the industry in the early '80s and it was a nightmare, frankly. You spend all this time writing documents and then you go to write the code and often you realize that it's really stupid and you totally change the code and put the documents down the memory hole.

Seibel: So that's code that is going into Mozilla; do you ever read other people's code, outside Mozilla, just for edification?

Eich: Open source is great. I love looking at other people's code that's in some other part of the world. I don't spend enough time on it but I do look at server frameworks or I look at things like Python and Ruby.

Seibel: The implementations of those things?

Eich: Implementations and also library code. I look at the Ajax libraries—and it's heartening to see how clever people can be and how this small set of tools—closures, prototypes, and objects—can be used to create reasonable, convenient, sometimes very convenient abstractions. They're not always hardened or safe but they're awfully convenient.

Seibel: When you read a big piece of code, how do you get into it?

Eich: I used to start top-down. If it's big enough you get function pointers and control flow gets opaque. I sometimes drive it in the debugger and play around with it that way. Also, I look for bottom-up patterns that I recognize. If it's a language processor or if it's got something that makes system calls that I understand, I can start looking at how those primitives are used. How does that get used by higher levels in the system? And that helps me get around. But really understanding it is this gestalt process that involves looking at different angles of top and bottom and different views of it, playing in the debugger, stepping through in the debugger—incredibly tedious though that can be.

If you can understand what's going on a little bit in the heap—chase pointers, walk through cons cells, whatever—that can be worth the trouble though it gets tedious. That, to me, is as important as reading source. You can get a long way reading source; you can also get stuck and get bored and convince yourself you understand something that you don't.

When I did JavaScript's regular expressions I was looking at Perl 4. I did step through it in the debugger, as well as read the code. And that gave me ideas; the implementation I did was similar. In this case the recursive backtracking nature of them was a little novel, so that I had to wrap my head around. It did help to just debug simple regular expressions, just to trace the execution. I know other programmers talk about this: you should step through code, you should understand what the dynamic state of the program looks like in various quick bird's-eye views or sanity checks, and I agree with that.

Seibel: Do you do that with your own code, even when you're not tracking down a bug?

Eich: Absolutely—just sanity checks. I have plenty of assertions, so if those botch then I'll be in the debugger for sure. But sometimes you write code and you've got some clever bookkeeping scheme or other. And you test it and it seems to work until you step through it in the debugger. Particularly if there's a bit of cleverness that only kicks in when the stars and the moon align. Then you want to use a conditional break point or even a watch point, a data break point, and then you can actually catch it in the act and check that, yes, the planets are all aligned the way they should be and maybe test that you weren't living in optimistic pony land. You can actually look in the debugger, whereas in the source you're still in pony land. So that seems important; I still do it.

Seibel: Is the way you discover a problem that you're stepping through looking at the source with your mental model of what's about to happen, and then you see it not happen?

Eich: You see it not happen, or—and this is my problem—I was in pony land. I'm getting older and more skeptical and I'm doing better, but there's still something that I was optimistic about. In the back of my mind this Jiminy Cricket is whispering, "You probably have a bug because you forgot about something." That kind of problem happens to me still.

And sometimes I know about it, I swear—somewhere in there I know I'm wrong. I have this sort of itch in my hind-brain—well, not in my hind-brain; I don't know where it is; the microtubules. Anyway, I kind of feel like there's something that I should watch out for, and being in debugger helps me watch out for it and it helps me force the issue or see that the test vector, though it covered the code in some sense, didn't cover all the combinations, because it's a huge, huge hyperspace. And if you just change this one value then you'd go into a bad place.

Seibel: In addition to reading code, lots of programmers read books about programming—are there any books that you would recommend?

Eich: I should be a better student of the literature. But I think it's sort of like music in that you have to practice it. And you can learn a lot reading other people's code. I did like Brian Kernighan's books; I thought they were neat, because they would build up a small amount of code, and start reusing it as you go, and modularizing. And Knuth's *Art of Computer Programming*, Volumes 1–3, especially the seminumerical stuff. Double-hashing—I love those parts. The lemma about the golden ratio with the proof left as an exercise.

But I'm a little skeptical of book learning for programming. Programming is partly engineering; there's maybe some math on a good day. And then there's a lot of practical stuff that doesn't even rise to the level of engineering in the sense of civil engineering and mechanical engineering. Maybe it'll be formalized more over time.

There's definitely a good corpus of knowledge. Computer science is a science. I remember somebody on Usenet 20 years ago said, "Science lite, one-third the rigor." There's still a lot of stuff that doesn't look like it really holds up over time—there are these publish-or-perish ten-page, ten-point-font papers that often have holes in them. The journal publications are better because you get to interact with the referee; it's not just a truth or dare. And they get reviewed more carefully. The areas of mechanized proofs, that's getting impressive. But it's still not reaching programmers. So there's something a little bit missing in computer science in my view that makes me skeptical of book learning. I should probably not go so far on this Luddite track. But there it is.

There is science there, and there are important things to learn. You could spend a lot of time studying them, too. I know a lot of people on the theoretical side of it from work on JavaScript language development, and a lot of them are hackers, too, which is good.Some of them don't program.

They're not really practical people. They have amazing insights, which can sometimes be very productive, but when you have to actually write programs and ship them to users and have them be usable and have them win some sort of market contest, you're far removed from theory. But I am interested in theory, and it does help improve our lives.

Seibel: There are other kinds of books too. There are books that introduce you to the craft of programming, without a lot of theory.

Eich: And that's the kind of book I like. We talked about Knuth's literate programming paper. And there was a whole area of programming as craft that I like. I like the Smalltalk books. Now that I think about it, those were pretty influential. The Adele Goldberg book. And before that, the *Byte* issue.

Seibel: With the hot-air balloon on the cover?

Eich: Yeah. That turned me around in a big way. That was big. That was like '80 or so. So I wasn't really doing a lot of programming then. I was thinking about it and I was reading about it and I was playing around on this old iron at undergraduate university. The purity of the Smalltalk environment, the fact that it was so highly bootstrapped—all that really hit me in a way that made me want to be involved in programming—languages and virtual machines. Going into Unix was physical machines and operating systems, and that was where the action was. But even then I was reading—there was a Springer-Verlag book that had a bunch of papers, and people back then were fantasizing about universal object file formats and Java byte-code, essentially, before its time. But yes, Smalltalk was huge. I didn't actually get to use it until years later at U of I, when they finally released something that ran on the Suns of the time and it was slow.

Seibel: On another topic, how do you recognize programming talent?

Eich: We hired somebody a while ago; he was a friend of one of the superbrains we'd hired. But this was a guy who was, I think, just undergrad or a bachelor's degree; I'm not sure if he even finished. He met a guy who was working for us and they're both OCaml hackers, and he was doing his own OCaml hacking on the side. And he was thinking about problems that we were seeing in my static analysis. When we interviewed him, I knew he was young but you couldn't tell. Some people thought, "Oh, yeah, he hasn't done much. You know, we should only hire rock stars; what are we talking to him for?"

I said, "No, you guys are looking at this wrong. This is like one of our bright interns. Get them while they're young. He's done a bunch by himself, he's gotten into OCaml; he knows not just the source language, but the runtime, and he's hacked native methods and he was writing an OCaml operating system, toy operating system. But this guy is good." And it wasn't that I gave him any particular programming test; it was just that I'd listened to him talk about what he'd done and why he'd done it. He wasn't just repeating pabulum about C++ patterns. We have kids like that, unfortunately. Nice people and adequate programmers, for what they were doing, Java Enterprise stuff. But we needed somebody different, and this guy was different.

So in the interview the main problem was overcoming people misreading his age or thinking he wasn't accomplished enough. But we hired him and he's just been a superstar. He's done a bunch of static analysis tooling, originally on this open-source Berkeley Oink framework, and then on GCC as plug-ins, working with the GCC guys. Now he's kicking our mobile effort into high gear, just doing poor man's profiling and `printf` of timestamps and finding out where the costs are and whacking them.

So when I interviewed him I knew there was talent. That he came recommended from somebody bright was good, because you know bright people like each other and can judge each other—generally there's not a dysfunctional, "Hire my friend, who's really not bright." They want to work with bright people. Maybe this sounds like I'm cheating, but that's one way I recognize talent. And I think that's why we're hiring superhackers. I think we're hiring up all the Valgrind hackers. Some of those guys can do anything; they don't fuck around.

Seibel: So is that something you often do in interviews: get them to talk about their own projects?

Eich: I do. I don't give people puzzles to solve. We have people who do that here. To the extent that we have to do that and we're using that to filter applicants, I worry.

Seibel: Is that even a good first-pass filter?

Eich: I'm skeptical. Google does that in spades, and they hire a bunch of very bright puzzle-solvers. But some of them, their street smarts are not necessarily there, and mature judgment. So I'm skeptical of it. I think we have to do it to some extent because you can end up getting someone who talks well, but actually isn't effective at programming, and so you want to see them think on their feet, you want to see if they've solved a problem before. So we give them fairly practical problems. Not esoteric puzzles or math-y things, but more like programming problems.

Check their C++ knowledge, because C++ is hairy. So it's sort of a sanity check, not enough to say, "Let's hire him." But if they pass it, that's good; if they don't, we worry. To say, "Let's hire them," we have to see something else, and that's the spark that involves particulars, like what they've done and their approach and what languages they've used.

Maybe I'm also sympathetic to the odd duck. I don't mind people who are a little different. I don't want to hire somebody who's hard to work with, but we need talent. We need people who think differently.

When I was an undergrad I was really affected by Pirsig's *Zen and the Art of Motorcycle Maintenance*. And I had been going through Plato and the early philosophers. I was, at that point, inclined more towards idealism in some philosophical sense. I thought little-endian byte order was superior to big-endian, because after all, the least significant digits are in the lowest address—there was some kind of harmony or geometry in that. But try reading a hex dump. Practical things matter; particulars matter. The famous School of Athens painting with Aristotle pointing down and Plato pointing up—I'm more on the pointing-down side now. As I get older I get more and more skeptical and more and more interested in what works.

When I'm interviewing people, when I'm looking for talent, it's very hard for me to not stick with particulars and practicalities. OK, so this guy knew OCaml—it meant he was smart, but should we hire him? Well no, but he also did things on his own and he thought on his feet when I talked to him, and he was already thinking about compilation or analysis problems that we were going to hire him to work on. But maybe the important thing there, the real story, was the network we were going through, the guy we hired, he was his friend.

Seibel: Do you still enjoy programming?

Eich: Yeah. It's a bit like an addiction; it's a little problematic. It's not just the programming part of getting the code to run; to me now it's more and more finding the right idea that has the New Jersey philosophy of a 90/10 trade-off—a sweet, sound theoretical core that isn't going to solve *all* your problems but when you fall on the 10 percent that loses, you don't go to hell. You can actually win this way and the code stays small enough and simple enough and there's some dance between theory and implementation. I like that. That still appeals to me; it still is fun; it keeps me up at night thinking about it when I should be sleeping.

Seibel: Are there parts of it that you don't enjoy as much anymore?

Eich: I don't know. C++. We're able to use most of its features—there are too many of them. It's probably got a better type system than Java. But we're still screwing around with '70s debuggers and linkers, and it's stupid. I don't know why we put up with it.

Impatience and hatred of primitive tools drives me to try to be a better programmer. Our code is riddled with assertions now and they are fatal. That's important to us. But this is something that has helped me, especially when I'm doing one of these allegedly sound, 90/10, sweet trade-off moves on the code that doesn't quite satisfy all the invariants. I forget something; an assertion will botch and then it's like, bing, I know what to fix.

Also I'm even now learning about my own weaknesses, where I'll optimize something too much. I'll have made some kind of happy pony land in my head, where I forgot some important problem. That's always a challenge because programmers have to be optimists. We're supposed to be paranoid, neurotic, Woody Allen types who are always worried about things, but really you wouldn't get anywhere in programming if you were truly paranoid.

Seibel: Do you feel at all that programming is a young person's game?

Eich: I think young people have enormous advantages, just physiological advantages to do with the brain. What they don't have is the wisdom! You get crustier and maybe you get slower but you do learn some painful lessons that you try to pass on to the next generation. I see them ignoring me and learning them the hard way, and I shake my fist!

But, apart from that, if you stay well-read and keep at it, your output doesn't necessarily have to be voluminous. While producing a lot of code is still important, what has interested me—and this is something that we talked about at Netscape when we talked about their track for principal engineer—is somebody who isn't management but still has enough leadership or influence to cause other programmers to write code like they would write without them having to do it, because you don't have enough hours in the day or fingers.

Having that ability to spread your approach and whatever you've learned about programming, and have that go through some kind of community and produce a corpus of code that's bigger than you could do, that's as satisfying to me as being the one that stays up all night writing too much code.

I'm still working too much, plus I've got small children. My wife is a good sport but I don't think she likes me traveling so much. But I'm doing some of that too. That's not programming, yet it somehow has become important. In the case of JavaScript we have to figure out how to move the language forward, and that requires some amount of not just evangelism, but getting people to think about what would happen if the language did move, how would you like it to move, where should it go. And then dealing with the cacophony of responses.

Not all programmers will say this, a lot of them are solitary, in the corner, but one of the things I realized at Netscape was that I liked interacting with people who actually use my code. And I would miss that if I went back into a corner. I want to be grounded about this. I'm secure enough to think I could go do something that was a fine sky castle for myself, but I'm realist enough to know that it would be only for myself and probably not fine for other people. And what's the point? "If I'm only for myself", you know, Hillel the elder, "what am I?"

I am not JavaScript. In the early days, it was such a rush job and it was buggy and then there was some Usenet post Jamie Zawinski forwarded me. He said, "They're calling your baby ugly." I have real kids now; I don't have to worry about that.

CHAPTER

5

Joshua Bloch

Now Chief Java Architect at Google, Bloch previously was a Distinguished Engineer at Sun Microsystems, where he led the design and implementation of the Java Collections Framework introduced in Java 2 and was involved in the design of several language additions in the Java 5 release. He has a BS from Columbia University and a PhD from Carnegie-Mellon University, where he worked on the Camelot distributed transaction processing system, which later became Encina, a product of Transarc, where he was a Senior Systems Designer. He wrote the 2001 Jolt Award–winning book Effective Java and coauthored Java Puzzlers and Java Concurrency in Practice.

As you might expect from someone whose job is to encourage the use of Java at Google, Bloch is a strong advocate of the language. Despite the recent flurry of interest in approaches to concurrency such as Software Transactional Memory or Erlang's message passing, Bloch thinks Java has "the best approach of any language out there" to concurrency and predicts a resurgence of interest in Java as more and more programmers are forced to deal with programming for machines with multicore CPUs.

Bloch is also a strong advocate of treating programming as API design, and we talked about how that affects his own design process, as well as whether Java has gotten too complex and why picking a programming language is like picking a bar.

Seibel: How did you get into programming?

Bloch: I'm tempted to say it's in the blood. My dad was a chemist at Brookhaven National Lab. When I was in fourth grade, he took a programming course. Back then, of course, machines were mainframes behind glass windows and you handed your deck of cards to the operator. It wasn't hands-on, but I was just thrilled by the idea of these electronic computing machines that would do stuff for you. So I learned a little bit of Fortran from him while he was taking that course.

Seibel: This would have been what year?

Bloch: I think it was 1971. The bug didn't really bite me until a couple years later. And what did it, of course, was timesharing. Long Island had a DECsystem-10, which was shared among all of the schools in Suffolk County. There was another one for Nassau County. It's amazing how many well-known people got their start on one of those two DECsystem-10s.

Once you have interactivity, the bug bites you. I was programming in BASIC, like everybody else back then, from about 1973 through 1976. That's when I got seriously into it. The amazing thing is, I still have programs from back then on Teletype paper—that's the medium that survived—and I look at them and I can sort of see that bits and pieces of my style haven't changed since then.

Seibel: So what was the first interesting program that you remember writing?

Bloch: Well, I remember on July 4th, 1977 writing a version of the classic Twenty Questions game called "animals." The program had a binary tree with yes-or-no questions at the interior nodes and animals at the leaves. When it first encountered a new animal, it "learned" the animal by asking the user for a yes-or-no question to distinguish the new animal from the one it had incorrectly guessed. The binary tree was stored on disk so the program kept getting "smarter" over time.

I remember thinking, "My gosh, this is cool: the program actually learns." That was one sort of *aha!* moment for me. Another thing I remember was in high school—10th grade, I think—on that DECsystem-10. We weren't allowed to write what would now be called instant-messaging programs—they were thought to be too big a drain on system resources.

Seibel: As they are, in fact, now.

Bloch: Don't get me started. IM ruins my life. No, email ruins my life—IM is just a distraction. Anyway, being the bratty kid that I was, I entered a project into the Long Island Math Fair on what I called "inter-job communication programs." I actually won a prize for it.

Seibel: And you actually wrote the programs?

Bloch: Yes. I wrote the programs, except for one that was contributed by a friend named Thomas De Bellis. The unique thing about Tom's program was that it was written entirely in BASIC. It was line-oriented, and used files to communicate. It wasn't fast or efficient, but it worked! I wrote two, one line-oriented and one character-oriented. I wrote them in MACRO-10, the PDP-10 assembly language. They used a kind of shared memory called the "high segment" for the communication.

I didn't know anything about concurrent programming back then. I remember not really understanding mutexes. But there were communication buffers, and independent agents trying to communicate with each other concurrently. So there were race conditions, and occasionally the program lost a character or two. I wasn't able to figure that out myself as a high-school student.

Seibel: You say that you saw aspects of your current style in your earliest programs. What are the bits that have stayed the same?

Bloch: My attempts to make my programs readable. As Knuth would say, a program is essentially a work of literature. For whatever reason, I realized even back then that a program has to be readable. And that hasn't changed.

Seibel: And what has changed?

Bloch: Well, it's hard to make your programs readable when you're restricted to single-character variable names. So I worry more about variable naming now. Obviously, as you use languages with new features, many things change. And things that you vaguely understood over the years really get slammed home.

For example, don't repeat yourself. I was freer with the copy-and-paste back then than I am now. Now I really try not to do it at all. That's a little bit of an overstatement, but only a little bit. Generally speaking, if I find myself copying and pasting, I think, "What's wrong with this design? How can I fix it?" So that's something that took a little while to get right. Basically I've become harder on myself over the years—that's what it takes to write good programs. You really can't accept bad habits from yourself.

Seibel: If you were going to go back in time and do it all over again, is there anything you wish you had really done differently? The BASIC didn't brain-damage you or anything?

Bloch: No, actually that's a funny thing. I think Dijkstra, God rest his soul, was entirely wrong about that. I know so many really good programmers who got their start programming BASIC because that's what was available to them.

I do think it's good to use lots of languages, though. By the time I was in college, I was programming a whole bunch of them. Each course you would do in a different language. In a numerics course or a science course, you'd use Fortran. If you were taking a programming course back then, it was Pascal or SAIL or Simula or something like that. In an AI course, it was Lisp.

But maybe I should have learned more languages. It's funny—I didn't really get into the object-oriented thing until late in the game. Java was the first object-oriented language I used with any seriousness, in part because I couldn't exactly bring myself to use C++.

Seibel: When was that?

Bloch: Starting in '96 when I joined Sun. I think it would have been good to learn those concepts a little earlier than I did. That said, I don't think all those concepts are good. OO is a funny thing. It means two things. It means modularity. And modularity is great. But I don't think the OO people can claim the right to that. You can look at older literature—for example Parnas's information hiding—and see that the notion of a kind of class as an abstraction predates object-oriented programming. And the other thing is inheritance and I consider inheritance a mixed blessing, as many people do by now.

Also I should have exposed myself to more areas, inside and outside of computer science. The more things you learn and the younger you learn them, the better off you are. One thing I've never really done much of is GUI programming and I should have forced myself to do that at some point. But for whatever reason, libraries [have] appealed the most to me over the years, writing the building blocks for other people to use. So I've been doing data structures and algorithms and so forth for decades.

Seibel: Are there any books that every programmer should read?

Bloch: An obvious one, which I have slightly mixed feelings about but I still think everyone should read, is *Design Patterns*. It gives us a common vocabulary. There are a lot of good ideas in there. On the other hand, there's sort of a mish-mash of styles and languages, and it's beginning to show its age. But I think it's absolutely worth reading.

Another is *Elements of Style*, which isn't even a programming book. You should read it for two reasons: The first is that a large part of every software engineer's job is writing prose. If you can't write precise, coherent, readable specs, nobody is going to be able to use your stuff. So anything that improves your prose style is good. The second reason is that most of the ideas in that book are also applicable to programs.

My desert-island list is a little bit odd. For example, a book that's terribly important to me is *Hacker's Delight*, by Hank Warren.

Seibel: That's the bit-twiddling book?

Bloch: Yes. I love bit twiddling and it's relevant to what I do. If you write libraries, compilers, low-level graphics, or crypto, this book is indispensable. Warren has taken what used to be an oral tradition, put it all in one place, and given it the rigorous mathematical treatment that it deserves. I was thrilled when that book was published.

Of course there's Knuth's *The Art of Computer Programming*. In truth, I haven't read the whole series or anything close to it. When I'm working on a particular algorithm, though, I go there to see what he has to say about it. And often it's exactly what I need—it's all in there.

But I simply don't have the capacity and speed to read through all of it, so I'd be lying if I told you I had. An old book that I think is great is *The Elements of Programming Style*, by Kernighan and Plauger. All the examples are in Fortran IV and PL/I, so it's a bit out-of-date. But it's amazing, given the age of the book, the ideas are all still current.

Another old one is Frederick Brooks's *The Mythical Man Month*. It's 40 years old and still as true today as when it was written. And it's just a joy to read. Everyone should read that. The main message of the book is "adding people to a late software project makes it later," and it's still true. But there are a lot of other important things in it. Some of the details are beginning to age, but everyone should read it anyway.

These days, everybody has to learn about concurrency. So *Java Concurrency in Practice* is another good bet. Although it has *Java* in the title, a lot of the material transcends any particular programming language.

Seibel: That's the one you worked on with Brian Goetz?

Bloch: My name is on the cover but the reason I felt free to mention it is that it's not really my book. The lead author is Brian and then the secondary author was Tim Peierls and the remaining ones are everyone who was on JSR-166, the Java concurrency people. But those are almost there for courtesy—we contributed material but not prose to the book.

Oh, one more book: *Merriam-Webster's Collegiate Dictionary, 11th Edition*. Never go anywhere without it. It's not something you actually *read*, but as I said, when you're writing programs you need to be able to name your identifiers well. And your prose has to be good. I'd feel lost without a good dictionary.

Seibel: Other than naming your variables better, and cutting and pasting less, is there anything else about how you approach programming that has changed as you gained experience?

Bloch: The older I get, the more I realize it isn't just about making it work; it's about producing an artifact that is readable, maintainable, and efficient. Generally speaking, I find that, contrary to popular belief, the cleaner and nicer the program, the faster it's going to run. And if it doesn't, it'll be easy to make it fast. As they say, it's easier to optimize correct code than to correct optimized code.

Some of the changes in my approach are specific to languages. Every language presents you with a toolkit. You want to use the right tool for the job, and what would be the right tool in one language may not be the right one in another. A trivial example: if you're writing in Java 5, using `enums` instead of `int` constants or Booleans can greatly simplify your program and make it safer and more robust.

Seibel: Given that, can you say anything about how to speed up the process of getting to fluency in a new language?

Bloch: I think it's a lot like spoken languages. One way is by knowing a lot of languages—if you already know Italian and Spanish and you want to learn Portuguese, you're not going to have a very hard time doing it. The more you know, the more you have to draw on.

When you're learning a new language, come in with all that you've learned, but remain open-minded. I know people who have sort of decided, "This is the way that all programs should be written." I won't mention any languages, but some languages, for whatever reason, cause people to get this way. Whenever they go to a new language, they criticize it to the extent it isn't like God's true language, whatever that happens to be. And when they use the new language, they try to program in God's true language to the extent that you can in the new language. Often you're missing what makes a language special if you do that.

It's like if the only tool you have is a hammer and someone gives you a screwdriver, and you say, "Well, this isn't a very good hammer but I guess I can hold the blade in my hand and whack with the handle." You have a crappy hammer when in fact you could have used it as a fine screwdriver. So, a combination of open-mindedness and a willingness to apply everything you already do know. And of course, code, code, code! The more you use the language, the faster you'll learn it.

Seibel: Why do people get so religious about their computer languages?

Bloch: I don't know. But when you choose a language, you're choosing more than a set of technical trade-offs—you're choosing a community. It's like choosing a bar. Yes, you want to go to a bar that serves good drinks, but that's not the most important thing. It's who hangs out there and what they talk about. And that's the way you choose computer languages. Over time the community builds up around the language—not only the people, but the software artifacts: tools, libraries, and so forth. That's one of the reasons that sometimes languages that are, on paper, better than other languages don't win—because they just haven't built the right communities around themselves.

Seibel: Java strikes me as interesting in that regard because it has two communities. There's the implementers and systems programmers—people who worked at Javasoft or Weblogic or places like that. Then there's all the people who use Java and app servers and prebuilt frameworks to build business applications. Those are very different bars.

Bloch: There are multiple communities associated with Java and with other programming languages too. When there aren't, it's usually a sign that the language is either a niche language or an immature language. As a language grows and prospers, it naturally appeals to a more diverse community. And furthermore, as the amount of investment in a language grows, the value of it grows.

It's like Metcalfe's law: the value of a network is proportional to the square of the number of users. The same is true of languages—you get all these people using a language and all of a sudden you've got Eclipse, you've got FindBugs, you've got Guice. Even if Java isn't the perfect language for you, there are all these incidental benefits to using it, so you form your own community that figures out how to do numeric programming in Java, or whatever kind of programming you want to do.

Seibel: Do you enjoy programming as much as you did when you were a kid?

Bloch: I do, although not necessarily in the same way. Like many kids, I think, to some degree programming was a refuge from aspects of life that I couldn't handle. And the other thing is, when you're young you have boundless energy and you can hack for hours and hours on end.

As you get older and have a family and kids and all that, you have other responsibilities, other important things in your life. And yet, there's still this undeniable high that comes from writing a program, watching the pieces fall into place and coming up with several beautiful lines of code that are readable, fast, and do what you want.

Seibel: Do you ever find that because of your greater awareness that it's not just enough to get it to work, that there are all these other issues, that it's almost more daunting?

Bloch: Absolutely. Books too, by the way. I definitely go into avoidance behaviors when starting things. Starting is the hardest part, whether it's a program or a book or anything else. On the other hand, sometimes you remind yourself, "Come on Josh; you've been doing this for three decades now, you know how to do it as well as most other people, so just go for it." And you just sort of remind yourself that, "Look, pretty much every other time you've tried to do this the results have been good, so they're probably going to be good this time too."

Seibel: So you just talked about how as your life experience broadens, it can be a distraction, but are there any things, experiences outside of programming, that you feel have made you a better programmer?

Bloch: Oh, absolutely. I think almost everything you do, if you do it well. Ideas transfer from all over the place. One example that comes to mind is, when I wrote my thesis, I did an analysis of a distributed data structure, the replicated sparse memory. And the basic idea that enabled me to do the analysis came from a chemistry course I had taken. It was the notion of a rate-balance equation: when you have a dynamic equilibrium in a system, you can write equations that say, "Things are entering a certain state at the same rate that they're leaving it." I got three simultaneous equations in three variables, solved them, and came up with results that precisely matched the observed behavior of this complicated distributed data structure. This was an idea I stole straight from chemistry and retargeted at computer science.

Many things that you see in life, whether in architecture—the way buildings are constructed, in language—the way that communication occurs, many of these ideas can be retargeted. And, of course, there's math. Math and programming are pretty darn similar. So keeping your eyes open and being willing to reuse ideas is a good thing.

Seibel: Do you know programmers who are great programmers but who aren't mathematical or well-educated in math? Is it actually important to have learned calculus and discrete math and all this stuff in order to be a programmer? Or is just more a kind of thinking that you could have even if you hadn't had that training?

Bloch: I think it's a kind of thinking that you could have if you hadn't had that training. But it sure helps. I worked with a guy by the name of madbot, Mike McCloskey. He's very mathematically inclined but hadn't taken number theory. He rewrote BigInteger. It used to be a veneer over a C package, and he rewrote it in Java with marching orders to make it run as fast as the C-based version. He actually pulled it off. In doing so he had to learn a heck of a lot of number theory. He couldn't have done it if he weren't mathematically inclined, but he wouldn't have had to learn it if he already knew it.

Seibel: But that was an inherently mathematical problem.

Bloch: You're right; it's a terrible example. But I believe that even for problems that aren't inherently mathematical, the kind of thinking that you learn in math is essential to programming. For instance, inductive proofs are so tied to recursive programming that you can't really understand one without understanding the other. You may not know the terms *base case* and *induction hypothesis*, but you have to understand these concepts if you're going to write correct recursive programs. So even if the domain is unrelated to math, a programmer who isn't comfortable with these concepts is going to have a harder time.

You mentioned calculus—I think it's less important. A funny thing has happened over the years. It used to be just assumed that if you were an educated person who had gone to college you had to know calculus. And there are a lot of beautiful ideas there—it's nice to be able to get your mind around infinity in that way.

But there's a discrete and a continuous way to get your mind around infinity. I think that for a programmer it's more important to have mastered the discrete way. For example, I just mentioned induction proofs. You can prove something true for all integers. It's kind of magical. You prove it for one integer and you prove that one implies the next and then you've proved it for all of them. And I think that is more important for a programmer than, let's say, understanding the notion of limits.

Luckily we don't have to make a choice. I think that there's plenty of room in the curriculum for both. So even if you're not going to use the calculus as much as you use the discrete mathematics, I think it should still get taught. But I think that the importance of the discrete stuff is greater than that of the continuous.

Seibel: You talked before about how writing prose has many similar characteristics to programming. While mathematics has always been closely associated with computers and programming, I wonder if once you're talking about developing things like web frameworks or a web application on top of a framework, if it requires skills more related to writing.

Bloch: Yes—earlier you mentioned that there were two distinct communities of Java programmers. The need for math is much greater in the community that writes libraries, compilers, and frameworks. If you write web applications on top of frameworks, you have to understand communication, both verbal and visual. I get infuriated at web sites when they drive me to do the wrong thing. It's clear that someone just hasn't thought about how someone approaching this thing will deal with it. So yes, the truth of the matter is that programming is at the confluence of a whole bunch of disciplines. And depending on which ones you excel at, you will be better at writing different applications. But even libraries, compilers, and frameworks have to be readable and maintainable. I contend that you'll have a hard time achieving that goal if you aren't a competent writer.

Seibel: What is your process for designing software? Do you fire up Emacs and start writing code and then move it around until it looks right? Or do you sit down on your couch with a pad of paper?

Bloch: I gave a talk called "How to Design a Good API and Why It Matters" at OOPSLA a couple years ago, and several versions of it are floating around the Web. It does a pretty good job explaining how I go about it.

The most important thing is to know what you're trying to build: what problem you're trying to solve. The importance of requirements analysis can't be overstated. There are people who think, "Oh, yeah, requirements analysis; you go to your customer, you say, 'What do you need?' He tells you, and you're done."

Nothing could be further from the truth. Not only is it a negotiation but it's a process of understanding. Many customers won't tell you a problem; they'll tell you a solution. A customer might say, for instance, "I need you to add support for the following 17 attributes to this system. Then you have to ask, 'Why? What are you going to do with the system? How do you expect it to evolve?'" And so on. You go back and forth until you figure out what all the customer really needs the software to do. These are the use cases.

Coming up with a good set of use cases is the most important thing you can do at this stage. Once you have that, you have a benchmark against which you can measure any possible solution. It's OK if you spend a lot of time getting it reasonably close to right, because if you get it wrong, you're already dead. The rest of the process will be an exercise in futility.

The worst thing that you can do—and I've seen this happen—is you get a bunch of smart guys into a room to work for six months and write a 247-page system specification before they really understand what it is they're trying to build. Because after six months, they'll have a very precisely specified system that may well be useless. And often they say, "We've invested so much in the spec that we have to build it." So they build the useless system and it never gets used. And that's horrible. If you don't have use cases, you build the thing and then you try to do something very simple and you realize that, "Oh my gosh, doing something very simple like taking an XML document and printing it requires pages upon pages of boilerplate code." And that's a horrible thing.

So get those use cases and then write a skeletal API. It should be really, really short. The whole thing should, usually, fit on a page. It doesn't have to be terribly precise. You want declarations for the packages, classes, and methods and, if it's not clear what they should do, then maybe a one-sentence description for each. But this is not documentation of the quality that you will end up distributing.

The whole idea is to stay agile at this stage, to flesh the API out just enough that you can take the use cases and code them up with this nascent API to see if it it's up to the task. It's just amazing, there are so many things that are obvious in hindsight but when you're designing the API, even with the use cases in mind, you get them wrong. Then when you try to code up the use cases you say, "Oh, yeah, this is fundamentally wrong; I have too many classes here; these should be combined, these need to be broken out," whatever it is. Luckily, your API doc is only a page long, so it's easy to fix it.

As your confidence in the API increases, *then* you flesh it out. But the fundamental rule is, write the code that uses the API before you write the code that implements it. Because otherwise you may be wasting your time writing implementation code that won't get used. In fact, write the code that uses the API before you even flesh out the spec, because otherwise you may be wasting your time writing detailed specs for something that's fundamentally broken. That's how I go about designing stuff.

Seibel: And how specific is this to designing things like the Java collections, which are a particular kind of self-contained API?

Bloch: I claim it's less specific than you might think. Programming of any complexity requires API design because big programs have to be modular, and you have to design the intermodular interfaces.

Good programmers think in terms of pieces that make sense in isolation, for several reasons. One is that you, perhaps inadvertently, end up producing useful, reusable modules. If you write a monolithic system and, when it gets too big, you tear it into pieces, there will likely be no clear boundaries, and you'll end up with unmaintainable sewage. So I claim that it's simply the best way to program, whether you consider yourself an API designer or not.

That said, the world of programming is very large. If programming for you is writing HTML, it's probably not the best way to program. But I think that for many kinds of programming, it is.

Seibel: So you want a system that's made up of modules that are cohesive and loosely coupled. These days there's at least two views on how you can get to that point. One is to sit down and design these intermodule APIs in advance, the process that you're talking about. And the other is this "simplest thing that could possibly work, refactor mercilessly" approach.

Bloch: I don't think the two are mutually exclusive. In a sense, what I'm talking about is test-first programming and refactoring applied to APIs. How do you test an API? You write use cases to it before you've implemented it. Although I can't run them, I am doing test-first programming: I'm testing the quality of the API, when I code up the use cases to see whether the API is up to the task.

Seibel: So you write the client code to use the API and then look at it and ask, "Is this code I would want to write?"

Bloch: Absolutely. Sometimes you don't even get to the stage where you can look at the client code. You try to write it and you say either, "I cannot do this at all because I forgot this piece of functionality in the API," or, "I can do this but it's going to be so tedious that this was not the right approach."

It doesn't matter how good you are; you can't get an API right until you've tried to code to it. You design something; try to use it; and say, "Oh, this is so wrong." And if you do this before you've wasted time writing all of the layers underneath it, that's a huge win. So what I'm talking about is test-first programming and refactoring the APIs, rather than refactoring the implementation code underneath the APIs.

As far as doing the simplest thing that will work, I'm all for it. The fundamental theorem of API design is, *when in doubt, leave it out*. It should be the simplest thing that is big enough to handle all the use cases that you care about. That doesn't mean "Just throw some sloppy code together." There are oodles of aphorisms to this effect. My favorite is one that's commonly misattributed to Thelonious Monk: "Simple ain't easy."

Nobody likes sloppy software. People who say, "Write the simplest thing that could possibly work and refactor mercilessly" aren't saying, "Write sloppy code," and they aren't saying, "Don't do upfront design work." I've talked to Martin Fowler about this. He's a huge believer in thinking about what you're going to do so your system has a reasonable shape and a reasonable structure. What he's saying is, "Don't write 247-page specs before writing a line of code," and I agree.

I do disagree with Martin on one point: I don't think tests are even remotely an acceptable substitute for documentation. Once you're trying to write something that other people can code to, you need precise specs, and the tests should test that the code conforms to those specs.

So there are some points of disagreement between the two camps, but I don't think the gulf is as wide as some people do.

Seibel: Since you mentioned Fowler, who's written a couple of books on UML, do you ever use UML as a design tool?

Bloch: No. I think it's nice to be able to make diagrams that other people can understand. But honestly I can't even remember which components are supposed to be round or square.

Seibel: Have you ever done full-on literate programming a la Knuth?

Bloch: No. I'm not against it in principle. I just haven't had occasion to do it. The other thing is—how can I put this delicately—I tend not to buy into religions, any religions, whole hog. Whether it's object-oriented programming or functional programming or Christianity or Judaism—I mine them for good ideas but I don't practice them in toto. There are a lot of great ideas in literate programming, but it's not the right bar: there aren't enough other programmers hanging out there. I could see maybe doing it once as an experiment.

What I do instead is I will cheerfully spend literally hours on identifier names: variable names, method names, and so forth, to make my code readable. If you read some expression using these identifiers and it reads like an English sentence, your program is much more likely to be correct, and much easier to maintain. I think that people who say, "Oh, it's not worth the time; it's just the name of a variable," just don't get it. You're not going to produce a maintainable program with that attitude.

Seibel: One way that programs differ from most literature—non-experimental literature anyway—is that there is no one order in which to read a program. How do you read a big program that you didn't write?

Bloch: Good question. The truth is I really want programs to be well-written. I know a few people with the ability to take an arbitrarily large and poorly written system and wrap themselves in the code till they get a total mental picture of the architecture. It's a really useful skill, but I've never been able to do it.

I want to be able to take small modules, read them, and understand them in isolation. If I'm trying to read a system that's tightly coupled so I have to read the whole thing in order to understand one part, it's a nightmare. I have to psych myself up even to *attempt* to read it, and I have to have access to all the code at the same time. I usually print everything out and sit on the floor surrounded by the printout, writing notes on it.

If I'm reading a well-written piece of code, I try to find a view from 10,000 feet: usually someone, somewhere has written a description of the shape of the entire system. If I can find it, I know what the important modules are, and I read them first, occasionally diving down into lower-level modules to aid my understanding.

Also, although code is written linearly down the page, the execution is not at all linear. If I'm lucky enough to have a piece of code that can be read from top to bottom, great. If not, it's important that I have access to tools that let me quickly locate methods that are being invoked, classes that are being extended, and so on. This lets me understand key execution paths through the code.

Seibel: Do you ever step through code as a way of understanding it?

Bloch: Absolutely! That is still my chosen method of debugging. Especially for concurrent code—there are too many states that the thing can be in for me to possibly enumerate all of them. I just stare at the code; step through it mentally; think of what invariants must hold at what time. For all of the fancy debugging tools at our disposal, there's nothing that can match the power of simply stepping through a program, in a debugger or by reading it and mentally executing the code. I've found many bugs that way and I use it as part of the writing process.

As I write the program, I say to myself, what it is that must be true here? And it's very important to put those assertions into the code, to preserve them for posterity. If your language lets you do it with an assert construct, use it; if not, put assertions in comments. Either way, the information is too valuable to lose. It's what you need to understand the program six months down the road, and what your colleague needs to understand the program any time at all.

Seibel: Do you feel like people understand invariants and how to use assertions as well as they ought?

Bloch: No. You probably know that assertions were the first construct that I added to the Java programming language and I'm well aware that they never really became part of the culture. Only a small fraction of Java programmers use them. I don't exactly know why that is. Talking of mathematics—invariants are very much a mathematical idea.

Seibel: But you don't have to have a lot of math to be able to understand it.

Bloch: You don't. But let me just play the devil's advocate. There's a certain precision of thinking that comes with doing math. I coached a Math Olympiad team for fourth and fifth graders. This is just the age at which some kids are starting to understand, at some level, the notion of a proof—

that a proposition can be demonstrably, unequivocally true rather than just, "I think it's true because here are a few examples where it seems to work."

In order to understand the notion of an invariant, you have to understand the notion of a proof. Unfortunately, there are plenty of adults who don't. And it's a style of thinking that is typically taught in mathematics classes.

Seibel: You'd almost wonder if maybe the better forum to teach that kind of thinking would be in programming. If you just taught programming as being about invariants—

Bloch: To a certain extent I agree, but you can go too far in that direction. Then we're back to Dijkstra. I'm sure you've read "On the Cruelty of Really Teaching Computing Science", which I think is as wrong as it could possibly be. Dijkstra says that you shouldn't let students even touch a computer until they've manipulated symbols, stripped of their true meaning, for a semester. That's crazy! There's a joy in telling the computer to do something, and watching it do it. I would not deprive students of that joy. And furthermore, I wouldn't assume that I could—computers are everywhere. Ten-year-olds are programming.

Seibel: As a Java guy at Google, do you think it could be used more? Leaving aside the force of history and historical choices, if somehow you could wave a magic wand and replace all of the C++ with Java, could that work?

Bloch: Up to a point. Large parts of the system could be written that way, and over time, things are moving in that direction. But for the absolute core of the system—the inner loops of the index servers, for instance—very small gains in performance are worth an awful lot. When you have that many machines running the same piece of code, if you can make it even a few percent faster, then you've done something that has real benefits, financially and environmentally. So there is some code that you want to write in assembly language, and what is C but glorified assembly language?

I'm not religious. If it works, great. I wrote C code for 20 years. But it's much more efficient, in terms of programmers' time, to use a more modern language that provides better safety, convenience, and expressiveness. In most cases, programmer time is much more valuable than computer time.

But that isn't necessarily so if you're running the same program on many, many thousands of machines. So there are some programs that we write where probably using less-safe languages to extract every ounce of performance is worth it. I think for most programs these days the performance of all modern languages is a wash and if anyone tells you that their language is ten times more efficient, they're probably lying to you.

But in terms of efficiency, in terms of use of engineers' time, it's far from a wash. More modern languages, first of all, are exempt from large classes of errors. Second of all, they have marvelous sets of tools which make engineers more efficient. To some degree it's cultural; it's what languages people learned in schools. But to some degree I think it's actually fundamental engineering at work. For example, if a language has a macro processor it's much harder to write good tools for it. Parsing C++ is a much trickier business than parsing Java.

Google is writing a lot more of its code in Java now than it used to. I don't know what the numbers are, but if the lines haven't already crossed, they will soon. So there's a big difference between how many lines of code do we have in each language versus how many cycles are getting executed in each language. And I think it would be a fool's errand and not particularly meritorious, either, to try and get the inner loops of the indexing servers written in Java. If you were starting a company to do this sort of thing today, you might write things largely in Java or in some other modern, safe language, and then escape it when you needed to. But we have this engineering infrastructure. Libraries and monitoring facilities and all of that stuff that makes it go. And finally Java is, if not an equal partner in this, it's reasonably usable within these systems, which is good. When I arrived that wasn't the case yet.

Companies establish their DNA very early on. It can make them tremendously successful, but it can also make it hard for them to escape when what served them well in the early days doesn't serve them so well any more. I remember being an intern at IBM Research in Yorktown Heights around 1982, seeing the culture still dominated by batch processing. Even when they were doing timesharing, they talked in terms of virtual card readers and virtual card punches. Everything was still 80-column records. With DEC, it was the timesharing mentality that they never escaped. And I suppose with Microsoft it's an open question whether they'll be able to move beyond the desktop-PC mentality.

Seibel: And 20 years from now people will be talking about how Google can't get past how to sell ads on the Internet.

Bloch: Absolutely. Anyway, there was this sort of cultural meme at Google that Java is slow and unreliable. And it's obvious where it came from: Blackdown Java on Linux, around 1999, was slow and unreliable. And old ideas die very hard. Although the truth is, Google uses Java for many sorts of business-critical functions, including, by the way, ads.

So at some level they understand that it's neither slow nor unreliable. But the actual search pipeline, which is the most intense in terms of machine cycles, that stuff is all basically C++ and there's an obvious reason having to do with the genesis of the company. And I think that will continue to affect us for quite some time.

Seibel: What are the tools you actually use to program?

Bloch: I knew this was coming; I'm an old fart and I'm not proud of it. The Emacs keystrokes are wired into my brain. And I tend to write smaller programs, libraries and so forth. So I do too much of my coding without modern tools. But I know that modern tools make you a lot more efficient.

I do use IntelliJ for larger stuff, because the rest of my group uses it, but I'm not terribly proficient. It is impressive: I love the static analysis that these tools do for you. I had people from those tools—IntelliJ, Eclipse, NetBeans, and FindBugs—as chapter reviewers on *Java Puzzlers*, so many of the traps and pitfalls in that book are detected automatically by these tools. I think it's just great.

Seibel: Do you believe you would really be more productive if you took a month to really learn IntelliJ inside out?

Bloch: I do. Modern IDEs are great for large-scale refactorings. Something that Brian Goetz pointed out is that people write much cleaner code now because they do refactorings that they simply wouldn't have attempted before. They can pretty much count on these tools to propagate changes without changing the behavior of the code.

Seibel: What about other tools?

Bloch: I'm not good with programming tools. I wish I were. The build and source-control tools change more than I would like, and it's hard for me to keep up. So I bother my more tool-savvy colleagues each time I set up a new environment. I say, "How do you do it these days?" They roll their eyes and help me and I use the environment until it doesn't work anymore.

I'm not proud of this. Engineers have things that they're good at and things they're not so good at. There are people who would like to pretend that this isn't so, that engineers are interchangeable, and that everyone can and should be a total generalist. But this ignores the fact that there are people who are stunningly good at certain things and not necessarily so good at other things. If you force them all to do everything, you'll probably make mediocre products.

In particular there are some people who, in Kevin Bourrillion's words, "lack the empathy gene." You aren't going to be a good API designer or language designer if you can't put yourself in the shoes of an ordinary programmer trying to use your API or language to get something done. Some people are good API and language designers, though. Then there are people who are stunningly good at the technical aspects of language design where they can say, "Oh, this will make the thing not LALR(1) and you need to tweak it in just such a way." That's an incredibly useful skill. But it's no substitute for having the empathy gene and knowing you have this awful language that's unusable.

I know other people who are stunningly good at extracting that last percentage of performance. You want to put them in a position where that's what they're doing. They'll be happy and they'll do good stuff for your company. I think you've got to figure out what your engineers are good at and use them for that. So that's my apologia for why I suck at tools. Lame, I know.

Seibel: Let's talk about debugging. What's the worst bug you ever had to track down?

Bloch: One that comes to mind, which was both horrible and amusing, happened when I worked at a company called Transarc, in Pittsburgh, in the early '90s. I committed to do a transactional shared-memory implementation on a very tight schedule. I finished the design and implementation on schedule, and even produced a few reusable components in the process. But I had written a lot of new code in a hurry, which made me nervous.

To test the code, I wrote a monstrous "basher." It ran lots of transactions, each of which contained nested transactions, recursively up to some maximum nesting depth. Each of the nested transactions would lock and read several elements of a shared array in ascending order and add something to each element, preserving the invariant that the sum of all the elements in the array was zero. Each subtransaction was either committed or aborted—90 percent commits, 10 percent aborts, or whatever. Multiple threads ran these transactions concurrently and beat on the array for a prolonged period. Since it was a shared-memory facility that I was testing, I ran multiple multithreaded bashers concurrently, each in its own process.

At reasonable concurrency levels, the basher passed with flying colors. But when I really cranked up the concurrency, I found that occasionally, just occasionally, the basher would fail its consistency check. I had no idea what was going on. Of course I assumed it was my fault because I had written all of this new code.

I spent a week or so writing painfully thorough unit tests of each component, and all the tests passed. Then I wrote detailed consistency checks for each internal data structure, so I could call the consistency checks after every mutation until a test failed. Finally I caught a low-level consistency check failing—not repeatably, but in a way that allowed me to analyze what was going on. And I came to the inescapable conclusion that my locks weren't working. I had concurrent read-modify-write sequences taking place in which two transactions locked, read, and wrote the same value and the last write was clobbering the first.

I had written my own lock manager, so of course I suspected it. But the lock manager was passing its unit tests with flying colors. In the end, I determined that what was broken wasn't the lock manager, but the underlying mutex implementation! This was before the days when operating systems supported threads, so we had to write our own threading package. It turned out that the engineer responsible for the mutex code had accidentally exchanged the labels on the lock and try-lock routines in the assembly code for our Solaris threading implementation. So every time you thought you were calling lock, you were actually calling try-lock, and vice versa. Which means that when there was actual contention—rare in those days—the second thread just sailed into the critical section as if the first thread didn't have the lock. The funny thing was that that this meant the whole company had been running without mutexes for a couple weeks, and nobody noticed.

There's a wonderful Knuth quote about testing, quoted by Bentley and McIlroy in their wonderful paper called "Engineering a Sort Function," about getting yourself in the meanest and nastiest mood that you can. I most certainly did that for this set of tests. But this tickled all of the things that make a bug hard to find. First of all, it had to do with concurrency and it was utterly unreproducible. Second of all, you had some core assumption that turned out to be false. It's the hallmark of the tyro that they say, "Yeah, well, the language is broken" or, "The system is broken." But in this case, yes, the bedrock on which I was standing—the mutex—was, in fact, broken.

Seibel: So the bug wasn't in your code but in the meantime you had written such thorough unit tests for your code that you had no choice but to look outside your code. Do you think there were tests that the author of the mutex code could have, or should have, written that would have found this bug and saved you a week and a half of debugging?

Bloch: I think a good automated unit test of the mutex facility could have saved me from this particular agony, but keep in mind that this was in the early '90s. It never even occurred to me to blame the engineer involved for not writing good enough unit tests. Even today, writing unit tests for concurrency utilities is an art form.

Seibel: We talked a bit before about stepping through code, but what are the actual tools you use for debugging?

Bloch: I'm going to come out sounding a bit Neanderthal, but the most important tools for me are still my eyes and my brain. I print out all the code involved and read it very carefully.

Debuggers are nice and there are times when I would have used a `print` statement, but instead use a breakpoint. So yes, I use debuggers occasionally, but I don't feel lost without them, either. So long as I can put `print` statements in the code, and can read it thoroughly, I can usually find the bugs.

As I said, I use assertions to make sure that complicated invariants are maintained. If invariants are corrupted, I want to know the instant it happens; I want to know what set of actions caused the corruption to take place.

That reminds me of another very difficult-to-find bug. My memory of this one is a bit hazy; either it happened at Transarc or when I was a grad student at CMU, working on the Camelot distributed transaction system. I wasn't the one who found this one, but it sure made an impression on me.

We had a trace package that allowed code to emit debugging information. Each trace event was tagged with the ID of the thread that emitted it. Occasionally we were getting incorrect thread IDs in the logs, and we had no idea why. We just decided that we could live with the bug for a while. It seemed innocuous enough.

It turned out that the bug wasn't in the trace package at all: it was much more serious. To find the thread ID, the trace package called into the threading package. To get the thread ID, the threading package used a trick that was fairly common at the time: it looked at some high-order bits of the address of a stack variable. In other words, it took a pointer to a stack variable, shifted it to the right by a fixed distance, and that was the thread ID. This trick depends on the fact that each thread has a fixed-size stack whose size is a well-known power of two.

Seems like a reasonable approach, right? Except that people who didn't know any better were creating objects on the stack that were, by the standards of the day, very big. Perhaps arrays of 100 elements, each 4k in size—so you've got 400k slammed onto your thread stack. You jump right over the stack's red zone and into the next thread's stack. Now the thread-ID method misidentifies the thread. Worse, when the thread accesses thread-local variables, it gets the next thread's values, because the thread ID was used as the key to the thread-local variables.

So what we took to be a minor flaw in the tracing system was actually evidence of a really serious bug. When an event was attributed to thread-43 instead of thread-42, it was because thread-42 was now unintentionally impersonating thread-43, with potentially disastrous consequences.

This is an example of why you need safe languages. This is just not something that anyone should ever have to cope with. I was talking to someone recently at a university who asked me what I thought about the fact that his university wanted to teach C and C++ first and then Java, because they thought that programmers should understand the system "all the way down."

I think the premise is right but the conclusion is wrong. Yes, students should learn low-level languages. In fact, they should learn assembly language, and even chip architecture. Though chips have turned into to these unbelievable complicated beasts where even the chips don't have good performance models anymore because of the fact that they are such complicated state machines. But they'll be much better high-level language programmers if they understand what's going on in the lower layers of the system.

So yes, I think it's important that you learn all this stuff. But do I think you should start with a low-level language like C? No! Students should not have to deal with buffer overruns, manual memory allocation, and the like in their first exposure to programming.

James Gosling once said to me, discussing the birth of Java, "Occasionally you get to hit the reset button. That's one of the most marvelous things that can happen." Usually, you have to maintain compatibility with stuff that's decades old; rarely, you don't, and it's great when that happens. But unfortunately, as you can see with Java, it only takes you a decade until you're the problem.

Seibel: Since you say that, is Java off in the weeds a little bit? Is it getting more complex faster than it's getting better?

Bloch: That's a very difficult question. In particular, the Java 5 changes added far more complexity than we ever intended. I had no understanding of just how much complexity generics and, in particular, wildcards were going to add to the language. I have to give credit where credit is due—Graham Hamilton did understand this at the time and I didn't.

The funny thing is, he fought against it for years, trying to keep generics out of the language. But the notion of variance—the idea behind wildcards—came into fashion during the years when generics were successfully being kept out of Java. If they had gone in earlier, without variance, we might have had a simpler, more tractable language today.

That said, there are real benefits to wildcards. There's a fundamental impedance mismatch between subtyping and generics, and wildcards go a long way towards rectifying the mismatch. But at a significant cost in terms of complexity. There are some people who believe that declaration-site, as opposed to use-site, variance is a better solution, but I'm not so sure.

The jury is basically still out on anything that hasn't been tested by a huge quantity of programmers under real-world conditions. Often languages only succeed in some niche and people say, "Oh, they're great and it's such a pity they didn't become the successful language in the world." But often there are reasons they didn't. Hopefully some language that does use declaration-site variance, like Scala or C# 4.0, will answer this question once and for all.

Seibel: So what was the impetus for adding generics?

Bloch: As is always the case for ideas that prove less wonderful than they seemed, it was believing our own press sheets. My mental model was, "Hey, collections are almost all homogeneous—a list of strings, a map from string to integer, or whatever. Yet by default they are heterogeneous: they're all collections of objects and you have to cast on the way out and that's nonsense." Wouldn't it be much better if I could tell the system that this is a map from strings to integers and it would do the casting for me and it would catch it at compile time when I tried to do something wrong? It could catch more errors—it would have higher-level-type information and that sounds like a good thing.

I thought of generics in the same way I thought about many of the other language features we added in Java 5—we were simply getting the language to do for us what we had to do manually before. In some cases I was dead on: the `for`-each loop is just great. All it does is hide the complexity of the iterators or the index variables from you. The code is shorter and the conceptual surface area is no larger. In a sense, it's even smaller because we've created this false polymorphism between arrays and other collections so you can iterate over an ArrayList or an array and not know or care which you're iterating over.

The main reason this thinking didn't apply to generics is that they represent a major addition to an already complex type system. Type systems are delicate, and modifying them can have far-reaching and unpredictable effects throughout the language.

I think the lesson here is, when you are evolving a mature language you have to be even more conscious than ever of the power-versus-complexity trade-off. And the thing is, the complexity is at least quadratic in the number of features in a language. When you add a feature to an old language you're often adding a hell of a lot of complexity. When a language is already at or approaching programmers' ability to understand it, you simply can't add any more complexity to it without breaking it.

And if you do add complexity to it, will the language simply disappear? No, it won't. I think C++ was pushed well beyond its complexity threshold and yet there are a lot of people programming it. But what you do is you force people to subset it. So almost every shop that I know of that uses C++ says, "Yes, we're using C++ but we're not doing multiple-implementation inheritance and we're not using operator overloading." There are just a bunch of features that you're not going to use because the complexity of the resulting code is too high. And I don't think it's good when you have to start doing that. You lose this programmer portability where everyone can read everyone else's code, which I think is such a good thing.

Seibel: Do you feel like Java would be better off today if you had just left generics out?

Bloch: I don't know. I still like generics. Generics find bugs in my code for me. Generics let me take things that used to be in comments and put them into the code where the compiler can enforce them. On the other hand, when I look at those crazy parameterized-type-related error messages, and when I look at generic type declarations like the one I wrote for Enum—

`class Enum<E extends Enum<E>>`—I think it's clear that the generics design wasn't quite mature enough to go in.

We're all optimists in our profession or we'd be forced to shoot ourselves. So we say, "Oh, yeah, of course we can do this. We've known about generics since CLU. This is 25-year-old technology." These days you hear the same argument applied to closures except it's 50-year-old technology. "Oh, it's easy; it doesn't add any complexity to the language at all."

Hell yes, it does. But I think many of us have learned from our experience with generics. You shouldn't add something to a language until you really understand what it's going to do the conceptual surface area—until you can make a convincing argument that working programmers will be able to use the new feature effectively, and that it will make their lives better.

If you look at how the man on the street has been reacting to generics, we certainly should have done something other than what we did. Does that mean we shouldn't have done generics at all? No, I don't think so. I think that generics are actually good. The fundamental argument that most collections are homogeneous, not heterogeneous, so it should be easy to deal with homogeneous collections is true. Furthermore casting is generally a bad thing. Casts can fail and casts don't make your program beautiful. So I think you should be able to say what kind of collection it is and then it should just automatically be enforced for you. But does that mean you have to suffer with all this complexity that we have today? No. I think we just didn't take the right cut at it.

Seibel: Was there real user pressure for generics? Were people complaining that the lack of generics was stopping them from writing software?

Bloch: Were real engineers bitching about the lack of generics? I think the unfortunate answer to that question is, no, they weren't. I think I was guilty of putting in something because it was neat. And because it felt like the right thing to do.

That said, a lot of engineering is from the gut. Had people been telling me to put in `foreach`? No. They hadn't been telling me to do that either. But I just knew that it was the right thing to do. And I was right—everybody likes it.

But I think a big sin in our area, in engineering, is doing stuff just because it's neat, because it's good engineering, whatever. If you're not solving real problems for real users—in this case, Java programmers—then you shouldn't add the feature.

There's this marvelous talk that James Gosling gave called "The Feel of Java," in which he said you need three real uses before you put anything in. You don't put anything in just because it's neat.

But people just want to put stuff in. What do engineers do? They write code. And if they are writing a library or writing a language, they want to put their stuff in. You need some presence, some guiding voice, to give you something that works well together and has made the right set of trade-offs between what you do and don't put in. Because there's simply more stuff that you could put in than you should put in to any given language. Does that mean that any of this stuff is bad? No, it doesn't. It just means that you make your choices and certain things shouldn't be mixed.

Seibel: I was reading *Java Puzzlers* and *Effective Java* and it struck me that there are a lot of little weird corners for a language that started out so simple.

Bloch: There are weird corners, yes, but that's just a fact of life; all languages have them. You haven't seen a book called *C Puzzlers*. Why not?

Seibel: Because it's *all* puzzlers.

Bloch: Yep. It would take up a shelf. In Java, the puzzlers are worth collecting precisely because you think of it as a simple language. Every language has its corner cases and Java has few enough that they're for the most part fun and interesting.

Seibel: Is there anything that you've learned about programming specifically from working on Java and thinking about its design?

Bloch: I've learned an awful lot of things. One thing I've learned—I wrote about this in the "Nearly All Binary Searches and Mergesorts Are Broken" blog entry—is that even writing small programs correctly is incredibly difficult. We're just fooling ourselves if we think our programs are, by and large, free of bugs. They're not. For the most part, we've written programs that are free enough of bugs to approximate the jobs that we want them to do.

I learned that, given how hard it is to write correct programs, we need all the help we can get. So anything that removes potential bugs from our plate is good. That's why I'm very much a believer in static typing and in static analysis—anything that can remove the possibility of a certain class of bugs from our plate is a very good thing. Anything that can make our jobs as programmers easier is a good thing.

My belief in the importance of good API documentation has been reinforced. Javadoc is one of the lesser-appreciated reasons for the success of the platform. Good API documentation has always been a part of Java's culture, and I believe it's because Javadoc has been there from day one.

My natural tendency to believe that simple is good has been reinforced. Over and over I see additions that are more complex proving themselves to be detrimental in the long—or short—run. When I'm designing stuff, I pay close attention to my "complexity meter:" when it starts bumping into the red zone, it's time to redesign stuff.

I've occasionally run into people who just don't believe that, who just say, "Well, you're stupid, Josh, you just don't get it; this is the right way to do it and I'm sorry if you don't understand it." I just don't buy that. I think that if things start getting complicated, there's probably something wrong with them and it's probably time to start looking for an easier way to do it.

There's a brilliant quote by Tony Hoare in his Turing Award speech about how there are two ways to design a system: "One way is to make it so simple that there are *obviously* no deficiencies and the other way is to make it so complicated that there are no *obvious* deficiencies."

The paragraph that follows is equally brilliant, though it isn't as well-known: "The first method is far more difficult. It demands the same skill, devotion, insight, and even inspiration as the discovery of the simple physical laws which underlie the complex phenomena of nature. It also requires a willingness to accept objectives which are limited by physical, logical, and technological constraints, and to accept a compromise when conflicting objectives cannot be met. No committee will ever do this until it is too late."

Seibel: Do you expect that you will change your primary language again in your career or do you think you'll be doing Java until you retire?

Bloch: I don't know. I sort of turned on a dime from C to Java. I programmed in C pretty much exclusively from the time I left grad school until 1996, and then Java exclusively until now. I could certainly see some circumstance under which I would change to another programming language. But I don't know what that language would be. I think it may not exist yet. I think the world is ripe for a new programming language but I also think that the inertia of a platform is so much higher now than it used to be. A modern platform isn't just a language and a few libraries; it's got loads of tools, a virtual machine—it's an enormous thing. The prospect of creating an entire new platform is much more daunting than it ever was before.

I don't know what's coming next. But I'd like to think that if changing my primary language was the correct thing to do, I could still do it. I want to keep my mind open to the possibility. I want to play around more with other languages. I haven't had the time to do that recently, but I want to take the time.

Seibel: What's your short list of ones you want to play with more?

Bloch: I want to try Scala, though I have some doubts as to whether it will be the next big thing. I have great respect for Martin Odersky. I think there a bunch of neat ideas in the language. But I also think it may be too complex and too oriented towards academics to succeed in the world at large. I have no right to say that, though, because I haven't learned it yet.

I should also play with Python. A real old one I want to play with is Scheme. I think that it would be fun to just take a couple of months and work my way through *Structure and Interpretation of Computer Programs* with my son. Everybody says it's such a great book. I bought it—that's the first step. But it'll take a while to do. I guess that's my current short list.

Seibel: These days lots of people are worrying about how we're going to write software that takes good advantage of the coming multicore CPUs.

Java is notable as the first mainstream language to provide built-in mechanisms for multithreading; do you feel like Java's approach is viable in a multicore world?

Bloch: I'm going to go one step further. I think it is the best approach of any language out there. It's funny because it seems very popular to talk about Java being dead now. I see it as histrionics, basically. But I think that right now the best existing multithreaded building blocks are in Java. I think Java is poised for a little resurgence. I'm not saying it is where we'll be headed for the next 20 years; that it is the best way to take care of these multicores. But I think of what's available today, it's head and shoulders above the competition.

Seibel: What do you see as the competition to Java?

Bloch: Well, I'm thinking C++ and C#.

Seibel: What about things like Erlang or Software Transactional Memory?

Bloch: So far as I know, STM doesn't yet exist in a practical form in any mainstream language. If STM proves to be worth its salt, I suspect it will appear in Java at about the same time it appears elsewhere.

Erlang's approach to concurrency is actors, and if they prove to be a big win, they can also be implemented in many languages. As you know, Odersky and company have already implemented them in Scala. I'm not convinced that actors are the best fit for multicore parallelism, but if they are, I suspect that someone will implement them in Java soon enough.

Seibel: So Java provides, as you say, building blocks that let you get portable access to threads provided by the OS and then some higher-level constructs with the `java.util.concurrent` API. But they're still pretty low-level constructs compared to something like Erlang or STM, aren't they?

Bloch: I'm not so sure. Some of Java's building blocks are low-level, like AtomicInteger; some are midlevel, like CyclicBarrier; and some are high-level, like ConcurrentHashMap and ThreadPoolExecutor. I believe that STM and actors could both find comfortable homes in Java's "concurrency building blocks" approach when and if people are convinced that they pull their weight.

Some form of transactional memory may become important in the future, perhaps as a building block for use by concurrency library designers. But I don't think STM will succeed as a tool that lets the application programmer stop worrying about locks and live in a beautiful world where threads don't interfere with one another. It's just not going to happen.

There are a bunch of reasons for this. Here's one I learned when I worked in transaction systems. When you try to do automatic locking or optimistic concurrency control based merely on reading and writing at the byte level, you end up with "false contention" between threads: you have physical conflicts that don't correspond to logical conflicts. If you're forced to think about what locks to acquire, you can do your best to ensure that you don't acquire any locks beyond what is required to enforce logical conflicts.

So, for example, if you have two threads, both of which are incrementing a counter, they should be allowed to proceed concurrently. They may be accessing the same piece of memory but they're not conflicting with each other from a logical perspective. If you have one thread that's reading a counter and one that's incrementing it, they're in conflict. But you can have arbitrarily many readers or arbitrarily many incrementers proceeding concurrently. This is the sort of thing that no system that I've seen to date can figure out of its own accord. The counter example may be artificial, but it's not uncommon that physical contention is far more restrictive than logical contention.

Another problem with STM is that there are all manner of operations that can't occur inside a transaction. I/O is the classic example. A third problem is that some STM schemes allow "doomed transactions" to view memory in inconsistent states, with potentially disastrous results. Again, these are problems that we struggled with back when we were building general-purpose distributed transaction systems. They have solutions, but all the solutions I know of add complexity or reduce performance.

Anyway, to the best of my knowledge, STM is still research. I think it's great that people are doing this research. But I simply don't believe in a silver bullet for concurrency, at least for the foreseeable future.

Seibel: OK, different topic: how do you prefer to work with other programmers?

Bloch: I'm actually quite flexible. I love "buddy programming" where you're working with someone else but not at the same keyboard. You're writing different parts of the system—you trade the code back and forth. You don't even have to be in the same hemisphere. Doug Lea and I have worked that way extensively over the years. One of us will write an interface and the other one will say, "Well this is great but this part sucks and I changed it this way."

Eventually we arrive at some interface that we like and I'll implement the nonconcurrent version and he'll implement the concurrent version and as we do that, we'll find out all the things that we did wrong and take another crack at the interface. And we'll read each other's code and he'll say, "Well, you can make this much faster this way," and I'll say, "You're right, Doug, you can." He's very good at making things go fast—he kind of communes with the VM. So that's one style that I like a lot. And that lends itself to remote collaborations.

I do like sitting at the same terminal with someone and working on code, but I haven't written many programs that way from the ground up. Typically it's in the context of a code review where I'll get some code to review and there'll be a lot of changes and I'll say, "Why don't we just sit together at a machine and bash it into shape?" That's good for a whole bunch of reasons. I think it's a great way to teach, to pass knowledge down from one generation of hacker to the next.

I don't like working in total isolation. When I'm writing a program and I come to a tricky design decision, I just have to bounce it off someone else. At every place I've worked, I've had one or more colleagues I could bounce ideas off of. That's critically important for me; I need that feedback.

Seibel: Is that for the feedback you get or just for the chance to talk it through?

Bloch: Both. There's so much craft in what we do—it's often the case that there's no one right solution, or if there is, it's not apparent until you've used it. You have to go from the gut and talking to someone with a different perspective can be very helpful.

I've known people who don't feel this way—who are willing to program in a vacuum. I think it hurts them. You will discover your bugs earlier—you really want to discover problems with a design long before it hits the point of code. So when you're wrestling with different approaches or even different features—should I support this and this or simply that—you just have to bounce it off other people. On the other hand, you can't take what each person says as gospel because you'll get conflicting opinions, and ultimately, you are responsible for your own work.

Seibel: That raises another age-old question—I think Weinberg wrote about this in *The Psychology of Computer Programming* in the '70s and the XPers talk about it today: should code be "owned" by one person who is the only person who ever touches it or should everyone on a project collectively own all the code so anyone can fiddle with anything?

Bloch: I believe that code ownership can't be denied. In a way, it's like motherhood—you give birth to the code that you write, and especially if it's large, complex, or original, it *is* yours. If you find yourself working in someone else's code, talk to them before mucking with their code. Especially if you think there's something really wrong with it, because you might be wrong. If you break someone else's code, that's not nice.

Of course, it's bad for an organization if a piece of code belongs to exactly one person because if that person leaves the organization, they're high and dry. So it's really important that multiple people learn about each piece of code and are able to work on it. But I think it's unrealistic to expect everyone to own all the code.

This also touches on what we were discussing earlier in terms of areas of expertise. There aren't that many people who can really write bit-twiddling code, so if you find yourself in the bowels of some code that's doing bit twiddling, you should talk to one of the few people at your company who can actually handle that stuff, if you're not one of them. People who do this stuff love it and are willing to spend whole days reducing an instruction sequence by one instruction or proving some identity that speeds up a computation. But it's so easy to break something. And it's so easy to write something that, let's say, works well for 2^{32} minus 1 of the 2^{32} possible inputs. A unit test may or may not test that one value where your new solution doesn't work. And if it doesn't and you broke it, you're the goat.

Seibel: Speaking of writing intricate code, I've noticed that people who are too smart, in a certain dimension anyway, make the worst code. Because they can actually fit the whole thing in their head they can write these great reams of spaghetti code.

Bloch: I agree with you that people who are both smart enough to cope with enormous complexity and lack empathy with the rest of us may fall prey to that. They think, "I can understand this and I can use it, so it has to be good."

Seibel: Is there something intrinsic in programming that's always going to draw people with that kind of mentality?

Bloch: Absolutely. We love brainteasers. But we have to temper this love with the knowledge that we're solving real problems for real people. And if we don't do that we are, essentially, whacking off. I think that part of the failure of the first company that I was involved in was due to the fact that we didn't understand that what we were doing wasn't pure engineering.

We weren't really thinking that the most important thing we could do was solve real problems for real customers. The moment you lose sight of that and who your customers are, you're dead meat. But I do think that it tends to conflict with the sort of people who are attracted to programming, who are the people who love brainteasers. But I think you can have your cake and eat it too. Keep that empathy gene on when you're designing your APIs, but then, in order to make them run bloody fast, you can freely descend into the puzzle palace.

You'll have plenty of opportunity to solve brainteasers when designing and optimizing algorithms and data structures, especially concurrent ones. You have to be able to think with mathematical precision about stuff that is quite complex, and you have to be able to come up with creative ways of combining primitives to achieve the desired effect.

But you have to know where you can and should apply that kind of thinking and where it will just produce a system that is unmaintainable or unusable.

Seibel: Are the opportunities for doing that kind of programming going away? A lot of this low-level stuff is implemented in the VM that you're using or the concurrency libraries that you're using. So for a lot of people, anymore, programming is about gluing stuff together.

Bloch: I totally agree. Well, in relative terms it's diminishing. The percentage of programmers who have to do this is way smaller than it used to be. Back when you bought a machine and it didn't even have an operating system on it, nevermind a programming language or any ready-written applications, yeah, everybody had to do that.

The world in which most programmers have to do this is vanishing or vanished. But in absolute terms there's probably as much need as there ever was for that sort of people. We want to have our cake and eat it too—we want to have the advantages of safe languages coupled with the speed of hand-tuned assembly code, so we need people to write these virtual machines and these garbage collectors and design these chips which are themselves basically works of software, albeit realized in hardware.

I think there's plenty of employment for people who like doing this stuff, but we have to carefully target them. I think if you have people who are pure puzzle solvers you have to couple them with management who can make sure that they are using their skills in the organization's best interests.

There's this problem, which is, programming is so much of an intellectual meritocracy and often these people are the smartest people in the organization; therefore they figure they should be allowed to make all the decisions. But merely the fact that they're the smartest people in the organization doesn't mean they should be making all the decisions, because intelligence is not a scalar quantity; it's a vector quantity. And if you lack empathy or emotional intelligence, then you shouldn't be designing APIs or GUIs or languages.

What we're doing is an aesthetic pursuit. It involves craftsmanship as well as mathematics and it involves people skills and prose skills—all of these things that we don't necessarily think of as engineering but without which I don't think you'll ever be a really good engineer. So I think it's just something that we have to remind ourselves of. But I think it's one of the most fun jobs on the planet. I think we're really lucky to have grown up at the time that we did when these skills led to these jobs. I don't know what we would have been doing a few generations back.

CHAPTER 6

Joe Armstrong

Joe Armstrong is best known as the creator of the programming language Erlang and the Open Telecom Platform (OTP), a framework for building Erlang applications.

In the modern language landscape, Erlang is a bit of an odd duck. It is both older and younger than many popular languages: Armstrong started work on it in 1986—a year before Perl appeared—but it was available only as a commercial product and used primarily within Ericsson until it was released as open source in 1998, three years after Java and Ruby appeared. Its roots are in the logic programming language Prolog rather than some member of the Algol family. And it was designed for a fairly specific kind of software: highly available, highly reliable systems like telephone switches.

But the characteristics that made it good for building telephone switches also—and almost inadvertently—made it quite well suited to writing concurrent software, something which has drawn notice as programmers have started wrestling with the consequences of the multicore future.

Armstrong, too, is a bit of an odd duck. Originally a physicist, he switched to computer science when he ran out of money in the middle of his physics PhD and landed a job as a researcher working for Donald Michie—one of the founders of the field of artificial intelligence in Britain. At Michie's lab, Armstrong was exposed to the full range of AI goodies, becoming a founding member of the British Robotics Association and writing papers about robotic vision.

When funding for AI dried up as a result of the famous Lighthill, it was back to physics-related programming for more than half a decade, first at the EISCAT scientific association and later the Swedish Space Corporation, before finally joining the Ericsson Computer Science Lab, where he invented Erlang.

In our several days of conversation over his kitchen table in Stockholm, we talked about, among other things, the Erlang approach to concurrency, the need for better and simpler ways of connecting programs, and the importance of opening up black boxes.

Seibel: How did you learn to program? When did it all start?

Armstrong: When I was at school. I was born in 1950 so there weren't many computers around then. The final year of school, I suppose I must have been 17, the local council had a mainframe computer—probably an IBM. We could write Fortran on it. It was the usual thing—you wrote your programs on coding sheets and you sent them off. A week later the coding sheets and the punch cards came back and you had to approve them. But the people who made the punch cards would make mistakes. So it might go backwards and forwards one or two times. And then it would finally go to the computer center.

Then it went to the computer center and came back and the Fortran compiler had stopped at the first syntactic error in the program. It didn't even process the remainder of the program. It was something like three months to run your first program. I learned then, instead of sending one program you had to develop every single subroutine in parallel and send the lot. I think I wrote a little program to display a chess board—it would plot a chess board on the printer. But I had to write all the subroutines as parallel tasks because the turnaround time was so appallingly bad.

Seibel: So you would write a subroutine with, basically, a unit test so you would see that it had, in fact, run?

Armstrong: Yes. And then you'd put it all together. I don't know if that counts as learning programming. When I went to university I was in the physics department at University College of London. I think we probably had programming from the first year. Then you had this turnaround of three hours or something. But again it was best to run about four or five programs at the same time so you got them back fairly quickly.

Seibel: In high school, was it an actual school course?

Armstrong: It was an after-hours course—computer club or something. We went to see the computer, I remember. Lots of serious-looking older men wearing white coats with pens stuck in their pockets wandering around, like, a church. It was a very expensive computer.

Seibel: You were studying physics; when did you shift to programming?

Armstrong: Well, as an undergraduate some of the courses involved writing programs and I really enjoyed that. And I got to be very good at debugging. If all else failed, I would debug people's programs. The standard debugging was one beer. Then it would go up—a two-beer problem or a three-beer problem or something like that.

Seibel: That was in terms of how many beers they had to buy you when you debugged their program?

Armstrong: Yeah, when I fixed their program. I used to read programs and think, "Why are they writing it this way; this is very complicated," and I'd just rewrite them to simplify them. It used to strike me as strange that people wrote complicated programs. I could see how to do things in a few lines and they'd written tens of lines and I'd sort of wonder why they didn't see the simple way. I got quite good at that.

When I really got to programming was after I finished my first degree and I decided I wanted to do a PhD. So I started to do a PhD in high-energy physics and joined the bubble chamber group there and they had a computer. A DDP-516, a Honeywell DDP-516. And I could use it all by myself. It was punched cards, but I could run the programs there—I could put them into the thing and press a button and *whoomp*, out came the answer immediately. I had great fun with that. I wrote a little chess program for it.

This was when real core memory was knitted by little old ladies and you could see the cores—you could see these little magnets and the wires went in and out. Frightfully expensive—it had something like a10MB disk drive that had 20 platters and weighed 15 kilos or something. It had a teletext interface—you could type your programs in on that.

And then came this "glass TTY" which was one of the first visual display units and you could type your programs in and edit them. I thought this was fantastic. No more punched cards. I remember talking to the computer manager and saying, "You know, one day everybody will have these." And he said, "You're mad, Joe. Completely mad!" "Why not?" "Well, they're far too expensive."

That was really when I learned to program. And my supervisor at the time, he said, "You shouldn't be doing a PhD in physics. You should stop and do computers because you love computers." And I said, "No, no, no. I've to finish this stuff that I was doing." But he was right, actually.

Seibel: Did you finish your PhD?

Armstrong: No, I didn't because I ran out of money. Then I went to Edinburgh. When I was reading physics we used to go and study in the physics library. And in the corner of the physics library there was this section of computer science books. And there were these brown-backed volumes called *Machine Intelligence,* Volumes 1, 2, 3, and 4, which came from Edinburgh, from the Department of Machine Intelligence there. I was supposed to be studying physics but I was eagerly reading these things and thought, "Oh, that's jolly good fun." So I wrote to Donald Michie, who was the director of the Department of Machine Intelligence at Edinburgh, and said I was very interested in this kind of stuff and did he have any jobs. And I got back a letter that said, well, they didn't at the moment but he would like to meet me anyway, see what sort of person I was.

Months later I got a phone call, or letter, from Michie, saying, "I'll be in London next Tuesday; can we meet? I'm getting the train to Edinburgh; can you come to the station?" I went to the station, met Michie, and he said,

"Hmmm! Well, we can't have an interview here—well, we'll find a pub." So we went to a pub and I chatted to Michie and then a bit later I got another letter from him, he says, "There's a research job at Edinburgh, why don't you apply for it." So I became Donald Michie's research assistant and went to Edinburgh. That was my transition between physics and computer science.

Michie had worked with Turing at Bletchley Park during the second World War and got all of Turing's papers. I had a desk in Turing's library, so all around me were Turing's papers. So I was a year at Edinburgh. After that Edinburgh kind of collapsed because James Lighthill, a mathematician, was hired by the government to go and investigate artificial intelligence at Edinburgh. And he came back and said, "Nothing of commercial value will ever come out of this place."

It was like one gigantic playpen kind of place. I was a founding member of the British Robotics Association and we all thought this was really going to have enormous relevance. But the funding agencies—Robotics! What's this stuff? We're not going to fund this! And so there was a period around '72, I guess, when all the funding dried up and everybody said, "Well, we had fun while we were here; better go and do something else."

Then it's back to being a physicist. I came to Sweden and I got a job as a physicist programmer for the EISCAT scientific association. My boss had come from IBM and he was older than me and he wanted a specification and he would go and implement it. We used to argue over this. He said, "What's bad about the job is we don't have a job description and we don't have a detailed specification." And I said, "Well, a job with no job description is a really good job. Because then you can form it how you like." Anyway, he left after about a year and I got the boss's job, the chief designer.

I designed a system for them and that was what I suppose you'd call an application operating system—it's something that runs on top of the regular operating system. By now computers were becoming quite reasonable. We had NORD-10 computers which were Norwegian—I think they were an attempt to get into the PDP-11 market.

I worked there for almost four years. Then I got a job for the Swedish Space Corporation and built yet another application operating system to control Sweden's first satellite, which was called *Viking*. That was a fun project—I've forgotten the name of the computer but it was a clone of the Amdahl computer. It still only had line editors. It didn't have full-screen editors. And all your programs had to be in one directory. Ten letters for the file name and three letters for the extension. And a Fortran compiler or assembler and that's it.

The funny thing is, thinking back, I don't think all these modern gizmos actually make you any more productive. Hierarchical file systems—how do they make you more productive? Most of software development goes on in your head anyway. I think having worked with that simpler system imposes a kind of disciplined way of thinking. If you haven't got a directory system and you have to put all the files in one directory, you have to be fairly disciplined. If you haven't got a revision control system, you have to be fairly disciplined. Given that you apply that discipline to what you're doing it doesn't seem to me to be any better to have hierarchical file systems and revision control. They don't solve the fundamental problem of solving your problem. They probably make it easier for groups of people to work together. For individuals I don't see any difference.

Also, I think today we're kind of overburdened by choice. I mean, I just had Fortran. I don't think we even had shell scripts. We just had batch files so you could run things, a compiler, and Fortran. And assembler possibly, if you really needed it. So there wasn't this agony of choice. Being a young programmer today must be awful—you can choose 20 different programming languages, dozens of framework and operating systemsand you're paralyzed by choice. There was no paralysis of choice then. You just start doing it because the decision as to which language and things is just made—there's no thinking about what you should do, you just go and do it.

Seibel: Another difference these days is that you can no longer understand the whole system from top to bottom. So not only do you have lots of choices to make, they're all about which black boxes you want to use without necessarily fully understanding how they work.

Armstrong: Yeah—if these big black boxes don't work properly, and you have to modify them, I reckon it's easier just to start from scratch and just write everything yourself. The thing that really hasn't worked is software reuse. It's appallingly bad.

Seibel: Yet you're the architect not only of Erlang but of an application framework, the Open Telecom Platform. Is it reusable?

Armstrong: To an extent it's reusable. But the same problem will occur. If that framework exactly solves your problem—if some programmer who doesn't know anything about the design criteria for OTP looks at it in a few years' time and says, "Oh, that's great; that's exactly what I want to do," then it's fine and you get this measure of reusability. If it's *not*, then you have a problem.

Fairly recently I've seen people say, "This is really kind of artificial, we're twisting the code to fit into this OTP framework." So I say, "Well, rewrite the OTP framework." They don't feel they can change the framework. But the framework's just another program. It's really rather easy. And I go into it and then it does what they want. They look at it and they say, "Yeah, well, that's easy." They accept that it's easy. But they say, "Well, our project management doesn't want us messing around with the framework." Well, give it a different name then or something.

Seibel: But do you think it's really feasible to really open up all those black boxes, look inside, see how they work, and decide how to tweak them to one's own needs?

Armstrong: Over the years I've kind of made a generic mistake and the generic mistake is to not open the black box. To mentally think, this black box is so impenetrable and so difficult that I won't open it. I've opened up one or two black boxes: I wanted to do a windowing system, a graphics system for Erlang, and I thought, "Well, let's run this on X Windows." What is X Windows? It's a socket with a protocol on top of it. So you just open the socket and squirt these messages down it. Why do you need libraries? Erlang is message based. The whole idea is you send messages to things and they do things. Well, that's the idea in X Windows—you've got a window, send it a message, it does something. If you do something in the window it sends you a message back. So that's very much like Erlang. The way of *programming* X Windows, however, is through callback libraries—this happens and call this. That's not the Erlang way of thinking. The Erlang way of thinking is, send a message to something and do something. So, hang on, let's get rid of all these libraries in between—let's talk directly to the socket.

And guess what? It's really easy. The X protocol's got, I don't know, 100 messages, 80 messages or something. Turns out you only need about 20 of them to do anything useful. And these 20 messages you just map onto Erlang terms and do a little bit of magic and then you can start sending messages to windows directly and they do things. And it's efficient as well. It's not very pretty because I haven't put much effort into graphics and artistic criteria—there's a lot of work there to make it look beautiful. But it's not actually difficult.

Another one is this typesetting system I did where the abstraction boundary I opened up is Postscript. As you get to that boundary you think, "I don't want to go through the boundary," because what's underneath is—you imagine—enormously complicated. But again, it turns out to be very easy. It's a programming language. It's a good programming language. The abstraction boundary is easy to go through and once you've gone through, there's a lot of benefit.

For my Erlang book, my publisher said, "We've got tools to make diagrams." But the thing I don't like about diagramming tools is it's really difficult to get an arrow to meet exactly. And your hand hurts. I thought, "The amount of time to write a program that spits out Postscript and then say, 'I want a circle there and the arrow goes exactly there,' and get the program right, isn't long." It takes a few hours. Doing diagrams with programs takes about the same time as doing them in a WYSIWYG thing. Only there are two benefits. Your hand doesn't hurt at the end and even when you blow the thing up to a magnification of 10,000, the arrow points exactly right.

I can't say beginner programmers should open up all these abstractions. But what I am saying is you should certainly consider the possibility of opening them. Not completely reject the idea. It's worthwhile seeing if the direct route is quicker than the packaged route. In general I think if you buy software, or if you use other people's software, you have to reckon with an extremely long time to tailor it—it doesn't do exactly what you want, it does something subtly different. And that difference can take a very long time to solve.

Seibel: So you started out saying software reuse is "appallingly bad," but opening up every black box and fiddling with it all hardly seems like movement toward reusing software.

Armstrong: I think the lack of reusability comes in object-oriented languages, not in functional languages. Because the problem with object-oriented languages is they've got all this implicit environment that they carry around with them. You wanted a banana but what you got was a gorilla holding the banana and the entire jungle.

If you have referentially transparent code, if you have pure functions—all the data comes in its input arguments and everything goes out and leaves no state behind—it's incredibly reusable. You can just reuse it here, there, and everywhere. When you want to use it in a different project, you just cut and paste this code into your new project.

Programmers have been conned into using all these different programming languages and they've been conned into not using easy ways to connect programs together. The Unix pipe mechanism—A pipe B pipe C—is trivially easy to connect things together. Is that how programmers connect things together? No. They use APIs and they link them into the same memory space, which is appallingly difficult and isn't cross-language. If the language is in the same family it's OK—if they're imperative languages, that's fine. But suppose one is Prolog and the other is C. They have a completely different view of the world, how you handle memory. So you can't just link them together like that. You can't reuse things. There must be big commercial interests for whom it is very desirable that stuff won't work together. It creates thousands of jobs for consultants. And thousands of tools to solve problems that shouldn't exist. Problems that were solved years ago.

I think it's really weird that we have very few programming languages that describe the interaction between things. I keep coming back to ways of gluing things together and ways of describing protocols. We don't have ways of describing this protocol in between things: if I send you one of them then you send me one of these. We have ways of describing packets and their types but we have very restricted ways of describing the protocols.

Programming is fundamentally different to the way we construct things in the real world. Imagine you're a car manufacturer. You buy components from subcontractors. You buy a battery from Lucas and you buy a generator from somewhere. And you bolt things together—you construct things by placing things next to each other. You build a house by putting the bricks on top of each other and putting the door *there*. That's how we make chips. You get a printed circuit board that basically just provides this connection. But you can think of making electronic things as you buy all these chips and you connect the legs of some to others with wires. And that's how you make hardware. But we don't make software like that. We should make software like that and we don't.

The reason we don't, has to do with concurrency. You see, the chips, when you put them next to each other, they all execute in parallel. And they send messages. They are based on this message-passing paradigm of programming, which is what I believe in. And that's not how we write software together. So I think one direction Erlang might take, or I would like it to take, is this component direction. I haven't done it yet, but I'd like to make some graphic front ends that make components and I'd like to make software by just connecting them together. Dataflow programming is very declarative. There's no notion of sequential state. There's no program counter flipping through this thing. It just is. It's a declarative model and it's very easy to understand. And I miss that in most programming languages.

That's not to say that what's inside an individual black box isn't very complicated. Take grep, for example. Seen from the outside—imagine a little square. The input is a stream of data, a file. You say `cat foo | grep` and grep has got some arguments, it's got a regular expression it's got to match. OK. And out of grep come all the lines that match that regular expression. Now, at a perceptual level, understanding what grep does is extremely simple. It has an input which is a file. It has an input which is a regular expression. It has an output which is a set of lines or a stream of lines that match the regular expression. But that is not to say that the algorithm inside the black box is simple—it could be exceedingly complicated.

What's going on inside the black boxes can be exceedingly complicated. But gluing things together from these complicated components does not itself have to be complicated. The use of grep is not complicated in the slightest. And what I don't see in system architectures is this clear distinction between the gluing things together and the complexity of the things inside the boxes.

When we connect things together through programming language APIs we're not getting this black box abstraction. We're putting them in the same memory space. If grep is a module that exposes routines in its API and you give it a `char*` pointer to this and you've got to malloc that and did you deep copy this string—can I create a parallel process that's doing this? Then it becomes appallingly complicated to understand. I don't understand why people connect things together in such complicated ways. They should connect things together in simple ways.

Seibel: Comparing how you think about programming now with how you thought when you were starting out, what's the biggest change in your thinking?

Armstrong: The big changes in how I think about programming have nothing to do with the hardware. Obviously it's a lot faster and lot more powerful but your brain is a million times more powerful than the best software tools. I can write programs and then suddenly, days later, say, "There's a mistake in that program—if this happens and that happens and that happens and this happens, then it will crash." And then I go and look in the code—yup, I was right. There has never been a symptom. Now you tell me a development system that can do that kind of stuff. So the changes that have happened as a programmer, they're mental changes within me.

There are two changes and I think they're to do with the number of years you program. One is, when I was younger quite often I would write a program and work at it until it's finished. When it was finished I would stop working on it. It was done, finished. Then I'd get an insight—"Ah! Wrong! Idiot!" I'd rewrite it. Again: "Yeah, it's wrong"—rewrite it.

I remember thinking to myself, "Wouldn't it be nice if I could think all of this stuff instead of writing it?" Wouldn't it be nice if I could get this insight without writing it. I think I can do that now. So I would characterize that period, which took 20 years, as learning how to program. Now I know how to program. I was doing experiments to learn how to program. I think I know how to program now and therefore I don't have to do the experiments anymore.

Occasionally I have to do very small experiments—write extremely small programs just to answer some question. And then I think through things and they more or less work as I expect when I program them because I've thought through them. That also means it takes a long time. A program that you write, you get the insight, you rewrite—it might take you a year to write. So I might think about it for a year instead. I'm just not doing all this typing.

That's the first thing. The second thing that's happened is intuition. When I was younger, I would do the all-night hacks, programming to four in the morning and you get really tired and it's macho programming—you hack the code in hour after hour. And it's not going well and you persevere and you get it working. And I would program when the intuition wasn't there.

And what I've learned is, programming when you're tired, you write crap and you throw it all away the next day. And 20 years ago I would program although I was getting a strong feeling that this isn't right—there's something wrong with this code. I have noticed over the years, the really good code I would write was when I'm in complete flow—just totally unaware of time: not even really thinking about the program, just sitting there in a relaxed state just typing this stuff and watching it come out on the screen as I type it in. That code's going to be OK. The stuff where you can't concentrate and something's saying, "No, no, no, this is wrong, wrong, wrong"—I was ignoring that years ago. And I'd throw it all away. Now I can't program anymore if it says, "No." I just know from experience, stop—don't write code. Stop with the problem. Do something else.

Because I was good at math and that sort of stuff at school, I thought, "Oh, I'm a logical person." But I took these psychology tests and got way high scores on intuition. And quite low scores on logical thinking. Not low—I can do math and stuff; I'm quite good at them. But because I was good at math I thought science was about logic and math. But I wouldn't say that now. I'd say it's an awful lot of intuition, just knowing what's right.

Seibel: So now that you spend more time thinking before you code, what are you actually doing in that stage?

Armstrong: Oh, I'm writing notes—I'm not *just* thinking. Doodling on paper. I'm probably not committing much to code. If you were to monitor my activity it'd be mostly thinking, a bit of doodling. And another thing, very important for problem solving, is asking my colleagues, "How would you solve this?" It happens so many times that you go to them and you say, "I've been wondering about whether I should do it this way or that way. I've got to choose between A and B," and you describe A and B to them and then halfway through that you go, "Yeah, B. Thank you, thank you very much."

You need this intelligent white board—if you just did it yourself on a white board there's no feedback. But a human being, you're explaining to them on the white board the alternative solutions and they join in the conversation and suggest the odd thing. And then suddenly you see the answer. To me that doesn't extend to writing code. But the dialog with your colleagues who are in the same problem space is very valuable.

Seibel: Do you think it's those little bits of feedback or questions? Or is it just the fact of explaining it?

Armstrong: I think it is because you are forcing it to move it from the part of your brain that has solved it to the part of your brain that has verbalized it and they are different parts of the brain. I think it's because you're forcing that to happen. I've never done the experiment of just speaking out loud to an empty room.

Seibel: I heard about a computer science department where in the tutor's office they had a stuffed animal and the rule was you had to explain your problem to the stuffed animal before you could bother the tutor. "OK, Mr. Bear, here's the thing I'm working on and here's my approach—aha! There it is."

Armstrong: Really? I must try that.

Seibel: Talk to your cats.

Armstrong: The cats—absolutely! I worked with this guy who was slightly older than me and very clever. And every time I'd go into his office and ask him a question, every single question, he would say, "A program is a black box. It has inputs and it has outputs. And there is a functional relationship between the inputs and the outputs. What are the inputs to your problem? What are the outputs to your problem? What is the functional relationship between the two?" And then somewhere in this dialog, you would say, "You're a genius!" And you'd run out of the room and he would shake his head in amazement—"I wonder what the problem was, he never said." So he's your bear which you explain the problem to.

Seibel: The doodling—is that writing little snippets of code or is it literally graphical doodles?

Armstrong: It's more bubbles with arrows. You know when you explain things to people on a white board—you draw bubbles and arrows and equations and notations. Not code. Code fragments—piddly bits of code sometimes because that's a compact way to express something. This is in the thinking period. Very occasional code experiments because I don't know how long it takes to do something. So I'll write ten lines of code and time something.

Seibel: You mean how long it takes for the computer to do it?

Armstrong: Yeah. Does that take a millisecond or a microsecond—I don't know. I can guess but I want to confirm that guess. And so I'm only looking at the bits I don't really know. But I have a great stock of experience programming Erlang so I know pretty much what things are going to do. Problem solving was the same years ago. It was, identify the difficult bits, write the small prototypes, identify the areas of uncertainty, writing very small bits of code. Essentially I do the same thing now but I have less reason to do these small experiments. If it's Erlang. If I'm doing Ruby or Java then I have to go back and do a lot of experiments because I don't know what's going to happen.

Seibel: Then somewhere in this thinking process you get to the point where you know how to write the code?

Armstrong: Yeah, then all the bits fit together. But maybe I can't explain it to anybody. I just get a very strong feeling that if I start writing the program now it'll work. I don't really know what the solution is. It's like an egg. The chicken's ready to lay the egg. Now I'm ready to lay the egg.

Seibel: And that's the point at which you need to go into flow and not be interrupted.

Armstrong: Yes, yes.

Seibel: So there are still presumably a lot of details to be sorted out at the code level which requires your concentration.

Armstrong: Oh yes. But then there are two types of those things. The stuff that really needs the concentration is the stuff that is not automatic—you've got to think about it. You've got this really tricky garbage collection—exactly what needs to be marked and exactly where—you've got to think hard about that. You know you'll find a solution because you've kind of bounded it in. And you know it's in the right little black box.

Michelangelo is doing the roof of the Sistine Chapel or something and he's got a whole team of painters helping him. So he would sketch the big picture first. These huge areas have got to be done in blue and green. So that's rather like writing a program. The first sketch is this broad sketch where everything's in the right place. Some of these places are going to be filled with uniform color and just can be filled in fairly rapidly—you don't have to think.

And then you get to the details of the eyes—that's tricky stuff. You know you can do it. And the eye is in the right place because the picture is OK. So you go and do the eye and the detail. That's not to say that's easy—that's the difficult bit, actually. You've got to really concentrate while you're doing the eye. You don't have to really concentrate while you're doing the forehead or the cheeks because they're fairly uniform. A bit of stubble here so you pay a sort of half concentration.

Then type it all in and get the syntax errors out and run a few little tests to make sure it works. And that's all rather relaxing. See a little compiler error there and you fix it. Once you're experienced at a language you don't even bother to read the diagnostic. It just says the line number—you don't read what it says. That line—oh, yeah. That's wrong, you retype it.

I gave a course in Erlang in Chicago. I was wandering around the class and I'd notice, there's something wrong. Oh, there's a comma missing there or that'll crash before that happens and you're not linked. My wife's very good at proofreading and she says errors spring out of the page at you. A missing comma or a spelling mistake—they literally spring out of the page at her.

And programming errors just spring out of the page if I look at other people's code, wandering around. It doesn't feel like conscious thought is involved—it's holistic. You see everything on the screen and there's the error, bumpf. So it's just a matter of correcting those surface errors.

One that's tricky is slight spelling errors in variable names. So I choose variable names that are very dissimilar, deliberately, so that error won't occur. If you've got a long variable like `personName` and you've got `personNames` with an "s" on the end, that's a list of person names, that will be something that my eye will tend to read what I thought it should have been. And so I'd have `personName` and then `listOfPeople`. And I do that deliberately because I know that my eye will see what I thought I'd written. But punctuation, I do see that—I do see the commas and the brackets as being wrong. And of course Emacs colors everything and auto-indents and the brackets are different colors. So this is really easy.

Seibel: At the point that you start typing code, do you code top-down or bottom-up or middle-out?

Armstrong: Bottom up. I write a little bit and test it, write a little bit and test it. I've gone over to this writing test cases first, now. Unit testing. Just write the test cases and then write the code. I feel fairly confident that it works.

Seibel: Back to a bit of your history, it was after the Swedish Space Corporation that you went to Ericsson's research lab?

Armstrong: Yes. And it was a very, very fortunate time to come, it must have been '84. I think I had come to the lab something like two years after it had started. So we were very optimistic. Our view of the world was, yes we'll solve problems and then we'll push them into projects and we will improve Ericsson's productivity. This view of the world wasn't yet tinged by any contact with reality. So we thought it would be easy to discover new and useful stuff and we thought that once we had discovered new and useful stuff then the world would welcome us with open arms. What we learned later was, it wasn't all that easy to discover new stuff. And it's *incredibly* difficult to get people to use new and better stuff.

Seibel: And Erlang was one of those new and useful things you expected them to use?

Armstrong: Yes. Absolutely. So what happened was, first of all it was just Prolog. I sort of made a little language and people started using it. And then Robert Virding came along and said, "Hey, this looks like fun." And he'd been reading my Prolog and he said, "Can I modify it a bit?" That's pretty dangerous because Robert says that and you end up with one comment at the top of the program that says, "Joe thought of this stuff and I've changed a bit," and then it's completely changed. So Robert and I just rewrote this stuff back and forth and we had great arguments—"Ahhh, I can't read your code, it's got blanks after all the commas."

Then we found somebody inside Ericsson who wanted a new programming language or wanted a better way of programming telephony. We met up with them once a week for about, I can't remember, six months, nine months. And the general idea was we would teach them how to program and they would teach us about telephony—what the problem was. I remember it was both frustrating and very stimulating. That changed the language because we had real people using it and that resulted in a study where they thought, "Yeah, this would be OK but it's far too slow"—they measure the performance of it and said, "It's gotta be 70 times faster." So then we said, "This phase is now over. We'll make it go 70 times faster and they'll carry on programming it and we have to do this in two years or something."

We had several false starts. And we had several really embarrassing moments. Big mistake: don't tell people how fast something is going to be *before* you've implemented it. But ultimately we figured out how to do it. I wrote a compiler in Prolog. And Rob was doing the libraries and things. We're now kind of two years in. Then I thought I could implement this abstract machine in C so I started writing my first-ever C. And Mike Williams came along and looked at my C and said, "This is the worst C I've ever seen in my entire life. This is appallingly bad." I didn't think it was *that* bad but Mike didn't like it. So then Mike did the virtual machine in C and I did the compiler in Prolog. Then the compiler compiled itself and produced byte-code and you put it in the machine and then we changed the grammar and the syntax and compiled the compiler in itself and came out with an image that would bootstrap and then we're flying. We've lost our Prolog roots and we're now a language.

Seibel: Has there ever been anything that you've found difficult to work into the Erlang model?

Armstrong: Yeah. We abstract away from memory, completely. If you were turning a JPEG image into a bitmap data, which depends on the placement of the data in a very exact sense, that doesn't work very well. Algorithms that depend on destructively upgrading state—they don't work well.

Seibel: So if you were writing a big image processing work-flow system, then would you write the actual image transformations in some other language?

Armstrong: I'd write them in C or assembler or something. Or I might actually write them in a dialect of Erlang and then cross-compile the Erlang to C. Make a dialect—this kind of domain-specific language kind of idea. Or I might write Erlang programs which generate C programs rather than writing the C programs by hand. But the target language would be C or assembler or something. Whether I wrote them by hand or generated them would be the interesting question. I'm tending toward automatically generating C rather than writing it by hand because it's just easier.

But I'd use an Erlang structure. I've got some stuff that does my family images and things. So I use ImageMagik with some shell scripts. But I control it all from Erlang. So I just write wrappers around it and call `os:command` and then the ImageMagik command. So it's quite nice to wrap up things in. Wouldn't want to do the actual image processing in Erlang. It'd be foolish to write that in Erlang. C's just going to be a lot better.

Seibel: Plus, ImageMagik is already written.

Armstrong: That doesn't worry me in the slightest. I think if I was doing it in OCaml then I would go down and do it because OCaml can do that kind of efficiency. But Erlang can't. So if I was an OCaml programmer: "OK, what do I have to do? Reimplement ImageMagik? Right, off we go."

Seibel: Just because it's fun?

Armstrong: I like programming. Why not? You know, I've always been saying that Erlang is bad for image processing—I've never actually tried. I feel it would be bad but that might be false. I should try. Hmmm, interesting. You shouldn't tempt me.

The really good programmers spend a lot of time programming. I haven't seen very good programmers who don't spend a lot of time programming. If I don't program for two or three days, I need to do it. And you get better at it—you get quicker at it. The side effect of writing all this other stuff is that when you get to doing ordinary problems, you can do them very quickly.

Seibel: Is there anything that you have done specifically to improve your skill as a programmer?

Armstrong: No, I don't think so. I learned new programming languages but not with the goal of becoming a better programmer. With the goal of being a better language designer, maybe.

I like to figure out how things work. And a good test of that is to implement it yourself. To me programming isn't about typing code into a machine. Programming is about understanding. I like understanding things. So why would I implement a JPEG thing like we talked about earlier? It's because I'd like to understand wavelet transforms. So the programming is a vehicle to understand wavelet transformations. Or why do I try to do an interface to X Windows? Because I wanted to understand how the X protocol worked.

It's a motivating force to implement something; I really recommend it. If you want to understand C, write a C compiler. If you want to understand Lisp, write a Lisp compiler or a Lisp interpreter. I've had people say, "Oh, wow, it's really difficult writing a compiler." It's not. It's quite easy. There are a lot of little things you have to learn about, none of which is difficult. You have to know about data structures. You need to know about hash tables, you need to know about parsing. You need to know about code generation. You need to know about interpretation techniques. Each one of these is not particularly difficult. I think if you're a beginner you think it's big and complicated so you don't do it. Things you don't do are difficult and things you've done are easy. So you don't even try. And I think that's a mistake.

Seibel: Several of the folks I've talked to have recommended learning different programming languages because it gives you different perspectives on how to solve problems.

Armstrong: Languages that do different things. There's no point learning lots of languages that all do the same thing. Certainly I've written quite a lot of JavaScript and quite a lot of Tcl and quite a lot of C and quite a lot of Prolog—well, an enormous amount of Prolog and an enormous amount of Fortran and an enormous amount of Erlang. And a bit of Ruby. A bit of Haskell. I sort of read all languages and I'm not fluent at programming them all. Certainly I can program in quite a lot of languages.

Seibel: No C++?

Armstrong: No, C++, I can hardly read or write it. I don't like C++; it doesn't feel right. It's just complicated. I like small simple languages. It didn't feel small and simple.

Seibel: What languages influenced the design of Erlang?

Armstrong: Prolog. Well, it grew out of Prolog, obviously.

Seibel: There's not a lot of Prolog discernible in it today.

Armstrong: Well, unification—pattern matching, that comes directly from Prolog. And the kind of data structures. Tuples and lists have slightly different syntax in Prolog but they're there. Then there was Tony Hoare's CSP, Communicating Sequential Processes. Also I'd read about Dijkstra's guarded commands—that's why I require that some pattern should always match, there shouldn't be a default case—you should explicitly require that some branch always match. I think those are the main influences.

Seibel: And where did you get the functional aspect?

Armstrong: Once you've added concurrency to Prolog you really just had to make sure it didn't backtrack after you'd done something. In Prolog you could call something and then backtrack over the solution to basically undo the effect of calling it. So you had to realize if this statement says, "Fire the missiles," and *whoom*, off they go, you can't backtrack over it and reverse that. Pure Prolog programs are reversible. But when you're interacting with the real world, all the things you do are one way. Having said, fire the missiles, the missiles fire. Having said, "Change the traffic lights from red to green," they change from red to green and you can't say, "Oh, that was a bad decision; undo it."

Now we've got a concurrent language and parallel processes and inside these processes we're doing full Prolog with backtracking and all that kind of stuff. So the Prolog became very deterministic with cuts everywhere to stop it from backtracking.

Seibel: Where the irreversible things would be sending messages to other processes?

Armstrong: Yes. But it's just a function call and maybe not of the function that fires the rockets but one that calls something else that calls something else that calls it so it's just a pain kind of trying to keep these two worlds separate. So the code you wrote inside a process became more and more functional, sort of a dialect of Prolog which was a functional subset. And so if it's a functional subset, might as well make it completely functional.

Seibel: Yet Erlang is pretty different from most functional languages these days in being dynamically typed. Do you feel like part of the functional language community?

Armstrong: Oh yes. When we go to functional programming conferences, I suppose we argue about our differences. We argue about eager evaluation and lazy evaluation. We argue about dynamic type systems and static type systems. But despite everything the central core of functional programming is the idea of nonmutable state—that *x* isn't the name of a location in memory; it's a value. So it can't change. We say *x* equals three and you can't change it thereafter. All these different communities say that has enormous benefits for understanding your program and for parallelizing your program and for debugging your program. Then there are functional languages with dynamic type systems like Erlang and functional languages with static type systems and they've both got their good and bad points.

It'd be really nice to have the benefits of a static type system in Erlang. Maybe in certain places we could annotate programs to make the types more explicit so the compiler can derive the types and generate much better code.

Then the static type people say, "Well, we really rather like the benefits of dynamic types when we're marshaling data structures." We can't send an arbitrary program down a wire and reconstruct it at the other end because we need to know the type. And we have—Cardelli called it a system that's permanently inconsistent. We have systems that are growing and changing all the time, where the parts may be temporarily inconsistent. And as I change the code in a system, it's not atomic. Some of the nodes change, others don't. They talk to each other—at certain times they're consistent. At other times—when we go over a communication boundary—do we trust that the boundary is correct? They might fib. So we need to check certain stuff.

Seibel: So early on you earned your beer by debugging other people's programs. Why do you think you were such a good debugger?

Armstrong: Well, I enjoyed debugging. At this point in the program you print out a few variables and things to see what's going on and they're all according to what you expect. And at this point in the program it's right. And somewhere later it's wrong. So you look halfway in between—it's either right or wrong and you just do this interval halving. Provided you can reproduce an error. Errors that are nonreproducible, that's pretty difficult to debug. But they weren't giving me that. They were giving me reproducible errors. So just carry on halving until you find it. You must ultimately find it.

Seibel: So do you think you just had a more systematic view?

Armstrong: Yeah, they gave up. I don't know why—I couldn't really understand why they couldn't debug programs. I mean, do you think debugging is difficult? I don't. You just stop it and slow it down. I mean, I'm just talking about batch Fortran.

OK, debugging real-time systems or garbage collectors—I remember once Erlang crashed—it was early days—and it crashed just after I'd started it. I was just typing something. It had built in sort of Emacsy commands into the shell. And I typed `erl` to start it and you get into a read-eval-print loop. And

I'd typed about four or five characters and made a spelling mistake. And then I backed the cursor a couple of times and corrected it and it crashed with a garbage collection error. And I knew that's a deep, deep, error. And I thought, "Can I remember exactly what did I type in?" Because it was only about 12 characters or something. I restarted and typed and it didn't crash. And I sat there for like an hour and a half trying probably a hundred different things. Then it crashed again! Then I wrote it down. Then I could debug it.

Seibel: What are the techniques that you use there? Print statements?

Armstrong: Print statements. The great gods of programming said, "Thou shalt put `printf` statements in your program at the point where you think it's gone wrong, recompile, and run it."

Then there's—I don't know if I read it somewhere or if I invented it myself—Joe's Law of Debugging, which is that all errors will be plus/minus three statements of the place you last changed the program. When I worked at the Swedish Space Corporation my boss was a hardware guy. We were up at Esrange, the rocket-launching site and satellite-tracking station in the north. And one time he was banging his head, debugging some bug in the hardware, plugging in oscilloscopes, and changing things. And I said, "Oh, can I help?" And he said, "No Joe, you can't help here—this is hardware." And I said, "Yeah, but it must be like software—the bug will be pretty near to the last change you made to the hardware." And he went, "I changed a capacitor. You're a genius!" He'd replaced one capacitor with a bigger capacitor and he unsoldered it and put the original one back and it worked. It's the same everywhere. You fix your car and it goes wrong—it's the last thing you did. You changed something—you just have to remember what it was. It's true with everything.

Seibel: So have you ever proved any of your programs correct? Has that kind of formalism ever appealed to you?

Armstrong: Yes and no. I've manipulated programs algebraically to just show that they were equivalent. Haven't really gone into theorem proving as such. I did a course in denotational semantics and things like that. I remember giving up. The exercise was given: `let x = 3 in let y = 4 in x plus y` show that the eager evaluation scheme given by the equations foo and the lazy evaluation scheme given by the equations bar, both evaluate to seven.

Fourteen pages of lemmas and things later I thought, "Hang on—x is three, y is four, x plus y; yeah seven." At the time I was writing the Erlang compiler. If it took lots of pages to prove that three plus four is seven then the proof that my compiler was in any sense correct would have been thousands and thousands of pages.

Seibel: Do you prefer to work alone or on a team?

Armstrong: I like a workplace of teams, if you see what I mean. I'm not antisocial. But I just like programming by myself. Certainly I like collaborating with people in the sense of discussing problems with them. I always thought the coffee break that you have when you got to work and out came all the ideas that you'd had on your walk to work was very valuable. You get a lot of insights then. Good to thrash your ideas out in front of the crowd. You're put in a position of explaining your ideas which, for me, moves them from one part of my brain to another part. Often when you explain things then you understand them better.

Seibel: Have you ever pair programmed—sat down at a computer and produced code with another person?

Armstrong: Yeah. With Robert, Robert Virding. We would tend to do that when both of us were kind of struggling in the dark. We didn't really know what we were doing. So if you don't know what you're doing then I think it can be very helpful with someone who also doesn't know what they're doing. If you have one programmer who's better than the other one, then there's probably benefit for the weaker programmer or the less-experienced programmer to observe the other one. They're going to learn something from that. But if the gap's too great then they won't learn, they'll just sit there feeling stupid. When I have done pair programming with programmers about the same ability as me but neither of us knew what we were doing, then it's been quite fun.

Then there are what I might call special problems. I wouldn't attempt them if I've got a cold or I'm not on good physical form. I know it's going to take three days to write and I'll plan a day and not read email and start and it's gonna be four hours solid. I'll do it at home so I know I won't be interrupted. I just want to do it and get into this complete concentrated state where I can do it. I don't think pair programming would help there. It would be very disruptive.

Seibel: What's an example of that kind of problem?

Armstrong: Figuring out bits of a garbage collector—it's the imperative coding—where you've got to remember to mark all those registers. Or doing some lambda lifting in the compiler, which is pretty tough—you relabel all the variables and then you've got four or five layers of abstract data types all messing around and frames with different stuff in them and you think, "I've got to really understand this, really think deeply about it." You want to concentrate.

I vary the tasks I do according to mood. Sometimes I'm very uninspired so I think to myself, "Ah, who shall I go and disturb now." Or I'll read some emails. Other times I feel, right now I'm going to do some hard coding because I'm in the mood for it. You've got to be sort of right to do the coding. So how's that going to work with two people? One of them is just not in a concentrating mode and wants to read his emails and things.

Seibel: You did do a kind of serial pair programming with Robert Virding, when you passed the code back and forth rewriting it each time.

Armstrong: Yeah. One at a time. I would work on the program, typically two or three weeks, and then I'd say, "Well, I've had enough, here you are, Robert." And he'd take it. Every time we did this, it would come back sort of unrecognizable. He would make a large number of changes and it'd come back to me and I'd make a large number of changes.

Seibel: And they were productive changes?

Armstrong: Oh, absolutely. I was delighted if he found better ways of doing things. We both got on very well.He used to generalize. I remember once I found a variable—I followed it round and round through about 45 routines and then, out it came, at the end, never even used. He just passed this variable in and out of 45 different functions. I said, "What's that for?

You don't use it." He said, "I know. Reserved for future expansion." So I removed that.

I would write a specific algorithm removing all things that were not necessary for this program. Whenever I got the program, it became shorter as it became more specific. And whenever Robert took my program it became longer, adding generality. I believe this Unix philosophy—a program should do what it's supposed to do *and nothing else*. And Robert's philosophy is it should be a general program and then the program itself should be a specific case of the general program. So he would add generality and then specialize it.

Seibel: That seems like a pretty deep philosophical divide. Was there any benefit to having the program go through those two extremes?

Armstrong: Oh yes. Every cycle it improved. I think it was a lot better because of that. And probably better than either of us could have done on our own.

Seibel: Can you talk about how you design software? Maybe take example of something like OTP.

Armstrong: OTP was designed by me and Martin Björklund and Magnus Fröberg. There were just the three of us did the original design. We met every morning at coffee and had a long conversation—about an hour to two hours—and we covered the white board in stuff. I'd take loads of notes—I wrote all the documentation immediately and they wrote all the code. Sometimes I'd write a bit of code as well. And when I was writing the documentation I'd discover, I can't describe this, we have to change it. Or they would run into me and say, "Nah, it doesn't work; this idea we had this morning, because of this, this, this, and this it doesn't work." At the end of the day we either got to the point where we got all the documentation and all the code or enough of the code and enough of the documentation that we knew it was going to work. And then we called it a day.

Some days it didn't work so we said, "OK, we'll do it again tomorrow." There wasn't enough time to do a second pass in a day. But about one pass in a day worked fine. Because it gives us about two hours to discuss it in the morning, about two hours to write the documentation or code it up. And if you spent four hours really thinking hard, that's a good day's work. So that worked very, very well. I don't know how long we worked like that for. Ten weeks, twelve weeks, something like that. And then we got the basic framework and then we had more people. We'd specified the architecture—now we could start growing it. We'd get three or four more programmers in.

Seibel: And then how did you divvy up the work for those new folks?

Armstrong: Well, we knew what were prototypes and what were final versions. I've always taken the view of system design, you solve the hard problems first. Identify the hard problems and then solve them. And then the easy problems, you know they'll just come out in the wash. So there's a bit of experience there in classifying them as easy and hard. I know IP fail-over or something like that is going to be fairly hard. But I know that parsing a configuration file is going to be easy. In the prototype you might just have a configuration file that you read. You don't syntax check it—you don't have a grammar. In the production version you might do it in XML and have a complete grammar and validate it. But you know that that's a mechanical step to do that. It will take a competent programmer several weeks, or whatever time it takes. But it's doable, it's predictable in time, and there shouldn't be any nasty surprises on the way. But getting the communication protocols right, and getting them working properly when things fail, that I would do in a small group.

Seibel: So in this case you wrote the documentation before, or at least while, the code was being written. Is that how you usually do it?

Armstrong: It depends on the difficulty of the problem. I think with very difficult problems I quite often start right by writing the documentation. The more difficult it is, the more likely I am to document it first.

I like documentation. I don't think a program is finished until you've written some reasonable documentation. And I quite like a specification. I think it's unprofessional these people who say, "What does it do? Read the code." The code shows me what it *does*. It doesn't show me what it's supposed to do. I think the code is the answer to a problem. If you don't have the spec or you don't have any documentation, you have to guess what the problem is from the answer. You might guess wrong. I want to be told what the problem is.

Seibel: Is the documentation you write at this stage internal documentation that another programmer would read or documentation for the user?

Armstrong: It's for user guides. It sort of switches me into a different mode of thinking. I just start, in order to do this, create a directory called that, put this file in there, rename this as that and that is guiding the structure. I've sort of pondered the question. I bet Knuth would say, "Well, all programs are literate programs." You don't write the code and then write the documentation. You write both at the same time, so it's a literate program. I'm not there. I don't think that. I don't know if his view is because he publishes his programs.

I don't know if it's a left-brain/right-brain shift, or what it is, but when you write the documentation you think about the program differently to when you write the code. So I guess writing literate programs forces that shift as you're doing it. Which might be very productive. I did do some literate Erlang though I haven't actually used it for a very long time. So that's an interesting idea—perhaps I should wake it up again and write some stuff using literate Erlang. I'm not against the idea but I'm sort of impatient and wanted to write the code and not the documentation. But if you really want to understand it then I think writing the documentation is an essential step.

If I were programming Haskell, I would be forced to think about the types pretty early and document them and write them down. If you're programming in Lisp or Erlang you can start writing the code and you haven't really thought about the types. And in a way, writing the documentation is thinking about the types in a way. I suppose you start off with "is a". You say, "A melody is a sequence of notes." Right. OK. A melody is a sequence of chords where each chord is a parallel composition of notes of the same duration. Just by defining terms in your documentation—a something is a something—you're doing a sort of type analysis and you're thinking declaratively about what the data structures are.

Seibel: Do you think overall programming languages are getting better? Are we on a trajectory where we learn enough lessons from the past and come up with enough new ideas?

Armstrong: Yes. The new languages are good. Haskell and things like that. Erlang. Then there are some funny languages that should really be used. Prolog is a beautiful language but not widely used. It sort of peaked; Kowalski called it a solution looking for a problem.

Seibel: Dan Ingalls mentioned Prolog as an example of the kind of idea that we should really revisit now that we've had a couple decades of Moore's Law.

Armstrong: Prolog is so different to all the other programming languages. It's just this amazing way of thinking. And it's not appropriate to all problems. But it is appropriate to an extremely large set of problems. It's not widely used. And it's a great shame because programs are incredibly short. I think I went into shock when I wrote my first Prolog program. It's a kind of shocking experience. You just walk around going, where's the program—I haven't written a program. You just told it a few facts about the system, about your problem. Here it is figuring out what to do. It's wonderful. I should go back to Prolog—drop Erlang.

Seibel: Are there other skills that are not directly related to programming that you feel have improved your programming or that are valuable to have as a programmer?

Armstrong: Writing is. There's some computer scientist that said, "Oh, if you're no good at English you'll never be a very good programmer."

Seibel: I think Dijkstra had something about that.

Armstrong: I've occasionally been asked to advise people at universities on choice of syllabus subjects for computer science courses, being as how I work for industry—what does industry want? And I say, "Well, turn 'em out being able to write and argue cogently." Most graduates who come out, and they've got degrees in computer science, writing's not their strong point.

I think it's actually very difficult to teach because it's very individual. Somebody's got to take your text and a red pen and explain to you what you did wrong. And that's very time consuming. Have you ever read Hamming's advice to young researchers?

Seibel: "You and Your Research"?

Armstrong: He says things like, "Do good stuff." He says, "If you don't do good stuff, in good areas, it doesn't matter what you do." And Hamming said, "I always spend a day a week learning new stuff. That means I spend 20 percent more of my time than my colleagues learning new stuff. Now 20 percent at compound interest means that after four and a half years I will know twice as much as them. And because of compound interest, this 20 percent extra, one day a week, after five years I will know three times as much," or whatever the figures are. And I think that's very true. Because I do research I don't spend 20 percent of my time thinking about new stuff, I spend 40 percent of my time thinking about new stuff. And I've done it for 30 years. So I've noticed that I know a lot of stuff. When I get pulled in as a troubleshooter, boom, do it that way, do it that way. You were asking earlier what should one do to become a better programmer? Spend 20 percent of your time learning stuff—because it's compounded. Read Hamming's paper. It's good. Very good.

Seibel: Do you find some code beautiful?

Armstrong: Yes. Why this is I don't know. The funny thing is, if you give two programmers the same problem—it depends on the problem, but problems of a more mathematical nature, they can often end up writing the same code. Subject to just formatting issues and relabeling the variables and the function names, it's isomorphic—it's exactly the same algorithms. Are we creating these things or are we just pulling the cobwebs off? It's like a statue that's there and we're pulling the cobwebs off and revealing the algorithm that's always been there. So are we inventing a new algorithm or are we inventing a structure that already exists? Some algorithms feel like that. I think it's more the mathematical algorithms. I don't get that feeling when I'm implementing a telephony protocol or something. That's not a statue that I'm pulling the cobwebs off.

Seibel: So that's similar to the beauty of math, because it's part of nature. Then there are other levels at which code sort of has an aesthetic.

Armstrong: Yeah. It's kind of feng shui. I like minimalistic code, very beautifully poised, structured code. If you start removing things, if you get to the point where if you were to remove anything more it would not work any more—at this point it is beautiful. Where every change that you could conceivably make, makes it a worse algorithm, at that point it becomes beautiful.

Seibel: You mentioned that when you and Robert Virding were passing the code back and forth how each of you changed the low-level details of formatting, stuff that programmers argue endlessly about.

Armstrong: That's not affecting the beauty of the algorithm.

Seibel: But it's part of the aesthetic. It's people's taste.

Armstrong: Yeah. But I wouldn't say, "This is ugly code because there's a blank after the comma." Ugly is when it's done with a linear search and it could have been done with a binary interval halving. Or it could have done logarithmically and it's done linearly. For the wrong reasons. Sure do it linearly if we know we're searching through a list of ten elements, who cares? But if it's a big data structure then it should have been done with a binary search. And so it's really not very pretty to do it in a linear form.The mathematical algorithms—that's like Platonic beauty. This is more like architecture. You admire a fine building—it's not a mathematical object. Not a solid or a sphere or a prism—it's a skyscraper. It looks nice.

Seibel: What makes a good programmer? If you are hiring programmers—what do you look for?

Armstrong: Choice of problem, I think. Are you driven by the problems or by the solutions? I tend to favor the people who say, "I've got this really interesting problem." Then you ask, "What was the most fun project you ever wrote; show me the code for this stuff. How would you solve this problem?" I'm not so hung up on what they know about language X or Y. From what I've seen of programmers, they're either good at all languages or good at none. The guy who's a good C programmer will be good at Erlang—it's an incredibly good predictor. I have seen exceptions to that but the mental skills necessary to be good at one language seem to convert to other languages.

Seibel: Some companies are famous for using logic puzzles during interviews. Do you ask people that kind of question in interviews?

Armstrong: No. Some very good programmers are kind of slow at that kind of stuff. One of the guys who worked on Erlang, he got a PhD in math, and the only analogy I have of him, it's like a diamond drill drilling a hole through granite. I remember he had the flu so he took the Erlang listings home. And then he came in and he wrote an atom in an Erlang program and he said, "This will put the emulator into an infinite loop." He found the initial hash value of this atom was exactly zero and we took something mod something to get the next value which also turned out to be zero. So he reverse engineered the hash algorithm for a pathological case. He didn't even execute the programs to see if they were going to work; he read the programs. But he didn't do it quickly. He read them rather slowly. I don't know how good he would have been at these quick mental things.

Seibel: Are there any other characteristics of good programmers?

Armstrong: I read somewhere, that you have to have a good memory to be a reasonable programmer. I believe that to be true.

Seibel: Bill Gates once claimed that he could still go to a blackboard and write out big chunks of the code to the BASIC that he written for the Altair, a decade or so after he had originally written it. Do you think you can remember your old code that way?

Armstrong: Yeah. Well, I could reconstruct something. Sometimes I've just completely lost some old code and it doesn't worry me in the slightest. I haven't got a listing or anything; just type it in again. It would be logically equivalent. Some of the variable names would change and the ordering of the functions in the file would change and the names of the functions would change. But it would be almost isomorphic. Or what I would type in would be an improved version because my brain had worked at it.

Take the pattern matching in the compiler which I wrote ten years ago. I could sit down and type that in. It would be different to the original version but it'd be an improved version if I did it from memory. Because it sort of improves itself while you're not doing anything. But it'd probably have a pretty similar structure.

I'm not worried about losing code or anything like that. It's these patterns in your head that you remember. Well, I can't even say you remember them.

You can do it again. It's not so much remembering. When I say you can remember a program exactly, I don't think that it's actually remembering. But you can do it again. If Bill could remember the actual text, I can't do that. But I can certainly remember the structure for quite a long time.

Seibel: Is Erlang-style message passing a silver bullet for slaying the problem of concurrent programming?

Armstrong: Oh, it's not. It's an improvement. It's a lot better than shared memory programming. I think that's the one thing Erlang has done—it has actually demonstrated that. When we first did Erlang and we went to conferences and said, "You should copy all your data." And I think they accepted the arguments over fault tolerance—the reason you copy all your data is to make the system fault tolerant. They said, "It'll be terribly inefficient if you do that," and we said, "Yeah, it will but it'll be fault tolerant."

The thing that is surprising is that it's more efficient in certain circumstances. What we did for the reasons of fault tolerance, turned out to be, in many circumstances, just as efficient or even *more* efficient than sharing.

Then we asked the question, "Why is that?" Because it increased the concurrency. When you're sharing, you've got to lock your data when you access it. And you've forgotten about the cost of the locks. And maybe the amount of data you're copying isn't that big. If the amount of data you're copying is pretty small and if you're doing lots of updates and accesses and lots of locks, suddenly it's not so bad to copy everything. And then on the multicores, if you've got the old sharing model, the locks can stop all the cores. You've got a thousand-core CPU and one program does a global lock—all the thousand cores have got to stop.

I'm also very skeptical about implicit parallelism. Your programming language can have parallel constructs but if it doesn't map into hardware that's parallel, if it's just being emulated by your programming system, it's not a benefit. So there are three types of hardware parallelism.

There's pipeline parallelism—so you make a deeper pipeline in the chip so you can do things in parallel. Well, that's once and for all when you design the chip. A normal programmer can't do anything about the instruction-level parallelism.

There's data parallelism, which is not really parallelism but it has to do with cache behavior. If you want to make a C program go efficiently, if `*p` is on a 16-byte boundary, if you access `*p`, then the access to `*(p + 1)` is free, basically, because the cache line pulls it in. Then you need to worry about how wide the cache lines are—how many bytes do you pull in in one cache transfer? That's data parallelism, which the programmer can use by being very careful about their structures and knowing exactly how it's laid out in memory. Messy stuff—you don't really want to do that.

The other source of real concurrency in the chip are multicores. There'll be 32 cores by the end of the decade and a million cores by 2019 or whatever. So you have to take the granules of concurrency in your program and map them onto the cores of the computer. Of course that's quite a heavyweight operation. Starting a computation on a different core and getting the answer back is itself something that takes time. So if you're just adding two numbers together, it's just not worth the effort—you're spending more effort in moving it to another core and doing it and getting the answer back than you are in doing it in place.

Erlang's quite well suited there because the programmer has said, "I want a process, I want another process, I want another process." Then we just put them on the cores. And maybe we should be thinking about actually physically placing them on cores. Probably a process that spawns another process talks to that process. So if we put it on a core that's physically near, that's a good place to put it, not on one that's a long way away. And maybe if we know it's *not* going to talk to it a lot maybe we can put it a long way away. And maybe processes that do I/O should be near the edge of the chip—the ones that talk to the I/O processes. As the chips get bigger we're going to have to think about how getting data to the middle of the chip is going to cost more than getting it to the edge of the chip. Maybe you've got two or three servers and a database and maybe you're going to map this onto the cores so we'll put the database in the middle of the chip and these ones talk to the client so we'll put them near the edge of the chip. I don't know—this is research.

Seibel: You care a lot about the idea of Erlang's way of doing concurrency. Do you care more about that idea—the message-passing shared-nothing concurrency—or Erlang the language?

Armstrong: The idea—absolutely. People keep on asking me, "What will happen to Erlang? Will it be a popular language?" I don't know. I think it's already been influential. It might end up like Smalltalk. I think Smalltalk's very, very influential and loved by an enthusiastic band of people but never really very widely adopted. And I think Erlang might be like that. It might need Microsoft to take some of its ideas and put some curly braces here and there and shove it out in the Common Language Runtime to hit a mass market.

CHAPTER

7

Simon Peyton Jones

One of the instigators, back in 1987, of the project that led to the definition of the programming language Haskell, Simon Peyton Jones is a Principal Researcher at Microsoft Research's lab in Cambridge, England. He edited the Haskell 98 Revised Report*, the current stable definition of the language; he is the architect and lead developer of the Glasgow Haskell Compiler (GHC), the "de facto standard compiler" according to haskell.org; and he gave Haskell its widely cited unofficial motto: "Avoid success at all costs."*

A high-powered researcher and former professor who never got a PhD, Peyton Jones values both the practical and the theoretically beautiful. He learned to program on a machine with no permanent storage and only 100 memory locations, and in college he worked on both writing high-level compilers for the school's big iron and building his own primitive computers out of parts he could afford on a student's budget. But he was drawn to functional programming by a professor's demonstration of how to build doubly linked lists without using mutation and the beauty of the idea of lazy evaluation. Peyton Jones saw the ideas of functional programming "as a radical and elegant attack on the whole enterprise of writing programs": a way, rather than "just putting one more brick in the wall," to "build a whole new wall." In 2004 the Association for Computing

Machinery elected him a Fellow, citing his "contributions to functional programming languages."

Among the topics we covered in this interview are why he thinks functional programming shows increasing promise of changing the way software is written, why Software Transactional Memory is a much better way of writing concurrent software than locks and condition variables, and why it is so difficult, even at a place like Microsoft Research, to do real studies of whether different programming languages make programmers more or less productive.

Seibel: When did you learn to program?

Peyton Jones: When I was at school. Intel had just about produced the 4004—the world's first microprocessor. We didn't have a 4004 or anything like it—it was really a chip that hobbyists could barely get at that stage. The only computer they had available was an IBM schools computer, which was a strange machine built out of spare parts from mainframes. It had no permanent storage whatsoever so you had to type in your program every time you ran it.

It had 100 storage locations, total, which would each store, I think, eight-digit decimal numbers. And this stored both your program and your data. So the name of the game of programming that was to simply to fit the program into 100 storage locations. I can't quite remember how I got to write my first program. I think I and one other enthusiast at the school spent a lot of time on the schools computer. This would have been when I was about 15, 1974, '73—that kind of era.

Then after we'd been programming this machine for a little bit we discovered there was a computer at the technical college in Swindon. So we spent an hour on a very slow bus one afternoon a week and went to Swindon where there was this enormous machine—an Elliot 803—which lived in half a dozen large, white, fridge-sized cabinets in a room all its own with a white-coated operator.

After a bit the white-coated operator learned that we could figure out how to use the machine so she went away while we played with this vast engine.

It worked with paper tape and teletype so you had your program on a paper tape. We wrote in Algol, so that was my first high-level language. You wrote your program on the tape, you edited on the tape. You wanted to change it, you had to run the tape through the teletype, make it print out a new tape, stop it at the right place, type the new bit—an extremely laborious way to edit your program. A kind of line editor with physical medium. So that was my first experience of programming. It was very motivating.

Seibel: That wasn't a course at school though.

Peyton Jones: Oh, no! Zero, absolutely no teaching about computers at school.

Seibel: So it was just—"Hey kids, here's a computer, knock yourself out."

Peyton Jones: Absolutely. It was there in a large locked cupboard and you could borrow the key and there it was with a screen and it just displayed a fixed display of what was in the registers and these decimal numbers of what was in memory locations. You could set the program and press Go. You could single-step it. That was really it. So it wasn't even assembly language programming because there was no ASCII characters at all. It was literally the machine code, displayed in decimal, not even in hexadecimal.

Seibel: But it had a screen?

Peyton Jones: It did have a television screen. That was its sole output medium.

Seibel: And what was the input?

Peyton Jones: It was a kind of touch keyboard. You touched these buttons and they sensed that your finger touched. So that was rather sophisticated—no mechanical keys. It was some kind of capacitive thing—you touched the key and there it was. There were a total of about 20 buttons.

Seibel: So these buttons were just for numbers?

Peyton Jones: Numbers and Go and Step. And "show me this memory location." It was really extremely primitive. And all the more exciting for that.

Seibel: I assume you had to plan your program, probably in excruciating detail, before you get up to this machine and start keying stuff in.

Peyton Jones: First of all you draw a flow diagram. Then you'd break it down into instructions. Then you'd encode the instructions into this strange digital format. And then you type in the numbers. You type in essentially an 800-digit number, which is your program. And then you press Go. If you were lucky you hadn't mistyped one of those 800 digits and you were in good shape. So we spent a lot of time just looking down the thing with one guy looking at the screen and checking and the other guy saying, "Go to the next location."

Then when I went to university at Cambridge, microprocessors were just beginning to take off. So there was a university computing club. There was a big university computing mainframe kind of machine, called Phoenix, with an extremely elaborate accounting system.

The time at which you used it was very significant. You were given a certain amount of units of the machine's currency and the more memory your program took, the more units you consumed; the longer your program took, the more units you consumed. But the lower the load was, the fewer units your program consumed. So as a result, us undergraduates, who didn't get a very large allocation, simply spent our nights there because from about 9:00 at night it became rather cheap to run your program.

So we would be there 9:00 to 3:00 a.m., writing our programs. And what did we write in mainly? BCPL, I think. So this again was completely hobbyist stuff. I was doing a maths degree at the time. So zero formal teaching in computer science.

There wasn't a whole undergraduate degree at that time either. That was 1976 to '79. There was a final year course so you could graduate in computer science. But you couldn't do three years of computer science—you had to do something else like maths or natural sciences beforehand. In fact I did maths and finished up with a year of electrical sciences. Mainly because I thought computing was my hobby—it'd be a bit like cheating to do it as your degree as well; degrees should be hard.

But maths turned out to be a bit too hard because Cambridge is stuffed with extremely brainy mathematicians so I switched to electrical sciences.

Seibel: And electrical sciences—that's what we'd call electrical engineering in the U.S.?

Peyton Jones: That's right. At that stage my same friend that I was at school with, Thomas Clarke, was also here at Cambridge. So Thomas and I built various computers. You would buy yourself a microprocessor and lots of 7400 series TTL and wire it up. Our biggest problem, I remember, was printers. Printers and screens. Those were the hard bits.

Seibel: Because they're expensive.

Peyton Jones: They're so expensive—yes. You could get the electrical parts for the kind of money students could afford but printers were typically big, fridge-sized line printer things. They had a lot of mechanics in them that made them completely out of our price bracket. That and storage devices—any kind of permanent storage device tended to be tricky. So we tended to have computers with a keyboard, a screen, and not much else. And some kind of primitive tape mechanism.

Seibel: You guys were building these computers from scratch in '76 to '79. Isn't that about the same time the Altair was coming out?

Peyton Jones: That's right. Hobbyist computers were definitely starting to come out. But we considered those to be rather cheating.

The thing about this machine that we built ourselves was that software was the problem. I think my most advanced program for this machine was Conway's Game of Life. That worked very nicely. But writing any kind of serious program, like a programming language, was just too much work because it had very limited permanent storage medium. And it was all typing in hexadecimal stuff—no assembler.

Seibel: So more raw machine code.

Peyton Jones: Of course the Cambridge mainframe understood BCPL so we were writing lots of BCPL programs. We were actually writing a compiler then for a programming language that we'd invented. We never completed this compiler—it was very elaborate. There were these two completely divorced worlds. Writing compilers in a high-level language for a mainframe and diddling with hardware on the other end.

Seibel: What was the first interesting program you remember writing?

Peyton Jones: A program to extract 24-digit square roots on this schools computer and fit it into 99 memory locations.

Seibel: So you had one spare!

Peyton Jones: That's right. It was some kind of Newton-Raphson approximation to do square roots. I was terribly proud of it. What after that? I suppose the next scale up must have been this compiler that we never completed. It was written in BCPL and it was extremely elaborate. We were extremely ambitious with it. There was no type system so we just had enormous sheets of printout with pictures, diagrams of structures and arrows between them.

Seibel: You mean in BCPL there was no type system.

Peyton Jones: Yeah, that's right. So essentially we wrote out our types by drawing them on large sheets of papers with arrows. That was our type system. That was a pretty large program—in fact it was over ambitious; we never completed it.

Seibel: Do you think you learned any lessons from that failure?

Peyton Jones: That was probably when I first became aware that writing a really big program you could end up with problems of scale—you couldn't keep enough of it in your head at the same time. Previously all the things I had written, you could keep the whole thing in your head without any trouble. So it was probably the first time I'd done any serious attempt at long-standing documentation.

Seibel: But even that wasn't enough, in this case?

Peyton Jones: Well, we had a lot of other things to do, like get degrees. This was all between 9:00 p.m. and 3:00 a.m.

Seibel: And is there anything you wish you had done differently about learning to program?

Peyton Jones: Well, nobody every taught me to program. I'm not sure I ever really missed that. Today I feel as if my main programming blank spot is that I don't have a deep, visceral feel for object-oriented programming. Of course I know how to write object-oriented programs and all that. But something different happens when you do something at scale. When you build big programs that last for a long time and you use class hierarchies in a complex way and you build frameworks—that's what I mean by a deep, visceral understanding. Not the kind of stuff that you'd learn immediately from a book.

I feel that as a lack because I don't feel I can really be authoritative about what you can and can't do with object-oriented programming. I'm always very careful in what I say, particularly not to be negative about imperative programming because it's an incredibly sophisticated and rich programming paradigm. But somehow because of the way my life developed, I never really spent several years writing big C++ programs. That's how you get some kind of deep, visceral feel and I never have.

Seibel: I think that feeling is usually revulsion.

Peyton Jones: That's right—but it's a well-informed revulsion rather than a superficial, "Oh, that sucks" kind of revulsion.

Seibel: So you finished your three years at Cambridge, then what?

Peyton Jones: Then I thought, "Alright, better do a little bit of work on computing." So I spent one year doing a postgraduate diploma in computer science—my sole formal education in computer science.

Seibel: Is that kind of like a master's degree?

Peyton Jones: Kind of like a master's degree. I had a great year. I suspect it was very similar to the computer science tripos, the undergraduate degree.

But it was intended for students who hadn't done any other computer science.

Seibel: Then you spent a couple years in industry before getting back into research. What were you doing then?

Peyton Jones: That was a very small process control and monitoring company. We built hardware and software that sat in microprocessor-based computers that were physically sitting in weigh scale controllers for conveyor belts. One thing I built watched a load cell on a conveyor belt that carried coal; it controlled the speed of the belt and listened to what the load cell was saying and adjusted the speed to make the flow rate what it should be. It was a little real-time operating system, which I wrote in a language called PL/Z. It was a little bit like Algol. I wrote it on a Z80 machine that ran a sort of cut-down Unix called Chromix.

It was a very small company—it was like half a dozen people. Varied up to 15 at times. But because it was small everything was quite volatile. Sometimes we had plenty of money, other times we had none. After two years I'd decided that the entrepreneurial life was not for me. This was my main insight about small companies: to be an entrepreneur you need to get energy from stressful situations involving money, whereas my energy is sapped by stressful situations involving money. My boss was the managing director of this company. The worse things got, the more energetic he would be. He'd come bouncing around and he'd have new technical ideas for software. He was just as happy as a bee. And I realized, that's what you need, because if it saps your energy, you spend your whole time in a slump.

So I decided that was all much too hard work and looked around for a job and ended up getting a job as a lecturer at University College London. And when I was there I had no PhD, I had no research training. So my head of department gave me time off to do research. Gave me a light teaching load so I could get my research gig started. But I hadn't the faintest idea what to do. So I would sit in my office with a blank sheet of paper and a sharpened pencil and wait for great ideas. And there was this sort of silence while I would sort of stare around the room waiting for great ideas to come. And nothing much would happen.

John Washbrook, who was himself a senior academic in the department, took me under his wing and he told me something that was very important. He said, "Just start something, no matter how humble." This is not really about programming, this is about research. But no matter how humble and unoriginal and unimportant it may seem, start something and write a paper about it. So that's what I did. It turned out to be a very significant piece of advice.

I've told that to every research student I've ever had since. Because it's how you get started. Once you start the mill turning then computer science is very fractal—almost everything turns out to be interesting, because the subject grows ahead of you. It's not like a fixed thing that's there that you've got to discover. It just expands.

Seibel: So you came back into academia but you never did get a PhD. How was that possible?

Peyton Jones: These days getting a faculty post without a PhD would be very hard. This must have been 1982, 1983. I applied to UCL because my sister was studying computer science there and she said, "Oh, there are a couple of lectureships at UCL, why don't you apply?" Much to my astonishment, I was appointed. I can only assume that at the time there must have been a desperate shortage and that anyone that could give a plausible account of himself, in a computing sense, could get hired. Because otherwise, how did they manage to hire somebody without a PhD?

After seven years at UCL I began to think maybe I should get a PhD. But it was a big hassle writing a thesis, really. But, it turns out at Cambridge you can get a PhD by special regulation, which means that you just submit your published work and, with luck, they say, "You are a fine person who should have a PhD." So I was just getting geared up to do that when I got appointed as a professor at Glasgow. Full professor. So by that time I was called "Professor" so nobody would know whether I had a PhD or not so I dropped the idea. Robin Milner doesn't have a PhD; it must be a distinguished company. I've stuck like that every since.

Seibel: These days, is getting a PhD valuable? Someone once told me a PhD is really a vocational degree—if you want to be a professor, you've got to get one but if you don't want to be a professor, there's no point. Do you think that analysis applies to computer science?

Peyton Jones: That part is certainly true. It's necessary but not sufficient if you want to stick with research as a career—either academic or at somewhere like Microsoft Research or Google's research labs—a serious industrial research lab. You really need a PhD to get past the starting post.

If you don't want to pursue a career in research, then I think it becomes a follow-your-heart kind of thing. You're five times as productive if you're working on something that makes you enthusiastic. So if you find yourself thinking, "I just love this and I'd just like to have some time to dig into it some more," a PhD is a fantastic opportunity to spend three years in Britain, or rather longer in the States, just studying something. It's an incredible freedom really because you're sort of a parasite on society. If you know you don't want to do full-time research as a career then the reason to do a PhD is because you're just enthusiastic and inquisitive and interested. But PhDs are rather strange anyway. They force you to work on your own and produce a substantial thesis that most people won't read—they'll read your papers. So it's an unusual research mode.

Once you've finished a PhD you start working much more collaboratively with lots of other people on typically smaller, more bite-sized pieces of work. I think in some ways a PhD is an odd preparation, even for research. Odder in Britain because of its compressed timescale. I think in the States you can be more collaborative for a while until you zero in on your own research program.

Seibel: Speaking of research and academics, functional programming is quite popular within the research community but I think a lot of people outside that community see functional programming as being driven by ideas that, while neat, can be very mathematical and divorced from day-to-day programming. Is that a fair characterization?

Peyton Jones: I think it's about half fair. I characterize functional programming—that is, purely functional programming, where side effects are somehow really relegated to a world of their own—as a radical and elegant attack on the whole enterprise of writing programs. Things that are radical are by definition not evolutionary from the state of where things are at.

Today "where things are at" is that big companies are pouring immense resources into ecosystems and editors and profilers and tools and programmers and skills and all that kind of stuff. The mainstream is, by definition, deeply practical. Meanwhile this radical and elegant stuff of functional programming has much less of that deep, infrastructural support. But at the same time that doesn't necessarily make it self-indulgent to pursue it. Because, after all, unless *some* people are working on radical and elegant things you're going to end up in a local optimum, incrementally optimizing the mainstream but stuck on a low hill.

So I think that one of the good things about the whole business of academic research is that professors can go off and do sort of loopy things without being asked how it's benefiting the bottom line. Some will do things that turn out to be fantastically important, and some less so; but you can't tell which is which in advance! So my big-picture justification for why it's worth some people, like me, spending a lot of time on purely functional programming, is that it shows promise. I don't want to claim that it's exactly the way that everyone will be writing programs in the future, but it shows promise. And actually I'll make the case that it shows *increasing* promise. I see it as, when the limestone of imperative programming is worn away, the granite of functional programming will be observed.

That said, I think purely functional programming started quite geeky and academic and mathematical. The story of the last, really, 20 years—all the time I've been working on it—has been a story of becoming increasingly practical, focusing not just on abstract ideas but trying to overcome, one by one, the obstacles that prevent real-life programmers using functional programming languages for real applications. The development of Haskell itself is an example of that.

It's good that there are a bunch of people out here, maybe slightly impractical, who are heading towards the mainstream and maybe the perspectives you learn over here in the purely functional world can inform and illuminate the mainstream. That, you can see, has happened. Lots of stuff about type systems and generics were originally developed in the context of functional programming languages. It was a kind of laboratory in which some of those ideas were developed. Generators and lazy streams are another example. Python has list comprehensions at the syntactic level. There are lots of individual things. Usually they've been rebranded and sometimes, to fit the mainstream context, they've been changed quite a bit. I don't want to claim a kind of exclusive genealogy but I do think a lot of ideas have nevertheless percolated across. So it's been useful.

Seibel: For you, what about the relation between research and actually programming?

Peyton Jones: Oh, they interact a lot. My area of study is programming languages. What are programming languages for in the end? They're to make it easier to program. They're the user interface of programming, in effect. So programming and programming language research are deeply related. One thing we're not good about is this: the proof of the pudding is in the eating, so you should watch programmers eating. That is, you should do proper, formalized studies of programmers programming and see what they do. And that's jolly expensive. And it's also more "squishy." It's harder to come up with unequivocal results.

So the culture of the programming-language community is much more, "prove that your type system is sound and complete," kind of stuff. We dodge, probably, the more important but much harder to answer questions about whether, in practice, they make people more productive. But they are questions that are really hard to give convincing answers to. Are you more productive writing a functional program or an object-oriented program to do the same thing? Even if you could spend a lot of money on doing serious experiments, I'm not sure you'd come up with results which people would actually buy.

Seibel: Do you guys do any, even small-scale experiments? You're working for Microsoft, who has plenty of cash, so why not get a team of experienced Haskellites and a team of experienced C# people and give them the same task and see what happens? That's the kind of test you would need, right?

Peyton Jones: Yeah, yeah, that's right. It's partly a question of money. But it's not just a question of money. It's also sort of time and attention. To do that kind of experiment your whole methodology is different. And you need to shift culturally as well. And, while Microsoft, from the outside, appears to have plenty of cash, in fact the story here is largely one researcher and his workstation. We can't just turn on money for any particular thing. Be nice if we could. Nearer the coalface, as it were, there are big usability labs in Redmond where they do perform experiments on things that are proto products. New versions of Visual Studio are extensively usability tested.

Seibel: Presumably that's more for the total user interaction, rather than for programming language issues.

Peyton Jones: Well, they also do some interesting work on testing APIs. Steven Clarke and his colleagues at Redmond have made systematic attempts to watch programmers, given a new API, talk through what they're trying to do. And they get the people who designed the API to sit behind a glass screen and watch them.

And the guys sitting there behind the glass screen say, "No, no, don't do that! That's not the right way!" But it's soundproof. That turns out often to be very instructive. They go and change their API. To be honest, programming language research is weak on that score. But it is partly because these are difficult questions to answer. And culturally we're not well adapted to do it. I regard it as a weakness. But not one that I personally feel terribly well equipped to address.

Seibel: So if researchers are coming up with interesting ideas about how to improve programming, are the best of those good ideas from research labs and universities percolating into practice fast enough?

Peyton Jones: Well, fast enough. I don't know. Whenever I talk to people who are actually involved in building products that customers want and are therefore prepared to pay for, I'm very conscious that many of the things that bother me just aren't on their radar at all.

They have to do something this week that their customers are going to value; they just don't have time to mess about with something that might work or that might even work in some ways but in total isn't yet ready for prime time.

There's a bit of a disconnect—it's sort of a chicken-and-egg problem there. Sometimes the ideas that are developed in research need quite a bit of engineering effort around the edges that isn't fundamental research in order to be directly useful.

I wouldn't like to imply that developers on the ground are being dopey about this, just not taking up good ideas that would benefit their lives. They're doing what they're doing for quite good reasons. There is sometimes a bit of a gap between research prototypes and stuff that you can build in reality. And I think that Microsoft is actually doing quite well here because Microsoft Research does fill that gap a bit and does have quite a bit of mechanism—incubation groups and so forth—whose aim is to put researchers and developers in closer touch with each other and perhaps to help provide some extra effort to lift things across the boundary. So MSR is kind of as good as it gets, I think, as far as crossing that boundary is concerned.

There are layers to this kind of onion. For a mainstream developer shop that's stuffed with Java, not only is functional programming a radically different way of thinking about programming but also there are lots of interop questions. And have you got enough books and are there enough libraries? So there's this whole ecosystem that goes with programming, people and skills and libraries and frameworks and tools and so forth.

If you have enough of those blockers you get sort of stuck. So I think different pieces of research technology in programming language live on different points on a spectrum. Some are more evolutionary from where we are. You can say, "It just plugs right into your existing framework, it works on unmodified Java, it's a static analysis that points you to bugs in your code and yipee!" That's much easier to absorb than, "Here's a whole new way of thinking about programming."

That said, I think that if we're specifically discussing functional programming then I do think that we have seen a qualitative sea change in people's attitude. Many more people have heard about functional programming than ever used to. Suddenly rather than *always* having to explain what Haskell is, sometimes people say, "Oh, I've heard about that. In fact I was reading about it on Slashdot the other week and I gather it's rather cool." That just didn't happen a few years ago.

But what's underlying that? Is it just a random popularity thing? Or maybe part of it is that more students have been taught about functional programming in university and are now in managerial or seniorish positions. Perhaps. But perhaps it's also to do with as we scale up software dealing with the bad consequences of unrestricted side effects and as we want to deal with more verification and parallelism, all those issues become more pressing. I think that leads to this greater level of interest. I think gradually the needle is moving across this cost/benefit tradeoff.

Seibel: When did you get introduced to functional programming?

Peyton Jones: I didn't learn about functional programming until something like my final year at Cambridge when I went to a short course given by Arthur Norman. Arthur Norman was a brilliant and slightly eccentric lecturer in the department. Wonderful guy, interested in symbolic algebra so he was big into Lisp as well. He gave a short course on functional programming in which he showed us how to build doubly linked lists without using any side effects at all. I vividly remember this because this was my first notion that you could do something that weird—you'd think if you build a doubly-linked list you have to allocate the cells and then you have to fill them in to make them point to each other. It looks as if you just *have* to use side effects somehow.

But he showed how, in a purely functional language, you could actually write it without using any side effects. So that opened my eyes to the fact that functional programming, which at that stage I knew very little about, was a medium you could really write quite interesting programs in rather than just little toy ones.

Seibel: I think a lot of people might look at that demonstration and say, "Oh, isn't that interesting," and then still go back to hacking BCPL. Why do you think you were able to take the leap so much farther, spending most of your career trying to show how folks can really use this stuff?

Peyton Jones: There was one other component, which was David Turner's papers on S-K combinators. S-K combinators are a way of translating and then executing the lambda calculus. I'd learned a little bit about the lambda calculus, probably by osmosis at the time. What Turner's papers showed was how to translate lambda calculus into the three combinators, S, K, and I. S, K, and I are all just closed lambda terms. So in effect it says, "You can translate these arbitrary complicated lambda terms into just these three." In fact, you can get rid of I as well because I equals SKK.

So there's this strange compilation step in which you take a lambda term that you can kind of understand and turn it into a complete mess of S's and K's that you can't understand at all. But when you apply it to an argument, miraculously, it computes the same answer as the original lambda stuff did. And that was another example of something that was very clever and, to me at the time, implausible. But nevertheless you could see that it would just always work.

I don't know quite what it was that turned me on about this. I found it completely inspirational. It's partly, I suppose, because, being interested in hardware, it felt like this is a way you could *implement* the lambda calculus. Because the lambda calculus doesn't look like it's an implementation mechanism at all. It's a bit of a mathematical way of thinking, a bit remote from the machine. This S-K stuff looks as if you could just run it and indeed you can.

Seibel: So, you had a sense that, OK, I'll just build a machine that has S and K hardwired and then all I've got to do is compile things to a series of S and K ops.

Peyton Jones: In fact that's exactly what my friends did. William Stoye and Thomas Clarke and a couple others, built this machine, SKIM, the SKI Machine, which directly executed S and K. For some reason I wasn't directly involved in that project. But at the time there was this feeling developing. John Backus's paper, called, "Can Programming Be Liberated from the von Neumann Style" was extremely influential at the time. It was his Turing Award lecture and he was this guy who had invented Fortran saying, in effect, "Functional programming is the way of the future."

Furthermore, he said, "Maybe we should develop new computer architectures to execute this stuff on." So this very high-level endorsement of this research area meant we cited that paper like crazy. And so SKIM was an example of such a thing. We thought maybe this unusual way of going about executing, or at least thinking about, programs turns into a completely different sort of computer architecture. That phase lasted from about 1980 to 1990—radical architectures for functional programming. I now regard it as slightly misdirected but nevertheless it was terribly exciting.

Lazy evaluation was another huge motivating factor. With the benefit of hindsight I now think lazy evaluation is just wonderful but at that time it was sort of pivotal. Lazy evaluation is this idea that functions don't evaluate their arguments. Again the motivating factor was something to do with it being beautiful or elegant and unusual and radical.

That's kind of good for catching the imagination: it looks as if this might be a way of thinking about programming in a whole new way. Rather than just putting one more brick in the wall, we can build a whole new wall. That's very exciting. I was strongly motivated by that. Was it just that it was a neat trick? In some ways I think neat tricks are very significant. Lazy evaluation was just so neat and you could do such remarkable different things that you wouldn't think were possible.

Seibel: Like what?

Peyton Jones: I remember my friend John Hughes wrote a program for me. For a project I was doing two implementations of the lambda calculus and comparing their performance, so John gave me some test programs. One of them was a program that computed the decimal expansion of e to arbitrary precision. It was a lazy program—it was rather beautiful because it produced *all* the digits of e.

Seibel: Eventually.

Peyton Jones: Eventually, that's right. But it was up to the consumer. You didn't have to say how many digits to produce in advance. You just got given this list and you kept hauling on elements of the list and it wouldn't give you another digit until it had spent enough cycles computing it. So that's not something that's very obvious to do if you're writing a C program. Actually you can do it with enough cleverness. But it's not a natural programming paradigm for C. You can almost only do it once you've seen the lazy functional program. Whereas John's program was just about four or five lines. Amazing.

Seibel: Other languages have since special-cased that kind of computation with, for example, generators in Python or something where you can yield values. Was there something that made you say, "Aha; there are lots of things that could be fruitfully looked at as an infinite series of computations from which we just want to draw answers until we're tired of it?" As opposed to saying, "Oh, that's an interesting technique for certain problems but not the basis for everything."

Peyton Jones: I think at this stage I wasn't as reflective as that. I just thought it was so cool. And fun. I think it's important to do what you find motivating and interesting and follow it. I just found it very inspiring. I don't think I really thought there are deep principled reasons why this is *the* way to do programming. I just thought it was a rather wonderful way to do programming. I like skiing. Well, why do I like skiing? Not because it's going to change the world—just because it's a lot of fun.

I now think the important thing about laziness is that it kept us pure. You'll have seen this in several of my talks probably. But I actually really like laziness. Given a choice I'd choose a lazy language. I think it's really helpful for all kinds of programming things. I'm sure you've read John Hughes's paper, "Why Functional Programming Matters." It's probably the earliest articulate exposition of why laziness might be important in more than a cute way. And his main story is that it helps you write modular programs.

Lazy evaluation lets you write generators—his example is generate all the possible moves in your chess game—separately from your consumer, which walks over the tree and does alpha-beta minimaxing or something. Or if you're generating all the sequence of approximations of an answer, then you have a consumer who says when to stop. It turns out that by separating generators from consumers you can modularly decompose your program. Whereas, if you're having to generate it along with a consumer that's saying when to stop, that can make your program much less modular. Modular in the sense of separate thoughts in separate places that can be composed together. John's paper gives some nice examples of ways in which you can change the consumer or change the generator, independently from each other, and that lets you plug together new programs that would have been more difficult to get by modifying one tightly interwoven one.

So that's all about why laziness is a good thing. It's also very helpful in a very local level in your program. You tend to find Haskell programmers will write down a function definition with some local definitions. So they'll say "f of x equals blah, blah, blah *where* . . ." And in the `where` clause they write down a bunch of definitions and of these definitions, not all are needed in all cases. But you just write them down anyway. The ones that are needed will get evaluated; the ones that aren't needed won't. So you don't have to think, "Oh, goodness, all of these sub expressions are going to be evaluated but I can't evaluate that because that would crash because of a divide by zero so I have to move the definition into the right branch of the conditional."

There's none of that. You tend to just write down auxiliary definitions that might be needed and the ones that are needed will be evaluated. So that's a kind of programming convenience thing. It's a very, very convenient mechanism.

But getting back to the big picture, if you have a lazy evaluator, it's harder to predict exactly when an expression is going to be evaluated. So that means if you want to print something on the screen, every call-by-value language, where the order of evaluation is completely explicit, does that by having an impure "function"—I'm putting quotes around it because it now isn't a function at all—with type something like string to unit. You call this function and as a side effect it puts something on the screen. That's what happens in Lisp; it also happens in ML. It happens in essentially every call-by-value language.

Now in a pure language, if you have a function from string to unit you would never need to call it because you know that it just gives the answer unit. That's all a function can do, is give you the answer. And you know what the answer is. But of course if it has side effects, it's very important that you *do* call it. In a lazy language the trouble is if you say, "`f` applied to `print "hello"`," then whether `f` evaluates its first argument is not apparent to the caller of the function. It's something to do with the innards of the function. And if you pass it two arguments, `f` of `print "hello"` and `print "goodbye"`, then you might print either or both in either order or neither. So somehow, with lazy evaluation, doing input/output by side effect just isn't feasible. You can't write sensible, reliable, predictable programs that way. So, we had to put up with that. It was a bit embarrassing really because you couldn't really do any input/output to speak of. So for a long time we essentially had programs which could just take a string to a string. That was what the whole program did. The input string was the input and result string was the output and that's all the program could really ever do.

You could get a bit clever by making the output string encode some output commands that were interpreted by some outer interpreter. So the output string might say, "Print this on the screen; put that on the disk." An interpreter could actually do that. So you imagine the functional program is all nice and pure and there's sort of this evil interpreter that interprets a string of commands. But then, of course, if you read a file, how do you get the input back into the program? Well, that's not a problem, because you can output a string of commands that are interpreted by the evil interpreter and using lazy evaluation, it can dump the results back into the input of the program. So the program now takes a stream of responses to a stream of requests. The stream of requests go to the evil interpreter that does the things to the world. Each request generates a response that's then fed back to the input. And because evaluation is lazy, the program has emitted a response just in time for it to come round the loop and be consumed as an input. But it was a bit fragile because if you consumed your response a bit too eagerly, then you get some kind of deadlock. Because you'd be asking for the answer to a question you hadn't yet spat out of your back end yet.

The point of this is laziness drove us into a corner in which we had to think of ways around this I/O problem. I think that that was extremely important. The single most important thing about laziness was it drove us there. But that wasn't the way it started. Where it started was, laziness is cool; what a great programming idiom.

Seibel: Since you started programming, what's changed about how you think about programming?

Peyton Jones: I think probably the big changes in how I think about programming have been to do with monads and type systems. Compared to the early 80s, thinking about purely functional programming with relatively simple type systems, now I think about a mixture of purely functional, imperative, and concurrent programming mediated by monads. And the types have become a lot more sophisticated, allowing you to express a much wider range of programs than I think, at that stage, I'd envisaged. You can view both of those as somewhat evolutionary, I suppose.

Seibel: For instance, since your first abortive attempt at writing a compiler you've written lots of compilers. You must have learned some things about how to do that that enable you to do it successfully now.

Peyton Jones: Yes. Well, lots of things. Of course that was a compiler for an imperative language written in an imperative language. Now I'm writing a compiler for a functional language in a functional language. But a big feature of GHC, our compiler for Haskell, is that the intermediate language it uses is itself typed.

Seibel: And is the typing on the intermediate representation just carrying through the typing from the original source?

Peyton Jones: It is, but it's much more explicit. In the original source, lots of type inference is going on and the source language is carefully crafted so that type inference is possible. In the intermediate language, the type system is much more general, much more expressive because it's more explicit: every function argument is decorated with its type. There's no type *inference*, there's just type *checking* for the intermediate language. So it's an explicitly typed language whereas the source language is implicitly typed.

Type inference is based on a carefully chosen set of rules that make sure that it just fits within what the type inference engine can figure out. If you transform the program by a source-to-source transformation, maybe you've now moved outside that boundary. Type inference can't reach it any more. So that's bad for an optimization. You don't want optimizations to have to worry about whether you might have just gone out of the boundaries of type inference.

Seibel: So that points out that there are programs that are correct, because you're assuming a legitimate source-to-source transformation, which, if you had written it by hand, the compiler would have said, "I'm sorry; I can't type this."

Peyton Jones: Right. That's the nature of static type systems—and why dynamic languages are still interesting and important. There are programs you can write which can't be typed by a particular type system but which nevertheless don't "go wrong" at runtime, which is the gold standard—don't segfault, don't add integers to characters. They're just fine.

Seibel: So when advocates of dynamic and static typing bicker the dynamic folks say, "Well, there are lots of those programs—static typing gets in the way of writing the program I want to write." And then the fans of static typing say, "No, they exist but in reality it's not a problem." What's your take on that?

Peyton Jones: It's partly to do with simple familiarity. It's very like me saying I've not got a visceral feel for writing C++ programs. Or, you don't miss lazy evaluation because you've never had it whereas I'd miss it because I'm going to use it a lot. Maybe dynamic typing is a bit like that. My feeling—for what it's worth, given that I'm biased culturally—is that large chunks of programs can be perfectly well statically typed, particularly in these very rich type systems. And where it's possible, it's very valuable for reasons that have been extensively rehearsed.

But one that is less often rehearsed is maintenance. When you have a blob of code that you wrote three years ago and you want to make a systemic change to it—not just a little tweak to one procedure, but something that is going to have pervasive effects—I find type systems are incredibly helpful.

This happens in our own compiler. I can make a change to GHC, to data representations that pervade the compiler, and can be confident that I've found all the places where they're used. And I'd be very anxious about that in a more dynamic language. I'd be anxious that I'd missed one and shipped a compiler where somebody feeds in some data that I never had and it just fell over something that I hadn't consistently changed.

I suppose static types, for me, also perform part of my explanation of what the program *does*. It's a little language in which I can say something, but not too much, about what this program does. People often ask, "What's the equivalent of UML diagrams for a functional language?" And I think the best answer I've ever been able to come up with is, it's the type system. When an object-oriented programmer might draw some pictures, I'm sitting there writing type signatures. They're not diagrammatic, to be sure, but because they are a formal language, they form a permanent part of the program text and are statically checked against the code that I write. So they have all sorts of good properties, too. It's almost an architectural description of part of what your program does.

Seibel: So do you ever write a program that you know is correct but somehow falls outside the bounds of the type checker?

Peyton Jones: This comes up when you're doing generic programming, where you want to write functions that will take data of any type and just walk over it and serialize it, say. So that's a time when types can be a bit awkward and an untyped language is particularly straightforward. It couldn't be easier to write a serializer in an untyped language.

Now there's a small cottage industry of people describing clever typed ways of writing generic programs. I think such things are fascinating. But it's somehow just isn't as simple as writing it in a dynamically typed language. I'm trying to persuade John Hughes to write a paper for the *Journal of Functional Programming* on why static typing is bad. Because I think it would be very interesting to have a paper from John, who's a mainstream, strongly typed, very sophisticated functional programmer, who is now doing a lot of work in untyped Erlang, saying why static types are bad. I think he would write a very reflective and interesting paper. I don't know quite where we'll end up.

I think I would still say, "Where static typing fits, do it every time because it has just fantastic maintenance benefits." It helps you think about your program; it helps you write it, all that kind of stuff. But the fact that we keep generating more and more sophisticated type systems is an indication that we're trying to keep pushing the boundary out to say more in the world—to cover more programs. So the story hasn't finished yet.

The dependently typed programming people would say, "Ultimately the type system should be able to express absolutely anything." But types are funny things—types are like a very compact specification language. They say something about the function but not so much that you can't fit it in your head at one time. So an important thing about a type is it's kind of crisp. If it goes on for two pages, then it stops conveying all the information it should.

I think the direction I'd like to see things go is to have still crisp and compact types which are a little bit weak, precisely so that they can be crisp, along with invariants, perhaps stated in a rather richer language than the inferable type system, but which are still amenable to static checking. Something I'm working on in another project is to try to do static verification for pre- and post-conditions and data-type invariants.

Seibel: Similar to Design by Contract in Eiffel?

Peyton Jones: That's right. You'd like to be able to write a contract for a function like, "You give me arguments that are bigger than zero and I'll give you a result that is smaller than zero."

Seibel: How do you go about designing software?

Peyton Jones: I suppose I would say that usually the dominant problem when I'm thinking about writing a program—thinking about writing some new piece of GHC—is not how to get the idea into code. But it's rather, what is the idea?

To take an example, at the moment we're in mid-flight for moving GHC's back end, the code generation part, to refactor it in a new way. At the moment there's a step in the compiler that takes essentially a functional language and translates it into C--, which is an imperative language. And that's a pretty big step. It's called C-- because it's like a subset of C. But it's really meant to be a portable assembly language. And it's not printed out in ASCII—it's just an internal data type. So this step in the compiler is a function from a data structure representing a functional program to a data structure representing an imperative program. How do you make that step?

Well, I have a pretty complicated bit of code that does that at the moment. But a couple of days ago I realized that it could be separated into two parts: first transform it into a dialect of C--, which allows procedure calls—inside a procedure, you can call a procedure. Then translate *that* into a sub-language that has no calls—only has tail calls.

Then the name of the game is figuring out, just what is the data type? This C-- stuff, what is it? It's a data structure representing an imperative program.And as you make the second step, you walk over the program, looking at each bit, one at a time. So your focus of attention moves down the control flow, or perhaps back up through the control flow. A good data structure for representing that is called a "zipper"—which is a very useful purely functional data structure for moving the focus around a purely functional data structure.

Norman Ramsey at Harvard found a way to use this for walking around data structures that represent imperative control flow graphs. So he and I and John Dias then spent a while reengineering GHC's back end to adopt essentially this factored technology. And in doing so making it much more general so we can now use this same back end as a back end for other languages.

A lot of our discussion was essentially at the type level. Norman would say, "Here's the API,"—by giving a type signature—and I would say, "That looks way complicated, why is it like that?" And he'd explain why and I'd say, "Couldn't it be simpler this way." So we spent a lot of time to'ing and fro'ing at the level of describing types.

But a lot of the time it wasn't really about programming as such—it was about, what is the idea? What are we trying to do with this dataflow analysis, anyway? You try to say in a clear way what this step of the program is meant to do. So we spent quite a lot of time just being clear on what the inputs and the outputs are and working on the data types of the inputs and the outputs. Just getting the data types right, already you've said quite a lot about what your program does. A surprisingly large amount, in fact.

Seibel: How does thinking about the types relate to actually sitting down and coding? Once you sketch out the types can you sit down and write the code? Or does the act of writing the code feed back into your understanding of the types?

Peyton Jones: Oh, more the latter, yes. I'll start writing type signatures into a file right away. Actually I'll probably start writing some code that manipulates values of those types. Then I'll go back and change the data types. It's not a two-stage process where we say, "Now I've done the types, I can write the code."

If anything I'm a bit ill-disciplined about this. This comes from not working as part of a large team. You can do things when you're working on code that one person can still get their head around that you probably couldn't in a much bigger team.

Seibel: You mentioned that in this latest code upheaval in GHC, things got much more general. GHC is a big program that's evolved over time so you've had the chance to benefit from generality and the chance to pay the cost of over-generality. Have you learned anything about how to strike the balance between over- and under- generalization?

Peyton Jones: I think my default is not to write something very general to begin with. So I try to make my programs as *beautiful* as I can but not necessarily as *general* as I can. There's a difference. I try to write code that will do the task at hand in a way that's as clear and perspicuous as I can make it. Only when I've found myself writing essentially the same code more than once, then I'll think, "Oh, let's just do it once, passing some extra arguments to parameterize it over the bits that are different between the two."

Seibel: What is your actual programming environment? What tools do you use?

Peyton Jones: Oh, terribly primitive. I just sit there with Emacs and compile with GHC. That's just about it. There are profiling tools that come with our compiler and people often use those for profiling Haskell programs. And we do that for profiling the compiler itself. GHC dumps a lot of intermediate output so I can see what's going on.

Debugging, for me, is often, the compiler isn't generating good code so I'm eyeballing the state of its entrails. Or, take this little source program; compile it this far; look at that. That's debugging for me. It's seldom single-stepping through the program—it's more looking at values of different parts in compilation.

I don't even have any very sophisticated Emacs jiggery-pokery. Which some people do. There's also a whole world of people out there who are used to Visual Studio and Eclipse kind of IDEs. I think a cultural barrier to adoption of functional programming languages is partly that we haven't got the IDE story sorted out. There's a bit of a chicken-and-egg problem here. At the moment the chicken is getting busier—there's more interest in functional programming generally. I'm hoping that will provoke work on the egg. It's a lot of engineering to build an IDE for Haskell. Even with Visual Studio as a shell or Eclipse as a shell, there's quite a lot of work in making a plugin that's really smooth and does everything right.

Seibel: GHC has a read-eval-print loop, GHCI. Do you tend program Haskell interactively?

Peyton Jones: Actually, I tend to mostly edit and compile. But other people just live their whole lives in GHCI.

Seibel: When it comes to testing, I suppose one of the nice things about functional languages is when you want to test some little function in the bowels of your program, you just have to figure out what form is its input going to be.

Peyton Jones: Well, for me, if the input data is simple enough that you could do that, it's probably not going to be the problem with my program. The problem with my program is going to be some fairly humongous input program that GHC is trying to compile and getting the wrong answer for it.

Testing is, I think, frightfully important for writing down properties and QuickCheck properties are really useful—QuickCheck is a Haskell library for generating random tests for a function based on its type. But I was trying to think why I don't use QuickCheck—which is a very nice tool—more. I think it's because the situations that cause me trouble are ones that I would find it difficult to generate test data for. In any case, there are loads of people out there generating programs that make GHC barf in one way or another. That's what GHC's bug tracker is about.

So typically I'm starting with something that's not right, already. Maybe the compiler could just fall over altogether or reject a program when it shouldn't. Or it could just generate suboptimal code. If it's just generating bad code, I'll look at the code at various stages in the compilation pipeline and say, "It looks good then; it looks good then. Bah, it's gone bad here; what's gone wrong?"

Seibel: So how do you actually look at it?

Peyton Jones: GHC has flags that let you say, in rather a batch-dumpy kind of way, "Just print out various things."

Seibel: Built-in print statement debugging?

Peyton Jones: Yes. And it's aided by the fact that the structure is like most compilers: it has this top-level structure of a pipeline of things that happen. If something's gone wrong in the middle of one of these passes, then that could be a bit trickier. But I tend to use rather unsophisticated debugging techniques. Just show me the program before and after this pass. Aaah, I see what's going wrong. Or sometimes I don't see what's going wrong so then I might scatter a few unsafe `printf`s around to show me what's actually going on.

There are various debugging environments for Haskell—a summer student, Pepe Iborra, did a nice one earlier this year which now comes with GHC, which is an interactive debugger of some kind. Which I've not used very much yet. Partly because we haven't had one for so long, because it's less obvious how do you single-step a functional program.

It's been a kind of interesting research question of how you go about debugging functional programs for some time. It's a bit embarrassing that we can't tick that box in a straightforward way, but that makes it an interesting research problem.

That was the long way around of saying that I tend to use terribly crude debugging techniques with unsafe `printf`s. And I'm not very proud of that. But for a long time we didn't have anything else. At least as far as GHC is concerned, I've evolved mechanisms that mean that's the shortest path to completion for me.

Seibel: That seems to be a common story. It sort of makes you wonder about the utility of writing better debuggers if so many people get by with print statement debugging.

Peyton Jones: There's a cultural thing though. On the .NET platform with debuggers that people have put tens or hundreds of man-years into engineering, I think it's a qualitatively different experience. I think debuggers do require perhaps more engineering cycles to get to work well. But if you put them in, you do get something that is really quite remarkably more helpful.

Maybe the people that you've been mainly talking to are more in the academic software mold. And also perhaps have grown up with sophisticated debugging environments less. I wouldn't like to draw any general lessons. I certainly wouldn't wish to denigrate or downplay the importance of good debugging environments. Particularly in these rather complicated ecosystems where there are many, many, many layers of software. GHC is a very simple system compared to a full-on .NET environment with layers of DOMs and UMLs and I don't know what kind of goop. The real world gets so goopy that more mechanical support may well be really important.

Seibel: Another approach to getting correct software is to use formal proofs. What do you think about the prospect of that being useful?

Peyton Jones: Suppose you declare that your goal is for everything to have a machine-checked proof of correctness. It's not even obvious what that would mean. Mechanically proved against what? Against some specification. Well how do you write the specification? This is now meant to be a specification of *everything* the program does. Otherwise you wouldn't have proved that it does everything that it should do. So you must have a formal specification for everything it should do. Well now—how are you going to write that specification? You'll probably write it in a functional language. In which case, maybe that's your program.

I'm being a bit fast and loose here because you can say some things in specification languages that you can't say in programs like, "The result of the function is that *y* such that *y* squared equals *x*." That's a good specification for a square-root function but it's not very executable. Nevertheless, I think to try to specify *all* that a program should do, you get specifications that are themselves so complicated that you're no longer confident that they say what you intended.

I think much more productive for real life is to write down some *properties* that you'd like the program to have. You'd like to say, "This valve should never be shut at the same time as that valve. This tree should always be balanced. This function should always return a result that's bigger than zero." These are all little partial specifications. They're not complete specifications. They're just things that you would like to be true.

How do you write those down? Well, functional languages are rather good at that. In fact this is exactly what happens when you write a QuickCheck specification; you write down properties as Haskell functions. Say we want to check that `reverse` is its own inverse—well, you might write `checkreverse` with type list of A to bool. So `checkreverse` of `xs` is `reverse` of `reverse xs` equals `xs`. So this is a function that should always return true. That's what a property function is. But it's just written in the same language—so that's nice.

Now you might hope to do some static checking on this. It might be hard or easy. But even having the property written down in a formal way is a real help. You can test it by generating test data, which is, indeed, just what QuickCheck does.

So rather than trying to write down specifications for *all* that a program does I think it's much more productive to write down partial specifications. Perhaps multiple partial specifications. And then check them either by testing or by dynamic checks or by static checks. You never prove that your program is right. You just increase your confidence that it's right. And I think that's all that anybody ever does.

Seibel: So you define however many properties, covering the things you care about. And then you can choose to confirm that those properties actually hold either statically or dynamically, depending on what's actually feasible. Because we may not know how to statically check them all?

Peyton Jones: Right. But in a functional setting, you have a better chance. But we've still been dragging our feet a bit about demonstrating that. Nevertheless—step one is to write down these properties in the first place.

But I think the big thing is to get away from this monolithic, all-or-nothing story about specification and to say that you can do useful static and dynamic tests on partial specifications. These will increase your confidence in the correctness of your program and that is all you can possibly hope for.

Even the allegedly complete specifications miss out—you know, it has to work in .1 of a second. Or must fit in 10KB of memory. Resource things are often not covered. Or timing things. There's endless little stuff that means the program might actually not function as desired even though it meets its formal specification. So I think we're kidding ourselves to say we've actually proved the whole thing is completely right. Best thing to do is to acknowledge that and say we're improving our confidence—that's what we're doing. And that can start quite modestly—you might have improved your confidence by 75 percent with only 5 percent of the effort. That'd be good.

Seibel: Let's talk about concurrency a little bit. Guy Steele asked me to ask you: "Is STM going to save the world?"

Peyton Jones: Oh, no. STM is not going to save the world on its own. Concurrency, and parallel programming generally, is a many-faceted beast and I don't think it will be slain by a single bullet. I'm a diversifist when it comes to concurrency.

It's tempting to say, "Use one programming paradigm for writing concurrent programs and implement it really well and that's it;" people should just learn how to write concurrent programs using that paradigm. But I just don't believe it. I think for some styles of programming you might want to use message passing. For others you might want to use STM. For others data parallelism is much better. The programmer is going to need to grapple with more than one way to do it.

But if you ask me, is STM better than locks and condition variables? Now you're comparing like with like. Yes. I think it completely dominates locks and condition variables. So just forget locks and condition variables. For multiple program counters, multiple threads, diddling on shared memory on a shared-memory multicore: STM. But is that the only way to write concurrent programs? Absolutely not.

Seibel: A criticism I've heard of STM was that when it really gets down to it, optimistic concurrency won't allow as much concurrency as you hope. I think the claim was you can fairly easily get in these situations where you're really not making progress.

Peyton Jones: You do have to worry about starvation. My favorite example here is of one big transaction that keeps failing to commit because a little transaction gets in there and commits first. So an example would be a librarian who's reorganizing their library. They start optimistically reorganizing their library. And they've got two-thirds of the way through and an undergraduate comes along and borrows a book. Well, he commits his transaction successfully because the library reorganization hasn't committed. The librarian gets to the end and discovers, ah, I saw an inconsistent view of memory because the library changed while I was reorganizing it so I just have to go back and start again.

Seibel: In a locks-and-condition-variables program it would probably go the other way—the librarian would lock the library and nobody could check out books until it's completely reorganized. So you would probably look at this problem and immediately say, "We can't lock the library until we're done," disallowing checkouts so we have to come up with some hairier locking scheme.

Peyton Jones: Right. Make a little sub-library or something—put the commonly borrowed books out there so undergraduates can borrow them while you lock the main library and reorganize it or something. So now you've got to think of an application-specific strategy and now you've got to express it in some way. Well, the same problem arises in both cases—you need an application-specific strategy so you can reorganize the library despite not wanting to block out all sorts of borrowing. Once you've done the hard thinking about how you wish to do it, now you've got to express that. What is the medium in which to express it? STM is a clear win. It's just much better than locks and condition variables for expressing concurrent programs.

Seibel: What if I don't even want to allow for the possibility that someone comes in and looks for the 21st most-requested book and gets blocked? In the physical world you can imagine that when someone checks out a book we swap in a proxy for the book that the librarian then reorganizes and whenever a book comes back we put it back wherever the proxy is now. But you are modifying the library which seems, in an STM world, like it would cause the librarian to have to retry his whole transaction.

Peyton Jones: But there's something that stayed the same—the key on the book is guaranteed not to change somehow, right? So there's a number of ways you could do this. One is you could say, "What you do when you replace it with a proxy is you don't modify the library at all"—that's unchanged. What you do is you modify the book itself. And you don't modify its key field—you only modify its value field, where it's currently living. Now the index can be reorganized while the book is somewhere else. That's cool—and you can express that perfectly naturally.

With STM, at the end the librarian looks through all the memory locations that he has read and sees if they contain now the same values that they did when he read them. So the locations that he has read will include the key field of the book because that determined where he put it. But he hasn't read the contents of the book. So he'll say, "Ah, this book—does this key field still contain 73; oh, yes it does."

But I don't want to minimize the problem of starvation because it's a bit insidious. You need good profiling tools that point you at transactions that are failing to commit because they keep getting bumped so that, rather than the program just silently not doing very much, you get some feedback about it. The same is true of a lock-based program. I hate it when those hourglasses appear.

Seibel: I guess in locked-based programs we've just learned to try hold locks for as short a duration as possible since that will give us the least contention.

Peyton Jones: Right. But, of course, then it's harder to program. Finer-grained locking is tricky to get right. I think this is one of the huge wins of STM, is it gives you the fine granularity of very fine-grained locking along with very simple reasoning principles.

Here's a reasoning principle that STM gives you that locks absolutely do not. I'll establish my top-level invariants—I've got a bunch of bank accounts, the total sum of money in all the bank accounts added together is *N*. Money moves between bank accounts—that's all. So there's my invariant. Any transaction assumes that invariant at the beginning and restores it at the end. How do you reason that it does? We look at any one transaction that says, "Take three out of that one and put three into that one." Good, invariant maintained. How is my reasoning in that done? Purely sequential reasoning. Once I've described some top-level invariants, I can reason completely sequentially about each transaction separately.

Seibel: Because you have transaction isolation.

Peyton Jones: Because they are put in isolation. So that's really rather a powerful reasoning principle. Because it says you can use your sequential reasoning about imperative code despite the fact that the program's concurrent. You've got to establish what those top-level invariants are, but that's good for your soul, too. Because then you know what things you are trying to maintain. If you get an exception thrown in the middle of a transaction, that's cool, too—that can't destroy the invariants because the transaction is abandoned without effect. I think this is fabulous. Then reasoning about performance issues is a different level—you've guaranteed a certain sort of correctness; now you want to make sure you haven't got any performance holes. Those are harder to get at—at the moment I don't know anything better than profiling and directed feedback tools for doing that.

Seibel: It strikes me that while optimistic concurrency has been used from time to time in persistent databases, it's never really gotten a foothold there compared to lock-based concurrency.

Peyton Jones: Of course STM can be implemented in all sorts of ways—optimistic concurrency is only one of them. You can lock as you go, which is more like a pessimistic concurrency model.

Seibel: But there's also a reason that lock managers are the hairiest part of databases.

Peyton Jones: Right. So the thing about STM is you want to make sure that one person, or one team, gets to implement STM and everybody else gets to use it. You can pay them a lot of money and shut them in a small dark room for a year to try to make sure they do a really good job.

But then that work is usable by everybody through a very simple interface. That's what I think is nice about it. What I want to avoid is having that level of expertise in everybody's head. The example that I used at a talk I gave yesterday—this comes from Maurice Herlihy—is a double-ended queue: insert and delete elements.

A sequential implementation of a double-ended queue is a first-year undergraduate programming problem. For a concurrent implementation with a lock per node, it's a research paper problem. That is too big a step. It's absurd for something to be so hard. With transactional memory it's an undergraduate problem again. You simply wrap "atomic" around the insert and delete operations—job done. That's amazing, I think. It's a qualitative difference. Now the people who implement the STM, they'd have to make sure they atomically commit a bunch of changes to memory as one. That's not easy to do, just with compare and swaps. It can be done but you have to be careful about it.

And then if there are performance problems to do with starvation then you may need to do some application-level thinking about how to avoid that. But then you express the results of your application-level thinking, again using STM. I do think for that kind of program it's a leap forward.

There was one other thing I wanted to mention—this goes back to functional programming. STM, of course, has nothing directly to do with functional programming at all. It's really about mutating shared state—that doesn't sound very functional.

But what happened is this, I went to a talk given by Tim Harris about STM in Java. I'd never heard about STM before; I just happened to go to his talk. He was describing an STM in which he had "atomic" but really not much else. You could implement these atomic transactions.

I said, "Wow, that seems really neat. Ah, so you need to log every side effect on memory. Every load and store instruction. Gosh, well there are a lot of those in Java." But in Haskell there are practically none because they occur in this monadic setting. So loads and stores in Haskell are extremely explicit—programmers think of them as a big deal.

So I thought, "Oh, we should just try replicating this atomic memory stuff in Haskell because it would be a very cool feature to have." And off we went—I talked to Tim about how to do this. Before long, because of the kind of framework that we had—this kind of pure, rather sparer framework that we had—we'd invented `retry` and `orElse`. `Retry` is this mechanism that allows you to do blocking within a transaction and `orElse` is the bit that allows you to do choice within a transaction. Neither of these are things that had occurred to him or his colleagues in developing transactional memory for Java because the rest of their context was rather more complicated.

So they hadn't really thought much about blocking. Or maybe they just assumed that the way you do blocking was you say, atomically, "Only run this transaction when this predicate holds." But that's very noncompositional—supposing you wanted to get something out of one bank account and put it in another, well, what's the condition that the transaction can run under? Answer: well, if there's enough money in the first bank account and there's enough space in the second—let's say that they're limited at both ends. So that's a rather complicated condition to figure out. And it gets even more complicated if there's a third bank account involved. It's very noncompositional—you have to look inside the methods and pull all their preconditions out to the front.

That's what he had and it kind of worked fine for small programs but clearly wasn't very satisfactory. So in a Haskell context we came up with this `retry`, `orElse` thing which we've since transplanted back into the mainstream imperative context and they're busy doing `retry` and `orElse` as well. That's great.

Seibel: So there's nothing actually inherent about Haskell that enabled that concept? It was just that you were able to think of it?

Peyton Jones: That's right. There was less crap, basically, so the cool idea stood out in higher relief. It became more disgusting that there was no way to do blocking without losing the abstraction. That's what led us to `retry` and `orElse`. I think a really good place for functional programming to be, or a role for it to play, is as a kind of laboratory in which to examine the beast. And then ideas can feed back. And this STM was a particularly clear example because there was a transition in both directions. Here there was a loop that actually got closed, which I thought was lovely.

Seibel: What's your desert-island list of books for programmers?

Peyton Jones: Well, you should definitely read Jon Bentley's *Programming Pearls*. Speaking of pearls, Brian Hayes has a lovely chapter in this book *Beautiful Code* entitled, "Writing Programs for 'The Book'" where I think by "The Book" he means a program that will have eternal beauty. You've got two points and a third point and you have to find which side of the line between the two points this third point is on. And several solutions don't work very well. But then there's a very simple solution that just does it right.

Of course, Don Knuth's series, *The Art of Computer Programming*. I don't think it was ever anything I read straight through; it's not that kind of book. I certainly referred to it a lot at one stage. Chris Okasaki's book *Purely Functional Data Structures*. Fantastic. It's like Arthur Norman's course only spread out to a whole book. It's about how you can do queues and lookup tables and heaps without any side effects but with good complexity bounds. Really, really nice book. Everyone should read this. It's also quite short and accessible as well. *Structure and Interpretation of Computer Programs*. Abelson and Sussman. I loved that. And *Compiling with Continuations*, Andrew Appel's book about how to compile a functional program using continuation passing style. Also wonderful.

Books that were important to me but I haven't read for a long time: *A Discipline of Programming* by Dijkstra. Dijkstra is very careful about writing beautiful programs. These ones are completely imperative but they have the "Hoare property" of rather than having no obvious bugs they obviously have no bugs. And it gives very nice, elegant reasoning to reason about it. That's a book that introduced me for the first time to reasoning about programs in a pretty watertight way. Another book that at the time made a huge impression on me was Per Brinch Hansen's book about writing concurrent operating systems. I read it lots of times.

Seibel: Do you still program a lot?

Peyton Jones: Oh yes. I write some code every day. It's not actually every day, but that's my mantra. I think there's this horrible danger that people who are any good at anything get promoted or become more important until they don't get to do the thing they're any good at anymore. So one of the things I like about working here and working in research generally is that I can still work on the compiler that I've been working on since 1990.

It's a big piece of code and there are large chunks of it that I'm really the person who knows most about it.

How much code do I write? Some days I spend the whole day programming, actually staring at code. Other days, none. So maybe, on average, a couple hours a day, certainly. Programming is such fun. Why would you ever want not to do it? Furthermore it keeps you honest—it's a good reality check to use your own compiler and to use the language that you advocate as well.

Seibel: And you still enjoy programming just as much as when you started?

Peyton Jones: Oh, yes, yes. That's the most fun thing. I think most programmers have the feeling that "there must be a good way to do this." One of the nice things about working in research is that instead of some manager standing over me saying, "This has to be done this week—just get it done," I can sit and look at something and say, "There must be a right way to do this."

So I spend a lot of time refactoring and moving interfaces around and writing new types or even just rewriting a whole blob to try to make it right. GHC is pretty large—it's not large by industrial standards; it's large by functional programming standards—it's about 80,000 lines of Haskell, maybe a bit more. And it's long-lived—it's 15 years old now. The fact that it's still actively developed is indicative that chunks have got rewritten. There are no untouchable bits. So it's both challenging and good fun to look at something and think, "What is the right way to do this?" And often I'll hold off for weeks on something but I just can't think of a nice way to do it. But that's tantalizing. Because there has to be a nice way.

Seibel: In those weeks, what happens?

Peyton Jones: Oh, I'm thinking about it in the back of my mind. And sometimes I'll have a go at it—I sort of run up the hill. And then I remember why it was so complicated and then usually some other displacement activity takes place. So sometimes I run up this hill several times. Sometimes I'm thinking about it in the background. And sometimes I think, "Well, time's up—just got to do something now." And maybe it's not quite as beautiful as it could be.

Seibel: Is it the kind of thing that you wake up in the morning and you say, "Ah, I've got it!" Or is it that you decide to take another run at it and this time you get to the top of the hill?

Peyton Jones: It's more like that. It's seldom that I just having a blinding insight in the morning. Another thing that happens as a researcher is you have the opportunity to reflect on what you've done and write it up. So quite often if something interesting has happened I try to write a paper about it. So an example of that is there's a paper called "The Secrets of the GHC Inliner," which is really a very implementation-oriented paper that describes some implementation techniques that we developed for a particular part of GHC's innards which we thought might be reusable for others. The chance that you have as an academic is to abstract from the code that, the fourth time around, you've finally kicked into a shape that feels good, and write about it so other people can reuse that same technique.

Seibel: What is programming to you? Do you think of yourself as a scientist or an engineer or a craftsman? Or something else entirely?

Peyton Jones: Have you read Fred Brooks's paper about this, the one called, "The Computer Scientist as Toolsmith"? I reread it recently. It's very nice. I think it's good to remember that we're concerned with building things. I think that's why programming is so interesting.

At the same time I'm really keen on trying to extract *principles* of enduring value. I have a paper about how to write a good paper or give a good research talk and one of the high-order bits is, don't describe an artifact. An artifact is an implementation of an idea. What is the idea, the reusable brain-thing that you're trying to transfer into the minds of your listeners? There's something that's useful to them. It's the business of academics, I think, to abstract reusable ideas from concrete artifacts. Now that's still not science in the sense of discovering laws. But it is a kind of abstraction into reusable thought-stuff out of the morass of real life that I think is very important.

Seibel: So what about engineering vs. craft. Should we expect to be like the guys who build bridges where, for the most part, bridges don't fall down? Or are we really more like the guys making pottery—except the pottery is just incredibly complex—where all you can do is apprentice yourself to someone and learn from them how they do it?

Peyton Jones: It's a bit of a false dichotomy. It's not truly an either-or choice. One thing that is hard, even for professional software engineers and developers, is to viscerally grok the size of the artifacts on which we work. You're looking at the Empire State Building through a 1-foot-square porthole, so it's difficult to have a real feel for how gigantic the structure you're looking at is. And how it's interconnected.

How big is GHC? I don't have a feel for that in the same sense I have a feel for how big this building is. So I don't think we're anywhere near where the engineers are with building bridges. Their design patterns have now been boiled down to where they can pretty much be sure that the bridge isn't going to fall down. We're nowhere near that with software. But I don't think that that's a reason for saying we just shouldn't worry about it at all.

In fact I think it's somewhere where functional programming has a lot to offer. Because I think fundamentally it enables you to build more robust structures. Structures that are easier to comprehend and test and reason about. And here is something that I think functional programmers are lagging on: we talk about reasoning about functional programs but we don't *do* it very much. I'd like to see much more by way of tools that understand Haskell programs and formally reason about them and give you guarantees beyond their types. We stand on a higher platform and we should be able to go further.

So that's about saying the material should become more robust. The more robust your materials, the less you need to concentrate on the minutia instead of the larger-scale structures. Of course that will just make us more ambitious to build larger structures until we get to the point where they fall apart again.

I think that's sort of an invariant. As soon as you can do it, you stretch to the point where you can't do it anymore. I suppose I don't really see it as, is it this or is it that? There will always be a strong crafty element, I think, just because we'll stretch our ambition. In the case of engineering structures, there are physical limits on how far you can stretch. Nobody's going to build a bridge that traverses the Atlantic any time soon. And that really might fall down if you built it. But that's not the reason people won't build it—it's just because it'd be too expensive. Whereas nowadays, with software, once you can build bridges over the Channel pretty quickly and cheaply, well then, that becomes a done deal and we now think that's pretty cheap so we'll now try the Atlantic. And now it falls apart again.

Seibel: Guy Steele was saying how Moore's Law has been true for his whole career and he suspects it won't be true for his son's whole career and was speculating a bit about what that's going to do to programming. I wonder will we eventually have to stop just saying, "If we can build a bridge over the Channel, we can build one over the Atlantic"?

Peyton Jones: No, no. Software's different I think. Because if you write software that's ten times as big that doesn't mean you have to run it on a computer that's ten times as fast. The program counter spends its time in a small portion of the code. Ninety percent of its time is spent in ten percent of the code or something. So the parts that are performance critical may be a relatively small part of the program.

It's true that what tends to happen is you slap abstraction on abstraction on abstraction and before you know it pressing a single button on the screen a great number of things happen all the way down the chain before you finally get to some registers being moved.

So we may have to work on ways of collapsing out those layers by sophisticated compiler transformations so not so much happens. The abstraction boundary may be useful for people but machines don't care. So I don't think just because we may reach the boundaries of what computers can do that necessarily software will immediately halt from getting more complicated. Because by that time they'll be pretty fast anyway. I think the primary limitation on software is not the speed of computers but our ability to get our heads around what it's supposed to do.

Seibel: What do you enjoy about programming?

Peyton Jones: For me, part of what makes programming fun is trying to write programs that have an intellectual integrity to them. You can go on slapping mud on the side of a program and it just kind of makes it work for a long time but it's not very satisfying. So I think a good attribute of a good programmer, is they try to find a beautiful solution. Not everybody has the luxury of being able to not get the job done today because they can't think of a beautiful way to do it.

But I really think it's a funny medium because it's so malleable. You can do virtually anything with it. But that means you can build ugly things as well as beautiful things and things that will be completely unmaintainable and undurable. I sometimes feel a bit afraid about the commercial world with, on the one hand, the imperatives of getting it done because the customer needs it next week and, on the other hand, the sheer breadth rather than depth of the systems that we build.

Systems are filled with so much goop—in order to build an ASP.NET web service-y thing you need to know about this API and this tool and you need to write in three different languages and you need to know about Silverlight and LINQ and you can go on doing acronyms forever. And each of them has a fat book that describes it.

This is a tension I don't know how to resolve. These are useful systems—they're not designed by accident. Each of them is there for a reason and each of them has a smart person who's thinking hard about how this thing should be architected. But nevertheless, each, individually, has a broad interface. It may or may not be deep but it's certainly broad. There's a lot of stuff you need to just have in your head. It's like learning a language—a human language—there's a large vocabulary.

For me, that's no fun. I never learned my multiplication tables. I always worked them out from first principles every time and I just developed enough tricks that I could do it quickly enough. When you do seven nines I still have to go, oh, seven nines, oh, seven tens and subtract, so it's sixty-three. Whereas other people just learnt them. And that's a relatively small thing. So I hate things were you just have to learn these big things. So instinctively I back away from these big goopy things. But at the same time I acknowledge that they're useful and important in practice. The question in my mind is, if you were able to take a bit longer to design some of these things, could they be designed with smaller, less complicated, and less ad hoc interfaces?

Seibel: Sometimes it seems that it's exactly *because* each of these blobs has some smart person or people working on it and each smart person wants their own little playground to play in, that things get so complicated.

Peyton Jones: I'm sure there's an element of that. But to put a more positive construction on it, if you like, it's a big, complicated world and there's a lot to get done. If you had a grand Olympian vision—if you had a very large brain and enormous throughput—you might be able to do something with less overlap and more overall coherence.

But in practice we have to factor these problems into little chunks. And then the little chunks each have somebody who looks after it and who's conditioned by the things they've done before and their heritage. So maybe they design something within that space that may not be as good as it could possibly be—they're pressed for time. And certainly by the time you look at the combination of everything it's maybe quite a lot less good than it could possibly be. And then before you know it you're locked into a legacy problem—that's another reason that things are not as good as they could possibly be.

So there's a tremendous legacy ball and chain that's being dragged around. It's one of the nice things about Haskell. When I gave a retrospective on Haskell at, I think it was POPL 2004 or something, I put up a slide that said one of the things we've learned to do in Haskell is to "avoid success at all costs." This is clearly a sort of meme because people remember that phrase and they quote it back to me.

It has a grain of truth in it because it means by not being too successful, too early, we've been able to morph Haskell quite a lot during its life. And part of the reason that I'm feeling a bit manic at the moment is because Haskell has become more successful and so I get more bug reports, more feature requests. And more people saying, "Don't break my program please." That didn't use to happen.

Seibel: You've mentioned writing beautiful code a couple of times. What are the characteristics of beautiful code?

Peyton Jones: Tony Hoare has this wonderful turn of phrase in which he says your code should obviously have no bugs rather than having no obvious bugs. So for me I suppose beautiful code is code that is obviously right. It's kind of limpidly transparent.

Seibel: What about those little jewels of code that you almost have to puzzle out how they work but once you do, it's amazing. Are those also beautiful?

Peyton Jones: Sometimes to say that it's obviously right doesn't mean that you can see that it's right without any mental scaffolding. It may be that you need to be told an insight to figure out why it's right. If you look at the code for an AVL tree, if you didn't know what it was trying to achieve, you really wouldn't have a clue why those rotations were taking place. But once you know the invariant that it's maintaining, you can see, ah, if we maintain that invariant then we'll get log lookup time. And then you look at each line of code and you say, "Ah, yes, it maintains the invariant." So the invariant is the thing that gave you the insight to say, "Oh, it's obviously right."

I agree completely that just looking at the bare code may not be enough. And it's not a characteristic, I think, of beautiful code, that you should be able to just look at the bare code and see why it's right. You may need to be told why. But after you have that, now with that viewpoint, that invariant, that understanding of what's going on, you can see, oh yeah, that's right.

Seibel: Does that put an upper bound on how big a piece of software can be and still be beautiful?

Peyton Jones: I don't know if it's a bound on its size. The insights that you need in order to reassure yourself that it's right, or at least right-ish, are along the lines of being more confident that it's correct. Any really, really big piece of software is bound to have shortcomings or indeed outright things that you just know are wrong with it. But it's not economic to fix them at the moment. It's certainly true of GHC and it's definitely true of Microsoft's software.

But what makes big software manageable is having some global invariants or big-picture statements about what it's supposed to do and what things are supposed to be true. So, to take GHC as another example, having this invariant that each of these intermediate programs should be well typed.

That can be checked, actually, at runtime if you like. That's quite a powerful invariant about what's going on. So I'm not sure it's really necessarily to do with size.

Certainly interconnectedness makes big programs eventually crumble under their own weight. Sometimes one of the luxuries that you get from working in research is that you can sometimes take a chunk of code and simply rewrite it in the light of your improved insights into what you were trying to achieve and how you might try to achieve it. We talked about this business of refactoring GHC's back end. If I was working in a more commercial setting, I might not be able to afford to do that. But I'm hoping that it will make GHC more maintainable and understandable in the long term.

Is there an upper bound on the size? I don't know. I rather suspect that as long as we can go on building good abstractions we can keep building bridges across the Atlantic. We have software that works—not perfectly, but surprisingly well considering how big it is.

Seibel: So the question is, can you build an edifice that's that large, and works, and is also beautiful.

Peyton Jones: It's hard for it to maintain its beauty. Bits are often beautiful or at least acceptably non-ugly when they're first built. In the face of protracted life—maintenance—it's quite difficult to maintain that. That's the worst thing about long-lived programs . . . that they gradually become ugly. So there's no moment at which they become disfigured but nevertheless after a while they just become crappy.

Seibel: And is the only way out to say, "OK, this thing has lived long enough, start over"?

Peyton Jones: I think that eventually you have to reengineer chunks of it. And if you can afford to reengineer a bit as you go along, then—if you don't do anything for ten years then the result may just be so daunting that you think, "I just have to throw it away and start again." If you can afford to reengineer a bit as you go along, like the human cells regenerating themselves—that's what I hope is happening to GHC.

The most depressing thing about life as a programmer, I think, is if you're faced with a chunk of code that either someone else wrote or, worse still, you wrote yourself but you no longer dare to modify. That's depressing.

CHAPTER

8

Peter Norvig

Peter Norvig is a broad thinker and a hacker at heart. He once wrote a program to find in Google's search logs series of three consecutive searches by the same user that, when put together, made a haiku (one of the most memorable: "java ECC / java elliptical curve / playboy faq").

On his web site Norvig has links to the usual stuff: books and papers he's written, slides from talks he's given, and various bits of his code. But there are also links to items he's had published in McSweeney's Quarterly Concern, his witty recounting of writing a program to generate the world's longest palindromic sentence, and his "Gettysburg Powerpoint Presentation," a send-up of Microsoft's PowerPoint software, which has been cited by Edward Tufte and which appears on the first page of results if you Google "PowerPoint."

He is now the Director of Research at Google, after having been the Director of Search Quality. Prior to that he had been the head of the Computational Sciences Division at NASA Ames Research Center and before that, an early employee at the late-'90s Internet startup Junglee. He won the NASA Exceptional Achievement Award in 2001 and is a Fellow of the American Association for Artificial Intelligence and the Association for Computing Machinery.

Between Google, NASA, and Junglee, Norvig has experience with both the "hacker" and "engineer" approaches to building software and talks in this interview about the advantages and disadvantages of each. As a former computer-

science professor and now an insider at one of the biggest industrial software shops in the world, he also has an interesting perspective on the relation between academic computer science and industrial practice.

Other topics in our conversation included how programming has changed in recent years, why no design technique can make up for not knowing what you're doing, and why NASA might be better off with less-reliable but cheaper software.

Seibel: When did you start programming?

Norvig: In high school. We had a PDP-8, I think it was, at my high school, and there was a class I took—we started in BASIC programming and I went from there.

Seibel: What year would that have been?

Norvig: I graduated high school in '74, so it must have been '72 or '73. I remember a couple of things, going back to those early days. I remember the teacher trying to teach shuffling of a deck of cards. Her algorithm was, use a random-number generator to pick two locations and then swap them and keep a bit vector that said, these were swapped, and keep going until they're all swapped. I remember my reaction being, "That's stupid. That's gotta be the stupidest thing in the world. It could take forever because there could be one pair that you never happen to choose." I didn't know enough then to say it's *n* squared when it could have been order *n*. But I knew that that was just wrong. Then I was able to come up with, I think, the Knuth algorithm of swapping from 0 to 52 and then from 0 to 51 and so on—an order *n* algorithm. And I remember the teacher defending her approach. That helped me think, "Well, maybe I have an aptitude for this programming stuff." It also helped me say, "Maybe teachers don't really know everything."

Seibel: Was it as soon as she described it that you just said, "Wow, this is wrong"? Or did you play with it for a while and then say, "Gosh it seems like we're doing a lot of work here"?

Norvig: I think I noticed right away. It's hard to know what I was really thinking back then but I think right away I noticed there's a finite possibility that this might not terminate. I'm not sure I knew as much about the expected runtime.

I also remember finding my father's back issues of *Scientific American* in the attic and going through them. There was this article by Christopher Strachey on software engineering in which he said that people are going to use these higher-order languages. And he had invented this language that there was never a compiler for—it was a paper language. And he said, "I'm going to write a checkers program using this language." I remember reading that—it was the first nontrivial program I had ever read because in school we were just learning how to shuffle and so on. I read it again recently and the first thing I noticed was that there's a bug in it. And it was great because you figure this is Christopher Strachey, he should know what he's doing, and it's *Scientific American*, they've got editors and so on—they should probably get those bugs out. But in the prose it says there's a function `make-move` which takes a board position and returns a move and then you look in the code and there's `make-move` and it takes a board position and an extra parameter. Apparently they wrote the prose first and then they wrote the implementation. And they found out you can't search infinitely deep so they added an extra parameter which was depth of search and you recurse down to a certain level and then you stop. They had added that in afterwards and hadn't gone back and fixed the documentation.

Seibel: So that was the first interesting code you read; what was the first interesting program you wrote?

Norvig: I guess it was probably the Game of Life. It was actually an assignment for the class. I quickly did the assignment, and of course then we didn't have the nice display screens. I didn't have my 30-inch monitor—I had the teletype with the yellow paper. I said, "This is a waste, printing out one small field"—they probably wanted us to do a ten-by-ten field—"and then printing out the next one and the next one." So I said, "Let's print out five generations in a row." And I remember that you couldn't have three-dimensional arrays in BASIC, and for some reason I couldn't even have a bunch of two-dimensional arrays. It's like they ran out of memory or something. So I had to figure out how am I going to have five or six across of these two-dimensional arrays, and that's when I discovered bit fields.

Seibel: So given the constraints on memory, you rolled your own storage for that much data. Had you been taught about bit arrays and figured out how to apply them, or did you go digging through the manual and discovered, "Oh, look, here's this PEEK and POKE" or whatever it was?

Norvig: Well, I was storing a zero or one in each of these locations, and I needed to store more stuff somewhere, and I said, "Oh, store other numbers there." In fact, I don't even remember if I did bit store. I might've done digits—decimal rather than binary—because the binary stuff hadn't really been exposed to us in an interesting way. And then I got to add in things, like, is it repeating and if so, with what cycle. You couldn't do that when you were just keeping one previous generation.

Seibel: When you were coming up as a programmer, did you do things specifically to improve your skill as a programmer, or did you just program?

Norvig: I think I just programmed. Certainly I would do things because they were fun. Especially when I was a grad student and I was less beholden to schedules. I'd say, "Oh, here's an interesting problem. Let's see if I can solve that." Not because it's progress on my thesis, but just because it was fun.

Seibel: And you studied computers in college but didn't major in computer science, right?

Norvig: When I started, the computer classes were part of the applied-math department. By the time I graduated there actually was a computer-science department, but I stuck with math as my major. It felt like doing all the requirements for a computer-science major was like majoring in IBM. You had to learn their assembly language, you had to learn their 360 operating system, and so on. That didn't seem like much fun. There were some courses that I liked and I took those, but I didn't want to go through all the requirements.

After college I worked for two years, for a software company in Cambridge. And after two years I said, "It took me four years to get sick of school and only two years to get sick of work, maybe I like school twice as much."

Seibel: What were you doing for them?

Norvig: Their main product was a software-design tool set, and they also did software consulting of various kinds. The founders had worked at Draper Labs in Cambridge on the *Apollo* mission and other things like that; they had air force connections and they were a government contractor. They had this idea of how software should be designed. I never believed in the whole idea, but it was fun.

I remember one of the projects we had there, at this company, was to write a flowchart drawer. The idea was that it would parse your program and generate a flowchart for it. Which was perfect because that's the way people always use flowcharts. You're supposed to write them ahead of time but you really never do—you write them after the fact. And it was clever in that it had a sort of partial grammar so you could take a program that wasn't even quite syntactically correct and it would gloss over the parts that it couldn't parse. It would have to know how to parse the IF statements because those made different blocks and so on but the other stuff it just said, "Well, whatever is there just throw it into a block." We got this contract to generate this thing and they specified that they wanted to run it on a Unix system. So we borrowed a machine at MIT and used all the Unix tools, yacc and stuff, for the compiler. And at the last minute they said, "No, we're going to install it on a VMS system." So all of the sudden, yacc wasn't there. But we said, "That's OK, we don't need it—we just needed it to generate the tables and that's done."

Seibel: As long as your grammar never changes, you're OK.

Norvig: Right, and so we delivered it and they were happy and then—of course—the grammar changed. And we didn't have access to any Unix machines anymore. So I ended up having to patch the grammar by understanding the tables and saying, "Here's a jump to this other state—OK, I'll invent a new state here and jump to that one instead."

Seibel: And was that really the right solution—did you ever consider just writing a new parser?

Norvig: I probably should have. But, you know, it was just this one little fix.

Seibel: And you didn't get caught in the trap of every three weeks they come around with a new change to the grammar?

Norvig: Well, then I went off to grad school. Somebody else had the problem and I don't know what happened.

Seibel: Not your problem anymore. So you got your PhD. Is there anything that you wish you had done differently about how you learned to program?

Norvig: I ended up in industrial settings, so maybe I would've wished to have done more of that earlier on. I did learn to do it, but I was in school and in grad school for a long time. That was a lot of fun, too, so I don't have any regrets.

Seibel: What were the things you had to learn about industrial programming?

Norvig: About having schedules, and keeping team members and customers and managers happy. When you're a grad student, you don't have to do that; just show up to your adviser every now and then.

I guess the biggest change was going from one person to a team and figuring out how those kinds of interactions work. That's something you don't normally get in school. I guess some of the schools are starting to bring that into the curriculum more. When I was in school, working as a team was called cheating.

Seibel: For people who are going into industry, are there other skills, beyond just the ability to write code, that people should develop?

Norvig: Getting along with people is the main thing. Being able to understand the customer is important: to know what it is you want to build and whether what you have is right. Being able to interact with them and then interact with your teammates. And interact with people higher up in the company and your customers when you go out and see them. There are all different social relations and they require different skills.

Seibel: Has programming become a more social activity than it used to be?

Norvig: I think so. I think the computer used to be more segregated. And in the old days it was mostly batch processing, so the interface was so much simpler. It was possible to do this kind of waterfall design where you said,

"The input is going to be this deck of cards, and the output is going to be a report that has this number in this column."

It probably wasn't a very good idea to specify it that way. Probably right from the start you should have had more interaction with the customer. But it seemed more separable. Now everything seems more fluid and interactive so it makes more sense to say, "Rather than have a complete specification from the start, just get customers in the room and start brainstorming."

Seibel: And do you remember any particular *aha!* moments where you noticed the difference between working on something by yourself and working on a team?

Norvig: I don't know if it was so much moments, but just this realization that you can't do everything yourself. I think a lot of programming is being able to keep as much as you can inside your head, but that only goes so far, at least in my head. Then you have to rely on other people to have the right abstractions so that you can use what they have. I started thinking about it in terms of, "How is this likely done?" rather than, "I know how this was done because I did it." If I were to have done this, how would I have done it? I hope that it's like that, and if it's not, figure out why not, and then figure out how to use it.

Seibel: Do you think that learning to work on teams that way also enables you to actually work on bigger things even by yourself when you're sort of a team spread across time?

Norvig: I think that's true and that's certainly something I see in the younger programmers that are coming out now. Another difference between now and then is it seems like it's much more assembling pieces now rather than writing everything from scratch. Now, for a school assignment, someone says, "OK, I needed a website, so I used Ruby on Rails for this, and I used Drupal for that part, and then I had this Python script, and then I downloaded this statistical routine," and it's all scripting to put together these pieces rather than writing everything from scratch. So I think understanding interfaces and how they go together is more important than all the details of the insides of these packages.

Seibel: And do you think that changes the kind of people who can be successful at programming now?

Norvig: I think the people that are really successful are the same—at least that's what I see around here. But, yeah, it is a little bit more of, "Can I quickly get an understanding of what I need," and less of, "I need complete understanding." I think some of it is bravado, this willingness to say, "I'm just going to go ahead and do it," the fearlessness of saying, "I don't understand everything that's going on, but I went into the documentation and I learned these three things. I tried it and it worked, so I'm just going to go ahead." That gets you to a certain point, but I think to really be a good programmer, you can't just do that. You have to understand a little bit more, and say, "Is it safe, what I'm doing here? Or what are the failure cases? Sure, I tried it once and it worked, but is it always going to work? How do I write test cases to show that and to understand it a little better, and then once I've done that, can I extract what I've done and publish a new tool that other people can use because I've put these pieces together in a certain way."

Seibel: How did you like to work on a team when you were a programmer? Is it better to take the problem and split it up so everybody gets their piece? Or do you like the XP model of pair-program everything and everybody owns all the code collectively?

Norvig: I guess it's more break it up. Steve Yegge's got this "Good Agile, Bad Agile" piece. I think he's about right. Ten percent of the time it is a really good idea to sit down together because you want that shared understanding. I think most of the time you're not going to be as effective.

If you have two good programmers, it's better for them to work independently and then debug each other's work afterwards rather than to say, "We'll take a 50 percent hit just for that added set of eyes."

I think it is important to get together when you're figuring out what it is you want to do both in terms of brainstorming what is the problem we're trying to solve and what is the functionality going to be here? You don't even know what the product is before you start. That you really want to do together. Then you get to the point of saying, "OK, now we know what we want to do. How are we going to divide it up?" That you want to do together. Once you have a pretty good idea, I think you're better off spending most of the time on your own. You want feedback, so I think you should require every piece of code to be reviewed by another set of eyes, but it doesn't have to be real-time, when you're writing it.

I remember the IBM master-programmer idea, and that just seemed like the dumbest thing I have ever heard of. Why would anybody want to subject themselves to being a gopher for the one real programmer?

Seibel: I'm surprised you think the master-programmer model is such a dumb idea. In your "Teach Yourself Programming in Ten Years" essay you make the point that programming is a skill that, like many skills, probably takes about a decade to really master. And lots of crafts had master/journeymen/apprentice kind of hierarchies. So maybe nobody *wants* to be the apprentice, but maybe it isn't crazy to say that somebody who's been through that decade-long learning experience should be doing different work than someone who's fresh out of school.

Norvig: I think the best part of the apprentice approach is that you get to watch the master, and I would like to see more of that. So I guess that's another use of pair programming. I can see that it'd be really good, if you were inexperienced, to watch somebody who's much more experienced. Particularly for the types of things that aren't taught as much, like debugging skills. Anybody can learn algorithms and so on, but they don't really teach debugging and watching someone, and saying, "Wow, I never thought of doing that," that's really useful.

But I think part of the reasons why you had master and apprentice is because the materials were rarer. When you were doing goldsmithing, there's only so much gold. Or when the surgeon's operating, there's only one heart, and so you want the best person on that and you want the other guys just helping. With coding, it's not like that. You've got plenty of terminals. You've got plenty of keyboards. You don't have to ration it.

Seibel: Speaking of things that aren't taught as much, you've been both an academic and in industry; do you feel like academic computer science and industrial programming meet in the right place?

Norvig: It's a big question. I don't think there's a lot of waste in computer-science curriculum. I think that it's mostly very good stuff to know. I think going to school is useful, but it's not everything that you need to be successful in the industry or to build systems. I do think that curriculum in many schools has been slow to adapt. There are a number of places where that comes into play: working in a team is not taught so much in school. This idea of being able to put the pieces together is not really taught there, but somehow the kids pick it up anyway, so maybe that's OK. At Google we're certainly interested in this large-scale cloud computing, parallel computing, and so forth. That's not taught so much, although I think there's a lot of interest in it. So I think they lag behind a little bit, but I think it's still useful.

Seibel: And are there any areas where academics are out in front of industry? Where industry is ignoring good stuff about how we ought to build software.

Norvig: I think to some degree. Probably the best example was the model checking where Intel wasn't really paying much attention and then they had this big recall and they lost a lot of money because they had a bug in their multiply. And then they started to pay attention, and they went to an academic and said, "What can you do to help us?" So there actually was something there. And now it's an integral part of what they do, so that was a good example. It seems like programming languages, probably not so much. There's a lot of work going on but you don't see a big impact of the newer programming languages. Operating systems, a little bit. We're supporting this RAD Lab at Berkeley with Dave Patterson and so on. They have some good ideas—how to make reliable systems. But it's certainly the case that industry has the larger, bigger problems. They may not have all the answers to them—but they're hitting them harder than in the university setting.

Seibel: So you don't think there are any ideas floating around academia that haven't been picked up by industry simply because people resist certain kinds of change—maybe a generation of self-taught PHP programmers are never going to warm to Haskell even if it might be a better way to write software?

Norvig: I guess I'm pretty skeptical. I think that if there were real advantages, people would be taking advantage of them. I don't think it's a perfect information market where everything instantly moves to the optimal solution, but I think it approximates that. Academics may be not seeing the whole problem that the industry has to deal with. And part of it is an education problem, but if you have a bunch of programmers who don't understand what a monad is and haven't taken courses in category theory, there's a gap.

And part of it's this legacy of we've got all these systems and you can't just throw them out all at once, so there's a transition. I'm sure there are places where industry should be more forward-looking about saying, "Sure, we can't make that transition today, but we should have a plan to say where are we going to be in ten years? It's not going to be where we are now and how do we get there?"

But you want improvements in areas that are going to make a big impact. And I think a lot of the times the level that programming languages are looking at is maybe too low a level to have as big an impact as language designers think it's going to. So if they say, "Oh look, in my shiny new language, these six lines of code become two lines of code." Well yeah, that's nice, and I guess that makes you more productive and it's easier to debug and maintain and so on. But maybe the code that you write is just a small part of the whole production system, and really the big headache is updating your data every day, and scraping the Web and getting this new data in, and putting it in the right format. So you have to remember that you're solving a very small part of the overall problem and that means there has to be a big barrier to make it worthwhile to make a switch.

Seibel: So leaving aside the utility language research, you feel like we have come a ways since computer science was like majoring in IBM.

Norvig: Yeah. I think it's a good curriculum now, and it's depressing that it's not being taken up by many students. Enrollments are down. Certainly there is a class of people who just love computers or computer design so much that that's where they end up. We're holding onto that group. But then there's a bunch of the best and the brightest who are going into physics or biology or something because those are the hottest fields. And then there's a bunch who are saying, "Well, I kind of like computers but there's no future in it because all of the jobs are outsourced to India anyway, so I'm going to do prelaw or something else so I can get a job." And I think that's a shame. I think they've been misinformed.

Seibel: You mean it's a shame because you think a lot of those people would enjoy being programmers, or because we need them?

Norvig: Both. Many people could enjoy lots of different things and if they enjoy two equally I don't want to say that they have to do computer science. But I think there is a mismatch. We need more good people and I think that they can have a big impact on the world and if that's what they want to accomplish, rationally we should be allocating more of the top people into computer science than we are now.

Seibel: In one of his papers Dijkstra talks about how computer science is a branch of mathematics and how computer-science students shouldn't even touch a computer for the first *n* years of their education and should instead learn to manipulate systems of formal symbols. How much mathematics do you think is required to be a competent programmer?

Norvig: I don't think you need the full Dijkstra level. And it's a particular type of math that he focuses on. It's discrete, logical proofs. I guess I'm coming from an area where that's less important and it's more probabilistic rather than logical. I rarely have a program that I can prove correct.

Is Google correct? Well, type in these words, you get back ten pages. If it crashes, then it's incorrect but if it gives you back these ten links rather than those ten links, there's no saying that one is right. You can have opinions on which are better than the other, but you can't go beyond that. I think that's quite different than what he had in mind. I think once you start solving these types of problems or the problem of having a robot car navigate through a city without hitting anybody, the logical proof gets thrown out pretty quickly.

Seibel: So is there any essential skill needed to be a good programmer? Different domains obviously have different requirements but ultimately is there some commonality to writing code regardless of the domain?

Norvig: You've got to be able to make progress and then improve on it. That's all you need to be able to do in life. You've got to have some idea and say, "Here's the direction to go," and then be able to say, "Now I've got to refine it." And refinement can be, "I didn't quite get it right; there are cases I didn't handle," or it can be, "Now that I understand it better, I'm going to write a tool so that it's more abstract and next time I can write a system like this more easily." Which I guess is that level of introspection to say, "Where was I going? How did I get there? Is there a better way to get there?"

Seibel: So do you think that that skill—essentially make it; debug it; iterate—is a kind of thinking that lots of people should learn, even people who aren't going to ultimately be programmers? If you were making a grade-school or junior-high or high-school curriculum, would you want everyone to be exposed to the idea of programming? Or is it too specialized a skill?

Norvig: I think it's specialized. I think it's one example of this type of thinking. But I'd be just as happy if you brought other examples like some type of mechanical problem. "Here's a bunch of pieces. How can I move some water from here to here and get it into this cup?" It doesn't have to be manipulating lines of code. It could be manipulating many kinds of pieces and seeing how they work together.

Seibel: And how far down should programmers go? In "Teach Yourself Programming in Ten Years," you talk about knowing how long it takes to execute an instruction vs. reading from disk and so on. Do we still need to learn assembly?

Norvig: I don't know. Knuth said, do everything in assembly, because it's just too inefficient to write in C. I don't agree with that. I think you want to know enough to know what instructions are inefficient, but that's no longer at the level of individual instructions. It's not just that this was a three-instruction sequence rather than a two-instruction sequence. It's, did you have a page fault or a cache miss? I don't think we need to know assembly language. You need architecture. You should understand what assembly language is, and you should understand that there's a memory hierarchy and missing from one level of the hierarchy to the next is a big performance penalty. But I think you can understand that at the abstract level.

Seibel: Are there any books that you think all programmers should read?

Norvig: I think there are a lot of choices. I don't think there's only one path. You've got to read some algorithm book. You can't just pick these things out and paste them together. It could be Knuth, or it could be the Cormen, Leiserson, and Rivest. And there are others. Sally Goldman's here now. She has a new book out that's a more practical take on algorithms. I think that's pretty interesting. So you need one of those. You need something on the ideas of abstraction. I like Abelson and Sussman. There are others.

You need to know your language well. Read the reference. Read the books that tell you both the mechanics of language and the whole enterprise of debugging and testing: *Code Complete* or some equivalent of that. But I think there are a lot of different paths. I don't want to say you have to read one set of books.

Seibel: Though your job now doesn't entail a lot of programming you still write programs for the essays on your web site. When you're writing these little programs, how do you approach it?

Norvig: I think one of the most important things is being able to keep everything in your head at once. If you can do that you have a much better chance of being successful. That makes a small program easier. For a bigger program, you need extra tools to be able to handle that.

It's also important to know what you're doing. When I wrote my Sudoku solver, some bloggers commented on that. They said, "Look at the contrast—here's Norvig's Sudoku thing and then there's this other guy, whose name I've forgotten, one of these test-driven design gurus. He starts off and he says, "Well, I'm going to do Sudoku and I'm going to have this class and first thing I'm going to do is write a bunch of tests." But then he never got anywhere. He had five different blog posts and in each one he wrote a little bit more and wrote lots of tests but he never got anything working because he didn't know how to solve the problem.

I actually knew—from AI—that, well, there's this field of constraint propagation—I know how that works. There's this field of recursive search—I know how that works. And I could see, right from the start, you put these two together, and you could solve this Sudoku thing. He didn't know that so he was sort of blundering in the dark even though all his code "worked" because he had all these test cases.

Then bloggers were arguing back and forth about what this means. I don't think it means much of anything—I think test-driven design is great. I do that a lot more than I used to do. But you can test all you want and if you don't know how to approach the problem, you're not going to get a solution.

Seibel: So then the question is, how should he have known that? Should he have gone and gotten a PhD and specialized in artificial intelligence? You can't know every algorithm. These days you have Google, but finding the right approach to a problem is a little different than finding a web framework.

Norvig: How do you know what you don't know?

Seibel: Exactly.

Norvig: So I guess it's two parts. One is to recognize that maybe there is a known solution to this. You could say, "Well, nobody could possibly know how to do this, so just exploring randomly is as good as everything else." That's one possibility. The other possibility is, "Well, probably somebody does know how to do this. I just don't know what the words are for it, so I have to discover those." I guess that's partly just intuition and saying, "It seems like the kind of thing that should be in the body of knowledge from AI." And then you have to figure out, how do I find it? And probably he could've done a search on Sudoku and found it that way. Maybe he thought that was cheating. I don't know.

Seibel: So let's say that *is* cheating—say you were the first person ever to try and solve Sudoku. The techniques that you ended up using would still have been out there waiting to be applied.

Norvig: Let's say I wanted to solve some problem in biology. I wouldn't know what the best algorithms were for doing gene sequencing or whatever. But I'd have a pretty good idea that there were such algorithms. Then I could start looking around. At another level, some of these things are pretty fundamental—if you don't know what dynamic programming is, then you're at a severe disadvantage. It's going to come up time and time again. If you don't know this idea of search in general—that you can make a choice and backtrack when you don't need it. These are all ideas from the

'60s. It was only a few years into programming that people discovered these things. It seems like that's the type of thing that everyone should know. Some things that were discovered last year, not everybody should know.

Seibel: So should programmers go back and read all the old papers?

Norvig: No, because there are lots of false starts and lots of mergers where two different fields develop completely different technology and terminology, and then they discover they were really doing the same thing. I think you'd rather have a story from the modern point of view rather than have to follow all the steps. But you should have them. I don't know what the best books are for that since I picked it up the hard way, piecemeal.

Seibel: So back to designing software. What about when you're working on bigger programs, where you're not going to be able to just remember how all the code fits together? Then how do you design it?

Norvig: I think you want to have good documentation at the level of overall system design. What's the thing supposed to do and how's it going to do it? Documentation for every method is usually more tedious than it needs to be. Most of the time it just duplicates what you could read from the name of the function and the parameters. But the overall design of what's going to do what, that's really important to lay out first. It's got to be something that everybody understands and it's also got to be the right choice. One of the most important things for having a successful project is having people that have enough experience that they build the right thing. And barring that, if it's something that you haven't built before, that you don't know how to do, then the next best thing you can do is to be flexible enough that if you build the wrong thing you can adjust.

Seibel: How much do you think you can you sit down and figure out how something ought to work, assuming it's not something that you've built before? Do you need to start writing code in order to really understand what the problem is?

Norvig: One way to think about it is going backwards. You want to get to an end state where you have something that's good and for some problems there's roughly one thing that's good. For other problems there are roughly millions and you can go in lots of different directions and they'd all be roughly the same. So I think it's different depending on which type of those types of problems you have.

Then you want to think about what are the difficult choices vs. what are the easy ones. What's going to come back to really screw you if you make the wrong architectural choice—if you hit built-in limitations or if you're just building the wrong thing. At Google I think we run up against all these types of problems. There's constantly a scaling problem. If you look at where we are today and say, we'll build something that can handle ten times more than that, in a couple years you'll have exceeded that and you have to throw it out and start all over again. But you want to at least make the right choice for the operating conditions that you've chosen—you'll work for a billion up to ten billion web pages or something. So what does that mean in terms of how you distribute it over multiple machines? What kind of traffic are you going to have going back and forth? You have to have a convincing story at that level. Some of that you can do with calculations on the back of the envelope, some of that you can do with simulations, and some of that you have to predict the future.

Seibel: It seems for that kind of question you'll be far more likely to answer correctly with either back-of-the-envelope calculations or simulation than writing code.

Norvig: Yeah, I think that's right. Those are the kind of things where the calculations are probably a better approach. And then there are these issues of some vendor says they're going to have a switch coming out next year that will handle ten times as much traffic; do you design to that? Do you believe them? Or do you design to what you have today? There are a lot of trade-offs there.

Then there are user-interface things where you just don't know until you build it. You think this interaction will be great but then you show it to the user and half the users just can't get it. Then you have to backtrack and come up with something new.

Seibel: Leaving aside designing user interactions, when is prototyping valuable? As opposed to just thinking about how something is going to work?

Norvig: I think it's useful to imagine the solution, to see if it's going to work. It's useful to see if it feels comfortable. You want a set of tools that are going to help you build what you have to build now and are going to help you evolve the system over time. And if you start out prototyping and all the sudden it feels clunky, then maybe you've got the wrong set of primitives. It'd be good to know that as soon as possible.

Seibel: What about the idea of using tests to drive design?

Norvig: I see tests more as a way of correcting errors rather than as a way of design. This extreme approach of saying, "Well, the first thing you do is write a test that says I get the right answer at the end," and then you run it and see that it fails, and then you say, "What do I need next?"—that doesn't seem like the right way to design something to me.

It seems like only if it was so simple that the solution was preordained would that make sense. I think you have to think about it first. You have to say, "What are the pieces? How can I write tests for pieces until I know what some of them are?" And then, once you've done that, then it is good discipline to have tests for each of those pieces and to understand well how they interact with each other and the boundary cases and so on. Those should all have tests. But I don't think you drive the whole design by saying, "This test has failed."

The other thing I don't like is a lot of the things we run up against at Google don't fit this simple Boolean model of test. You look at these test suites and they have `assertEqual` and `assertNotEqual` and `assertTrue` and so on. And that's useful but we also want to have `assertAsFastAsPossible` and assert over this large database of possible queries we get results whose score is precision value of such and such and recall value of such and such and we'd like to optimize that. And they don't have these kinds of statistical or continuous values that you're trying to optimize, rather than just having a Boolean "Is this right or wrong?"

Seibel: But ultimately all of those can get converted into Booleans—run a bunch of queries and capture all those values and see if they're all within the tolerances that you want.

Norvig: You could. But you can tell, just from the methods that the test suites give you, that they aren't set up to do that, they haven't thought about that as a possibility. I'm surprised at how much this type of approach is accepted at Google—when I was at Junglee I remember having to teach the QA team about it. We were doing this shopping search and saying, "We want a test where on this query we want to get 80 percent right answers." And so they're saying, "Right! So if it's a wrong answer it's a bug, right?" And I said, "No, it's OK to have one wrong answer as long at it's not 80 percent." So they say, "So a wrong answer's *not* a bug?" It was like those were the only two possibilities. There wasn't an idea that it's more of a trade-off.

Seibel: But you are still a believer in unit tests. How should programmers think about testing?

Norvig: They should write lots of tests. They should think about different conditions. And I think you want to have more complex regression tests as well as the unit tests. And think about failure modes—I remember one of the great lessons I got about programming was when I showed up at the airport at Heathrow, and there was a power failure and none of the computers were working. But my plane was on time.

Somehow they had gotten print-outs of all the flights. I don't know where—there must have been some computer off-site. I don't know whether they printed them that morning or if they had a procedure of always printing them the night before and sending them over and every day when there is power they just throw them out. But somehow they were there and the people at the gates had a procedure for using the paper backup rather than using the computer system.

I thought that was a great lesson in software design. I think most programmers don't think about, "How well does my program work when there's no power?"

Seibel: How does Google work when there's no power?

Norvig: Google does not work very well without power. But we have backup power and multiple data centers. And we do think in terms of, "How well does my piece work when the server it's connecting to is down or when there are other sorts of failures?" Or, "I'm running my program on a thousand machines; what happens when one of them dies?" How does that computation get restarted somewhere else?

Seibel: Knuth has an essay about developing TeX where he talks about flipping over to this pure, destructive QA personality and doing his darnedest to break his own code. Do you think most developers are good at that?

Norvig: No. And I had an example of that in my spelling corrector. I had introduced a bug in the code that measured how well I was doing and simultaneously had made some minor change in the real code. I ran it and I got back a much better score for how well it was doing. And I believed it! If it had been a much worse score I would have never said, "Oh, this minor change to the real function must have made it much worse." But I was willing to believe this minor change made the score much better rather than being skeptical and saying, "Nah, couldn't have made that much difference, there must be something else wrong."

Seibel: How do you avoid over-generalization and building more than you need and consequently wasting resources that way?

Norvig: It's a battle. There are lots of battles around that. And, I'm probably not the best person to ask because I still like having elegant solutions rather than practical solutions. So I have to sort of fight with myself and say, "In my day job I can't afford to think that way." I have to say, "We're out here to provide the solution that makes the most sense and if there's a perfect solution out there, probably we can't afford to do it." We have to give up on that and say, "We're just going to do what's the most important now." And I have to instill that upon myself and on the people I work with. There's some saying in German about the perfect being the enemy of the good; I forget exactly where it comes from—every practical engineer has to learn that lesson.

Seibel: Why is it so tempting to solve a problem we don't really have?

Norvig: You want to be clever and you want closure; you want to complete something and move on to something else. I think people are built to only handle a certain amount of stuff and you want to say, "This is completely done; I can put it out of my mind and then I can go on." But you have to calculate, well, what's the return on investment for solving it completely? There's always this sort of S-shaped curve and by the time you get up to 80 or 90 percent completion, you're starting to get diminishing returns. There are 100 other things you could be doing that are just at the bottom of the curve where you get much better returns. And at some point you have to say, "Enough is enough, let's stop and go do something where we get a better return."

Seibel: And how can programmers learn to better recognize where they are on that curve?

Norvig: I think you set the right environment, where it's results-oriented. And I think people can train themselves. You want to optimize, but left to yourself you optimize your own sense of comfort and that's different from what you really should be optimizing—some people would say return on investment for the company, others would say satisfaction of your customers. You have to think how much is it going to benefit the customer if I go from 95 percent to 100 percent on this feature vs. working on these ten other features that are at 0 percent.

At Google, I think it's easy because we have this "launch early and often" philosophy. And because of the way the company is, for a number of reasons: one, most of our products we don't charge any money for so it's easy to say, well, go ahead and ship it; how much could they complain? The other one is we're not stamping CDs and putting them in a box so if there's something that's not complete today or even if it has a bug, it's not a disaster. Most of the software is on our servers so we can fix it tomorrow and everybody gets the update instantly. We don't have this nightmare of installing updates. So it makes it easier for us to say, "We're just going to launch things and get some feedback from the users and fix the stuff that needs to be fixed and don't worry about the other stuff."

Seibel: If you're working on the design of a big system what are the tools you use—do you sit down with a pad of graph paper or a UML drawing tool?

Norvig: I never liked any of these UML-type tools. I always thought, "If you can't do it in the language itself that's a weakness of the language." I think a lot of what you're doing, you're dealing at a higher level. At Google a lot of what we do is figuring out how to break things up and parallelize them. We're going to necessarily run this on multiple machines but we've got so many users and, for many applications, so much data; how's that going to work? So we're thinking more at the level of machines and racks of machines rather than at the level of functions and interactions. Once you get that straightened out, then you can start diving into individual functions and methods.

Seibel: And so that level of description is just prose?

Norvig: Yeah, mostly. Sometimes people draw pictures. They'll say, "We'll have this server here that will be serving these kinds of requests and then it's connected to this server and then we'll use these various tools for storage and big distributed hash tables and other types of things. We'll choose these three tools off the shelf and then we'll argue about whether we have to build a new one; which of these existing ones works or do we need something else?"

Seibel: And how do you evaluate that kind of design?

Norvig: You show it to the people who've done it before. They say, "Oh, it looks like you'll need a cache here—it's going to be too slow but there should be a lot of repeat requests, so if you install a cache of this size here that should help a lot." You have a design review where people look over it and say whether they think it makes sense and then you start building it and testing it.

Seibel: And you guys have formal design reviews? You worked at NASA where they had a very formal design review.

Norvig: Nothing formal like NASA. The stakes are lower for us because, as I say, it's easy for us to have a failure and recover from that. At NASA usually the first failure is fatal so they were much more careful. We don't worry about that much. It's more of a consultation, I think, rather than a review.

There are people who officially read design documents and comment on them. You go through that and get your design approved. But it's still much more informal than the NASA thing. That's at the instigation of the project. During the course of a project there are periodic reviews, but they don't really dig into the code. It more says, "How do you stand? Are you ahead of schedule? Behind schedule? What are your big problems?"—at that level.

Then the launch process is the most formal of them all. Then, there is a checklist—it's very formal in terms of security issues. If we launch this, is someone going to be able to go in and do cross-site scripting to take over something else? That's fairly strict.

Seibel: You told me once that when Guido van Rossum came here he had to get checked out on Python and Ken Thompson had to get checked out on C, to make sure they could meet very explicit coding standards. Do you have design standards that are equally explicit?

Norvig: No. Some of the coding standards go into some design issues, but you get a lot more leeway there. But there certainly are policies, so you need to be certified before you can start contributing code. Every check-in has to be reviewed by somebody else and verified.

Seibel: So every code check-in into the p4 depot is reviewed before it goes in?

Norvig: You can do experimental stuff on your own, and there is an exception process where you can check something in and have be reviewed at a future date. But you're supposed to minimize those.

Seibel: So is this essentially the equivalent of the classic desk check: "Here's my code; someone else look at it and read it and say, 'Yeah, this is righteous.'"

Norvig: Yeah. In fact that was Guido's first project. We had used the standard diff tools to do that, and it was kind of clunky, so Guido wrote this distributed system with fancier display and coloring and so on that allowed you to do reviews of check-ins better.

Seibel: A of companies say they should do reviews but it's very rarely followed through on. You must, at some level, train people how to do that.

Norvig: I think it was something that had always been done and so people accept it. Well, I shouldn't say that completely. Some people it takes a while to get used to it. One of the typical failure cases is a new hire comes in and they're not used to doing this kind of thing so they just start an experimental branch and they have all their code in there and you keep on telling them, "Gee, you don't have any check-ins yet." And they say, "Yeah, yeah, yeah, I'm just cleaning it up—I'll check it in tomorrow." And then another week goes by and another week goes by and eventually they have this one gigantic check-in. And then it's a problem that too much time has gone by, it's hard to evaluate it all at once, and some of the things they're comparing against have changed out from underneath them. Then they see what a headache it is and they learn not to do that.

Seibel: So that's on the coding side. Are there skills that the reviewers develop?

Norvig: There certainly are people who are known for being better reviewers than others. There's a trade-off of when you submit a review—do you try to get somebody who will give you a lot of good feedback or do you try to get somebody who will just say "OK" as quickly as possible?

Seibel: So what makes the better reviewers better?

Norvig: Well, that they catch more things. Some of it is the trivial stuff of you indented the wrong number of spaces or whatever but some of it is, "I think this design would be cleaner if you moved this from here over to there." So some people will do more of that and others won't bother.

Seibel: Sort of related to that, does every good programmer turn into a good architect when they grow up? Or are there some people who are brilliant coders but only at a certain level and they should never be allowed to do bigger designs?

Norvig: I think different people have different skills. One of our best search people is by no means our best programmer, in terms of how the code looks. But if you say, "Here's this new factor that we have—you know, how many times people click on this page after they've done such and such—how do we fold that into our search results?" He'll say, "Oh, on line 427 there's this variable alpha and you should take this new factor and raise it to the second power and multiply it by 1.5 and add it to alpha." Then you experiment for a couple months trying different things and you find out he was right except it should have been 1.3 instead of 1.5.

Seibel: So that suggests he just has this very good mental model of how the software works.

Norvig: He understands the code perfectly. Other people can write code better but he understands all the implications of what goes where.

Seibel: Do you think those are related? It often seems that people who write the worst spaghetti code are the ones who can hold the most in their head—that's the only way they could possibly write code like that.

Norvig: Yeah, I think that may be.

Seibel: So the reviews here are less formal here than at NASA. What are the other differences between the "engineering" and "hacker" ethos, in the best sense of both those words?

Norvig: One big difference is organizational structure and how software is accepted. Google was founded as a software company, and they went out and hired a CEO who has a PhD in computer science from Berkeley, hired a VP of Sales who has a computer engineering background—it's throughout the whole company. At NASA they're rocket scientists! They aren't software guys. They say, "Software is this necessary evil. Straight line code, I can sort of understand; if it's got a loop in it, that's kind of iffy. Then if there's a branch statement *inside* the loop, ooooh, that's getting away from what I can solve with a differential equation in control theory." So they're distrustful.

Seibel: As well they should be!

Norvig: As well they should be, yeah. And they're distrustful of innovation. So you can say, "Look at this great new prototype I have," and they'll say, "That's fantastic; I'd love to fly that on my mission—as soon as it's been proven on two other missions." And you go to everybody else and they all say the same thing.

Don Goldin came in as NASA administrator and he said, "We've got to do this better, faster, cheaper. These space missions cost too much. It'd be better to run more missions and some of them would fail but overall we'd still get more done for the same amount of money." And that was undeniably true. Unfortunately it was not politically true. It's not OK to lose a spacecraft. Because the public understands very well, NASA lost a spacecraft. They don't really know that there's any difference between a $100 million spacecraft and a billion dollar spacecraft. It's not like you get to lose ten of the $100 millions instead of one billion. So it was never quite true.

Seibel: What is the worst bug you've ever had to track down?

Norvig: Well, I guess the most consequential bugs I was involved with were not mine, but the ones I had to clean up after: the Mars program failures in '98. One was foot-pounds vs. newtons. And the other was, we think, though we're not 100 percent sure, prematurely shutting off the engines due to a software problem.

Seibel: I read one of the reports on the Mars Climate Orbiter—that was the one that was the foot-pounds vs. newtons problem—and you were the only computer scientist on that panel. Were you involved in talking to the software guys to figure out what the problem was?

Norvig: That was pretty easy, post hoc, because they knew the failure mode. From that they were able to back it out and it didn't take long to figure that one out. Then there was this postmortem of why did it happen? And I think it was a combination of things. One was outsourcing. It was a joint effort between JPL in Pasadena and Lockheed-Martin in Colorado. There were two people on two different teams and they just weren't sitting down and having lunch together. I'm convinced that if they had, they would have solved this problem. But instead, one guy sent an email saying, you know, "Something not quite right with these measurements, seems like we're off by a little bit. It's not very much, it's probably OK, but—"

Seibel: That was all during the flight?

Norvig: Right. During the flight they had chance and chance to catch it. They knew something was wrong and they sent this email but they did not put it into the bug-tracking system. If they had, NASA has very good controls for bug tracking and at later points in the flight somebody would have had to OK it. Instead it was just an informal email that never got an answer back, and JPL said, "Oh, I guess Lockheed-Martin must have solved this problem." And Lockheed says, "Oh, JPL's not asking anymore—they must not be concerned."

So it was this communications problem. It was also a software reuse problem. They have extremely good checks for the stuff that's mission-critical, and on the previous mission the stuff that was recorded in foot-pounds was non–mission-critical—it was just a log that wasn't used for navigation. So it had been classified as non–mission-critical. In the new mission they reused most of the stuff but they changed the navigation so that what was formerly a log file now became an input to the navigation.

Seibel: So the actual problem was that one side generated a data file in foot-pounds and that data file was fed into a piece of software that was calculating inputs to the actual navigation and was expecting newtons?

Norvig: Right. So essentially the other root cause was too many particles from the sun. The spacecraft is asymmetrical and it's got these solar panels. Particles twist the spacecraft a little bit so you've got to fire the rockets to twist it back. So this new hire at Lockheed went to the rocket manufacturer, and they had all their specifications in foot-pounds, so he just said, "I'll go with that," and he recorded them that way, not knowing that NASA wanted them in metric.

Seibel: I was struck, reading that report, by the NASA attitude of, "Well, the problem was due to this software bug but we had so many other chances to notice that the ship wasn't where we expected, and we should have. We should have fixed it anyway even though the numbers we were dealing with were totally bogus because of some stupid software glitch." I thought that was admirable.

Norvig: Yeah, they were looking at the process.

Seibel: Is it actually common for there to be software bugs of that magnitude, which we never hear about because all the other processes keep everything online?

Norvig: Yeah, I think so. Look at all the software bugs on your computer. There are millions of them. But most of the time it doesn't crash.

Seibel: Yet you hear about how the shuttle flight software costs $1,500 a line or something because of the care with which they write it and which is allegedly bug-free. Is that just a lie?

Norvig: No, that's probably true. But I don't know if it's optimal. I think they might be better off with buggy software.

Seibel: With cheaper software and better operations?

Norvig: Yeah, because of the amount of training they have to give to these astronauts to be able to deal with the things the software just can't do. They put these astronauts in simulators and give them all these situations and when things go bad you've got this screen and stuff is scrolling through it and you can't pause the screen, you can't go back, you can't get a summary of what the important things are. The astronauts just have to be trained to know, "When I see this happening, here's what's really going on." There are a hundred messages in a row saying, "This electrical thing has faulted," and you train them to say, "OK, that must be because this one original one faulted and then there was a cascade downstream and all the other ones are reported." Why can't you do that in software rather than train the astronaut? They don't try because they don't want to mess with it.

Seibel: On a different topic, what are your preferred debugging techniques and tools? Print statements? Formal proofs? Symbolic debuggers?

Norvig: I think it's a mix and it depends on where I am. Sometimes I'm using an IDE that has good tracing capability and sometimes I'm just using Emacs and don't have all that. Certainly tracing and printing. And thinking. Writing smaller test cases and watching them go, and breaking the functionality down to see where the test case failed. And I've got to admit, I often end up rewriting. Sometimes I do that without ever finding the bug. I get to the point where I can just feel that it's in this part here. I'm just not very comfortable about this part. It's a mess. It really shouldn't be that way. Rather than tweak it a little bit at a time, I'll just throw away a couple hundred lines of code, rewrite it from scratch, and often then the bug is gone.

Sometimes I feel guilty about that. Is that a failure on my part? I didn't understand what the bug was. I didn't find the bug. I just dropped a bomb on the house and blew up all the bugs and built a new house. In some sense, the bug eluded me. But if it becomes the right solution, maybe it's OK. You've done it faster than you would have by finding it.

Seibel: What about things like assertions or invariants? How formally do you think about those kinds of things when you're coding?

Norvig: I guess I'm more on the informal side. I haven't used languages where that's a big part of the formal mechanism, other than just type declarations. Like loop invariants: I've always thought that was more trouble than it was worth. I occasionally have a problem where this loop doesn't terminate, but mostly you don't, and I just feel like it slows you down to do the formal part. And if you do have a problem, the debugger will tell you what loop you're stuck inside. I guess if you're writing high-dependability software that's embedded in something that it's really important that it doesn't fail, then you really want to prove everything. But just in terms of getting the first version of the program running or debugging it, I'd rather move fast towards that than worry about the degree of formal specification you need later.

Seibel: Have you ever done anything explicit to try and learn from the bugs that you've created?

Norvig: Yeah, I think that's pretty interesting and I wish I could do more with that. I'm actually in a discussion now to see if I can do an experiment, company-wide and then maybe for the world at large, to understand more some of these issues. How do you classify bugs, but also what are some factors in terms of productivity? How do you know? Is there a certain type of person? What are the factors of that person that makes them more productive? And I think it's more interesting what the controllable factors are that make somebody do better. If giving them a bigger monitor increases productivity by such and such a percent, then you should probably do it.

Seibel: People are going to hate you when you discover that actually, really tiny monitors make people more productive.

Norvig: Right. And if providing quiet is important, then you should probably do that, but on the other hand, if providing communication between team members is important, then you should do that, and how do you balance those two?

I just started thinking about what's the right way to do that. How do you set up an experiment? What do you track? Do we have numbers already that we could make use of just by adding in some kind of questionnaire? Do we have to set up an experiment?

Seibel: It's often claimed that there are orders of magnitude differences in productivity between programmers. Yet I read somewhere some criticism of those claims, saying the studies that found that were done quite some time ago, and a lot of things have changed about programming since then that could have accounted for the differences—such as some people in the study were still using batch processing techniques while other people were using timesharing programming environments.

Norvig: I don't think that's all of it, because I think there were some differences within the same organization using more of the same tools. I also remember there were criticisms of some of the studies of finding correlation, but not knowing cause and effect. If you found that the programmers in the big corner offices were more productive, is that because you reward the good programmers with the offices, or is it because the offices makes them better? You can't really come to a conclusion.

Seibel: Do you still enjoy programming as much as when you were starting out?

Norvig: Yeah, but it's frustrating to not know everything. I'm not doing it as much, so I forget a little bit. And there are all these new things. I really should redesign my web site and it should have JavaScript on the client side. It should have PHP or something like that, and I just haven't gotten up the momentum to learn all that stuff and be able to do it.

Seibel: Do you think programming is a young person's game?

Norvig: I think it helps in some ways. We certainly have a range of people here that are exceptionally good at all levels and all ages. I think the advantage of being young is it's important to grasp the whole program, the whole problem, in your head—being able to concentrate. And I think that's easier when you're younger, because your brain is better at it, or maybe it's just that you have less distractions. If you have kids, and family, and so on, you just can't devote as many consecutive hours as when you don't. So that's part of it. But on the other hand, you've got this range of experience, so you can make up for that in some ways by being able to do more because you know how to do it.

Seibel: One of the aspects of the modern style of programming, as you were saying, is that programmers have to absorb things quickly. How do you tackle the problem of understanding a big pile of code, none of which you've ever seen before?

Norvig: I think you do a mix of statically and dynamically. You start reading the code and trying to make sense of it and then you get some traces of what calls what, and where most of time is spent, and what's the flow through it. Then try to do something. Say, "I'm going to make this trivial little change." Or go to the issues database and say, "I'll take this one." In order to do that, I have to learn a little piece of it. There's only a little piece, but you get that done and you move on to the next one.

Seibel: Have you ever done literate programming a la Knuth?

Norvig: I never used his tools per se. I've certainly written macros and so on. And I've used the Java docs and things like that. In many ways, Lisp programming encourages you to make your own system as you go, and so it ends up being literate in that way. You find your own macros for your own application-specific programming, and part of that is the documentation, part of it's the data, and part of it's the code, so I've certainly done that. Then more recently, in whatever language I'm using, whether it's Java, or Python, or whatever, I've certainly been careful to write test cases, and document around that.

You look at Knuth's original *Literate Programming*, and he was really trying to say, "What's the best order for writing a book," assuming that someone's going to read the whole book and he wants it to be in a logical order. People don't do that anymore. They don't want to read a book. They want an index so they can say, "What's the least amount of this book that I have to read? I just want to find the three paragraphs that I need. Show me that and then I'll move on." I think that's a real change.

Seibel: I wonder if there isn't a way to write modern-style literate programming. Certainly Knuth's tools give you an index and beautiful cross-referencing. I wonder if perhaps a modern approach to literate programming just would organize the book differently—both as a whole program and as a bunch of pieces that you can understand in bits?

Norvig: I don't know. I think he was solving a problem that doesn't exist anymore to a large degree. Part of it was because he wanted to put it in a linear order rather than in a web-like or a searchable order. I think part of it was the limitations. I think he was using Pascal originally. And there it's pretty strict in terms of what had to be declared first and not necessarily in the order you want. Modern languages are more free in that order, so I think it's less of an issue now.

Seibel: You mentioned reading Strachey's checkers code in *Scientific American*. And in your "Teach Yourself Programming in Ten Years" essay, you talk about the importance of reading code. What code did you read coming up?

Norvig: I read a lot of the Symbolics's code, because that was available when I was at Berkeley.

Seibel: Was that just because it was available and was interesting? Or were you reading it to try to understand some behaviors you were observing?

Norvig: Both. I sometimes just tried to figure out how things work and sometimes I needed it to solve a problem.

Seibel: So when you're reading just for general edification, how do you approach that?

Norvig: I think it's probably interest-driven. "Gee, this file system allows you to read files across the net using the same protocol that you use locally on your machine—I wonder how it does that?" And so you'll say, "Maybe it's in the open function." You look there, and say, "Oh, that calls this other thing." And you look there, and eventually you say, "Oh, this is how it does it."

Seibel: Have you read any of Knuth's literate programs in book form?

Norvig: I've certainly picked up the books and flipped through them. I could say I glanced at them, but I haven't studied them.

Seibel: What about *The Art of Computer Programming*? Some of the people I've talked to on this have absolutely read it from cover to cover. Some people have it on the shelf and use it as a reference. And some people just have it on the shelf.

Norvig: At one point I had it as my monitor stand because it was one of the biggest set of books I had, and it was just the right height. That was nice because it was always there, and I guess then I was more prone to use it as a reference because it was just right in front of me.

Seibel: But you had to lift up the monitor every time you wanted to look at it?

Norvig: No, I had the box set. You had to pull hard, but you could pull one of the box. Now I'm less likely to use any book for reference—I'm just likely to do a search.

Seibel: Just because it's more convenient?

Norvig: It's convenient. I think it's also that I'm probably more goal-oriented. Knuth is good if you say, "I want to know everything about this subject." But usually I'm saying, "I want to know if A is better than B," or, "I want to know the asymptotic complexity of this, and once I've got that, I don't need all the details of how we got there."

Seibel: As a programmer, do you consider yourself a scientist, an engineer, an artist, or a craftsman?

Norvig: Well, I know when you compare the various titles of books and so on, I always thought the "craft" was the right answer. So I thought art was a little pretentious because the purpose of art is to be beautiful or to have an emotional contact or emotional impact, and I don't feel like that's anything that I try to do. Certainly I want programs to be pretty in some ways, and sometimes I feel like I spend too much time doing that. I've been in a position where I've had the luxury to say, "Gee, I have time to go back and pretty this up a little bit." And places where I've been able to write for a publication, you spend more time doing that than you would if it was just for your own professional growth.

But I don't think of that as art. I think *craft* is really the right word for it. You can make a chair, and it's good looking, but it's mostly functional—it's a chair.

Seibel: How do you recognize a great programmer, particularly when you're hiring? You guys have hired a lot of programmers and you obviously try to hire really good programmers. How do you do it?

Norvig: We still don't know.

Seibel: Google is somewhat famous for asking puzzle questions in interviews. Do you think that's a good approach?

Norvig: I don't think it's important whether people can solve the puzzles or not. I don't like the trick puzzle questions. I think it's important to put them in a technical situation and not just chitchat and get a feeling if they're a nice guy. Though it is important to have someone that you can get along with. But you really have to see, can they technically do what they said they can do. And there are a lot of different ways to demonstrate that. And many times you can see it from the résumé. I think our best signal is if somebody has worked with one of our employees before and the employee can vouch for them. But we still try to draw it out on-site during the interview. It's more you want to get a feeling for how this person thinks and how they work together, so do they know the basic ideas? Can they say, "Well, in order to solve this, I need to know A, B, and C," and they start putting it together. And I think you can demonstrate that while still failing on a puzzle. You can say, "Well, here's how I attack this puzzle. Well, I first think about this. Then I do that. Then I do that, but geez, here's this part I don't quite understand." For some people that little part clicks and for some it doesn't. And you can do fine if it doesn't click as long as you've demonstrated the basic competency and fluency in how you think about it. And then you really want to have people write code on the board if you're interviewing them for a coding job. Because some people have forgotten or didn't quite know and you could see that pretty quickly.

Seibel: So is that just a negative indicator? If they can't write reasonable code, that's a bad sign. But if they don't stumble over that hurdle, it's hard to tell whether they're actually going to write really good code in a larger context.

Norvig: Right. You could tell to a certain degree but at other levels you can't. And we've studied this pretty carefully because we've gotten a lot of applications and we look at it at two levels. One, we say, from all the résumés we get, are we interviewing the right set of people? And then, from the interviews we get, are we hiring the right set of people?

Seibel: So how do you measure that? You don't know about the one you didn't talk to or didn't hire.

Norvig: Yeah, so that's hard. At both levels, you've only got half your sample, so it's this biased problem, but I guess basically what we're doing is saying, "Of the people that we interviewed and did well, what did their résumé look like," and try to find more of those. Is having so many years of experience important? Is working on an open-source programming project important? How does that compare to winning a programming contest?

Seibel: Do you really take all these things and shove them into a database?

Norvig: Yes, we do, and when we're doing the hiring, we have these scores that come up that say, "The résumé predictor says such and such, and the interview predictor says such and such." We don't take them as gospel, but they're just another piece of input along with all the other feedback we have.

Seibel: Do the people who are doing the interviews have those numbers beforehand?

Norvig: No, we only see that when they're in the hiring committee, once we've gathered all the feedback. One of the interesting things we found, when trying to predict how well somebody we've hired is going to perform when we evaluate them a year or two later, is one of the best indicators of success within the company was getting the worst possible score on one of your interviews. We rank people from one to four, and if you got a one on one of your interviews, that was a really good indicator of success.

Seibel: But you had to do well enough on something else that you actually got hired?

Norvig: Right, so that's the thing. Ninety-nine percent of the people who got a one in one of their interviews we didn't hire. But the rest of them, in order for us to hire them somebody else had to be so passionate that they pounded on the table and said, "I have to hire this person because I see something in him that's so great, and this guy who thought he was no good is wrong, and I've got to stand up for him and put my reputation on the line."

Seibel: So you're surrounded by top-notch programmers here at Google. Given how pervasive computers and software are in our society, do you think everybody needs to understand a bit about programming just to get along in or understand the world they live in?

Norvig: You probably want an educated person to understand how software is made to the same degree they understand how a car is made. The other interesting thing is, how much does an informed citizen have to *be* a programmer? Certainly the average person now can do word processing and many of them can do spreadsheets, and so if you're a little bit experienced with spreadsheets, you're starting to be a programmer.

Lots of attempts at end-user programming, and programming for everyone, haven't been very successful. I don't know how easy it is. Is there a way of thinking that people have that we've gotten all the people that it's easy to teach, and the other ones are going to be really hard, or is it just that we've missed the model and there's some simple model in place of many people that could influence programming if we created it?

Seibel: A lot of people that I have talked to for this book, and elsewhere, got into computers both because they just enjoyed it and because they felt like it would change the world. Some of the folks I talked to for this book did that in the past and now are depressed by how little they feel the world has changed as a result. How do you feel about that?

Norvig: Well, I'm in the right place. We have hundreds of millions of users and we can make a difference for them, and we can launch new services for them quickly. I think that's great. I can't imagine anything else I could be doing to have that level of impact.

CHAPTER

9

Guy Steele

*Guy Steele is a true programming polyglot. When I asked him what languages he has used seriously he came up with this list: COBOL, Fortran, IBM 1130 assembly, PDP-10 machine language, APL, C, C++, Bliss, GNAL, Common Lisp, Scheme, Maclisp, S-1 Lisp, *Lisp, C*, Java, JavaScript, Tcl, Haskell, FOCAL, BASIC, TECO, and TeX. "Those would be the main ones, I guess," he added.*

He had a hand in the creation of both of the major surviving general-purpose Lisp dialects: Common Lisp and Scheme. He served on the standards bodies that defined Common Lisp, Fortran, C, ECMAScript, and Scheme and was recruited by Bill Joy to help write the official language specification for Java. He is now at work designing Fortress, a new language for high-performance scientific computing.

Steele's academic career included an AB from Harvard and an SM and PhD from MIT. While at MIT he collaborated with Gerald Sussman on a series of papers now known as "The Lambda Papers," which included the original definition of the Scheme programming language. He has also been a chronicler of hacker culture as one of the original compilers of the Jargon File and editor of the book version, The Hacker's Dictionary (subsequently updated and expanded by Eric S. Raymond as The New Hacker's Dictionary). And he played an important role in the birth of Emacs and was one of the first programmers to port Donald Knuth's program TeX.

Steele is a Fellow of the Association for Computing Machinery and the American Academy of Arts and Sciences and a member of the U.S. National Academy of Engineering. He won the ACM's Grace Murray Hopper Award in 1988 and Dr. Dobb's Excellence in Programming Award in 2005.

In this interview he talks about designing software and the relation between writing and programming, and he gives one of the best explanations I've ever heard of the value—and limitations—of formal proofs of correctness.

Seibel: How did you get involved in programming?

Steele: Well, when I was in elementary school I remember being fascinated by science and math and I read books such as Irving Adler's House of Numbers; it was one of my favorites. And I liked kiddie science fiction like, say, the Danny Dunn series and that kind of thing. So I had this general interest in science and math. In reading everything I could about science and math, I read a little bit about these newfangled computers that were coming up as well.

Seibel: And when would that have been?

Steele: I was in elementary school from 1960 through '66. But I think the real turning point was when I got to Boston Latin School—it would have been in the equivalent of the ninth grade. A friend asked me, "Have you heard about the new computer in the basement?" I thought this was the newest story after the one about the fourth-floor swimming pool and the school only has three stories. But he said, "No really, it exists."

It turns out that T. Vincent Learson had arranged for an IBM 1130 minicomputer to be in the basement of the Boston Latin School. He was an alum and a very generous one apparently. My friend proceeded to show me a Fortran program of about five lines and I was immediately fascinated.

Then I went to one of our math teachers and asked if I could have some books to study. He gave me some books and thought they'd keep me busy for a month but they actually lasted a weekend. I taught myself Fortran over Thanksgiving weekend—so it was a long weekend—of 1968. After that I was completely hooked.

My Latin School friends and I had a fascination with IBM because of the IBM 1130 and we took to visiting the IBM office downtown every couple of months and talking with the people there and occasionally ordering publications with what little money we had.

There was also a bookstore downtown that had books about exotic languages like PL/I, and we'd occasionally buy books there. So, through Latin School we got to know IBM equipment. We just had the 1130 but we drooled over System 360. We read about it and didn't really have access to one.

Then I became involved at MIT in the spring of 1969 in the High School Studies Program. This was great—go on Saturday mornings and have college students teach you all this cool stuff. I took courses in group theory and computer programming and I forget what all else. I became rather heavily involved and therefore got to feel on very familiar turf at MIT. Through the High School Studies Program, we had access to both IBM 1130s and DEC PDP-10s. So that's how we got to know the Digital Equipment line.

As high-school students we became aware of the DEC office in Central Square that tended to cater to the MIT students. They didn't blink when high-school students walked in and asked for reference manuals. It was great. When I was a junior or senior at Latin School, a friend of mine and I typed up a proposal to DEC to implement an APL for the PDP-8. And they took the proposal seriously. They looked at it for a week and then they said, "Well, we don't think this is a good idea, but thanks for the offer."

Seibel: What was the first interesting program you wrote?

Steele: Well, I learned Fortran first so I think things really got interesting when I started to learn IBM 1130 assembly language. And I guess the earliest interesting program I can remember was something that would generate keyword-in-context indexes. IBM provided these so-called quick indexes for their manuals that, given a keyword, you could look it up in the index and it was alphabetized according to keyword but on either side of the keyword you would see several other words of context surrounding that word.

Seibel: Context from where the word appeared?

Steele: Where the word had appeared in the original publication. So down the middle column were the words that had been alphabetized and sticking out on either side would be chunks of context. So I thought I'd tackle that problem, doing it on the 1130. And considering that the 1130 had only 4,000 words of memory, it was clear that I was going to have to keep the records on disk. So I took this opportunity to learn about efficient out-of-core sorting techniques. What was interesting about this program was not so much the generation of the KWIC index but implementing a multiway out-of-core merge sort. And it was reasonably effective. Unfortunately my in-core sort was bubble sort because I wasn't that sophisticated. I should have also done a merge sort in core but I hadn't quite figured that out at the time.

Seibel: How long do you think it was from when you first realized there really was a computer in the basement to when you were writing this program? Was it months? Weeks?

Steele: It would have been within the first two years. I don't remember whether it was in the first year. I learned Fortran in the fall of '68. And I remember that APL was my third language so I must have learned the assembly language somewhere around Christmastime or shortly after. I know I learned APL in the spring of '69 because that's when the Spring Joint Computer Conference came to Boston.

IBM had an exhibit on the show floor touting all manner of IBM products but the APL 360 in particular, and I hung around that booth. At the end of the trade show they were about to throw the stack of paper away that had been used for demos on the Selectric terminal. At just the right moment I walked up and asked, "Are you going to throw that away?" And the lady looked at me, puzzled, and said, "Here, it's yours," as if she was giving me this big Christmas present. Which she was.

Seibel: What was on that paper?

Steele: It was fan-fold paper from a Selectric terminal on which they had been demonstrating APL for the past two days. Just little programming examples of whatever they had happened to type in. And from that and the brochure they had on the trade-show floor, I taught myself APL.

Seibel: So you were very comfortable at MIT but you ended up going to Harvard and working at MIT. What happened?

Steele: By the time I was applying to colleges I applied to MIT, Harvard, and Princeton and really wanted to go to MIT. I got accepted at all three. The headmaster of Boston Latin School was Wilfred L. O'Leary, an old-school classicist, a wonderful gentleman. He called up my parents and said, "Do you realize that your son is actually considering going to Tech when he has an acceptance at Harvard?!" So he twisted their arms and they twisted my arm and I decided to go to Harvard after all.

Then my parents were on my case to get a summer job and not just sit around the house—you know, the classic syndrome. I knew I was interested in computing and didn't want to flip burgers. So I interviewed for keypunching jobs, figuring that was something I'd be reasonably qualified to do. But nobody wanted to hire me, in part because I wasn't 18 yet. I didn't figure that out until later. They just listened to my story and said, "Don't call us, we'll call you."

Then around the beginning of July I heard that Bill Martin at MIT was looking for Lisp programmers. I thought, "Aha, I know Lisp." I'd hung around MIT so much and had obtained copies of Lisp documentation from the Artificial Intelligence Lab and I would sneak into the labs and play with the computers. The doors were open in those days—the Vietnam protests had not yet happened, which is what caused them to put locks on the doors. And I had spent my senior year implementing my own Lisp for the IBM 1130.

So I showed up at Bill Martin's office, this skinny kid out of nowhere, and poked my head in and said, "I hear you're looking for Lisp programmers." And he didn't laugh at me. He just looked at me and said, "Well, you have to take my Lisp quiz." "OK. How about now?" So I sat down and spent two hours working on a list of questions and puzzles. When I was done I gave him the papers and he spent ten minutes looking them over and said, "You're hired."

Seibel: Was Lisp one of the things you had actually studied in this High School Studies Program?

Steele: A little bit, though it was more Fortran and some other things.

Seibel: Did you have any important mentors when you were starting out?

Steele: At Latin School I'd primarily have to credit the math teachers with encouraging me just the right amount. In the ninth grade Ralph Wellings, who lent me those books over the Thanksgiving weekend, struck a deal with me. He said, "I notice you've been getting 100 percent on all your math quizzes." He said, "I'll let you spend four math classes a week in the computer room if on the fifth day you take the quiz and get 100 percent. If you ever get less than 100 percent then the deal is over." So that was incentive. I proceeded to ace quizzes for the rest of the year—I studied math especially hard and that gave me access to the computer. Even better, the next year my math teacher would not offer the same deal, which was appropriate because I did not know the math for that year. So they judged it about right. So I had good teachers that gave me what I needed to learn all kinds of things.

Seibel: And then, as you got more involved in computers, were there particular folks who helped you along the way?

Steele: Well, certainly Bill Martin, who hired me. And Joel Moses, who was in charge of the Macsyma project into which I was hired at MIT.

Seibel: And you ended up working on that project throughout college?

Steele: Yes, I was an employee of MIT all the time I was at Harvard. It was a full-time job in the summers and it became a afternoon job during the school year. I'd do my best to arrange my classes to be in the mornings at Harvard, then I could take the T down to MIT and get in two or three hours of programming before heading home.

Seibel: And that was all working on Macsyma in Lisp?

Steele: Yeah. My specific job was to be the maintainer of the Maclisp interpreter. JonL White had been in charge of both the interpreter and the compiler and he became pretty much the compiler guru, and I took care of the interpreter, and it was a pretty good split. So JonL White was a mentor of mine. All the people on the Macsyma project kind of took me under their wing. I also got to know some of the people in the AI Lab. So by the time I applied to MIT for graduate school it was pretty easy to get accepted because they already knew me and what I was doing.

Seibel: Did you get your undergrad degree in computer science?

Steele: Yeah. I set out to be a pure math major and arranged my courses appropriately and then discovered that I had no intuition whatsoever for infinite dimensional Banach spaces. That's what did me in. Fortunately, just out of interest, I had taken enough computer courses on the side that I was well-positioned to make the switch in major. To be precise, what I switched to was an applied math major. Computer science was part of applied math, and applied math was part of the engineering department at Harvard.

Seibel: At Harvard what kinds of machines were you dealing with?

Steele: DEC PDP-10s. There was a PDP-10 on campus, but I think that was mostly used for the graduate work. Undergraduates had access to teletype terminals to a commercial system that Harvard was renting or leasing or something.

Seibel: Is there anything you would do differently about how you went about learning to program? Is there anything you wish you had done earlier?

Steele: It's not as if I set out with a particular goal in mind. I have no regrets about the particular path I took. Looking back I think I was the fortunate beneficiary of a number of interesting coincidences or blessings.

This experience of being, in effect, both at MIT and Harvard at the same time I now realize was a very unusual experience. I could run back and forth and say, "The professor at the other end of the river says this." And this one will say, "Oh, he's full of it; here's the way you should think about it." That gave me a very broad education, very quickly.

Having access to MIT as a high schooler was another relatively unusual thing. And to be allowed to play with million-dollar computers when I was 15, back when a million dollars was real money. So no, I certainly don't have any complaints or regrets or wishes that I had done anything differently. I also tend to be a laid-back kind of guy and to take things as they come.

Seibel: What has changed the most in the way you think about programming now, vs. then? Other than learning that bubble sort is not the greatest sorting technique.

Steele: I guess to me the biggest change is that nowadays you can't possibly know everything that's going on in the computer. There are things that are absolutely out of your control because it's impossible to know everything about all the software. Back in the '70s a computer had only 4,000 words of memory. It was possible to do a core dump and inspect every word to see if it was what you expected. It was reasonable to read the source listings of the operating system and see how that worked. And I did that—I studied the disk routines and the card-reader routines and wrote variants of my own. I felt as if I understood how the entire IBM 1130 worked. Or at least as much as I cared to know. You just can't do that anymore.

Seibel: Were there books that were important to you when you were learning to program?

Steele: In the '70s, absolutely: Knuth, *The Art of Computer Programming*.

Seibel: Did you read those cover-to-cover?

Steele: Pretty close to cover-to-cover, yes. I worked as many exercises as I felt I was capable of tackling. Some called for higher math or other things I didn't understand, and I'd sort of gloss or skip over those. But the first two volumes and much of the third I read pretty carefully. The Aho, Hopcroft, and Ullman algorithms book—that's where I learned how to do sorting for real, I think. I'd have to step across to my library to try to remember other ones. I'm a pack rat—I've saved all these books. But those are the ones that I would cite off the top of my head.And books about Lisp. The Triple-I Lisp book edited by Berkeley and Bobrow: kind of a scatter-shot collection of papers, but I learned a lot of interesting stuff from that. And then I started reading *SIGPLAN Notices* and *Communications of the ACM*. Back in those days *CACM* had real technical content and was well worth reading.

I should mention two things. First, I did science fairs when I was at Latin School and I made a point of doing projects about computer science. One of the judges one year said, "Have you considered becoming a student member of ACM?" I don't know his name. But I have been very thankful ever since. That was a good thing for me.

And when I got to Harvard, if I had a spare hour to kill in the morning I would go over to Lamont Library and I would do one of two things: I would read my way backwards through *Scientific American* and I would read my way forward, from the beginning, in *Communications of the ACM*. So I was, in particular, trying to pick up all of Martin Gardner's columns on mathematical games. And I just read whatever interested me out of *CACM*. In 1972 there was only about 15 years of that journal, so it didn't take that long to plow through them all.

Seibel: It also must have been easier then than it would today in the sense that the same way you could understand whole systems, one person could hope to understand the whole field.

Steele: Yeah, you could hope to understand the whole field. There were lots of one-page articles. You know: "Here's a clever new hashing technique." I read a lot.

Seibel: I often find older papers are hard to get into since they're tied to the particulars of old hardware or languages.

Steele: Well, necessity is the mother of invention—an idea arises because it's needed in a particular context. Then a little later it's recognized that that idea is the important thing. And then you need to strip away the context so the idea can be seen and that takes some years. "Here's a clever technique for reversing the bits of a word," and they give something in 7090 assembly language. And there's an interesting mathematical idea there but they haven't quite abstracted yet.

Seibel: I guess that's Knuth's job, right?

Steele: Knuth and people like him, absolutely.

Seibel: Presumably people who study computer science in school get guided through all that stuff. But there are also a lot of programmers who came into it without formal training, learning on the job. Do you have any advice for how to tackle that problem? Where do you start and how do you get to the point where you can actually read these technical papers and understand them? Should you start at the beginning of the ACM and try to get up to the present?

Steele: Well, first of all, let me say that that exercise of reading through *CACM* from early on wasn't my plan to become a great computer scientist by reading everything there was in the literature. I read it because I was interested in stuff and felt internally motivated to tackle that particular set of material. So I guess there are two things: one is having the internal motivation to want to read this stuff because you're interested or because you think it will improve your skills.

Then there is the problem of how do you find the good stuff? And of course the view of what is the good stuff changes from decade to decade. Stuff that was considered the really good stuff this year may be kind of dated in ten years. But I guess you go to a mentor who's been through it and say, what do you think was the good stuff? For me the good stuff was Knuth; Aho, Hopcroft, and Ullman. Gerald Weinberg on *The Psychology of Computer Programming*, which I think is still very readable today. Fred Brooks's *Mythical Man-Month* gave me some insights.

In those days I haunted the computer-science book section of the MIT bookstore and just made a point of going through there once a month and browsing through the bookshelves. Of course now you walk into a bookstore and there's a computer section that's ten times as big, but most of it is about how to do C or Java this year. But there will be a smaller section of books about the theoretical background, algorithms, that kind of thing.

Seibel: There's another kind of reading, which I know you think is important—reading code. How do you find your way into a big pile of code you didn't write?

Steele: If it's a piece of software that I know how to use and just don't know how the insides work, I will often pick a particular command or interaction and trace it through.

Seibel: The execution path?

Steele: Yes. So if I were walking up to Emacs, I'd say, "OK, let's take a look at the code that does 'forward a character'." And I won't completely understand it but at least it'll introduce me to some data structures it uses and how the buffer is represented. And if I'm lucky I can find a place where it adds one. And then once I've understood that, then I'll try "backwards a character." "Kill a line." And work my way up through more and more complicated uses and interactions until I feel that I've traced my way through some of the more important parts of the code.

Seibel: And would "tracing" mean looking at the text of the source code and mentally executing it, or would you fire it up in a debugger and step through it?

Steele: I've done it both ways—I've done it with a stepping debugger mostly on smaller codes back in the '70s or '80s. The problem nowadays is from the time a program first fires up until it begins to do anything interesting can already be a long initialization process. So perhaps one is better off trying to find the main command loop or the central control routine and then tracing from there.

Seibel: And once you find that, would you set a break point and then step from there or just do it by mental execution?

Steele: I'd be inclined to do it by desk-checking—by actually reading the code and thinking about what it does. If I really need to understand the whole code then at some point I might sit down and try to read my way all the way through it. But you can't do that at first until you've got some kind of framework in your head about how the thing is organized. Now, if you're lucky, the programmer actually left some documentation behind or named things well or left things in the right order in the file so you actually can sort of read it through.

Seibel: So what is the right order in the file?

Steele: That's a very good question. It strikes me that one of the problems of a programming language like Pascal was that because it was designed for a one-pass compiler, the order of the routines in the file tended to be bottom-up because you had to define routines before you use them. As a result, the best way to read a Pascal program was actually backwards because that would give you the top-down view of the program. Now that things are more free-form, you really can't count on anything other than the programmer's good taste in trying to lay things out in a way that might be helpful to you. On the third hand, now that we've got good IDEs that can help you with cross-referencing, maybe the linear order of the program doesn't matter so much.

On the fourth hand, one reason I don't like IDEs quite so much is that they can make it hard to know when you've actually seen everything. Walking around in a graph, it's hard to know you've touched all the parts. Whereas if you've got some linear order, it's guaranteed to take you through everything.

Seibel: So when you write code these days would you present more of a top-down organization with the high-level functions before the lower-level functions on which they depend?

Steele: I'd try to present the high-level ideas. The best way to present that might be to show a central command-and-control routine with the things it dispatches to beneath it. Or, it might be that the important thing is to show the data structures first, or the more important data structures. The point is to present the ideas in an order such that they tell a story rather than just being a pile of code thrown together.

One of the wonderful things about working at MIT was that there was a lot of code sitting around that was not kept under lock and key, written by pretty smart hackers. So I read the ITS operating system. I read the implementations of TECO and of Lisp. And the first pretty printer for Lisp, written by Bill Gosper. In fact I read them as a high-school student and then proceeded to replicate some of that in my 1130 implementation.

I would not have been able to implement Lisp for an 1130 without having had access to existing implementations of Lisp on another computer. I wouldn't have known what to do. That was an important part of my education. Part of the problem that we face nowadays, now that software has become valuable and most software of any size is commercial, is that we don't have a lot of examples of good code to read. The open source movement has helped to rectify that to some extent. You can go in and read the source to Linux, if you want to. Reading the source to TeX was a valuable exercise just because it was a large body of well-thought-out, well-debugged code.

Seibel: I usually have the best luck reading code when I have a very specific need to know how something works; what is your mindset reading a program like TeX?

Steele: Sometimes I've got a specific goal because I'm trying to solve a problem. There have been exactly two times, I think, that I was not able to fix a bug in my TeX macros by reading *The TeXbook* and it was necessary to go ahead and read *TeX: The Program* to find out exactly how a feature worked. In each case I was able to find my answer in 15 minutes because *TeX: The Program* is so well documented and cross-referenced. That, in itself, is an eye-opener—the fact that a program can be so organized and so documented, so indexed, that you can find something quickly.

The other thing I learned from it is how a master programmer organizes data structures, how he organizes the code so as to make it easier to read. Knuth carefully laid out *TeX: The Program* so you could almost read it as a novel or something. You could read it in a linear pass. You'd probably want to do some jumping back and forth as you encountered various things. Of course, it was an enormous amount of work on his part, which is why very few programs have been done that way.

Seibel: And when you get to the end, what are you going to take away?

Steele: I'll have a pretty good idea of how it's organized and I may have come away with some ideas about how to organize my own code better. I don't think I'll ever be able to write in the style of Knuth any more than I could write in the style of Faulkner or Hemingway. Nevertheless, having read novels by those writers will influence my own thinking about English style a little bit. Maybe I'll make a conscious decision *not* to write like Hemingway for some reason or another. It's a valuable experience. Not to mention just the enjoyment of going through a well-written novel or a well-written piece of code.

Seibel: Have you ever written literate programs?

Steele: Not in nearly the disciplined way that Knuth has. It has influenced my style in that I think about those issues—I will often actually write a paragraph of prose before beginning to write a subroutine. But I don't do it in nearly as disciplined a style. And sometimes I wonder whether he does, either, when he's doing exploratory programming before he readies it up for publication. I don't know what his process looks like there.

Seibel: So you've tried it but it didn't strike you as something that made programming much more productive or enjoyable?

Steele: In part I didn't feel like doing a lot of tool building for myself. The tools he had built were organized around Pascal and then C. Pascal I could see but I was quite aware of the flaws in C and I wasn't sure that using literate programming tools would suffice to overcome them. If he had built literate programming tools for Common Lisp I might have jumped over to them much more quickly.

Seibel: Leaving aside literate programs and back to reading code, do you find that you can read usually well-written programs from beginning to end? Or is it always a hypertext that you have to find your way through?

Steele: I don't necessarily object to hypertext. But I think if a program is well written, there will be something about its structure that will guide me to various parts of it in an order that will make some kind of sense. You know, it's not just what the program does—there's a story. There's a story about how the program is organized, there's a story about the context in which the program is expected to operate. And one would hope that there will be something about the program, whether it's block comments at the start of each routine or an overview document that comes separately or just choices of variable names that will somehow convey those stories to you. And one would hope that a good programmer, a really good programmer, will have given thought to conveying those stories in addition to the story of *what* the program actually does.

Seibel: What code have you read most recently just for fun?

Steele: It's hard to find good code that's worth reading. We haven't developed a body of accepted literature that says, "This is great code; everybody should read this." So it tends to be one-page snippets, often in papers, rather than chunks of code out of existing stuff. Probably the code I've read most recently is the stuff that my own team has been producing as part of the Fortress implementation. And parts of the Java libraries.

Probably the last substantial body of code I read just for fun was written by George Hart. He's a mathematician, a specialist in polyhedra. And he has a very interesting piece of code that will generate and display complex polyhedra using VRML within a browser. And so he's got this enormous body of JavaScript code that constructs VRML code and then feeds that to the VRML displayer.

I decided to try to enhance it in various ways so I went in and read his code thoroughly. And then proceeded to try to make various enhancements to it and understand what was going on: try to make some somewhat funkier polyhedra and so forth. I also managed to make several bad errors—there was a relaxation algorithm that tries to spread out the vertexes of the polyhedra to make it prettier and easier to display, and occasionally I'd introduce mathematical instabilities which would cause grotesque things to happen. Tremendous fun, and I was doing this purely for my own edification. That was probably six or seven years ago.

Seibel: How much did the reading and the modification intertwine? Can you read sitting at a table with a printout or at a computer without executing it to see what happens if you twiddle that little bit there?

Steele: Well I did, in fact, print out the code on paper. I would sit at a desk and read it. And very often mark it up and make annotations and ask myself questions and things like that. And then I'd go back to the computer and start typing in things and see how it behaved. And tracing it.

Seibel: In this case you wanted to modify it, so that's what you did. But could you get some benefit or enjoyment out of just reading the code? Print it out, read it, maybe scribble some questions on it, and then put it down?

Steele: Yes. If I had stopped at that point, it would have been a worthwhile exercise, just having read the code. It taught me something about VRML; it taught me something about JavaScript, which is that it doesn't have as many abstractions as I would like. The dynamic typing was a little bit too free-form for my taste—in an object-oriented language.

Seibel: So let's talk a little bit about designing software. You're not coding as much these days as you used to, but how did you go about designing a new piece of software? Do you sit down at a computer and start coding or do you sit with a pad of graph paper, or what?

Steele: I'm being very cautious here because it's all too easy to have a revisionist memory and say, "Oh, well, back in the '70s this is the way I should have done it so that must be the way I did it." I'm trying to remember actual things I did.

Sometimes I would draw flowcharts—I did have an IBM flowcharting template and pads of such paper. And I learned to program before the structured programming era, so some of my designs were structured and some of them weren't. As I became aware of structured programming I recognized some of the good ideas in that and I think during the '70s my assembly language programming became more structured in nature and I was thinking explicitly of making if/then/else paths and loops and things like that and I thought more about the structure of my assembly-language code.

I would often make lists describing the kinds of inputs I wanted to be able to give to a program and then write down a description of what kind of output I wanted. Or I would sometimes make up short examples. I recently found an example of one of the earliest APL programs that I ever wrote. I was probably 15 or 16 at the time. And what I had was a piece of APL code—this was the first thing I jotted down on paper before I'd actually tried it out. And enclosed was another piece of paper, which was an example of what I thought the input/output interaction would look like. It has bugs in it and doesn't match the code and so forth but at least I was struggling to try to produce some examples of what I thought it would be like to use this program. It was exactly what I thought the terminal transcript would look like, on a printing terminal. Here's a series of interactions that I think we can cause with this program.

Once I started working on the Maclisp project, that provided a structure. Nearly everything I did was a new function being added to an already existing large collection of functions. There were already plenty of examples of what documentation of functions ought to look like so it was just a matter of adding to that pile.

Seibel: You said you took over the interpreter from JonL, who had been doing both the interpreter and the compiler.

Steele: We'd collaborate on the design work. I was the junior member so he'd say, "Here's a function we should have and here's how it should work; why don't you go code it." Or, more often, we'd get requests from the Macsyma implementers saying, "We need something to do this," and JonL and I would put our heads together and say, "Well, why don't we design an interface that looks this way," and I then would go off and code it.

Seibel: So those were new language features being added to Maclisp that had to be implemented in the interpreter and the compiler?

Steele: Yeah, language features. Many of a systems-oriented flavor—they needed to be able to control resources or allocate pages. I implemented a new data type called a "hunk," which was probably the biggest disaster in language design we ever put in. It was essentially a cons cell with more than two pointers. It was a desperation move because we were running out of address space on the PDP-10. Recall that the 10 only had an 18-bit address space. In a list, 50 percent of the pointers were dedicated to just maintaining the structure of the list, whereas with a threaded set of hunks, maybe only one-eighth of the pointers were dedicated to the threading of the chunks so you'd get better memory usage that way.

Seibel: So you had this stream of requests for features—given that it was incremental, how did you maintain some kind of coherence? If you just keep adding one thing in the most obvious way, eventually you end up with a big pile of kludges that barely holds together.

Steele: There were one or two big reorgs. I think probably the most notable one was the complete redesign and reimplementation of all the input/output operations in the language. This was the so-called New I/O design, something I undertook in, I want to say, 1975 or '76, somewhere in there. The goal was that the old I/O system allowed for only one input stream and one output stream, plus being able to interact with the console. We realized that it would be a lot more flexible if we could have actual Lisp objects that stood for I/O channels and then we could have as many as 15 I/O channels open.

The other thing that was pushing this was that Maclisp was beginning to be ported to other operating systems. Every site had its own variant of the PDP-10 operating system. When we looked at all the customers we had, we realized there were a half a dozen different operating systems we wanted to support: TENEX, TWENEX, ITS, TOPS-10, WAITS, and the CMU variant.

So there was a summer when I sat down with JonL and we designed a new set of APIs. We didn't call them APIs at the time, but it was descriptions of functions that could be used to create file objects, open and close them, do things like "delete" and "rename" in a systematic way, and get directory listings.

Then there was a point where I took a fresh listing of all of Maclisp on paper and retreated to my parents' summer home for a week with six sets of operating-systems manuals and the listing and spent six hours a day scribbling corrections and changes in the code.

I had to figure out for each feature, such as the "rename" function, how is that done, because the details of how you interact with the operating system to rename a file were very different among those six operating systems. But it tended to fall into three clusters—the TOPS-20 variants, the TOPS-10 variants, and ITS.

I spent a solid week doing that, and notice, doing design and implementation without sitting at a computer terminal. This was all desk work. And then after a week of that, I came back to MIT and spent the next month typing it all in and debugging and testing it.

Seibel: Why did you do it that way?

Steele: I did it that way because for every function I had to write, it would have to be preceded by an enormous amount of research. As I say, I'd have to read the specification for six operating systems. And I would have to spend an hour doing that and then write the 30 lines of code, probably times three. It didn't seem to make sense to be sitting in front of a terminal when it wasn't going to be buying me that much. It's not as if I could Google something or access online documentation. I wasn't spending most of the time typing. Better to use that desk space for the paper documents in front of me.

Seibel: Are there situations today where you think turning off the computer and clearing your desk is the right approach?

Steele: Yeah, I still do that. In fact, I find that I literally have to turn off the computer because if the fan is whirring behind me there's the lure of "Check your email, check your email." So I'll turn it off or at least put it to sleep, come over to this table on the other side of the room, and spread out my papers and think. Or work at the whiteboard or something.

Seibel: I read something where you paraphrased Fred Brooks's saying about flowcharts and tables, saying, "Show me your interfaces and I won't need your code because it'll be redundant or irrelevant." When you're working in a language like Java, do you start your designs from interfaces?

Steele: Yeah, I've become much more interface-oriented than I used to be. Descriptions of the inputs and actions and outputs of methods with no code. I love writing that stuff. I also enjoy writing the code that implements it, but I do less of that nowadays than I used to. And of course it's important to have had an experience doing that so you don't design impossible specifications. You should have an idea what the implementation is going to look like as you design the interface. You should at least have an idea for the implementation. Then if someone comes along with a better one, that's fine.

Seibel: Other than the possibility of implementing it at all, how do you decide whether your interfaces are good?

Steele: I usually think about generality and orthogonality. Conformance to accepted ways of doing things. For example, you don't put the divisor before the dividend unless there's a really good reason for doing so because in mathematics we're used to doing it the other way around. So you think about conventional ways of doing things.

I've done enough designs that I think about ways I've done it before and whether they were good or bad. I'm also designing relative to some related thing that I've already designed before. So, for example, while looking at the specifications for numeric functions in Java, I'd already done numeric functions for Common Lisp. And I'd documented numeric functions for C. I knew some of the implementation pitfalls and some of the specification pitfalls for those things. I spent a lot of time worrying about edge cases.

That's something I learned from Trenchard More and his array theory for APL. His contention was that if you took care of the edge cases then the stuff in the middle usually took care of itself. Well, he didn't say it that way; I guess that's the conclusion I draw from him.

To turn it around, you want to design the specification of what's in the middle in such a way that it naturally is also correct on the boundaries, rather than treating boundaries as special cases.

Seibel: During your time at MIT you were somehow involved in the birth of Emacs. But the early history of Emacs is a bit hazy. What is your version of the story?

Steele: My version of the story was that I was playing standards guy. What had happened was there was this display mode that turned TECO into something like a WYSIWYG editor. On our 24X80 screens, 21 lines of what was in the buffer would be shown on the screen and the bottom 3 lines were still a TECO command line.You'd be typing in these TECO commands and only when you hit the double almode would they then be executed. Then there was the real-time edit mode, where it was suggested that a TECO command throw you in this other mode whereby instead of waiting for you to type the double altmode, TECO would react immediately to single character commands. If you type one character, it would do the command. You type another character, it would do the command. And most printing characters were self-inserting. Then the control characters were used to move forward, back, up, and down. It was a very, very primitive—it looked like a very primitive version of Emacs.

Then came the breakthrough. The suggestion was, we have this idea of taking a character and looking it up in a table and executing TECO commands. Why don't we apply that to real-time edit mode? So that every character you can type is used as a lookup character in this table. And the default table says, printing characters are self-inserting and control characters do these things. But let's just make it programmable and see what happens. And what immediately happened was four or five different bright people around MIT had their own ideas about what to do with that. Within just a few months there were five completely incompatible GUI interfaces to TECO.

Seibel: So they were just customizing, essentially, the key-bindings?

Steele: That's right. And they each had their own ideas about what should be concise because you do it most often and what you can afford to be longer. So one guy, for example, was really concerned about typing in Lisp code and began to experiment with finding balanced parenthesized expressions. And another guy was more interested in text, so he was interested in commands that would move over words and convert between uppercase and lowercase and capitalize them. And that's where those commands in Emacs came from.

Different people had different ideas about how the key-bindings ought to be organized. As a systems-support guy for Lisp, I was often called to people's terminals and asked to help them. And I fairly quickly noticed that I couldn't sit down at their TECOs and help them modify their programs because I'd be faced with a set of key-bindings and I had no idea what they were going to do.

Seibel: Was one of these guys Richard Stallman?

Steele: No, Stallman was the implementer and supporter of TECO. And he provided the built-in real-time edit mode feature, although I think Carl Mikkelsen had worked on the early version of it. He provided the key-bindings feature that made all of this possible.

Anyway, there were something like four different macro packages and they were incompatible, and I decided to play standards guy, or community reconciliation guy. I saw something that had been lost in our community, which was the ability to easily help each other at our terminals. I said, "OK, we've had some experimentation; we've seen a bunch of ideas. What if we could agree on a common set of key-bindings and draw the best ideas from each of these things?"

I literally had a pad of paper and ran around the building, talking to these guys, visiting each of them several times, and tried to get some kind of consensus. I was trying to get consensus on what the content ought to be and then I drew on their designs and tried to organize the actual choice of key-bindings so as to make them a little more regular and a little more mnemonic. And not being a human-factors guy at all, I didn't think at all about convenience for touch typists. I was principally concerned with mnemonic value. And so that's why Meta-C and Meta-L and Meta-U stand for capitalize and lowercase and uppercase.

Seibel: Which is sort of ironic given the way the commands move out of your brain and into your fingers. I'm sure you have experienced the phenomenon of having someone ask you what is the key-binding for something that you use a thousand times a day, and you can't say.

Steele: Actually my wife had that experience. Maybe one of the reasons I was less aware of it is that I'm not a particularly good touch typist. But she'd been away from Emacs for 20 years and then I made one available on her Macintosh. And she sat down, typed in some stuff, and then said, "How do I save this? I forget how to save a file." And then she realized her fingers had done it and she didn't know what she'd typed. So she did it again and *watched* her fingers and said, "Oh yes, Control-X Control-S." But she literally couldn't remember what the commands were.

Seibel: So you made this standard set of key-bindings. How did that go over? Were people happy with it?

Steele: Well, people worked through it. Then I then sat down and proceeded to begin an implementation of it. And we had another idea that came into the mix at the same time and it was the idea that you could make TECO macros run a lot faster if you squeezed out the spaces and deleted all the comments. The way the TECO interpreter worked, interpreting one character at a time, when you encountered a comment it had to spend the time skipping over that comment. So we had this idea of this very primitive TECO compiler that was mostly just squeezing out the white space and the comments and doing a few other minor things to put it in a form that would run a little bit faster.

So I began in an initial way to try to construct a version of this macro compressor, which I think was actually based on an earlier idea that Moon had had. I don't think I originated that idea. I began to think about how to organize the initial dispatch and organize some of the first few routines borrowing on the existing implementations of other macro packages—I was trying to synthesize them. And about that point Stallman came along and said, "What are you doing? This looks interesting." He immediately jumped in and he could implement ten times as fast as I could, partly because he knew TECO inside out.

So I worked seriously on the implementation of Emacs probably for only about four or six weeks. At which point it became clear that Stallman understood what the program was. I wanted to get back to doing graduate-student things. So Stallman did the other 99.999 percent of the work. But I played a role in catalyzing it and beginning the implementation.

Seibel: On a different subject, academic computer science is very mathematical these days. How important is it for working programmers to be able to understand, say, the math in Knuth? Versus saying, "I need to sort things; I'm going to flip through Knuth and skip to where he says, 'This is the best algorithm' and implement that"?

Steele: I don't know. There are parts of Knuth that I don't understand because I don't have the mathematical training. Particularly if it involves higher or continuous math. I'm a little weaker on that. I think my strengths are in things like combinatorics and permutations, group theory, things like that. And I find myself using that over and over and over again. Maybe that's because that's the particular hammer I have at hand. I don't think that every programmer needs that. But I think that mathematics formalizes concepts that programmers do need to work with every day.

I'll give you an example from my recent programming-language work on parallel languages, this Fortress project that I've got going. Suppose you want to add up a bunch of numbers. Well, one thing you can do is you can initialize a register to zero and add in the numbers one at a time—a classic sequential technique.

Notice that this depends on the addition operation having an identity. You needed to start with zero. Trivial little observation, but it's there.

Now here's another strategy—you can lay out all the numbers in a row and then add them up pairwise, giving you a bunch of sums, and keep adding pairwise until you've only got one number left. And of course if at any point you've got an odd number of them you just leave that one over extra and let it go to the next stage and so forth. Well, that works fine, too. And if you're using floating-point numbers it may actually give you a little bit better accuracy, although with the bookkeeping overhead it's sometimes not worth it.

Notice that this will give you the same answer, at least if you're working with integers, as starting with zero and adding them one at a time. This depends on the fact that addition is associative. In other words, it doesn't matter in what way you group the numbers.

And then there's a third strategy. Suppose you've got a bunch of processors. You could parcel out the pairs to the processors and distribute that work. The "start with zero and add them one at a time" algorithm is hard to parallelize, but with the bunching in pairs, you've in effect made a tree and you can assign processors different parts of the tree, and they can do their parts independently, and only at the end do they need to interact and you get the sum.

OK, so that's cool. Here's another parallel strategy that's more like the first one: pick some register and initialize it to zero, and then let processors compete for grabbing numbers and adding them into that common place. This involves questions of synchronization, but you will still get the same answer. But this depends on addition being both associative and commutative. That is, not only does it not matter how you group the numbers, it also doesn't matter in what order you process the numbers.

Mathematicians have big, scary words like "identity" and "associativity" and "commutativity" to talk about this stuff—it's their shorthand. But programmers need to know about ideas like, it doesn't matter in what order you do it. And they need to know about ideas like, it's OK if you regroup things. So to that extent I claim that mathematical ideas are important at some level to programmers.

Seibel: Obviously that's a good example to give because anyone who understands arithmetic can understand it. But do you find that there are kind of higher-level concepts that come back into programming in the same way?

Steele: Now suppose I'm generating a report. The typical thing is you make a bunch of print statements and you depend on doing them in order and things get printed out in the order you said. Well, in this multicore world maybe I would like to break up the generation of the report and parcel it out to processors. Well, how about concatenating strings? Can I use the same techniques I used for adding up numbers? Turns out it is associative but not commutative—that tells me exactly which tricks will work for the strings and which ones won't.As a language designer worrying about designing parallel programming languages, I find these concepts and a vocabulary for them very useful.

Seibel: Speaking of being a language designer, how have your ideas about language design changed over time?

Steele: I think that the biggest change in my thinking is what I set down in that talk "Growing a Language" at OOPSLA almost ten years ago, in 1998. Back in the '70s people would invent languages and make a complete design and implement it and you'd be done. Or you wouldn't be done, but you had this idea that there is this complete thing.

So Pascal was an invention. Things were in it for a reason and things were left out for a reason but it was a complete design. And if it turned out that it wasn't complete—if it turned out that string processing wasn't that great, well, too bad: Wirth had designed the language. And PL/I got designed and Ada got designed. And maybe Ada and C++ were close to the last of that generation. And C++ not so much, because it did sort of evolve over time.

I realized as languages got more complicated they were really too big to design all at once and that languages would necessarily from now on undergo evolution because they were too big to design all at once or to implement all at once. And that caused a change in how I approached programming-language design and thinking about it.

Seibel: So you think Java was not designed that way?

Steele: I think maybe Java was not and should have been. Java has evolved through the Java Community Process. That has addressed more API than core language issues. And while features have been added to the language over the last 12 or 13 years, I think the team that designed Java in the early '90s thought they were designing a complete language for a specific self-contained purpose. You know, they were aiming at set-top boxes.

Seibel: Right.

Steele: They hadn't even envisioned at that point programming the World Wide Web or having as huge a user base as it has turned out to have. And so I thought they were designing a fairly small, self-contained kernel language on top of which you would then build a bunch of APIs and use it for various things. And that was the model and that's the way it's worked out. And part of my thoughts about "Growing a Language" came out of observing that process, that Java turned out to be a little bit too small and people wanted more features to get to other things.

In particular there was pressure for the kind of `for` loop that could iterate through an enumeration. That is a feature that got added to the language. There was pressure from the high-performance scientific computing community to put in more features to support floating point and stuff like that. That pretty much got rejected by the Java Community Process, and I think that was more for social reasons than technical reasons.

But there is this demand for adding to the language and then there was a social process that gated that in various ways. And so I got to thinking that maybe for a really successful programming language, you need to design and plan for the social process as much as you design the technical features of the language and think about how those two things are going to interact. And Fortress is our first experiment with that, or at least my first experiment with that. And it's still early in the game—it's only a half-done experiment.

Seibel: Don't you think Common Lisp, which you were involved with, stakes out a position in how one does that?

Steele: Yes, that was the other early example as over against something like Java that got me thinking about these "growing a language" issues. I'm certainly familiar with the history of Lisp and how its macro facilities in particular made it somewhat easier for it to evolve over time and for people to make contributions.

Seibel: It seems like recently three languages, all of which you were involved with at some level, have gone through or are going through a painful redesign. Scheme just went through R6RS; JavaScript—

ECMAScript—is going through the ES4 vs. ES3.1 debate. And Java is struggling with whether or not and how to add closures.

Steele: For example, yes.

Seibel: Are these examples of languages that didn't have enough built-in technical or social wherewithal to grow easily and so had to go through these painful growth processes? Or is this how it always happens?

Steele: Well, if a language doesn't die, it is going to grow. There are always evolutionary pressures because needs change and people will want to modify the tool to suit where they are now as opposed to where they were five years ago. My conjecture isn't about whether a language *will* grow or not but rather about technical choices you can make in the early design of the language that may facilitate the growth in certain ways later on. And I think some languages have turned out to be easier to grow than others because of technical differences among them. And also in part because of differences among the social contexts.

Seibel: So what are the examples that have grown easily?

Steele: Well, I think Lisp is an example of a language that has grown easily because of the flexibility of its macro mechanism. And to some extent in part because of the social attitudes of the group that constructed it.

Scheme, by contrast, has had a much more painful growth path. And that's in part because the Scheme community developed a culture early on that they would not put anything in the language unless everyone agreed on it. Or close to everyone. So it was more of a blackball culture. Whereas with the community that turned into Common Lisp, majority was enough to satisfy everyone. And people were more willing to accept things they weren't crazy about in order to get other things.

Seibel: How much does a choice of language really matter? Are there good reasons to choose one language over another or does it all just come down to taste?

Steele: Why shouldn't taste be a good reason?

Seibel: Well, I may like vanilla ice cream and you like chocolate, but we don't *fight* about it. But people fight about programming languages.

Steele: Well, that's the human social phenomenon of wanting to belong to the winning side. And, no, I don't think it's worth fighting over, but I think it's reasonable to have opinions about what is a more effective tool for a given task.

The one thing I am reasonably convinced of is that it's a mistake to think that one language solves all problems better than any other language, or even equally well. I really think that there are application areas for which particular languages are better suited.

I feel perfectly free, when doing algorithm design, to use a hodgepodge of different languages. As long as I'm just communicating with myself I will go to a whiteboard and write fragments of Java and Fortran with APL mixed in. It doesn't bother me in the least as long as I can sort out what I've written afterwards. For a particular piece of the algorithm the notation is buying me something that I think another language wouldn't be nearly as clear or useful for.

The problem is, if you come up with a notation that's good at one small set of ideas, you still want to put that in the context of a complete programming language and you have to build something around it and make it complete and if you don't do a good job of everything, then you end up with a lopsided language that's great at this one idea and kind of clunky for the other stuff.

On the other hand, it's really hard to make a language that's great at everything, in part just because there are only so many concise notations to go around. There's this Huffman encoding problem. If you make something concise, something is going to have to be more verbose as a consequence. So in designing a language, one of the things you think about is, "What are the things I want to make very easy to say and very easy to get right?" But with the understanding that, having used up characters or symbols for that purpose, you're going to have made something else a little bit harder to say.

Seibel: One way to resolve that is the way Lisp does—make everything uniformly semiconcise. Where the uniformity has the advantage of allowing users of the language to easily add their own equally uniform, semiconcise, first-class syntactic extensions. Yet a lot of folks resist the s-expression syntax. The smug Lisp weenie view of the world is, "Some people just don't get it; if they did they would see the brilliance of the solution." Are you a smug enough Lisp weenie to think that if people really understood Lisp they would not be put off by the parentheses?

Steele: No. I don't think I've got the standing to be smug. If anything, because I have learned so many languages I think I understand better than a lot of people the fact that different languages can offer different things. And there are good reasons to make choices among them rather than to hold up one language and say, "This is the winner."

There are certain kinds of projects that I would not want to tackle with anything other than Lisp because I'm interested in the set of tools it provides me. For instance, ready-made input/output—if I'm willing to conform to Lisp's syntax, then I've already got readers and printers built that are adequate for some kinds of jobs. This in turn allows you to do some kinds of rapid prototyping. On the other hand, if it's important that I customize the I/O to an existing specific format, then Lisp might not be such a good tool. Or else I might have to build some kind of transducer in some language, Lisp or otherwise, to get it over to the Lisp world.

Seibel: What languages have you used seriously? It must be a long list for you.

Steele: I earned my first money programming in COBOL. I was still a high-school student and subcontracted to someone who was doing a report-card generator system for another school system, so there wasn't any conflict of interest there. I used Fortran, IBM 1130 assembly language, PDP-10 machine language, APL. I guess I can't claim to have used SNOBOL seriously. Certainly C, C++, Bliss, the DECsystems implementation language that came out of Carnegie Mellon. GNAL, which is based on Red, I've used quite seriously.

Several different varieties of Lisp, including Common Lisp, Scheme, Maclisp. The version of Lisp that Dick Gabriel and I built for the S-1, S-1 Lisp, which was one of the four or five that merged to make Common Lisp. I developed Connection Machine Lisp but I'm not sure I could be said to have done serious coding in it. That was, I think, in turn implemented in *Lisp. *Lisp is not to be confused with Connection Machine Lisp; they are two distinct languages.

I did some serious coding in C*, which was another language we developed for the Connection Machine. Java, of course. And some scripting languages. I've done some extensive work in JavaScript, in Tcl.

I've done serious programming in Haskell, taking "serious" to mean I've worked with a language for more than a month and tried to write a substantial piece of code in it. Oh, FOCAL, an early interactive language on the DEC computers, similar to . . . a little bit like BASIC, a little bit like JOSS. I've done substantial coding in BASIC, now that I think about it. And TECO, the Text Editor and Corrector, of course was used to program the first version of Emacs and I regard that as a programming language for that purpose. I wrote enormous amounts of TECO code. And TeX, also regarded as a programming language. Those would be the main ones, I guess.

Seibel: I'm guessing from what you said earlier that the answer to the question of "What's your favorite programming language?" would have to be "mu."

Steele: I've got three children; you might as well ask me which is my favorite. They're all great—they've got different skills and different personalities.

Seibel: Are there any programming languages which you just don't enjoy using?

Steele: I get some kind of pleasure out of each language. But there are certainly certain languages that I find more frustrating than others. I enjoyed TECO at the time; I don't think I'd want to go back. It had quite a number of difficulties—it was very difficult to come back in a month and read what you'd written.

I'm not sure that I've written enough Perl code to be taken seriously as a detractor, but I have not been attracted to the language. I have not been attracted to C++. I have written some C++ code. Anything I think I might want to write in C++ now could be done about as well and more easily in Java. Unless efficiency were the primary concern.

But I don't want to be seen as a detractor of Bjarne Stroustrup's effort. He set himself up a particular goal, which was to make an object-oriented language that would be fully backwards-compatible with C. That was a difficult task to set himself. And given that constraint, I think he came up with an admirable design and it has held up well. But given the kinds of goals that I have in programming, I think the decision to be backwards-compatible with C is a fatal flaw. It's just a set of difficulties that can't be overcome. C fundamentally has a corrupt type system. It's good enough to help you avoid some difficulties but it's not airtight and you can't count on it.

Seibel: Do you think languages are getting better? You keep designing them, so hopefully you think it's a worthwhile pursuit. Is it easier to write software now because of advances that we've made?

Steele: Well, it's much easier now to write the kinds of programs we were trying to write 30 years ago. But I think our ambitions have grown tremendously. So I think programming is probably a more difficult activity than it was 30 years ago.

Seibel: And what are the things that are making it more difficult?

Steele: I think we've got people now who are just as smart as the people we had 30 years ago and they are being pushed to the limits of their abilities as people were 30 years ago—I've chosen 30 years ago as an arbitrary baseline because that's when I got out of school. But the difference is that—as I remarked earlier—it's not possible to understand everything that's going on anymore. Or even to think you can. So I think that the programmers of today are up against a more difficult environment—still exercising the same amounts of ingenuity but in an environment that's harder to understand. So we try to make more elaborate languages to help them deal with the uncertainty of those environments.

Seibel: It's interesting that you say, "more elaborate languages." There's a school of thought—one that you're certainly aware of as it could be called the Scheme school of thought—that the only way to manage complexity is to keep things, including our programming languages, very simple.

Steele: I think it's important that a language be able to capture what the programmer wants to tell the computer, to be recorded and taken into account. Now different programmers have different styles and different ideas about what they want recorded. As I've progressed through my understanding of what ought to be recorded I think we want to say a lot more about data structures, we want to say a lot more about their invariants. The kinds of things we capture in Javadoc are the kinds of things that ought to be told to a compiler. If it's worth telling another programmer, it's worth telling the compiler, I think.

Seibel: Isn't most of the stuff in Javadoc, other than the human-readable prose, actually derived from the code?

Steele: Some of it is. But some of it isn't. Relationships between parameters are not well captured by Java code. For instance, here's an array and here's an integer and this integer ought to be a valid index into the array. That's something you can't easily say in Java. That's an important concept and in Fortress you are able to say such things.

Seibel: And they're compiled into runtime asserts or statically checked?

Steele: Whatever is appropriate. Both. In the case of Fortress we are trying to be able to capture those kinds of relationships. We talked about algebraic relationships earlier, the idea that some operation is associative. We want to be able to talk about that very explicitly in Fortress. And I don't expect that every applications programmer is going to stop and think, "You know, this subroutine I just invented is associative."

But library programmers really care about that a lot. Partly because if they're going to use sophisticated implementation algorithms, the correctness of the algorithm hinges crucially on these properties. And so where it does depend crucially on those properties, we want a way to talk about them in a way the compiler can understand. I conjecture that that is an important approach to finding our way forward, to capture in the language important properties of programming.

Seibel: What about the role of the language in making it impossible to make mistakes? Some people say, "If we just lock this language down enough it'll be impossible to write bad code." Then other people say, "Forget it;

that's a doomed enterprise, so we might as well just leave everything wide open and leave it to the programmers do be smart." How do you find that balance?

Steele: The important thing is just to realize that it is a trade-off that you make. And you can't hope to eradicate all bad code. You can hope to discourage certain kinds of likely errors by requiring "Mother, may I?" code; in order to do something difficult, you have to write something a little more elaborate to say, "Yes, I really meant this." Or you can purposely make it difficult or impossible to say a certain thing, such as, for example, to corrupt the type system. Which has its pluses and minuses—it's really hard to write device drivers for bare metal in a completely type-safe language just because the levels of abstraction are wrong for talking to the bare metal. Or you can try to add in stuff that lets you say, "This variable really is this device register at absolute address XXXX." That in itself is a kind of unsafe feature.

Seibel: Have any of the newer languages provided any interesting surprises?

Steele: Python's kind of nice in the way that it's organized. I think I disagreed with Guido's decision not to use a garbage collector early on. I think he's since recanted that decision—I could have predicted they would probably want one eventually. They made some interesting syntactic choices including the decision to rely on indentation, and the way they use colons at the end of certain statements is kind of cute. And the specific ways in which they support objects and closures is kind of interesting.

Seibel: Most Lispers would think of the closures as being sort of deficient; the lambda is pretty limited.

Steele: Right. Well you know, he was making a certain set of compromises based on implementability and explainability and other things. And it was an interesting set of choices. And it was not the set of choices I would have made, but he was serving a particular user community and trying to get certain things done and I can appreciate why he made the choices the way he did. Haskell is a beautiful language. I love Haskell. I don't use it that much.

Seibel: So you're in the midst of designing a language and you love Haskell, but Fortress isn't a pure functional language?

Steele: On the other hand, now Haskell has discovered monads and they have dragged in the I/O monad and now the transactional-memory monad. There's a theory that it's functional and maybe that does give you a leg up. On the other hand it's feeling more and more imperative. And I can't resist thinking of the White Knight in *Through the Looking Glass*—"I was thinking of a plan to dye one's whiskers green, and always use so large a fan that they could not be seen." And in some ways, monads strike me as that fan, where you're dragging in the I/O and trying to hide it again—are the side effects really there, or are they really not?

Although I will say that about once a month I get the feeling that I wish that in designing Fortress we had started with Haskell and tried to move it toward Fortran and Java, rather than starting with Fortran and Java and trying to move it toward Haskell. We are finding ourselves taking more and more of a functional approach as we design the Fortress libraries as we encounter the difficulties of trying to make efficient parallel data structures.

Seibel: You obviously write a lot in English and care about that craft as well. Do you find writing prose and writing code to be similar mental exercises?

Steele: Well, they feel different in that I'm very aware that the primary reader for English prose has a very different kind of processor than a computer. So I can't use recursion in quite the same way, for example. For sophisticated readers I can use it a little bit. But there's a constant awareness of how a reader is going to process the text and understand it.

Something I worry about a lot when I write, that I'm less worried about with a computer, is about the ways in which English is ambiguous. I'm constantly worrying about ways in which the reader might misinterpret what I've written. So I've actually spent a lot of time consciously crafting the mechanics of my prose style to use constructions that are less likely to be misinterpreted.

My favorite *Saturday Night Live* sketch, even more than the bees or the wild and crazy guys, was a sketch where Ed Asner was on and he played the manager of a nuclear power plant going on vacation for two weeks. He walked out the door, saying, "Goodbye, everybody, I'm going. Remember, you can't give too much coolant to the nuclear reactor." And they spend the next three minutes arguing over what he meant.

Seibel: So when you're writing English, you're obviously writing for a human reader and you seem to contrast that to writing software, which is for a computer. But lots of people—such as Knuth—make a big point that when you're writing code you're writing as much for human readers as for the computer.

Steele: Oh, that's true.

Seibel: So do the lessons of writing English for a human reader help you with that aspect of code?

Steele: Well, sure. When I'm writing code, one of the foremost things in my mind is, will this get the computer to do what I want? And so it's a matter of, "Will it be understood even one way?" Rather than not at all. Then there's the question of often there's more than one way to write something correctly. And at that point I begin worrying about the human reader. And I also worry about efficiency.

There's a trade-off there, typically. If efficiency is important, I'll often resort to a trick. And then I realize that will mislead a human. And you have to comment it or do something to flag that, to make it more readable. But yes, very often in things like choices of variable names and the way code is laid out and so forth, the emphasis is more on the human reader, and you think about how you can use details of the code formatting that don't matter to the computer to provide the necessary signals to the human reader.

Seibel: As our languages get better, or at least more programmer-friendly, compared to the days of assembly language on punch cards, it seems like it's easier to write correct programs—you get a lot of help from compilers that flag errors for you and so forth. Is it possible to allow the focus on readability to come first, if only slightly ahead, of correctness? After all, as the Haskell folks are fond of saying, "If your Haskell program type checks, it can't go wrong."

Steele: I think that's a terrible pitfall. There are so many ways for a compilable program to have errors in it that you really do need to worry about correctness all the time. And if it's not correct you'll mislead not only the computer but your human readers, too.

Programming is a highly unnatural activity, I'm convinced, and it must be carefully learned. People are used to their listeners filling in the gaps. I suppose we lean on compilers to do that in a little way—you say, "I need a variable named 'foo'," you don't worry about exactly what register and so forth. But I think that most people are not used to being very precise and rigorous in their communications. But when we are describing processes to be carried out, little details do matter because a change in a small detail can affect the gross outcome of the process.

I think people are used to using recursion in a limited way—I think Noam Chomsky demonstrated that. But in practice people rarely go even three deep—and when they do it's usually in a tail-recursive way. The discipline of understanding recursion is actually a very difficult learned art. And yet that is actually one of our most powerful programming tools, once you've learned the discipline and wrapped your head around it. So I really think you can't afford to take your eye off the correctness ball.

Seibel: Yet lots of people have tried to come up with languages or programming systems that will allow "nonprogrammers" to program. I take it you think that might be a doomed enterprise—the problem about programming is not that we haven't found the right syntax for it but that people have to learn this unnatural act.

Steele: Yeah. And I think that the other problem is that people like to focus on the main thing they have in mind and not worry about the edge cases or the screw cases or things that are unlikely to happen. And yet it is precisely in those cases where people are most likely to disagree what the right thing to do is.

Sometimes I'll quiz a student, "What should happen in this case?" "Well, obviously it should do this." And immediately someone else will jump in and say, "No, no, it should do that." And those are exactly the things that you need to nail down in a programming specification of some process.

I think it's not an accident that we often use the imagery of magic to describe programming. We speak of computing wizards and we think of things happening by magic or automagically. And I think that's because being able to get a machine to do what you want is the closest thing we've got in technology to adolescent wish-fulfillment.

And if you look at the fairy tales, people want to be able to just think in their minds what they want, wave their hands, and it happens. And of course the fairy tales are full of cautionary tales where you forgot to cover the edge case and then something bad happens.

Seibel: *Fantasia* and the perils of recursion, for instance.

Steele: *Fantasia* and recursion, yes. Or, "I wish I was the richest man in the country"—well, that makes everybody else extremely poor and you're the same as you were before. That kind of thing happens in fairy tales because people forget that there's more than one way to do something. And if you just think about your main wish and don't think about the details, that leaves a lot not tied down.

Seibel: So the lesson from fairy tales is that the Gandalfs of the world got there by hard labor, learning the incantations, and there's no shortcut to that?

Steele: Yeah. I'll give you another example—suppose I were to tell my smart computer, "OK, I've got this address book and I want the addresses to always be in sorted order," and it responds by throwing away everything but the first entry. Now the address book is sorted. But that's not what you wanted. It turns out that just specifying something as simple as "a list is in sorted order and I haven't lost any of the data and nothing has been duplicated" is actually a fairly tricky specification to write.

Seibel: So are there language features that make programmers—folks who have mastered this unnatural act—more productive? You're designing a language right now so you've obviously got some opinions about this.

Steele: I said earlier that I think you can't afford to neglect correctness. On the other hand, I think we can design tools to make it easier to achieve that. We can't make it trivial, but I think we can make it easier to avoid mistakes of various kinds. A good example is overflow detection on arithmetic, or providing bignums instead of just letting 32-bit integers wrap around. Now, implementing those is more expensive but I believe that providing full-blown bignums is a little less error-prone for some kinds of programming.

A trap that I find systems programmers and designers of operating-systems algorithms constantly falling into is they say, "Well, we need to synchronize some phases here so we're going to use a take-a-number strategy. Every time we enter a new phase of the computation we'll increment some variable and that'll be the new number and then the different participants will make sure they're all working on the same phase number before a certain operation happens." And that works pretty well in practice, but if you use a 32-bit integer it doesn't take that long to count to four billion anymore. What happens if that number wraps around? Will you still be OK or not? It turns out that a lot of such algorithms in the literature have that lurking bug. What if some thread stalls for 2 to the 32nd iterations? That's highly unlikely in practice, but it's a possibility. And one should either mitigate that correctness problem or else do the calculation to show that, yeah, it's sufficiently unlikely that I don't want to worry about it. Or maybe you're willing to accept one glitch every day. But the point is you should do the analysis rather than simply ignoring the issue. And the fact that counters can wrap around is a lurking pitfall that doesn't hurt most programmers but for a very few it lays traps in their algorithms.

Seibel: Speaking of glitches, what was the worst bug you've ever had to track down?

Steele: I'm not sure I can dig up a worst one, but I can tell you a few stories. Certainly, dealing with parallel processes has produced the most difficult-to-deal-with bugs.

When I was a teenager programming on the IBM 1130 was the one time in my life when the solution to a bug came to me in a dream. Or as I woke up. I had been puzzling over a bug for a couple days, couldn't figure it out. And then suddenly sat bolt upright in the middle of the night and realized I knew what the problem was. And it was because I had overlooked something in an interface specification.

It had to do with concurrent processes. I was writing a decompiler so that I could study the IBM disk operating system by decompiling it. And to this end it would take binary data on the disk and print it in a variety of formats including as instructions, as character codes, as numbers, and so on. And in order to convert the characters, I was feeding the data to various character-conversion routines, one of which was designed for use after reading card codes from a card reader. And I had overlooked the tiny footnote in the specification that said, "We assume that before you call the procedure, the buffer in which the card data will be read has all over the low order bits cleared." Or maybe had them set.

Anyway, the 12 bits from the card-code column were going into the high 12 bits of the 16-bit word and they were using the low bit for a clever trick whereby you could call the card-reader routine asynchronously and it would asynchronously load the buffer and the conversion routine would follow behind, using that low bit to determine whether the next card column had been read in or not. And if it had been read it would then convert that character. Thereby, as soon as the card was read, very shortly thereafter the conversion would finish—they were overlapping the cost of the card conversion with the time it took to read the card. And I was feeding it raw binary data that wasn't obeying this constraint. And I had just overlooked this—I thought it was yet another card-conversion routine but it turned out this one had something special about its interface—it was relying on those low-order bits, which ordinarily you wouldn't think about. It was interpreting what was in the buffer as saying, "Oh, the data has not yet arrived from the card reader." In principle I knew this, but it wasn't occurring to me. And then, as I say, it came to me while I was asleep. So that was an odd case.

The other really interesting story I can think of was while I was the maintainer of the Maclisp system and Maclisp supported bignums—integers of arbitrary precision. They'd been around for several years and were considered pretty well debugged and shaken out. They'd been used for all kinds of stuff in Macsyma, and Macsyma users were using them all the time. And yet a report came in from Bill Gosper saying, "The quotient of these two integers is wrong." And he could tell because the quotient was supposed to be very near a decimal multiple of pi.

These were numbers about a hundred digits each and it really wasn't feasible to trace through the entire thing by hand because the division routine was fairly complicated and these were big numbers. So I stared at the code and didn't see anything obviously wrong. But one thing that caught my eye was a conditional step that I didn't quite understand.

These routines were based on algorithms from Knuth, so I got Knuth off the shelf and read the specification and proceeded to map the steps of Knuth's algorithm onto the assembly-language code. And what caught my eye in Knuth was a comment that this step happens rarely—with a probability of roughly only one in two to the size of the word. So we expected this to happen only once in every four billion times or something.

From that I reasoned to myself, "These routines are thought to be well shaken out, thus this must be a rare bug; therefore the problem is likely to be in the rarely executed code." That was enough to focus my attention on that code and realize that a data structure wasn't being properly copied. As a result, later down the line there was a side-effect bug where something was getting clobbered. And so I repaired that and then fed the numbers through and got the right answer and Gosper seemed to be satisfied.

A week later he came back with two somewhat larger numbers and said, "These don't divide properly either." This time, properly prepared, I returned to that same little stretch of ten instructions and discovered there was a second bug of the same kind in that code. So then I scoured the code thoroughly, made sure everything was copied in the right ways, and no errors were ever reported after that.

Seibel: That's always the trick—that there's going to be more than one.

Steele: So I guess there's lessons there—the lesson I should have drawn is there may be more than one bug here and I should have looked harder the first time. But another lesson is that if a bug is thought to be rare, then looking at rarely executed paths may be fruitful. And a third thing is, having good documentation about what the algorithm is trying to do, namely a reference back to Knuth, was just great.

Seibel: When it's not just a matter of waking up in the middle of the night and realizing what the problem is, what are your preferred debugging techniques? Do you use symbolic debuggers, print statements, assertions, formal proofs, all of the above?

Steele: I admit to being lazy—the first thing I will try is dropping in print statements to see if it will help me, even though that is probably the least effective for dealing with a complicated bug. But it does such a good job of grabbing the simple bugs that it's worth a try. On the other hand, one of the great revelations in the evolution of my thinking about programming was when I was working on that one project in Haskell. Because it was a purely functional language, I couldn't just drop in print statements.

This forced me to go 100 percent to a regimen of unit testing. So I proceeded to construct thorough unit tests for each of my subprocedures. And this turned out to be a very good discipline.

This has influenced the design of Fortress to try to include features that would encourage the construction of unit tests. And recording them alongside the program text, rather than in separate files. To that extent we borrowed some ideas of say, Eiffel's Design by Contract and similar things where you can put preconditions and postconditions on procedures. There are places where you can declare test data and unit-test procedures, and then a test harness will take care of running those whenever you request.

Seibel: Since you just mentioned Design by Contract, how do you use assertions in your own code?

Steele: I have a tendency to drop in assertions, particularly at the beginnings of procedures and at important points along the way. And when trying to—maybe "prove" is too strong a word—trying to justify to myself the correctness of some code I will often think in terms of an invariant and then prove that the invariant is maintained. I think that's a fruitful way to think about it.

Seibel: How about stepping through code in a debugger? Is that something you'll do if all else fails?

Steele: It depends on the length of the program. And of course you can have tools that will help you to skip sections you don't need to step through because you're confident that those parts are OK. And of course Common Lisp has this very nice STEP function, which is very helpful. I've stepped through a lot of Common Lisp code. The ability to skip over particular subroutines whose details you trust, of course, buys you a lot. Also the ability to set traps and say, "I really don't need to look at this until this particular loop has gone around for the seventeenth time." And there were hardware tools to support that on the PDP-10, which was nice, at least at MIT. They tended to modify their machines in those days, to add features. And there's a lot to be said for watching the actual execution of code in various ways.

Seibel: Do you ever try to formally prove your code correct?

Steele: Well, it depends on the code. If I'm writing code with some kind of tricky mathematical invariant I will go for a proof. I wouldn't dream of writing a sorting routine without constructing some kind of invariant and proving it.

Seibel: Peter van der Linden in his book *Expert C Programming* has a sort of dismissive chapter about proofs in which he shows a proof of something, but then, ha ha, this proof has a bug in it.

Steele: Yes, indeed. Proofs can also have bugs.

Seibel: Are they at least less likely to have a bug than the code which they are proving?

Steele: I think so, because you come at it in a different way and you use different tools. You use proofs for the same reason you use data types, or for the same reason that mountain climbers use ropes. If all is well, you don't need them. But they increase the chance of catching it if something does go wrong.

Seibel: I suppose the really bad case would be if you had a bug in your program and then a compensating bug in your proof. Hopefully that would be rare.

Steele: That can happen. I'm not even sure it's necessarily rare, because you tend to construct the proof to match the structure of the code. Or conversely, if you've got a proof in mind as you're writing the code, that tends to guide your construction of the program. So you really can't say the code and the proof are totally independent, in the probabilistic sense. But you can bring different tools and different modes of thought to bear.

In particular, the details of the programming tend to take a local point of view and the invariants tend to focus on the global point of view. It's in doing the proof that you cause those two things to interact. You look at how the local steps of the program affect the global invariant you're trying to maintain.

One of the most interesting exercises in my career was the time I was asked to review a paper for *CACM* by David Gries on proving a garbage-collector algorithm correct, a parallel garbage collector. Susan Owicki was a student of Gries's and she developed some tools for proving parallel programs correct, and he decided to apply these techniques to a version of a parallel garbage collector that had been developed by Dijkstra. The whole piece of code fit on, I think, a half a page. And then the entire rest of the paper was the proof of correctness.

I cranked through the proof and tried to verify every step for myself. And what makes it tricky is, in effect, every statement in the program has the potential to violate any invariant because it's a parallel program. So the Owicki technique involves cross-checking these at all points. And it took me about 25 hours to go through, and in the process I found a couple of steps I couldn't push through. So I reported this and it turned out they did represent bugs in the algorithm.

Seibel: So they were bugs in the algorithm which the proof missed since the result of the proof was, Q.E.D. this thing works.

Steele: Yes, the proof presented was a faulty proof. Because something had been overlooked somewhere. It was some detail of formula manipulation—the formula was almost right but not quite. And I think it was a matter of correcting the order—the sequence of two statements or something.

Seibel: So it took you 25 hours to analyze the proof. Could you have found the bug in the code in just 25 hours if you just had the code?

Steele: I doubt I would have even realized there was a bug. The algorithm was sufficiently intricate that I would probably have stared at the code and said, "Yeah, this makes sense to me" and not have spotted this very obscure interaction. It was a multistep sequence that was necessary—a highly unlikely interaction.

Seibel: And so that kind of interaction basically gets abstracted by the process of making the proof so you don't have to come up with this scenario of what if this happens and then this and then this to realize that there's a problem.

Steele: Exactly. In effect the proof takes the global point of view and covers all the possibilities, summarizing it in a very complicated formula. And you have to do formula crunching to push it through. So the author resubmitted the paper and it came back for rereviewing and even though I had done the entire exercise, it took me another 25 hours to reverify the proof. This time it all seemed to be sound.

I reported that and the paper was published and nobody's found a bug in it since. Is it actually bug-free? I don't know. But I think having gone through the exercise of the proof gives me a lot more confidence that the algorithm is now sound. And I'm hoping that I wasn't the only reviewer who actually did the complete cranking through of the proof.

Seibel: There's a Dijkstra quote about how you can't prove by testing that a program is bug-free, you can only prove that you failed to find any bugs with your tests. But it sort of sounds the same way with a proof—you can't prove a program is bug-free with a proof—you can only prove that, as far as you understand your own proof, it hasn't turned up any bugs.

Steele: That's true. Which is why there is a subspecialty in the discipline having to do with mechanical proof verification. And the hope is that you then reduce the problem to proving that the proof verifier is correct. Which is—if you can write a small enough verifier—actually a much more tractable problem that verifying the proof of any rather large program.

Seibel: And then the manually proved mechanical verifier would do the 25 hours of work you did of grinding out a verification of a specific proof of some other piece of code?

Steele: Yes. Exactly.

Seibel: Is there anything that you would like to talk about?

Steele: Well, we haven't talked that much about the beauty in programs, and I wouldn't want that to go without remark. I have read some programs that really strike me as having a kind of beauty to them. TeX is one example, the source code for TeX. METAFONT a little less so and I don't know whether it's just because I use the program less or there's something subtly different about the organization of the code or about the design of the program that I like less. I really can't decide.

There are certain algorithms that strike me as just wonderful. I have seen little pieces of program that were marvels of code compression back in the days when that mattered—when you had only a megabyte of memory, whether you used 40 words or 30 really mattered, and people would really work hard sometimes to squeeze a program down. Bill Gosper wrote these little four-line wonders that would do amazing things if you then connected an amplifier to the low bits of some accumulator while it was twiddling the bits.

This may seem like a terrible waste of my effort, but one of the most satisfying moments in my career was when I realized that I had found a way to shave one word off an 11-word program that Gosper had written. It was at the expense of a very small amount of execution time, measured in fractions of a machine cycle, but I actually found a way to shorten his code by 1 word and it had only taken me 20 years to do it.

Seibel: So 20 years later you said, "Hey Bill, guess what?"

Steele: It wasn't that I spent 20 years doing it, but suddenly after 20 years I came back and looked at it again and suddenly had an insight I hadn't had before: I realized that by changing one of the op codes, it would also be a floating point constant close enough to what I wanted, so I could use the instruction both as an instruction and as a floating point constant.

Seibel: That's straight out of "The Story of Mel, a Real Programmer."

Steele: Yeah, exactly. It was one of those things. And, no, I wouldn't want to do it in real life, but it was the only time I'd managed to reduce some of Gosper's code. It felt like a real victory. And it was a beautiful piece of code. It was a recursive subroutine for computing sines and cosines.

So that's the kind of thing we worried about back then. When I programmed on the IBM 1130, there was this concept of a boot card, which is a single card you put on the front of your deck. You hit a start button on the computer and the hardware would automatically read the first card and put it in the first 80 locations in memory. And then start execution at a given location. And the job of that card was then to be a real card-reader routine to read the rest of the cards, and then that's how you got yourself bootstrapped.

What made it hard on the IBM 1130 was that cards have only 12 rows and it was a 16-bit computer word. So the 12 bits were scattered throughout the 16 bits of instructions, which meant that some instructions couldn't be represented on the card. Therefore any instructions that couldn't be represented on the card had to be built by using other instructions that were on the card. So you had this very complicated trade-off—"What instructions can I use, and if I use this instruction; I'm going to need several other instructions on the card just to build it"—and this presented a tremendous amount of pressure and you only got 80 words to write your routine, and so you do tend to use things like reusing instructions as data, using a piece of data for more than one thing. If you can manage to put this little subroutine *there* in memory, then its address can also be used as a data constant. This is what it took—it was origami and haiku and all that as a style of programming. And I spent several years doing that.

Seibel: Do you think that people who went through that discipline are better or worse programmers in the current environment?

Steele: They got experience at dealing with resource constraints and trying to measure them accurately.

Seibel: Well, learning to measure them accurately is a good thing. But it can also cut both ways where you develop habits of programming that are now maladaptive.

Steele: It's easy to become too fixated on optimizing something just because you can, even though it's not what you need to work on. That's indeed true. I'm glad that my son had the experience of programming TI calculators when he was in high school. Because again, those had moderately severe memory constraints. And so he had to learn how to represent data in compressed forms to get it to fit in the calculator. I wouldn't want him to spend his whole programming career that way, but I think it was a useful experience.

Seibel: Back to code beauty—that kind of haiku, origami programming is beautiful for the reason that any intricate little thing is beautiful.

Steele: Yes. But I should emphasize that that piece of Gosper's code is beautiful not only because you can compress it in this way—one of the reasons it's so small to begin with is because it's based on a beautiful mathematical formula, a triple angle formula for the sine function. And that recursion can be expressed very concisely on this particular architecture because that architecture was designed to support recursion in a way that other machines of its day weren't. So there are several different aesthetics melding together, combined in this one routine.

Seibel: You also mentioned Knuth's TeX, which is obviously a much larger program. What is it that makes that program beautiful?

Steele: He took a very, very complicated program with lots of special cases and reduced it to a single, very simple paradigm: sticking boxes and glue together. That was an immensely critical breakthrough. It turns out to be flexible not only for typesetting text but for all manner of other things as well that have to do with laying things out visually, two-dimensionally, on a page. I wish that more GUI interfaces were based on boxes and glue for laying out buttons and things like that.

Seibel: So there is beauty to be appreciated once you understand what boxes and glue means, you can say, "Yeah, that's a deep and righteous idea and I appreciate the beauty of that and see how it would apply outside this one program." Is there further aesthetic quality that you get—and can only get—by reading through the source code and seeing how that theme plays out? Or is it more that you read the whole thing and then at the end you say, "Wow, that was really all based on this one simple, but not simplistic, idea."?

Steele: It's a combination of those. And Knuth is really good at telling a story about code. When you read your way through *The Art of Computer Programming* and you read your way through an algorithm, he's explained it to you and showed you some applications and given you some exercises to work, and you feel like you've been led on a worthwhile journey. And you've seen interesting sights along the way. Wandering through the code of TeX I feel much the same way. I've learned some things about programming. And some parts of them are mundane and perfunctory and so forth. And other ones you say, "Wow, I didn't think of organizing it that way." It's a little of each.

Seibel: At the other end of the spectrum from code beauty, software is also full of painful historical warts that we can't get rid of, like differing line-ending conventions.

Steele: Yes. We spent hours and hours in the Common Lisp committee just debating the treatment of end of line in order to accommodate both Unix, which used just newline, and the PDP-10 systems, which used CRLF. And getting the definition of newline just right so it worked on both those operating systems was a nightmare.

Seibel: So for the people who are reading this book and are going to be writing some of the software of the future, is there any way to avoid that stuff? Is there any way we can be smarter? Or is it just the nature of evolutionary design?

Steele: Yeah. And not knowing the future. If I could change one thing—this is going to sound stupid—but if I could go back in time and change one thing, I might try to interest some early preliterate people in not using their thumbs when they count. It could have been the standard, and it would have made a whole lot of things easier in the modern era. On the other hand, we have learned a lot from the struggle with the incompatibility of base-ten with powers of two.

CHAPTER

10

Dan Ingalls

If Alan Kay is Smalltalk's father, Dan Ingalls is its mother—Smalltalk may have started as a gleam in Alan Kay's eye, but Ingalls is the one who did the hard work of bringing it into the world. Starting with the first implementation of Smalltalk, written in BASIC and based on one page of notes from Kay, Ingalls has been involved in implementing seven generations of Smalltalk from the first prototype to the present-day open source implementation, Squeak.

Originally a physicist, Ingalls started programming with Fortran, made a business selling a profiler he wrote while in grad school, and eventually found his way to Xerox PARC, where he joined Kay's Learning Research Group, which built Smalltalk and explored the use of computers in children's education.

While at PARC, Ingalls also invented the BitBlt operation used in bit-mapped graphics and coded it in microcode for PARC's Alto computer, allowing the high-performance bit-mapped graphics that enabled UI innovations such as pop-up menus that we now all take for granted. (At one of Ingalls's in-house demonstrations of the Smalltalk system, a pop-up menu caused the subject of my next chapter, L Peter Deutsch, to leap to his feet and exclaim, "Did you just do what I thought you did?")

Now a Distinguished Engineer at Sun Microsystems, Ingalls is working on Lively Kernel, a Smalltalk-like programming environment that runs completely in the browser using JavaScript and browser-provided graphics. He received the

Association for Computing Machinery Grace Murray Hopper Award in 1984 and the ACM Software System Award in 1987 for his work on Smalltalk. In 2002 he won the Dr. Dobb's Excellence in Programming Award.

In our conversation, we talked about the importance of interactive programming environments, why it was a lucky thing he never learned Lisp, and why it's better to build flexible, dynamic systems and then lock them down rather than building static systems and then trying to add dynamic features.

Seibel: To start at the start, how did you get involved in programming?

Ingalls: Let's see. I grew up being an inventor in my basement, and physics was the closest I could come to that so that was my college major. I went to Harvard and there was a course on programming in Fortran, which I took.

Seibel: What years would that have been?

Ingalls: I was at Harvard from '62 to '66. My two programming experiences were this course on Fortran and there was a great lab in the basement of one of the buildings where I took a course on analog computers. It makes you think completely differently—you've got this big patch panel and then just a bunch of circuits that are integrators, differentiators—things that you can wire together to solve all sorts of problems in real time. But it began with Fortran and I loved it from the get-go. I tried to see how much shorter I could make programs, and stuff like that.

As a result I decided that maybe I was interested in electrical engineering. So I came out to Stanford in double E and took some computer-science courses there and really enjoyed that. I didn't spend that much time with double E. I got into Don Knuth's course and he had a graduate course on program measurement and I loved that. I actually worked on a program that would analyze other programs and dropped out of Stanford to make a business out of it. I got my master's the next year, and then dropped out. So we're in '68 now, I guess.

Seibel: So it was a PhD program you dropped out of?

Ingalls: Right, in the radio science department at Stanford, which was part of double E.

Seibel: So the program you made a business out of—what was it?

Ingalls: Well, it started out with Knuth, as a part of a seminar I took. The seminar was to measure programs and look at their dynamic behavior.

Seibel: Meaning, profiling?

Ingalls: Yeah. So there was a program that would gobble up a Fortran program and insert counters at every branch point. I made a fancier version of it that also had a timer-interrupt process so that it would keep track of how much real time was spent in various parts of the program.

Seibel: So basically a sampling profiler?

Ingalls: Right. And what was notable about these was that until that time profiling had typically been in terms of memory locations, and it took a quantum mechanic to know what the results were telling you, whereas this came out in terms of your source code and you could see, "Oh, it's spending all its time here." This was immediately usable to the user. I recognized, "Whoa! people could be using this."

Seibel: So you ran your business for a while—is that what you were doing up until you went to Xerox PARC?

Ingalls: Pretty much. In fact, that's how I ended up at PARC. I wound up spending a bunch of time in local service bureaus. There was a Control Data one and an IBM one. And I would take my program around to these various places and make sure that it ran on their particular computer.

Seibel: And this was profiling Fortran code still?

Ingalls: Yeah. But I found out an interesting thing. Who were the big Fortran users? They're big scientific computation users. And who are they all working for? They're all working for the government. Do they care how efficient their program is? Not really. What they really want to do is to show that the computer is overloaded and that they need a new computer and more money. I showed this at a couple of companies and they said, "Jeez, if you had this for COBOL it would be great."

Seibel: Because no one's going to give them more money to buy big iron for COBOL.

Ingalls: Exactly. So I wrote the same thing for COBOL. This was my immersion into COBOL. I remember writing the completion routine that would put together the statistics from the timer interrupts. The completion routine wanted to be written in the same language as the thing you're measuring so that it could all be loaded in together. I may be the only person who's ever written a hash table in COBOL.

Anyway, that sold great. I can remember several sales calls where I'd go out and as a demo I'd run it on one of their programs and, in the course of the demo, would show them how to save more money than the program cost.

In the process of going around to these service bureaus, I wound up at the CDC service bureau in Stanford industrial park—typically you're working late at night because that's when it was less expensive—there was another guy there who had a Fortran program to do speech recognition. He had various speech samples and his program analyzed the spectra and grouped the phonemes and stuff like that. I started talking to him and I said, "Well, jeez, you want to run my program on yours?" So we did that and parted company.

He called me up a couple of weeks later and said, "I've been hired by Xerox to do a speech-recognition project and I've got no one to help me with the nitty-gritty; would you like to work with me?" So I started consulting with him. That was George White, who went on for a long time to do speech recognition. That's how I got in with Xerox and also with Alan Kay, because it turned out that my office was across the hall from Alan's and I kept hearing conversations that I was more interested in than speech recognition.

Seibel: Was the domain of speech recognition not that interesting or was it something about the programming involved?

Ingalls: Oh, it was interesting—it was fascinating. I ended up building up a whole personal-computing environment on this Sigma 3 minicomputer. It used card decks and Fortran was the main thing I had to work with. Out of that I built an interactive environment. I wrote a text editor in Fortran and then something so we could start submitting stuff remotely from a terminal. It wound up being a nice little computing environment, just done in this sort of strange way.

Seibel: This desire for an interactive environment is a theme that's come up a bunch of times in your career. For example, you wrote the first Smalltalk in BASIC because that was the interactive environment you had at hand. Where did you get that idea that given a problem to solve, the first thing you need is an interactive programming environment?

Ingalls: That's a good question. I think anything where you get immediate gratification feeds on itself by definition.

Seibel: So what was that first place that you had that immediate gratification?

Ingalls: There were a couple of experiences. I had a chance to work with a semi-interactive PL/I. And a friend of mine was working at an IBM where they had an interactive APL environment. I can't remember which of those was first. I really remember the APL one. That affected me in a number of ways because of both the immediacy of interaction—seeing your results come back—and the expression evaluation, which is really different from Fortran's statement-oriented programming.

You still see that now, it's amazing—the whole C/C++/Java tradition, although it goes in an object-oriented direction, is still statement-oriented. But if it's convenient to make expressions, it really makes the experience different. To me it brings the mathematics to life more. Anyway, it was one of those two. When I got to Xerox there wasn't much interactive except the Lisp guys' stuff. I happened not to be into Lisp. Things would have been different if I were, I expect.

Seibel: How so?

Ingalls: I think I would have gone completely in that direction. And by not having gone in that direction, it left me wanting to do that kind of thing in a different way. I think what I worked on with Alan had that same kind of nice, lively, expression feel, but it included the notion of objects and messages more naturally.

I think if I had been as comfortable in a system like Lisp, I never would have bothered. I would have tried working around it to get objects, but starting with the notions of objects from the get-go and then making that nice and interactive and convenient was, I think, a contribution.

Seibel: Alan Kay has said that both Lisp and Smalltalk have the problem that they're so good they eat their children. If you had known Lisp, then Smalltalk would have been the first eaten child.

Ingalls: Maybe so.

Seibel: So that's a nice example of the advantage of some ignorance; it leaves some room for creativity. But sometimes it feels like ignorance is endemic in this industry—that people are unaware of things and wheels are constantly being reinvented with pointy corners.

Ingalls: That's true.

Seibel: Should we be trying to fix that? Is it just a price that we have to pay so that people can have room for creativity? Or would we be better off if people were a little more aware of what else is going on?

Ingalls: I'm an embrace-diversity guy. The example we just went through, I think, says, "No, let people go whatever way they want." There will be waste from ignorance, but natural selection will take care of straightening things out. And you will get these occasional sports that take you into the future.

I can think of lots of areas where trying to standardize, trying to all go in one direction, has suppressed creativity. I work at a company that's supported by Java, so I'm not going to go very far with this, but it is the case that when Java came out—the easiest way I had of measuring it was looking at what went on at OOPSLA—when Java came out not only did work slow down and even maybe come to a halt on other object-oriented programming languages but even in dynamic programming in general. I think that was a loss.

But it wasn't permanent. People finally realized "Oh, wait a minute, Java has all these great strengths and we're using it for this and that but we were on to other good things with dynamic programming languages and it's time to get back to that." But that's an example that's easy for me to see because I'm involved in it.

In a much bigger sense I hate to see computer-science departments that feel their role is to prepare people to work in an industry and the industry is going that way and therefore we have to teach our students that way. It's exactly the wrong thing to do. What you should be doing with your students is teaching them to think generally—think outside the box and plot the *other* courses we should be pursuing.

It's not a simple problem because there *is* great value to having that whole standard out there. Having thousands of programmers who have worked on thousands of routines and they're very solid—you can get your work done that way.

It's a little bit the difference between computer science in the service of production and computer science in the service of moving the intellectual content forward. I've been having fun with the Lively Kernel, which is, in a way, trivial. There's nothing new about it—I'm using all stuff that was there before. It's built on JavaScript and the graphics you can get in a browser. But it's been really fun because it's another kernel like Squeak. Because JavaScript is all there in the browser and the graphics is all there in the browser, the work on the kernel is very tiny. It's just, how do you bring the graphics to life and how do you build up a little computing environment.

Whenever you do something like that, small enough, then anybody can understand it. If you take a few things out of the equation, like the language and the graphics, then the question is, what is the kernel? And I think that's an interesting question.

I'm hoping that this—not particularly my stuff—but this kind of investigation might reinspire computer science to do some studies about how do you make a kernel, what other kernels could we build that are even simpler, even more uniform.

It's like what math did. Math found by symbolizing things that you could simplify a lot of stuff. Then, because of that, you could start to think about bigger constructs. That's my hope.

Seibel: When you say a kernel, you're talking about a programming kernel. What's the core of the Lively Kernel?

Ingalls: What I mean by a kernel, typically, is you put together enough stuff that it can, in some sense, build itself or build other useful things. Squeak is one that really can build itself. The Lively Kernel presumes the existence of JavaScript and some graphics, but it ends up with the ability to edit the graphics so that you can make new graphical things and to edit the programs so you can make new programs. So it's enough to build all the applications that you might want to build in a browser.

I think in playing this game you get to hide layers that you want to. The question is, where is your playing field. In Squeak the whole language is part of the kernel so it's got its own compiler and byte-code interpreter. And it's got its whole graphics system—it's got BitBlt and all the stuff around that.

It looks like those are an important part of any kernel but you *can* take them out. You can say, "Let's assume that we have a dynamic language; let's assume that we have graphics." In my old thinking, I would have thought, "Well, there is nothing else." But it's not true. What's left is, how do you put the graphics together to make an interesting user interface environment? And how do you bring programs and scripts up to the level that you can change them?

I was forced, by trying to come up with something that would run without installation, in a browser, to take what was in the browser. What's in the browser? Well, we've got JavaScript and we've got a graphics environment. It was a chance to step back from all this and say, "Well, yes there are language kernels, there are graphics kernels, and then there's this other kind of self-supporting user-interface environment kernel."

Seibel: In both Lively Kernel and Squeak, from the little that I've played with them, part of that kernel that's not the language or the graphics is this notion of a UI that's always programmable—it's got these little handles and so forth that you can do programmatic things with.

Ingalls: Right.

Seibel: I found that pretty confusing. Am I programming? Am I using this application? Sometimes I wished there were a bit more of a distinction.

Ingalls: Yup. This is another of those double-edged swords. I don't think there's a simple answer. At the very bottom, it's a wonderful thing that we've built computers that totally allow for change. It's all random-access memory; it's all programmable. To me it's important to keep that liveliness, that malleability, that changeability. If you have a system that's dynamic and changeable, it's much easier to then draw boundaries and say, "You can't change stuff inside of here" than it is to start out with something that's not dynamic and changeable and then try to make it that way.

If you look at web programming right now, it started out with this text-markup language and then JavaScript came into the picture to try and make it dynamic. It would have been so much easier to start out with something that was like the dynamic graphics everyone knew about in those days and then make stuff fixed and printable when you needed to.

Seibel: Well, easier for everybody except someone who just wanted to put some text on the Web.

Ingalls: I suppose that's true. But it's easier for someone to put a layer, like HTML, on top of that. I think it's better to have the underlying systems be as dynamic as possible. Then you can put on syntax or type restrictions, or this, that, and the other that make it into a fixed thing. Absolutely there are situations when people are just using a system—you want things to be fixed that don't need to be flexible. And yes it does seem that if people perceive that it's flexible, it's scary to them. If you take the Lively Kernel as it is right now, it's not at all something that an end user would want. Nobody wants to suddenly see their window tilted at 20 degrees.

Seibel: Or to inspect the code of the button they're trying to press.

Ingalls: Right, right. Really it's a demo to try to inspire people who want to go that direction. It's also very simple so somebody could put in a layer that would make it usable and not changeable in those various weird ways. But yeah, there's a real trade-off between having things be flexible and general and having things be codified and able to be used as a cookbook and always do what you expect.

Seibel: Do you really think the current Lively Kernel, or some near-term evolution of it, will become a way people are going to build apps, or is this really a thought experiment out of Sun Labs to show people a way of thinking?

Ingalls: Well, it's definitely a thought experiment. It offers a couple of sweet spots that might actually survive as real products in some sense. It's got the ability to very quickly do something like, if you wanted to make a red heart and put a message in it and make it throb, and then store that as a web page, you can do all that from within it, never having installed any software. So you get the Lively Kernel and you build this little dynamic thing with a little bit of scripting in it and it's got the WebDAV protocol to go out and create and store a new web page.

That's something that's simple and useful and if the scripting were equally simple, the way the tile scripting is in eToys, I think that a lot of people could have fun playing with that. So that's sort of a gimmick. But if you take that about two levels more, you're into stuff that's actually educational—you could build simple dynamic models that you could interact with. It's a lot like Flash but it's simpler and more integrated with programming.

From there, I just think of it as being possibly a nice environment for embedding lots of little dynamic, educational examples. A decade or two ago there was HyperCard and lots of teachers were able to understand that and do useful things in it. It's really strange that that whole experience didn't naturally go right into the Web. I think there's still a role to be filled there with tools as simple as HyperCard and as immediate as the Web. It would be cool if it went that way.

Seibel: You've famously been involved in five or seven or however many generations of Smalltalk implementations. Let's start with the first Smalltalk that you did in BASIC. You had a couple pages of notes from Alan Kay that you had to make real. What did you do?

Ingalls: I just started typing in code. I think the first thing was to validate the execution model. There were just a couple of basic structures that were needed, the equivalent of a stack frame. So I just made, it must have been an array, in BASIC, to do that and put together enough that would execute a piece of code.

Typically with something like that—the word that's coming to mind is you "breadboard" it—you just do what you need to do to put a structure in place that's the structure you think you're going to want to interpret and then try to make it work. I remember the first thing we got to run was six factorial. It's a really simple example but it involves the process of dynamic lookup and creating new stack frames. And then once you've got that working, you come to understand how things are going to go and you find out what's difficult.

Eventually you figure out where the time's going and so you improve all those things. Then, in this particular case, once that worked there was the problem of putting a layer on it which is essentially a parser so you can type text into it and get it to go into that structure that you breadboarded. Then you've got a little environment and you start learning things.

Then you say, "OK, I see how this works, I'm going to write it in assembly code," or whatever else. Then you suddenly realize, "Oh, yeah, we need automatic storage management. So how are we going to do that?" It's one thing after another.

Seibel: So have there ever been things where that sort of just-in-time development either failed to work, or you knew it would not work and you had to do a design in some different way?

Ingalls: Well, you always do what you can and when you're stuck you always turn away and reflect.

In the spectrum of implementers, I probably err on the side of just making things happen. A lot of that is because I get so much of a thrill bringing things to life that it doesn't even matter if it's wrong at first. The point is, that as soon as it comes to life it starts telling you what it is.

And you find out that, yes, maybe you could have done the storage management completely differently, but the really important things you're learning have nothing to do with that. The first Smalltalks I did used reference counting for garbage collection; probably it would have been better to use something else. For a while there was a certain amount of pain associated with reference counts. But that didn't matter—the point was the system was up and alive and running and we were learning all this other great stuff about how you put together things with objects, what it's like to do numerics in an object-oriented style—all that other real progress.

Seibel: I don't know that you're that far out on the spectrum, at least among the people I've talked to for this book. Though Don Knuth did write TeX in pencil in a notebook for six months before he typed in a line of code and he said he saved time because he didn't have to bother writing scaffolding to test all the code he was developing because he just wrote the whole thing.

Ingalls: I believe that. There are people who operate completely differently. But for a given person I think that's just how they have to operate. I know I've wasted some time one way or another. But there's also this side of it, and it's sort of the archetypal aspect of exploratory programming, which is if it gets you more quickly to an environment that you can learn from, you may find out that some of your original goals don't even matter. What's much more important is that other thing over there. And that becomes a whole new focus.

Coming back to this need to reflect and get things right, there have been a couple of times when I've done that. The example that comes to my mind is BitBlt. When I decided to do the thing that became BitBlt, it had this challenge to it that I had to sit and noodle for a night or two. Which is, how are you going to efficiently move all these bits on bit boundaries across word boundaries? That was a case where there weren't any alternatives out in the world for me to work with. And so I thought about that and thought about that and came up with a simple model. It wasn't somebody else's spec but I had looked at all the places we were doing line drawing and text display and scrolling so I had a spec in my mind for what it needed to do.

Seibel: Maybe you can explain the basic problem that BitBlt was designed to solve.

Ingalls: The disconnect between wanting to think about the display as just a 1000×1000-pixel screen and the fact that the memory is organized word by word. If you want to pick up these four bits and put them down *there*, they may be in a different part of the word where you put them down. In fact they might straddle two words. If, on the screen, you're trying to move this thing to there, it may be that you're going to have to pick up pieces from two separate words *here* and lay them down *there*. And when you lay them down you have to store an entire word. So you're going to have to insert that into what was there before and mask around it. So it's a mess.

Then there's the screen raster—the line-by-line aspect of the screen that gives you two dimensions. BitBlt handles the possibility that the source and destination may have differing numbers of words per scan line.

That was a challenge where there was a clear spec for what needed to happen, and it was also one of these things where you tried to have a very general kernel, because if you do this right, it will not only give you moving things from one part to another, but it will allow you to do overlapping scrolls. And it will also allow you to blend pixels. There's all this opportunity for generalization.

I tested it and made sure it ran first in Smalltalk, then in assembly, then put it into microcode for the Alto. When finally done, we could do these operations at essentially the full speed of the memory without any delay due to all the yucky masking and shifting because that could all be hidden under the memory-cycle time.

Having microprogrammed computers around was a wonderful motivation because it was clear that if there was a little kernel that would do what was needed, then that could be put in microcode and the whole thing would run fast. So I was always motivated to do that.

The thing I came up with for all of this, it actually came to me as an image rather than anything else, which is, it's like a wheel. If you think of the source and the destination and word boundaries, it's like there's a wheel picking up whole words *here* and then dropping them off *here*, and there would only be one shift required—that was the picture that came to me. Then it was just a matter of putting that into code.

So at the center of the BitBlt operation there's essentially one long shifter, which is picking up words from the source and dropping them in the destination. That was the thing I had to sit down and think about. But once you had that you could do storing of constants this way, you could do the laying down of text, the extraction of glyphs from a font, and putting them down at any pixel location.

Seibel: Back to the BASIC implementation of Smalltalk: that was sort of the primordial Smalltalk, before even Smalltalk-72?

Ingalls: Right. The minute that worked I set off and did this whole assembly-language version—because that's what I had on the Nova—that was fairly complete. So we used that to debug a bunch of stuff and then, in parallel with that, the Alto was being built. As soon as it was available, we moved over and started running on the Alto. That became Smalltalk-72.

Seibel: So Smalltalk-72 was written in assembler—where along the line did it become self-hosting? You often hear that one of the great things about Smalltalk was that so much of it was implemented in itself.

Ingalls: That was a long time later. Smalltalk-72 had a big pile of assembly code with it. And Smalltalk-76 did, too. The big difference from Smalltalk-72 to Smalltalk-76 was that I came up with the byte-code engine for Smalltalk that had the keyword syntax and it was compilable. Also that classes and even stack frames were real objects, to your point about self-description.

Seibel: Where did you get the idea to write a byte-code interpreter?

Ingalls: That was a mechanism. The big thing that I was grappling with was that Smalltalk-72 parsed on the fly and for two reasons, at least, we needed to be able to compile something that had those kinds of semantics but that didn't require parsing everything on the fly.

So I came up with the Smalltalk-76 syntax, which is pretty much the Smalltalk-80 syntax. Then the question is, what do you compile that into that will run effectively this way? The only place where it got complicated was in doing what we called remote evaluation—variables you declare up here but they get evaluated down here. This is what ended up as blocks in Smalltalk, which are like closures in other systems.

Seibel: Why not just compile to machine code?

Ingalls: We were still very space-conscious and this stuff wound up incredibly compact compared to anything else around. And it needed to be that compact because we were still trying to run this on Altos that had 96K. Then they came out with the big one, which was 128K. The compactness was important.

Seibel: Meaning the generated code would be smaller because the byte codes were richer than native machine instructions?

Ingalls: Yeah. I also just plain loved the idea and was inspired by Peter Deutsch's work on the byte-code engine for Lisp. I was further inspired by this synergy—it's another one of these kernels that could fit in microcode. From the beginning I envisioned it as going into the microcode of the Alto.

Seibel: And the microcode was RAM so you could put the Smalltalk kernel in there and then switch to Lisp and put the Lisp byte-code interpreter in there.

Ingalls: Yup.

Seibel: Then what was the next evolution?

Ingalls: Smalltalk-76 inherited all the same sort of graphics baggage—a lot of special code for line drawing, text display, and so on. But at that time I had done BitBlt, so I rewrote the kernel so all the graphics just used BitBlt and Smalltalk, so that made the kernel much smaller. That was Smalltalk-78, which was the first one we ran on a microprocessor—on an 8086.

But that still wasn't Smalltalk in Smalltalk. The Smalltalk in Smalltalk wasn't until Squeak. Smalltalk-80 had a virtual machine spec that was published in the book, but all the implementations were in C or assembly code.

Seibel: What about the compiler?

Ingalls: The compiler was written in Smalltalk. Actually, when we were doing the Smalltalk-80 books, Dave Robson and I—it was mainly his work—wrote a Smalltalk emulation of the byte-code interpreter. As part of the Smalltalk-80 release we wanted to help people build their own virtual machines. We had discovered that one of the most useful aids was a trace of exactly what byte-codes get executed in what order when you first start up the system.

So he wrote an emulator in Smalltalk, because our Smalltalk was getting fast enough that that was a reasonable thing to do, and produced all those traces that would help people debugging.

Seibel: And you wanted to help people write Smalltalk virtual machines because the point of Smalltalk-80 was to be an escape pod so Smalltalk could go out into the world even if PARC decided not to do anything with it?

Ingalls: That's right. Then I left the industry and when I came back, I wanted to do a Smalltalk for a new project. At that time things were running so fast that, "Wait a minute; why don't we just try running the Smalltalk version of it and see what that does?" But the "aha!" was, it shouldn't be hard to mechanically translate that to C and then it would be as fast as the other engines. If you wanted to change something about the virtual machine you could change that in Smalltalk—you could try it out in Smalltalk and then push a button, and it would suddenly be in the production interpreter.

Seibel: So you took this Smalltalk interpreter written in whatever subset of Smalltalk it happened to be written in and wrote a special-purpose compiler that knows how to compile that subset into C?

Ingalls: And the C translator was simply a subset of the Smalltalk compiler—we just had to make the parse trees print out in C. This was actually something we had done before at Xerox—Ted Kaehler had written a virtual memory in Smalltalk, and then we used the same trick to translate that to BCPL. Same thing.

Seibel: When Smalltalk-80 got out in the world there were Smalltalk companies; objects were a big thing; *Byte* did its issue all about Smalltalk.

The promise was that objects were going to be these reusable components and that programmers would just go down to Ye Olde Object Shoppe and buy some objects and plug them into their program. Has that promise been kept?

Ingalls: I think yes and no.

Seibel: So in what ways has it happened?

Ingalls: Look at the world of Java—it's that kind of a world. There are huge bodies of software that work well together because of those kinds of interfaces. I think that was all a real step forward. There were several things going on in Smalltalk that did end up in the world more or less. One of them is object-oriented design and interfaces. The other is dynamic languages and user interfaces. It didn't take over and you can look at various little places in history where things could have been done differently and it might have had a better chance. But I don't think that's a big thing lost or gained. The world moves forward slowly. Other things got done that were better. Natural selection takes care of it all.

Seibel: But natural selection can also select some pretty grotesque outcomes.

Ingalls: Oh yeah, Beta and VHS, it's true. But ultimately, nothing that's really good ever gets really lost.

Seibel: Another aspect of Smalltalk that Alan Kay has particularly emphasized in recent years is that it wasn't supposed to be about objects; it was about message passing. C++ and Java don't have message passing in nearly the same way Smalltalk did. Why is that such a core idea?

Ingalls: Because it gives you real separation. Alan's latest phrase—which is appropriate, I think—is it should be like the Internet all the way down. We worry about where we have security and various sorts of security mechanisms in programs and there are all sorts of things wrong with them. But the Internet-style separation is a real layer that there's no way around.

So why is message passing such a good thing? That's the reason: it separates the inside from the outside, 100 percent. At least, done right it does. And there are other systems that have gone farther with this and I think we'll see more in that space.

Seibel: So nothing good ever gets really lost. Are there ideas, from Smalltalk or anywhere else, that you wish had been adopted by the mainstream?

Ingalls: I don't really have wishes for the mainstream—I have things I want to do or that I would like to be easy. My one wish for the mainstream, in the context of computer science, is that people would go back to first principles a little bit more about ways to leverage computing in the intellectual space.

We've gotten incredibly good with the programming systems and the languages we know. What if we were that good with logic programming? And had it integrated well? I think we would be doing extraordinarily more stuff in much more of a human-oriented space. It does go in the direction of artificial intelligence. You have to know that at some point we're going to cross a threshold where computers will be doing a better job thinking about stuff than we do.

I wonder sometimes if we're unconsciously holding that off. A lot of progress was made, up until 1980, in that area. And the computers are orders of magnitude faster and bigger now. On the latest computer I got, if I run the Smalltalk music synthesis, in Smalltalk, it can compute the radio signal for a radio station. This is hard for somebody who, at one point, could watch simple arithmetic being computed.

So you take that and put it against all sorts of possibilities in logic programming, in rule-based systems, and artificial intelligence, and you have to know there's lots of progress to be made there. I would like to see the kind of thinking that led to the Lively Kernel—what is a kernel apart from the language and the user interface? What other kernels are there? What if you build a kernel around logic programming and what kinds of things can you do with that? I don't think that people are playing around with, tinkering with that stuff enough. Because, Lord, the machines we have today—if you have a minor breakthrough there you could do incredible stuff.

Seibel: Smalltalk was originally envisioned as a platform for use in education, right?

Ingalls: It was envisioned as a language for kids—children of all ages—to use Alan's original phrase. I think one of the things that helped that whole project, and it was a long-term project, was that it wasn't like we were out to do the world's best programming environment. We were out to build educational software, so a lot of the charter was more in the space of simplicity and modeling the real world.

Something about having this educational goal made it easy to keep inspiring the lower-level stuff to be as simple as possible. So there were lots of things we did that didn't run as fast as you might like. The first Smalltalk-72 system was really slow—the second revision on it ran about 20, 25 times faster. But we had it running, by God, and we were able to use it with kids and learned a huge amount before even trying a second version.

We focused a lot on getting some cool graphics to work, bitmapped graphics, music, and putting it together in a fairly simple language. What we learned from that did actually make a seriously good language. So after Smalltalk-72, we did Smalltalk-76, which was essentially Smalltalk-80. And I saw that that could be a serious programming environment for the industry. There was some tension there with Alan because he wanted to not get scattered in that direction.

It wasn't too much longer before he left Xerox, and so we pursued those separate paths. But that was because we had discovered some things. For instance, our turnaround time for making changes in the system from the beginning was seconds, and subsecond fairly soon. It was just totally alive. And that's something which I, and a bunch of the other people, got a passion for. Let's build a system that's living like that. That's what Smalltalk became. So that then became a new goal, which then spun Smalltalk-80 off. Squeak was a return to that, but with the doing-it-in-itself bit added.

Seibel: So you and Kay followed, as you say, separate paths. Did you become disenchanted with the original Smalltalk vision?

Ingalls: No, not at all. I've talked about my training as a physicist, and I think it's in my nature to look at the world—how it works, how forces are, how the planets move, how the winds blow, and all that stuff—as asking questions about it and really being in touch with the phenomenon. In the physical world, at least, that's easy. You can zero in and come away with an understanding of, "Yes, that's how it works."

In computers I think there's the same kind of thing. You should be able, in a computing environment, to zero in on music and musical synthesis and sound and just understand how the whole thing works. It should be accessible. The same thing with graphics. It's put together very much the same way. You've got atomic things, which are the various graphical effects, and then you've got structural things you put them together with. The same thing's the case for numerical calculation.

When I take somebody new with Smalltalk, I'll say, "What interests you, taking text apart? Playing with numbers? Looking at graphics? Or playing with music?" And then we start there and do a deep dive on that. It's very much still a part of my passion, and I'm sure Alan's too, to take people through some deep dive in a direction that they're motivated about so they come away with what Alan calls powerful ideas—the "aha!" that lets you see this amazing variety is really a couple of small, general things at work.

You can see that in music. You can see it in graphics. You can see it in numbers and text manipulation. And it's really exciting to me to make that available and accessible.

The Squeak environment is really a computer scientist's environment. The eToys environment is a kids' environment, but not as comprehensive as it could be, and I still feel there's a thing we haven't done out there, which would allow you equally intuitively to dive in and get a physical understanding of those powerful ideas.

I'm still as passionate about that as anything. Why I'm here doing this stuff—JavaScript and the browser—is that we're getting pretty close to being able to put Squeak-like material on a web page that you can browse from any browser and interact with in some nice, self-revealing way. That's part of this whole picture. I'm sure it's going to change. Browsers are going to change. We'll get other languages besides JavaScript, and I'm still totally in touch with Alan and his group, who are doing another take on this going deeper down and trying to solve some of these other things more seriously. But it's absolutely still the same vision.

Seibel: You mention four disciplines: music, graphics, mathematics, and text. Those are about as old as humanity. Clearly there are powerful ideas there that are independent of computers—the computer just provides a way to explore them that might be hard without the computer. Is there also a set of interesting, powerful ideas inherent in the computer? Is programming or computer science another deep discipline—a fifth area—that we can only do now that we have computers?

Ingalls: Yes, I think that's what I am getting at. The curriculum I've always envisioned is one in which you start with one of these and maybe from the motivation of going deep in one of those areas, you move over to one of the other ones that's less familiar and do a similar thing there. And a lesson to be learned is that the way in which you get to those simpler, deeper structures that generate that whole field is similar in every case.

There's an algebra of graphics. It's primitive objects, superposition translation, rotation. Or music. It's notes and temporal sequences and chordals—same thing. And I think this goes back to seeing how the wind works and how the planets move. It's an invitation to go down and find out how things work and learn the things that make up the algebra—the processes and the primitive things. So yes, that fifth area, as you call it, is just what's common about all of these things.

Seibel: Would you expect someone who has played with three or four of these areas to end up learning how to program? Or is that just one of the things that could happen if their interest happened to go down a particular channel?

Ingalls: I think it's just one of the things that could happen. Hopefully you've sharpened their thinking skills. Both by introducing them to stuff and by getting them excited about stuff in some way or another. But there are people who are going to like programming and there are people who are not. I've got a 12-year-old son and all he wants to do is do 540s on skis, and there's a time and a place for everything.

Seibel: Back to some nitty-gritty: how do you test your software?

Ingalls: It depends what I'm doing. I always set it up for the most immediate gratification. So when trying to do something new, I just think of what would be the first piece of success that's achievable. And it's different in every case. If I had a more normal life, in more normal programming teams, I'd probably be totally into the current way of team programming. But for me, it's much more self-induced—even down to a question of my attention span. If I think I could get this working over the weekend, then that's the chunk I pick and that's the thing that I go flat out for, ignoring all the other things. It's hard for me to generalize this except to say, there's a place you want to get to, you pick a piece of it that would be gratifying and that would demonstrate that you're on the path and that you can fit into the time until you next get pulled off to do this at home or that at work.

Seibel: Since you've picked something that's going to have some kind of gratifying result at the end, that's your first test—an acceptance test: does it draw a window on the screen or whatever? What about finer-grained tests?

Ingalls: If it's the first time you've made it possible to pick something up and drag it over and drop it down, there's a framework that you need to have working there. Is the framework factored so that someone else coming along will see that these are the tests? That's something that I have not typically done. This may just be the luxury of my generation—nobody would get away with that these days. But I'm an old fart and they're not going to make me do it. But I think the underlying feeling is still the same. The Squeak code used to be full of comments that are executable and things to check. For instance, in lots of the BitBlt tests, there are these little things that will pick something up from one place on the screen, do something to it, and put it back, and if you see anything change on the screen, it's not working right and the comment says so. That's a straightforward test.

Seibel: So let's talk about working with others. The Learning Research Group at PARC sounded like a pretty close-knit group. How did you collaborate on the code itself?

Ingalls: Just by being close. And occasional mayhem. It was never a big group and we each had our own areas. There's a lot of team programming expertise that's grown up and I'm not up on it at all. Right now, in the Lively Kernel, the kernel part has been just me and one other guy, Krzysztof Palacz. And we sort of have our separate areas that we work on. We actually do use a code repository now, and there are other guys on the team who are doing more application stuff and a little bit in the kernel. And I see that it's nice having a shared repository that works—that's great. The next step for the Lively Kernel is to integrate it with the repository—you can change stuff in the Lively Kernel but it's only that running version; it doesn't get pushed out to the repository and become a part of the future. That's the next step we need to do.

Seibel: Have you ever done pair programming?

Ingalls: I'm trying to think of examples. Usually I've been on my own or working on a separate part. There are lots of projects on which I've worked with others, and many intense pair debugging sessions.

Seibel: Are there any techniques for managing that kind of collaboration? When everybody goes off to each do their own work, there's always the potential of things not quite fitting together.

Ingalls: Either you agree on some interface, or often I'll build some framework that's incomplete but that works for one example and then it's obvious to someone else where their stuff would fit in. Or they've done that and it's obvious to me where my stuff fits in. It's usually been in that concrete way, rather than any kind of spec because we've usually been working on something that nobody wrote down. It's all kind of been following the needs of the moment.

Seibel: You've worked at a lot of levels from down in the bits of BitBlt and writing microcode up to fairly high-level stuff in Smalltalk. How much do programmers need to know about the various levels of software and hardware they're dealing with?

Ingalls: That's a good question. To think outside the box, you've got to *be* a little outside the box. If there's something to be taken advantage of that you don't see in your normal exposure to a language, then you've got to have some intuition outside and some understanding of that and the ability to work in a system that has control over that.

In the context of language design, maybe you're going to want to work with the processors that are out there so maybe you don't need to know a lot about them, other than, for decent performance, how caching works and that kind of stuff. I think you have to stand back and say, "What boundaries is this going to cross?"

Seibel: Leaving aside how much you need to know eventually, when it comes to learning to program, some people say you should start with a high-level language and learn certain universal concepts. Other people say you need to start with assembly and work your way up so you understand what's going on. Do you buy that?

Ingalls: No, I don't think I necessarily buy that. That's how I learned it and I was fascinated with it. And I think there will always be people who are fascinated with this level or that. But I don't think there's any one way, just like there's any one way to do art.

I think there are other things that are equally exciting and probably more appropriate nowadays still to be explored. Lord, we were thinking of doing artificial intelligence a quarter of a century ago. The machines are immeasurably faster and we're doing almost nothing in that space—we're still doing very close to Fortran. Prolog has been out there for a long time; there's all sorts of stuff that can be done with logic programs. If you ought to learn about assembly and find out how that works, you ought to be doing some immersion in things that are more outside the box and that are really a possible piece of the future.

So I'm not saying, "not assembly language." I'm saying, you should learn some of these other powerful techniques so when you think about how to go forward, you can take advantage of them. In terms of a place to start, immediate gratification has always worked for me. When I want to teach somebody Smalltalk, I usually start with a little dialog: "What interests you most? Are you interested in how to play with text or things you can do with numbers or things you can do with music, or things you can do with graphics?" And start with any one of those.

There's all kinds of fun stuff you can do taking text apart and putting it together. There's all kinds of fun stuff you can do with numbers and different bases and floating-point and fixed. And the same thing with music: you can start with notes and put them together in melodies and chords. And with graphics: superpositions and rotations. Any one of those is a rich space to explore. I really think different people think differently that way. Similarly, if you're going to teach somebody to program a computer, maybe you work with expression evaluation, maybe you work with logic programming. Maybe you do some stuff in user interface. People will light up in one area and that's where they should go deep.

Seibel: As I understand it, the original purpose of Smalltalk was to teach a kind of programming literacy. Is that something everyone should have, just the way everyone is expected to be able to read and write and do a little bit of math? Should everyone have some ability to program a computer just because it's a useful way of thinking?

Ingalls: It's very hard for me to say that anyone *should* do anything, because I've met people that I think are better than me in this way or that way that know nothing about programming. In terms of literacy, the stuff that's under there is logic and math and yes, people should be able to think logically. But I'd never say that somebody should know how to program, I don't think. There's stuff we do in everyday life that's like programming. You need to know about procedures with steps, that kind of thing.

Computers incorporate some powerful ideas and can bring some powerful ideas to life. The wonderful thing about computers is they bring mathematics to life. So they can be a great tool that way. Now, my feeling about the powerful ideas that are necessary to lead a good life, it's not clear how many of them are in this space.

Seibel: Seymour Papert wrote in *Mindstorms* about debugging as an important element of an intellectual toolkit—the idea that the name of the game is not to get the right answer but to get *an* answer and then debug it.

Ingalls: Oh, absolutely! People should learn to think clearly and to question. And to me it's very basic. If you grow up in a family where when the cupboard door doesn't close right, somebody opens it up and looks at the hinge and sees that a screw is loose and therefore it's hanging this way vs. if they say, "Oh, the door doesn't work right; call somebody"—there's a difference there. To me you don't need any involvement with computers to have that experience of what you see isn't right, what do you do? Inquire. Look. And then if you see the problem, how do you fix it? To me that's so basic and human and comes so much from parent to child.

Computers are certainly a medium for doing that. But they're just computers. There's a lot of that that will transfer, but to me it's really big and basic and human, so it's not like we're going to enlighten the world just by teaching them computers.

Seibel: Do you remember the first interesting program you wrote?

Ingalls: Oh, let's see. In each programming experience, there was something that was out of the box. When I discovered VisiCalc, I wrote a spreadsheet to translate English to pig Latin in VisiCalc. That was, to me, interesting, because it used the spreadsheet metaphor as a parallel programming approach. Parsing text that way was fun and enlightening.

Seibel: So VisiCalc had primitives for taking apart strings?

Ingalls: Yeah, you could take apart strings. Maybe what I actually had was Lotus 1-2-3, not VisiCalc, because I'm not sure that VisiCalc had string primitives. I got one of those little Poqet PCs—it was the first truly handheld PC. It ran on two penlights, and I put 1-2-3 on it, and I had a plane flight across the country and I thought, "What can I do in this time?"

Seibel: That must've been well after you learned to program, because there obviously weren't Poqet PCs when you were starting out.

Ingalls: That was later on. The really interesting thing that I did in Fortran was I got a hold of Val Schorre's paper on META II—just a wonderful, really simple compiler compiler and wrote an implementation of that in Fortran. So all of a sudden this meant you could have other languages in a Fortran-only environment. That was the most interesting thing I did in Fortran, because it used Fortran to escape from the world of Fortran.

Seibel: That seems to be a bit of a theme: the pig-Latin spreadsheet, then this, and a hash table in COBOL for your profiler—is there a part of you that just likes cutting against the grain?

Ingalls: I don't feel like it's against the grain, but whenever I have a computing environment to play with, I like to try new things in it. That's what's been so much fun about doing the Smalltalk systems I did. You start from pretty much scratch and your job is to figure out what to assemble and get working first that will help you to do the next step and build stuff up from there.

In these cases, it was a matter of getting outside the box. That's a way of asserting that you've mastered the thing—if you can do some things that you wouldn't have thought you could do in it.

Seibel: Can you identify any big changes in the way you think about programming now?

Ingalls: That's a good question. One thing is we've got lots of computer cycles to spend. So I'm comfortable now, as the pejorative saying goes, pissing away cycles to get something done cleanly. But the basic thing hasn't changed for me at all, which is trying to get clear about what the kernel or kernels are that I have to work with and the goal that I'm trying to achieve.

It's changed a little bit in that I'm no longer the quantum mechanic in the group that I work in. I'm more at a higher level—that just means that I'm spending a little bit more time on goals and politics than on code. It's got more to do with creating a context. Until this later phase of my life, I've been lucky to be in an existing context where I didn't have to create it. But every once in a while I still get down and write serious code.

Seibel: I was looking at one of your papers from the '70s about your Fortran profiler. In the preamble you were very enthusiastic about how that tool changed your programming from figuring out what you were going to write, writing it, and debugging it, to figuring out what you were going to write, writing a really simple version, profiling it, then optimizing it. Do you still work that way?

Ingalls: I definitely go for effects first, bits on the screen or whatever it is, because that's so motivating, and you often learn something new about what you had wanted to do just by getting a chance to glimpse where it's going.

Then if profiling is what's needed, you profile. Or it may turn out you weren't doing the right thing—that wasn't quite what you wanted to do, so you changed the goals, or you change how you're doing it. But when it's a matter of performance, I still operate the same way. We did a really nice profiler in Smalltalk, and then Squeak, that gave you good feedback that way.

Part of that is about performance but part of it is about just structure and architecture. You may find that some things are hardly ever used and maybe you could just get rid of them by doing things differently. It's just a different perspective on the thing.

Seibel: It seems that virtually every programmer has a copy of Knuth's *The Art of Computer Programming*. Some people have it and it's just on their shelf. Some people have it and use it as a reference. And some people have it and really read it cover-to-cover. You actually studied with Knuth at Stanford; how much of it have you read?

Ingalls: I loved working with Don and I taught his MIX course for one quarter at Stanford, too, which was also enlightening. I think I'm pretty different from Don, but what I like about him is he's got a great mathematical mind but also loves to go deep into the bits—the pragmatic parts of things. I, too, love to get into the pragmatic side of things but I'm not as rigorous as Don.

I was trained in physics and to me the problems I work on, or how I work on them, is really much more a physical thing. When I'm talking about other perspectives on programs, I'm really thinking that there's a thing there that you can touch and feel it vibrate.

If you take the way he worked on TeX, it was very mathematical and beautiful and elegant. Compare that with, say, the first Smalltalk engines: they were very ad hoc. I just put together what was needed. It may be that after a few go-rounds, I started to get some sort of mathematical picture of it, or we did, but it's different in that regard.

So the truth is, I read a fair amount of his basic data structures stuff, but I'm not a big reader—I'm very much of a doer. If I have a flaw, it's that I will often do my own of X, Y, or Z rather than reading the literature and knowing about it. It's usually worked to my advantage I think, but who knows?

Seibel: How much math do you think programmers need to know? Dijkstra claimed that computer science is just a branch of mathematics. And understanding *The Art of Computer Programming* requires a fair bit of math.

Ingalls: You've got to have a logical mind. But I spent a lot of time in the country in Virginia while learning about computers. I always thought that if I wanted to start a computer company in the mountains of Virginia, I'd go find the mechanics. Except in certain fairly esoteric parts, the math isn't near as important as logic and intuition.

I think of a lot of it as being more architectural: the way the graphics work together with the models; the way things need to be updated or cached. That's not esoteric mathematics. That said, I do view it as being very much a part of the field of mathematics. To me, the really exciting thing about computers is they allowed mathematics to become a synthetic, not just an analytic art. What I have so much fun doing day to day is a mathematical kind of thing, but it's creative, generative, synthetic.

Seibel: You say you're not a big reader. Are there any books you'd recommend?

Ingalls: No. And I'm sure I'm in the minority this way. I was not a big reader as a kid. I would occasionally read things thoroughly and not be interrupted until I was done. There are some papers, absolutely, and I guess with them come some books. Val Schorre's paper on META II is one of them. There is the LISP 1.5 book. There's APL, but I didn't find Iverson's book to be at all a good way to learn it. A mathematician probably would have. I can't even remember what I read to learn about it from. But I loved it. So I think spending a bit of time in that language would be like a book to read. Likewise, Smalltalk.

Seibel: So do you still enjoy programming as much as you used to when you started?

Ingalls: Yeah, the programming itself. The last couple of years have been interesting because I've been taken away from the environment that I got so used to—Smalltalk and then Squeak—where the tools are just really great. I've had to step back a little bit, working with JavaScript in browsers and conventional development environments. It sometimes takes me longer to debug stuff than it used to, but the basic process of getting an idea and making it happen I still really enjoy.

Seibel: Do you feel at all that programming is a young person's game?

Ingalls: Not really, no. There's something about being able to survey all the stuff that's going on, and some of that endless energy that I don't feel I have the way I used to. But I still love to just take a problem and sit down and pore over it until it's right. There's an analogy here: I tried to learn to play piano fairly late in life. People said, "Oh, you should learn when you're young. You learn so much quicker." Although I didn't go very far, my conclusion was that it isn't that young people learn that much faster; it's just they have more time. When I would put time in, I made progress.

I feel a bit the same thing with programming. When I look back on earlier times in my life, I had all the time I wanted. I would just work and work. Now there are other things going on in my life and I've got responsibilities that aren't just programming. That undermines a bit of that intense focus.

Seibel: Leaving aside the amount of time you get to spend on it, doesn't programming require a certain intensity and focus? People talk about flow and how if you get interrupted every 15 minutes, you never get anything done because it takes that long to even start getting the stuff in your brain sorted out.

Ingalls: That reminds me of something I said to somebody way back at PARC. I was starting to have some other responsibilities besides just hacking Smalltalk, but we were also making a lot of progress in making it a really productive system. I kidded that I was racing to improve the Smalltalk environment so that I could continue to get reasonable work done in increasingly short amounts of time. So I'd gotten to where in 15 minutes I could sit down and actually do something useful.

The other part of it is that you work with other people. I work with younger people and it's great—maybe I spend a bit more time thinking at the level of goals and politics and arranging to make things happen, and they're making up for what I lack in available time for that deep, deep dive.

Seibel: You have a reputation of being a great guy to work for, when you're leading a project. How do you lead a team that makes people productive and happy?

Ingalls: I love what I do. And it's fun to share with other people. These activities can go arbitrarily deep or wide, so it's easy to find things for various people to work on. I've just always enjoyed doing that with other people. There have been times when it's worked better or not—there are very different phases to this kind of work. There are times when you see everything that needs to be done and it's just a matter of getting people to do it. And there are other times when you don't really know what needs to be done and you're trying to find out. Those are really different phases.

Seibel: Do you have any tips on how to be a good technical leader?

Ingalls: The first thing is being clear about what you're trying to do. The job is to get a clear vision. If you've been around, you can see actually how you're going to implement that, so you can start to see how that would work out in terms of what various people can do and how it would all fit together.

There have been times when I've been working on a project where I could see everything. It felt really powerful because whenever anybody was stuck I could tell them immediately what the next step was, or how to get around it. And people feel that, too, if you know where you're headed. They can immediately sense it's all there—he's got it. And that's empowering for the team as well.

Seibel: Does having too clear a picture of what you want ever *disempower* people—since you've got everything in your head, there's nothing fun for them to do?

Ingalls: Well, you can leave it open how they do their part of it and you maybe only step in with micromanagement where it's needed. And often things turn out better. I was lucky to work with a great crew of people for a long time whom I trusted. Trust is part of it, trust for the people that you're working with. The other thing is just confidence. When the picture's clear, it's easy to be confident about it. I think the kind of thing that makes for bad micromanagement is you're worried and you're insecure, and so you're feeling like you have to nail everything down.

Seibel: Have you ever had a really great team leader when you were a worker bee?

Ingalls: The best boss in my life has been Alan Kay. I worked under him at Xerox for some very formative years, and that was an interesting combination, because he knew what he wanted but he hardly ever said how I should do things. But he was technically savvy about all of it so he was a good critic. I and the guys who came to work with me were really productive so I think he felt enough progress that he didn't have to interfere much. He made an umbrella for me, for us, and he really had a picture of what he wanted to do.

Seibel: When folks are working in a group, is it better for coders to each own a piece of a system? Where "This is my code and no one touches it" vs. the team owns the code and anybody can touch anything.

Ingalls: I don't know. The way we work now on the Lively Kernel project is different people have different areas they work on, but there aren't any fences. It's more a matter of expertise, or focus, or goals. I'm trying to think of these periods that seemed really successful, how that worked. I've never worked in big teams, so it's generally been that people pretty much worked solely on a piece of code.

Seibel: Another topic, debugging: what's the worst bug you've ever had to track down?

Ingalls: It was a garbage-collection bug. Garbage collection is the worst thing because the manifestation of the problem is long after the cause has come and gone. Being able to track down an obscure bug like that makes me think of breaking codes. My father was in the Office of Strategic Services, and they worked in teams, and a lot of what they did was just gathering information, just trying to be up on things. Then a code would come in with a fragment of something they had seen in a newspaper and they would put it together that way.

It was the same thing with being able to track this down. What I brought to it was just having all this intuition of what can cause what to happen in these situations. This particular one, I was in it deep down for at least a day. When I finally got it done, I was elated, and my son, who was, I think, four at the time, made me a "Determined Debugger Award."

Seibel: This was in Smalltalk, I assume. Did you have a symbolic debugger that you could use, or were you looking at hex dumps of memory?

Ingalls: This was lower level than the nice Smalltalk debugger. I really can't tell you the details of this one, but the kind of thing is you get an error somewhere, which would actually take you to the low-level debuggers. So you're looking at memory like a bunch of octal locations. Then you find things like one object pointing into another object in the way it shouldn't. So you're trying to think of, "How could that happen?" You have all these little clues and little patterns of this can cause that, this can cause that, and so then you try to figure them out.

Seibel: So that was at a very low level. When you're developing in the nice Smalltalk environment, I assume you use symbolic debuggers. Do you ever resort to print statements?

Ingalls: I don't know of anybody who does that if they have the choice of using a good debugger. Because where do you put the `print` statement? You put it *there*. Well, wouldn't you just like to *be* there, looking at everything, instead of just printing it? Now I do a fair amount of print statement–style debugging because it's often the case I don't have a good enough JavaScript debugger.

Seibel: What made the Smalltalk debugger so nice?

Ingalls: Well, you could stop anywhere in the program and you could actually look at all the bindings of all the variables. You could execute fragments, evaluate expressions right in the middle of the context.

Seibel: At any particular point in the stack frame?

Ingalls: Yep, and you could make significant changes and then proceed. And you could get to an error, have it on the screen, save the entire state of the system, ship it to somebody else who was on a Windows machine and not a Mac, and they could fire up that same image, be where you were, make a fix, and proceed. So just complete preservation of state across different machine representations.

Seibel: Invariants are another sort of debugging tool. Some people are very big on formal preconditions, and postconditions on all their methods and class invariants, and some people are more ad hoc about how they think about things. How do you think about them?

Ingalls: I'd probably go in the less formal camp. Mainly out of that original feeling of having things be as absolutely simple as possible. I feel the same kinds of things about types. Types are essentially assertions about a program. And I think it's valuable to have things be as absolutely simple as possible, including not even saying what the types are. I think as you get more serious about a system, it's nice to be able to add all that stuff, and there are ways of having your cake and eating it, too, such as inferring the types and not having to see them except when you want to see them.

And types are only one thing in a spectrum that includes units and all sorts of other assertions you can put on there. That's part of the fascinating area we have to explore with this synthetic mathematics. I think increasingly we can take areas of computation and document them more and more with living documentation, real programming documentation, so there are assertions there that really help you that you don't usually see, but if you're stuck, you can start to bring them in and test various things about it.

Seibel: Do you have an opinion one way or the other on formally proving programs correct?

Ingalls: It's never been an occupation of mine. I'm inclined to focus on the architectural part that makes it easier to make assertions about things. So if you are allowed to do all sorts of dangerous things in a program, then when you sit down to do the formal proof, it's very hard because at every step you've got to say, "Well, this could happen, that could happen, that could happen." If the architecture is clean, then the formal proof may almost be obvious just by reading the code. You'll say, "Well, this could only come from there. We're safe."

Seibel: Have you ever used C++?

Ingalls: No. Nor C.

Seibel: But you did BCPL and assembly, so it's not like you've never used low-level languages.

Ingalls: Right. And I actually have done some C to debug things generated by Squeak. But I remember when we did Squeak, part of my purpose was to have a system that you really could be master of without having to know anything *but* Squeak. So I made it my purpose to not ever learn that. John Maloney did the translator from Squeak to C in order to give us a practical implementation. The truth is, I would go in and look at that C code but I pretty much made sure that you didn't need to do any of that.

Seibel: You must've looked at C++ when it came out, as you were part of the group that—other than perhaps the Simula folks—can best claim to have invented object-oriented programming.

Ingalls: I didn't get that much into it. It seemed like a step forward in various ways from C, but it seemed to be not yet what the promise was, which we were already experiencing. If I had been forced to do another bottom-up implementation, instead of using machine code I would've maybe started with C++. And I know a couple of people who are masters of C++ and I love to see how they do things because I think they don't rely on it for the stuff that it's not really that good at but totally use it as almost a metaprogramming language.

Seibel: Let's talk about code reading. How do you get into a new piece of code?

Ingalls: It's hard for me to answer in the abstract. You start out knowing what it does or is supposed to do. I guess I go at it pretty much top-down—I just try to understand what the pieces are and how they work together. See what classes and methods are defined and what they're doing. Then it depends on why we're looking. It could be it's just something new and we want to find out about it. It could be that it's performing badly and then you do a profile of it and look at that.

Seibel: We talked about Knuth before. His other passion is literate programming. Have you ever written literate code or read any?

Ingalls: I like to work that way with something where I've got the time to finish it off. When I first write stuff, there are no comments. As soon as I have it working, I'll write some comments. And if I like what I've done or it seems like it would be hard to figure out, I'll write more comments. But I don't believe in putting comments beside everything. And I kind of feel like the better a language is, the less you need comments. You use reasonable variable names. That's why I liked the keyword parameters in Smalltalk. It really makes things pretty readable.There's this wonderful little hack that you can do in various places in JavaScript. It's a little bit expensive, but JavaScript has this curly bracket object notation, and so you can use keywords and they actually looks like Smalltalk keywords because they end with colons, so you can have your multiple arguments be in a curly brace expression. It actually makes nice-looking programs.

Seibel: Hmmm. That's kind of beautiful and disgusting at the same time.

Ingalls: Yeah, right.

Seibel: Have you convinced anyone else to adopt that style?

Ingalls: The truth is I found somebody else doing that before I thought of it myself.

Seibel: Do you consider yourself a scientist, an engineer, an artist, or a craftsman?

Ingalls: Really, all of those. I think my education as a physicist was good for me. A lot of that just has to do with looking at problems like physical problems, trying to isolate the forces on a body. It's the same kind of thing you use for looking at what all the ways are that something's being used in the system, how it could be affected. And it's a very physical feeling I have about stuff that's also really spatial—how things work together and how things that might be different could be the same and how that would make a better architecture.

I remember one of the early talks I had to give about Smalltalk; I said, "What we do in this group is like the scientific method, which is you make an observation, you come up with a theory to explain it, and you perform an experiment to verify it." And that's very much what we did in the successive generations of Smalltalk. We had a theory for how to make something work. We built a system that worked that way. We used it for a while and we found out, "Oh, it'd be good if we did this and this and this differently," and we built a new one. So we kept going around that circle, which is just like scientific research and progress.

I feel like an artist when I'm working because I have this idea in my head and I just want to make it real. I imagine a sculptor having the same feeling, bringing a piece to life.

In this context, I view engineer and craftsman as being almost identical. It's just that an engineer is a craftsman in a technological field. There are times when I feel that way, too, but they are different times—a very different time. It's when I'm doing something low-level. From my history, I worked on the deepest parts of BitBlt or the Smalltalk byte-code engine and those are very craftsman-like things. And I had the luxury to do those over again a couple of times to get them really right and that's a craft.

Seibel: The difference I see between engineers and craftsmen is the engineers are the folks who say, "We should be like the guys who build bridges. Bridges don't fall down. They have a repeatable engineering process." The craftsmen say, "This is more like woodworking. The wood is unique every time and there are rules of thumb but no method that can guarantee certain results."

Ingalls: So in that regard I may be less of an engineer. I think that the ways in which I stress systems are different. I know there are people who do serious enterprise programming systems. That's not a focus or a passion of mine. Of the four you mentioned, the engineer is probably the least, then craftsman, and then this funny combination between artist and scientist at the top.

Seibel: You mentioned that you left industry for a while and then you came back. Were you tired of computers or was it just other things in life?

Ingalls: It was other things in my life. It was also a nice break, and I picked a good time for it, because when I came back, it didn't seem to me like things had changed that much, except everything was a hundred times faster.

Seibel: Do you have any recommendations for people who want to be programmers?

Ingalls: Well, I think a decent course in computer science should be good. The way I would organize that is to learn several different languages that have various different strengths. Smalltalk's got a lot of strengths but it's not the answer to everything. There's logic programming. There's functional programming. Actually, you can do Smalltalk in a functional style, and so that's covered there pretty much. But like what I said about Lotus 1-2-3 and translating English to pig Latin, I think it's worth it to take several different computing environments and then pick a problem to solve in them, which either reveals the strength of the language or encourages you to somehow escape from it.

Seibel: Do you think programming—and therefore the kind of people who can succeed as programmers—has changed? Can you be a great programmer operating at a certain high level without ever learning assembly, or C, and maybe without ever learning the algorithms you would get from reading Knuth, because these days you're using some high-level language that includes a lot of those algorithms in libraries?

Ingalls: Different people have different levels that they need to go to to feel good about what they're working with. So I think somebody can be entirely confident maybe using a collections library without having programmed it themselves. It just means they're operating at another level. Lord knows, I wouldn't expect anybody who intends to work with graphics to have had to write BitBlt. You don't have to do NAND gates; you can use assembly language. I think you can work at any of these levels. If the challenge calls on you for it, you're going to have to go deeper, and if your interest is sparked, you will want to go deeper.

Seibel: So do you think most programmers today, who may be working at a fairly high level, in a different environment would have learned assembly and microcode? Or do you think the kind of talents that people need to be successful programmers are changing?

Ingalls: Yes and no. It is in a way the same up and down at any level and hopefully it will come to appear even more so. But there are areas right now where I think there's more putting together according to formula and other areas where there's dealing with things that are much more primitive.

I was a physicist; I had mathematician friends and I did not feel like I was at all the same kind of brain as they were. But we both did good things. I think that's going to be the case in computers, too. The people who are working on program provers are different from the people who are working on graphics systems, I think. And so people are going to find their strengths and the place they want to work and the place that they're not comfortable working. I think there's some nature as well as nurture going on here, and there always will be.

It may be that some of these systems have enough levels and parts to them that a given person may be mainly comfortable and productive working in one kind of area rather than another, but I think it's all the same stuff. There's logical thought and there's structural thought. And there's human stuff and creativity. A given person has a given mix of that from their nature and their nurture, and to me, it hasn't changed much. People are trying to do presumably bigger, better stuff, but it seems to me to still be pretty much the same.

Seibel: Related to that, as more and more fields rely on computing in more and more ad hoc ways, there are folks who want to find a way for "nonprogrammers" to program. Do you think that'll happen, or will domain experts, say biologists, always have to team up with programmers to build custom software to solve their problems?

Ingalls: I think there will be that kind of collaboration because the biologist isn't interested in programming it. He's interested in finding out this or that. Then there's somebody who understands how this stuff is being worked on on the computers who can help him do that. I think the thing that lets a nonprogrammer program is an application.

Seibel: I worked on a project that tried to provide a programming environment for biologists on the theory that the software they would need would always be ad hoc. You couldn't build an application and be done with it because the biologists didn't really know what they needed until they got down to some piece of biological data and said, "What I really want to know is X," and the only way to extract X from that data was, essentially, to write a program.

Ingalls: Yeah, it would be nice if we could have some computing environment with all your information in it so you could somehow figure out how to get to it all just by its self-revealing nature. But I think that there are people who are going to be interested in that and people who aren't.

Seibel: Is there anything I haven't asked about that you thought I might?

Ingalls: Often, reading about famous people, the side of it that I'm interested in is, how do they make their life work? All the things that weren't their passion, and how did they deal with that, and with their family, and with their finances, and balancing that. Or did they just hole up and say, "To hell with everything else," and let it just come crumbling down until they had their work done?

Seibel: Do you feel like there were times in your life where your passion for programming ran amok to the detriment of other parts of your life?

Ingalls: Yeah, there are times when it's been hard on others because I'm focused and need to stay focused. It's a risk with anybody who's got a passion for what they're doing. I think either you learn to moderate it somewhat or the other thing you do is communicate it so that everybody around you knows that you're dealing with this thing, and you'll probably be done in a week, but until then Daddy's somewhat inaccessible.

Seibel: And then you win your "Dad the Determined Debugger" award.

Ingalls: Exactly; right. The other thing is, the more you can reflect the satisfaction from progress back out to all the people who have dealt with you during that time, at least they have a sense that Daddy's doing something good, and we'll all be happy when it's done.

CHAPTER

11

L Peter Deutsch

A prodigy, L Peter Deutsch started programming in the late '50s, at age 11, when his father brought home a memo about the programming of design calculations for the Cambridge Electron Accelerator at Harvard. He was soon hanging out at MIT, implementing Lisp on a PDP-1, and hacking on and improving code written by MIT hackers nearly twice his age.

As a sophomore at UC Berkeley, he got involved with Project Genie, one of the first minicomputer-based timesharing systems, writing most of the operating system's kernel. (Ken Thompson, inventor of Unix and the subject of Chapter 12, would also work on the project while a grad student at Berkeley, influencing his later work on Unix.) After participating in a failed attempt to commercialize the Project Genie system, Deutsch moved to Xerox PARC, where he worked on the Interlisp system and on the Smalltalk virtual machine, helping to invent the technique of just-in-time compilation.

He served as Chief Scientist at the PARC spin-off, ParcPlace, and was a Fellow at Sun Microsystems, where he put to paper the now famous "Seven Fallacies of Distributed Computing." He is also the author of Ghostscript, the Postscript viewer. In 1992, he was part of the group that received the Association for Computing

Machinery Software System Award, for their work on Interlisp, and in 1994 he was elected a Fellow of the ACM.

In 2002 Deutsch quit work on Ghostscript in order to study musical composition. Today he is more likely to be working on a new musical composition than on a new program, but still can't resist the urge to hack every now and then, mostly on a musical score editor of his own devising.

Among the topics we covered in our conversation were the deep problems he sees with any computer language that includes the notion of a pointer or a reference, why software should be treated as a capital asset rather than an expense, and why he ultimately retired from professional programming.

Seibel: How did you start programming?

Deutsch: I started programming by accident when I was 11. My dad brought home some memo from the Cambridge Electron Accelerator, which was being built at the time. There was a group that did design computations and some memo of theirs accidentally found its way to him. I saw it lying around his office and it had some computer code in it and there was something about it that caught my imagination.

It turned out the memo was actually an addendum to another memo so I asked him if he could lay his hands on the original memo. He brought that home and I said, "Gee, this stuff is really interesting." I think I might actually have asked him if I could meet the guy who had written the memos. We met. I don't really remember the details any more—this was 50 years ago. Somehow I got to write a little bit of code for one of the design calculations for the Cambridge Electron Accelerator. That's how I got started.

Seibel: So that was when you were eleven. By 14 or 15 you were playing on the PDP-1s at MIT, where your dad was a professor.

Deutsch: When I was 14, I found my way to the TX-0 and to the PDP-1 shortly thereafter. I remember getting a hold of a copy of the Lisp 1.5 programmers' manual. I don't remember how. It was a very early version—it was actually mimeographed—the old purple ink. There was something about Lisp that caught my imagination. I've always had a kind of mathematical bent, and Lisp just seemed sort of cool. I wanted to have one to play with and I couldn't get my hands on the Building 26 mainframe. So I did my Lisp implementation on the PDP-1.

Seibel: Do you remember at all how you designed your PDP-1 Lisp?

Deutsch: I'm smiling because the program was so small. Have you seen the listing? It's only a few hundred lines of assembler.

Seibel: I've seen it; I didn't try to understand it. Was it just a matter of transliterating the thing in the 1.5 manual into assembly?

Deutsch: No, no, no. All that was in the 1.5 manual was the interpreter. I had to write a reader and tokenizer and I had to design the data structures and all that stuff. My recollection was that I did that the way I actually have done most of my programming, which is to do the data structures first. When I was young enough that my intuition would point me in the right direction—I won't say infallibly, but close enough—that was a really good approach.

In the last couple of years I've noticed that I've gotten rusty—my intuition doesn't work so well anymore. I've been doing a substantial project off and on for several years now to do a good open-source music score editor. I've been fiddling with that off and on for several years now and I find that letting my intuition steer me to the right data structures and then just writing everything out from there just doesn't work anymore.

Seibel: Do you think your intuition is actually worse or did you used to have more stamina for making it work even if your intuition was actually a bit off?

Deutsch: I think it's some of each but I think it's more the former. I think what intuition is, really, is an unconscious process for synthesizing a solution out of a large amount of data. And as I've gotten further and further away from being immersed in the stuff of software, the data that goes into that synthesis has become less and less accessible.

I've heard it said that to be a master at something you have to have, pretty much at your command, something like 20,000 specific cases. What's happened is the 20,000 specific cases of software design that passed in front of my face in my 45 years in the industry are just gradually becoming less and less accessible, the way memories do. I think that's pretty much what's going on.

Seibel: Do you remember what it was about programming that drew you in?

Deutsch: With the benefit of 50 years of hindsight, I can see that I have always been drawn to systems of denotative symbols—languages. Not only languages of discourse—human languages—but languages in which utterances have effects. Programming languages certainly fall right into that category.

I think that also has something to do with why the career that I've switched into is musical composition. Music is a language, or a family of languages, but what you say in those languages not only has denotation, maybe, but it also it has effects on people. Music is kind of interesting because on the spectrum of formality it falls between natural languages and computer languages. It's more formal and structured than a natural language, but it doesn't have nearly the structure or formality of a computer language. That, I think, may have to do with why I went into music and not poetry. I think poetry is not structured enough for me.

But the short answer really is, I just gravitated to this stuff right away.

Seibel: Do you remember the first interesting program you wrote?

Deutsch: The first program that I wrote because the content interested me was actually the second program that I wrote. The first program I wrote was some piece of calculation having to do with the Cambridge Electron Accelerator. The second program was a floating-point-output-formatting program.

Seibel: Which is a pretty hairy problem.

Deutsch: Well it is on a binary machine. It's not a hairy problem on a decimal machine, and I was working on a decimal machine. You just slide the string around and decide where to put the decimal point. You have to decide whether to use the E or F format. But in those days, everything was a lot harder—I was writing in assembly language on a batch-processing machine—so this was not a trivial problem. It wasn't a hard problem but it wasn't a trivial one. That was the first program that I wrote because I wanted to.

Seibel: So you were hanging out at MIT during high school and then you went to Berkeley for college. Did you want to escape the East Coast?

Deutsch: Sort of. I realized that it would be really good for me to go to someplace that was far away from my parents. The three places that I considered seriously were, I think it was University of Rochester, University of Chicago, and Berkeley. That was a no-brainer—only one of the three has reasonable weather. So that's how I ended up at Berkeley. And it was one of the best things that ever happened in my life.

I was at Berkeley and I found Project Genie pretty quickly after I arrived and stayed with that project until—well there was Project Genie and then there was Berkeley Computer Corporation and then there was Xerox.

Seibel: Presumably at Berkeley you started working on bigger projects than your PDP-1 Lisp implementation.

Deutsch: Oh, yeah. Considerably larger projects at Project Genie. To begin with I wrote pretty much the whole operating-system kernel. The kernel was probably pushing 10,000 lines.

Seibel: How did that change—an order-of-magnitude difference in size—change your design process?

Deutsch: I'm trying to remember what was in the kernel. It was still a small enough program that I could approach it as a whole. There were obviously functional divisions. I know I had a clear mental model of which sections of the program were allowed to interact with which of the key data structures. But in fact there weren't very damn many data structures. There was a process table; there were ready lists. There were I/O buffers and there was some stuff for keeping track of virtual memory. And then there was an open file table, per process. But the descriptions of all the system data structures probably could have fit on, in terms of C struct definitions, probably could have fit on two pages. So we're not talking about a complicated system.

Seibel: What's the biggest system that you've worked on that you remember how it was designed?

Deutsch: I've been the primary mover on three large systems. Ghostscript—not counting the device drivers, which I didn't write most of—was probably somewhere on the order of between 50,000 and 100,000 lines of C.

On the ParcPlace Smalltalk virtual machine I worked only on the just-in-time compiler, which was probably 20 percent of it, and that was probably in the low single-digit thousands of lines of C. Maybe 3,000, 5,000—something like that.

And the Interlisp implementation, as much of it as I was concerned with, was probably a couple thousand lines of microcode, and maybe—I'm guessing now—maybe another 5,000 lines of Lisp. So Ghostscript is probably the largest single system I've ever been involved with.

Seibel: And other than the device drivers written by other people, you basically wrote that by yourself.

Deutsch: Up to the end of 1999, I basically wrote every line of code. At the beginning I made a few architectural decisions. The first one was to completely separate the language interpreter from the graphics.

Seibel: The language being PostScript?

Deutsch: Right. So the language interpreter knew nothing about the data structures being used to do the graphics. It talked to a graphics library that had an API.

The second decision I made was to structure the graphics library using a driver interface. So the graphics library understood about pixels and it understood about curve rendering and it understood about text rendering but it knew as little as I could manage about how pixels were encoded for a particular device, how pixels were transmitted to a particular device.

The third decision was that the drivers would actually implement the basic drawing commands. Which, at the beginning, were basically `draw-pixmap` and `fill-rectangle`.

So the rendering library passed rectangles and pixel arrays to the driver. And the driver could either put together a full-page image if it wanted to or, for display, it could pass them through directly to Xlib or GDI or whatever. So those were the three big architectural decisions that I made up front and they were all good ones. And they were pretty much motherhood. I guess the principle that I was following was if you have a situation where you have something that's operating in multiple domains and the domains don't inherently have a lot of coupling or interaction with each other, that's a good place to put a pretty strong software boundary.

So language interpretation and graphics don't inherently interact with each other very much. Graphics rendering and pixmap representation interact more, but that seemed like a good place to put an abstraction boundary as well.

In fact I wrote a Level I PostScript interpreter with no graphics before I wrote the first line of graphics code. If you open the manual and basically go through all the operators that don't make any reference to graphics, I implemented all of those before I even started designing the graphics. I had to design the tokenizer; I had to decide on the representation of all the PostScript data types and the things that the PostScript manual says the interpreter has to provide. I had to go back and redo a lot of them when we got to PostScript Level 2, which has garbage collection. But that's where I started.

Then I just let my experience with language interpreters carry me into the design of the data structures for the interpreter. Between the time that I started and the time that I was able to type in `3 4 add equals` and have it come back with `7` was about three weeks. That was very easy. And by the way, the environment in which I was working—MS-DOS. MS-DOS with a stripped-down Emacs and somebody's C compiler; I don't remember whose.

Seibel: This was a task that you had done many times before, namely implementing an interpreter for a language. Did you just start in writing C code? Or fill up a notebook with data-structure diagrams?

Deutsch: The task seemed simple enough to me that I didn't bother to write out diagrams. My recollection was that first I sort of soaked myself in the PostScript manual. Then I might have made some notes on paper but probably I just started writing C header files. Because, as I say, I like to design starting with the data.

Then I had some idea that, well, there'd have to be a file with a main interpreter loop. There'd have to be some initialization. There'd have to be a tokenizer. There'd have to be a memory manager. There'd have to be something to manage the PostScript notion of files. There'd have to be implementation of the individual PostScript operators. So I divided those up into a bunch of files sort of by functionally.

When I took the trouble of registering the copyright in the Ghostscript code I had to send them a complete listing of the earliest Ghostscript implementation. At that point it was like 10 years later—it was interesting to me to look at the original code and the original structure and the original names of various things and to note that probably 70 or 80 percent of the structure and naming conventions were still there, 10 years and 2 major PostScript language revisions later.

So basically that's what I did—data structures first. Rough division into modules. My belief is still, if you get the data structures and their invariants right, most of the code will just kind of write itself.

Seibel: So when you say you write a header file, is that to get the function signatures or the structs, or both?

Deutsch: The structs. This was 1988, before ANSI C—there weren't function signatures. Once ANSI C compilers had pretty much become the standard, I took two months and went through and I made function signatures for every function in Ghostscript.

Seibel: How has your way of thinking about programming or your practice of programming, changed from those earliest days to now?

Deutsch: It's changed enormously because the kinds of programs that I find interesting have changed enormously. I think it's fair to say that the programs that I wrote for the first few years were just little pieces of code.

Over time I've considered the issues of how do you take a program that does something larger and interesting and structure it and think about it, and how do you think about the languages that you use for expressing it in a way that manages to accomplish your goals of utility, reliability, efficiency, transparency?

Now I'm aware of a much larger set of criteria for evaluating software. And I think about those criteria in the context of much larger and more complex programs, programs where architectural or system-level issues is where all the hard work is. Not to say that there isn't still hard work to be done in individual algorithms, but that's not what seems most interesting to me any more—hasn't for a long time.

Seibel: Should all programmers grow up to work at that level?

Deutsch: No. In fact, I was just reading that an old friend of mine from Xerox PARC, Leo Guibas, just received some fairly high award in the field. He has never really been a systems guy in the sense that I've been; he's been an algorithms guy—a brilliant one. He's found a way to think about certain classes of analysis or optimization algorithms in a way that's made them applicable to a lot of different problems, and that has yielded new tools for working with those problems. So, it's wonderful work. Programmers should be able to grow up to be Leo Guibas, too.

There's a parallel between architectural principles and the kinds of algorithmic design principles that Leo and people like him use to address these hard optimization and analysis problems. The difference is that the principles for dealing with algorithmic problems are based a lot more directly on 5,000 or10,000 years' worth of history in mathematics. How we go about programming now, we don't have anything like that foundation to build on. Which is one of the reasons why so much software is crap: we don't really know what we're doing yet.

Seibel: So is it OK for people who don't have a talent for systems-level thinking to work on smaller parts of software? Can you split the programmers and the architects? Or do you really want everyone who's working on systems-style software, since it is sort of fractal, to be able to think in terms of systems?

Deutsch: I don't think software is fractal. It might be nice if it were but I don't think it is because I don't think we have very good tools for dealing with the things that happen as systems get large. I think the things that happen when systems get large are qualitatively different from the things that happen as systems go from being small to medium size.

But in terms of who should do software, I don't have a good flat answer to that. I do know that the further down in the plumbing the software is, the more important it is that it be built by really good people. That's an elitist point of view, and I'm happy to hold it.

Part of what's going on today is that the boundary between what is software and what isn't software is getting blurred. If you have someone who's designing a web site, if that web site has any kind of even moderately complex behavior in terms of interacting with the user or tracking state, you have tools for building web sites like that. And working with those tools—as I understand it, not having used them—accomplishes some of the same ends as programming, but the means don't look very much like writing programs.

So one of the answers to your question might be that over time a larger and larger fraction of what people used to think of as requiring programming won't be "programming" any more and pretty much anybody will be able to do it and do a reasonable job of it.

You know the old story about the telephone and the telephone operators? The story is, sometime fairly early in the adoption of the telephone, when it was clear that use of the telephone was just expanding at an incredible rate, more and more people were having to be hired to work as operators because we didn't have dial telephones. Someone extrapolated the growth rate and said, "My God. By 20 or 30 years from now, every single person will have to be a telephone operator." Well, that's what happened. I think something like that may be happening in some big areas of programming, as well.

Seibel: Can programmers be replaced that way?

Deutsch: Depends on what you want to program. One of the things that I've been thinking about off and on over the last five-plus years is, "Why is programming so hard?"

You have the algorithmic side of programming and that's close enough to mathematics that you can use mathematics as the basic model, if you will, for what goes on in it. You can use mathematical methods and mathematical ways of thinking. That doesn't make it easy, but nobody thinks mathematics is easy. So there's a pretty good match between the material you're working with and our understanding of that material and our understanding of the skill level that's required to work with it.

I think part of the problem with the other kind of programming is that the world of basically all programming languages that we have is so different in such deep ways from the physical world that our senses and our brains and our society have coevolved to deal with, that it is loony to expect people to do well with it. There has to something a little wrong with you for you to be a really good programmer. Maybe "wrong with you" is a little too strong, but the qualities that make somebody a well-functioning human being and the qualities that make somebody a really good programmer—they overlap but they don't overlap a whole heck of a lot. And I'm speaking as someone who was a very good programmer.

The world of von Neumann computation and Algol-family languages has such different requirements than the physical world, that to me it's actually quite surprising that we manage to build large systems at all that work even as poorly as they do.

Perhaps it shouldn't be any more surprising than the fact that we can build jet airliners, but jet airliners are working in the physical world and we have thousands of years of mechanical engineering to draw on. For software, we have this weird world with these weird, really bizarre fundamental properties. The physical world's properties are rooted in subatomic physics, but you've got these layers: you've got subatomic physics, you've got atomic physics, you've got chemistry. You've got tons of emergent properties that come out of that and we have all of this apparatus for functioning well in that world.

I don't look around and see anything that looks like an address or a pointer. We have objects; we don't have these weird things that computer scientists misname "objects."

Seibel: To say nothing of the scale. Two to the 64th of anything is a lot, and things happening billions of times a second is fast.

Deutsch: But that doesn't bother us here in the real world. You know Avogadro's number, right? Ten to the 23rd? So, we're looking here around at a world that has incredible numbers of little things all clumped together and happening at the same time. It doesn't bother us because the world is such that you don't have to understand this table at a subatomic level.

The physical properties of matter are such that 99.9 percent of the time you can understand it in aggregate. And everything you have to know about it, you can understand from dealing with it in aggregate. To a great extent, that is not true in the world of software.

People keep trying to do modularization structures for software. And the state of that art has been improving over time, but it's still, in my opinion, very far away from the ease with which we look around and see things that have, whatever it is, 10 to the 23rd atoms in them, and it doesn't even faze us.

Software is a discipline of detail, and that is a deep, horrendous fundamental problem with software. Until we understand how to conceptualize and organize software in a way that we don't have to think about how every little piece interacts with every other piece, things are not going to get a whole lot better. And we're very far from being there.

Seibel: Are the technical reasons things that could be changed, or is it just the nature of the beast?

Deutsch: You'd have to start over. You'd have to throw out all languages that have the concept of a pointer to begin with because there is no such thing as a pointer in the real world. You'd have to come to grips with the fact that information takes space and exists over time and is located at a particular place.

Seibel: As you made the progression from writing small pieces of code to building big systems, did you still write small pieces of code the same way and just add a new perspective about bigger systems, or did it actually change the way you did the whole thing?

Deutsch: It changed the way I did the whole thing. The first significant programs I wrote would be the ones on the UNIVAC at Harvard. The next little cluster would be the work that I did on the PDP-1 at MIT. There were really three different programs or systems that I think of dating from that era, in the early-1960s timeframe, around when I was in high school.

There was a Lisp interpreter that I built for a stock PDP-1. I did some work on the operating system for Jack Dennis's weird modified PDP-1. And I wrote a text editor for Dennis's PDP-1.

Those three systems I still wrote basically monolithically. The difference from my old programs on the UNIVAC was I had to start doing data-structure design. So that was the first big shift in what kind of programming I was doing.

I was starting to be aware of what I would call functional segmentation but I didn't think of it as having any particular significance. I was aware that you could write certain parts of the program and not have to think about other parts of the program while you were doing it, but the issues about interfaces, which really become paramount as programs get big, I don't recall those being of concern.

That transition happened with my the next big cluster of work, which was the work that I did at Berkeley, mostly as an undergraduate, on Project Genie: the 940 timesharing system and on the QED text editor. And I wrote an assembly-language debugger but I don't remember much of anything about it.

The piece that had the most system flavor to it was the operating system. It's not fair to say that I wrote the whole operating system; I didn't. But I essentially wrote the whole kernel. This was done in assembly language. We're talking about programs that are getting to be a little larger here, probably on the order of 10,000 lines of assembler. It had a process scheduler. It had virtual memory. It had a file system. In fact, it had several file systems.

There, there were more complex questions of data-structure design. The one that I remember is there was an active process table. And there was a question as to how to design that and how the operating system should decide when a process was runnable or not—that kind of thing. There were structures for keeping track of the virtual memory system. But some issues of interface started to emerge. Not within the operating system itself, because the operating system was so small that the kernel was designed essentially as a single piece, as a monolith.

But there were two important areas where issues of software interface started to emerge. One of them was simply the interface between user programs and the kernel. What should the system calls be? How should the parameters be laid out? I know that in the first few versions of the 940 TSS, the basic operations for reading and writing files were the equivalent of the Unix `read` and `write` calls, where you basically gave a base address and a count. Well, that was all very well and good, but a lot of the time that wasn't what you wanted. You basically wanted a stream interface. And in those days, we didn't have the concept that you could take an operating-system facility and then wrap user-level code around it to give you some nicer interface in the way `getc` and `putc` get built on top of `read` and `write`. So what we actually did was in later versions of the operating system, we added operating-system calls that were the equivalent of `getc` and `putc`.

The other place where issues of interface started to show up were—again, based on the MULTICS mode—from the beginning we had a strong distinction between the kernel and what today we would call the shell. This was early enough in the development of operating systems that we didn't realize that you could, in fact, build a shell with essentially no special privileges. The shell was a user-mode program, but it had a lot of special privileges. But there were some issues about what facilities the kernel had to give the shell—what things the shell should be able to do directly and what things it should have to make kernel calls for.

We saw interface-design choices just emerging from the task. That was the point in my career at which I dimly started to become aware that interfaces between entities really needed to be designed separately, that the interfaces between them were also an important design issue.

So responding to your question about whether the way I programmed in the small changed as I started to work with larger systems, the answer is, yes. As I built larger and larger systems, I found that when sitting down to write any piece of code, more and more the question I would ask myself first is, "OK, what's the interface between this and everything around it going to look like? What gets passed in? What gets passed out? How much of a task should be on which side of an interface?" Those kinds of questions started to become a larger and larger part of what I was dealing with. And they did affect the way that I wrote individual smaller chunks of code, I think.

Seibel: And this was a natural consequence of working on bigger systems—eventually the systems get big enough that you just have to find some way to break them apart.

Deutsch: That's right. In that sense I agree that software is fractal in that decomposition is an issue that happens at many different levels. I was going to say I don't think that the kinds of decomposition at bigger grains are qualitatively the same as the kinds of decomposition that happen at smaller grains. I'm not sure. When you're doing decomposition at a smaller grain you may not be thinking, for example, about resource allocation; when you're doing decomposition at a larger grain you have to.

Seibel: Have you worked with people who, in your opinion, were very good programmers, yet who could only work at a certain scale? Like they could work well on problems up to a sort of certain size but beyond that, they just didn't have the mentality for breaking systems apart and thinking about them that way?

Deutsch: I've worked with programmers who were very smart but who didn't have experience at larger-scale programming. And for Ghostscript, I did have some pretty serious disagreements with two of the engineers who were brought into the team as it was getting handed over to the company that I started. Both very smart and hardworking guys, both experienced. I thought they were very good programmers, good designers. But they were not system thinkers. Not only were they not used to thinking in terms of the impact or ramifications of changes; they to some extent didn't even realize that that was an essential question to ask. To me the distinction is between people who understand what the questions are that you have to ask in doing larger-scale design and the people who for whatever reason don't see those questions as well.

Seibel: But you think those people—when they're not trying to be the architect of a whole system—do good work?

Deutsch: Yeah. The two engineers that I'm thinking of both did really great work for the company. One of them was working on something that was large and rather thankless but important commercially. And the other one redid some substantial chunks of my graphics code and his code produces better-looking results. So these are good, smart, experienced guys. They just don't kind of see that part of the picture—at least that's my take on it.

Seibel: Are there particular skills that you feel made you a good programmer?

Deutsch: I'm going to give you a very new-age answer here. I'm not a new-age kind of guy generally speaking, although I went through my period of really long hair. When I was at what I would consider the peak of my abilities, I had extremely trustworthy intuition. I would do things and they would just turn out right. Some of that was luck. Some of it, I'm sure, was experience that had simply gotten internalized so far down that I didn't have conscious access to the process. But I think I just had a knack for it. I know that's not a very satisfying answer but I truly believe that some of what made me good at what I did was something that was just there.

Seibel: In your days as a precocious teenager hanging out at MIT, did you have had a chance to observe, "Wow, this guy's really smart but he doesn't know how to do this thing that I know how to do."?

Deutsch: No, I didn't. Well, OK, I do remember when I started rewriting the text editor on Dennis's PDP-1; I must have been 15 or 16. The original code had been written by one or two of the guys from the Tech Model Railroad Club group. Those were smart guys. And I looked at the code and I thought a lot of it was awful.

I would not say it was a difference between me and the people I was working around. It was a difference between the way I thought code should be and the code that I saw in front of me. I would hesitate to generalize that into a statement about the people.

I've always been really comfortable in what I would call the symbolic world, the world of symbols. Symbols and their patterns have always just been the stuff I eat for lunch. And for a lot of people that's not the case. I see it even with my partner. We're both musicians. We're both composers. We're both vocal performers. But I come at music primarily from a symbolic point of view. I do a lot of my composition just with a pencil and a pad of paper. The notes are in there but I'm not picking them out on the piano. I hear them and I have a plan.

Whereas he does most of his composition on his guitar. He plays stuff and fools around with it, maybe plunks around at the piano a little bit, runs through it again. And he never writes anything down. He'll write down the chord sequences, maybe, if pressed, and I guess at some point he writes down the words. But he doesn't come at composition kind of from the symbol-based mindset at all.

So some people go that way, some people don't. If I was going to draw lessons from it—well again, I'm kind of an elitist: I would say that the people who should be programming are the people who feel comfortable in the world of symbols. If you don't feel really pretty comfortable swimming around in that world, maybe programming isn't what you should be doing.

Seibel: Did you have any important mentors?

Deutsch: There were two people One of them is someone who's no longer around; his name was Calvin Mooers. He was an early pioneer in information systems. I believe he is credited with actually coining the term *information retrieval.* His background was originally in library science. I met him when I was, I think, high-school or college age. He had started to design a programming language that he thought would be usable directly by just people. But he didn't know anything about programming languages. And at that point, I did because I had built this Lisp system and I'd studied some other programming languages.

So we got together and the language that he eventually wound up making was one that I think it's fair to say that he and I kind of codesigned. It was called TRAC. He was just a real supportive guy at that point for me.

The other person that I've always thought of as something of a mentor is Danny Bobrow. He and I have been friends for a very long time. And I've always thought of him as kind of a mentor in the process of my career.

But in terms of actually how to program, how to do software, there wasn't anybody at MIT. There wasn't really anybody at Berkeley. At PARC, only one person really affected the way that I did software, and he wasn't even a programmer. That was Jerry Elkind, who was the manager of the Computer Science Lab at PARC for a while.

The thing that he said that made a profound effect on me was how important it is to measure things; that there'll be times—maybe more times than you think—when your beliefs or intuitions just won't be right, so measure things. Even sometimes measure things you don't think you need to measure. That had a profound effect on me.

When I want to do something that's going to involve a significant amount of computation or significant amount of data, one of the things that I always do now is measure. And that's been the case since I was at PARC, which was starting about 35 years ago.

Seibel: You were the only person I contacted about this book who had a really strong reaction to the word *coder* in the title. How would you prefer to describe yourself?

Deutsch: I have to say at this point in my life I have even a mildly negative reaction to the word *programmer*. If you look at the process of creating software that actually works, that does something useful, there are a lot of different roles and a lot of different processes and skills that go into achieving that end. Someone can call themselves a programmer and that doesn't tell you very much about what set of skills they actually bring to bear to that process.

But at least the word *programmer* is pretty well established as covering a pretty wide range. "Coder" is strongly associated with the smallest and most narrowly focused part of that whole endeavor. I think of *coder*, in relation to the process of producing software that actually works and does something useful, as being maybe slightly above *bricklayer* in the process of constructing buildings that actually work.

There's nothing wrong with being a coder. There's nothing wrong with being a bricklayer, either. There's a lot of skill that goes into doing it well. But it represents such a small corner of the whole process.

Seibel: What is an encompassing term that would work for you? Software developer? Computer scientist?

Deutsch: I have a little bit of a rant about *computer science* also. I could make a pretty strong case that the word *science* should not be applied to computing. I think essentially all of what's called *computer science* is some combination of engineering and applied mathematics. I think very little of it is science in terms of the scientific process, where what you're doing is developing better descriptions of observed phenomena.

I guess if I was to pick a short snappy phrase I would probably say *software developer*. That covers pretty much everything from architecture to coding. It doesn't cover some of the other things that have to happen in order to produce software that actually works and is useful, but it covers pretty much all of what I've done.

Seibel: What doesn't it cover?

Deutsch: It doesn't cover the process of understanding the problem domain and eliciting and understanding the requirements. It doesn't cover the process—at least not all of the process—of the kind of feedback loops from testing to what happens after the software has been released. Basically "software developer" refers to the world within the boundaries of the organization that's developing the software. It says very little about the connections between that organization and its customers or the rest of the world, which, after all, are what justifies the creation of software in the first place.

Seibel: Do you think that's changing? These days there are people advocating trying to connect earlier with the customer or user and really making that part of the software developer's job.

Deutsch: Yes, XP certainly does that. I'm not a big fan of XP, and it's for two reasons. XP advocates very tight coupling with the customer during the development process on, I guess, two grounds. One is that this results in the customer's needs being understood and met better. That may well be true. I don't have firsthand knowledge of it but I'm a little wary of that because the customer doesn't always know what the customer's needs are.

The other reason that XP, I think, advocates this tight coupling with the customer is to avoid premature generalization or overdesign. I think that's a two-edged sword. Because I've seen that process go astray in both directions: both premature generalization and premature specialization.

So I have some questions about XP in that respect. What happens after the project is "done"? Is it maintainable? Is it supportable? Is it evolvable? What happens when the original developers have left? Because XP is so documentation-phobic, I have very grave concerns about that.

That's an issue I've had with a number of people who are very much into rapid prototyping or any form of software development that doesn't treat it as engineering. I seriously question how well software not built from an engineering point of view lasts.

Seibel: Can you give an example of when you've seen generalization or specialization go awry?

Deutsch: When I was in the peak years of my career, one of the things that I did extremely well, and I can't claim that I did it in a completely systematic way, was to pick the right level of generality to cover several years' worth of future evolution in directions that might not have been completely obvious.

But I think in retrospect the one example of premature specialization was the decision in Ghostscript, at an architectural level, to use pixel-oriented rather than plane-oriented representation of color maps. To use bitmaps and to require the representation of a pixel to fit in a machine long.

The fact that it used a chunky rather than planar representation meant that it turned out to be very awkward to deal with spot color—where you have printers that may, for specific jobs, require colors that are not the standard CMYK inks. For example silver, gold, or special tints that have to be matched exactly.

If you look at a pixelized color image there are more or less two ways of representing that in memory. You can represent it in memory as an array of pixels where each pixel contains RGB or CMYK data for the spot on the image. That's typically the way display controllers work, for example.

The other way, which is more common in the printing industry, is to have an array that contains the amount of red for each pixel and then another that contains the amount of green for each pixel, then another that contains the amount of blue, etc., etc. If you're processing things on a pixel-by-pixel basis, this is less convenient. On the other hand, it doesn't impose any a priori constraint on how many different inks or how many different plates can go into the production of a given image.

Seibel: So if you have a printer that can use gold ink, you just add a plane.

Deutsch: Right. This certainly is not common in consumer-grade printers or even typically in office printers. But in offset printing it is relatively common to have special layers. So that was one area of insufficient generalization.

So that's an example where even with a great deal of thought and skill I missed the boat. It doesn't illustrate my point well; in a sense it undermines my point because, in this case, even careful foresight resulted in insufficient generalization. And I can tell you exactly where that insufficient foresight came from—it came from the fact that Ghostscript was basically done by one very smart guy who had no acquaintance with the printing industry.

Seibel: Meaning you.

Deutsch: Right. Ghostscript started out as strictly a screen previewer for previewing PostScript files because there wasn't one and PDF didn't exist yet. If I was going to draw a moral from that story, it's that requirements always change, they always are going to at least attempt to change in directions you didn't think of.

There are two schools of thought as to how you prepare yourself for that. One school of thought, which I think is probably pretty close to the way XP looks at it, that basically says that because requirements are going to change all the time, you shouldn't expect software to last. If the requirements change, you build something new. There is, I think, a certain amount of wisdom in that.

The problem being the old saying in the business: "fast, cheap, good—pick any two." If you build things fast and you have some way of building them inexpensively, it's very unlikely that they're going to be good. But this school of thought says you shouldn't expect software to last.

I think behind this perhaps is a mindset of software as expense vs. software as capital asset. I'm very much in the software-as-capital-asset school. When I was working at ParcPlace and Adele Goldberg was out there evangelizing object-oriented design, part of the way we talked about objects and part of the way we advocated object-oriented languages and design to our customers and potential customers is to say, "Look, you should treat software as a capital asset."

And there is no such thing as a capital asset that doesn't require ongoing maintenance and investment. You should expect that there's going to be some cost associated with maintaining a growing library of reusable software. And that is going to complicate your accounting because it means you can't charge the cost of building a piece of software only to the project or the customer that's motivating the creation of that software at this time. You have to think of it the way you would think of a capital asset.

Seibel: Like building a new factory.

Deutsch: Right. A large part of the sell for objects was that well-designed objects are reusable, so the investment that you put into the design pays itself back in less effort going down the road.

I still believe that, but probably not quite as strongly as I did. The things that I see getting reused these days are either very large or very small. The scale of reuse that we were talking about when we were promoting objects was classes and groups of classes. Except in situations where you have a collection of classes that embody some kind of real domain knowledge, I don't see that happening much.

What I see getting reused is either very small things—individual icons, individual web page designs—or very big things like entire languages or large applications with extension architectures like Apache or Mozilla.

Seibel: So you don't believe the original object-reuse pitch quite as strongly now. Was there something wrong with the theory, or has it just not worked out for historical reasons?

Deutsch: Well, part of the reason that I don't call myself a computer scientist any more is that I've seen software practice over a period of just about 50 years and it basically hasn't improved tremendously in about the last 30 years.

If you look at programming languages I would make a strong case that programming languages have not improved qualitatively in the last 40 years. There is no programming language in use today that is qualitatively better than Simula-67. I know that sounds kind of funny, but I really mean it. Java is not that much better than Simula-67.

Seibel: Smalltalk?

Deutsch: Smalltalk is somewhat better than Simula-67. But Smalltalk as it exists today essentially existed in 1976. I'm not saying that today's languages aren't better than the languages that existed 30 years ago. The language that I do all of my programming in today, Python, is, I think, a lot better than anything that was available 30 years ago. I like it better than Smalltalk.

I use the word *qualitatively* very deliberately. Every programming language today that I can think of, that's in substantial use, has the concept of pointer. I don't know of any way to make software built using that fundamental concept qualitatively better.

Seibel: And you're counting Python- and Java-style references as pointers?

Deutsch: Absolutely. Yes. Programs built in Python and Java—once you get past a certain fairly small scale—have all the same problems except for storage corruption that you have in C or C++.

The essence of the problem is that there is no linguistic mechanism for understanding or stating or controlling or reasoning about patterns of information sharing and information access in the system. Passing a pointer and storing a pointer are localized operations, but their consequences are to implicitly create this graph. I'm not even going to talk about multithreaded applications—even in single-threaded applications you have data that's flowing between different parts of the program. You have references that are being propagated to different parts of the program. And even in the best-designed programs, you have these two or three or four different complex patterns of things that are going on and no way to describe or reason about or characterize large units in a way that actually constrains what happens in the small.People have taken runs at this problem. But I don't think there have been any breakthroughs and I don't think there have been any sort of widely accepted or widely used solutions.

Seibel: They aren't, perhaps, widely used, but what about pure functional languages?

Deutsch: Yes, pure functional languages have a different set of problems, but they certainly cut through that Gordian knot.

Every now and then I feel a temptation to design a programming language but then I just lie down until it goes away. But if I were to give in to that temptation, it would have a pretty fundamental cleavage between a functional part that talked only about values and had no concept of pointer and a different sphere of some kind that talked about patterns of sharing and reference and control.

Being a compiler and interpreter guy, I can think of lots of ways of implementing a language like that that doesn't involve copying around big arrays all the time. But the functional people are way ahead of me on that. There are a lot of smart people who've been working on Haskell and similar languages.

Seibel: Wouldn't the Haskell guys come back and say, "Yes, that's our monads and the way that it's clearly differentiated is in the type system?"

Deutsch: You know, I have never understood Haskell monads. I think I stopped tracking functional languages at ML.

If you look at E—this is not a language that anyone knows about to speak of—it's this language which is based on a very strong notion of capability. It's related to Hewitt's actor languages and it's related to capability-based operating systems. It has ports, or communication channels, as the fundamental connection between two objects, the idea being that neither end of the connection knows what the other end of the connection is. So this is very different from a pointer, which is uni-directional and where the entity that holds the pointer has a pretty strong idea what's at the other end of it. It's based on very strong opacity.

My sort of fuzzy first-order idea is that you have a language in which you have functional computations and you do not have sharing of objects. What you have is some form of serialized ports. Whenever you want to talk to something that you only know by reference, it's part of the basic nature of the language that you are aware that whatever that thing out there is, it's something that's going to be dealing with multiple sources of communications and therefore it has to be expected to serialize or arbitrate or something. There's no concept of attribute access and certainly no concept of storing into an attribute.

There are languages in which you have opaque APIs so the implementations can maintain invariants; it still doesn't tell you anything about the larger patterns of communication. For example, one common pattern is, you have an object, you hand it off to some third party, you tell that third party to do certain things to it, and then at some point you ask for that object back. That's a pattern of sharing. You, the caller, may never have actually given up all pointers to the object that you handed off. But you agree with yourself not to make any references through that pointer until that third party has done whatever you asked them to.

This is a very simple example of a pattern of structuring a program that, if there were a way to express it linguistically, would help people ensure that their code was conformant with their intentions.

Maybe the biggest reason why I haven't actually undertaken this effort to design a language is that I don't think I have enough insight to know how to describe patterns of sharing and patterns of communication at a high enough level and in a composable enough way to pull it off. But I think that is why constructing software today is so little better than it was 30 years ago.

My PhD thesis was about proofs of *program correctness*. I don't use that term anymore. What I say is you want to have your development system do as much work as possible towards giving you confidence that the code does what you intend it to do.

The old idea of program correctness was that there were these assertions that were your expressions of what you intend the code to do in a way that was mechanically checkable against the code itself. There were lots of problems with that approach. I now think that the path to software that's more likely to do what we intend it to do lies not through assertions, or inductive assertions, but lies through better, more powerful, deeper declarative notations.

Jim Morris, who's one of my favorite originators of computer epigrams, once said that a type checker is just a Neanderthal correctness-prover. If there's going to be a breakthrough, that's where I see it coming from—from more powerful ways of talking declaratively about how our programs are intended to be structured and what our programs are intended to do.

Seibel: So, for instance, you could somehow express the notion, "I'm passing a reference to this object over to this other subsystem, which is going to frob it for a while and I'm not going to do anything with it until I get it back."

Deutsch: Yes. There was some experimental work being done at Sun when I was there in the early '90s on a language that had a concept similar to that in it. And there was a bunch of research done at MIT by Dave Gifford on a language called FX that also tried to be more explicit about the distinction between functional and nonfunctional parts of a computation and to be more explicit about what it meant when a pointer went from somewhere to somewhere.

But I feel like all of this is looking at the issue from a fairly low level. If there are going to be breakthroughs that make it either impossible or unnecessary to build catastrophes like Windows Vista, we will just need new ways of thinking about what programs are and how to put them together.

Seibel: So, despite it not being qualitatively better than Smalltalk, you still like Python better.

Deutsch: I do. There are several reasons. With Python there's a very clear story of what is a program and what it means to run a program and what it means to be part of a program. There's a concept of module, and modules declare basically what information they need from other modules. So it's possible to develop a module or a group of modules and share them with other people and those other people can come along and look at those modules and know pretty much exactly what they depend on and know what their boundaries are.

In Smalltalk it is awkward to do this—if you develop in Smalltalk in the image mode, there never is such a thing as the program as an entity in itself. VisualWorks, which is the ParcPlace Smalltalk, has three or four different concepts of how to make things larger than a single class, and they've changed over time and they're not supported all that well by the development tools, at least not in a very visual way. There's little machinery for making it clear and explicit and machine-processable what depends on what. So if you're developing in the image mode, you can't share anything with anybody other than the whole image.

If you do what's called *filing out*—you write out the program in a textual form—you have absolutely no way of knowing whether you can read that program back in again and have it come back and do the same thing that it does because the state of the image is not necessarily one that was produced, or that can be produced, by reading in a set of source code. You might have done arbitrary things in a workspace; you might have static variables whose values have been modified over time. You just don't know. You can't reliably draw lines around anything.

I'm on the VisualWorks developers' list and the stuff that I see coming up over and over again is stuff that cannot happen in languages that don't use the image concept. The image concept is like a number of other things in the rapid-prototyping, rapid-development world. It's wonderful for single-person projects that never go outside that person's hands. It's awful if you want software to become an asset; if you want to share software with other people. So I think that's the real weakness of the Smalltalk development approach and a serious one.

The second reason I like Python is that—and maybe this is just the way my brain has changed over the years—I can't keep as much stuff in my head as I used to. It's more important for me to have stuff in front of my face. So the fact that in Smalltalk you effectively cannot put more than one method on the screen at a time drives me nuts. As far as I'm concerned the fact that I edit Python programs with Emacs is an advantage because I can see more than ten lines' worth at a time.

I've talked with the few of my buddies that are still working at VisualWorks about open-sourcing the object engine, the just-in-time code generator, which, even though I wrote it, I still think is better than a lot of what's out there. Gosh, here we have Smalltalk, which has this really great code-generation machinery, which is now very mature—it's about 20 years old and it's extremely reliable. It's a relatively simple, relatively retargetable, quite efficient just-in-time code generator that's designed to work really well with non type-declared languages. On the other hand, here's Python, which is this wonderful language with these wonderful libraries and a slow-as-mud implementation. Wouldn't it be nice if we could bring the two together?

Seibel: Wasn't that sort of the idea behind your pycore project, to reimplement Python in Smalltalk?

Deutsch: It was. I got it to the point where I realized it would be a lot more work than I thought to actually make it work. The mismatches between the Python object model and the Smalltalk object model were bad enough that there were things that could not be simply mapped one-for-one but had to be done through extra levels of method calls and this, that, and the other.

Even at that, Smalltalk with just-in-time code generation was, for code that was just written in Python, still in the same range as the C-coded interpreter. So the idea that I had in mind was that if it had been possible to open-source the Smalltalk code generator, taking that code generator and adapting it to work well with the Python object model and the Python data representation would not have been a huge deal.

But it can't be done. Eliot Miranda, who's probably the most radical of my buddies associated with VisualWorks, tried, and Cincom said, "Nope, it's a strategic asset, we can't open-source it."

Seibel: Well, you're the guy who says software should be treated as a capital asset.

Deutsch: But that doesn't necessarily mean that it's always your best strategy to prevent other people from using it.

Seibel: So in addition to being a Smalltalker from way back, you were also an early Lisp hacker. But you're not using it any more either.

Deutsch: My PhD thesis was a 600-page Lisp program. I'm a very heavy-duty Lisp hacker from PDP-1 Lisp, Alto Lisp, Byte Lisp, and Interlisp. The reason I don't program in Lisp anymore: I can't stand the syntax. It's just a fact of life that syntax matters.

Language systems stand on a tripod. There's the language, there's the libraries, and there are the tools. And how successful a language is depends on a complex interaction between those three things. Python has a great language, great libraries, and hardly any tools.

Seibel: Where "tools" includes the actual implementation of the language?

Deutsch: Sure, let's put them there. Lisp as a language has fabulous properties of flexibility but really poor user values in terms of its readability. I don't know what the status is of Common Lisp libraries is these days, but I think syntax matters a lot.

Seibel: Some people love Lisp syntax and some can't stand it. Why is that?

Deutsch: Well, I can't speak for anyone else. But I can tell you why I don't want to work with Lisp syntax anymore. There are two reasons. Number one, and I alluded to this earlier, is that the older I've gotten, the more important it is to me that the density of information per square inch in front of my face is high. The density of information per square inch in infix languages is higher than in Lisp.

Seibel: But almost all languages are, in fact, prefix, except for a small handful of arithmetic operators.

Deutsch: That's not actually true. In Python, for example, it's not true for list, tuple, and dictionary construction. That's done with bracketing. String formatting is done infix.

Seibel: As it is in Common Lisp with `FORMAT`.

Deutsch: OK, right. But the things that aren't done infix; the common ones, being loops and conditionals, are not prefix. They're done by alternating keywords and what it is they apply to. In that respect they are actually more verbose than Lisp. But that brings me to the other half, the other reason why I like Python syntax better, which is that Lisp is lexically pretty monotonous.

Seibel: I think Larry Wall described it as a bowl of oatmeal with fingernail clippings in it.

Deutsch: Well, my description of Perl is something that looks like it came out of the wrong end of a dog. I think Larry Wall has a lot of nerve talking about language design—Perl is an abomination as a language. But let's not go there.

If you look at a piece of Lisp code, in order to extract its meaning there are two things that you have to do that you don't have to do in a language like Python.

First you have to filter out all those damn parentheses. It's not intellectual work but your brain does understanding at multiple levels and I think the first thing it does is symbol recognition. So it's going to recognize all those parenthesis symbols and then you have to filter them out at a higher level. So you're making the brain symbol-recognition mechanism do extra work.

These days it may be that the arithmetic functions in Lisp are actually spelled with their common names, I mean, you write plus sign and multiply sign and so forth.

Seibel: Yes.

Deutsch: Alright, so the second thing I was going to say you have to do, you don't actually have to do anymore, which is understanding those things using token recognition rather than symbol recognition, which also happens at a higher level in your brain.

Then there's a third thing, which may seem like a small thing but I don't think it is. Which is that in an infix world, every operator is next to both of its operands. In a prefix world it isn't. You have to do more work to see the other operand. You know, these all sound like small things. But to me the biggest one is the density of information per square inch.

Seibel: But the fact that Lisp's basic syntax, the lexical syntax, is pretty close to the abstract syntax tree of the program does permit the language to support macros. And macros allow you to create syntactic abstraction, which is the best way to compress what you're looking at.

Deutsch: Yes, it is.

Seibel: In my Lisp book I wrote a chapter about parsing binary files, using ID3 tags in MP3 files as an example. And the nice thing about that is you can use this style of programming where you take the specification—in this case the ID3 spec—put parentheses around it, and then make that be the code you want.

Deutsch: Right.

Seibel: So my description of how to parse an ID3 header is essentially exactly as many tokens as the specification for an ID3 header.

Deutsch: Well, the interesting thing is I did almost exactly the same thing in Python. I had a situation where I had to parse really quite a complex file format. It was one of the more complex music file formats. So in Python I wrote a set of classes that provided both parsing and pretty printing.

The correspondence between the class construction and the method name is all done in a common superclass. So this is all done object-oriented; you don't need a macro facility. It doesn't look quite as nice as some other way you might do it, but what you get is something that is approximately as readable as the corresponding Lisp macros. There are some things that you can do in a cleaner and more general way in Lisp. I don't disagree with that.

If you look at the code for Ghostscript, Ghostscript is all written in C. But it's C augmented with hundreds of preprocessor macros. So in effect, in order to write code that's going to become part of Ghostscript, you have to learn not only C, but you have to learn what amounts to an extended language. So you can do things like that in C; you do them when you have to. It happens in every language.

In Python I have my own what amount to little extensions to Python. They're not syntactic extensions; they're classes, they're mixins—many of them are mixins that augment what most people think of as the semantics of the language. You get one set of facilities for doing that in Python, you get a different set in Lisp. Some people like one better, some people like the other better.

Seibel: What was it that made you move from programming to composing?

Deutsch: I basically burned out on Ghostscript. Ghostscript was one of my primary technical interests starting in 1986 and it was pretty much my only major technical project starting somewhere around 1992–'93. By 1998, roughly, I was starting to feel burned out because I was not only doing all the technical work; I was also doing all the support, all the administration. I was a one-person business, and it had gotten to be too much. I hired someone to basically build up a business, and he started hiring engineers.

Then it took another two years to find the right person to replace me. And then it took another two years after that to get everything really handed over. By 2002, I had had it. I didn't want to ever see Ghostscript again.

So I said, "OK, I'll take six months to decompress and look around for what I want to do next." At that point I was 55; I didn't feel particularly old. I figured I had one more major project left in me, if I wanted to do one. So, I started looking around.

The one project that kind of interested me was an old buddy of mine from the Xerox days, J. Strother Moore II, is, or was, the head of the computer-science department at the University of Texas at Austin. His great career achievement was that he and a guy at SRI named Bob Boyer built a really kick-ass theorem prover. And he built up a whole group around this piece of software and built up these big libraries of theorems and lemmas about particular domain areas.

So they had this thriving little group doing theorem proving, which was the subject of my PhD thesis and which had always interested me. And they had this amazing result on the arithmetic unit of the AMD CPU. So I thought, "Hey, this is a group that has a lot of right characteristics: they're doing something that I've always been interested in; they're run by a guy that I know and like; their technology is Lisp-based. It'll be really congenial to me."

So, I went down there and gave a talk about how, if at all, could theorem proving have helped improve the reliability of Ghostscript? By that time, we had a big history in the bug tracker for Ghostscript. So I picked 20 bugs, more or less at random, and I looked at each one and I said, "OK, for theorem-proving technology to have been helpful in finding or preventing this problem, what would have had to happen? What else would have had to be in place?"

The conclusion I came to is that theorem-proving technology probably wouldn't have helped a whole lot because in the few places where it could have, formalizing what it was that the software was supposed to do would've been a Herculean job.

That's the reason why theorem-proving technology basically has—in my opinion—failed as a practical technology for improving software reliability. It's just too damn hard to formalize the properties that you want to establish.

So I gave this talk and it was pretty well received. I talked with a couple of the graduate students, talked with J. a little bit, and then I went away. I thought to myself, "The checklist items all look pretty good. But I'm just not excited about this."

I was kind of flailing around. I've sung in a chorus for years. In the summer of 2003 we were on a tour where we actually sang six concerts in old churches in Italy. My partner was with me on that trip and we decided to stay in Europe for two or three weeks afterwards.

We went to Vienna and did the things you do in Vienna. The old Hapsburg Palace has now been divided—part of it—into ten different little specialized museums. I saw in the guidebook that there was a Museum of Old Musical Instruments.

I went to this museum, and it's in this long hall of high-ceilinged old salons. And it starts with, I don't know whether they're Neolithic, but very old musical instruments, and it progresses through. Of course, most of their musical instruments are from the last couple of centuries in Western Europe. I didn't actually make it all the way through; I was like one or two salons from the end and I was standing there and here was a piano that had belonged to Leopold Mozart. And the piano that Brahms used for practicing. And the piano that Haydn had in his house.

And I had this little epiphany that the reason that I was having trouble finding another software project to get excited about was not that I was having trouble finding a project. It was that I wasn't excited about software anymore. As crazy as it may seem now, a lot of my motivation for going into software in the first place was that I thought you could actually make the world a better place by doing it. I don't believe that anymore. Not really. Not in the same way.

This little lightning flash happened and all of a sudden I had the feeling that the way—well, not the way to change the world for the better, but the way to contribute something to the world that might last more than a few years was to do music. That was the moment when I decided that I was going to take a deep breath and walk away from what I'd been doing for 50 years.

Seibel: But you do still program.

Deutsch: I can't help myself—I can't keep myself from wanting to do things in ways that I think are fun and interesting. I've done a bunch of little software projects of one sort or another over time, but only two that I've paid ongoing attention to over the last several years.

One has been spam-filtering technology for my mail server. I wouldn't say it was fun but it had a certain amount of interest to it. Based on the logs that I look at every now and then, the filter is actually picking up—depending on who's ahead in the arms race at any given moment—somewhere between 80 and 95 percent of the incoming spam.

The other substantial piece of software that I keep coming back to is a musical-score editor. And the reason that I do that is that I have done a fair amount of investigation of what's available out there. I used Finale at a friend's house a few times. It sucks. The quality of that system is so bad I can't even tell you. I got a copy of Sibelius. I actually got a Mac laptop primarily so that I could run Sibelius. And discovered that the way that they did the user interface, it is the next thing to unusable if you don't have a Num Lock key. Mac laptops do not have a Num Lock key. And there were some other things about the user interface that I didn't like. So, I decided to roll my own.

I've been through four different architectures and I finally got one that I like pretty well. But it's been kind of an interesting learning experience. That's an interactive application that's large and complex enough that these system issues do come up, these issues of interfaces.

After having gone through four different architectures I wound up with an architecture for the rendering side of the program—which I think is by far the hardest part—based on equational programming. You define variable values in terms of equations then you let the implementation decide when to evaluate them.Turns out that's not too hard to do in Python. It's been done at least two other times that I know of. I like the way I do it because it has the least boilerplate.

So yeah, so I still do a moderate amount of programming and I still have fun with it. But it's not *for* anybody and if I don't do programming for weeks at a time, that's OK. When that was what I did professionally, I always wanted to be in the middle of a project. Now, what I want to always be in the middle of is at least one or two compositions.

Seibel: You said before that you thought you could make the world a better place with software. How did you think that was going to happen?

Deutsch: Part of it had nothing to do with software per se; it's just that seeing anything around me that's being done badly has always offended me mightily, so I thought I could do better. That's the way kids think. It all seems rather dreamlike now.

Certainly at the time that I started programming, and even up into the 1980s, computer technology was really associated with the corporate world. And my personal politics were quite anticorporate. The kind of computing that I've always worked on has been what today we would call personal computing, interactive computing. I think part of my motivation was the thought that if you could get computer power into the hands of a lot of people, that it might provide some counterweight to corporate power.

I never in my wildest dreams would have predicted the evolution of the Internet. And I never would've predicted the degree to which corporate influence over the Internet has changed its character over time. I would've thought that the Internet was inherently uncontrollable, and I no longer think that. China shows that you can do it pretty effectively.

And I think there's a good chance that if Microsoft plays its cards right, they will have a lock on the Internet. I'm sure they would love to, but I think they might be smart enough to see the path from where they are to having what effectively is control of essentially all the software that gets used on the Internet.

So I'm not really much of an optimist about the future of computing. To be perfectly honest, that's one of the reasons why it wasn't hard for me to get out. I mean, I saw a world that was completely dominated by an unethical monopolist, and I didn't see much of a place for me in it.

CHAPTER

12

Ken Thompson

Ken Thompson is the original bearded Unix hacker. He has spent a career working on whatever he finds interesting, which has, at various times, included analog computing, systems programming, regular expressions, and computer chess.

Hired as a researcher at Bell Labs to work on the MULTICS project, after Bell Labs pulled out of MULTICS, Thompson went on, with Dennis Ritchie, to invent Unix, an endeavor for which he fully expected to be fired. He also invented the B programming language, the precursor to Dennis Ritchie's C.

Later he got interested in computer chess, building Belle, the first special-purpose chess computer and the strongest computerized chess player of its time. He also helped expand chess endgame tablebases to cover all four- and five-piece endgames.

When working on Bell Lab's Plan 9 operating system, he devised the now ubiquitous UTF-8 Unicode encoding.

In 1983, Thompson and Ritchie received the Turing Award for their "development of generic operating systems theory and specifically for the implementation of the Unix operating system." He was also awarded the National Medal of Technology and the Institute of Electrical and Electronics Engineers Tsutomu Kanai Award, both for his work on Unix.

In this interview he talked about his early love of electronics, a rather unorthodox academic career that had him teaching courses while he was still a student, and why modern programming scares him.

Seibel: How did you learn to program?

Thompson: I was always fascinated with logic and even in grade school I'd work on arithmetic problems in binary, stuff like that. Just because I was fascinated.

Seibel: Did you turn them in that way?

Thompson: No, no. But I worked out the algorithms for adding in different bases, what carry means, and what each column means and things like that. Then I had a little calculator, a decimal calculator. It was like a decimal abacus. Instead of one and two it had a slide from zero to nine. It had a subtract one from a previous column down and an add one from the previous column up. So you'd put a stylus in, like a four, and run it up and hook over if you want to carry. And I built some binary stuff based on that and how that generalized to *n*-ary.

Seibel: Where did you even get that notion of binary arithmetic?

Thompson: In the class at the time I actually started doing this, they introduced binary.

Seibel: Were you a victim of the "new math?"

Thompson: No, no. I was victim of bad math. I moved every year or so and I was in some really, really horrible schools and then some good schools. So I would have to do two years of work in one year and then I'd be off a year. I was just loafing through math, so I had a horrible math primary education. And this one class they just described binary arithmetic. I took that and extended it to any base and played with that. So that's kind of where I got started.

Seibel: And that was in grade school?

Thompson: Yeah, seventh grade. Then around senior year in high school, somewhere around in that time, I was into electronics a lot, building radios and amplifiers and oscillators and theremins. And I got hooked on analog computing. It was really marvelous. Electronics was my passion during all that time. I went into double E at Berkeley, and there I saw real digital computers for the first time in my junior year.

Seibel: And so what year would that have been?

Thompson: I went to junior semester early, so it was three semesters in. I started school in September '60, so it would be the fall or spring of '62. They had an analog computer which I had a great time with. And they had a G15, a drum computer. They had one lab class on it and then it was open. Anybody could play with it, but no one did, so it was free. And I used it essentially exclusively. I wrote programs on it, on my own, to scale an analog computer—analog computing is almost all scaling.

Seibel: Scaling in the sense of?

Thompson: Time scaling and amplitude scaling. Basically what you do is you build it to do a function. You put some input in and then you get a function of that input out and you concatenate these things with feedback. And at every point in this process you can't go too high or you'll clip.

Likewise there's time scaling—you halve the frequency at different places or double the frequency in different places. And when you do that, a bunch of the linear scaling changes also. So if you have a simple job that doesn't need scaling, analog is really great. But as soon as you need scaling it becomes very, very complex. And so I wrote digital computer programs to scale the analog computer setups. Without computing the actual wave forms, you compute the amplitude and frequency of the wave form at every point. And then it tells you when you're out of range for whatever operation you're doing at that time.

Seibel: And the programs on the digital computer were written in assembly or Fortran?

Thompson: They were assembly mostly. There was an interpreted language that turned out to be too slow. That's why I was forced to go to assembly and actually learn what the computer was.

Seibel: So load in your program, hit the run button, and away you go. Was it using punch cards?

Thompson: No, no. It was a Flexowriter, which is like a Teletype and paper tape. And you'd store it on paper tape and talk to it on the Flexowriter.

Seibel: Did they actually teach you assembly in that lab?

Thompson: Nah.

Seibel: What was your next exposure to programming?

Thompson: This G15 had an interpreter called Intercom 501. And the double-E class would program it in Intercom. There was a graduate student that I was friends with that wrote an interpreter for Intercom on the big IBM machine, the big campuswide computing facility. I got a listing of that and on vacation, Christmas or something, I read it and just dissected it. I didn't know the language it was written in. which happened to be NELIAC. And it was just a marvelously written program. And I learned programming, NELIAC, Intercom, and how to interpret something—everything—from that. I just sat and I read it for probably the entire vacation, a week. And then came back and asked him questions about it, nagging little bugs kinds of things. After that I knew how to program and I was pretty good at it. Then I got jobs programming.

I was basically working my way through school, work-study and then odd jobs. I was a research assistant—a grunt for a graduate student to get programming done for his thesis. And I was a TA. I did programming for the computer center. Part of the computer-center stuff was to sit in a little booth and have people come in and say, "I only changed one thing." "Well, let's look at that one thing and see what happened to you."

Seibel: Did that hone your debugging skills or was it all just incredibly stupid stuff?

Thompson: It honed that type of debugging—you understood common errors really well after that. Somebody who had spent days working on their program would come in and you'd say, "Right there!"

Seibel: And your degree was in double E? Did they offer a computer-science degree at that point?

Thompson: No, all over the United States at the time computer science was trying to come out, and it was coming out in two ways. It was coming out theoretically through math, or practically through double E. In Berkeley, computer science at that point was almost exclusively inside of electrical engineering. Math was trying, but they just weren't politically astute enough to compete with these old grizzled guys.

Seibel: Berkeley obviously ended up being known for things like the Berkeley Systems Lab—building things—as opposed to being renowned for contributions to theory.

Thompson: Yes, absolutely. This is the genesis of either a theoretical computer-science department, like Cornell, or the Berkeley kind of computer science. It really gives the flavor to the place. So I spent one year in graduate school there, not because I had any ambitions for anything. It's just because I had nothing else to do and I was having a good time.

Seibel: Immediately after college?

Thompson: Yeah. To be honest, I was working at the university and I didn't even apply for graduate school. One of the professors essentially applied for me and told me I was in graduate school.

Seibel: Still in double E?

Thompson: Right. My senior year and my graduate year were just immense fun. I didn't do anything that I didn't want to do. There were no requirements, no nothing. To graduate I took a summer course in American history or something, some requirement, to get a degree. But outside of that, my senior year and my graduate year I taught about half of the courses I took.

The basic theory of computing was just coming out then. Shell sort came out and no one could figure out why it was faster than *n*-squared sort. And so everyone was doing tests on it and trying to figure out—it's pretty easy to see it sorts, but nobody knows why it's fast. And they were taking the asymptote and figuring out why it was *n* to the 1.3 or something like that. And that's just not a natural number. And from that—shell sort and the intellectual attraction to shell sort and why it was fast—came all this speed order of computing. And the first *n* log *n*s and divide and conquer and all that struck. It was an amazing, exciting era.

I had friends, a bunch of these very junior professors—a math professor I was real close to, and a double-E professor I was close to, and the graduate student that I worked for, and others. They would invent a class for me, and then I would teach the class.

Seibel: Were you officially taking the class or were you actually on the books as teaching it?

Thompson: No, no, I wasn't on the books as teaching it. They were all double-E 199, which meant individual research or group research or something. And they would invent a class and give it a title and then turn it over to me. And there'd be three or four students there.

Seibel: Of which, officially, you were one.

Thompson: Yes.

Seibel: Did you like teaching?

Thompson: To an extent. I've gone back and taught twice. Taken a year off and taught one year at Berkeley in '75–'76 and one year in Sydney in '88. It's fun. I really, really enjoy it. I was doing research in the labs and I went to Berkeley to teach and to learn the classes I was teaching from the bottom up since I never had a computer-science education. A normal visiting teacher teaches one class. I taught five classes. Some classes I taught twice and I thought they were the best because the first year I was learning and the second time I taught it I knew where it was going and I could present it organized and be two steps ahead of the students. The third class was just boring. I taught one class three times and it was just wrong. So I could never be a teacher because you end up teaching your class over and over and over. I could never do that. But I love the teaching: the hard work of a first class, the fun of the second class. Then the misery of the third.

Seibel: What was the first interesting program you wrote?

Thompson: The first long computational program I wrote was solving the pentaminos problem. Do you know it?

Seibel: The tile game, right?

Thompson: It's a tile game. And I ran it on an IBM 1620 that was in the physics department. I knew where all the underground computers were in the place, and I had them all running at night doing my jobs. Plus, at the main computer center I probably had 20 accounts under different rocks. There are 12 pentaminos. These are different tile pieces made out of 5 squares. And there are 12 different such shapes.

Seibel: Sort of like Tetris tiles.

Thompson: Yes. But every piece has five squares. If you put them all together on the board there are two configurations that are—I don't know—appealing. One is the most square, which is ten-by-six, and then the second is eight-by-eight with a two-by-two hole in the middle. And I solved all configurations of those two boards of how you place the pieces for those boards. And I did it generically by laying out a pattern of the boards and then laying out pattern pieces, and then it would fit the pieces in the patterns. It didn't know it was pentaminos.

Seibel: This was basically brute-force search?

Thompson: Brute force.

Seibel: And so this was also in assembly probably?

Thompson: I have to think. Yeah, it was probably assembly. I can't remember.

Seibel: You must have learned Fortran somewhere along the line.

Thompson: Yeah, well, I had to teach Fortran in the computer center and debug the Fortran programs. I never programmed in it. I wrote a Fortran compiler for Unix early, and B was an attempted Fortran compiler that got away from me.

Seibel: I thought B was your translation of BCPL.

Thompson: It sort of was. It started off as—I didn't know what it was. Semantically, it turned out to be BCPL. As I started it, it was going to be Fortran. And at that point I got my first description of BCPL. And I liked the clean semantics. And that's when I abandoned Fortran and it turned into essentially C syntax and BCPL semantics.

Seibel: Is there any really big differences in how you think about programming or how you practice programming from when you learned to now? Do you feel like your programming has matured in some way or you got better at it or you learned things that make you look back and say, "Oh, man, I didn't know what I was doing back then."?

Thompson: No, not really. Sometimes I look back at stuff I did and say, "Wow. I was much better then." The period from when I spent that week reading that program to maybe when I was 30, 35 years old, I knew, in a deep sense, every line of code I ever wrote. I'd write a program during the day, and at night I'd sit there and walk through it line by line and find bugs. I'd go back the next day and, sure enough, it would be wrong.

Seibel: Do you think when you were 35 you could still remember the stuff you had written a decade before?

Thompson: Yes. Then I started being selective about what I'd remember.

Seibel: Is there anything you would have done differently about learning to program? Do you have any regrets about the sort of path you took or do you wish you had done anything earlier?

Thompson: Oh, sure, sure. In high school I wish I'd taken typing. I suffer from poor typing yet today, but who knew. I didn't plan anything or do anything. I have no discipline. I did what I wanted to do next, period, all the time. If I had some foresight or planning or something, there are things, like typing, I would have done when I had the chance. I would have taken some deeper math because certainly I've run across things where I have to get help for math. So yeah, there are little things like that. But if I went back and had to do it over I'm sure that I just wouldn't have it in me to do anything differently. Basically I planned nothing and I just took the next step. And if I had to do it over again, I'd just have taken the next step again.

Seibel: After school you got hired directly into the Bell Labs; how did that happen? It doesn't sound like you were a classical academic researcher at that point in your career.

Thompson: I just drifted. It was hard to describe. I certainly wasn't in school in any real sense. In the formal sense, yes, I was. One of my professors, who is actually a very good friend, sicced the Bell Labs recruiter on me. But I wasn't looking for a job. In fact, I had absolutely no ambitions; nothing. And he made me appointments to see him in his little recruiting booth, and I either slept through them or told him I wasn't interested. And he kept after me. At some point he called me and said that he wanted to come over and see me. So he came over to my apartment. And said that he wanted me to come out and interview at Bell Labs. I told him no. And he said, "It's a free trip. You can do what you want to out there." And I say, "Well, up front I'll just tell you that I'm not interested in a job. I'll be glad to go for a free trip 'cause I have friends on the East Coast. I'll go visit them." And he says, "Fine." So that was the interview that I got into. And I went and spent my two days at Bell Labs and then rented a car and went up and down the East Coast visiting my high-school friends that were spread out all over everywhere.

Seibel: Obviously there was something that the folks at Bell Labs saw in you and said, "We should get this guy into our lab."

Thompson: I don't know their side of it. My side of it is that these are people that I was reading the papers of in the classes I was taking/teaching. And I knew them by name and reputation. And they were still doing fun things. To me, work was work and these guys weren't working. They were having a good time. Just like school.

Seibel: And so what kind of things did you do when you first arrived there?

Thompson: Bell Labs was in the MULTICS project and I was hired in to work on MULTICS. And I did. I played with the machines, booted up MULTICS, and did my little piece of it. At some point, Bell Labs decided that MULTICS wasn't for them, and they backed out of the project.

But they had these MULTICS machines which were special-purpose machines that were just sitting around idle until someone could cart them away. So for approximately a year I had this machine that was monstrous. There are maybe two or three of us that used it. So I started doing operating-system stuff, trying to get a little operating system up and running.

It was insanely hard because it was a real complex computer. But I got it up where it would sit there and say hello on 50 Teletypes around the building. And then it went out the door. So I shopped around then and found some other unused machines and essentially built Unix on these very, very small PDP machines.

Seibel: Did you have the time to do that because your bosses knew that that's what you were doing and said this is a good research project, or was it just because you were in between jobs?

Thompson: No, I was sort of incorrigible, to be honest. I suspected that I would eventually get fired, but it didn't bother me. We were supposed to be doing basic research but there was some basic research we should be doing and some basic research we shouldn't be doing. And just coming out of the ashes of MULTICS, operating systems was one of those basic research things we *shouldn't* be doing. Because we tried it, it didn't work, it was a huge failure, it was expensive; let's drop it. So I kind of expected that for what I was doing I was going to eventually get fired. I didn't.

Seibel: How do you design software? Do you scribble on graph paper or fire up a UML tool or just start coding?

Thompson: Depends on how big it is. Most of the time, it sits in the back of my mind—nothing on paper—for a period of time and I'll concentrate on the hard parts. The easy parts just fade away—just write 'em down; they'll come right out of your fingertips when you're ready. But the hard parts I'll sit and let it germinate for a period of time, a month maybe. At some point pieces will start dropping out at the bottom and I can see the pyramid build up out of the pieces. When the pyramid gets high enough in my mind, then I'll start at the bottom.

Seibel: But you're not just building leaves—you know the structure they're going to fit into.

Thompson: Suppose someone is describing something to me from postulates like, "Here's a computer and here are the op codes." I can visualize the structure of programs and how things are efficient or inefficient based on those op codes, by seeing the bottom and imagining the hierarchy. And I can see the same thing with programs. If someone shows me library routines or basic bottom-level things, I can see how you can build that into different programs and what's missing—the kinds of programs that would still be hard to write. So I can envision that pyramid, and the problem is to try and decompose it and get the bottom pieces.

Modern programming scares me in many respects, where they will just build layer after layer after layer that does nothing except translate. It confuses me to read a program which you *must* read top-down. It says "do something." And you go find "something." And you read it and it says, "do something else" and you go find something and it says, "do something else" and it goes back to the top maybe. And nothing gets done. It's just relegating the problem to a deeper and deeper level. I can't keep it in my mind—I can't understand it.

Seibel: So why not still read bottom-up? The leaves are there, somewhere.

Thompson: Well, you don't know what are leaves and what aren't. If it's well described you can read the English and get it and then you don't have to read the code. But if you're actually just given a bunch of code and told, "Read it and try and make it better or try and make it do something else," then typically I read it top-down.

Seibel: Do you ever write down anything before you start writing code?

Thompson: I usually write down data structures before I write down code. I don't write down algorithms—no flowcharts, or stuff like that. But the stuff you have to refer to on almost every line of code—data structures.

Seibel: If you're writing a C program, does that mean C code that would define those data structures?

Thompson: No, little boxes with arrows and stuff.

Seibel: So you've got this big picture, the pyramid. How much do you stick to that plan once you start coding?

Thompson: I don't stick to code. If I find a different partitioning halfway through, I'll just hack and go over it. A lot of people I know, when they write a line of code, it's concrete from then on for the rest of life, unless there's a bug. Especially if they write a routine with an API and scribble the API somewhere on an envelope or an API list—then that's it. It'll never change, no matter how bad it is. And I've always been totally willing to hack things apart if I find a different way that fits better or a different partitioning. I've never been a lover of existing code. Code by itself almost rots and it's gotta be rewritten. Even when nothing has changed, for some reason it rots.

Seibel: How do you decide when code needs to be thrown away?

Thompson: When it's hard to work on. I do it much quicker than most people do. I'll throw away code as soon I want to add something to it and I get the feeling that what I have to do to add it is too hard. I'll throw it away and start over and come up with a different partitioning that makes it easy to do whatever I wanted to do. I'm really quick on the trigger for throwing stuff out.

Seibel: Is that true working with other people's code as well?

Thompson: It depends on whether I have control. If I have control, sure, it doesn't matter. If I don't have control, it's someone else's code, then I'll suffer. Or not do it.

Seibel: In the case where you've inherited someone's code there's a danger in rewriting it that maybe you missed some subtlety to the way it works or overlooked some bit of functionality that it had. Have you ever been bitten by that?

Thompson: Well, you get bitten, but that's just part of debugging. If there's something you forgot or didn't do, when you realize it you do it. That's just part of debugging. It's not complete when you first write something. You extend it.

Seibel: Once you've built a system, do you go back and document it in any way?

Thompson: It depends on what it's for. If it's for me, no I won't. I'll put in a usage line if I forget the arguments. And I'll put in a comment at the header about what the whole thing does. But very, very brief. If it's part of a system or a library or something that's meant to be published, then I'll take the time to document it. But otherwise, no.

Documenting is an art as fine as programming. It's rare I find documentation at the level I like. Usually it's much, much finer-grained than need be. It contains a bunch of irrelevancies and dangling references that assume knowledge not there. Documenting is very, very hard; it's time-consuming. To do it right, you've got to do it like programming. You've got to deconstruct it, put it together in nice ways, rewrite it when it's wrong. People don't do that.

Also, I prefer bottom-up documentation and that's usually not the way it's written. If some program relies on other programs or files or data structures, I like to see clear a reference to those where I can go off and read those and they don't refer back.

Seibel: So you'd like to understand code the way you would like to write it, which is from the bottom up?

Thompson: Yeah. It's the way I can put a handle on it in my mind and remember. Otherwise I read it and I may understand it right after I read it but then it's gone. If I understand the structure of it, then it's part of me and I'll understand it.

Seibel: In your Turing Award talk you mentioned that if Dan Bobrow had been forced to use a PDP-11 instead of the more powerful PDP-10 he might have been receiving the award that day instead of you and Dennis Ritchie.

Thompson: I was just trying to say it was serendipitous.

Seibel: Do you think you benefited to being constrained by the less powerful machine?

Thompson: There was certainly a benefit that it was small and efficient. But I think that was the kind of code we wrote anyway. But it was more the fact that it was right at the cusp of a revolution of minicomputers. The 10 was the big mainframe run by the computer center. Computing going autonomous instead of centralized was, I think, the really serendipitous part of it. And that rode in on the PDP-11.

Seibel: Didn't Unix also benefit from being written in C while OSs like TENEX and ITS were written in assembly and couldn't jump to different hardware as easily as Unix?

Thompson: There were good system-programming languages that things were written in to some extent.

Seibel: Such as?

Thompson: NELIAC was a system-programming version of Algol 58.

Seibel: Was Bliss also from that era?

Thompson: Bliss I think was after. And their emphasis was trying to compile well. I think it was pretty clear from the beginning that you shouldn't kill yourself compiling well. You should do well but not really good. And the reason is that in the time it takes you to go from well to really good, Moore's law has already surpassed you. You can pick up 10 percent but while you're picking up that 10 percent, computers have gotten twice as fast and maybe with some other stuff that matters more for optimization, like caches. I think it's largely a waste of time to do really well. It's really hard; you generate as many bugs as you fix. You should stop, not take that extra 100 percent of time to do 10 percent of the work.

Seibel: You've presumably heard of the essay, "Worse Is Better" by Richard Gabriel.

Thompson: No.

Seibel: He contrasted what he called the MIT style, where correctness trumps everything else, and the New Jersey (i.e. Bell Labs) style, where simplicity of implementation is highly valued. His theory was that the New Jersey style, which he also called "Worse Is Better" made it possible to get stuff out and running and from there it will get improved.

Thompson: I think MIT has always had an inferiority complex over Unix. I gave a Unix talk at MIT and I was introduced by Michael Dertouzos, I think. He expounded on why Unix wasn't written at MIT and why it should have been. Why they had the opportunity, they had the people, they had everything, and why it wasn't done there. And it dawned on me that there was a rivalry in their minds. Not in my mind at that point. We did Unix and they did MULTICS, which was this monster. This was just clearly the second-system syndrome.

Seibel: Where MULTICS was the second system after the MIT's Compatible Time-Sharing System?

Thompson: Yes. So overdesigned and overbuilt and over everything. It was close to unusable. They still claim it's a monstrous success, but it just clearly wasn't.

Seibel: My understanding was that a lot of the MIT hackers viewed MULTICS that same way. They preferred ITS and the Lisp-based systems that they built. It seems there was a real fork post-MULTICS. Unix came out, as you well know, and at MIT these Lisp guys went off and did their things on PDP-10s and built Lisp-based systems which, eventually I guess, begat the Lisp machines.

Thompson: Yeah, yeah. I knew all those guys. I thought it was a crazy job. I didn't think that Lisp was a unique enough language to warrant a machine. And I think I was proved right. All along I said, "You're crazy." The PDP-11's a great Lisp machine. The PDP-10's a great Lisp machine. There's no need to build a Lisp machine that's not faster. There was just no reason to ever build a Lisp machine. It was kind of stupid.

Seibel: Are there any features of MULTICS that you did like but that never made it into Unix?

Thompson: The things that I liked enough to actually take were the hierarchical file system and the shell—a separate process that you can replace with some other process. Before that all systems had some sort of "executive"—that was the typical word for it—which was a built-in processing language. Per-process execution. Every time you type to the shell and it creates a new process and runs whatever you typed and when that dies you come back so that you're at arm's length from the thing you're running.

Seibel: So those are all things you did take; there's nothing you left behind that you now regret?

Thompson: No.

Seibel: From what I've read about the history of Unix, it sounds like you used the design process that you described earlier. You thought about it for a while and then your wife and kid went away for a month and you said, "Oh, great—now I can write the code."

Thompson: Yeah.... A group of us sat down and talked about a file system. There were about three or four of us. The only person who's not well known is a guy named Rudd Canady. In those days at Bell Labs the amenities were great—you could call a telephone number and get a transcription. You know, leave a message and say you want it written up and it'll appear the next day in your inbox as sheets of paper. And Canady, after we talked about the file system on the blackboard for a little while, picked up the phone, called a number, and read the blackboard into the phone.

It came back and it was about as close to a design document as we got except that it had homonyms that you wouldn't believe. So I went off and implemented this file system, strictly on a PDP-7. At some point I decided that I had to test it. So I wrote some load-generating stuff. But I was having trouble writing programs to drive the file system. You want something interactive.

Seibel: And you just wanted to play around with writing a file system? At that point you weren't planning to write an OS?

Thompson: No, it was just a file system.

Seibel: So you basically wrote an OS so you'd have a better environment to test your file system.

Thompson: Yes. Halfway through there that I realized it was a real time-sharing system. I was writing the shell to drive the file system. And then I was writing a couple other programs that drove the file system. And right about there I said, "All I need is an editor and I've got an operating system."

Seibel: What's the worst bug you've ever had to track down?

Thompson: Basically bugs where memory gets corrupted. It never happens anymore. I don't know why. But in the early days we were always working with experimental hardware of various sorts, and there'd be some hardware bug.

Seibel: So memory would get corrupted by the hardware screwing up, not by a runaway pointer?

Thompson: It could be pointer. It could be hardware. Or a combination. The one I'm actually thinking of, the worst example, was the on PDP-11. It didn't have multiply but you could buy a multiply unit and plug it in, but it was an I/O peripheral. You would store a numerator and a denominator and say go. You'd busy-loop and then pull out the answer, the quotient and the remainder. And this thing was built for a non-memory-managed PDP-11 and we got the first experimental hardware for a memory-managed PDP-11 and this multiply unit didn't fit with the memory management well.

So you'd store into this thing and then you'd busy-test. And during certain aspects of the busy test it would send a physical address down instead of a virtual address and some piece of memory would get clobbered with a numerator of what you were trying to divide by. And it'd be ages before you'd find it, and it'd be different places. That's by far the hardest one I'd ever had to find.

Seibel: How did you track it down?

Thompson: There was a program that I wrote that was going after a world record for the number of digits of e. Previous world records were limited not by computation—by cycles per second—but by I/O. I came up with a new algorithm where it was computation-bound and I/O became trivial. It was monstrously heavy on multiply and divide. And we noticed that the machine just crumbled whenever I put on my program. And therefore we got the connection.

Seibel: So that gave you the clue that there was a problem with the multiplier; did you ultimately track it down to some root cause?

Thompson: At some point we got it to where you store in the multiplier in the multiply unit, and you pull it back and it wasn't there. We reported that to DEC and DEC couldn't find it, and they didn't want to deal with it. Their normal people didn't want to deal with this hybrid machine. In those days you actually got the circuit diagrams of the machines, and we actually found the bug in the circuit diagrams. Then we just called DEC and said, "Connect that wire and that wire."

Seibel: So, thankfully, hardware mostly doesn't flake out on us that way these days.

Thompson: Yeah. That's why I think they're rare. Plus things are isolated from each other more—if you go bizarrely wild you'll get a fault. Also you did it in assembly language—it's really easy to have the wrong thing in some register through some subroutine call. When you have a high-level language where the arguments all have to match up, these things become more and more rare.

In the early days, in assembly language, you'd find them a lot. If it was software, as opposed to a combination of software/hardware, usually it would happen in one spot—the same spot would be corrupted. There'd be some correlation of the bug with something. And you could sit there and put a monitor in the operating system. And every so often, or very often, you'd check and see if the error occurred, and stop as quick as you can, and see what's going on elsewhere, and chase them down that way. So you could attack them.

This one you couldn't attack. It wasn't until I wrote this intensive multiply/divide program that it saw the frequency of the error went way, way up. Instead of crashing once every couple of days you'd crash once every couple of minutes. And then as soon as you got something that would crash the machine you had a fighting chance to find it.

Seibel: So some folks today would say, "Well, certainly assembly has all these opportunities to really corrupt memory through software bugs, but C is also more prone to that than some other languages." You can get pointers off into la-la land and you can walk past the ends of arrays. You don't find that at all problematic?

Thompson: No, you get around that with idioms in the language. Some people write fragile code and some people write very structurally sound code, and this is a condition of people. I think in almost any language you can write fragile code. My definition of fragile code is, suppose you want to add a feature—good code, there's one place where you add that feature and it fits; fragile code, you've got to touch ten places.

Seibel: So when there's a security breach that turns out to be due to a buffer overflow, what do you say to the criticism that C and C++ are partly responsible—that if people would use a language that checked array bounds or had garbage collection, they'd avoid a lot of these kinds of problems?

Thompson: Bugs are bugs. You write code with bugs because you do. If it's a safe language in the sense of run-time-safe, the operating system crashes instead of doing a buffer overflow in a way that's exploitable. The ping of death was the IP stack in the operating system. It seems to me that there'd be more pings of death. There wouldn't be pings of "take over the machine becoming superuser." There'd be pings of death.

Seibel: But there is a difference between a denial-of-service attack and an exploit where you get root and can then do whatever you want with the box.

Thompson: But there are two ways to get root—one is to overflow a buffer and the other is to talk the program into doing something it shouldn't do. And most of them are the latter, not overflowing a buffer. You can become root without overflowing any buffers. So your argument's just not on. All you've got to do is talk su into giving you a shell—the paths are all there without any run-time errors.

Seibel: OK. Leaving aside whether it results in a crash or an exploit or whatever else—there is a class of bugs that happen in C, and C++ for the same reason, that wouldn't happen in, say, Java. So for certain kinds of applications, is the advantage that you get from allowing that class of bugs really worth the pain that it causes?

Thompson: I think that class is actually a minority of the problems. Certainly every time I've written one of these non-compare subroutine calls, `strcpy` and stuff like that, I know that I'm writing a bug. And I somehow take the economic decision of whether the bug is worth the extra arguments. Usually now I routinely write it out. But there's a semantic problem that if you truncate a string and you use the truncated string are you getting into another problem. The bug is still there—it just hasn't overflown the buffer.

Seibel: When you're debugging, what tools do you use?

Thompson: Mostly I just print values. When I'm developing a program I do a tremendous amount of printing. And by the time I take out, or comment out, the prints it really is pretty solid. I rarely have to go back.

Seibel: And what kinds of things do you print out?

Thompson: Whatever I need; whatever is dragging along. Invariants. But mostly I just print while I'm developing it. That's how I debug it. I don't write programs from scratch. I take a program and modify it. Even a big program, I'll say "main, left, right, print, hello." And well, "hello" isn't what I wanted out from this program. What's the first thing I want out, and I'll write that and debug that part. I'll run a program 20 times an hour that I'm developing, building up to it.

Seibel: You print out invariants; do you also use asserts that check invariants?

Thompson: Rarely. I convince myself it's correct and then either comment out the prints or throw them away.

Seibel: So why is it easier for you to print that an invariant is true rather than just using `assert` to check it automatically?

Thompson: Because when you print you actually see what it is as opposed to it being a particular value, and you print a bunch of stuff that aren't invariants. It's just the way that I do it. I'm not proposing it as a paradigm. It's just what I've always done.

Seibel: When we talked about how you design software, you described a bottom-up process. Do you build those bottom-up pieces in isolation?

Thompson: Sometimes I do.

Seibel: And do you write test scaffolds for testing your low-level functions?

Thompson: Yeah, very often I do that. It really depends on the program I'm working on. If the program is a translator from *A* to *B*, I'll have a whole bunch of *A*s lying around and the corresponding *B*s. And I'll regress it by running in all the *A*s and comparing it to all the *B*s. A compiler or a translator or a regular-expression search. Something like that. But there are other kinds of programs that aren't like that. I've never been into testing much, and those kinds of programs I'm kind of at a loss. I'll throw in some checks, but very often they don't last in the program or around the program because they're too hard to maintain with the program. Mostly just regression tests.

Seibel: By things that are harder to test, you mean things like device drivers or networking protocols?

Thompson: Well, they're run all the time when you're actually running an operating system.

Seibel: So you figure you'll shake the bugs out that way?

Thompson: Oh, absolutely. I mean, what's better as a test of an operating system than people beating on it?

Seibel: Another phase of programming is optimization. Some people optimize things from the very beginning. Others like to write it one way and then worry about optimizing it later. What's your approach?

Thompson: I'll do it as simply as possible the first time and very often that suffices for all time. To build a very complex algorithm for something that's never run is just stupid. It's just a waste of time. It's a bug generator. And it makes it impossible to maintain because you've got to have 50 pages of math to tell the next guy what you're actually doing.

Ninety-nine percent of the time something simple and brute-force will work fine. If you really are building a tool that is used a lot and it has some sort of minor quadratic behavior sometimes you have to go in and beat on it. But typically not. The simpler the better.

Seibel: Some people just like bumming code down to a jewel-like perfection, for it's own sake.

Thompson: Well, I do too, but part of that is sacrificing the algorithm for the code. I mean, typically a complex algorithm requires complex code. And I'd much rather have a simple algorithm and simple code than some big horror. And if there's one thing that characterizes my code, it's that it's simple, choppy, and little. Nothing fancy. Anybody can read it.

Seibel: Are there still tasks which, for performance reasons, people still have to get down to hand-tuned assembly code?

Thompson: It's rare. It's extremely rare unless you can really get an order of magnitude and you can't. If you can really work hard and get some little piece of a big program to run twice as fast, then you could have gotten the whole program to run twice as fast if you had just waited a year or two. If you're writing a compiler—certainly 99 percent of the code you produce is going to be run once or twice. But some of it's going to be in an operating system that's run 24 hours a day. And some of it's going to be in the inner, inner loop of that operating system. So maybe 0.1 percent of the optimization you put into a compiler here is going to have any effect on your users. But it can have profound effect, so there maybe you want to do it.

Seibel: But that would be a result of generating better code in the compiler rather than writing the compiler itself in assembly.

Thompson: Oh, yes, yes.

Seibel: And presumably part of the reason writing programs directly in assembly is less important these days is because compilers have gotten better.

Thompson: No. I think it's mostly because the machines have gotten a lot better. Compilers stink. You look at the code coming out of GCC and it's awful. It's really not good. And it's slow; oh, man. I mean, the compiler itself is over 20 passes. It's just monstrously slow, but computers have gotten 1,000 times faster since GCC came out. So it may seem like it's getting faster because it's not getting slower as much as computers are getting faster underneath it.

Seibel: On a somewhat related note, what about garbage collection? With Java, GC has finally made it into the mainstream. As Dennis Ritchie once said, C is actively hostile to garbage collection. Is it good that folks are moving toward garbage-collected languages—is it a technology that deserves to finally be in mainstream use?

Thompson: I don't know. I'm schizophrenic on the subject. If you're writing an operating system or a C compiler or something that's used by lots and lots of people, I think garbage collection is a mistake, almost. It's a cheat for you where you can do it by hand and do it better—much better. What you're doing is your sloughing your task, your job, making it slower for your users. So I think it's a mistake in an operating system. It almost just doesn't fit in an operating system. But if you are writing a hack program to do a job, get an answer and then throw the program away, it's beautiful. It takes a layer of stuff you don't want to think about, at a cost you can afford, because computers are so fast, and it's nothing but a win-win-win position. So I'm really schizophrenic on this subject.

Part of the problem is there are different garbage-collection algorithms and they have different properties—massively different properties. So you're writing some really general-purpose thing like an operating system—if you're going to write it in a language that garbage-collects underneath, you don't even have the choice of the algorithm for the operating systems. Suppose that you just can't stand big real-time gaps and you have a garbage collector that runs up to some threshold and then does mark and sweep. You're screwed before you start.

So if you're doing some general-purpose task that you don't know who your real users are, you just can't do that. Plus, garbage collection fights cache coherency massively. And there's no garbage-collection algorithm that is right for all machines. There are machines where you can speed it up by a factor of five or more by messing around with the cache. They should be tied to the machine much more than they are. Usually they treat them as separate algorithms that have nothing to do with machines, but the cache coherency is very important for garbage-collection algorithms.

Seibel: Do you think of yourself as a scientist, an engineer, an artist, a craftsman, or something else?

Thompson: I don't know. I hate to use the word *scientist* because I think it's elitist. And implies a PhD. There's no certificate that says "scientist" on it when you complete the scientist course, so I don't like the term or use it. Engineer, I do have a degree that says "engineer" on it, so I can use the word *engineer*. And when I fill out an occupation I either put engineer or programmer because I can justify those. But mostly I just don't worry about it.

Seibel: Well, leaving aside what you call yourself, who do you feel the most affinity with? Is it a physicist, a guy who builds bridges, a painter, or a carpenter?

Thompson: Kind of the lower things. I believe a craftsman but with a certain amount of artistry to keep it alive.

Seibel: How do you identify talented programmers?

Thompson: It's just enthusiasm. You ask them what's the most interesting program they worked on. And then you get them to describe it and its algorithms and what's going on. If they can't withstand my questioning on their program, then they're not good. If I can attack them or find problems with their algorithms and their solutions and they can't defend it, being much more personally involved than I am, then no. At the same time you can get a sense of enthusiasm. It's not something you ask directly, but in the conversation you'll come with this enthusiasm-ometer, and that is tremendously helpful for me. That's how I interview. I've been told that it's devastating to be on the receiving side of that.

Seibel: I would imagine. It's sort of like an oral exam. Do you suppose you've ever run into people who just didn't have the personality that can deal with that, independent of their programming ability?

Thompson: No, I don't think it's independent of programming. It would be if I started asking them classical computer-science kind of questions, but that's not what I'm asking them. I'm asking them to describe something they've done that they've spent blood on. I've never met anybody who really did spend blood on something who wasn't eager to describe what they've done and how they did it and why. I let them pick the subject. I don't pick the subject, so I'm the amateur and they're the professional in this subject. If they can't stand an amateur asking them questions about their profession, then they don't belong.

Seibel: What are you doing here at Google?

Thompson: Infrastructure. Operating-systems kind of stuff. Glue between the pieces. I have a charter for anything I want. The challenge is to get a bunch of unreliable machines to work like a reliable multiprocessor machine. I guess that's the closest thing.

Seibel: Isn't the point of Google's famous MapReduce machinery that it's shared-nothing message-passing rather than a shared memory?

Thompson: Well, it's a process that has well-known semantics and no feedback loops. If you have a reliable structure to do that, you can fit a lot of problems into that structure.

Seibel: And are you working on things within that kind of framework?

Thompson: No, it's just trying to keep the burden of reliability off the individual programmers. It's a real tough challenge. All the software here has layers and layers and layers of what happens if this doesn't work, what happens if that doesn't work. What happens if I don't work—who kills me and who starts up, who does what. I would guess way more than 50 percent of the code is the what-if kind.

Seibel: So your goal is to have that half of the code go away?

Thompson: Well, it would be hidden somewhere. It would apply in a systematic way to the other code. Hopefully. It's a hard job.

Seibel: Do you like working here at Google?

Thompson: Parts of it I like, very much. But parts of it are just ponderous because there's money involved in bugs and there's money involved in lots of the stuff. The size is unimaginable. Like day one you kind of get something crippling along and day two you've got two million users. You just can't imagine such a thing.

Seibel: And you're actually on the production side. As opposed to being in Google Labs, which might be more akin to your past at Bell Labs.

Thompson: But I'm not actually production either. I'm in projects that will become production. But I don't babysit them after they've gone. Probably my job description—whether I follow it or not, that's a different question—would be just to find something to make life better. Or have some new idea of new stuff that replaces old stuff. Try to make it better. Whatever it is that's wrong, that takes time, that causes bugs. If there's anything in the structure of Google, anything that you can put your finger on that could be done better, try to do it better.

Seibel: I know Google has a policy where every new employee has to get checked out on languages before they're allowed to check code in. Which means you had to get checked out on C.

Thompson: Yeah, I haven't been.

Seibel: You haven't been! You're not allowed to check in code?

Thompson: I'm not allowed to check in code, no.

Seibel: You just haven't gotten around to it, or you have philosophical objections to the Google coding standard?

Thompson: I just haven't done it. I've so far found no need to.

Seibel: So you're doing your stuff in your own sandbox? Do you mostly do your stuff in C?

Thompson: I write mostly in C. I do all my test stuff and toy stuff in C while Google is C++, strictly C++. It's no big deal programming in C++, but I don't like it. I resist it.

Seibel: You were at AT&T with Bjarne Stroustrup. Were you involved at all in the development of C++?

Thompson: I'm gonna get in trouble.

Seibel: That's fine.

Thompson: I would try out the language as it was being developed and make comments on it. It was part of the work atmosphere there. And you'd write something and then the next day it wouldn't work because the language changed. It was very unstable for a very long period of time. At some point I said, no, no more.

In an interview I said exactly that, that I didn't use it just because it wouldn't stay still for two days in a row. When Stroustrup read the interview he came screaming into my room about how I was undermining him and what I said mattered and I said it was a bad language. I never said it was a bad language. On and on and on. Since then I kind of avoid that kind of stuff.

Seibel: Can you say now whether you think it's a good or bad language?

Thompson: It certainly has its good points. But by and large I think it's a bad language. It does a lot of things half well and it's just a garbage heap of ideas that are mutually exclusive. Everybody I know, whether it's personal or corporate, selects a subset and these subsets are different. So it's not a good language to transport an algorithm—to say, "I wrote it; here, take it." It's way too big, way too complex. And it's obviously built by a committee.

Stroustrup campaigned for years and years and years, way beyond any sort of technical contributions he made to the language, to get it adopted and used. And he sort of ran all the standards committees with a whip and a chair. And he said "no" to no one. He put every feature in that language that ever existed. It wasn't cleanly designed—it was just the union of everything that came along. And I think it suffered drastically from that.

Seibel: Do you think that was just because he likes all ideas or was it a way to get the language adopted, by giving everyone what they wanted?

Thompson: I think it's more the latter than the former.

Seibel: It seems there are a lot of people who say, "Gosh, C++ is terrible." Yet everyone uses it. For instance, it's one of Google's four official languages. Why do folks continue to use it if it's so bad?

Thompson: I don't know. I think it's losing at Google. Now there are more people who don't like it than like it.

Seibel: And they switch to Java?

Thompson: I don't know. There's almost no replacement for it. They complain, but they don't switch. Graduate students coming out—the people who are hired by Google—know it. So it's hard to do anything else. That's the reason it keeps going—it saves a tremendous amount of education, re-education. It gets people productive faster.

Seibel: Are there other languages that you enjoy, or have enjoyed, programming in?

Thompson: All of the funny languages at one point I've taken a step in. Like for solving equations and stuff: Maple and Macsyma, things like that. For strings, SNOBOL. Anyway, I've played with dozens and dozens of languages, if they do something that's interesting.

Seibel: And are there development tools that just make you happy to program?

Thompson: I love yacc. I just love yacc. It just does exactly what you want done. Its complement, Lex, is horrible. It does nothing you want done.

Seibel: Do you use it anyway or do you write your lexers by hand?

Thompson: I write my lexers by hand. Much easier.

Seibel: Have you ever done any literate programming, a la Donald Knuth?

Thompson: No. It's a great idea, but it's almost impossible to do in practice.

Seibel: Why?

Thompson: It's two representations of the same program that are often out of phase and conflict with each other. And there's no way to resolve it. If something is written well in a programming language, then it's readable. It suffices. The comments don't need to be that parallel. The comments are maybe for algorithms, or if you do something tricky it'd probably be more in the form of a warning or something. I'm not a big, gross comment kind of guy. It's legendary.

Seibel: When I interviewed him, Knuth said the key to technical writing is to say everything twice in complementary ways. So I think he sees that as a feature of literate programming, not a bug.

Thompson: Well if you have two ways, one of them is real: what the machine executes. One of them is not. Only if one is massively more brief way than the other is it worthwhile. If it's the same volume, you read the one that works. If one is much more terse, much less precise, and you can get out of it what you need, then that's great. But very often you can't get out of it what you need—you really need the nitty-gritty and then you go to the other. Depending on what you're after, you read one or the other. But to try to have microscopic descriptions of an algorithm, one in the programming language and one in English—maybe Knuth can do it, but I can't.

Seibel: Have you ever read any of his literate programs?

Thompson: Just his stuff in the early papers. Nothing recent.

Seibel: And are there books that you think are particularly important—that either were important to you or that you would recommend people to read?

Thompson: I don't read beginning programming books, so I have trouble recommending such things. If I have to learn a new language or something I'll try to find a book. I prefer much denser books that just give me the syntax and semantics rather than chatting me up and telling me what's good style and what's bad style.

When I taught, I would have to select a textbook for my course and would read all of the textbooks in the area and have to make a selection. So at two points in time, I knew the basic literature for those courses. But outside that I don't read.

Seibel: When you were inventing Unix you had your plan to do the four pieces that would actually give you an operating system. Then your wife and kids went away, leaving you free to hack for a month. I assume you put in some long hours in that month. Why do we do that? Is it necessary? Is it just because it's fun?

Thompson: You do it when you're driven. I don't think I could have *not* done it. The other thing is when the wife and kid are around you have this synchronizing to a 24-hour cycle. When they go away, I don't have a 24-hour cycle. There's nothing that keeps me and the sun together. And so I typically sleep on a 27- or 28-hour cycle, sleeping 6 hours. So I drift. When I get to sleep until I wake up I'm in better shape to work than if I get to sleep and get up when the kid starts screaming.

Seibel: So that's when you're driven by a project and you wake up wanting to get to the computer to start writing more code. But people also work long hours because we have this idea that we've got to get this product out the door and the way to do it is for everyone to work 80, 100 hours a week.

Thompson: That generates burnout. Excitement programming, I never ever felt stress. I've been in other situations too where deadlines—external deadlines—generate stress. That's not fun; I don't like that.

Seibel: You burn out at the end, which is obviously bad, but in terms of getting things done in the short term, does it work?

Thompson: Usually you're in a position where such a thing is continual. That as soon as that deadline is over another one starts coming up over the horizon. If you're constantly under deadlines like that, then the next one you'll have less enthusiasm and pretty soon you just can't live like that. I can't.

Seibel: Tied up with trying to meet deadlines is being able to estimate how long things are going to take. Can you estimate how long it's going to take to write a given piece of code?

Thompson: It depends on whether I'm writing it for me or writing it for production. I can if I'm writing for me. I can live with the quirks. I can not do the extra ten percent. I can avoid the gaping holes that I know are in there. Things like that. I can produce it and then clean it up at leisure and still use it. Maybe that's a different definition of *finished*. But if you're doing it for production then usually there are other people involved and coordination—I can't estimate that.

Seibel: In one 1999 interview you said you didn't think much of Linux, and got the Linux guys all up in arms. What do you think of it now about a decade later, and it's taking over the world?

Thompson: It's much more reliable—there's no doubt about that. And I've looked at the code occasionally. I don't look at it as much as I used to. I used to, for Plan 9. They were always ahead of us—they just had massively more resources to deal with hardware. So when we'd run across a piece of hardware, I'd look at the Linux drivers for it and write Plan 9 drivers for it. Now I have no reason to look at it. I run Linux. And I occasionally look at code, but rarely, so I can't really tell whether the quality has gotten better or not. But certainly the reliability has gotten better.

Seibel: Do you ever read code just for fun?

Thompson: In the past I used to; less so now. When I first came here I did it just to try and get the feel of the place. You've got to. There's so much unsaid that you've got to know.

Seibel: Would you pick a program and completely understand it, or were you just sort of looking for how do they do things around here?

Thompson: A little bit of both. I'd certainly try to pick the big libraries at first. I'd look at the main programs of some of the things. The programming style here at Google is so bizarre. They take a subroutine call, package it as an RPC, and store it somewhere static. Which means anybody can call it at any time for any reason. And then they call generic listening kind of code and somebody somewhere gets a message, goes off and finds that, and makes that subroutine call.

Seibel: So that's a mechanism for distributed computation.

Thompson: Yeah. That's all this place does. It's very hard to read. So you go off and you start reading the binding code. And then this code. And then the general IPC. That gets you a handle into where you can actually start reading stuff and understanding stuff. Before that, you can't understand a thing.

Seibel: When you work on a team, what's the structure that you like?

Thompson: Just working with good, compatible people.

Seibel: When you're working with compatible people, do you favor strong code ownership: "I wrote this piece of code; it is mine and I'm responsible for it," or more shared ownership: "We all own this code together and anyone can do what they see fit."?

Thompson: I've always worked halfway in between. There's somebody who owns it and if you have a problem with it, you mail them or tell them and their job is to fix it. And then at some point they disappear, they don't want it, they don't fix it, they're not responsive—then you fix it. The catchphrase is, "You touched it last." You own it. So it's halfway between. You don't have a bunch of people going in and modifying the code willy-nilly. It's all filtered through an owner. But that owner can change pretty easily.

Seibel: These days there are folks who advocate pair programming, meaning two people working at one keyboard. Have you ever worked that way?

Thompson: Something small can be done like that. Very often I'll be typing and somebody else, who will obviously be faster at it than I, will sit down and they'll type and I'll talk. I've done that on orders of minutes to hours, very few hours, to get one thing done that both of us could have done separately.

Seibel: And did you find that the result was better or it got done faster?

Thompson: The result isn't better. Probably debugging is faster—as you're typing, someone can catch a bug over your shoulder. So I think it will generate fewer bugs as you go. But I didn't find it as a philosophy as a way to go—it just happens.

Seibel: Do you still enjoy programming?

Thompson: Yes. I like small programs. Small, meaning you can do it in a month. If you're trying to do some monster task that takes a year, I can't keep in it that long.

Seibel: Was that always the case, or have you lost the energy for longer projects?

Thompson: I don't know. It depends on the actual thing. Something big that takes years, like an operating system, you subdivide that and there are lots of fun pieces, so that counts as multiple small things as opposed to one big thing. But there are lots of things that are just one big thing, and those I think I've always found difficult. I need gratification, feedback. And if you have to sit there and work and work and work for days, months and see nothing except a pile of code, then I have trouble doing that.

Seibel: You've mostly worked in research and it seems you've had a lot of latitude to work on what you like, but did it change when it become a job? Did it take any of the fun out of it?

Thompson: No. It's always been fun, and mostly because I just selected what I wanted to do. And even when it was a job, back in college, there were tons and tons of jobs available. It seemed to me that there were tons of people who were doing something, whatever it is, and they needed some little programming task done on the side to aid them. So they were perfect for me. They were little tiny jobs that I could get into, get in and out in days and pick and choose which one I wanted to take.

I think my first one was a humanities professor cataloging Homer's work. And he had *The Iliad* and *The Odyssey* on cards. He wanted word frequencies and counts—essentially statistical analysis of these two works. And that was fun. It was text processing, which just wasn't done by computers in those days. So that was my first odd job.

Seibel: In a 1999 interview you talked about how you had told your son he should go into biology instead of computers because you thought computers were played out. That was almost ten years ago. How do you feel about that now?

Thompson: I feel the same. Nothing much new has happened in computers that you couldn't have predicted. The last significant thing, I think, was the Internet, and that was certainly in place in '99. Everything has expanded—the speed of individual computers is still expanding exponentially, but what's different?

Seibel: Reading the history of Unix, it seems like you guys basically invented an operating system because you wanted a way to play with this computer. So in order to do what today might be a very basic thing, such as write a game or something on a computer, well, you had to write a whole operating system. You needed to write compilers and build a lot of infrastructure to be able to do anything. I'm sure all of that was fun for its own sake. But I wonder if maybe the complexity of modern programming that we talked about before, with all these layers that fit together, is that just the modern equivalent of, "Well, first step is you have to build your own operating system"? At least you don't have to do that anymore.

Thompson: But it's worse than that. The operating system is not only given; it's mandatory. If you interview somebody coming out of computer science right now, they don't understand the underlying computing at all. It's really, really scary how abstract they are from what a computer is or even the theory of computing. They just don't understand it.

Seibel: I was thinking about your advice to your son to go into biology instead of computing. Isn't there something about programming—the intellectual fun of defining a process that can be enacted for you by these magical machines—that's the same whether you're operating very close to the hardware at a very abstract level?

Thompson: It's addictive. But you wouldn't want to tell your kid to go into crack. And I think it's changed. It might just be my aging, but it seems like when you're just building another layer on top of another layer on top of another layer, you don't really get the benefit of writing, say, a DFA. I think by necessity algorithms—new algorithms are just getting more complex over time. A new algorithm to do something is based on 50 other little algorithms. Back when I was a kid you were doing these little algorithms and they were fun. You could understand them without it being an accounting job where you divide it up into cases and this case is solved by this algorithm that you read about but you don't really know and on and on. So it's different. I really believe it's different and most of it is because the whole thing is layered over time and we're dealing with layers. It might be that I'm too much of a curmudgeon to understand layers.

CHAPTER

13

Fran Allen

Planning to be a math teacher but needing to pay off her student loans, in 1957 Fran Allen took what she intended to be a temporary job as a programmer at IBM Research. Her first assignment: teach resistive IBM scientists the newly invented language Fortran.

Instead of returning to teaching, Allen stayed at IBM for 45 years and worked on a series of compiler projects, including the compilers for the STRETCH-HARVEST machine and the ambitious but never-built ACS-1 supercomputer as well as her own PTRAN project, which developed techniques for automatic parallelization of Fortran programs and developed the Static Single Assignment intermediate representation, which is now widely used in both static and just-in-time compilers.

In 2002 Allen was awarded the Turing Award for her "pioneering contributions to the theory and practice of optimizing compiler techniques," becoming the first female recipient in the 40-year history of the prize. She was also the first woman to be named an IBM Fellow, IBM's top technical honor. She is also a fellow of the IEEE and the Association for Computing Machinery and a member of the National Academy of Engineering, the American Academy of Arts and Sciences, and the American Philosophical Society.

Over her career, Allen has observed the changing role of women in computing, from her earliest days when women were specifically recruited by companies like

IBM for the new and ill-defined job of "programmer," to later decades when the field became largely male-dominated.

In our conversation she talks about what that transition was like as well as why it is important to increase the diversity in the field and how C has grievously wounded the study of computer science.

Seibel: How did you get involved in programming? I know you started out planning to be a math teacher but took a job at IBM in order to pay your student loans.

Allen: To be a fully certified teacher in New York state required a master's degree. I had an undergraduate degree in mathematics, a minor in physics, and had taught for two years. Then I went to the University of Michigan and focused very much on mathematics. At the University of Michigan, in order to get a master's degree, one had to take two courses outside one's field, so I took a course on computing. Computer science didn't exist then, in 1957. It was ten years later that it started to emerge seriously. But they had a couple of courses in the engineering school.

Seibel: What did they teach you?

Allen: They had an IBM 650 machine, which was quite a different machine than what we're used to today, and the students learned to program that machine. That involved not only learning all about the machine itself and coding in, essentially, assembly language but also running your programs on the machine. It was a really hands-on experience.

Seibel: So you would punch your deck, take it to the machine yourself, and feed it through yourself?

Allen: Right. And then go and fix it. It was a drum machine—the drum was constantly spinning and that's where your instructions were. So the way one got it to run fast involved spacing the placement of the instructions on the drum so as it turned the next instruction would be in the right place.

Seibel: Then the IBM recruiters came around. What was it about working at IBM that appealed to you?

Allen: Well, I just needed a job. I had this debt and the recruiter came on campus and it was in the right geographical area, back in New York state. So I filled out an application and really didn't realize much about what group I was interviewing with, the fact that it was IBM Research. I was kind of clueless about that.

A few weeks later I got a call while I was interviewing for a faculty job at a teacher's college in southern Illinois. I was really getting desperate—it was time to get a job and I didn't have one. So I got that call while I was on the road and took the job, sight unseen, and got the papers to report at what turned out to be the research laboratory in Poughkeepsie.

So I went there and got started as a programmer. IBM was expanding rapidly into computing and there weren't any computer-science courses, so they were hiring people from wherever they had found them.

Seibel: What kind of training did they give you?

Allen: Well, it was a kind of a learn-as-you-go, as I recall. There was an orientation to the company but I don't recall there was any programming class per se, which is odd in retrospect. I suppose there were some classes, depending on what your background was. It was all very informal.

The first assignment I got, because I'd been a math teacher, was to teach the scientists and other programmers Fortran. I had joined in July of 1957 and Fortran had been issued as a product on April 15 that same year. And IBM Research—the group I was in—had an edict that by September all the programming had to be done in Fortran. That was the way to convince their own people, just as they were trying to get outside people to, to use it.

Seibel: So these were scientists within IBM, doing their own scientific computation?

Allen: Yes. The machine they had was the 704 machine and that's what Fortran was originally designed for and optimized to. They were used to writing in assembly code right on the machine, doing the same thing I had done at the University of Michigan, running their own programs—scheduling some time and running the programs. They did not believe that it would be possible for any high-level language to do nearly as well as what they could do programming the machine itself.

Seibel: And that was the last time scientists adopted a new language, because they're still using Fortran, right?

Allen: That's right. Well, it was an unhappy class. But in the end, it was an amazing experience for all of us because Fortran was not only a language, but they had provided a compiler which was extremely advanced, and laid the foundations for the structure of compilers today.

Seibel: The next big project that you worked on, that I know about, was the Stretch computer. Did you work on anything in between this time and the Stretch project?

Allen: There were two projects that I was involved with between Fortran and the Stretch compiler. One of them was the Monitored Automatic Debugging system, which was down at the assembly level for the 704. I really enjoyed that.

It was a very early operating system. There were three of us who worked on it. We installed some buttons on the computer, because you could do that, at that time and one was a panic button. When the program appeared to loop one could just push the panic button. Then we wrote the debugger, and one of my tasks was to take the assembly-language program and produce the column binary—rotate the output of it. When you used a card reader the data was row-binary, which means each row contained the bits that were associated with the instruction, but on tape things were read differently, so it needed to be column-binary. I still have the program.

One of the things I remember really enjoying is reading the original program—and considering it very elegant. That captured me because it was quite a sophisticated program written by somebody who had been in the field a while—Roy Nutt. It was beautifully done.

Seibel: What makes a program beautiful?

Allen: That it is a simple straightforward solution to a problem; that has some intrinsic structure and obviousness about it that isn't obvious from the problem itself. I picked up probably a habit from that of learning about programming and learning about a new language by taking an existing program and studying it.

Seibel: How do you read code? Let's say you're going to learn a new language and you find a program to read—how do you attack it?

Allen: Well, one example was one of my employees had built a parser. This was later on for the PTRAN project. And I wanted to understand his methods. It's actually probably the best parser in the world—now it's out in open source, and it's really an extraordinary parser that can do error correction in flight.

I wanted to understand it, so I took it and read it. And I knew that Philippe Charles, the man who had written it, was a beautiful programmer. The way I would approach understanding a new language or a new implementation of some very complex problem would be to take a program from somebody that I knew was a great programmer, and read it.

Seibel: And how do you get into a piece of code like that? Do you trace through the execution? Or read from top to bottom and just build a structure in your mind? It's a sort of tricky reading problem.

Allen: Well, it is a tricky reading problem, but I usually had some intuition about or learned what the structure of the solution was, and then would go in and start maybe in the middle and look for the kernel piece. And it was a wonderful way to learn not only the algorithms that were used but how to use the language in an elegant way.

Seibel: Do you have any favorite debugging war stories?

Allen: There were a couple. I remember one from the MAD system. The machine operator called me in the middle of the night because it wouldn't run a program that had been submitted for running overnight. There was a way in which we did automatic checksumming to ensure that the data was right because the machines themselves didn't have much error detection, and no error correction.

I couldn't figure it out on the phone. It took a little while, but suddenly I realized that the way I had built the checksumming piece of the system did not handle a particular case. Even when the program was correct it couldn't pass that barrier because of the way I had calculated the checksum. And I called the man back and there was a way of getting around it.

Then there was another one where—this one I remember because I was very pleased with myself—I had an employee on Stretch who preferred to work all night. He came in in the morning and he was a very intimidating man—giant guy and a very serious fellow. And he threw a debug listing across my desk—a dump of the program—a huge, thick thing. And he pointed to one particular bit in that dump, and he said, "Why is that bit set?" He had been worrying all night on it. And oddly enough, I knew why. It wasn't a bug but it was something that he didn't know what it was there for and had been assuming that that was the cause of the error.

Seibel: So that was later; you said there was another project between MAD and the Stretch.

Allen: Yes. It was for a scientist here that was doing wiring diagrams for the hardware. It had to do with laying out wires on what passed for chips at that time. It was a mathematical solution we were implementing and it had a lot of constraints, of course, because of the size of the real estate. I was working as a programmer on that. There were two of us, maybe three—all women.

Seibel: And then it was on to the Stretch project, which was a big one.

Allen: From my experience with Fortran and knowing that compiler very well, I got drafted from Research to go and work on the next big project at IBM—the Stretch machine. It started in 1955—it got the name Stretch in '56 I guess—and was going to be 100 times faster than anything else in the world—an absolutely amazing machine.

It was well recognized that the compiler was going to be key to the success of the machine and that the biggest challenge to achieve that performance was going to be access to memory and that the compiler played a big role in that.

Seibel: Because dealing with the memory latency was going to be more complex than programmers writing assembly by hand were going to be able to handle?

Allen: Yes. And because the memory-latency problem was being solved by a lot of concurrency in the hardware—very complex concurrency. And the memory organization itself was multiway-interleaved and it was unpredictable what order data would be delivered to the computational unit. Six accesses could be in flight at the same time. There were pipelines in the computational unit itself and there was an ability for multiple instructions to be in execution at the same time. And the most complicated unit on the machine was a look-ahead unit, because they had precise interrupts as part of the architectural design, so not only did it have to keep track of all the concurrency going forward, but they had to back it out when there was an interrupt.

It was an extremely complicated machine and a wonderful one to program. The compiler had a very big challenge in order to take advantage of it. It was a wonderfully challenging project.

So a bunch of us were drafted out of Research to come and work on the compiler and the operating-system software itself. The compiler itself was as grandiose as the machine. I ended up, because of my previous exposure to the Fortran optimizer, involved with the optimizer for the Stretch machine—the Stretch Harvest, as it turns out. The outlines of the compiler were established by a different committee but there were four of us who were given the charge of filling in the details, including the interfaces in the compiler and what the specs were for that and taking charge of the different pieces of it. I had the optimizer, and somebody else had the parser, the register allocator, and the interface with the assembly program.

Seibel: How was the project structured in terms of the technical people working on it?

Allen: Well, there were around three people who laid out the overall design of the compiler—we're going to have a parser, we're going to have this and that, and then where it fit. And there was somebody above them—this was a product, so there were more layers of decision-making and management.

Then they needed to have project overseers for each of the big components. So they asked four of us, three of us being women, to get involved, to get together as a team and design the interfaces.

Seibel: And then were there other programmers working on the actual implementation?

Allen: Yes. I had a group of 17, all doing programming.

Seibel: What was the relation between the design phase and the coding? You four got together and sorted out the interfaces between the parts. Did that all happen before your 17 programmers started writing code, or did the coding feed back into your design?

Allen: It was pretty much happening as we went. Our constraints were set by the people we reported to. And the heads of the different pieces, like myself, reported to one person, George Grover, and he had worked out the bigger picture technically. And a lot of it was driven by the constraints of the customers. There was a lot of teamwork and a lot of flexibility at the time, in part, because we were kind of inventing as we went. But under a deadline. So there was not as much management hierarchy, but just being more part of the team.

Seibel: Did the people below you ever write code that would then force the realization that some of the higher-up decisions about how the pieces were going to fit together had to be revisited?

Allen: Yes, how this interface is not going to work. Keeping track of how things were coming together was a part of it. We would meet as a team, the four of us. But most of our time was spent on trying to build the component that we were responsible for—there was a lot of freedom.

Software engineering came much later. There wasn't software engineering and there weren't big processes set up yet. On a subsequent project, the 360, run by Fred Brooks, which I wasn't involved with, the software was a huge crisis. The engineering on the 360 was doing pretty well around '63. And some engineers moved over from building the machines—hardware engineers—guys that just knew nothing about software—to run the software because it was so out of hand. And it was really a mess.

After the 360 got shipped one of the people—I don't know that he'd been involved with the 360—wrote a letter to the higher-ups in IBM proposing a software-engineering discipline called Cleanroom. He made statement that if you followed all these set of processes he was laying out, you could write perfect programs. And because of what management had been through—this is my version—they bought the whole thing.

Seibel: Because the 360 project had been so painful?

Allen: That's right. So IBM product development moved very strongly over to the Cleanroom processes—a whole set of processes. One of the things was that there would be somebody that would set objectives and there would be another group that did the design. And the designers would specify the design to the detail that the programmers could write to the designs. And these groups were not interactive—you just did this cleanly enough, and perfect software came out.

Seibel: On the 360 project, Brooks was in charge of both software and hardware, right?

Allen: Yes, I think he had the whole thing. But he replaced some of the software heads with people with hardware experience. And it was really the right thing to do because the hardware people already had a wonderful discipline around building hardware—the chip design and the testing process and all of that. And that was an older and much more rigorous ways of expressing designs. We software people were just making it up.

Seibel: So you feel that, at least on that project, that they brought something to the software-development process that saved the project?

Allen: It was absolutely necessary, but it was so painful for the software people to have these guys—all guys—move in, knowing nothing about software, and just impose design reviews, design specs, all of this stuff.

Seibel: So it did help save that project. Did that embolden folks to take this next step to the Cleanroom process that was sort of a step too far?

Allen: Yeah, I think it did. That was the sequence. And the Cleanroom process, the waterfall process, came in through management with a very strong advocate for it.

Seibel: And that advocate was from the hardware side?

Allen: No, the advocate was from the software side. But I don't think that he had been part of the 360 project, in the depths of trying to rescue that. But some of us who already had some experience with software structure were appalled at the statements at the time. But sometimes one has to make bold claims in order to sell something.

Seibel: Did you ever work on a project where that kind of process was used?

Allen: Oh, yes. And found it frustrating because in its early stages, a designer and the programmer could not interact. One of the problems was—probably still is—that the life cycle of a piece of software is very long. And at that time, if you were building a big piece of software, it took months and months or years. And the environment changed and the requirements changed. And the customers really did have the say in what they wanted in the end.

Seibel: Would you then push changes all the way down through the process? Or did people start short-circuiting the process, going directly to the programmers and saying, "All right, we figured out the customer needs *X*"?

Allen: Yeah. One could never really write specs that were going to be adequate and useful at a detail level over the years of the life cycle. That was a problem. And now we have another process, of course—just do it and throw it away, kind of.

Seibel: Well, it was Brooks, in his famous book, who said, "Build one to throw away because you're going to."

Allen: Yes. And in fact, that is true—I very much believe that. But lots of times, that has led, in my opinion, to not thinking at all before you start building.

I always like to have a picture—a model. Often a flowchart and some specification about the interfaces. We were heavy users, of course, of flowcharts at that time because one didn't get access to the machine that often and that was a very nice model for thinking through how parts of the system would interact, what would be done, and specifying what would be done where, and the functionality of the various components. I don't know what the analog of that is now.

Seibel: Even with flowcharting, there are formal flowcharts produced as documentation and then there are the flowcharts you draw on a blackboard to try and understand something. Was it more of the former or the latter?

Allen: In some cases, it would be formal flowcharts. Often in the kernels of things there were some very complex pieces and one would do that. Otherwise, it was just informal and a way of working at solving a problem. Blackboards would be covered and become the record for the month or whatever period of time.

Seibel: So the big project you led was the PTRAN compiler project, which was when you first started working on explicit concurrency, as opposed to the implicit concurrency in the CPU pipelines and so forth. When you started that, that was a new thing, both for you and for IBM.

Allen: It was new for IBM, but we were very, very late coming into it. The great work that initiated it from a real pragmatic point of view was at Illinois starting in '69 and '70.

Seibel: And what language did the PTRAN compiler compile? Was it straight Fortran with no added constructs for parallelism?

Allen: That's right, that's where we started from. What I wanted to do was to do the same thing we'd done for optimization: The user writes a sequential code in the language in a way that's natural for the application and then have the compiler do the optimization and mapping it to the machine and taking advantage of concurrency.

In PTRAN, the idea was still to take the "dusty decks," as we called them, referring to an existing code base, and to automatically take advantage of the hardware's parallel components.

Seibel: So, essentially, that was targeting what today we would think of as symmetric multiprocessors?

Allen: Yeah, could be. There are many, many models of parallelism, which is one of the difficulties. I think that that can be greatly simplified. But multicore is one of the things that really are particularly interesting, for me at least. But there are many models of parallelism.

We actually built it from existing work, particularly Dave Kuck's. Some work from NYU. We hired a group of newly minted PhDs from these places that already had built up a lot of expertise. We had a quite a lot of significant results, both on the practical and on the theoretical side—we worked on both at the same time. I'm a very strong believer that one wants to be able to take the practice into identifiable algorithms, and theory, and ways of thinking about how to solve the problems and also to take the algorithms into practice to see how really valuable they are, and how they apply. I think our field is best done when it works on both sides on the same projects.

Seibel: On the PTRAN project, you were leading a team. Were you still coding at all by then?

Allen: I wasn't doing the coding, but I was very close to it. As an example, when the Static Single Assignment work was done, I didn't see how it could be implemented in any reasonable time. I mean, it was a very good algorithm, but I didn't see an implementation that was bounded in time and space in some real way. So I had that challenge out there. I had to see that code. I needed it. It had to be implemented. It couldn't be just a paper—a very nice paper, a famous paper—that shows graphs and complexity bounds.

If we can't implement it in a real system, that challenge would still be out there. It wasn't going to be as useful as I wanted it to be. Finally, one of my people had an encoding. And I walked through that, every piece of that code, and looked at the data structures that were used. And it was astounding. I said, "This is it. It works."

Seibel: So you were looking at all of the pieces that were going to go into the whole system?

Allen: Yes, yes, yes.

Seibel: You also were managing all these people? Or were you a technical architect with someone else managing the group?

Allen: No, I was the research manager for the group. There were about 10 or 12 core people and we divided the work up so that each person really had ownership of a piece of it.

Seibel: People have been debating at least since Gerald Weinberg's book *The Psychology of Computer Programming* whether it's better for people to "own" code, so they take responsibility for it, or to have people work more collaboratively so you avoid having silos that only one person understands. It sounds like you thought dividing up the ownership was the way to go?

Allen: We worked collaboratively, but the collaboration was about the state of the system, of the implementation. And some people were very good at the implementation, and so they'd own a piece—some piece of the optimizer or the intra-procedural analysis was definitely one or two people. But also, there were a number of people that were doing a lot of the theory work, or the abstract work of writing the papers, and writing a lot of the papers and algorithms. And it was the bringing together of those two special parts that I think really made the group so strong.

This was a period of a lot of work going on in the analysis and transformations for parallelism. So what I tried to do was, for each of the people that were doing theory to get them to write some code, express it in code as a part of the system. And the people who were just doing the other part, well I'd try to get them to write things up so they were more generally available.

Seibel: A lot of programmers will do anything to avoid becoming a manager. Was managing something that you also enjoyed?

Allen: Well, Research in the earlier times did not distinguish—doing management was not a promotion, not a salary raise. It was just somebody had to manage this piece of work, and "OK, don't you want to do it?" Or, "You're the obvious one to manage this piece of work." And it was technical management; there wasn't much people management involved. But in Research people are RSMs, Research Staff Members, the day they enter, and for the rest of their career mostly. All my colleagues, that's what we are. So one moved in and out of management without any stigma attached.

Seibel: So presumably the people who got chosen to manage were the ones who were actually good at it. How did you pick up those skills?

Allen: Well, I was sent to management school. Everybody was, back when I was first appointed. But I think it goes back to when I grew up on the farm. I was the oldest of six kids and there were five of us in a row, so my parents were pretty overwhelmed. So it was a natural role for me in some ways.

Seibel: One of the difficulties of the kind of technical management that you were doing is finding the balance between having your own technical opinions about how stuff should be done and giving people room to put their own ideas in.

Allen: I think I had some hard lessons on the Stretch project. I remember some of the people on the project came in and said to me one day that we ought to be using list and hash functions. Well, we knew about list programs but hashing was new. So a couple of my people came and said they wanted to use hashing for the symbol table. And I said, "No, we can't do that. We don't know how to do that." Yadda, yadda, yadda. The next Monday I came in and they had done it. They had torn down the system and rebuilt it with hashing. It worked, and it was much faster. So that was a big lesson to me. I should be much more open to some brand-new ideas.

Seibel: So sometimes—maybe even often—your people actually know what they're talking about and you shouldn't interfere too much because you might stomp out a good idea. It's trickier when you're really right and their idea really is a little bit flawed but you don't want to beat up on them too much.

Allen: There was some of that. It was often where somebody came in with a knowledge of some area and wanted to apply that knowledge to an ongoing piece of project without having been embedded in the project long enough to know, and often up against a deadline.

I ran into it big time doing some subcontracting work. I had a group of people that was doing wonderful work building an optimizer based on the work we've done here for PL/I, a big, different language. But one of the people working for the subcontractor had just discovered object-oriented programming and decided that he would apply it to the extreme. And I couldn't stop him, even though I was the contract overseer, and the project was destroyed. Ultimately, what did it was PL/I has lots of pointers and tracing a pointer is done all the time, and it took 11 instructions to trace the value, to find the value of one pointer consistently.

Seibel: You mean in the generated code.

Allen: In the generated code and in the compiler itself because it was bootstrapping the compiler. Every time you made a step you had to check that the thing's valid. And you were checking, and rechecking, and rechecking. It still happens today. Some of these lessons we haven't learned well. And I guess I was not dealing with it very well, because I should have just pointed out what the cost of applying object-oriented technology in that kind of situation. It was just hopelessly slow, so the whole thing got canceled.

Seibel: When were you most directly building a product for IBM, with production deadlines that had to be met?

Allen: Certainly, the Stretch project was that way. And I've worked in product development two or three times, and been in the situation where one has week-by-week code reviews right up against deadlines. I have a lot of respect for those processes and how important they are for the end result and for the team that's doing it. It can be very painful to sit there every Friday and do code reads with people explaining why they're doing what they're doing and finding other people's errors.

Seibel: Painful, but worthwhile?

Allen: Absolutely worthwhile. On the PTRAN project, towards the end when we were shipping a piece of it to the products, a half a day was devoted to explaining errors in our code, their code, whatever it was, every week. That went on for ten months, I think. Devoted Friday afternoon to it.

Seibel: When you were working in those settings did you feel like you had a process that let you estimate how long it's going to take to build X amount of software with any kind of accuracy?

Allen: Well, they did. The product-development people certainly did. It was all tracked, and I'm sure it still is. Part of it would be to statistically get a handle on the quality of the code. How many bugs showed up this week, yeah. I liked the environment of a product lab because it's sort of where things get real.

Seibel: When you were hiring programmers what did you look for?

Allen: Well, I had a lot of connections in the universities. NYU had some fabulous compiler-writer faculty—that group was really well-trained to write compiler code.

Seibel: So you could hire people recommended by the professors you knew and trusted. How about when you have to interview someone who doesn't come with a recommendation from someone you trust—how do you figure out in the course of a couple of hours whether they are going to be a good programmer?

Allen: I always start with interviewing anybody for IBM Research by trying to find out what they're excited about. That's kind of a basic threshold for me. And it doesn't matter whether it has anything to do with programming or computers. If they can't get enthusiastic about something, they're not going to get charged up in a group.

Sometimes one takes a high risk. I took a high risk on a guy whose thesis adviser wrote that he was very dyslexic. He didn't work out so well here because he didn't fit in some ways, but he started his own company and I still go to him for advice, for insights on how to do things technically. He just knows things. So that wasn't a mistake. It was a mistake in terms of the project, but not in terms of his relationship with a lot of us.

Seibel: Lately you've been involved in mentoring—there's a mentoring award here at IBM that is named for you. Do you have any ideas about how new programmers should be brought along into being better programmers?

Allen: That aspect of mentoring, I don't get very close to these days. What I do do, though, is encourage a young person starting out to not jump into becoming a manager, which is very tempting for people who have a talent in that direction. Get a reputation for technical work. Whether it's a nice piece of science, an algorithm, or writing great code—whatever it is, establish a strong reputation there first. That'll serve you well if you do want to go to managing projects and so forth, to have learned the discipline of what it takes to do that and how to function in that way.

Seibel: Is it possible to have a great manager who's actually not very technically skilled, but is very good at organizing the efforts of others?

Allen: Yes, as long as he doesn't think he's good at the technology, and is able to distinguish between who is and who isn't in the people that work for him.

Seibel: That's probably the trickiest thing. For you, what distinguishes the really best programmers?

Allen: Well, I always like to find the people who can turn a light bulb on over my head. That's really important for me because I spend a lot of time thinking about systems, so I like to have people that will be able, at least in Research, to show me something new and interesting or a new way of looking at something—a new way of solving a problem.

Also, I rely on what other people think. I've been wrong plenty and it's a real learning experience when I find myself thinking more highly of somebody than the group does. If you have a good group, it's a very good way of sorting out who's doing good work.

Seibel: When do you think was the last time that you programmed?

Allen: Oh, it was quite a while ago. I kind of stopped when C came out. That was a big blow. We were making so much good progress on optimizations and transformations. We were getting rid of just one nice problem after another. When C came out, at one of the SIGPLAN compiler conferences, there was a debate between Steve Johnson from Bell Labs, who was supporting C, and one of our people, Bill Harrison, who was working on a project that I had at that time supporting automatic optimization.

The nubbin of the debate was Steve's defense of not having to build optimizers anymore because the programmer would take care of it. That it was really a programmer's issue. The motivation for the design of C was three problems they couldn't solve in the high-level languages: One of them was interrupt handling. Another was scheduling resources, taking over the machine and scheduling a process that was in the queue. And a third one was allocating memory. And you couldn't do that from a high-level language. So that was the excuse for C.

Seibel: Do you think C is a reasonable language if they had restricted its use to operating-system kernels?

Allen: Oh, yeah. That would have been fine. And, in fact, you need to have something like that, something where experts can really fine-tune without big bottlenecks because those are key problems to solve.

By 1960, we had a long list of amazing languages: Lisp, APL, Fortran, COBOL, Algol 60. These are higher-level than C. We have seriously regressed, since C developed. C has destroyed our ability to advance the state of the art in automatic optimization, automatic parallelization, automatic mapping of a high-level language to the machine. This is one of the reasons compilers are . . . basically not taught much anymore in the colleges and universities.

Seibel: Surely there are still courses on building a compiler?

Allen: Not in lots of schools. It's shocking. there are still conferences going on, and people doing good algorithms, good work, but the payoff for that is, in my opinion, quite minimal. Because languages like C totally overspecify the solution of problems. Those kinds of languages are what is destroying computer science as a study.

Seibel: But most newer languages these days are higher-level than C. Things like Java and C# and Python and Ruby.

Allen: But they still overspecify. The core thing is that it specifies location of data. If you look at these other languages, they stayed away from specifying the location of data and how to move it, where to put it in the machine. It was ultimately about its value at any point.

Seibel: But very few languages other than C and C++ have raw pointers anymore. Java has garbage collection and the data moves around. Would you say that's still overspecified?

Allen: Yes. I believe that there's an opportunity to do what we have done with computation in the optimization world with data. We don't manage data very well. We don't have good ways of managing data automatically—establishing locality of data that's going to be used together.

There are lots of threads of research now which are very exciting. But I think what's missing is the bigger, bolder concepts. A lot of this is happening within a space that is bounded by what exists already or the current thinking. It's not going to change overnight by any means—there are millions of lines of code out there. But we do need to start trying to break the boundaries of, "This'll be done here and that'll be done there."

Seibel: Your career has been largely in high-performance computing. Yet by 2019, or whatever, we're supposed to have 1,000 cores in a notebook computer. Does that mean high-performance computing and everyday computing will merge? Or will high-performance computing always be out there doing things in a sufficiently different way?

Allen: Well, it kind of depends on where one is on the scale. To go to the petaflop, which is our current goal in high-performance computing—I don't know how that's going to go. Certainly the game in performance is going to be at the multicore because it's driven by reducing energy and lots of good things and solving some problems with the basic physics.

And there's a competitive element that's just going to drive it. But harnessing those multicores pushes the problem out of the hardware space into the software space. And that is where we're not prepared to make any progress as far as I can see. To harness these multicores—I think that's where the new language levels are going to have to break in. We should do an end-to-end look at it. But it's going to take some very new thinking.

I think these first 50 years—60 years maybe; ENIAC was in '44, '43—we've built up not only a wonderful, amazing legacy—just astounding—but also some artifacts that we need to get rid of. It'll take a very long time to replace these and I think it's a little hard to predict how that will evolve. But it'll evolve very fast if we can get some new thinking going in the right places. We know how to do computations on a lot of stuff. We don't know how to deliver the data to the computation elements in the machine.

Seibel: Can you give a simple example of what you mean by bringing the data to the computation in contrast to what we know how to do now?

Allen: To me it means taking over the management of the data, Basically, how we do it now is by reference—it's moved by hardware, or by the underlying operating systems and support systems. And often the references are at an element level.

Seibel: You mean in the sense that you can have a pointer into the middle of a struct or an array?

Allen: Yeah, into an element of it. And that brings, depending on the protocols of the hardware and of the architecture itself, the value to where it can be used as part of the computation.

But another way to do that would be to organize locations of data in their relative positions as a target of optimization. The other part of it is that very often what is good for one computation is poor for another. One organization, even of simple things like matrices, is bad when you're actually accessing it in a different way. So it's a combination of the order of the accessing against the location. It may require some architectural work, and hardware work, but I think that one can do this if we put some of the referencing, addressing capabilities back out in the hardware itself. There are machines where one has the ability, at the point data comes into the memory, to do quite a lot of transformations. Mapping can happen there.

Computation speed is what we measure, mostly, in high-performance computing so we go through all kinds of things to increase that speed. Feeding that computational unit is one of the big issues that we face, but we never made it a first-order problem to solve. We leave it to the hardware.

Seibel: In your Turning Award lecture you said something along the lines of, "We're at a crossroads here and we might miss it. We might go down the wrong path and then be going down it for quite a while."

Allen: Yeah.

Seibel: So the right path, in your view, is getting back to that kind of work in automatic parallelization?

Allen: Right, but it has to be done against a higher-level language than we have now.

Seibel: And the wrong path is finding better ways for people to express parallelism explicitly?

Allen: Well, I think we would eventually realize that we've created more of a mess than we had. But we do need higher-level languages and there certainly are domain-specific languages, and ways of developing things, which are really quite wonderful.

But we have to be willing to try and take advantage of that, but also take advantage of the integration of systems and the fact that data's coming from everywhere. It's no longer encapsulated with the program, the code. We're seeing now, I think, vast amounts of data, which is accessible. And it's numeric data as well as the informational kinds of data, and will be stored all over the globe, especially if you're working in some of the bioinformatics kind of stuff. And we have to be able to create a platform, probably composed of a lot of parts, which is going to enable those things to come together—computational capability that is probably quite different than we have now. And we also need to, sooner or later, address usability and integrity of these systems.

Seibel: Usability from the point of the programmer, or usability for the end users of these systems?

Allen: Of the end users of these systems. It's a resource, a giant resource. And the integrity of the correctness of the systems. I worked on project for the NSA on risk management, quite a few years ago, and it suddenly dawned on me that we often, in high-performance computing, do not need to compute to the accuracy that we have. We do not need all the data to be able to make progress on a solution. And so there's some nice work going on in the data side, I think, with accommodating good enough answers. I see these multicores—they're a wonderful opportunity—to go back and to take another look at lots of things.

Seibel: Do you think of yourself as a scientist, an engineer, an artist, or a craftsman?

Allen: I think of myself as a computer scientist. I was involved in my corner of the field in helping it develop. And those were interesting times—the emergence of computer science—because there was a lot of question about, "Is this a science? Anything that has to have *science* in its name isn't a science." And it was certainly unclear to me what it meant.

But compilers were a very old field—older than operating systems. Some day want I to really look it up. The word *compiler* comes actually from the embedding of little snippets of instructions to execute. Like an add would be spelled out in very primitive terms for the machine. If you want to do an add, then it would go to its library that defined that and expand it.

But assemblers were also using symbolics. I'm not sure this is accurate, but I used to believe that the first early use of symbolics for names of variables came from a man named Nat Rochester, on a very early IBM machine, the 701 around 1951. He was in charge of testing it and they wrote programs to test the machine. In the process of doing that, they introduced symbolic variables. Now, I've seen some other things since that make me believe that there were earlier ways of representing information symbolically. It emerged in the early '50s, I think, or maybe even in the '40s. One would have to go back and see exactly how things were expressed in the ENIAC, for one thing.

Seibel: So somewhere along the line, you realized you had become a computer scientist, developing theories about compiler optimization and so forth. But you started out as a programmer, hired to write code. By the time of the PTRAN project you were managing a team of people who were actually writing the software. Why did you make that switch?

Allen: Well, probably two reasons—one, I wasn't a very good programmer. I tended to make quite a few mistakes—unlike the conventional wisdom at the time that said that women make good programmers because they pay attention to details. I didn't fit that category. So I tended to be kind of disinterested in getting all the details right and I was much more interested in the way systems work.

My interest in mathematics was very abstract. If I had had enough money to go on to get a PhD, I would have become a geometer. I loved the rigor of that process. That's what I really most enjoy, puzzling through systems—puzzling through the engineering kinds of things without necessarily knowing the details of what one would need to know to be an engineer, which is quite a different area.

Seibel: The way you contributed technically to the PTRAN project, it sounds like you had the big architectural picture of how the whole thing was going to work and could point out the bits that it wasn't clear how they were going to work.

Allen: Right.

Seibel: Do you think that ability was something that you had early on, or did that develop over time?

Allen: I think it came partially out of growing up on a farm. If one looks at a lot of the interesting engineering things that happened in our field—in this era or a little earlier—an awful lot of them come from farm kids. I stumbled on this from some of the people that I worked with in the National Academy of Engineering—a whole bunch of these older men came from Midwestern farms. And they got very involved with designing rockets and other very engineering and systemy and hands-on kinds of things. I think that being involved with farms and nature, I had a great interest in, how does one fix things and how do things work?

Seibel: And a farm is a big system of inputs and outputs.

Allen: Right. And since it's very close to nature, it has its own cycles, its own system that you can do nothing about. So one finds a place in it, and it's a very comfortable one.

Seibel: You mentioned earlier that when you were working on the Stretch compiler, that three of the four people leading the compiler effort were women. Can you talk about how that came about?

Allen: This was in '59, something like that. Women were playing a big role at that time as programmers. And IBM has always been a great, great company on that. I saw some history recently, that IBM's diversity policies go back to 1899, just consistently, all through these periods when there wasn't much attention being paid to that—very explicit policies.

Seibel: Do you think the number of women on that project was due to explicit management policies—that they were saying IBM should hire more women?

Allen: I don't think they said, "We must hire more women." They just hired whoever was qualified, and it wasn't just women. These were really hard times for African-Americans, and IBM really stepped out. One story that's not very well known is there was segregated housing in Poughkeepsie at that time, regarding blacks, and IBM got it changed.

Seibel: You told a story in an interview once about one time you arrived at a conference. And they looked at you and said, "Fran Allen?"

Allen: "You're a woman."

Seibel: "We have you rooming with Gene Amdahl."

Allen: Oh, yes, that one. This was an IBM conference, when we were moving the System Y project that was going on here to the West Coast into product development and had renamed it ACS. We had a big conference at the Harriman Estate across the river. It was all, with one or two exceptions, IBM people. There was a person from the West Coast who was charged with organizing it and he didn't know any of us. He'd done it alphabetically.

Seibel: So they sorted you out and found you a room by yourself?

Allen: Yeah, a maid's room up in the garret.

Seibel: Did you publish papers under Fran or Frances?

Allen: F.E. Allen. And I don't recall why I did that. I think it was fairly common, at the time at least, to just use first initials.

Seibel: You also mentioned before that when you started, people thought women would be good programmers because women were thought to be detail-oriented. These days the conventional wisdom is that it's men who have a bizarre ability to focus on things, usually to the detriment of everything else, and that's why most programmers are men.

Allen: Right.

Seibel: You must have observed many shifts in attitudes along those lines.

Allen: Well, today they wouldn't say great programmers, but they're great on teams because they like to collaborate. It shifted to women collaborate and they work together well. So that's today's analog of that earlier assumption that women were quite detail-oriented.

Seibel: Despite the number of women in that Stretch compiler group, you must have also have had times in your career when you were working almost entirely with men. Was it a different kind of experience working in a group with lots of women?

Allen: Yes. I think it was, but it was not only lots of women—a lot of my peers were truly peers in the sense that they were mostly all the same age because of this big hiring that was going on at the point I was hired. We were pretty much all the same age and pretty much of the same background. So it was a very collegial group. And also, the whole area was so new—so much was unknown. We didn't know what we didn't know, but it wasn't as if there were a lot of people around us that had years of experience or knew a whole lot more.

Seibel: So what happened? The field is not full of women anymore; when did that change?

Allen: It took me quite a few years to identify the cause. It happened in the late '60s, at least in the environments that I was in. I had left Research to be involved with the ACS project and went to California. Then I came back to the Research division and found it a very, very different environment than the one I had left essentially eight years earlier.

There was a significant glass ceiling. There were processes in place, lines of management. And the management structures had changed and decision-making had become much more formal, particularly about what projects to do and how to do them. And the number of women had changed and the position of women in the organization had significantly changed, and not for the good. And I was not happy about it, obviously.

In 1970, '71, '72, I was 19 years or 18 years into a career that was just full of fun and opportunity. I never saw myself as advancing, but I felt I had the freedom to do what I felt was right and to work on interesting things in roles that I would enjoy. And I came back and found out that wasn't the case.

Seibel: Do you think that glass ceiling had, in fact, been there before and you hadn't bumped up against it yet? Or had something changed?

Allen: It really hadn't been there previously. Recently I realized what was probably the root cause of this: computer science had emerged between 1960 and 1970. And it mostly came out of the engineering schools; some of it came from mathematics.

And the engineering schools were mostly all men in that period. And the people IBM was hiring had to meet certain requirements: have certain degrees and have taken certain courses in computer science. And so they were almost all men because they were the ones that satisfied the requirements—because it was a discipline now. The other thing that seemed to have happened is that it was a profession—there were a lot of processes in place and chains of management that implemented the processes and kept everything running smoothly. So it was a very different place.

Seibel: I'm pretty sure sexism in society at large was pretty rampant in the '50s and '60s. Yet in that period you were working in groups that had lots of women in them. Why was it so open to women then?

Allen: Software was the newest-of-the-new stuff that was going on. And it's also probably still to this day considered a soft part of the science. And that's where women gravitated. Early on they were programmers on ENIAC and at Bletchley Park. Women were the computers—that was their name. But in engineering and physics and the harder, older sciences there weren't as many women. It was just divided that way, early on.

Then women started to come out of the engineering schools. Now the undergraduate percentage of women in engineering is somewhere around 20 percent. Carnegie Mellon would be much higher than that—they have made a special effort. But in computer science, it's essentially 8 percent. There's no domain that is as bad as computer science for women right now in terms of numbers. "Bad" is the wrong word—it's low.

Seibel: To play devil's advocate, why does it matter whether we achieve, say, Anita Borg's goal of "50/50 by 2020," meaning 50 percent women in computer science by the year 2020? Why does it matter whether this one particular field be representative of the population at large?

Allen: It's such a transformative field for society as a whole. And without the involvement of a diverse group of people, the results of what we do are not going to be appealing or useful to all aspects of our society. A piece of our challenge is to make computing, and all that it enables, accessible to everyone. That's an ideal. But it's really where it's going—the work at MIT on the $100 computer and the way we're trying to enable commerce at a very low level through computing in the remote areas of underdeveloped countries.

Seibel: So clearly the closer you get to the end user, the easier it is to imagine that people with diverse experiences are going to bring different ideas about how those users might like to interact with a computer. Again playing devil's advocate, what do you say to someone who says, "That's all well and good when we're talking about designing applications, but when you're designing compiler optimizations, who cares about a diversity of point of view?" Is it still valuable to have a diverse staff even when you're working on extremely technical aspects of software, like optimizing compilers?

Allen: Yes. In fact, that was one of the keys to the PTRAN group. A lot of women were attracted to the group, partly because there were other women there already. But it also made the group a very congenial group. And it was because of the mix—it wasn't because there were women there, but because of the mix. These people came from other organizations here, but also other educational backgrounds.

I had people that came in from NYU—the Courant Institute—who had their own way of thinking about doing things because they'd come through the same graduate school. And then I had a couple people from MIT. One in particular—a woman—was on the very theoretical side and a very wonderful thinker in a different way. The Illinois people had some different characteristics. So even taking out the gender differences or other cultural differences, the fact that they came from these different places provided, in and of itself, a much stronger group.

Seibel: I suppose if we get to the point where undergraduate computer science is split 50/50 by gender we could actually lose some of that experiential diversity, if everyone is going through the same sort of CS degree.

Allen: What makes some of the new graduates very appealing to, say, IBM, is that they're not staying in one discipline. They move from one discipline to another. And they can be deeply technical but very diverse disciplines. Often it's done purposefully—a person decides that they want to connect some big fields. I've talked to some people like that—they see a connection between working in linguistics and working in computing. They're very appealing as an employee.

Seibel: So how are you feeling about the "50/50 by 2020" project?

Allen: Pretty discouraged about it.

Seibel: What are the steps that should be taken to get to that goal? Do you need to change math education in junior high school? As I understand it, that's where a lot of girls drop out of math and science—before that girls still love math.

Allen: That's been a popular belief, but I don't believe it. Look at the Westinghouse competitions. Women are winning those. And there are a lot of women in engineering—taking all the tough sciences and mathematics in high schools. At my little high school in Croton, New York, we had a Westinghouse person nationally come in fifth. And they have a nice science program. Six of the seven people in it this year at the senior level are women doing amazing pieces of individual science.

What's happening with those women is that they're going into socially relevant fields. Computer science could be extremely socially relevant, but they're going into earth sciences, biological sciences, medicine. Medicine is going to be 50/50 very soon. A lot of fields have belied that theory, but we haven't.

Seibel: What is it, then, about computer science that is so unappealing?

Allen: A lot of people think it's the games and the nerdiness of sitting in front of a computer all day. It's going to be interesting how these new social networks online will have an effect. I don't know. But I feel it's our problem to solve. It's not telling the educators to change their training; we in the field have to make it more appealing.

We have to give the field an identity that expands it further than the identity it seems to have now—a much more human identity. We haven't articulated why we like this field and what's exciting about it and what's exciting about the future and why it's a great field to be in.

Seibel: So why do you like it?

Allen: Part of it is that there's the potential for new ideas every day. One sees something, and says, "Oh, that's new." The whole field gets refreshed very frequently. It's very exciting to think about what the potential for all of this is and the impacts it can have.

Isaac Asimov made a statement about the future of computers—I don't know whether it's right or not—that what they'll do is make every one of us much more creative. Computing would launch the age of creativity. One sees some of that happening—particularly in media. Kids are doing things they weren't able to do before—make movies, create pictures. We tend to think of creativity as a special gift that a person has, just as being able to read and write were special gifts in the Dark Ages—things only a few people were able to do. I found the idea that computers are the enablers of creativity very inspiring.

Seibel: You have been the first woman in many categories—first Turing Award winner, first IBM Fellow. Do you feel like there were women before you who were overlooked?

Allen: Oh, yes, absolutely.

Seibel: So when you won the Turing, did you think to yourself, "Gee, there's another woman who should have won this a long time ago?"

Allen: Well, the very first thing I thought about was how wonderful it was. And then I started to think about all the many other women who were never recognized at all for their work. In many cases, their work was stolen. I thought about the women who had done some very amazing things that have not been recognized, even by their peers. When I approach them and say, "You need to join some professional organizations—I'll write some recommendations for you," they kind of shy away from that.

Seibel: So you think that part of the problem is they don't get recognized because they're not putting themselves in a place to be recognized as easily.

Allen: Right.

Seibel: Are there any particular folks that you would like to name—to give a little recognition now?

Allen: Well, there's Edith Schonberg, who is a great computer scientist. In terms of technical work, it's just one first after another on some of her papers. She's had work stolen—absolutely brutally stolen. She wrote a paper on debugging of parallel code, which is a very hard problem. It was not accepted at a conference and somebody who had been on the program committee made three papers out of it. That kind of thing. It happens in our field and we don't have good ways of dealing with it.

Seibel: And it happens more to women?

Allen: Yes, I think it does. They were often viewed as not going to put up a fight—that they were more isolated and don't have the advocates who will deal with a famous thief. He was a famous thief, known but nobody dared touch it. And there are plenty of others way back from the Stretch days. There was a woman who essentially was the inventor of multiprogramming and credit was taken by somebody who eventually became a Turing Award winner.

Seibel: Would you have rather won the Turing Award, but not had to have been the first woman? There were a lot of newspaper stories: "Woman Wins the Turing Award," which I imagine might be a little annoying. If another woman had won it ten years ago, and been the first, and you could have just won it when you did, do you think you would've preferred that?

Allen: Well, I can't say preferred or not preferred. I feel I won it for a very good set of reasons. And it took a long time because it was not always clear what I was doing in some sense. I always worked with a group. Worked with some great, famous people often. And the work could easily be attributed to somebody else—to John Cocke, who distributed ideas everywhere. Lots of people have received accolades and awards because they picked up on something from him, as we all did.

But I was very glad to get it and partly because it was late for a woman to get it. I felt it was an embarrassment for the community that there were 50 men in 40 years, or whatever it was. So I felt it was certainly overdue for some woman to achieve it, and I was perfectly happy to be the first. But I steered a little bit clear of making a big deal out of that aspect of it. I tried to focus a lot more on the length of my career and the whole history of it.

Seibel: How does it feel to have spent your whole career at IBM?

Allen: Working for IBM Research was one of the most fortunate things that ever happened to me because IBM Research sits between industry and academia. I have a picture of a stone wall that I'm standing on and can look either way and find interesting problems and opportunities in both ways.

Seibel: From your vantage point on this stone wall, do you feel there is enough going back and forth between the academy and industry?

Allen: Well, NSF published a wonderful report with a one-page graph a few years ago which showed where several billion-dollar industries come from, like graphics, the Internet, high-performance computing, transistors. These billion-dollar industries were down the y-axis and on the x-axis was a timeline showing when it started, what was the role of industry, by lab, and what was the role of academia.

Some started in industry; some started in academia. Together, these two entities had contributed pretty much equally into building these multiple billion-dollar industries. I think the real important thing is to protect the interplay so that there's a lot of cross-channeling of ideas, and of technologies, and methods, and investments to see it continuing.

Right now, with the focus that the U.S. has on maintaining innovation, and the importance of it, I think we're doing pretty well in terms of interaction, working together, and solving problems together. And solving the problems that keep us from solving problems—intellectual property being one of them.

Seibel: IBM is not exactly blameless there.

Allen: Not at all.

Seibel: You must have your name on patents.

Allen: No, none. Part of it is that software wasn't patentable. The other thing was that I was often working at the leading edge of things and the best way to get it into IBM was to publish it and some other company would pick it up. I was much more interested in getting it into products than to getting a patent on things.

Seibel: So that was easier than convincing someone within IBM to build a product based on your research?

Allen: We have a much better way of doing things now. But there was a long way, sometimes, between a good idea in research and a product.

Seibel: Since receiving the Turing Award has caused you to reflect a bit on your whole career, is there anything that you've realized ties it all together?

Allen: I think my career and the way I do things—the one word that kind of sums it up is "exploring." I love exploring the edges—of ideas, of projects, and the physical earth, whatever it is—people too—and that I find very exciting.

But there's a flip side in that I'm a starter, not a finisher. I get attracted to new things. The field of compilers was just a marvelous field because the computers continued to present challenges. And the problems being solved continued to be increasingly challenging.

CHAPTER

14

Bernie Cosell

In 1969 when the first two nodes of the ARPANET—the network that would become the core of the Internet—came on line, every packet that flowed over 50 kilobit/second leased lines was routed through two specialized computers called Interface Message Processors, or IMPs. The IMPs were designed and built by Bolt Beranek and Newman (BBN), and the software that ran the IMPs had been written by a team of three programmers, one of whom was Bernie Cosell, who had left MIT three years before, at the beginning of his junior year, to join BBN.

Originally hired as an application programmer on a project building one of the earliest timesharing systems, Cosell quickly moved to the systems programming side of things and was soon "czar of the PDP-1 timesharing system" responsible for finishing the operating-system code and keeping the system running.

Over a 26-year career at BBN, Cosell would work on a little bit of everything, earning a reputation within BBN as a master debugger and "fixer" who could be thrown onto a struggling project to make the software work. And he hacked just for fun: to hone his Lisp skills he wrote DOCTOR, a version of Joseph Weizenbaum's ELIZA, based on Weizenbaum's description in a journal article. Written in BBN-LISP, which spread around the ARPANET along with the TENEX operating system, Cosell's version of DOCTOR also had a wide distribution—wider than Weizenbaum's original—inspiring new implementations and related programs.

In 1991 Cosell left BBN and bought a sheep farm in Virginia, where he now lives with his wife Lynn, three dogs, innumerable cats, and lots of sheep. He does some programming for a local ISP, hacks a bit on his own projects, and teaches a few courses in programming and computer security but is glad he no longer works as a full-time programmer. Ironically, as a result of his move to the country, Cosell—one of the fathers of the Internet—now has only dial-up access from his home.

In this interview we talked about how he won his reputation as a master debugger, the importance of writing clear code, and how he convinced the other programmers on the IMP project to stop patching the binary.

Seibel: When did you first get involved with programming?

Cosell: In high school. I don't know if it was true or not but the rumor was that our high school was the first high school in the country to actually have its own computer. IBM donated a 1620 to our high school. I think it arrived either the year before I arrived, or the year I arrived at high school in '59.

Seibel: And what high school was it?

Cosell: Bronx High School of Science in New York. I believe the previous generation of students were using Columbia University's 650. But the head of the math department was very pleased that he had his own computer. In fact, he was writing a book on programming and this was back when there weren't many books on programming. I ended up debugging all of his examples. Almost the only thing I remember about high school is learning to program.

Seibel: What were you programming then? Assembly on punch cards?

Cosell: Yeah. Well, it was punch cards but the 1620 also had a console. It had an IBM Selectric typewriter that was the input/output console, and you could input programs from that. To show you the era it was, they chose not to put arithmetic hardware in it. It had table-lookup arithmetic: there was an area of memory and when you wanted to do an addition, one digit gave you the row, one digit gave you the column, and the value was there. And part of every program was loading that part of memory with the addition and multiplication tables.

So you could actually type from the typewriter but mostly we punched cards and loaded them in. There was a Fortran for it but I never did very much Fortran. Mostly, I programmed in 1620 assembler.

The other thing I learned in high school is how to wire plug boards. Someplace along the route, we had something like an old 403 calculating printers and I learned how to wire a plug board. It was such a primitive art, even at the time, but it turned out to be useful. At BBN, like ten years after I was in high school, we actually needed somebody to wire a plug board and I just said, "Oh, give me the manual on that thing." And I read the manual and made an old standalone accounting-machine printer do a primitive protocol to serve as a line printer on our PDP-1.

Seibel: And in between high school and BBN you went to MIT?

Cosell: I graduated from high school and entered MIT in '63. I was a solid math major at MIT, taking an odd computer course. Computers were still an occasional class taught out of the electrical engineering department; you couldn't major in computer science. Folks were just starting to build the first time-sharing systems on the 709 or 7094, whatever they had at the computer center, but I was pretty busy doing math.

I took some EE courses and logic courses and I took the odd computer course and seemed to be OK at it. I didn't understand what the really good programmers did because I was just a little kid. But I seemed to be able to program.

I did fall in with a group called the Tech Model Railroad Club. I really thought that was great. Relay logic was right up my alley. They had a railroad layout completely done with relay logic and stepping switches. Through that, I got slightly in touch with the people at RLE—Research Lab of Electronics. This was still in the era where we spent all of our time in the basement of Building 26 typing up punch cards on the keypunch, which we would then hand to the shaman, who would give us listings back the next day. Then I started hanging out at Project MAC. Basically, when I was supposed to have been doing lots of math lessons, I discovered I was spending more and more time hanging out in the computer places.

And after RLE, you went over to Tech Square. I met people like Richard Greenblatt and Bill Gosper. But I was just drifting through that world; I don't think I was doing much programming. Like I remember how I got involved with Project MAC: I was really taken by *Spacewar!* on the PDP-1. But I didn't approach it as a hacker or a programmer—"Let me see the source code. How did you do that?" I just thought the game was the neatest thing. I was just a gamer at that point, as opposed to a programmer, and I had heard that the guys over at Project MAC had done a super version of *Spacewar!*, that they had fancy consoles, and they had a spare PDP, so I wandered up there. So I got to meet Peter Samson in his great failed attempt to solve the New York City subway system, to ride the whole system on one ticket as fast as possible.

I was probably a sophomore, deeply entrenched in the usual sophomore things, watching all of these guys who were clearly adept and clearly knew what they were doing. I was writing little programs to solve a maze. The frog had to hop from lily pad to lily pad and get out of the middle of the pond. I remember writing that program and helping other students from my dorm get theirs working. But that's where I was at. I had no clue what happened after I handed my deck in.

As I look back, I would say that at that point, I was learning the craft of programming. I could sort of make computers do what I wanted. But the light hadn't gone off. I hadn't internalized it; I didn't really understand what was happening. It was all a little bit magical and strange. And that was how I was drifting through college. The thing that really made me a programmer was going to work at BBN.

One of the guys I had met at college, who had graduated and worked at BBN said, "Come out here." He took me out one night in the middle of the night because BBN was a 24-hour-a-day, 7-day-a-week weird place. It was sort of an extension of the MIT labs. People could come and go at all hours. And he was part of the night crew. So we went out one evening. It was all too mysterious and marvelous to understand; I just had no clue what he was showing me. Not long after that, he suggested that they hire me. And so they had me out, interviewed me, and hired me.

Seibel: This was when you were three years into MIT?

Cosell: Correct. In September of my junior year they hired me part-time. I believe I made it until October before I dropped out and went to work full-time at BBN.

In retrospect, I wasn't very good. I had seen a PDP-1 but I had no idea how to program one. I didn't know anything about time-sharing. That, of course, was not surprising, since there were probably maybe 50 people on the planet who knew what time-sharing was.

But BBN was working on a project with Massachusetts General Hospital to experiment with automating hospitals and I got brought onto that project. I started out as an application programmer because that was all I was good for. I think I spent about three weeks as an application programmer. I quickly became a systems programmer, working on the libraries that they were using. And not long after that, the two systems gurus, the guys that had written much of that PDP-1 time-sharing system, took me under their wing and designated me their heir apparent. That winter they both left BBN to go back to grad school. By January I was the czar of the PDP-1 time-sharing system—I was responsible for the whole mess.

But in that little interval, a whole series of lightbulbs lit up. All of a sudden, I understood time-sharing. I understood real-time systems. Once I understood it, I absorbed the time-sharing system. And everything's been downhill for me after that.

The project was quite ambitious for its time. The idea was that there would be a Model 33 Teletype—noisy and clunky and uppercase only—on each ward. There would be a Model 33 Teletype in each doctor's office. There would be a Model 33 Teletype in the pharmacy. And there would be, I guess, a Model 33 Teletype in the admissions office. And our little time-sharing system was going to coordinate all of that.

When a patient got in, they would be assigned a bed. The doctor would schedule lab tests. At which point, the nurse's Teletype would say, "Take these samples. Put this number on it." The lab would get a message saying, "Run these tests." If the doctor prescribed something, the pharmacy would be told and the cart would be ready.

It was amazing to have those little noisy, silly things on the wards. Having that level of professional dealing with these clunky things was really pretty offensive, so there was a lot of resistance. But I was sort of immune to all of that, because I had gravitated off to the systems part of the world.

And I had decided it was really important that the system not stop. I don't know if they told me that or not, but I decided that we had to prove—I had to prove—that time-sharing could work. That it was a good enough and solid enough thing that you would consider running a hospital with it. I thought about what happened if a patient needed medication and the system crashed? Or worse, the system lost the prescription and the patient never got dosed? Or the system juggled prescriptions and the nurses had actually started trusting the system? So I started thinking the system should not crash. This system should be good as Unix 30 years later.

But there was no real-time debugging. When the system crashed, basically the run light went out and that was it. You had control-panel switches where you could read and write memory The only way to debug the system was to say, "What was the system doing when it crashed?" You don't get to run a program; you get to look at the table that kept track of what it was doing. So I got to look at memory, keeping track on pieces of graph paper what it was doing. And I got better at that.

In retrospect, I got scarily better at that. So they had me have a pager. This was back in the era when pagers were sort of cool and only doctors had them. It was a big, clunky thing and all it would do is beep. No two-way. No messages. And it only worked in the Boston area, because its transmitter was on top of the Prudential Center. But if I was within 50 miles of Boston, it worked.

And basically, I was a trained little robot: when my pager went *beep, beep, beep*, I called in to find out what the problem was. What was bizarre was that with no paper, in a parking lot, on a pay phone I could have them examining octal locations, changing octal locations and then I would say, "OK, put this address in and hit run," and the system would come back up. I don't know how the hell I managed to do that. But I could do those kinds of things. I took care of the time-sharing system for probably a good two or three years.

Seibel: At this point, you had presumably written a lot of the code despite having originally inherited the system.

Cosell: Yeah. The operating system was not done when I got it. It was buggy and there were pieces of it that were not finished when Steve Weiss and Bob Morgan went off to grad school. I did something that they hadn't done—it was one of the things that I got known for around BBN, which is, I made things work.

I really believed that computers were deterministic, that you could understand what they were supposed to do, and that there was no excuse for computers not working, for things not functioning properly. In retrospect, I was surprisingly good at keeping the system running, putting in new code and having it not break the system.

That was the first instance of something I got an undeserved reputation for. I know that my boss, and probably some other of my colleagues, have said I was a great debugger. And that's partly true. But there's a fake in there.

Really what I was was a very careful programmer with the arrogance to believe that very few computer programs are inherently difficult. I would take some piece of code that didn't look like it was working and I would try to read it. And if I could understand, then I could usually see what was wrong or poke around with it and fix it. But sometimes I would get a piece of code—often one that other people couldn't make work—and I would say, "This is way too complicated."

So I would think through what it was supposed to do, throw it away, and write it again from scratch. Some of the folks I worked with—like Will Crowther—who are terrific programmers, couldn't tolerate that. They would believe that by doing that, I would probably have fixed the 2 bugs that were there and introduced 27 new bugs. But the fact is, I was good at that. So I would rewrite stuff completely and it would be organized differently than the original programmer had organized it because I had thought about the problem differently. Typically, it was simpler than it used to be, or at least simpler to my eyes. And it would work.

So I got this reputation—I fixed these mysterious bugs that nobody else could fix. Fortunately, they never asked me what the bug was. Because the truth of the matter is if they'd have asked, "How did you fix the bug?" my answer would have been, "I couldn't understand the code well enough to figure out what it was doing, so I rewrote it."

I did that a lot on the PDP-1 time-sharing system. There were chunks of the code that I would read and would say, "This doesn't do what I think this part of the program is supposed to be doing," or "It's weird." So I'd rewrite it. The only thing that kept me working there, with that attitude, was that I had a good track record. That's one of the things, that if you're not good at it, you make chaos. But if you are good at it, the world thinks that you can do things that you can't, really.

Seibel: When you left MIT, was it a hard decision at all, deciding to drop out of school?

Cosell: No. In retrospect, it was surprisingly easy. I was hating school. It was making me crazy. MIT is really a pressure-filled place. And BBN was like the Promised Land. It was wonderful. They played with computers; the company was so laid back. It was more like Project MAC than Project MAC. This was back in an era when people routinely brought their dogs in with them. So pets were padding up and down the halls; people were working day and night.

I started working part-time because I almost always had a part-time job while I was at MIT. And it just instantly felt like home. I couldn't believe it. My MIT stuff went completely to hell so I dropped out of school and went to full-time. Then I got settled in at BBN and was much more mellow and got my head in a better place. So the following fall, which would have been my senior year, I actually re-enrolled back at MIT. And I got back in again. So that all worked out.

Seibel: Did you feel like your MIT education was a good complement to your work experience?

Cosell: The programming courses that I took when I was an MIT undergraduate stood me in good stead in some abstract way, but didn't actually teach me very much. Mostly what did was the environment at BBN. Nobody, other than maybe Steve Weiss, was really mentoring me, but I was sucking what I needed to know from everybody.

Seibel: Obviously there were fewer computer books available then than there are now, but are there books that you found particularly useful or books that you think programmers should read?

Cosell: Hard for me to say what programmers should do now. There was certainly nothing I can remember from back then in terms of how to program. The closest was when I got my copy of Knuth's *The Art of Computer Programming* and sort of digested them from cover to cover. But I would hardly recommend that as a tutorial text for people.

Seibel: You read Knuth straight through?

Cosell: Oh, it was hot stuff. I was in my prime back then. So each volume as it came out we mostly read and sucked into our heads cover to cover.

Seibel: That requires a fair bit of mathematical sophistication. Do you think most programmers need to be able to read Knuth cover to cover like that?

Cosell: I brought up Knuth as an example. I would not teach students Knuth per se for two reasons. First, it's got all this mathematical stuff where he's not just trying to present the algorithms but to derive whether they're good or bad. I'm not sure you need that. I understand a little bit of it and I'm not sure I need any of it. But getting a feel for what's fast and what's slow and when, that's an important thing to do even if you don't know how much faster or how much slower.

The second problem is once students get sensitive to that, they get too clever by half. They start optimizing little parts of the program because, "This is the ideal place to do an AB unbalanced 2-3 double reverse backward pointer cube thing and I always wanted to write one of those." So they spend a week or two tuning an obscure part of a program that doesn't need anything, which is now more complicated and didn't make the program any better. So they need a tempered understanding that there are all these algorithms, how they work, and how to apply them. It's really more of a case of how to pick the right one for the job you're trying to do as opposed to knowing that this one is an order *n*-cubed plus three and this one is just order *n*-squared times four.

If they're interested in that it's nice to know that Knuth is there, but no ordinary person needs to know that. But they need to know the wisdom in there. They need to know the data structures. They need to not be stunned when they see me building linked lists in Perl. When you know all of those data structures you can pick the right one. You don't have to pick the fastest one. You don't have to pick the one that's cutest to implement. You can actually pick the one that best serves your data because you know the alternatives. Don't tell Don that I fought through but didn't have a lot of use for a lot of the gruesome numerical calculations he did to reduce those combinatorics. But boy, did I learn a lot about data structures, and that was good stuff.

Seibel: Do you have any advice for the many programmers who are self-taught?

Cosell: Write a lot of programs. That's certainly what worked for me. Looking at the various courses I've taken, writing programs is what really did it. Not programming just to while away the hours but specifically, "I ought to learn something about this; why don't I try writing a little program to do it?" That really does it.

You can't see how these things work and how they interact until you've done it some. You don't know what programming practices are dangerous until you've seen which ones make your programs take weeks to debug and then seen a good programmer fix it in five minutes. I don't think you can get that from classes. Classes can give you a lot of stuff, but in the end programming is a craft you have to perfect by plying it.

If you're lucky, you can do it at work. But even in a work environment, where you're learning on the job, I think that to really be good you have to learn faster than your job will make you learn things. You have to supplement what your job is asking you to do. If your job requires that you do a Tcl thing, just learning enough Tcl to build the interface for the job is barely adequate. The right thing is, that weekend start hacking up some Tcl things so that by Monday morning you're pretty well versed in the mechanics of it.

Seibel: How much of your own programming did you do for fun versus consciously doing things to learn particular techniques?

Cosell: Mostly I viewed computer programming as a means to get neat things done and I learned how to program in order to make things happen. There were things that seemed broken to me that I could fix. I thought it would be fun to do some Lisp programming not because I wanted to learn Lisp but because some of my friends across the bridge were big Lisp guys and it was all a little mysterious to me. So I wrote some programs and that just seemed like the natural thing for me to do as opposed to sitting at Dan Murphy's knee and having him give me lectures on CONS and CDR and CAR.

Seibel: Are there areas in formal computer science that you think are particularly useful for people who ultimately want to work as programmers?

Cosell: There are a bunch of things. I know a lot of schools do a terrible job of it, but I think getting a good course in object-oriented programming in its abstract form. One of the things I fought about with some folks at a local college here was teaching object-oriented programming using C++. I asked how they make sure their students understand the distinctions between the philosophical concept of object-oriented programming versus the idiosyncrasies and weirdnesses of C++'s implementation of it.

One other thing I think schools can do is the stuff that's in Knuth. I'm surrounded by people who think linked lists are magic. They don't know anything about the 83 different kinds of trees and why some are better than others. They don't understand about garbage collection. They don't understand about structures and things.

Then the next volume: sorting and searching. If the programming language didn't have a sort function, they wouldn't have a clue about different types of sorting, or how to search for things, when you should build indexes, what it means that the database we're using stores things in a B-tree. I think a good course would give them background not in, how do you write a linked list in C—that's a craftsman thing—but what do linked lists do in an abstract sense?

Seibel: Perhaps the most famous project you worked on was the beginning of the ARPANET, when you, Will Crowther, and Dave Walden wrote the software for the original ARPANET IMPs. How did that come about?

Cosell: In Frank Heart's group, our division, Frank viewed all of his programmer guys as this basic stable. He picked and chose how to move people from project to project. When my projects ran out, Frank would figure out what I should work on next. As opposed to the real consulting guys who would start flying to Washington and writing proposals; I was spared having to do that. Somehow, Frank had decided that I was to be the third guy on the IMP project.

I was working on another project in the fall of '68 when Dave and Willy and those guys had started. I think the contract had been awarded but wasn't going to start until January. When I joined the project, not much was done. I think they had scraped out some of the code, but nothing was really cycling yet. When I came on board and Dave and Willy had started blocking out how the system was going to be organized and had taken hunks that they were starting to write. I just fit in and claimed a piece or two for myself. We all had different skills but we were all going to know how every line of code worked for the thing because it wasn't that big a program. Complicated, but not that big.

And I know they couldn't have gotten very much done when I joined because they were still doing offline assemblies, which involved taking a paper tape into the Honeywell room where there was a 516 and running paper tapes through, making an assembly listing by having it punch an entire box of paper tape, which they would then have to carry to another machine because there was no line printer on the Honeywell machine to make an assembly listing. It was really pretty cumbersome doing the software management for that. One of the first concrete things I did on the project was I wrote a cross assembler for our PDP-1.

Then on the PDP-1 we could edit the files, assemble the files, make assembly listings of the files, run TECO macros over things. The only thing that got punched out was the comparatively small paper tape of the binary executable program, which would then go into the Honeywell machine.

Seibel: Was that the biggest challenge of writing the IMP software: making it go fast?

Cosell: Oh, that's interesting. Well, let's see. We didn't think very much about how big it was because the idea was that the system was going to have to have a lot of space for buffering. And the code wasn't going to be that big. And if the code was, say, ten percent larger than it could be if you squeezed it down, that would just mean that there would be a few fewer buffers. So we weren't quite so much worried about counting how many instructions everything took.

Seibel: In terms of how much space it would take.

Cosell: Right. How much space. But we were concerned with speed, whether we were going to keep up with the bandwidth. And how do you organize a system so that it degrades gracefully and, in particular, degrades in a way that it can dig itself out of a hole as opposed to just collapsing and dying?

The second thing was just making the system work. There was a lot of untried, untested stuff. Were the protocols going to work? Will had come up with some ideas for the routing algorithm—was that going to work? There were still a lot of underlying questions. A question about congestion control. Did we know for sure that if everybody in the world sent packets to one poor guy that we would actually refuse the packets in the right order and dig himself out?

Seibel: So that was basically because nobody had ever tried to solve this problem before.

Cosell: Exactly right. It was a research project at that point—a lot of theory. A lot of people had written dissertations. A lot of people thought they knew what was going on. At that point, the rubber had to meet the road. We had to actually see whether the queuing theory was going to work, whether the routing algorithm could oscillate.

The third big challenge was simply how do you debug the thing. All of a sudden, you can't talk to Cincinnati, Ohio. What went wrong? How do you figure it out? You call Cincinnati, Ohio, and you get a sleepy night watchman at 3:00 in the morning walking up to this little blinking box in the corner. What does he look at? What do you do? And even if you get the system back up, what went wrong? How do you fix it? Remember, I was a big things-don't-crash, things-are-going to-keep-working guy.

I know that one of the things that impressed Will was there was some bug that they could not find and I found it. It turns out it was a bug in the handling of some protocol for the modems and it was sending the wrong packet at the wrong time. I put together a series of patches so that I could put a marker in a packet and when it saw that particular packet, it installed a patch on the system that looked for this other thing happening and as soon as it saw it, it stopped the system. Then once it stopped the system, we could use debuggers to figure out what was going on. Once I had done that, it took about two minutes to find the bug because the offending packet was still in memory; it hadn't been written over.

I don't remember the exact problem, but it was one of these problems that was not fatal. There was a bad pointer corrupting memory and the corruption wasn't causing any trouble, but thousands and thousands of machine cycles later, the program crashed because some data structure was corrupt. But it turns out the data structure was used all the time, so we couldn't put in code that says, "Stop when it changes." So I thought about it for a while and eventually I put in this two- or three-stage patch that when this first thing happened, it enabled another patch that went through a different part of the code. When that happened, it enabled another patch to put in another thing. And then when it noticed something bad happening, it froze the system. I managed to figure how to delay it until the right time by doing a dynamic patching hack where one path through the code was patched dynamically to another piece of the code. And I was lucky because I guessed the right thing and we immediately found the problem.

Seibel: What enables that kind of intuition?

Cosell: On the systems I'm very good with like that, like the IMP system when I had it all in my head, or the PDP-1 time-sharing system, even though the system is a multiprogramming, multilayered, interrupt-driven system, I have all the dynamics of the system in my head. I know what order things are supposed to happen. I know somehow what's not supposed to happen, when things are supposed to not be happening. That lets me build up a model for, "How could this thing possibly have happened?"

And at least some of those were two-machine problems, which also required some odd creativity to find. That is, the trouble is something goes wrong on my machine and the evidence of it shows up on yours. I can't stop—my machine has already processed 6,000 more packets by the time yours hits the trap that says, "I got a bogus packet." So now what do you do? We'd work through, the three of us, finding ways to track those things down and fix them and basically make the system pretty solid.

Seibel: Did you build in debugging code?

Cosell: No.

Seibel: So you had many different tricky bugs, each of which you had to track down in a unique way?

Cosell: As far as I can remember, we didn't build in any debugging stuff. I mean, these days, I always point out that you've got to make programs so that they are testable. And the only way to make a program testable is to think about that before you write the first line of code. You can't retrofit block points and assert points and test points that work efficiently and do the right thing if you wait until the program is working.

But I'm sure that we didn't think about any of that. We were just trying to write this incredibly complicated real-time thing that had to be fast. It was a hard enough problem. We didn't put in any real consistency checks; who would want to waste time for that? So these things were all ad hoc patches. Jump off into a spare part of memory, run through some hand-coded stuff to check this or that or the other, jump back, and continue.

In fact, it was even formalized. One of the things—I'm pretty sure I wrote it—was a patcher where you could submit a patch to the system and it would pull one buffer out of circulation and use it to hold the code and link up to that and then link back. We used to do that kind of stuff but it was all ad hoc. We would find some bug and we would crack our heads trying to figure out what it could be.

A lot of the times, just understanding what the bug is points you at the right piece of code. Now you read it more critically and you fix it. Other times, you need to collect more data. Other times, you need to bang your head against the wall trying to catch that little bit of evidence that illuminates the thing. And we did some of all of that.

Remember, we're running on a machine that's got no console, no nothing. In general, the patches would stash away some data and then halt the machine. Then we would probably use the front panel because I don't think there was a debugger we could run from the terminal that wouldn't trash the machine. So we'd look through the appropriate areas of memory from the front console, doing examines and deposits to go figure out what was going on.

Seibel: So that's literally a row of lights?

Cosell: Yeah, a row of lights. Bit per light.

Seibel: And toggle switches to put in the address?

Cosell: Right. Actually, this is better. The PDP-1 had toggle switches. This one had, as I recall, push buttons.

Seibel: How did the three of you work together?

Cosell: One of the things that I remember doing shows a little bit of the style difference. Will was a brilliant intuitive programmer. All of the hardest problems that most people couldn't understand how to do at all, he would find ways to do.

Like the AI engine in Adventure that he did in Fortran of all things. And the routing algorithm and all sorts of stuff in the dynamics of the IMP system, Will had cobbled together. One of the things about a real-time system is everything has to be timed out. You can't wait forever for anything because there's no forever in a real-time system.

And a bigger and bigger collection of time-outs were growing up all over the program. I tried to understand them and had a hard time doing it. So in one of my revisions of the source code, I tried to make an algebra for all of the time-outs. For example, the total time-out to get an acknowledgement for a message should be eight times the time-out for a single packet to transit the net plus something. Or, the total time-out for a message to track the net is the maximum diameter of the net times the maximum time for the packet to make one hop.

I was sort of trying to find out what the basic constants in Will's mind were when he put things together. When two time-outs had the same time were they supposed to be the same or were they coincidentally the same? Who knows? How many places do you have to change when you want to change one of the constants? If you discover dynamically that you're not waiting long enough for something to happen and it is timing out when it shouldn't, you know that you can't just change that one time-out because these things are interrelated.

So I made a whole bunch of sharp sign defines, basically, to try to find the smallest number of independent constants. I remember doing that because it was just really scary. It was one of the places where I was dabbling in things that really nobody understood because a lot of those constants Will had put in intuitively and we had tuned to make work, one by one. The time-out isn't big enough and so we would make it bigger, not doing it by first principles or algebra, but just tuning it until it works.

Seibel: Did you find bugs that way or did you just put it on a more solid footing so that as things changed, you could change things in a way that wouldn't require endless retuning?

Cosell: I don't recall finding any bugs. But there were undoubtedly some places where there were timers that now had different values than they used to, but not operationally significant ones, just defensively different ones. It was less so that you could change it if you have to; really it was so that it made the program easier to understand. I hated having a program that had 200 randomly chosen independent constants scattered throughout it and knowing that they have something to do with the heartbeat of the network. I think it simplified some of the code. It made it easier to fathom what was going on. It also let us use more symbolic constants. Eight times diameter plus pulse time or something like that would be understandable.

Will was sort of the advanced idea man. I remember complaining to Frank Heart about this once, that he got to work on the projects right out of the box because BBN was doing a lot of very cutting-edge stuff and he was terrific at finding ways to do things that couldn't be done before.

He was not as good at getting 100 percent done nailed-down code. He was really good at getting 75 or 80 percent pretty good code that worked most of the time. Will had already gone on to, I think, the TIP, and Dave and I were still working on the IMP system and that's when I redid the routing algorithm because it had funny constants and I didn't understand it. So it was still Will's routing algorithm but recoded with my style. And I think it was a little more solid. At least I understood if it was going to oscillate, *why* it was going to oscillate, because *I* made it oscillate.

One of the places where Will Crowther and I absolutely differed—and I had to put in hours and hours of work and even then he was skeptical—was he believed that when you reassemble a program you add more bugs than you remove. So he used to keep notebooks with pages and pages of patches. He would go as long as he could patching the existing system before he had to reassemble. Those patches were of patches on top of patches and so complicated that often his prediction was a self-fulfilling prophecy. It was hard, after all of that, to get it just right so that it turned out to be what the patches were actually saying.

Seibel: So you had an original source listing that you could feed to an assembler—

Cosell: Right, and a binary image that was running. Then we would have a paper tape—or sometimes we'd just do it by hand—that plants a jump here out to a little area where these three lines of code were replaced by these five lines of code and then it transfers back to the subsequent thing so when you execute this code it goes off to the patch, executes some stuff, and comes back.

Seibel: So the paper tape held the binary version of the patch?

Cosell: Yeah. Later on, when I built a little interactive debugger that had the examine and deposit functions I was so fond of, we actually could build a little text tape that looked like, "Go to location 12785, value, value, value, value. Blank line. Go to location 12832, value, value, value, value, value." If you had to load the program from scratch you loaded the program and then you loaded the patch tape when you were done.

Seibel: So at that point you didn't actually have any source code that would assemble into the current state of the running binary?

Cosell: Exactly right. One of the troubles was we had different copies of the listings. One of the listings will have an inked mark at some place in the code where two lines will be crossed out and next to it the replacement code. Now, did every copy of the listing get that? Will was very good because he had his notebook and the final say was not a particular listing but his notebooks. That was his approach.

My approach was that the system should always run out of the box. I do not want to mark on the assembly listing. When I first came on the project it was hard to get all of his patches in. We would work all day and then I would edit and reassemble the system overnight so that the next morning we had another clean tape and we would start with that. It turns out when you're doing it overnight you only have two or three changes and they're located so you can read the code as you change it and it makes sense. Of course, that settled down right away.

So we almost never again had a problem of fixing a bug creating a new one other than if the patch was wrong. But Will and I were at odds about that because he was really very fond of patching and staying away from assembler if you could, partly because it took a lot of time whereas he can patch and just go on, and partly because he didn't trust the cycle because the editing was too scary.

Seibel: Do you consider your work on the IMP one of your important technical achievements?

Cosell: Oddly enough no. It was an interesting, hard program, but I'd written Doctor, I was doing Lisp stuff, I'd been czar of the hospital computer system. Certainly at that point the neatest thing I had worked on was understanding every line of code in this cutting-edge time-sharing system. This thing was just a little stand-alone communications processor. It didn't have as many interrupt channels as we had on the PDP-1. It didn't have to deal with what do you do when you only have 32 swapping slots and you have 40 people logged on.

The three of us got along famously, so it was fun and it was challenging. There were things about debugging it and implementing it that were hard to do. But hard to say that I would've thought it was the crown of my career. It was just the next program. The other thing that was anticlimactic about the IMP system was how bounded it was. The PDP-1 was basically hard. It was a time-sharing system and it had to evolve over time.

The thing about the IMP system that was so neat is how we did it in such a disciplined fashion. They started officially in January; I joined the project in February and in September it was done. Small value of "done"—we were still working on it fixing bugs and stuff but it got released in September and didn't stop. Not long after that Will went on to his next project and Dave and I continued with it and somebody new came in.

The person I have to give a lot of credit to is Frank Heart. I don't understand how he hit on the management style of mostly letting us be as crazy as we were. I'm hard-pressed to remember a software-review meeting. I'm hard-pressed to remember being hassled for documentation when the three of us had the program in our heads and couldn't be bothered with a lot of that stuff. There was a level of trust and confidence that the three of us were going to do this thing and he left us alone. In retrospect, having been a project manager, that's a stunning thing; that's just bizarre. No weekly staff meetings, no PERT charts on the board. Willy was of course keeping track of what needed to be done and bugs we found and stuff, but the lack of oversight structure for that was pretty impressive. Throwing us together and telling us to go do it was, I think, a stroke of management bravery.

Another thing that Frank did, on other projects, was design reviews. He had the most scary design reviews and I actually carried that idea forward. People would quake in their boots at his design reviews. This was sort of like taking your orals for your dissertation. He would have a hand-picked collection of people in the audience and you would have to present your design. The people he picked were always good. The thing that made his design reviews so scary is he knew when you were bluffing.

I'm sure you've done design reviews where you didn't work on some part of it real well and so you kind of slide past that part. You think you got this right but you didn't really do the analysis so you don't know quite what's going on. He had an instinct, and it was abetted by having a good crew in there, of catching you when you were bluffing, catching you when you hadn't thought it through.

The parts that you did absolutely fine hardly got a mention. We all said, "Oh." But the part that you were most uncomfortable with, we would focus in on. I know some people were terrified of it. The trouble is if you were an insecure programmer you assumed that this was an attack and that you have now been shown up as being incompetent, and life sucks for you.

The reality—I got to be on the good side of the table occasionally—was it wasn't. The design review was to help you get your program right. There's nothing we can do to help you for the parts that you got right and now what you've got is four of the brightest people at BBN helping you fix this part that you hadn't thought through. Tell us why you didn't think it through. Tell us what you were thinking. What did you get wrong? We have 15 minutes and we can help you.

That takes enough confidence in your skill as an engineer, to say, "Well that's wonderful. Here's my problem. I couldn't figure out how to do this and I was hoping you guys wouldn't notice so you'd give me an OK on the design review." The implicit answer was, "Of course you're going to get an OK on the design review because it looks OK. Let's fix that problem while we've got all the good guys here so you don't flounder with it for another week or two."

What you wanted to do with a design review was double-check that the parts that he thought he had right he did have right and potentially give him some insight on the parts that he didn't. Once I apprehended that—I was only like 20 or 21—that seemed so obviously right, such an obvious good use of the senior talent doing the review.

Of course, the design review for the client is different. The design review for the client is all, "We know it all. It's all going to be perfect." But the internal design review was an opportunity and I was always surprised by how many people were absolutely scared about the prospect of a design review. These are good people but they just said, "My design is going to be torn to shreds." It's hard to convince them that it's won't get torn to shreds if it's any good, that these guys are not vindictive. They're going to try to continue the BBN mystique of getting it all right.

It's also hard to tell them that you will never again in your career get this collection of people willing to spend an hour helping you think through your design. You're going to be on your own after this, and that was just a wonderful experience.

Seibel: How often were these design reviews? At the beginning of a project or throughout?

Cosell: There weren't multiple design reviews; the design review was basically once when the design was considered done.

Seibel: So the design was done before you had really started the coding part?

Cosell: Yeah, right. Yeah. Probably some of the coding had been done because a lot of people, including me, have to start blocking up little bits of code to see how a thing is actually going to work out. But typically we are in a cycle where we have to propose things and then we get funded later to do them. So what we have to do is propose to the client, "This is what we're going to do," and you want a good understanding because the client at this point is going to give you so much time and so much money and expect it to work. So it was typically at that point, we are about to finalize the proposal, we are going to have the technical description of what we're going to do. Now we sit down for the design review to make sure we understand it. I don't recall Frank stepping into contracts once they were afoot. Certainly the projects I was working on I can't remember an ongoing project review including Frank.

Seibel: You just mentioned Doctor. What was that?

Cosell: When I was working on the PDP-1 time-sharing system, Dan Murphy and his friends were working on their PDP-1, bringing up this Lisp system. So I thought I would learn Lisp. That spring, Joe Weizenbaum had written an article for *Communications of the ACM* on ELIZA. I thought that was way cool. And I believed, as I likely still believe now, that anything I can understand, I can make a computer do. He described how ELIZA works and I said, "I bet I could write something to do that." And so I started writing a Lisp program on Dan Murphy's PDP-1 system at BBN. I had a Model 33 Teletype that was in my PDP-1 computer room connected to Dan Murphy's

PDP-1 so I could play on his computer from my computer room and pretend to be working on my system. I wrote that program and got it up and working. Playing with it was an all-BBN project. People would leave me comments: "It would be better if you did this" or, "I tried this, and it didn't work." That actually helped spread Weizenbaum's idea beyond its boundaries. It was written, at first, in the PDP-1 Lisp. But they were building a Lisp on the PDP-6 at that point—or maybe the PDP-10. But it was the Lisp that had spread across the ARPANET. So Doctor went along with it, it turns out.

I got a little glimmer of fame because Danny Bobrow wrote up "A Turing Test Passed". That was one of the first times I actually got some notice for my stupid hacking: I had left Doctor up. And one of the execs at BBN came into the PDP-1 computer room and thought that Danny Bobrow was dialed into that and thought he was talking to Danny. For us folk that had played with ELIZA, we all recognized the responses and we didn't think about how humanlike they were. But for somebody who wasn't real familiar with ELIZA, it seemed perfectly reasonable. It was obnoxious but he actually thought it was Danny Bobrow. "But tell me more about—" "Earlier, you said you wanted to go to the client's place." Things like that almost made sense in context, until eventually he typed something and he forgot to hit the go button, so the program didn't respond. And he thought that Danny had disconnected. So he called Danny up at home and yelled at him. And Danny has absolutely no idea what was going on. Except Danny knew about my terminal. So he came in and tore the typescript off of the thing, to save it.

It was a very slick version of Weizenbaum's thing. We improved the scripts a little bit. Lots of generations of hackers worked on it. And as I say, it traveled around the Net. And now, I guess, there's a version of it written in Emacs macros. But that was my trial by fire in becoming a serious Lisp programmer.

Seibel: So I'm curious—I've observed that often the programmers that write the hairiest, most complicated code are the ones who can keep a ton of details in their mind. You obviously had the ability to keep details in your mind but still cared a lot about making code simple and clear.

Cosell: I have to admit that I did both. I would make things simple in the large. But when I say that programs should be easy, it's not necessarily the case that specific pieces of the functionality of the program have to be easy. I could write some very complicated code to do the right thing, right there, code that people would cringe at and not be willing to touch. But it was always in an encapsulated place.

Most of the bad programs I ran into, the ones where I threw things out and recoded them, there wasn't a little island of complexity you could try to understand and fix, but the complexity had oozed through the program.

I have a couple of rules that I try to impress on people, usually people fresh out of college, who believe that they understand everything there is to know about programming. The first is the idea that there are very few inherently hard programs. If you're looking at a piece of code and it looks very hard—if you can't understand what this thing is supposed to be doing—that's almost always an indication that it was poorly thought through. At that point you don't roll up your sleeves and try to fix the code; you take a step back and think it through again. When you've thought it through enough, you'll find out that it's easy.

We just did that recently at work. They were working on some big design project and it was just getting more and more convoluted. So we had a meeting and started shedding away things. I said, "That seems too complicated." And all of a sudden, we had a block diagram for how the thing would work. And everybody was stunned because they understood how each block could possibly do its job. We hadn't done the dull things where you have to write it all down but they understood that the interfaces were clean and they could make progress. I've done this business long enough to understand that there are some very hard problems. But very few. It's invariably the case that when they think about it harder, it gets easier and all of a sudden it's easy to program correctly.

The other rule is to realize that programs are meant to be read. Even though I'm guilty of writing pages of TECO macros back in my early days, I very quickly—probably when I was working on the PDP-1 time-sharing system and the complexity of the time-sharing system started to sink in—came to the belief that computer-program source code is for people, not for computers. Computers don't care. I think it's a good thing that Perl has both "if" and "unless." Because it turns out that when you're getting an intuition for what something is supposed to be doing, saying "if not some condition" doesn't connote the same idea as saying "unless the condition."

The binary bits are what computers want and the text file is for me. I would get people—bright, really good people, right out of college, tops of their classes—on one of my projects. And they would know all about programming and I would give them some piece of the project to work on. And we would start crossing swords at our project-review meetings. They would say, "Why are you complaining about the fact that I have my global variables here, that I'm not doing this, that you don't like the way the subroutines are laid out? The program works."

They'd be stunned when I tell them, "I don't care that the program works. The fact that you're working here at all means that I expect you to be able to write programs that work. Writing programs that work is a skilled craft and you're good at it. Now, you have to learn how to program." Some of these guys were fabulously good programmers and they'd never once read a line of anybody else's code. In fact, some of them never even read their own code, so they never had the pain of seeing what happens six months later.

Some would rebel. Some were absolutely convinced that they were good programmers and I was just some over-the-hill old guy that didn't know what he was doing. I know I would have said the same thing not long ago: "The program works. What is your problem?" When I say, "You don't get credit because the program works. We're going to the next level. Working programs are a given," they say, "Oh." Then they talk to other people and discover that that's basically the BBN standard. You can't explore a new idea in doing something if you are not craftsman enough to make the computer do what you had in your mind.

I had a preference of how I liked my global variables and how I liked my subroutines organized and I got into a multiday battle with one guy where he said, "Look, it works just fine" and he was such a good programmer that I didn't want to pull rank. I felt it important that he understand that I was not just being a tyrannical turkey; that there was a reason why I wanted him to do it this other way. He didn't realize how hard it is to understand a program with a single C subroutine that's 42 pages of code long.

Seibel: Yikes!

Cosell: I argued with him because I'm a big fan of call-once subroutines where the only function of the subroutine is to abstract some little part of a parent subroutine. When you read the parent subroutine—in my approach to programming—and you get to this place in the code and you get distracted with the details of this big nexus of stuff, I like to pull that whole clump out. Now you have a single thing that says, "Sort the table and find the best route," even though this is the only place it's called. Someone optimizing the code would say, "That shouldn't be a subroutine. Put that in line." But it's a little subroutine where I can isolate it. It's obvious what the inputs are. You can see the algorithm, and only be concerned with that. He hated when I used to say, "Your routines are too complicated. Your routines are spanning big chunks of the design" He'd say, "That's OK because I can do it all in one routine."

He rebelled but eventually he did it my way. Then the next task he had was to take a big piece of code from one of the programmers working on an earlier effort and make it fit into our system. He worked on that for almost a week. He so hated the other guy's program that he complained to my boss that there aren't strict enough programming standards in the division. And the other guy was programming the way he had wanted to program but with a different spin. So he saw what happens when one very intense, very good programmer doesn't segment it down. You get one very long program—it's not that the program was spaghetti code but there were just so many levels of complexity in this one linear suite. He almost pissed me off because, as I say, he went over my head to demand that the department had to have standards to not allow that thing to happen.

Seibel: Not realizing that his own previous code would've probably fallen afoul of the same standards?

Cosell: No. He got that. He was a convert. It's sort of like the guys who give up smoking and are the most pains in the butt about other people still smoking. He became one of the strongest guys on my project. He used to nag me when I wasn't careful enough—when I compromised. My project was the first project of its type he had ever worked on. Communications, real time, all this stuff—all new to him. But he was a smart guy and he went through this little epiphany and came out of it the programmer I always thought he was going to be. Last I heard, he was doing wonderfully. With him it worked out. Other people didn't like working with me because they found me too overbearing; I can't imagine why.

Seibel: Did you have particular rules for how much or how little to comment?

Cosell: I don't put a lot of comments in my code because I think you should be writing your code so that it is readable and your algorithms and thoughts are clear in the code. I put comments that say this routine is supposed to do this, and usually some description of how you call it—what do you do when you get exceptions, what the order of the arguments is, and things like that. But the code itself should clearly express what you are doing.

The only place I tend to put comments in my code is when my instinct says, "This particular piece of code, even though it works, doesn't clearly state what I'm trying to accomplish." And so I put a comment in the code to say, "This code sorts the table," if it may not look like your standard table-sorting code because, as it turns out, I can take advantage of something.

I have never been a fan of structured programming listings where every subroutine has to have 18 lines of comment at the beginning and the arguments are in the right order. I don't do a consistent segmentation of my programs. Some of my subroutines are complicated and some are simple. I do worry about things like layout; I'm part of the contingent that argues about curly braces.

One of the reasons is because I read code to understand what it does as opposed to reading code to see what each little piece of it is. So when I see an `if` statement, for example, I see the condition. I'm now thinking yea or nay on that condition, and if I want to skip the `if` statement I like having a program organization that lets my eye flip down to the end of the `if` statement without me having to process a lot of syntax. So I'm one of those old-fashioned guys that likes lined-up, open and close braces.

If you made column five go away, my code would look like, "operator, open brace, close brace; operator, open brace, close brace," which lets me see the sequence of operators. Another part of that is related to something I mentioned before: if the open brace is too far from the close brace then often it's doing too much, in which case I can pull it out. Sometimes even if it's not doing too much I'll still pull it out because I can't apprehend what that little branch is doing if there's too much crap in there.

I try very hard to hide the crap, to move the crap someplace so that I can follow the flow of the code, so I can build the picture in my head of what the code is doing. I have a lot of trouble reading some programming styles because I have too much trouble trying to absorb the block structure. It's interesting that the guy that did Python was clearly of a similar mind. He eliminated the syntax wars because he doesn't have open and close braces. When you see an `if` the open curly brace is always there implicitly and the closed curly brace is also implicitly there and if you need to find the next thing, it's lined up under the `if`. I use an editor in C and in Perl, and I assume that editors in Python do the same thing, where you can click on a button and it shrinks the whole thing so you only see the outer structure.

I don't like to fight these style wars on the basis that one style is ugly. I like to believe I fight the style wars is because it interferes with me understanding the code. I was always pretty good at that. Unless you could convince me you're better at understanding code than I am, you have a tough fight convincing me your way is better.

Seibel: Certainly coming in cold to new code and debugging it is a particular skill that not every good programmer has, which it sounds like you did.

Cosell: Indeed. And there are two aspects of that. There was another guy. His name was Steve Butterfield. And he was also a good fixer, but the antithesis of me. Steve was about the best I have seen at not having any clue how a program worked and fixing it. He could dive into a program and change some little ugly piece down in the bowels of the code to make it do something different. Big, complicated programs, Steve could leap in and fix little things leaving them, to my view, functionally better but worse off.

I always tried to make the whole program better and that would often mean that even though there was one little problem, I would try to understand the whole program. I would try to find the problem by reasoning down from the top and finding it as opposed to saying, "Oh, this isn't working. Do surgery here." So there were some things where I just took too long and spent too much time trying to import the whole thing into my head, when a more directed approach just to go fix it would do.

But usually when Steve left a project, it was hard to revise the code to make it do stuff. Whereas I tried to keep things good, but it meant that if a program was really big and awful, I would spend a lot of time spinning my wheels before I felt comfortable diving in. But that didn't happen very often because often when I debug things, I don't do it by debugging.

As I mentioned before, there were many bugs that I never had any clue where they were. I just get to a point where I say, "This piece of code is supposed to be doing this. This does not look like it's doing that. I mean, how could anybody have written this complicated bit of code to do this simple thing?" So I'd rip it out and replace it with a routine that does the simple thing I thought that piece of code was supposed to do. And the program magically works. In retrospect, what had happened is that the program had evolved and this little routine kept getting changed. Rather than being replaced when the program evolved, somebody was patching it to do different things and missed once.

I never debugged any of that stuff. I hack on it for a day or two doing all of this typing and nobody would have a clue of what I'm doing and the program would get fixed. What a debugger! That is very dangerous because Will's dictum is basically right, that if you rewrite a hundred lines of code, you may well have fixed the one bug and introduced six new ones. And at least the one bug you, knew what to look for; you now have to start looking for the six new ones. And I was just fortunate because I had a very good track record over the years of managing to write code that, for the most part, worked.

Seibel: So you must have had some strategies for reading code. Even if there's no bug but just a big pile of code that you're going to work on, how did you tackle that?

Cosell: Not very well, it turns out. One of the reasons why I tend to rewrite chunks of code rather than fix them is because I reach points where I can't manage to figure it out anymore. I don't read the code as if it were a book. I try to figure out what the program is doing and then get hints about the code from the top down.

In parallel with reading the program I think about how would I solve this problem. Which means I'm looking for certain specific pieces so I can say, "Oh, here's where the program does it." Then I can say, in my usual arrogant way, that the guy that wrote this did it wrong. Or at least I now understand that they're doing this some other way.

So I would go top-down. But some of the guys I knew were spectacularly good at bottom-up. They would start reading little subroutines and eventually find the one subroutine they needed. But mostly for those kinds of things I was a top-down kind of guy. That is, I'm looking at the program trying to figure out what the other programmers *should* have done. That was one of the things that led me to sometimes fix bugs where I didn't know what the bug was. I'd hit a place where I say, "This piece of code—as I understand this program now—is supposed to be doing this" and then either the code I'm looking at doesn't do that or the code is so complicated and seems to be doing six other things and it's not making sense to me.

In either case my usual response at that point is to fix that piece of code so that it agrees with what I thought was supposed to be happening there in the program. You can see how fabulously dangerous that can be because there is no one correct way to organize a program and if the program was perfectly well organized but in a different way than I wanted, I have now just killed the program and now have an incredible avalanche of stuff to fix. But I was pretty lucky with that. Usually when I said, "This looks wrong and I'm going to fix it" it got fixed. And that was even true from the early days.

The first big program I worked on, the PDP-1 time-sharing system, I was just a raw programmer doing college-undergrad programming problems and I moved through the hospital project very quickly, from doing applications to coming under the wing of the systems guys. Even though I was six months into being a professional programmer I was perfectly willing to say that this little piece of the remote process swapper doesn't look like it's right and I would rewrite it.

Seibel: In addition to the danger of introducing new bugs, another risk is that you may have misapprehended what the program is supposed to do.

Cosell: That's right. The path I took was, if you will, not for the faint at heart. At the time I was 19 years old and that seemed like the only way to do things. I had two convictions, which actually served me well: that programs ought to make sense and there are very, very few inherently hard problems. Anything that looks really hard or tricky is probably more the product of the programmer not fully understanding what they needed to do and pounding it with a hammer 'til they got code that looked like it did the right thing.

I don't know why I had those two convictions. I arrived at BBN with no skill per se, but I had those principles in the back of my head for some reason. I thought I ought to be able to understand anything and it shouldn't be so hard. I found that even for the time-sharing system and the IMPs—for all of those class of programs, that proved to be true. In general once I had the right understanding of what a program was supposed to do, the pieces would fall into place. The pieces that didn't belong would stand out like a miscolored piece in a jigsaw puzzle.

Another principle was I always wanted clean listings. I wanted the thing to be just right. When you have to fix a bug in a program you never, ever fix the bug in the place where you find it. My rule is, "If you knew then what you know now about the fact that this piece of code is broken, how would you have organized this piece of the routine?" What were you thinking about wrong before? Fix the code so that can't happen. When you finish with a routine I want every routine you work on to look as if it was just written. I do not want to see any evidence of afterthoughts or things gone wrong followed by something to correct the error or a mysterious piece of code saying, "This routine returns the wrong value every now and then so I've got to fix it." I don't want to see any of that. I want to see code that looks like through some divine inspiration you got it exactly right the first time.

Then I compound that with one other little trick. I got this when I was working on D.O.D. projects. They'll never fund a new project. Both BBN and the government have too much invested in the current program, even when it has limitations that are awful that need to be fixed. The most common one is something that you did that was right when the program started is now hopelessly wrong because the program's use or requirements or something have evolved. What you'd like to do is rip out that part of the program and just fix it. And they say, "What is that going to improve?" You say, "It's not going to improve anything but it'll make the program better for next week." Not going to get permission to do that.

The method I took is the sneaky way and this has worked very well for me for a lot of programs. I do a design of the future version of the program. Knowing what I know now, this is how the program would have looked, now at the program level rather than at a subroutine level. Now when you go to fix a bug and you have a choice on how to fix it, fix it moving toward the better model. Don't just fix it in the shortest way. Don't just fix it in the way that fits, but move it toward the other model so that over several months instead of the program getting more and more mired in patches fixing up the stuff that was old and wrong, all the critical parts of the program all of a sudden look like they're the new way of doing things. Often you can get to the point where there are so few places left that still do things the old way that you can slip in and get those fixed because you're now not damaging the whole program.

So when they ask, "How long is it going to take you to put this change in?" you have three answers. The first is the absolute shortest way, changing the one line of code. The second answer is how long it would be using my simple rule of rewriting the subroutine as if you were not going to make that mistake. Then the third answer is how long if you fix that bug if you were actually writing this subroutine in the better version of the program. So you make your estimate someplace between those last two and then every time you get assigned a task you have a little bit of extra time available to make the program better. I think that that makes an incredible difference. It makes for programs that evolve cleanly. It's amazing to have a program that's still in version one but it's like Washington's hammer. It's now a really sleek new thing because all the key parts have gotten fixed without any project manager having to actually authorize you to go rip out the guts and go fix it.

Seibel: Have you heard of refactoring?

Cosell: No, what is that?

Seibel: What you just described. I think now there's perhaps a bit more acceptance, even among the project managers of this idea.

Cosell: Oh, that's good because I used to need a bug that—I used to need a reason to change the piece of the code to do what you just said because I could never get permission just to rewrite it to make it cleaner. So I would have to wait till a bug or an improvement request came along touching that part of code, but then I would do exactly that. I guess the thing about refactoring is that you have spend some time thinking about what the right target is because it won't do to refactor and have different people aiming in different directions or to have the target not be the right thing.

I never did that with a name; it just seemed like the only way I could do two things: manage the complexity *and* get a program that you didn't have to throw out and code over. The PDP-1 taught me that. It ran for a lot of years and it was such a huge project. It took three or four guys to write the first two versions of it and there was no way to throw it out, but it had to get better.

Seibel: How do you hire programmers? How do you recognize the talented ones?

Cosell: I couldn't ever get into the standard interviewing paradigm. People talk about—and I think Microsoft was famous for this—giving them little problems to solve. I seem to have taken a more intuitive approach. I basically glanced at the guy's—or girl's—résumé to get a feel for whether they felt like my type of person. Often the résumés were useless because they were just college seniors about to graduate. You read between the lines that this fancy-looking project was really a class project for some course in something or other. But I used to talk to them and just get a feel whether they had somehow the kind of inquiring, curious, precise kind of mind that I had grown to expect people around me to have.

What were their other interests, their nonprofessional interests? Did they show both aptitude for picking things up, and curiosity? It was kind of slapdash how I did all of that. I had this idealized image of a BBN-quality person, some vague thing about aptitude, curiosity, quickness of learning, interested in lots of different things, and kind of broadly based. I used to go on a hunt to see if I got the impression that this person was going to be BBN-quality folk.

Seibel: As you mentioned, Microsoft is famous for asking puzzle-type questions. And you like puzzles. What do you think of that as a way of gauging someone's potential?

Cosell: Carefully chosen, I think it has potential. Not because the person solves the puzzle, but if it gives you a glimmer as to how they organize something to approach it. I have never used it. I would certainly not have handed somebody one of the little tchotchke puzzles and watched them while they tried to put it back together again. The problem is that a lot of these puzzles require different styles of solution, and either you know that or you don't. That's not so good because I don't want somebody who's really good at doing a sliding-block puzzle because they happen to know some good tricks for doing that.

BBN spent a lot of its time sailing in unknown waters, doing things that hadn't been done, that we didn't know how to do. And that requires both a degree of daring, because it's not so easy, and a degree of skill in order to not founder. That's the kind of thing I'm looking for, not looking for somebody with a knack for solving a particular puzzle but, thrown into this complicated thing that they have a need to deal with, can they approach it reasonably?

A case in point was when the Rubik's Cubes arrived. We had just heard rumors about this wonderful puzzle and one of the guys was on a business trip to England and brought back a satchel of them. No books, no documentation, not yet a phenomenon in the U.S. at all. Just a strange little group theoretic puzzle. And we started to play with it. Several of us solved the puzzle in different ways, but it was interesting that we were able to cope with a puzzle like that. It's just that that group of BBN people back then had the right stuff. That was what I used to look for.

I don't know whether Microsoft's little quizzes—and I've heard that Google has an aptitude test too, or something—I don't know if those can give you a hint that this person has the right spark. But that's what I used to look for. Does this person look like they're ready to be BBN-quality folk? Often I would say no. They're perfectly good, they're terrific engineers, but as we're talking I'm not getting that spark. My approach was to look for the spark, and I don't know how I did it.

Seibel: Do you think programming is a young person's game?

Cosell: I think that may be the case. I can even see, as I look back at some of the projects I worked on toward the end of my career at BBN, that the people I had doing the work for me were doing things that I couldn't possibly have done. One of the guys working for me thought that using Tcl would be a neat thing for part of the interface, so in a day and a half he learned enough Tcl to bring the thing up and make it work, which I don't think I could've done. It was amusing for me to think in the back of my head, "Gee, I used to be able to do things like that."

I think that the actual production of code—of working, logical, good code—requires an intensity and a mental agility in terms of picking up new things that I, at least, find hard to do now. The other side of the coin is that you get a certain wisdom about things that you certainly didn't have when you were younger. I know better now how to do things. So I find a better mix is to be able to give young and active people guidance. I think that by and large the sort of programming that I've been talking about is similar to the old saw about mathematics, that most mathematicians do most of their best work well before they're 30. The kind of intensity, the kind of focus that you need to do really cutting-edge mathematics is probably similar to what you need to do the kind of crazy programming I used to do back when I was young.

Seibel: One part of the intensity is that it's simply physically draining to work long hours. Are long hours necessary or are they just a side effect of the fact that we love it?

Cosell: I think that's a personality side effect. The question of whether you can put something down and come back to it or whether you are compelled to stick with it and finish it is more of a personality thing. There were certainly many people I knew of at BBN out in the brilliant end of the spectrum who were perfectly able to work normal hours and not be interested in coming in on weekends. Then, of course, there were the other people who were at the lunatic fringe—for a while I was sleeping in the computer room because it took me too long to drive back to my apartment. I would just take a nap in the computer room and I have no idea how crazy people thought I was for doing that. But I don't think that is necessary; I think it's a byproduct of the fact that doing the kind of thing that we do is pretty exciting, especially when it starts to come together.

One of the really good guys at BBN ended up working a perfectly normal schedule *and* finished his PhD dissertation just by being astoundingly disciplined. He worked every Saturday on his thesis and he worked evenings on this and that. Part of it, I guess, is being organized. It is much easier to do something if you can do it all the way through, at which point you don't have to think about being organized or careful or putting it down and picking it back up, because when you're done you can forget about it. I've been learning that recently since my life is more normal now. I program around the cracks, putting things down and picking things back up. I find that if I don't work on it again for two to three weeks it's surprisingly hard to pick it back up. Often when I am lagging on some little personal programming thing and I really want to get it done, I try to say, "OK, I'm going to be like the people who exercise. I'm going to do it a couple hours every morning." That mostly doesn't work for me. What happens is at some point I get bored with having it not be done and I'll spend a day or two on it and get it done.

I can, in bursts, get the kind of focus I used to have, but not so well anymore. So I think that makes this kind of special, fancy programming—what the true hackers do—more of a young person's game. I have to admit almost all of the people I know who did stellar things when they were young did it intensely. It's hard for me to think of any folks in the really stellar category who did it just a couple hours a day as if it were a job. Almost everyone I know would do it with this burst of maniacal focus and intensity and then get it done. But the focus is hard. It really wears you out. It certainly used to wear me out.

Seibel: Would you consider yourself a scientist, an engineer, an artist, a craftsman, or something else?

Cosell: A blend of those, obviously. I don't consider myself a scientist, as I understand what scientists do. I'd like to believe I consider myself a combination of an artist and a craftsman. The way I do engineering is as a combination of art and craft.

Seibel: Let me first ask about the engineering part. There are certainly folks, like Watts Humphrey and the folks at the Software Engineering Institute, who say programming should be an engineering discipline just like building bridges. People can build bridges and they can predict how long it's going to take, and the bridges, for the most part, don't fall down.

Cosell: Exactly right. The analogy is very good except they put a non sequitur in the middle of it. It turns out that the guy that designs the bridge so it won't fall down is not the guy that strings the cables or that inspects the cables to make sure the steel was right or pours the concrete or does any of those other things.

Programming is in that regard an engineering discipline. You have to know what to do. You have to know what your capabilities are. At the level I was working, I had to be able to envision how the pieces were going to fit together. I had to have some intuition for what things were fast and what things were slow, what things were hard to build, what things were easy to build, and come up with, at the engineering level, a model of what I thought was going to happen.

The artist part decides that the design should be elegant. Those fit together because in computer programs the artistry affects the longevity of it. Part of what I call the artistry of the computer program is how easy it is for future people to be able to change it without breaking it. That doesn't have anything to do with constructing its functionality but with its life as an existing thing.

Seibel: So for you the beauty of code is tied up with the fact that people are going to have to change it.

Cosell: One or two things I wrote were black boxes that just had to run as long as the computer cycled, but most of them were code that generations of people were able to hammer on and mostly not keep breaking. When I talk about the artistry and the beauty of it, what I'm talking about is the idea that when you write a program you have a huge amount of discretion. How you organize your routines, how you lay them out on the page, where you decide to put comments, how you name your variables, whether you like your subroutines to all have uniform calling sequences or situational-appropriate code.

So you have to look at the program through the eyes of a new programmer sometime down the road. What's the structure of the program? What are you doing? How are you doing it? And why are you doing it? The artistry is how the next guy that reads the program and understands that this subroutine was supposed to do this—he gets the message that it's not right for him to go and muck it up to do something else and that he should keep the structure of the program.

Seibel: What about the tension between clarity and efficiency? Sometimes the simplest, easiest-to-read code isn't the fastest.

Cosell: Programmers are the worst optimizers in the world. They always optimize the part of the code that's most interesting to optimize, and almost never get the part of the code that actually needs optimization. So you get these little nuts of very difficult code that have no point. I always tell the people working with me, "Code it as lucidly, as easy to read, as crystal-clear as you can. Do it the simple way. And then if it needs to be sped up, we'll deal with that later. If you've done it right, we can draw a little box around this piece."

Eons ago one of the versions of Emacs had one page of the source code that was a gigantic skull and crossbones in comments that said something like: "Seriously twisted code follows this thing." It was some piece of the innermost guts of the search code or something like that that they had optimized the hell out of. That's a place where I can see that this piece is really tough. So there's a big black box around it saying, "Don't stray in here, unless you know what you're doing."

But programs we write these days are bigger and clumsier, in terms of the elegance I learned when I was doing PDP-1, and slower. And that's fine. It turns out it doesn't matter. Now, the guys doing video synthesis and the guys doing the CGI animation stuff, clearly those guys don't have that luxury. That takes some beaucoup careful programming. I could not do that anymore; I am way over the hill for that. But I could do that once. And I understand the guys that do that. But most of the programs we do are just routine crap.

At some college they had a two-semester course from September right through May and you had you work on some fairly hard program at the beginning. What they didn't warn you was in April they were going to make you work on the program again, having now really run you through the hoops on other things. The idea was for you to be stunned at how hard it was to remember whatever it was you thought you understood perfectly clearly just six months ago.

Seibel: So all that stuff that you did at the last weekend before it was due comes back to haunt you.

Cosell: That's right. I thought that was a brilliant scheme. It's teaching them a lesson that is hard to get except in the real world.

Seibel: When I talked to Ken Thompson I asked him about whether there were inherent problems in C that lead to security problems and he basically said that's not the problem. You teach courses on computer security—what do you think of that?

Cosell: I would hate to cross swords with him, but I say in my computer-security class that the biggest security problem to befall modern computers is C. It was designed to be a systems-programming language and it was such a comfortable systems-programming language that all the hotshots used it. We built operating systems out of it. We built real-time systems out of it.

I remember the wars in the days of Pascal. The argument was that computers should help you; that C was too dangerous a language. The two big voices I remember were Wirth and Dijkstra. On the other side was every systems programmer I know, including me. I wrote everything in C. So C sort of steamrolled the zillions of languages back then.

The government tried mandate Ada and they wouldn't let contracts unless they were in Ada. C steamrolled over those. It was just amazing. But as I look at it now, I am still stunned almost every day that it borders on the impossible to write a program of any real complexity in C and not have a security problem. The amount of care it takes for a programmer to never do a read into a buffer without explicitly making sure it can't run over the end of the buffer, to never free a block of memory at the wrong time so a pointer way elsewhere in the program becomes stale, to never store something that's the wrong size and happens to step on the next value—those problems can be so hard to find.

It has been such a boon in systems programming. The idea that we would write our systems in assembler and all our applications in Pascal sent shivers down my spine. I don't think that was the right answer. But writing both systems and applications in C, I would have to say has proven just not to work very well. It's just too hard.

It's kind of like the problems we had with interrupt bugs. You could argue that there's no real magic in writing a program with sequence breaks or interrupts. There's no real problem with that. It takes a little bit of understanding and a little bit of care. But I know for a fact that very good programmers who understand all of that put those bugs in their programmer. A programmer like me would have to come and fix it and I had to do the Niklaus Wirth–style thing of inventing the computer language that wouldn't let them make interrupt bugs.

For the IMP system I wrote a complicated set of assembler macros, so you could declare what you were doing. When you came in on an interrupt, you wrote a declaration that says, "I am on modem input" or "I am on the high-priority clock or the low-priority clock." And then when it assembled your program, it actually tagged every instruction with which interrupt level it was running on and then there was a postprocessor that I probably wrote in TECO macros, honest to God, that processed that and looked for time-sharing problems. It would look for a variable that was accessed by two different levels and it would say, "There is an interrupt conflict." Now all of a sudden, the time-sharing bug would go away. Other programmers could understand that if they put the right declarations in, these macros would keep them from making timing bugs. I got a trip to Hungary to present how you could get programmers who don't really understand real-time issues to be able to write solid real-time programs by using this technique to abstract out the conflict problems.

That's a little bit the way I feel about C. I'm sure that there are good programmers, perhaps including me, who can write good C programs. But it's just harder than it has to be. In the modern environment it's gotten harder because the environment is so much more difficult—the number of places where C's weaknesses can be exploited or overlooked, the amount of care it takes. That's one reason why I'm very comfortable writing in Perl. Perl is slow. I'm sure it's one of the slower languages, but in essence it repairs all of the security problems of programming in C. What happens when you index off the end of the array in Perl? It makes more array.

It knows what its pointers point to, so you can never misreference a pointer because you only say to go through it and it tells you where it's going. So I'm much more comfortable building security-necessary applications in Perl because I have a world full of Perl people pounding on the core and it's been stable for so many years. I don't think we're going to find too many allocate bugs or pointer bugs, and they're hard to exploit from random Perl code anyway. I don't have to trust the programmers around me to get every pointer check right.

And even then we get programs like the classic one where somebody wrote a web page that was looking up somebody in a table and some hacker put something in the input that looked like, "Joe;drop all tables." That still happens. That's obviously not C's fault, but it shows programmers just can't be careful enough. They don't see all the places. And C makes too many places. Too scary for me, and I guess it's fair to say I've programmed C only about five years less than Ken has. We're not in the same league, but I have a long track record with C and know how difficult it is and I think C is a big part of the problem.

As these applications get more complicated, and built on more and more complicated libraries—and nobody will ever understand the security cracks in the libraries because they're so immensely complicated—probably we'll have to move toward application-development languages that are more fault-free. Processors are becoming blindingly fast and memory is becoming ridiculously cheap. I don't know what tomorrow's language is. I don't think C or its derivatives such as C++ are going to really be the right vehicle for heavy-duty program application—even system development—going forward.

Java didn't feel right. My old reflexes hit me. Java struck me as too authoritarian. That's one of the reasons why I mentioned that Perl felt so good, because it's got the safety and the checks but it is so damn multidimensioned that the artist part of me has a lot of free board to express things clearly and to think about the right way to do things. I have some freedom.

When I first messed with Java—this was when it was little baby language, of course—I said, "Oh, this is just another one of those languages to help not-so-good programmers go down the straight and narrow by restricting what they can do." But maybe we've come to a point where that's the right thing. Maybe the world has gotten so dangerous you can't have a good, flexible language that one percent or two percent of the programmers will use to make great art because the world is now populated with 75 million run-of-the-mill programmers building these incredibly complicated applications and they need more help than that. So maybe Java's the right thing. I don't know.

Seibel: When I spoke with Fran Allen, who worked at IBM on Fortran compilers, she was quite upset about C from a completely different perspective, which was it made it impossible to write really highly optimizing compilers because it was so low-level.

Cosell: Now, she's in a different camp. She's working on compilers; she sees C as this awful, clunky step down that you can't do anything with. Whereas we were working with bit-twiddling assemblers and C was like a breath of fresh air. So of course most of the very best programmers back then were not the guys writing BASIC programs and not so much writing Fortran programs doing calculations. The real heavy hitters were of course the guys doing all the assembly code. So we went to C because C was like breath of fresh of air. If you think C has problems with array checks, try writing your array loops in assembler. So in that regard, it was a great boon.

I don't want to say that C has outlived its usefulness, but I think it was used by too many good programmers so that now not-good-enough programmers are using it to build applications and the bottom line is they're not good enough and they can't. Maybe C is the perfect language for really good systems programmers, but unfortunately not-so-good systems and applications programmers are using it and they shouldn't be.

Seibel: Do you think that the nature of programming has changed as a consequence of the fact that we can't know how it all works anymore?

Cosell: Oh, yeah. That's another thing that makes me a little bit more dinosaurlike. Everything builds assuming what came before. I remember on our old PDP-11, 7th edition Unix, we were doing some animation and graphics. That was a big deal. It was hard to program. The displays weren't handy. There were no libraries.

Each generation of programmers gets farther and farther away from the low-level stuff and has fancier and fancier tools for doing things. The good part is they can do cleverer things. The baseline is so good that the next thing is spectacular and that then becomes the baseline and two years later it becomes even better. The trouble is that these baselines are getting more and more complicated. The PDP-1 instruction set was like a walk in the park compared to some of the stuff that's happening.

I would hate to be the guys at Microsoft who have to build these operating systems that run on the quad-core multiprocessor. Video cards have grown to the point where they have multiple megs of memory, and complete pipeline parallel processors on them that can do array and vector things on the fly. So you now use your video card as this very fancy data processor. I keep thinking how hard it must be to program these things.

We had a thing called an IMLAC, which is one of the early machines that actually had a nice integrated vector display on it the way the old PDP-1 did but it was a mini computer. There was a program for that that had you sitting on a little cart doing a 3-D display of a maze. So you saw the walls coming by. You could peek around corners. I was fascinated because it did hidden-line suppression. This is in the era where guys are writing articles in *Communications of the ACM* about algorithms. I have a whole book about how to use symmetric coordinates and somebody's algorithm for figuring out where two lines cross so you know where a line crosses a plane so you know that that's where you have to stop the line because it now becomes hidden.

Doing the hidden-line thing was a big deal back then and that program did it. I was just stunned by that program. That was big deal code—singular stuff. Now, as far as I can tell, the video cards take 3-D coordinates and the video cards do the hidden-line suppression. Eight, nine years ago things like texture mapping and ray tracing were big deals. Hard to do in code. It took your program hours to get the glint off of a sphere.

And now I discover that video cards do the ray tracing. So on the one hand you have these guys working at NVIDIA and stuff who must be doing incredibly complicated stuff and you have the modern programmer who no longer can be content just writing a thing with little line-drawn walls—he has to master this incredible 3-D video environment that's built on libraries that have gotten more and more complicated. They're easier than it would be to write the code yourself, but I can't fathom how people can absorb all of that these days. It just seems so huge to me.

I run into that just with doing Tk. I've been trying to do a little Tk program and I am stunned by how complicated Tk is and how many hooks it's got, and it's what you need to do in order to make the button be bigger or smaller or here or there. Mastering that thing is just a huge thing. Understanding the PDP-1 time-sharing system was simple by comparison.

So I don't envy modern programmers, and it's going to get worse. The simple things are getting packaged into libraries, leaving only the hard things. That stuff is getting so complicated, but the standards that people are expecting are stunning. One of the ones they showed me stunned me. He was showing me Google Maps that will do routes for you. One of the things you can do is you can grab a piece of the route with your mouse and drag that piece of the route somewhere else to tell Google that you want the route go there. Then it remaps the route so that it goes through where you just dragged the point. Now I know what's going on in there: a pile of JavaScript code for the mouse tracking. When you let go of the mouse it has to do an Ajax XML request to tell momma system that he just put this point on the route. The route then has to do incremental updates. Calculating the route. I can't even imagine how they do that code so well. People complain that you get routed through people's backyards and stuff like that, but the optimal-route problems are one of the classic problems of computer science. How to take this arbitrary graph and find the shortest path through a graph. Just stunning.

At one level I'm thinking, "This is way cool that you can do that." The other level, the programmer in me is saying, "Jesus, I'm glad that this wasn't around when I was a programmer." I could never have written all this code to do this stuff. How do these guys do that? There must be a generation of programmers way better than what I was when I was a programmer. I'm glad I can have a little bit of repute as having once been a good programmer without having to actually demonstrate it anymore, because I don't think I could.

This is a good time to be an over-the-hill programmer emeritus, because you have a few props because you did it once, but the world is so wondrous that you can take advantage of it, maybe even get a little occasional credit for it without having to still be able to do it. Whereas if you were in college—if you major in computer science and you have to go out there and you have to figure out how you are going to add to this pile of stuff—save me.

CHAPTER

15

Donald Knuth

Of all the subjects of this book, Donald Knuth perhaps least needs an introduction. For the past four decades he has been at work on his multivolume masterwork The Art of Computer Programming, the bible of fundamental algorithms and data structures, which American Scientist included on its list of the top 12 physical-sciences monographs of the century, in the company of works by Russell and Whitehead, Einstein, Dirac, Feynman, and von Neumann. He popularized the use of asymptotic (a.k.a. Big-O) notation in analyzing algorithms, invented LR parsing, and defended goto statements from Dijkstra's criticism.

But he is not simply a theorist. After finishing Volume III of The Art of Computer Programming in 1976, Knuth took what was supposed to be a year off to write the typesetting software TeX and METAFONT so he could see his books typeset to his own satisfaction. Ten years later he was done, having along the way invented a new style of programming, "literate programming," and an algorithm for breaking paragraphs of text into lines for typesetting that is still pretty much the state of the art.

His numerous awards have included the first Association for Computing Machinery Grace Murray Hopper Award (1971), the Turing Award (1974), and the National Medal of Science (1979). In 1990 he stopped using email, explaining that his job was not "to be on top of things" but "to be on the bottom of things" deeply understanding and explaining large areas of computer science so he could explain them in his books.

In this interview we talked about Knuth's enthusiasm for literate programming, his ambivalence about black boxes, and what he sees as a regrettable "overemphasis on reusable software."

Seibel: When did you learn to program?

Knuth: I was a freshman at Case Institute of Technology. This was the fall of 1956 and during that quarter or semester they got a computer.

Seibel: This was the IBM 650?

Knuth: It was the 650, yeah. That was the first computer that they made more than a hundred of. I think they had thousands of them but maybe not ten thousand. But it was the first mass-produced computer, so even Case got one.

I was employed in the statistics lab sorting cards. I would tabulate data for the statisticians and that helped supplement my scholarship. There was this room on the first floor with a window in it and you could see this machine behind the window with lights flashing. It looked pretty fascinating.

One afternoon a guy from the lab went to the blackboard and was explaining to the three of us freshmen what this machine did. I found a manual for the machine and they had example ten-line programs. It seemed to me they were kind of stupid—it looked like there was a way to improve even those little programs.

And it turned out it was possible to go at night and touch the machine. This was unusual. I think Dartmouth and Case were the only universities that let undergraduates touch machines. Other places they had professionals and you submitted decks of cards and got your answers the next day. But at Case it was hands-on. They just said, "Oh, yeah, watch out for this; you don't want to do that; it'll mess up the machine," so we had a really nice chance to play with it.

Anyway, I got to see if one of my little changes to the program would also work, and it did. So I said, "My goodness, this is pretty amazing. I'm only a freshman and I can do better than what was in this book—this might be something I have talent for." Well, it turned out I did have a talent for it but not in the way I thought, because almost anybody in the world could have done better than that program in that particular manual.

The machine was a decimal machine, so it wasn't quite as strange as if I had to learn binary arithmetic, although I played with binary arithmetic a little bit when I was in high school. But the fact that it was decimal made it somehow more human or something—comfortable. I can still remember the machine language—*sixty-five is reset-add-lower*—it helps me making up passwords and things now.

Seibel: Uh-oh; you just revealed your secret there.

Knuth: Yeah, right. Then I decided I would write a little program to calculate the prime factors of a number. It was about 100 lines long. I would come at night when nobody else was using the machine, and debug it. And I found more than 100 bugs in my 100-line program. But 2 weeks later I had a program that would find prime factors of any 10-digit number that you dialed into the console switches.

That was how I learned programming—basically taking one program that I made up myself and sitting at a machine over a period of some weeks, and kept getting it to work a little better and a little better.

My second program was converting between binary and decimal. But my third program was a program to play tic-tac-toe and that was what really made me a programmer.

I had to use data structures for that. I made three versions of tic-tac-toe, one of which was self-learning so that it would start out knowing nothing about the game and then it would remember every time it lost a game that the moves it made were suspicious and the moves that the opponent made were good, and it would upgrade the quality of certain positions and downgrade the quality of other positions, and then after you played 400 games it would do a fairly decent job of tic-tac-toe.

Seibel: It seems a lot of the people I've talked to had direct access to a machine when they were starting out. Yet Dijkstra has a paper I'm sure you're familiar with, where he basically says we shouldn't let computer-science students touch a machine for the first few years of their training; they should spend all their time manipulating symbols.

Knuth: But that's not the way he learned either. He said a lot of really great things and inspirational things, but he's not always right. Neither am I, but my take on it is this: Take a scientist in any field. The scientist gets older and says, "Oh, yes, some of the things that I've been doing have a really great payoff and other things, I'm not using anymore. I'm not going to have my students waste time on the stuff that doesn't make giant steps. I'm not going to talk about low-level stuff at all. These theoretical concepts are really so powerful—that's the whole story. Forget about how I got to this point."

I think that's a fundamental error made by scientists in every field. They don't realize that when you're learning something you've got to see something at all levels. You've got to see the floor before you build the ceiling. That all goes into the brain and gets shoved down to the point where the older people forget that they needed it.

Seibel: I've asked the people I've talked to for this book about how much they've read *The Art of Computer Programming*. Most have used it as a reference but a few said they've read it cover to cover. Should every programmer be able to read your books? It's pretty mathematically intense stuff.

Knuth: I sometimes wonder if *I* can read them. I'm trying to organize a lot of wisdom that surrounds the topic that I'm discussing and I gather it from all these places where it appeared in parts and put it into some unity that can be carried forward, and gets the history right, and corrects bugs and obscurities in the original sources.

Like in the parts that I'm writing now, I'm starting out with stuff that's in math journals that is written in jargon that I wouldn't expect very many programmers to ever learn, and I'm trying to dejargonize it to the point where *I* can at least understand it. I try to give the key ideas and I try to simplify them the best I can, but then what happens is every five pages of my book is somebody's career.

In other words, there's still so much more beyond any five pages of my book that you can make a lifetime's worth of study, because there's just that much in computer science. Computer science doesn't all boil down to a bunch of simple things. If it turned out that computer science was very simple, that all you needed to do was find the right 50 things and then learn them really well, then I would say, "OK, everybody in the world should know those 50 things and know them thoroughly."

But it isn't that way. I've got thousands of pages and exercises, and I write it down and put it in the book so that I don't have to have it all in my head. I have to come back to it and learn it again. And I have the answers to the exercises because I know that ten years from now I won't remember how to do the darn thing and it will take me a long time to reconstruct it. So I give myself at least the clues to how to reconstruct stuff.

I'm constantly torn between saying, "Well, this is too complicated; you'd better not talk about it at all," and the other feeling that people are saying, "But all you've put in your book is just so trivial; there's nothing good." I can argue at any particular time that I should cut everything out or that I have way too little.

What it really boils down to is, all of the really cool things that can be explained in a half a page have to be in my book, on some half a page. And all the things I've seen that are just too good to be left out. So I find out that the section I just wrote about binary decision diagrams, it turned out that I had more than 260 exercises because there just was more and more stuff that seemed to me there would be more than a trivial audience for. But I'm not saying everybody is the audience for all 260 of these things. Still, I know there are a large number, for each of these, that are going to appreciate it.

I consider it amazing that some people do go cover to cover in my books. In most cases I know that people are going to pick and choose the parts that they like. But they know that if they dig further then they'll get something that has only one subset of jargon describing it instead of all different kinds of notations and terminology—if I didn't write the books it would be much harder for people to find stuff out. That's what turns me on.

Also, I try to explore the territory in a way that is most relevant to a practical programmer rather than the most academic cachet for getting something published that's theoretically interesting but wouldn't really be used in a real program.

The things that I leave out are where somebody has a data structure that saves a factor of log log *n* only when *n* gets bigger than two to the million. And there are lots and lots of papers that are doing that. They're playing games where in principal, if computers were godlike, then we could have algorithms that are faster. But even an algorithm like a balanced tree or AVL tree, I don't use in my own programs unless I know that it's going to be a really big tree.

Seibel: What do you use?

Knuth: I use an ordinary binary search tree with a little trick for randomizing it that I just put in.

Seibel: Speaking of practical work, in the middle of working on *The Art of Computer Programming* you took what turned into a ten-year break to write your typesetting system TeX. I understand you wrote the first version of TeX completely away from the computer.

Knuth: When I wrote TeX originally in 1977 and '78, of course I didn't have literate programming but I did have structured programming. I wrote it in a big notebook in longhand, in pencil.

Six months later, after I had gone through the whole project, I started typing into the computer. And did the debugging in March of '78 while I had started writing the program in October of '77. The code for that is in the Stanford archives—it's all in pencil—and of course I would come back and change a subroutine as I learned what it should be.

This was a first-generation system, so lots of different architectures were possible and had to be discarded until I'd lived with it for a while and knew what was there. And it was a chicken-and-egg problem—you couldn't typeset until you had fonts but then you couldn't have fonts until you could typeset.

But structured programming gave me the idea of invariants and knowing how to make black boxes that I could understand. So I had the confidence that the code would work when I finally would debug it. I felt that I would be saving a lot of time if I waited six months before testing anything. I had enough confidence that the code was approximately right.

Seibel: And the time savings would be because you wouldn't spend time building scaffolding and stubs to test incomplete code?

Knuth: Right.

Seibel: Other than the fact that they're so nicely typeset now, do you think your books would be very different if you hadn't spent ten years writing TeX?

Knuth: Good question. The experience of using structured programming in a not purely academic way—in other words, I'm not just thinking about invariants in toy programs, but in real programs—probably had a fair influence on how I'm describing algorithms in the new stuff I write now. Or if it hasn't, it should.

I wouldn't have known about caching and trends in the way computers change and things like that if I was just going on in the same mold of going from the literature to writing my books. While I was writing Volumes I, II, and III, I wasn't writing programs like TeX that that would be more typical of a large programming practice. They would be toy programs. So it gave me more of a perspective on numbers and quantity.

It's really amazing, though, when you're writing a book, the influences that will make you choose different words. It's mysterious how it gets in there. That's the most important influence of writing TeX—that it gave me a different kind of a mental take on things so that my sentences come out different. They'll be a little bit less hedgy. There is a tone that comes out in the whole thing, of confidence or something.

Seibel: Do you think you were a dramatically better programmer when you finished TeX than when you started?

Knuth: Well, yes, because of literate programming.

Seibel: So you had better tools, but had you actually improved your skills?

Knuth: I learned a terrific amount while I was doing it. One of the things I learned was how much software occupies the brain. It was a much more difficult task than I expected. I couldn't teach classes full-time and write software full-time. I could teach classes full-time and write a book full-time but software required so much attention to detail. It filled that much of my brain to the exclusion of other stuff. So it gave me a special admiration for people who do large software projects—I would never have guessed it without having been faced with that myself.

Seibel: So programming is harder than writing books, and somewhere I read something where you said that it's impossible to estimate how long it will take to write books. Does that then mean that it's even harder to estimate how long programming will take?

Knuth: Yeah, right. That's a very good corollary.

This year I've written probably three major programs which are pushing one hundred pages of code—literate code, with 8.5×11 pages. Two of them are related to each other, so it's more like two and a half major programs. And about 150 small programs. Probably more than I did the previous year. So I programmed galore this year on small programs but also, a couple of them were things that took a month or more to do.

Seibel: And did you expect them to take a month?

Knuth: Well, I expected one of them to take a month. I knew that it wasn't going to be easy but I didn't know how much richness there was going to be, so I added more features as I got to using them. I think it is always going to be true that a person who manages programmers should not expect it to be predictable.

Seibel: In addition to writing *The Art of Computer Programming* and TeX, you're also the inventor of—and advocate for—literate programming, a way of writing code so it can be more easily read by people. And you wrote `WEB` and `CWEB`, tools that implement literate programming languages based on Pascal and C.

Knuth: So you say *advocate*—it's sort of my shtick to say that this is good. But I also am the kind of guy that's uncomfortable preaching or trying to convert someone. I think programming is a lot like religion; people have their beliefs. Some people like to force their beliefs on others. Others say, you know, here's what I think; I can't prove that this is the best thing, but it sure works for me. Then you hope that other people will try it and come to the same conclusion. But I don't like going out and telling people what they ought to believe.

Seibel: Well, maybe you can explain why you like it so much and how it differs from illiterate programming.

Knuth: The first rule of writing is to understand your audience—the better you know your reader the better you can write, of course. The second rule, for technical writing, is say everything twice in complementary ways so that the person who's reading it has a chance to put the ideas into his or her brain in ways that reinforce each other.

So in technical writing usually there's redundancy. Things are said both formally and informally. Or you give a definition and then you say, "Therefore, such and such is true," which you can only understand if you've understood the definition.

Or you'll say, "We define *a* equals the such-and-such to be the set of all leading elements." So this informal term, *the set of all leading elements*, is complemented by the mathematical description of how we constructed the set *a*.

So literate programming is based on this idea that the best way to communicate is to say things both informally and formally that are related. And it just provides a natural framework for switching between the natural language, English, and the formal language, C or Lisp or whatever is your formal language, and putting this together. So that, to me, has to be a win for documentation.

Now, the other thing is, as I write the program, I don't have to present it in the form that the compiler wants to see it. I present it in the form that I think is easiest for a reader to understand.

You can write your code bottom-up and make subroutines that give you bigger and bigger things and your confidence builds because now you can do more things. Other people write top-down; they start out and say, "Well, I have this problem to solve, so first I'll do this and then I'll do this."

When I write a literate program I can choose between these as I like. And almost always the way my final program comes out is in the order in which I actually thought of the things myself. So I'll start out and I'll say, "I have this problem to solve, so first I'm going to have to solve this and then I'm going to have to solve that."

But then I say, "Now let's start building some tools bottom-up." We have the goal in mind but we build a few bottom-up tools and then we'll go back and do a little top-down. But in what order we do this is, first I write about what I thought about the first day I had to work on this problem. And then, the next chapter would be the thing I decided to tackle next.

And I start to tackle the thing that's most worrying to me but that I'm also ready to solve at the moment. Instead of postponing something 'til an evil day, if I'm ready to do it now, I get that out of the way. But it's a different order—it's neither top-down nor bottom-up. It's psychologically, "What do I find is the thing that's going to make me most satisfied to get done next and I'm ready to do it?" It doesn't have too many unknowns in it.So the freedom to put the program into that human-understandable order is very important to me.

Now, why hasn't this spread over the whole world and why isn't everybody doing it? I'm not sure who it was who hit the nail on the head—I think it was Jon Bentley. Simplified it is like this: only two percent of the world's population is born to be super programmers. And only two percent of the population is born to be super writers. And Knuth is expecting everybody to be both.

I don't think we're going to increase the total number of programmers in the world to more than two percent—I mean programmers who really resonate with the machine and that's their bread and butter that they've been born to do. But now that people are blogging, I've seen a great rise in the average ability of ordinary everybody to express themselves. So the second part of that that argument isn't so strong anymore.

I tried it only a limited amount at Stanford. I worked with a group of undergraduates. They would write their programs on a summer project and I introduced them to this idea of literate programming. There were only seven of them working with me that summer. And six of them loved it to the point that they're still using it today. The seventh one hated it. His idea of writing a literate program was to take an ordinary program and put a wrapper around it and say, "This is module one," and so on. Of course, Stanford admits people who are good writers, so this isn't a random sample.

Seibel: Have you ever written a literate program where you dramatically reorganized it into a different order for explication? It's hard for me to imagine that stream of consciousness is *always* the best organizing principle.

Knuth: It just hardly ever happened. I can't remember going back and really changing the order of the chapters. It just always seemed like there was almost only one choice what to attack next. I can't explain it exactly, but it just seemed that one would segue into the next.

Seibel: Do you write literate code for programs that no one but you will ever see?

Knuth: Exactly. This is what literate programming is so great for—I can talk to myself. I can read my program a year later and know exactly what I was thinking.

Seibel: Does that always work?

Knuth: Well, it's often a lot harder to understand a year later than before. But compare that to what I had without it. It doesn't make the complicated thing trivial ,but it's just way better than any other method I know.

I just printed out a small subset of a large collections of subroutines that are all written in C that are pretty much state of the art for manipulating BDDs—Boolean decision diagrams. This is the opposite of CWEB—this is what almost everyone in the world does when they're developing packages now. They do it by means of fairly disciplined commenting conventions that are understood by a large community. And the code is not real difficult to understand because it's separated out into a logical form and you've got these header files and I can see the data structures and there are comments on each part of the data structure explaining what it's doing. So this is another style of programming that works.

Yet I can't help but think that it's considerably below what can be achieved with literate programming. Because of lots of intangible things that I can't prove. The most convincing to me was that I believe that I've written some programs that I *could not* have written at all without literate programming. For example, the MMIX simulator would have been such an intellectual challenge that if I had to do it in the conventional style, I don't think I ever would have finished it. Just separating it out into subroutines wasn't enough to simplify it to make it intellectually manageable.

This is a simulator that takes an extremely general specification of a computer: what functional units it has, how many instructions can execute at a time, the caching strategies, how the bus works, how the output works, how are you doing branch prediction, and how you maintain the pipeline.

So you can imagine a computer that would have six division units and a pipeline of certain stages and this will simulate it. Would you be able to calculate prime numbers faster if you had this machine? You don't have to build the machine.

I'm not saying it's impossible to take that program and put it into subroutines, but I would never have finished it that way. And also it's only 170 pages and it is possible to understand it—I'm not the only person in the world who understands it.

Seibel: I read your literate reimplementation of the game *Adventure* and noticed that it seemed somewhat monolithic. It seemed like the literate style, because it lets you interpolate things, draws you away from breaking things down into subroutines.

Knuth: This is true. Instead of calling a subroutine, it's like inline subroutines all the way through. The idea of a subroutine is there but it's not in your final program as a subroutine. It's more like a macro in some ways. But the thing is, at the conceptual level, the subroutine-calling mechanism isn't necessary if you have some other way to do it in the language you're using.

In *Adventure* I don't think I actually removed subroutines from Don Woods's Fortran program—I was taking his Fortran program and putting it into English and C. But it's true that when you look at my code for TeX, the number of subroutines that you're in, on the subroutine stack, might be 4 or 5 whereas a program written by somebody else, without literate programming, it might be 50 or 100.

What I try to work on is units that correspond to the way I have it in my head, rather than the way a logician might want it to be in some formal system. My programs are supposed to match my intuition more than somebody else's rigid framework.

Of course, eventually it has to go into a computer, which is rigid, which has its precise rules of understanding. But to me the idea of the right kind of a program is something that matches the way I think as closely as possible rather than something that matches the machine as closely as possible. I have to find the way to do the conversion, but my source text tries to stay closer to my brain than to the machine.

I also believe that literate programming is a powerful style of documentation that can be used to communicate across groups of people. I had many people who understood the code for TeX well enough to construct scenarios where it would fail. I think more people, at one point in their life, understood that program than any other program of its size,

Seibel: Did you ever find, even with that, that you still had people who had read the thing and then sent you questions that made you think, "Wow, they really missed something here"?

Knuth: Of course. That always happens, but it's a mistake in my exposition. Let me give you a simple example. In *The Art of Computer Programming* I'm talking about the early history of bit-oriented operations and I have the following sentence: "The Manchester Mark I computer, built about the same time as the EDSAC, included not only bitwise *and* but also *or* and *exclusive or*. When Alan Turing wrote its first programming manual in 1950 he remarked that bitwise *not* can be obtained by using *exclusive or* in combination with a row of ones."

Now, in my sentence I'm saying, "Alan Turing wrote its first programming manual," meaning the first programming manual for the Manchester Mark 1. But four or five readers independently said, I must have meant "his:" "When Alan Turing wrote *his* first programming manual in 1950".

Well, actually, he had written other programming manuals, so what I said was correct but it was misinterpreted by people. So now I say, "When Alan Turing wrote the first programming manual for the Mark I, in 1950. . . ."

Mathematical things; similarly I'll get people who miss it. So then I'll say, you know, I actually said it correctly, but I know I still have to change it and make it better.

Seibel: When you publish a literate program, it's the final form of the program, typically. And you are often credited with saying, "Premature optimization is the root of all evil." But by the time you get to the final form it's not premature—you may have optimized some parts to be very clever. But doesn't that make it hard to read?

Knuth: No. A good literate program will show its history. A good literate program will say, "Here's the obvious way to do it and then why we don't follow that road?"

When you put subtle stuff in your program, literate programming shines because you don't just have the code that does it but also your documentation. You say, "This is a dirty trick here, it work's because—" and then you state very carefully the reasons and the assumptions.

I'll use dirty tricks for two reasons. One is, if it's really going to give me a performance improvement and my application is one that the performance improvement is going to be appreciated. Or sometimes I'll say, "This is tricky; I couldn't resist being tricky today because it's so cute." So just for pure pleasure. In any case, I document it; I don't just put it in there.

Seibel: Would that be more in the prose?

Knuth: It's in the prose part. I don't show the code that I've taken out. I could.

Seibel: Is there any facility in CWEB for actually including code that isn't part of the application, so rather than just document it in the prose, you can say, "Here's a really dirt-simple version of this function."

Knuth: You just have the code but you never use it. It comes out in the documentation saying this code is never used.

Seibel: So it would just be a fragment that you would never reference?

Knuth: Yeah. Also, I have code in there that I can then invoke from the debugger. I can say, "Call such-and-such with such-and-such parameters." The subroutine is never actually called in the program itself, but it's there in the documentation. So I can stop a program in the middle and I can call this subroutine and it'll take a look and see how it's doing, see how big things have gotten.

Seibel: So by the same token you could write, "Section one—here's a naive implementation of this algorithm; section two—here's a slightly souped-up version of section one; and section three, here's the one we actually use which you would never understand if you hadn't read the first two sections."

Knuth: Exactly. I have some programs on the Web that solve the 15 puzzle. And I go through 3 different versions. And I say, "Read version one or you'll never understand version two. And read version two or you'll never understand version three."

I write a whole variety of different kinds of programs. Sometimes I'll write a program where I couldn't care less about efficiency—I just want to get the answer. I'll use brute force, something that I'm guaranteed I won't have to think—there'll be no subtlety at all so I won't be outsmarting myself. There I'm not doing any premature optimization.

Then I can change that into something else and see if I get something that agrees with my brute-force way. Then I can scale up the program and go to larger cases. Most programs stop at that stage because you're not going to execute the code a trillion times. When I'm doing an illustration for *The Art of Computer Programming* I may change that illustration several times and the people who translate my book might have to redo the program, but it doesn't matter that I drew the illustration by a very slow method because I've only got to generate that file once and then it goes off to the publisher and gets printed in a book.

But right now I'm working on combinatorial algorithms, which are, by definition, humongous-size problems. So in order to have interesting examples in my book I've got to write programs that solve problems that readers will say, "Oh, yeah, I couldn't have done that just by simple methods, so I need to learn something about the art of programming or it'll take 100 years to solve this problem by the brute-force method."

Combinatorial algorithms are fascinating because one good idea can save you ten orders of magnitude in running time. But I don't sneer at ideas that save you twenty percent when you're doing it a trillion times. Because if you can save a hundred nanoseconds in a loop that's being done a trillion times, I think you're saving a day. If the code is going to be used a lot it can really pay off so you've got to go to subtle tricks that aren't easy to understand.

About a year ago I saw a review in *Computing Reviews*—the guy was reviewing a book; the title was *Programming Tricks* or something like this. And the thrust of the review was, "If I ever caught any of the programmers working for me using any of these tricks, I would fire them." And so naturally I went out and looked at the book because I thought, "This is a book I want to see and learn from. Unfortunately, the tricks weren't actually that good."

Seibel: Were they really firing offenses?

Knuth: They were very weak, actually. It wasn't presented systematically and everything, but I thought they were pretty obvious. It was a different culture entirely. But the guy who said he was going to fire people, he wants programming to be something where everything is done in an inefficient way because it's supposed to fit into his idea of orderliness. He doesn't care if the program is good or not—as far as its speed and performance—he cares about that it satisfies other criteria, like any bloke can be able to maintain it. Well, people have lots of other funny ideas.

People have this strange idea that we want to write our programs as worlds unto themselves so that everybody else can just set up a few parameters and our program will do it for them. So there'll be a few programmers in the world who write the libraries, and then there are people who write the user manuals for these libraries, and then there are people who apply these libraries and that's it.

The problem is that coding isn't fun if all you can do is call things out of a library, if you can't write the library yourself. If the job of coding is just to be finding the right combination of parameters, that does fairly obvious things, then who'd want to go into that as a career?

There's this overemphasis on reusable software where you never get to open up the box and see what's inside the box. It's nice to have these black boxes but, almost always, if you can look inside the box you can improve it and make it work better once you know what's inside the box. Instead people make these closed wrappers around everything and present the closure to the programmers of the world, and the programmers of the world aren't allowed to diddle with that. All they're able to do is assemble the parts. And so you remember that when you call this subroutine you put *x0*, *y0*, *x1*, *y1* but when you call this subroutine it's *x0*, *x1*, *y0*, *y1*. You get that right, and that's your job.

Seibel: Many people will agree with you that, yes, it's more fun to write the code yourself. But other than the fun—

Knuth: It's not only fun. The job of a mathematician is to make proofs but almost never, when you're solving a mathematical problem, do you find a theorem for which the hypotheses are exactly what you need for the problem you're solving. Almost always you've got something that's *sort of like* the theorem that's in the book. So what you do is you look at the proof of that theorem and you say, "Oh, here's how I have to change that proof in order to prove the hypothesis that I really have." So mathematical books are packed with theorems, but you never plug in exactly the theorem—you want to see that proof because it's one time in a hundred when you'll find just the theorem that you wanted. I think it's exactly the same with software.

Seibel: Yet isn't software—I think you've said it yourself—about the most complex thing human beings have ever made?

Knuth: It was Dijkstra, I think, first, but yeah. It's because the complexity of putting something together is so nonuniform. Pure mathematics tends to have a few rules that are applied universally—three or four axioms that describe a system. Computer programs have many parts—step one is different from step two is different from step three. It brings together all these things and they have to fit in an intricate way.

Seibel: So given that complexity, it seems like at some point you have to take some black boxes and say, "OK, we know how this thing works, and we can use it." If we were forced to look inside every black box, we'd never finish.

Knuth: I'm not saying black boxes are useless. I'm saying that if I'm not allowed to open 'em up—if I have to do everything with a library or something like this, I would come up with much, much worse results and much slower.

Seibel: Slower-running or slower-developing?

Knuth: Both. Well, OK, I can get programs to work in a hurry, so I can't claim that. It's just taking me longer because I have to search through more reference manuals and find the right parts, so it's more of a search problem than a creative problem.

Seibel: A while back the guy who wrote the standard Java collection libraries wrote an article about how there had been a bug in their implementation of binary search for nine years. Basically they took the min and the max and added them together and divided by two. But, of course, if that addition overflows, that's a bug. So, it's bad the standard library had a bug in it, but they found it eventually and fixed it. If everyone wrote binary search themselves, the percentage of binary searches that would be wrong would probably be quite high.

Knuth: That's true. And that's just one of a huge number of examples. Binary search is a particular example that we started out our programming classes in the '70s. The first day of class everyone writes a program for binary search and we collect them and the TAs take a look. And you find that fewer than ten percent are correct. And there are four or six different bugs. But not with respect to the overflow that you mentioned, which is a new one—it didn't occur in my classes that we thought adding these two numbers might be a problem.

But this black-box idea—why do I hate it so much? We're talking arithmetic, so say you have a program for matrix multiplication. You have a matrix multiply black box and then you change the data type from real to complex and so then you've got a complex matrix multiply box and it takes $4 \times n^3$ steps instead of n^3 steps. If the real case takes a certain time, t, then the complex case takes time $4t$. But if you're allowed to open the box, then you'll only need three real matrix multiplications instead of four because there's an identity that will describe the product of two complex matrices. That's just one small example—it just goes on and on.

I'll have a priority queue or I'll have some kind of a heap structure; whatever it is—binary search—I'll have a good source for the algorithm but it won't quite fit what I want, so I'll adapt it every time. And I think I'll be better off. I know I'm going against a lot of people who think their job is to write things that everybody is going to use, so if there are any bugs in it, they get to fix 'em and everybody else's program will start working better now. OK. I'm unhappy with that kind of world. I like to see their program.

When I wrote Volume I of *The Art of Computer Programming* people didn't realize that they could use linked lists in their own programs, that they could use pointers for data structures.

If you had a problem that had something beyond arrays, you would go to somebody's package, or an interpreted language like IPL-V or Lisp. There were also Fortran versions and you could get these subroutines and then you would learn how to use that package and you would do your program in that. It was completely preposterous for somebody to teach an ordinary programmer how to include linked lists in their program. Everything was supposed to be done by these canned routines.

But general packages have got to have all of this extra machinery in order to handle cases that only come up for a small number of the users. So my book sort of opened people's eyes: "Oh my gosh, I can understand this and adapt it so I can have elements that are in two lists at once. I can change the data structure." It became something that could be mainstream instead of just enclosed in these packages.

Well, I'm seeing the same thing now that I'm writing about BDD structures. At the moment there are three or four packages of subroutines that work with BDDs but the thrust of what I'm writing now for *The Art of Computer Programming* is that you too can program simple versions of BDDs for lots of applications and it'll go very far. You can use them for lots of different kinds of problems where you don't need all the bells and whistles of these other packages and these things you can do are easy to understand and easy to put into programs you're writing yourself.

Earlier this year I finished my section on bitwise tricks and techniques and these are things that have been a black art in the hacker community for years. I decided it's time to say that there's a theory of these things that you can understand the ideas, how they fit together. You can use them yourself with confidence. And you can build on things and do amazing things that last year you didn't know how to do well at all. It went through the underground until now; it's something that we might as well teach to people—something that deserves to be common knowledge.

I write a lot of programs and I can't claim to be typical but I can claim that I get a lot of them working for a large variety of things and I would find it harder if I had to spend all my time learning how to use somebody else's routines. It's much easier for me to learn a few basic concepts and then reuse code by text-editing the code that previously worked.

Seibel: How has the way you think about programming changed from those earliest days to now?

Knuth: We already talked about literate programming—that's a radical departure, that I'm viewing myself as an expositor rather than trying to just put together the right instructions. Dijkstra came out with that same evolution. In the end his programs were even more literate than mine in the sense that they didn't even go into the machine. They were *only* literate.

And he was one of the people largely responsible for structured programming, where we saw patterns that we could use to scale up our program so that we could make larger programs and still keep our head straight. You write a program that's ten times as big but you don't have to lose ten times as much sleep over it because you have tools that allow you to put things together reliably in a larger system. That was definitely different.

So that's one important aspect, the idea of the abstractions that we have to understand, the abstractions that allow us to deal with large systems and still be pretty confident that we're in control and we know what we're doing, even though they're a mind-bogglingly complex things.

There are lots of other things that look like they're important changes but to me they don't seem to make that much difference. These are the surface, the different type of syntactic sugar and the different dialects of languages that we have. There are many different flavors that appeal to different personality types. Some people are more logical than I am, for example. They really like to have lots of parentheses, and things matching up and saying that, "I'm now going to start something," and then at the end you say, "I'm now going to finish it." And that's not as appealing to me. That's not the way I think. But that's the way other people think and there's no one best way to think.

To me one of the most important revolutions in programming languages was the use of pointers in the C language. When you have nontrivial data structures, you often need one part of the structure to point to another part, and people played around with different ways to put that into a higher-level language. Tony Hoare, for example, had a pretty nice clean system but the thing that the C language added—which at first I thought was a big mistake and then it turned out I loved it—was that when `x` is a pointer and then you say, `x + 1`, that doesn't mean one more byte after `x` but it means one more node after `x`, depending on what `x` points to: if it points to a big node, `x + 1` jumps by a large amount; if `x` points to a small thing, `x + 1` just moves a little. That, to me, is one of the most amazing improvements in notation.

Seibel: So that's certainly powerful compared to what preceded it. But since then, a lot of people have decided that having raw pointers to memory is pretty dangerous and that they'd rather have references that behave a lot like pointers but without some of the dangers.

Knuth: Pointers have gone out of favor to the point now where I had to flame about it because on my 64-bit computer that I have here, if I really care about using the capability of my machine I find that I'd better not use pointers because I have a machine that has 64-bit registers but it only has 2 gigabytes of RAM. So a pointer never has more than 32 significant bits to it. But every time I use a pointer it's costing me 64 bits and that doubles the size of my data structure. Worse, it goes into the cache and half of my cache is gone and that costs cash—cache is expensive.

So if I'm really trying to push the envelope now, I have to use arrays instead of pointers. I make complicated macros so that it looks like I'm using pointers, but I'm not really. In a way it's a small thing and it's going out of fashion. But to me it was an important idea in notation at the lower levels; when I'm working and debugging and so on I'm still very grateful to Thompson and Ritchie. I don't know who came up with that particular one.

Seibel: Are there any other important parts of your programming toolkit?

Knuth: Change files are something that I've got with literate programming that I don't know of corresponding tools in any other programmers' toolkits, so let me explain them to you.

I had written TeX and Metafont and people started asking for it. And they had 200 or 300 combinations of programming language and operating system and computer, so I wanted to make it easy to adapt my code to anybody's system. So we came up with the solution that I would write a master program that worked at Stanford and then there was this add-on called a *change file* which could customize it to anybody else's machine.

A change file is a very simple thing. It consists of a bunch of little blobs of changes. Each change starts out with a few lines of code. You match until you find the first line in the master file that agrees with the first line of your change. When you get to the end of the part of the change that was supposed to match the master file, then comes the part which says, "Replace that by these lines instead."

Maybe the change says, "Replace these six lines by these twelve lines. Or by no lines. As soon as you get a match, you stick in the twelve that you changed. Then you go onto the next one." You've got to write the changes in order—it doesn't do anything intelligent for matching; it just says, "Go until you find the first line of the next change that has to match some line in the master file."

It's a system that only takes an hour to program and it's good enough for the purpose. Then all the tools that we have for literate programming, the weave and tangle programs, will take the master file and the change file.

So every so often I'd have to release a new master program. All these hundreds of people around the world had their change files—maybe their six lines that were supposed to match mine no longer matched, so they might have to make some changes. But they wouldn't have to do very much. Every time I would correct a bug it would almost automatically work—the bug fix would also apply to their program. This solved the problem very simply and it worked. Anybody could figure it out and do it.

The extreme example of this was when TeX was adapted to Unicode. They had a change file maybe 10 times as long as the master program. In other words, they changed from an 8-bit program to a 16-bit program but instead of going through and redoing my master program, they were so into change files that they just wrote their whole draft of what they called Omega as change files, as a million lines of change files to TeX's 20,000 lines of code or something. So that's the extreme.

But now I use change files all the time because I'm writing programs for myself that I'm using writing my book—I've got lots of problems that I want to solve and I want to experiment with different versions. Like yesterday I wanted to find out how big a Boolean circuit is for multiplication of *n*-bit numbers. I have a program that takes any Boolean function and finds out how big its BDD is. So I've got a program that takes any Boolean function and computes its BDD.

In my original program you input the truth table of the function online—it says, "Give me a truth table," and I type in a hexadecimal number, because I had a lot of small functions that I'm using as examples. But it only works for small functions, the ones that I want to type in the truth table.

Then I've got a big function like, "Multiply all pairs of 8-bit numbers." This is a function of 16 variables—there are 8 bits in *x* and 8 bits in *y*. So I write a little change file that takes out this interactive dialog and replaces it with a program that makes a truth table for multiplication.

Then I changed that by saying, "Let's read the bits from right to left instead of from left to right, which gives you a different BDD." Or, "Let me try all Boolean functions of six variables and I'll run through them all and find out which one has the largest BDD." But all of these are customizations of my original thing.

I'll have maybe 15 variants of that program that are easily understood. This was an unexpected spin-off from literate programming because of our need for sending out master files to a lot of people that were changing it for their own system; I'm now using it in a completely different way.

Seibel: It seems sort of obvious why that would be useful for you in the kind of work you're doing, where you want to do a lot of variations on different themes.

Knuth: Yeah, I'm writing a book.

Seibel: Do you think this mechanism could be more broadly applicable?

Knuth: I have no idea. I'm not sure how it would work if I was in a team of 50 people. But I hope that the idea of an individual programmer writing programs in order to learn something is not a dying breed.

Seibel: In your earliest days you were writing machine code; then you found structured programming, which provided literally a structure for organizing programs. And then you invented literate programming, which gave you another way to structure programs. Since the invention of literate programming, has there been anything else that's as dramatically changed the way you think about programming?

Knuth: I've got better debugging tools for literate programming; that's basically all.

Seibel: OK, let's talk about debugging. What better tools do you have now?

Knuth: It turned out that the inventors of the GNU debugger realized that you could have preprocessors writing programs. So you can correlate the low-level stuff to a high-level source in a completely different language. So I'm writing in CWEB but I still never have to look at the lower-level things because it'll flash my CWEB source as I'm stepping through the program.

Seibel: So that's a facility built into GDB which CWEB takes advantage of?

Knuth: And was built into GDB because it was built into C to have __LINE__ directives. We had to work to make use of the __LINE__directives, but it works beautifully. The computer is sitting there with a binary instruction but GDB knows that this came from something in my WEB source file even though WEB came 10, 20 years after C. So it was a very good, very forward-looking part of their design to make that work.

Seibel: So you use GDB. What other debugging techniques do you use?

Knuth: I'll add a lot of code that will check to see if my data structures, with all their redundancies, are properly done. This sanity checking might slow the whole thing down by a factor of 100 if I turn it on.

For instance, I had a complicated data structure that involves reference counts. So I'm writing some pretty complicated programs, and getting these reference counts correct is mystifying. Every once in a while I have to increase the reference count or decrease the reference count. But when a pointer is in a register or is a parameter to a subroutine, does that count as a reference in the data structure or not? So I've got the sanity check written that goes through the millions of counts seeing how many references are really made and are the numbers correct? Then I'll do a little computation and check the whole thing. That way errors will be detected billions of steps before they would surface in a crash.

There was a program that does multiplication in a new way, so I tried it exhaustively. I made 256 numbers and I multiplied each of them by each other one, but after each one I would do a sanity check. I multiply 2 by 3—fails! So I fixed that. And then something else. Finally I got it to where all 256 by 256 were working and getting the right answer.

So that's an important debugging technique for me. Maybe ten percent of the code is devoted to something that I don't need except when I'm debugging. And the sanity-check code also documents the data structure.

I'll also write something that gives a nice symbolic form of a data structure so I don't have to decode a whole bunch of binary things. Then, if necessary, I can print out a data structure in some decent structured form or I can dump it out in a file and I can write another program that analyzes it to find out what's going wrong.

Seibel: Related to invariants and various kinds of assertions, folks like Dijkstra would argue that we've got to put very formal assertions at every step of our program so that we can then prove our programs correct. I've read where you've talked about wanting to prove your programs "informally correct;" what's your take on the idea that we should go beyond that and formally prove things correct?

Knuth: On one hand you have this impossibility of ever having something proved. Somebody will say they have a program that's verified and it's only verified because it met its specifications according to some verifier. But the verifier might have a bug in it. The specifications might have bugs in them. So you never know that the program is correct. You have more reason to believe it, but you never get to the end of the loop. It's theoretically impossible.

The very first paper by Tony Hoare about formal proof, "Proof of a Program: FIND," was a great achievement and advanced the state of the art. But there were two or three bugs in that proof. It hadn't occurred to them that you had to verify that subscripts lie in-bounds or something like this. There's always a chance for gaps. Still, he had verified it much more than anybody else had at that point.

Now, the program that I did yesterday—I have no idea how I would state all of the assertions that are there. I would never get done because I wouldn't have any more confidence in my assertions than I would in the program.

Or TeX, for example, is a formal mess. It was intended to be for human use, not for computer use. To define what it means for TeX to be correct would be incomprehensible. Some methods for formal semantics are so complicated that nobody can comprehend the definition of *correctness*.

Seibel: When you were working on TeX you wrote a really horrendous torture test of the program.

Knuth: Right.

Seibel: How do you get in the frame of mind to do that? Programmers often tend to want to protect their baby, and so they don't test as hard as they could.

Knuth: Well, I've been a nitpicker all my life. So if I can get my kicks out of finding errors then I just have to make sure that I forget that I was the author of the program. I try to imagine that somebody else was the author. But otherwise it's fairly easy for me to get into attack mode. I don't know why.

For example, some of the best work I did for Burroughs Corporation was to debug their hardware designs. Their engineers would show me the specs for their computer and I would look at it and I would try to construct examples where they would be off by 1 or something. I got more than 200 bugs out of their B-5000–series machines before they went into production, although it had passed the simulators.

Seibel: So essentially you were inventing programs that were correct according to the semantics of the language but the machine would then execute incorrectly?

Knuth: Right. Certainly if their floating point isn't calculating the right product of two numbers, I would try to find examples of numbers where the floating point didn't work. But also there were cases where they were implementing a stack in hardware and they had cases where registers would be empty or not at the top of the stack and I would find scenarios where their logic would get screwed up.

Seibel: Did you have a systematic way of doing that? How did you find them?

Knuth: Am I just a mean guy? I don't know. But if I'm trying to prove something—a theorem in mathematics—instead of proving that it's correct, it's easier for me, usually, to say, "Well, find a counterexample." I can get psyched up to find a hole in this or explain why it doesn't work. And then when I can't find any holes, then I see the proof.

I think it's just my personality that I like to attack things and find errors. My juices are working when I'm playing the game as the opponent rather than if I'm just sitting there trying to say, "Oh, yeah; now why is this working?"

Seibel: It's curious that that's what gets you going, yet your life's work is explaining things. Do you think that approach somehow feeds into how you explain things?

Knuth: The only thing I can claim for my explanations is that I try to match a natural brain process of seeing things in two different ways at a time in order to understand something better. I think the key is usually to have a stereo view instead of a one-dimensional view. I don't know how that affects this attacking business.

But when you're attacking—when you're playing the game, trying to defeat something—it arouses competitive hormones or something that just stimulates the brain in a way that probably just means that I'm trying more than one way to get at it. A good explanation is a similar thing. A good explanation somehow combines different viewpoints.

Seibel: Another thing that came out of working on TeX, which you described in "The Errors of TeX," was a log of every error that you found in the program. Folks like the Software Engineering Institute people say that part of a mature software-engineering process is keeping track of all your bugs and learning how to prevent the same kind of errors in the future. But you said that having kept this log, it doesn't help you prevent future errors.

Knuth: Yeah. Though it's hard to say that I wouldn't have been even worse without the log.

Seibel: But you didn't feel like, "Ah, now that I've seen this I won't do it again."

Knuth: I just got to recognize my sins. People keep coming back for absolution, if you know theological terms.

Seibel: So you find yourself now making bugs in your programs and then saying, "Oh, I've done it again, that same kind of bug."

Knuth: Yeah.

Seibel: So why is that? Is there something about the nature of the mistakes that makes it hard to distill a lesson that will prevent making them again?

Knuth: I think it's probably more that I'll try harder things. I always try things that are at my limit. If I had to go back and write those kinds of programs again, the easier ones, I wouldn't make so many mistakes. But now that I know some more, I'm trying to write harder stuff. So I make mistakes because I'm always operating at my limit. If I only stay in comfortable territory all the time, that's not so much fun.

Seibel: So if you just kept writing typesetting systems for the rest of your life?

Knuth: Yeah, I would get those pretty good. But we keep raising the bar and then we stumble on it. We're dealing with—as we said earlier—things that are on the edge of what human beings can handle and more complicated than have been done before.

If we restrict ourselves to the things that are really easy, then that's not satisfactory because our appetite is always to push the boundary and go until it gets to something we can barely do. And once we've got to there, then we're going to want to push that boundary and so on.

So inevitably we're going to have bugs unless we decide we're never going to write anything that stretches our capabilities. So how are we going to do it better? Every three years there'll be another buzz word as to something that's going to solve all these problems and make it really work. *Extreme programming* was one the last two or three years. Before that there was something else. Somebody will come up with another supposedly silver bullet and there'll be a lot of people jumping on that bandwagon and then they'll find, "Oh, it's still hard."

Seibel: Has the kind of person who can be a good programmer changed over time?

Knuth: Pretty much a constant in my experience, over a long period of years, is that every time I'm exposed to 100 people from some population or other, except majors in computer science, 2 of them are programmers in the sense that they really resonate with the machine. Wasilla, Alaska, has 10,000 people, so it's probably got 200 programmers.

Seibel: So has programming changed enough that the kind of person who falls in that two percent has changed? Or is it still really the same?

Knuth: I don't know—you can use the word *programming* in different senses. We're always making tools that are intended to make more of a match between people's brains and getting something done in a computer. I'm mostly talking about the way a machine really works when the machine is being pushed to the envelope rather than just getting an answer out.

We've got machines that are so powerful now that people who aren't really good at programming, in my esoteric sense, are able to get answers out of these machines that would have taken a huge expert to do on old machines. But with the new machines, the people that I'm talking about are going to be doing the problems that couldn't be handled by the old machines.

So there's that change and then there's the change that I'm really worried about: that the way a lot of programming goes today isn't any fun because it's just plugging in magic incantations—combine somebody else's software and start it up. It doesn't have much creativity. I'm worried that it's becoming too boring because you don't have a chance to do anything much new. Your kick comes out of seeing fun results coming out of the machine, but not the kind of kick that I always got by creating something new. The kick now is after you've done your boring work then all of the sudden you get a great image. But the work didn't used to be boring.

Seibel: But you still find the kind of programming you do interesting?

Knuth: Oh my God, yes. I've got this *need* to program. I wake up in the morning with sentences of a literate program. Before breakfast—I'm sure poets must feel this—I have to go to the computer and write this paragraph and then I can eat and I'm happy. It's a compulsion; that I have to admit.

OK, let me show you the program I wrote yesterday. I'm multiplying huge integers that are way bigger than the universe—they're special integers that you can compress the representation down, and so I can deal with them even though I couldn't represent them in an ordinary notation, and I've been multiplying these integers that are inconceivably large and I've been squaring them and finding out how they look after squaring them. I'm very puzzled about what's going on, but this is exciting to me.

Seibel: You're an academic but also have worked on big systems and have done some work in industry. How do you see the relation between academic computer science and industrial practice?

Knuth: It's gone in waves. In the '60s the academics were way ahead of the industry and the programs that were produced in industry, except for maybe airline-reservation systems, were laughable to everybody in universities.

By 1980 the situation had pretty much reversed and the programs that were being written by people in universities were laughed at by the people in industry because the universities had gone into theological mode and you weren't allowed to use goto statements. I'm exaggerating to simplify, but basically there were no-nos in university programs that were keeping people's hands tied, and the people in industry didn't have to worry about that.

But then in universities people came up with some better ideas about networking and dealing with large pieces of data and so on, and got ahead. So it goes back and forth. But the trend in a lot of the algorithm and data-structure community has not been to my liking when they have lots of data structures that are just . . . *baroque* is the only word I can think of. They're intricate and clever and you have to admire them for the intellectual challenge, but I find them sterile. They don't connect with life; they're working in another world. It's an OK world and it's got its structure, and they're friendly and nice people, but it doesn't appeal to me personally and it doesn't really relate to practice.

I don't know why it's important to me if something relates to practice or not. There are mathematicians who never think about anything finite, and they hardly ever come down to countably infinite—they publish terrific papers just talking about kinds of infinity that are mind-boggling and they're able to make sense out of it and that gives them satisfaction. And there are similar things like that in algorithms. But for me I'm turned on much more by the ideas that I would be able to use in my machine.

Seibel: In 1974 you said that by 1984 we would have "Utopia 84," the sort of perfect programming language, and it would supplant COBOL and Fortran, and you said then that there were indications that such language is very slowly taking shape. It's now a couple of decades since '84 and it doesn't seem like that's happened.

Knuth: No.

Seibel: Was that just youthful optimism?

Knuth: I was thinking about Simula and trends in object-oriented programming when I wrote that, clearly. I think what happens is that every time a new language comes out it cleans up what's understood about the old languages and then adds something new, experimental and so on, and nobody has ever come to the point where they have a new language and then they want to stop at what's understood. They're always wanting to push further.

Maybe someday somebody will say, "No, I'm not going to be innovative; I'm just going to be clean and simple, and I'm going to stick to it." Pascal was started with that philosophy but then didn't continue. Maybe we'll get to a time when somebody will say, "Let's set our sights lower and really try to make something that's going to be stable." It might be a good idea.

Seibel: Isn't part of the problem that while there are misfeatures, there are also missing features and if a thing is missing you've got to make up something to fill that gap.

Knuth: Yeah, that's right. It's got to be extensible somehow. Java didn't make itself extensible in a good way.

Seibel: You've designed some languages yourself—probably the most widely used of which is TeX.

Knuth: So TeX is a programming language but I had to put in those features kicking and screaming. Guy Steele, Terry Winograd, Leslie Lamport, and different people needed things when they were using TeX as a front end for their material. I think Terry Winograd was writing a book on the syntax of natural languages, so he had some really powerful macros that he wanted to write in order to make the diagrams in his book. That pushed TeX a lot towards becoming a programming language in the earliest days.

Seibel: Do you ever wish you had focused more on the design of the language, as a language?

Knuth: I don't know. I guess so. In a way I resent having every language be universal because they'll be universal in a different way. It's a little bit like Unix having 30 definitions of regular expressions under one roof—depending on which part of Unix you're using you've got a slightly different flavor of regular expressions. If every tool that you have includes a Turing machine inside, is this really the way to go? I was really thinking of TeX as something that the more programming it had in it, the less it was doing its real mission of typesetting.

When I put in the calculation of prime numbers into the TeX manual I was not thinking of this as the way to use TeX. I was thinking, "Oh, by the way, look at this: dogs can stand on their hind legs and TeX can calculate prime numbers."

Seibel: But people use the fact that it's a Turing-complete programming language to do typesetting-related computations. If it wasn't Turing-complete they would be unable to do those things.

Knuth: Yeah, that's right. I wrote a programming language for simulation in the '60s that I had to work hard to kill because it had a lot of users, but then when Simula came out I liked Simula better and I told people to stop using my SOL language. Mostly I don't consider that I have great talent for language design.

With TeX I was interacting with hundreds of years of human history and I didn't want to throw out all of the things that book designers have learned over centuries and start anew and say, "Well, forget that guys; you know, we're going to be logical now." In this case, the name of the game was mostly to take an enormously complicated problem and find a fairly small set of primitives that would support it. Instead of having 1,000 primitives, I have 100 primitives or something like that. But going down to 50 primitives, 10 primitives—which we would do if we wanted to be mathematically clean—I believe wouldn't work. The problem of making books goes too much into the complexity of the world, which just doesn't want to be simplified.

Seibel: I haven't really done a study, but it seems like the vast majority of mathematical and scientific papers are typeset with TeX these days. There must have been things you've seen typeset in TeX that made you think, "Wow, my program played a part in this."

Knuth: Well, the proof of Fermat's Last Theorem was one of those. It's one of the most famous mathematical papers. And it happens all the time that I see books that I know wouldn't have been written if the authors had had to go through channels the way they used to. It's again a little bit of the black-box thing.

It used to be, you would have to type something up and that would go into a compositor and it would come back in galley proofs, and so on. You're going through all kinds of levels of people who aren't mathematicians and then coming out with the product at the end. So you don't dare do anything that would confuse any of the people in that line.

But if you can see yourself what it's going to look like, and you can make up a notation that isn't in somebody's style sheet because it just happens to be the right one for your problem, then you're encouraged to do a much better job.

So this brings me great satisfaction all the time when I know that people have been able to cut through this and their creativity goes directly to the reader.

Seibel: Do you feel like programmers and computer scientists are aware enough of the history of our field? It is, after all, a pretty short history.

Knuth: There aren't too many that are scholars. Even when I started writing my books in 1963, I didn't think people knew what had happened in 1959. I was reading in *American Scientist* last week about people who had rediscovered an algorithm that Boyer and Moore had discovered in 1980. It happens all the time that people don't realize the glorious history that we have. The idea that people knew a thing or two in the '70s is strange to a lot of young programmers.

It's inevitable that in such a complicated field that people will be missing stuff. Hopefully with things like Wikipedia, achievements don't get forgotten the way they were before. But I wish I could also instill in more people the love that I have for reading original sources. Not just knowing that so-and-so gets credit for doing something, but looking back and seeing what that person said in his own words. I think it's a tremendous way to improve your own skills.

It's very important to be able to get inside of somebody else's way of thinking, to decode their vocabulary, their notation. If you can understand something about the way they thought and the way they made a discovery, then that helps you make your own discoveries. I often read source materials of what brilliant people have said about this stuff in the past. It'll be expressed in unusual ways by today's conventions, but it's worth it to me to penetrate their notation and to try to get into their idea.

For example I spent a good deal of time trying to look at Babylonian manuscripts of how they described algorithms 4,000 years ago, and what did they think about? Did they have while loops and stuff like this? How would they describe it? And to me this was very worthwhile for understanding about how the brain works, but also about how they discovered things.

A couple of years ago I found an old Sanskrit document from the 13th century that was about combinatorial math. Almost nobody the author knew would have had the foggiest idea what he was talking about. But I found a translation of this document and it was speaking to me. I had done similar kinds of thinking when I was beginning in computer programming.

And so to me reading source materials is great enrichment for my own life and creativity.

I was unable to pass that on to any of my students. There are people alive now in computer science who are doing this well—a few. But I could count on the fingers of one hand the people who love source materials the way I do.

I've got lots of collections of source code. I have compilers, the Digitek compilers from the 1960s were written in a very interesting way. They had their own language and they used identifiers that were 30 characters long but very descriptive, and their compilers ran circles around the competition at the time—this company made the state-of-the-art compilers of 1963 or '64.

And I've got Dijkstra's source code for the THE operating system. I haven't read that. I've just skimmed it so far but I collected it because I'm sure it would be interesting to read if I had time.

One time I broke my arm—fell off a bike—and I had a month where I couldn't do anything much, so I read source code that I had heard had some clever ideas in it that hadn't been documented. I think those were all extremely important experiences for me.

Seibel: How do you tackle reading source code? Even reading something in a programming language you already know is a tricky problem.

Knuth: But it's really worth it for what it builds in your brain. So how do I do it? There was a machine called the Bunker Ramo 300 and somebody told me that the Fortran compiler for this machine was really amazingly fast, but nobody had any idea why it worked. I got a copy of the source-code listing for it. I didn't have a manual for the machine, so I wasn't even sure what the machine language was.

But I took it as an interesting challenge. I could figure out `BEGIN` and then I would start to decode. The operation codes had some two-letter mnemonics and so I could start to figure out "This probably was a load instruction, this probably was a branch." And I knew it was a Fortran compiler, so at some point it looked at column seven of a card, and that was where it would tell if it was a comment or not.

After three hours I had figured out a little bit about the machine. Then I found these big, branching tables. So it was a puzzle and I kept just making little charts like I'm working at a security agency trying to decode a secret code. But I knew it worked and I knew it was a Fortran compiler—it wasn't encrypted in the sense that it was intentionally obscure; it was only in code because I hadn't gotten the manual for the machine.

Eventually I was able to figure out why this compiler was so fast. Unfortunately it wasn't because the algorithms were brilliant; it was just because they had used unstructured programming and hand optimized the code to the hilt.

It was just basically the way you solve some kind of an unknown puzzle—make tables and charts and get a little more information here and make a hypothesis. In general when I'm reading a technical paper, it's the same challenge. I'm trying to get into the author's mind, trying to figure out what the concept is. The more you learn to read other people's stuff, the more able you are to invent your own in the future, it seems to me.

We ought to publish code. The Lions Book is available. And Bill Atkinson's programs are now publicly available thanks to Apple, and it won't be too long before we'll be able to read that. That's well-documented code with lots of pioneering graphics algorithms in it.

Seibel: Certainly with open source there's a lot more code out there to read than there use to be.

Knuth: Yeah, that's right. But the more varieties of different kinds of notations are still useful—don't only read the people who code like you.

APPENDIX

A

Bibliography

The Art of Computer Programming, Donaid Knuth (Addison-Wesley, 1997)

Beautiful Code: Leading Programmers Explain How They Think, Andy Oram, Greg Wilson (eds.) (O'Reilly, 2007)

Byte, Vol. 6, No. 8, "Smalltalk issue," August 1981

Code Complete, Steve McConnell (Microsoft Press, 1993)

Compiling with Continuations, Andrew W. Appel (Cambridge University Press, 1992)

The Design and Analysis of Computer Algorithms, Alfred V. Aho, John E. Hopcroft, and Jeffrey D. Ullman (Addison-Wesley, 1974)

Design Patterns: Elements of Reusable Object-Oriented Software, Eric Gamma, Richard Helf, Ralph Johnson, and John M. Vlissides (Addison-Wesley Professional, 1994)

A Discipline of Programming, Edsger W. Dijkstra (Prentice Hall, Inc., 1976)

Effective Java, Joshua Bloch (Prentice Hall, 2008)

The Elements of Programming Style, Brian Kernighan and P.J. Plauger (Computing McGraw-Hill, 1978)

Elements of Style, William Strunk and E.B. White (Longman, 1999)

Expert C Programming, Peter van der Linden (Prentice Hall PTR, 1994)

Founders at Work, Jessica Livingston (Apress, 2007)

Hacker's Delight, Hank Warren (Addison-Wesley, 2002)

Higher-Order Perl, Mark Jason Dominus (Morgan Kaufmann, 2005)

Java Concurrency in Practice, Brian Goetz, Tim Peierls, Joshua Bloch, Joseph Bowbeer, David Holmes, and Doug Lea (Addison-Wesley, 2006)

Java Puzzlers: Traps, Pitfalls, and Corner Cases, Joshua Bloch and Neil Gafter (Addison-Wesley, 2005)

The Lisp 1.5 Programmer's Manual, John McCarthy (MIT Press, 1962)

Literate Programming, Donald Knuth (Center for the Study of Language and Information, 1992)

Machine Intelligence 1, N.L. Collins and Donald Michie (eds.) (Oliver and Boyd, 1967)

Machine Intelligence 2, Ella Dale and Donald Michie (eds.) (Oliver and Boyd, 1968)

Machine Intelligence 3, Donald Michie (ed.) (Edinburgh University Press, 1968)

Machine Intelligence 4, Bernard Meltzer and Donald Michie (eds.) (Edinburgh University Press, 1969)

Magic House of Numbers, Irving Adler (HarperCollins, 1974)

"META II a Syntax-Oriented Compiler Writing Language," D.V. Schorre in *Proceedings of the 1964 19th ACM national conference,* (ACM, 1964)

Mindstorms: Children, Computers, and Powerful Ideas, Seymour A. Papert (Basic Books, 1993)

The Mythical Man-Month: Essays on Software Engineering, Frederick P. Brooks (Addison-Wesley Professional, 1995)

Principles of Compiler Design, Alfred Aho and Jeffrey Ullman (Addison-Wesley, 1977)

"Proof of a Program: FIND", C.A.R. Hoare in *Communications of the ACM,* Vol. 14, Issue 1 (ACM, 1971)

Programming Pearls, Jon Bentley (ACM Press, 1999)

Purely Functional Data Structures, Chris Okasaki (Cambridge University Press, 2008)

A Retargetable C Compiler: Design and Implementation, David Hanson and Christopher Fraser (Addison-Wesley Professional, 1995)

Smalltalk-80: The Interactive Programming Environment, Adele Goldberg (Addison-Wesley, 1983)

Smalltalk-80: The Language & Its Implementation, David Robson and Adele Goldberg (Addison-Wesley, 1983)

Structure and Interpretation of Computer Programs, Harold Abelson and Gerald Jay Sussman (MIT Press, 1996)

TeX: The Program, Donald Knuth (Addison-Wesley, 1986)

The Programming Language LISP: Its Operation and Applications, Edmund Berkeley and Daniel Bobrow, eds. (MIT Press, 1966)

The Psychology of Computer Programming: Silver Anniversary Edition, Gerald Weinberg (Dorset House, 1998)

The TeXbook, Donald Knuth (Addison-Wesley Professional, 1986)

Writers at Work: The Paris Review Interviews, Malcolm Cowley (Penguin, 1977)

Zen and the Art of Motorcycle Maintenance: An Inquiry into Values, Robert Pirsig (Bantam, 1984)

I

Index

A

B

C

D

M

Made in the USA
Columbia, SC
09 February 2021

32632343R00346